# The Complete Reference™

# Microsoft® SharePoint® 2010 Web Applications

Charlie Holland

New York   Chicago   San Francisco
Lisbon   London   Madrid   Mexico City
Milan   New Delhi   San Juan
Seoul   Singapore   Sydney   Toronto

The **McGraw·Hill** Companies

Cataloging-in-Publication Data is on file with the Library of Congress

McGraw-Hill books are available at special quantity discounts to use as premiums and sales promotions, or for use in corporate training programs. To contact a representative, please e-mail us at bulksales@ mcgraw-hill.com.

### Microsoft® SharePoint® 2010 Web Applications: The Complete Reference™

Copyright © 2011 by The McGraw-Hill Companies. All rights reserved. Printed in the United States of America. Except as permitted under the Copyright Act of 1976, no part of this publication may be reproduced or distributed in any form or by any means, or stored in a database or retrieval system, without the prior written permission of publisher, with the exception that the program listings may be entered, stored, and executed in a computer system, but they may not be reproduced for publication.

Trademarks: McGraw-Hill, the McGraw-Hill Publishing logo, The Complete Reference™, and related trade dress are trademarks or registered trademarks of The McGraw-Hill Companies and/or its affiliates in the United States and other countries and may not be used without written permission. All other trademarks are the property of their respective owners. The McGraw-Hill Companies is not associated with any product or vendor mentioned in this book.

1234567890   DOC DOC   109876543210

ISBN      978-0-07-174456-0
MHID      0-07-174456-8

| | | |
|---|---|---|
| **Sponsoring Editor** | **Copy Editor** | **Composition** |
| Roger Stewart | Lisa Theobald | Apollo Publishing |
| **Editorial Supervisor** | **Proofreader** | **Illustration** |
| Patty Mon | Susie Elkind | Apollo Publishing, Lyssa Wald |
| **Project Editor** | **Indexer** | **Art Director, Cover** |
| LeeAnn Pickrell | Karin Arrigoni | Jeff Weeks |
| **Acquisitions Coordinator** | **Production Supervisor** | **Cover Designer** |
| Joya Anthony | James Kussow | Jeff Weeks |
| **Technical Editors** | | |
| Craig Porter, Mike Catignani | | |

Information has been obtained by McGraw-Hill from sources believed to be reliable. However, because of the possibility of human or mechanical error by our sources, McGraw-Hill, or others, McGraw-Hill does not guarantee the accuracy, adequacy, or completeness of any information and is not responsible for any errors or omissions or the results obtained from the use of such information.

For Nicola, Cameron, and Fraser

## About the Author

**Charlie Holland** (Scotland, UK) is a freelance software developer with 15 years' experience developing software for some of the world's best-known companies, including IBM, Microsoft, Sony, and Hewlett Packard. As a SharePoint aficionado since the early days of SharePoint Team Services and SharePoint Portal Server 2001, since the beta release of SharePoint 2007, Charlie has been exclusively engaged in designing and delivering applications based on the features offered by the SharePoint platform for a number of UK clients. Charlie holds MCTS, MCPD, MCT, MCITP, CTT+, and MCSE Microsoft certifications. You can find Charlie online at http://www.chaholl.com or http://twitter.com/chaholl and feedback or questions are always welcome.

## About the Technical Reviewers

**Craig Porter** (Scotland, UK) is an MCTS-certified freelance SharePoint all-rounder. Craig has been involved in SharePoint development, administration, architecture, and consultancy for the past 10 years, having delivered a number of SharePoint projects both large and small and of varying requirements and complexity. Craig first got involved in SharePoint in late 2000 when asked to contribute to a prerelease beta version of SharePoint Portal Server 2001, then known as Tahoe. Since then, Craig has dedicated his working life to getting the most out of the SharePoint platform and understanding its many intricacies. You can find Craig's web site at http://collaborativetechnologysolutions.co.uk.

**Mike Catignani** (Scotland, UK) is technical director and founder of Solutions Developed, a company specializing in SharePoint implementations. The company completed its first SharePoint deployment in 2003 for The Deer Commission of Scotland and has been actively involved in delivering SharePoint solutions ever since. Mike is very proud of the solutions he's delivered for many major blue chip companies such as Daimler, HSBC, Bacardi, Ministry of Defence (UK), and the UK's Emergency Fire and Rescue Service, in addition to many other organizations perhaps not so well known but equally important. Mike holds many IS qualifications, including the Microsoft accreditations MCSD and MCT. To learn more about Mike, visit his web site at www.solutionsdeveloped.co.uk.

# Contents at a Glance

| Part I | Introduction to SharePoint 2010 Development | |
|---|---|---|
| 1 | The Microsoft SharePoint 2010 Platform | 3 |
| 2 | Developing with SharePoint 2010 | 9 |
| **Part II** | **Presentation Layer** | |
| 3 | Presentation Layer Overview | 33 |
| 4 | Client Object Model | 53 |
| 5 | InfoPath Forms Services | 79 |
| 6 | Enterprise Content Management | 107 |
| 7 | User Interface Customization | 133 |
| **Part III** | **Application Services** | |
| 8 | Application Services Overview | 153 |
| 9 | Service Application Framework | 169 |
| 10 | Word Automation Services | 203 |
| 11 | Workflow | 223 |
| 12 | Excel Services | 265 |
| **Part IV** | **Data Access Layer** | |
| 13 | Data Access Overview | 311 |
| 14 | LINQ to SharePoint and SPMetal | 337 |
| 15 | Business Connectivity Services | 387 |
| 16 | Enterprise Search | 423 |
| 17 | User Profiles and Social Data | 443 |
| 18 | Business Intelligence | 463 |
| **Part V** | **Configuration** | |
| 19 | Packaging and Deployment Model | 493 |
| 20 | PowerShell | 517 |
| | Index | 527 |

# Contents

Acknowledgments .................................................... xv
Introduction ........................................................ xvii

| Part I | **Introduction to SharePoint 2010 Development** |
|---|---|
| Chapter 1 | **The Microsoft SharePoint 2010 Platform** ........................... 3 |

        SharePoint Architecture ................................................. 4
        User Features ........................................................... 5
            Office Integration ................................................. 5
            Office Web Applications .......................................... 6
            SharePoint Workspace ............................................ 6
            Standards Compliant Web Interface .............................. 6
        Summary ............................................................... 7

| Chapter 2 | **Developing with SharePoint 2010** ................................. 9 |
|---|---|

            Visual Studio 2010 and SharePoint Designer 2010 ................. 10
            TypeMock Isolator ................................................ 10
            Red Gate .NET Reflector .......................................... 10
            U2U CAML Query Builder ........................................ 10
            Sysinternals DebugView ........................................... 11
        Development Server Configuration ..................................... 11
            Additional Development Environment Configuration ............. 12
            Debugging and Unit Testing SharePoint Applications ............. 12
        SharePoint Fundamentals ............................................. 14
            Creating a Web Application ...................................... 14
            Creating a Site Collection ........................................ 15
            Creating a Site .................................................. 15
        Server Object Model ................................................. 17
            Administration and Configuration Classes ........................ 20
            Site Provisioning and Content Access Classes .................... 21
            Saving Changes Using the Server Object Model ................... 25
            Best Practice Guidelines ......................................... 25
            Error Handling .................................................. 27
        Developer Toolbar ................................................... 28
        Sandboxed Solutions ................................................. 29
            Debugging Sandboxed Solutions .................................. 30
            Managing Sandboxed Solutions .................................. 30
        Summary .............................................................. 30

## Part II  Presentation Layer

**Chapter 3  Presentation Layer Overview** .......................................... 33
    Page Types .................................................................. 33
        Application Pages ..................................................... 33
        Site Pages ............................................................. 34
    Ghosting/Unghosting ........................................................ 35
    Executing Server-Side Code ................................................. 35
    Mobile Pages .............................................................. 40
    Ribbon .................................................................... 40
        Ribbon Architecture .................................................. 40
        Extending the Ribbon ................................................ 42
        Handling Events from the Ribbon .................................... 46
        Disabling Controls ................................................... 47
        Complex Event Handling ............................................. 47
    Summary .................................................................. 52

**Chapter 4  Client Object Model** ...................................................... 53
    Architecture .............................................................. 53
    Demonstration Environment Setup ........................................... 55
        Host Silverlight in SharePoint ........................................ 55
        Using the Silverlight Web Part ....................................... 59
        Referencing the JavaScript Client Object Model ....................... 60
    Available Client-side Objects .............................................. 61
        ClientContext ........................................................ 61
        Operation Batching .................................................. 64
    Retrieving Data ........................................................... 65
        In-place Load ........................................................ 65
        Queryable Load ...................................................... 71
    Adding Data .............................................................. 71
    Updating Data ............................................................ 72
    Deleting Data ............................................................. 74
    Using the Status Bar, Notifications, and the Dialog Framework ............. 75
        The Status Bar ....................................................... 75
        Notifications ......................................................... 76
        Dialogs .............................................................. 76
    Summary .................................................................. 77

**Chapter 5  InfoPath Forms Services** .................................................. 79
    InfoPath Overview ........................................................ 79
    InfoPath Forms Services ................................................... 79
        BrowserForm Web Part ............................................... 81
        Using InfoPath Forms in SharePoint .................................. 86
    Accessing Data in InfoPath Forms .......................................... 96
        Data Connection Libraries ........................................... 99
        Modifying UDC Files ................................................ 99
    Responding to Events in InfoPath Forms .................................... 101
        Using the Rules Engine .............................................. 101
        Adding Code-Behind ................................................. 103
    Summary .................................................................. 105

**Chapter 6  Enterprise Content Management** .......................................... 107
    Managed Metadata ........................................................ 107
        Configuring the Managed Metadata Service ............................ 108

|   |   |   |
|---|---|---|
| | Managed Metadata Field | 109 |
| | Metadata Navigation | 111 |
| | Content Organizer | 112 |
| | Large Libraries | 114 |
| Document Management | | 114 |
| | Content Management Users | 114 |
| | Multi-user Editing | 115 |
| | Item-Level Permissions | 115 |
| | Workflows | 115 |
| | Document Sets | 116 |
| | Document IDs | 118 |
| | Document Metadata | 120 |
| | Records Management | 120 |
| Digital Asset Management | | 120 |
| | Media Content Types | 120 |
| | Rich Media Content | 121 |
| | Disk-based Caching | 121 |
| | Remote BLOB Storage | 122 |
| Web Content Management | | 122 |
| | Page Model | 122 |
| | Publishing | 124 |
| | Content Deployment | 130 |
| | Web Parts and Fields | 131 |
| | Content Query Web Part | 131 |
| Summary | | 131 |

**Chapter 7  User Interface Customization . . . . . . . . . . . . . . . . . . . . . . . . . . . . . . . . . . . . . . . . 133**

|   |   |   |
|---|---|---|
| Working with Pages | | 133 |
| | Master Pages | 133 |
| | Creating a Custom Master Page | 134 |
| | Delegate Controls | 136 |
| | Cascading Style Sheets | 137 |
| | Themes | 137 |
| Adding Custom Functionality | | 140 |
| | Web Parts | 140 |
| | Improving the Property Editing Experience: Editor Parts | 144 |
| | Visual Web Parts | 145 |
| Summary | | 149 |

## Part III  Application Services

**Chapter 8  Application Services Overview . . . . . . . . . . . . . . . . . . . . . . . . . . . . . . . . . . . . . . . 153**

|   |   |   |
|---|---|---|
| Handling Events | | 153 |
| | Event Hosts | 154 |
| | Event Receivers | 154 |
| | Receiver Base Classes | 154 |
| | Synchronous and Asynchronous Events | 155 |
| | Security Context | 156 |
| | Event Properties | 157 |
| | Packaging and Deployment Events | 158 |
| Creating Event Receivers | | 159 |
| | Enabling or Disabling Event Firing | 163 |

| | | |
|---|---|---|
| | | Binding Events ............................................. 165 |
| | | E-mail Events ............................................. 167 |
| | Summary ..................................................... 167 |
| **Chapter 9** | **Service Application Framework** ................................... 169 |
| | Implementation ............................................... 169 |
| | | Server-side Implementation ................................ 169 |
| | | Client-side Implementation ................................ 171 |
| | | Client/Server Communication .............................. 173 |
| | Configuring Service Applications ................................ 173 |
| | | Connecting to Remote Applications ......................... 174 |
| | | Topology Service ......................................... 175 |
| | Demonstration Scenario ........................................ 175 |
| | | Prerequisite: Generating a New AppId ....................... 175 |
| | | Creating a New SharePoint Project .......................... 176 |
| | | Adding Server-side Configuration Classes .................... 176 |
| | | Adding Client-side Configuration Classes .................... 179 |
| | | Adding Windows Communication Foundation Components ....... 181 |
| | | Implementing Translation Functionality ...................... 183 |
| | | Installing Service Application Components ................... 185 |
| | | Provisioning Service Application Instances ................... 187 |
| | | Using Service Application in Front-end Components ............ 196 |
| | | Managing Service Applications .............................. 199 |
| | Summary ..................................................... 202 |
| **Chapter 10** | **Word Automation Services** ....................................... 203 |
| | Word Automation Services ...................................... 203 |
| | | Creating Conversion Jobs .................................. 204 |
| | | Checking Status of Conversion Jobs ......................... 205 |
| | OpenXML ..................................................... 206 |
| | | Getting Started with OpenXML ............................. 206 |
| | Demonstration Scenario ........................................ 207 |
| | | Architecture .............................................. 207 |
| | | Creating a Custom Content Type ........................... 208 |
| | | Customizing the DocumentSetProperties Web Part ............ 210 |
| | | Creating a Custom Job Definition ........................... 214 |
| | | Combine Documents Using OpenXML ....................... 215 |
| | | Converting an OpenXML Document to an Alternative Format ... 217 |
| | | Customizing Document Set Welcome Page .................... 219 |
| | | Create a Document Library ................................. 220 |
| | | Create a Document Template ............................... 220 |
| | Summary ..................................................... 222 |
| **Chapter 11** | **Workflow** ...................................................... 223 |
| | Workflow Foundation Fundamentals .............................. 223 |
| | | Types of Workflow ........................................ 224 |
| | | Making Workflows Work ................................... 225 |
| | | Custom Workflow Activities ................................ 226 |
| | | External Activities via Pluggable Workflow Services ............ 227 |
| | | Creating Workflows ....................................... 227 |
| | Demonstration Scenario ........................................ 228 |
| | | Prerequisites ............................................. 229 |

|  |  |  |
|---|---|---|
|  | Designing a Workflow Using Visio 2010............................. 231 |  |
|  | Using the Microsoft SharePoint Workflow Template................ 232 |  |
|  | Implementing a Visio Workflow Using SharePoint Designer.......... 233 |  |
|  | Using Visio Services to Visualize Workflow State.................. 238 |  |
|  | Creating a Pluggable Workflow Service............................ 240 |  |
|  | Creating a Sample WCF Calculation Service...................... 241 |  |
|  | Creating a Pluggable Workflow Service......................... 250 |  |
|  | Calling a SharePoint-Hosted WCF Service...................... 256 |  |
|  | Creating a Workflow Using Visual Studio 2010...................... 257 |  |
|  | Using the Visual Studio Workflow Designer..................... 258 |  |
|  | Creating a Workflow Using SharePoint Designer..................... 262 |  |
|  | Summary................................................. 264 |  |
| **Chapter 12** | **Excel Services**............................................. **265** |  |
|  | Excel Capabilities on SharePoint 2010............................. 266 |  |
|  | Excel Application Services.................................. 266 |  |
|  | Excel Client Service...................................... 266 |  |
|  | Excel Web App......................................... 269 |  |
|  | PowerPivot............................................ 270 |  |
|  | Configuring Excel Services..................................... 270 |  |
|  | Service Application Settings................................ 271 |  |
|  | Demonstration Scenario....................................... 273 |  |
|  | Set Up Adventure Works Sample Database...................... 273 |  |
|  | Create a Sample Site...................................... 273 |  |
|  | Create a Workbook for Use with Excel Services.................... 274 |  |
|  | Configure a Data Connection................................ 276 |  |
|  | Configure a PivotTable to Act like an External Data List............. 276 |  |
|  | Using Named Ranges in Excel Services......................... 277 |  |
|  | Perform Calculations Using PivotTable Values.................... 278 |  |
|  | Add a PivotChart........................................ 280 |  |
|  | Publish to Excel Services................................... 281 |  |
|  | Create a User Interface Using the Excel Web Access Web Part........ 281 |  |
|  | Adding Interactivity Using a Slicer............................ 282 |  |
|  | Using the Excel Services REST API............................... 285 |  |
|  | Excel Services REST API Syntax.............................. 285 |  |
|  | Retrieving a PivotTable Using REST........................... 286 |  |
|  | Using REST-Generated Content Within a Web Part Page............ 287 |  |
|  | User-Defined Functions....................................... 288 |  |
|  | Attributes Used when Creating UDFs.......................... 288 |  |
|  | Usable Data Types Within UDFs.............................. 289 |  |
|  | Creating a UDF Using Visual Studio 2010....................... 289 |  |
|  | Configuring UDFs for Development........................... 292 |  |
|  | Using UDFs Within Excel................................... 293 |  |
|  | Debugging UDFs......................................... 294 |  |
|  | Configuring UDFs for Production............................. 295 |  |
|  | Using the JavaScript Object Model................................ 297 |  |
|  | A Whirlwind Tour of Excel JSOM............................. 297 |  |
|  | Adding a Content Editor Web Part Containing JavaScript............ 298 |  |
|  | Creating JSOM Content in an External File..................... 299 |  |
|  | Using Data Connection Libraries................................. 300 |  |
|  | Restricting Data Connection Types............................ 301 |  |

Adding Connections to Data Connection Libraries .................. 302
Connecting to Data Using Alternative Credentials ................. 304
Configuring the Secure Store Service........................... 305
Summary ...................................................... 308

# Part IV  Data Access Layer

## Chapter 13  Data Access Overview ............................................. 311
Content Types ................................................. 311
    Content Type Inheritance ................................. 312
    Content Type Metadata ................................... 316
    Enterprise Content Types ................................. 318
Columns....................................................... 321
    Field Types .............................................. 323
    Validation ............................................... 330
Lists and Document Libraries................................... 331
    Views .................................................... 332
    Queries .................................................. 332
Performance ................................................... 333
    List Throttling .......................................... 334
    Column Indexes.......................................... 335
Summary ...................................................... 336

## Chapter 14  LINQ to SharePoint and SPMetal................................ 337
Overview of LINQ ............................................. 338
    Locating Data Using an Iterator .......................... 339
    Locating Data Using an Anonymous Delegate............. 340
    Locating Data Using a Lambda Expression ................ 340
    Locating Data Using LINQ ............................... 341
LINQ to SharePoint............................................ 341
    Microsoft.SharePoint.Linq.DataContext ................... 342
Demonstration Scenario ........................................ 344
    Create a Data Structure Using SharePoint 2010 ........... 346
    Creating Entities Using SPMetal ........................... 353
Adding Data Using LINQ ...................................... 358
    Add Data Generation Buttons to LinqSampleApplication ........... 358
Deleting Data Using LINQ ..................................... 361
    Deleting Sample Data .................................... 361
    Ensuring Referential Integrity............................. 362
Querying Data Using LINQ to SharePoint ..................... 365
    Query Limitations ....................................... 366
    Performing a Simple Query............................... 367
    Result Shaping Using LINQ .............................. 370
    Joining Tables Using LINQ ............................... 371
Combining LINQ to SharePoint and LINQ to Objects ........... 373
    Performing an In-Memory Subquery ...................... 373
Updating Information Using LINQ to SharePoint................ 375
    Disconnecting Entities.................................... 375
    Reconnecting Entities .................................... 376
    Handling Concurrency Errors when Updating Data................ 378
    Resolving Change Conflicts............................... 381
Summary ...................................................... 385

## Contents

| | | |
|---|---|---|
| Chapter 15 | **Business Connectivity Services** | **387** |
| | Business Data Catalog in MOSS 2007 | 387 |
| |     Components of BCS | 388 |
| | Demonstration Scenario | 391 |
| |     Prerequisites | 392 |
| | Connecting to BCS Data Using SharePoint Designer | 392 |
| |     Associations | 392 |
| |     Stereotypes | 392 |
| |     Create an External Content Type | 394 |
| |     External Data Picker Control | 400 |
| | Building a .NET Connectivity Assembly | 404 |
| |     Pluggable Connector Framework | 405 |
| |     Business Data Connectivity Model Project | 405 |
| | Using BCS Data in External Data Columns | 418 |
| |     Profile Pages | 419 |
| |     Default Actions on External Content Types | 420 |
| | Summary | 422 |
| Chapter 16 | **Enterprise Search** | **423** |
| | Components of Enterprise Search | 423 |
| |     Architecture | 423 |
| |     Indexing Components | 424 |
| |     Query Components | 429 |
| |     Front-End Components | 435 |
| | Summary | 442 |
| Chapter 17 | **User Profiles and Social Data** | **443** |
| | Folksonomies, Taxonomies, Tagging, and Rating | 444 |
| | User Profile Service Application | 445 |
| |     Synchronization | 445 |
| |     User Properties | 446 |
| |     Subtypes | 447 |
| |     Audiences | 448 |
| |     Organizations | 449 |
| | My Sites | 450 |
| |     My Profile | 452 |
| |     My Network | 461 |
| |     My Content | 462 |
| | Summary | 462 |
| Chapter 18 | **Business Intelligence** | **463** |
| | Microsoft Business Intelligence Solution | 464 |
| |     Business User Experience | 464 |
| |     Business Productivity Infrastructure | 464 |
| |     Data Infrastructure | 464 |
| | SharePoint Server 2010 Business Intelligence Platform | 465 |
| |     Excel Services | 465 |
| |     Business Intelligence Web Parts | 465 |
| |     PerformancePoint Services | 469 |
| |     PowerPivot | 480 |
| |     Reporting Services | 485 |
| | Summary | 489 |

## Part V  Configuration

**Chapter 19  Packaging and Deployment Model** .................................... **493**
    Working with Packages .................................................. 493
        Package Structure............................................. 494
        Package Designer............................................. 494
        Deploying Assemblies......................................... 496
    Features .............................................................. 496
        Feature Designer ............................................. 497
        Activation Dependencies...................................... 497
        Feature Scope................................................ 498
        Feature Activation Rules ..................................... 498
        Feature Properties ........................................... 499
        Feature Elements ............................................ 499
        Feature Receivers ........................................... 501
        Upgrading Features .......................................... 508
    Site Definitions ....................................................... 512
        Creating Site Definitions Using Visual Studio .................... 512
    Summary ............................................................. 515

**Chapter 20  PowerShell** ........................................................... **517**
    PowerShell Primer.................................................... 517
        Using Objects ............................................... 518
        Using Functions ............................................. 520
    PowerShell for SharePoint ............................................. 521
        Connecting to SharePoint Remotely ........................... 521
        PowerShell Permissions ...................................... 522
        Working with Site Collections and Sites ......................... 522
        Working with Lists and Libraries............................... 523
        Working with Content ....................................... 524
        Working with Timer Jobs..................................... 524
    Summary ............................................................. 525

**Index** .............................................................................. **527**

# Acknowledgments

Before embarking on this book, I did some research to get an idea of what was involved in such a project. Almost without exception, people told me that the amount of effort required to write a book is always much more than originally anticipated.

As a working systems architect and software developer, I often spend much of my time writing technical documents, and, like many of those who have gone before me, I arrived at the conclusion that writing a book is pretty much like that. The only difference is the length of the document. Logical, don't you think? If only it was that simple!

SharePoint is a huge product, and part of my motivation in writing this book was to enjoy an opportunity to develop a broader knowledge of the platform. Like many developers, I've been involved in a number of SharePoint projects over the years, but despite that, I've never delved into some aspects of the platform in a meaningful way.

Faced with the task of writing a book on these subjects, I turned to a number of technical experts for help, including my technical reviewers on this project, Mike Catignani and Craig Porter. Without the invaluable input of these guys and others such as Martin Hinshelwood, Andrew Woodward, Spencer Harbar, Andre Vermeulen, Peter Holpar, and Nick Swan, I would have found it practically impossible to provide coherent explanations of some of the functionality of the platform. Over and above the assistance provided by this group of technical experts, I also found Twitter to be an indispensable tool for getting answers to the most arcane questions even several months before the release of the product. If that isn't a case study in the power of social computing, then I don't know what is.

While getting to the bottom of the technical aspects of the SharePoint platform was undoubtedly the biggest challenge from my perspective, there is so much more to writing a book than simply writing the text. As a project that extended over many months and involved many people, putting my writings together into the finished package that you currently hold in your hands is the work of a team of dedicated professionals. I would like to express my thanks and appreciation for the work of the entire team at McGraw-Hill in making this book possible. I would particularly like to thank Joya Anthony and Roger Stewart for their patience in dealing with my flexible approach to deadlines.

Many months ago (in fact, it almost seems like a lifetime now), I made contact with Matt Wagner (www.fresh-books.com) with a view to writing a SharePoint book. I'd like to thank Matt for his efforts in hooking me up with McGraw-Hill. Without the great work that Matt did on my behalf, this book would not have been written.

Writing a book while working full time and dealing with the demands of a young family can be a very taxing experience, and without the full support of my family, I can honestly say that there is no way that this project would have been completed. I'd like to thank my wife, Nicola, for patiently listening to me rambling on about SharePoint 2010 and how many chapters I had to complete for months on end. For a long time, it seemed that the job would never be done, but we got there in the end, and looking back, I appreciate the many evenings and weekends that my family sacrificed in order to make this book a reality.

# Introduction

## Who Should Read This Book

Microsoft SharePoint 2010 is a large and complex product that serves many audiences and provides a range of functionality covering areas such as search, document management, and business intelligence. Each of the many specialist areas that make up SharePoint 2010 warrants a book in its own right to cover the functionality exposed from the perspective of all audiences. This book takes a comprehensive look at the entire platform as it relates to a specific audience.

Aimed primarily at software developers with experience in developing software using the Microsoft .NET Framework, this book covers Microsoft SharePoint as a software development platform. It places particular emphasis on aspects of the product that can be leveraged by developers to create custom applications such as user interface customizations and application layer services. It also provides reusable code samples and real-world demonstration scenarios, plus high-level technical information that is appropriate for getting technical architects, software testers, and project managers up to speed with the capabilities of the platform.

## How to Use This Book

With great many features and services available in the SharePoint 2010 platform, it's highly unlikely that any single application will use all of them. Nevertheless, it's important for you to understand which tools are available before you embark on the design of an application.

To make gaining such an understanding as easy as possible, this book is divided into five parts. Part I deals with the fundamentals: what is SharePoint, how does it work, and what tools do I need to get started? This part gives you an idea of what's involved in developing applications that leverage the SharePoint platform. The remainder of the book is designed to be used as a reference for the tools and technologies that are most appropriate for the task at hand.

The next three parts are named after the three layers that we commonly need to consider when designing an application: Presentation, Application Services, and Data Access. Each part contains an overview chapter that covers the key concepts and tools that are most appropriate for delivering functionality within that layer. The other chapters within each part build on the knowledge gained in the part overview and address a particular feature or service in detail.

The final part covers aspects that are common to every project: packaging, deployment, and configuration.

Many of the chapters in this book feature demonstration scenarios that are effectively mini-applications that illustrate a specific feature. For the most part, the code samples found in this book can be executed in isolation, making it easy for you to work through the book as a means of learning how to use the SharePoint platform.

# What This Book Covers

This book consists of 20 chapters organized into 5 parts.

## Part I: Introduction to SharePoint 2010 Development

**Chapter 1: The Microsoft SharePoint 2010 Platform**   This chapter provides an introduction to the SharePoint 2010 product, describing the product history and providing a high-level description of how the product is implemented within an organization. In addition, to help you build an understanding of how the product is accessed from a user perspective, I describe a number of user touch points. Understanding these touch points will help you build up a picture of SharePoint as a flexible software development platform offering practically limitless opportunities to leverage tools and technologies with which many users are already familiar.

**Chapter 2: Developing with SharePoint 2010**   This chapter looks at the basics of the SharePoint architecture. We look at the key objects in the server object model as well as important best practice guidance that ensure that applications targeting the SharePoint platform run as efficiently and effectively as possible.

## Part II: Presentation Layer

**Chapter 3: Presentation Layer Overview**   This chapter provides an overview of the presentation layer technologies in SharePoint 2010. In addition to covering the different types of pages that can be hosted within a SharePoint application, Chapter 3 also looks at customizing the ribbon and discusses how code can be added to hosted pages.

**Chapter 4: Client Object Model**   One of the new additions in SharePoint 2010 is the Client Object Model. This new API allows developers to create rich user interfaces by writing client-side code that interacts directly with the SharePoint object model. Chapter 4 covers the key programming conventions of the Client Object Model as well as providing coverage of the new user feedback interfaces that are available when using the JavaScript Client Object Model.

**Chapter 5: InfoPath Forms Services**   InfoPath Forms Services was introduced in Microsoft Office SharePoint Server 2007 (MOSS 2007) as a tool to allow nontechnical users to create web-based data capture forms. With SharePoint 2010, InfoPath Forms Services is available with all editions of the product and is the preferred mechanism for customizing data capture forms throughout the user interface and creating custom data entry forms. This chapter looks at the main uses of InfoPath forms and provides a number of reusable examples.

**Chapter 6: Enterprise Content Management**  In addition to providing a user interface for the creation of web pages, Enterprise Content Management (ECM) also encompasses the management of electronically stored documents and other files. SharePoint 2010 offers many tools and techniques for use in this area, and this chapter provides an overview of the key technologies available on the platform, including managed metadata, content deployment, workflows, and the SharePoint publishing page model.

**Chapter 7: User Interface Customization**  This chapter closes Part II by looking at how the user interface can be customized. Since SharePoint is fundamentally based on ASP.NET, many of the customization techniques will be familiar to web developers; however, a number of SharePoint-specific aspects should also be considered, from both a design perspective and a development perspective. This chapter covers the development of web parts and provides detail on the new themes capability introduced in SharePoint 2010.

## Part III: Application Services

**Chapter 8: Application Services Overview**  This chapter provides an overview of the application services that are available on SharePoint 2010. Setting the scene for further explanation of these services in subsequent chapters, Chapter 8 provides an in-depth look at one of the most basic of application services: event handling. For the most part, the entry point to any application service is the triggering of an event, either directly via the user interface or indirectly via another server-side workflow process. This chapter helps you understand and develop skills required to respond to SharePoint events in a manner most appropriate for a given application design.

**Chapter 9: Service Application Framework**  SharePoint 2010 introduces a new service application framework that can be used by developers to create scalable, reusable, load-balanced services. Although for the most part the clients for these services will commonly be SharePoint applications, the Service Application Framework is by no means limited to services in SharePoint; in fact, the flexibility of the Service Application Framework means that hosted services can be deployed using a range of technologies and can, therefore, be accessed by practically any client application. This chapter provides an in-depth discussion of the key components of the Service Application Framework and offers a reusable example that can act as the basis for any custom service application.

**Chapter 10: Word Automation Services**  Several new services are available in SharePoint 2010, and providing full coverage of all of them is beyond the scope of this book. However, one common requirement when you are developing SharePoint applications is to process data that's stored in Microsoft Office documents. Chapter 10 provides a sample application that leverages the new Word Automation Services functionality together with OpenXML to combine information stored in Microsoft Word documents into a read-only Adobe Acrobat file. In earlier versions of SharePoint, such functionality would require the services of a third-party component and possibly the server-side automation of the Microsoft Word application. With SharePoint 2010, such tasks can be performed more robustly using Word Automation Services.

**Chapter 11: Workflow**  There's more to workflow than approving expense forms. Workflow provides a new programming paradigm and is a viable alternative for many business applications. Chapter 11 looks at how SharePoint 2010 enables workflow-based application development. It demonstrates how SharePoint-hosted workflows can communicate easily with external systems. SharePoint Designer allows nontechnical users to customize workflows without having to delve into the code. This chapter looks at how developers can create custom actions that can then be used by nontechnical users to model business processes. As well as discussing the capabilities offered by Visual Studio and SharePoint Designer, this chapter introduces Visio Services and looks at how Visio can be used to model business processes that can be imported into SharePoint and implemented as a workflow with full Visio visualization support.

**Chapter 12: Excel Services**  At first glance, it may seem that nothing much has changed in Excel Services between MOSS 2007 and SharePoint 2010. This is not the case, however, as a number of improvements have been made, most notably the introduction of a JavaScript Object Model and a REST API, both of which enable the creation of a highly interactive user experience. Chapter 12 provides comprehensive coverage of Excel Services, from connecting to data sources, to utilizing the JavaScript Object Model to update values in an Excel chart.

# Part IV: Data Access Layer

**Chapter 13: Data Access Overview**  Many years ago, when I began studying computer science, a professor insisted that all application design should begin with the data. This made sense 20-odd years ago when applications were commonly nothing more than data capture tools, but things have moved on a bit since then: although the data is still a critical element in any application design, it's not necessarily the be-all and end-all. In modern application design, the ability to access data from ever-changing data sources is much more important than the actual structure of the data itself, and this is certainly true with the SharePoint platform. A number of data access strategies are included in SharePoint, and Chapter 13 kicks off Part IV by providing an overview of how data is represented in SharePoint and the various approaches you can take when designing a data access layer. Subsequent chapters address the various methods for working with data in more detail.

**Chapter 14: LINQ to SharePoint and SPMetal**  As discussed in Chapter 13, the underlying data structure of SharePoint is dynamic—that is, it can represent data from a range of sources. One consequence of this flexibility is that, prior to the release of SharePoint 2010, programmatically using data was not strongly-typed, often leading to code that could be difficult to maintain or refactor. With SharePoint 2010, the introduction of LINQ and SPMetal, a tool for generating strongly typed data access objects, means that more maintainable code is within easy reach of any developer. Chapter 14 provides an overview of LINQ and the technologies that enable it before moving on to look at using SPMetal and the capabilities provided by LINQ to SharePoint.

**Chapter 15: Business Connectivity Services**  MOSS 2007 introduced the Business Data Catalog as a tool to surface line-of-business data in SharePoint applications. With SharePoint 2010, the Business Data Catalog has evolved to Business Connectivity Services

(BCS), a number of services that allow SharePoint and non-SharePoint applications to use data from practically any source. While the Business Data Catalog was limited to read-only access to data, BCS provides full read/write capability, and, furthermore, by using external content types, a SharePoint application can work with external data in exactly the same way as it would with data that's stored and managed within a SharePoint list. Chapter 15 provides an overview of the components of BCS before introducing a demonstration scenario that provides the basis for the reusable code samples used in the chapter.

**Chapter 16: Enterprise Search**   The SharePoint data model is flexible enough to represent practically any type of data from any source. However, the ability to represent all this data gives rise to another problem: how do users find what they need? The enterprise search functionality in SharePoint Server 2010 addresses this problem by providing a scalable, flexible architecture for indexing content and responding to search queries. Furthermore, by customizing the user interface components for capturing search queries and processing results, you can develop customized search applications. Chapter 16 provides details of the three main components of enterprise search—indexing components, query components, and front-end components—and provides reusable code samples for each component, describing how each can be customized and used in custom code.

**Chapter 17: User Profiles and Social Data**   With the growth of social computing giants such as Facebook, MySpace, and Twitter, it has become apparent that social computing is the killer app that web observers have been searching for since the medium came into widespread use some 20 years ago. Although social computing is all about communication, the very nature of the tool gives rise to rich personalization opportunities, and it is via this personalization that content and data become relevant to the audience using it. This relevance sets up the virtuous cycle that fuels the widespread adoption of social computing. Users no longer need to search for content; instead, by analyzing their social graph, they can have content presented to them automatically. How does this relate to SharePoint? The answer is in the built-in social data capabilities of the platform. From an application design perspective, the two key aspects of social computing are the generation of social data, by allowing users to create connections and specify their interests and activities, and the analysis of social data, by using the data gathered to provide rich personalization. The SharePoint platform addresses both of the aspects, and Chapter 17 looks at the tools and technologies behind each one, providing reusable examples of how a custom application can be enabled to provide custom social data.

**Chapter 18: Business Intelligence**   This chapter closes Part IV by looking at the Business Intelligence capabilities of the SharePoint platform. Chapter 12 provided an in-depth discussion of Excel Services, and Chapter 18 builds on this to look at related technologies such as PerformancePoint Services, PowerPivot, and Reporting Services. By combining these tools and technologies, you can use SharePoint not only as a portal for displaying Business Intelligence data, but also as a repository for user-generated reports and data sources. Chapter 18 provides examples of each technology and describes the key features of each, which makes it possible for application developers to determine which technology is most appropriate for the task at hand.

## Part V: Configuration

**Chapter 19: Packaging and Deployment Model**    Chapter 19 kicks off the final part by looking at the packaging and deployment model in SharePoint 2010. Throughout the various examples in the book, the built-in packaging and deployment capabilities of Visual Studio 2010 are used implicitly; however, when it comes to embarking on real-world projects, you'll need a proper understanding of the packaging and deployment model. This chapter covers the core elements of the model, such as packages, features, and site definitions. The feature framework is emphasized as the recommended approach to packaging and deploying solutions in SharePoint 2010. In addition to covering the creation of new solutions, the chapter also looks at the new functionality introduced in SharePoint 2010 to accommodate upgrades.

**Chapter 20: PowerShell**    This chapter provides an overview of the system administration capabilities exposed via PowerShell. In previous versions of SharePoint, a SharePoint-specific tool, STSADM, was used to provide command-line access to various system administration and configuration functionality. With SharePoint 2010, the recommended approach, in line with Microsoft's overall strategy for command-line system administration, is to use PowerShell. While STSADM is still available in SharePoint 2010, a number of functions can be performed only using PowerShell. Users unfamiliar with PowerShell, or those who have used STSADM for many years, may be resistant to learning PowerShell; to aid the transition, the chapter begins with an introduction to the core syntactical elements of PowerShell before moving on to provide examples of how it can be used to manage SharePoint.

# PART I

# Introduction to SharePoint 2010 Development

**CHAPTER 1**
The Microsoft SharePoint 2010 Platform

**CHAPTER 2**
Developing with SharePoint 2010

# CHAPTER 1

# The Microsoft SharePoint 2010 Platform

So what is SharePoint? And more important, what is the SharePoint 2010 Platform and how can it be used to develop applications?

The SharePoint product has been around for some time, with the first version being released in 2001 as SharePoint Portal Server 2001. Things have moved on a bit since then. Following the acquisition of NCompass Labs, a content management system (CMS) vendor, Microsoft launched a new product, Content Management Server 2001. In 2003, Microsoft launched SharePoint Portal Server 2003 as well as an updated version of Content Management Server. These products were ultimately combined to become Microsoft Office SharePoint Server 2007 (MOSS) in late 2006.

While this was going on Microsoft also acquired ProClarity, a business intelligence (BI) vendor, and Groove, a peer-to-peer collaboration tool vendor. In 2007, Microsoft released PerformancePoint, a BI solution that was integrated with SharePoint and derived from the technology acquired from ProClarity. With MOSS 2007, Groove still existed as a stand-alone product, but now in SharePoint 2010, the features of Groove have been integrated into the platform. So, in answer to the question "What is SharePoint?" SharePoint 2010 is a fully integrated platform that is made up of the best bits of many tried-and-tested products.

There's more to SharePoint than a collection of useful business tools, however. Creating such tight integration is no easy feat, and to make it happen, the good people at Microsoft have effectively deconstructed each of the products and pieced them back together into a software development platform that is based on the .NET Framework. In a sense, the SharePoint 2010 Platform is the .NET Framework with a whole host of reuseable application services such as content management, business intelligence, offline synchronization, and workflow.

How can it be used to develop applications? The answer is simple: open Visual Studio and start typing in the language of your choice. Of course, you'll need to learn about a few new object models and you'll need a good understanding of the platform architecture, but fundamentally developing applications using the SharePoint platform is exactly the same as developing applications using the .NET Framework. There are no new languages to learn and the improved tooling in SharePoint 2010 means that most of the work can be done in Visual Studio.

The aim of this book is to provide the necessary guidance to allow developers who are already comfortable with the .NET platform and the Visual Studio toolset to make full use of the SharePoint platform when developing custom applications.

SharePoint is more than a document management tool, a content management tool, or an application that allows users to create collaborative web sites. Behind all of this, SharePoint is a new kind of operating system that runs across an entire organization and provides the tools and services that information workers need on a day-to-day basis.

Organizations will always have line-of-business applications, but what about the myriad administrative applications—the Access databases, Excel spreadsheets, custom .NET application for tracking widget returns? What about the business data that's stored in an incalculable number of Word documents and PDF files on desktop PCs and network file shares? What about the holiday request forms that get filled in and stuck in a filing cabinet somewhere? The SharePoint platform provides the tools and technologies to manage all of these processes and all of this data in a single unified manner. Building applications that leverage this platform provides an unparalleled level of visibility and integration—all using the familiar toolset of Microsoft Visual Studio 2010.

# SharePoint Architecture

The SharePoint platform is delivered via a *server farm* architecture, shown in the following example:

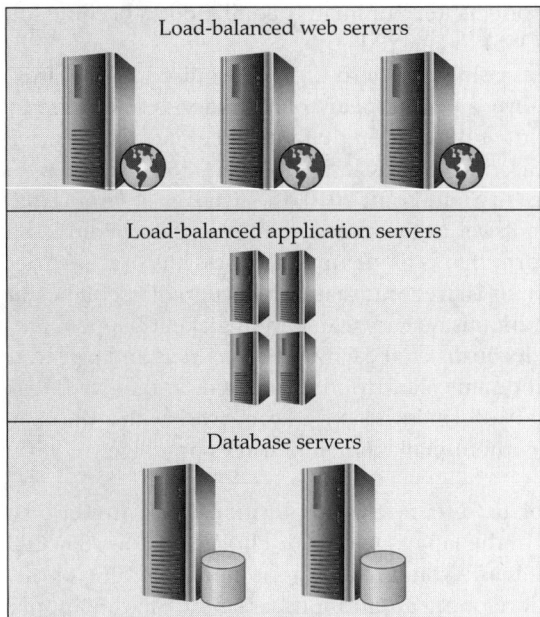

Example SharePoint 2010 Farm

Each farm can have one or more servers and can be scaled out to meet requirements. As you'll see in Chapter 9, at its most fundamental, the SharePoint platform is a collection of centrally managed services that are automatically installed and configured on the various servers within the farm. Among these services, one of the most prevalent is the web service that uses Internet Information Services (IIS) on each server to deliver the web user interface that is commonly associated with SharePoint. In Parts III and IV of this book, we'll look at a few of the additional services that are delivered via the SharePoint farm in more detail.

As well as leveraging IIS to deliver a web user interface, the SharePoint platform also makes use of Microsoft SQL Server as its primary data store. A number of separate databases are used to maintain data for each of the services on a farm; however, the global configuration for the farm itself is stored in a single database. New servers must connect to this database to be added to the farm.

# User Features

This book will focus predominantly on the developer features that are available on the SharePoint platform. To highlight how users can interact with SharePoint and therefore with any applications that are created using the SharePoint platform, let's take a brief look at the key user features.

## Office Integration

One of the key features of SharePoint from a user's perspective is the tight integration with Office applications such as Microsoft Word. This integration is even more visible in the 2010 version of these applications. Within the options in the new backstage area, shown next, users can easily share documents to SharePoint sites. Furthermore, when users create a personal site on a SharePoint farm, they can automatically set the web site as the default save location for all new documents.

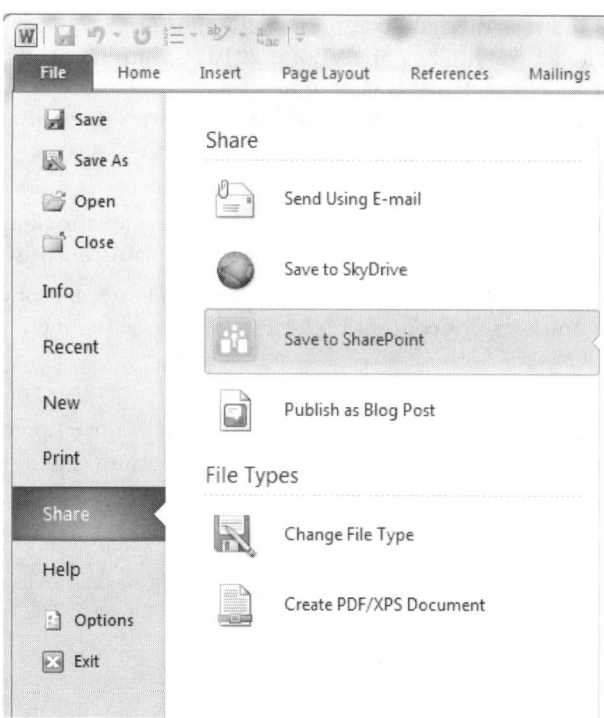

Along with file-level integration, the SharePoint 2010 platform also provides application-level integration. For example, by using Excel Services, a workbook that's been created in Excel can be published to a web site and accessed as a web page by other users, even those who don't have the Excel client application installed. The same is also true for Access databases, which can be published as fully interactive web applications, and Visio services, which allow diagrams created in Visio to be connected to business data surfaced via the SharePoint platform.

## Office Web Applications

Although not part of the standard SharePoint product, Office Web Applications can optionally be deployed as a SharePoint farm service. The Office Web Applications product provides web-based versions of Microsoft Office applications such as Word and Excel, so users can experience the same editing and presentation functionality of Office client applications without having the application installed locally.

## SharePoint Workspace

One new addition to the Microsoft Office suite is the SharePoint Workspace. As mentioned, in 2007 Microsoft acquired Groove, a peer-to-peer document collaboration tool. With SharePoint 2010, the functionality of Groove has been integrated into the SharePoint platform; the SharePoint Workspace product is a client-side tool that allows offline access to data and documents stored on a SharePoint site.

## Standards Compliant Web Interface

As well as the ability to deliver a comprehensive enterprise content management solution, the web interface presented by SharePoint 2010 is compliant with the Web Content Accessibility Guidelines 2.0 (WCAG 2.0) at level AA. The four principles of WCAG and a few examples of the features in SharePoint that address them are listed here:

### Perceivable

- A number of changes in the generated makeup for the SharePoint 2010 user interface describe content and media and explain controls.
- A new master page in SharePoint 2010 makes better use of Cascading Style Sheets (CSS) and presents content in the appropriate sequence.

### Operable

- In designing key user interface elements such as the ribbon, keyboard interaction has been a central aim to provide compatibility and usability.
- Proper heading structures have been added to pages to provide informational, organizational, and navigational benefits.

**Understandable**

- The SharePoint platform makes use of language packs to support multiple languages throughout the user interface. Using features such as variations, you can also implement business processes that ensure that user-generated content is also available in multiple languages.
- SharePoint supports browser settings to zoom content and operating system features to increase font sizes.

**Robust**

- Much of the markup produced as part of the SharePoint user interface is delivered as well-formed Extensible Markup Language (XML), greatly enhancing cross-browser support. In addition, the new rich text editor, which is used to create user content, has a function to convert its content into Extensible Hypertext Markup Language (XHTML). This ensures that user-generated data can also be used across browsers.

# Summary

This chapter has been a gentle introduction to SharePoint. You've learned what SharePoint is and where it came from and at the same time gained some understanding of how it can be used. You've also looked at how SharePoint is deployed from an infrastructure perspective as well as gained an understanding of the key user features that make SharePoint an ideal choice for many application development projects.

With this basic foundation in place, we will move on to look at how SharePoint works and, more importantly, how it can be leveraged for building custom applications.

# CHAPTER 2

# Developing with SharePoint 2010

This book is about developing applications using SharePoint 2010. That's a pretty broad definition, so I'll refine that a bit just to make it clear on where we're going. Along with the end-user role and the system administration role, there are two aspects to the SharePoint development role. First, there's the no-code, configuration-based aspect. Generally speaking, this is manifested in the web interface and to a certain extent in the capabilities of SharePoint Designer. Within this aspect, nontechnical users can build business applications by combining various platform building blocks such as web parts and out-of-the-box features. For the sake of simplicity, I'll refer to this aspect as the "SharePoint product."

In the second aspect, we developers dig a little deeper and determine how the underlying platform works so that we can create our own building blocks. This allows us to extend the functionality that's available to nontechnical users, allowing them to create applications that are more suited to the tasks at hand. We'll refer to this aspect as the "SharePoint platform."

This book's focus is the SharePoint platform. It's fair to say that to use the platform properly, we need to have some understanding of the product. As you work through this book, you'll pick up a good understanding of how the product works and what it can do, but the primary focus is on the platform.

This chapter covers the key objects in the SharePoint server object model. You'll encounter these objects in practically all of the chapters that follow, so you don't need to get to know their intimate details for now. They're covered here as a means of explaining the core SharePoint architecture from a software development perspective.

## Platform Development Tools

One of the big improvements in SharePoint 2010 is its tooling. In previous versions, platform developers were forced to rely on home-grown or community-supported tools to get any serious development efforts off the ground. Using Visual Studio 2010, developing solutions that target the SharePoint platform is much easier because of a number of new SharePoint-specific integrated development environment (IDE) tools and project templates. As you work through this book, you'll see most of these in action.

## Visual Studio 2010 and SharePoint Designer 2010

In addition to Visual Studio 2010, many improvements have been added to SharePoint Designer 2010. When it comes to doing any design work in SharePoint, SharePoint Designer has always been the way to go. Using the combination of Visual Studio and SharePoint Designer provides practically all the tools that we need to develop SharePoint platform applications.

## TypeMock Isolator

Having said that, there are still a few areas that aren't addressed by the combination of Visual Studio and SharePoint Designer. For example, when it comes to test-driven development, isolating dependencies to test custom SharePoint code can be challenging. Common practice would mandate the use of a mocking framework, but many of the classes in the SharePoint object model are sealed, making them difficult to mock. To address this particular problem, TypeMock Isolator provides a dependency isolation tool that is both integrated with Visual Studio 2010 and able to mock SharePoint sealed classes. In effect, we can write automated unit tests for SharePoint without actually touching the SharePoint platform.

## Red Gate .NET Reflector

The sheer complexity of the platform is another area where a third-party product can help, and this issue will be the source of much frustration for any developer building a complex business application on the SharePoint platform. Of course, plenty of documentation is available to help, but there will come a time when a piece of code just doesn't behave as you expected.

Experienced developers will be aware of .NET Reflector, a tool that is capable of disassembling .NET assemblies to expose their inner workings. When things don't behave as expected, the only way we can move forward is to disassemble the application binaries and try to work out what's going on. This works well, but it can be time-consuming and difficult to track what's going on in disassembled code. To make this process much easier, Red Gate provides the .NET Reflector Pro product. The product runs as an add-in to Visual Studio 2010 and allows developers to debug third-party assemblies. Or in other words, when things don't go according to plan, we can step in to the SharePoint assemblies and track down exactly where the problem lies in the same ways we use to debug our own code. I think it's fair to say that without Reflector Pro, this book would have been much shorter!

## U2U CAML Query Builder

Although I don't use a lot of it in this book, the built-in query language of the SharePoint platform is Collaborative Application Markup Language (CAML). It's covered in more detail in Part IV of the book. CAML is an XML dialect and can therefore be created using any text editor; however, sometimes the syntax and more often the field names aren't quite as straightforward as they could be. To make it easier to create CAML queries, the good people at www.u2u.be have created a free tool—the CAML Query Builder.

## Sysinternals DebugView

A lot of the code we write when developing SharePoint applications runs behind the scenes. It can be difficult to connect a debugger to the process in which much of this code runs without causing system instability. Furthermore, when an application is deployed to a farm environment, the problem is compounded by the fact that our code is running in more than one server. A few solutions to this problem are possible. The SharePoint platform provides a Unified Logging Service (ULS) that is intended to be a central source for all tracing and logging information, and this works well when tracing information needs to be included in context with other SharePoint-generated messages. The drawbacks to this approach are the relative complexity of using the ULS logs and the sheer volume of data produced in the logs. In my experience, the easiest way to debug programming errors in a complex application is to make use of Sysinternals DebugView. By simply adding Trace.Write and Debug.Write statements throughout our code, we can view the output at runtime using the DebugVew user interface.

> **NOTE** Although I use Trace.Write and Debug.Write extensively when creating SharePoint code, for the sake of brevity these statements have been removed from the code samples in this book.

SharePoint 2010 provides a few new tools that make it much easier to troubleshoot performance issues or debug code that runs in a user-initiated process such as a web page.

## Development Server Configuration

For development purposes, SharePoint 2010 can be installed on either a 64-bit Windows 7 or Windows Vista SP1 client machine or a 64-bit Windows 2008 or Windows 2008 R2 server.

> **NOTE** For full details on how to set up the development environment, see http://msdn.microsoft.com/en-us/library/ee554869.aspx.

While writing this book, I used a Windows 2008 Virtual Machine running on VMware workstation. I used the following tools:

- SharePoint Server 2010 Beta 2
- Visual Studio 2010 Beta 2 & Release Candidate
- Office 2010 Beta 2
- Visio 2010 Beta 2
- SharePoint Designer 2010 Beta 2
- Red Gate .NET Reflector Pro
- TypeMock Isolator

In Chapter 18 on Business Intelligence, I used a separate virtual machine with the same configuration and tools, except I used SQL Server 2008 R2 November CTP to enable use of PowerPivot.

## Additional Development Environment Configuration

In addition to installing the software listed previously, you'll need to take a few additional steps to follow the examples in this book.

### Defining an SPRoot Environment Variable

By performing a standard installation of SharePoint, most of the program files are installed at C:\Program Files\Common Files\Microsoft Shared\Web Server Extensions\14\. For many examples in the book, you need to add or edit these files. Rather than continually referencing the full path, you can define an environment variable that can be used as a shortcut.

Take the following steps:

1. Open a command prompt window.
2. Enter the following command:

```
setx SPROOT "C:\Program Files\Microsoft Shared\Web Server Extensions\14\
```

---

**NOTE** The omission of quotation marks at the end of the command line is intentional.

### Using Office Applications in Windows 2008 Server

Because Windows Server 2008 is not deigned to be a client operating system, some of the integration features of products such as Word 2010 don't work as you would expect. All Office 2010 applications come with a new backstage area that, among other things, allows users to publish documents easily to SharePoint document libraries. For this feature to work correctly on Windows 2008, the Desktop Experience feature must be enabled. To enable the Desktop Experience feature, take the following steps:

1. Open the Server Manager application.
2. Select the Features node, and then click the Add Features button link.
3. In the Add Features Wizard dialog, select the Desktop Experience feature.

## Debugging and Unit Testing SharePoint Applications

SharePoint 2010 is a 64-bit application. Therefore, all the code that we write that will run within SharePoint-managed processes must also be 64-bit. This detail can cause a bit of confusion, especially when you're trying to debug console applications or run automated unit tests.

To illustrate this point, suppose we have the following simple event receiver:

```
public class DemoEventReceiver : SPItemEventReceiver
    {
        public override void ItemAdding(SPItemEventProperties properties)
        {
          using (SPWeb web = properties.OpenWeb())
          {
            web.Title = "Some New Title";
            web.Update();
```

                }
            }
        }

We could create the following unit test using TypeMock Isolator:

```
[TestMethod()]
    public void ItemAddingTest()
    {
      DemoEventReceiver target = new DemoEventReceiver();
      SPItemEventProperties properties = Isolate.Fake.Instance<SPItemEventProperties>();
      using (SPSite site = new SPSite("http://sp2010dev2/"))
      {
        using (SPWeb web = site.RootWeb)
        {
          Isolate.WhenCalled(() => properties.OpenWeb()).WillReturn(web);
          target.ItemAdding(properties);
          Assert.AreEqual(web.Title, "Some New Title");
        }
      }
    }
```

When running this test within Visual Studio, a System.IO.FileNotFound exception is thrown, suggesting that the web application could not be found.

This error is misleading; if the site URL is correct, most likely the error is being thrown because we're trying to use the SharePoint object model from within a 32-bit application. Although Visual Studio supports 64-bit code, by default many projects are created in 32-bit mode, particularly console applications, as you'll see later. Also, the test runner within Visual Studio runs as a 32-bit application, meaning that unit tests cannot connect to SharePoint objects. Although you can force the test runner to use 64-bit, this uses a different test runner that runs as a .NET 4 application; as a consequence, SharePoint is not supported, since it is based on .NET 3.5.

All is not lost, however; when creating unit tests, it's generally considered good practice to isolate all dependencies, and with clever use of TypeMock, we can change our unit test as follows:

```
[TestMethod()]
    public void ItemAddingTest()
    {
      DemoEventReceiver target = new DemoEventReceiver();
      SPItemEventProperties properties = Isolate.Fake.Instance<SPItemEventProperties>();
      SPWeb fakeWeb = Isolate.Fake.Instance<SPWeb>();
      Isolate.WhenCalled(() => properties.OpenWeb()).WillReturn(fakeWeb);
      target.ItemAdding(properties);
      Assert.AreEqual(fakeWeb.Title, "Some New Title");
      Isolate.Verify.WasCalledWithAnyArguments(() => fakeWeb.Update());
    }
```

This time, the test passes as expected, because even though our code is being fully tested, since we're using mocked SharePoint objects rather than real objects, the test runner can execute our test in 32-bit mode.

## SharePoint Fundamentals

Now that you're up and running, you're ready to get into some serious development. Before we start looking at each of the functional areas in depth, let's spend a bit of time getting to know the fundamentals of the Server Object Model and the SharePoint product in general.

### Creating a Web Application

On the SharePoint platform, sites are provisioned on a farm according to a hierarchy. At the top level of the hierarchy is the *web application*. A web application is a web site in Internet Information Services 7 (IIS7), and web applications are automatically provisioned on all front-end servers within a farm. SharePoint content is stored in a content database, and when attached at the web application level, multiple content databases can exist within a single web application.

Within a SharePoint farm, most farm level configuration is performed using a Central Administration web site. As part of the SharePoint 2010 installation process, this web application will be provisioned using a random port number. However, to make it easy to find, a shortcut will be placed in the Start menu in the Microsoft SharePoint 2010 Product folder.

1. Click the SharePoint 2010 Central Administration link to open the Central Administration site.

2. From the Application Management section, select Manage Web Applications, as shown here:

3. In the Contribute section of the Web Applications tab, select New to create a new web application.

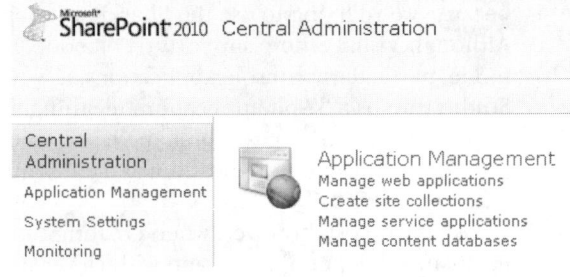

4. In the Create New Web Application dialog, select Create A New IIS Web Site and type **SP2010Dev** in the Name field. Accept the defaults for all other settings, and then click OK at the bottom of the page to create the web application.

5. After the new web application has been created, a dialog confirming success appears, as shown. Click OK to close the dialog.

## Creating a Site Collection

The next step in the site provisioning hierarchy is the *site collection*. This collection of sites exists mainly as an administrative container. Each site collection can make use of a single content database, although more than one site collection can exist in the same content database. As a result, each web application can contain many site collections spread across a number of content databases. From a backup and restore perspective, the site collection is the lowest level of granularity.

Follow these steps to create a site collection:

1. Navigate to the home page of the Central Administration site. In the Application Management section, select Create Site Collections.

2. In the Web Application drop-down, ensure that the SP2010Dev web application is selected. (This will appear as http://<servername>:<portNumber>.)

3. Type **SharePoint 2010 Demo** as the title, and then select Blank Site as the site template. Add an appropriate username in the Primary Site Collection Administrator box. Generally, this will be the username you use to log in to the server that provides full administrative privileges on all sites within the site collection.

4. Click OK to complete the process. A confirmation message will be displayed when the process has completed. Take note of the URL that is displayed for our new site collection, because you'll need it in the next example.

**New in 2010**

Although we've set out to create a site collection, we've also selected a site template and named our web site. Each site collection must have at least one root site; when we're creating a new site collection, we must also specify the details for this site. In some situations, however, the details of the root site are unknown; in such situations, you can create a site collection and allow the type of root site to be determined when the first administrative user connects. To achieve this, select the Select Template Later option in the Custom tab of the Template Selection section, as shown here:

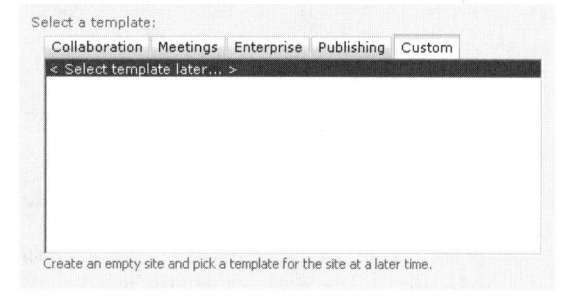

## Creating a Site

The final item in the provisioning hierarchy is the *site*. When creating a site collection, one or more sites are automatically provisioned. Each site collection must have a root site, but you can add more sites to a site collection if they are required. Furthermore, sites can also contain child sites.

Although the site collection is the lowest level of granularity in terms of backup and restore functionality, you can import or export an individual site. While import/export appears to achieve the same results as backup/restore, there are differences between these options, and backup/restore is the recommended approach when it comes to handling a significant volume of data.

Although we use the Central Administration web site to create web applications and site collections, creating web sites is performed from the root site of a site collection or via SharePoint Designer. We'll see the SharePoint Designer method in various examples in this book; for now, we'll use the root site method.

1. Connect to the URL of the site collection that we created earlier.
2. In the upper-left corner of the page, click the Site Actions menu, and then select New Site:

3. The Create dialog displays a number of different templates from which we can choose when creating our new site. For the purposes of our demonstration, select Team Site and type the Title as **Team Site** and the URL as **TeamSite**, as shown:

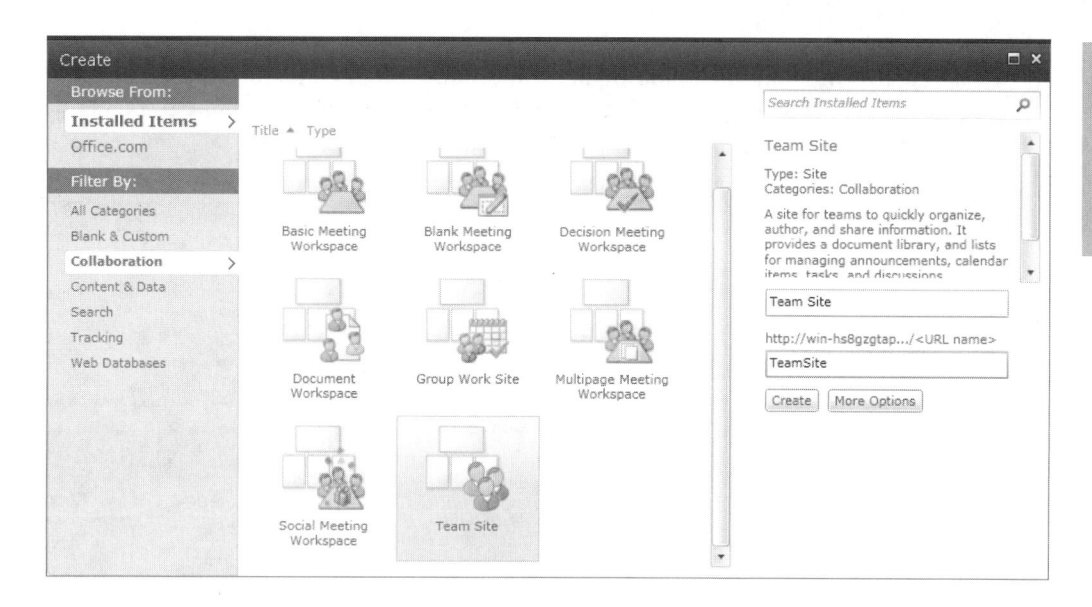

4. Click the Create button to provision the new site.

Our new site is created as a child of our site collection root site. We can add more child sites to our team site, allowing us to build a hierarchy of sites all contained within the same site collection. Next to the Site Actions button is a folder icon, and by clicking this we can view a navigation control that shows where we are within our site collection:

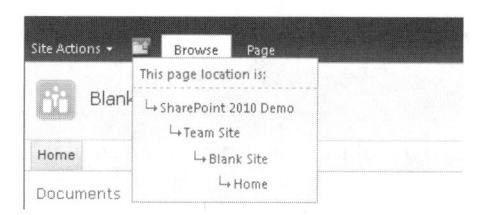

## Server Object Model

Many years ago, back when software shipped with printed manuals, I occasionally dabbled in a bit of development with Microsoft Access 2.0. Although the developers' manual that Microsoft provided with Access covered the ins and outs of the product in great detail, the thing that I found most useful was the pseudo-class diagram that was printed on the back cover. In my opinion, there's no easier way to find your way around a new object model. Bearing that in mind, the following illustration is my SharePoint 2010 hierarchy. Of course, the actual object model is far more complicated, but as a tool, this will help you get up to speed quickly.

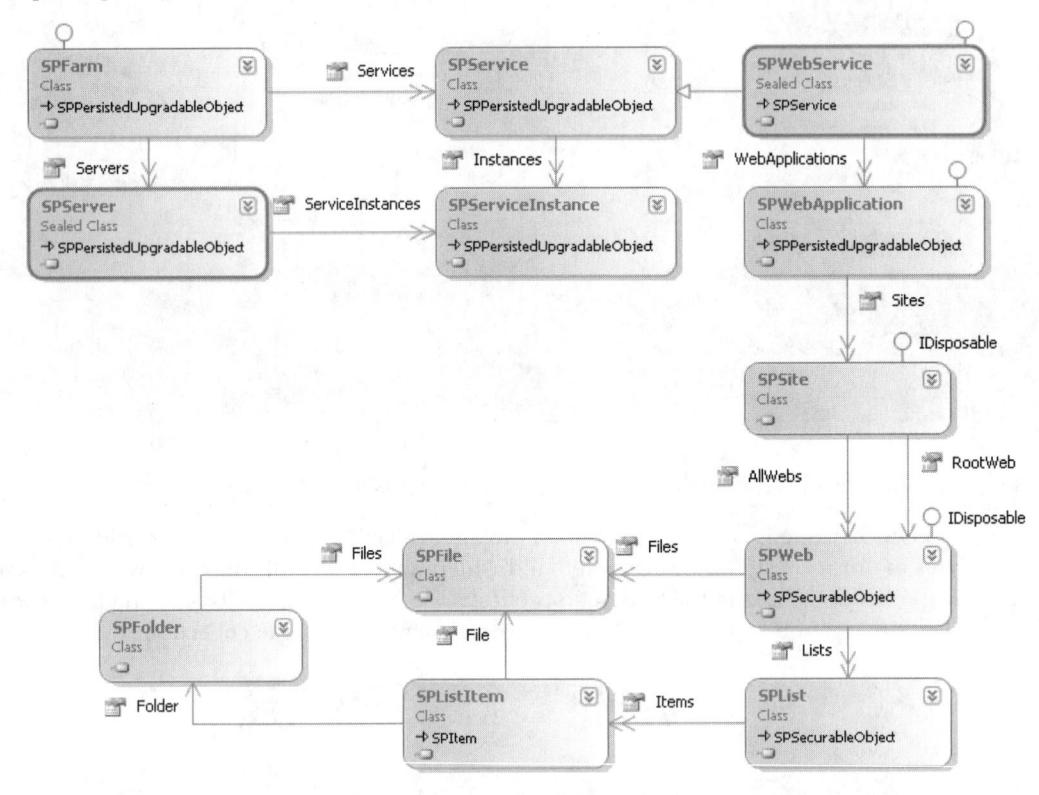

We'll work through the objects on the diagram to build an understanding of what each one represents and how you might use it in development. We'll use a console project to execute our code samples. Take the following steps:

1. In Visual Studio 2010, choose File | New | Project.
2. In the New Project dialog, select Console Application. Name the new project **Chapter2**, as shown. Ensure that the framework is set to .NET Framework 3.5. Click OK.

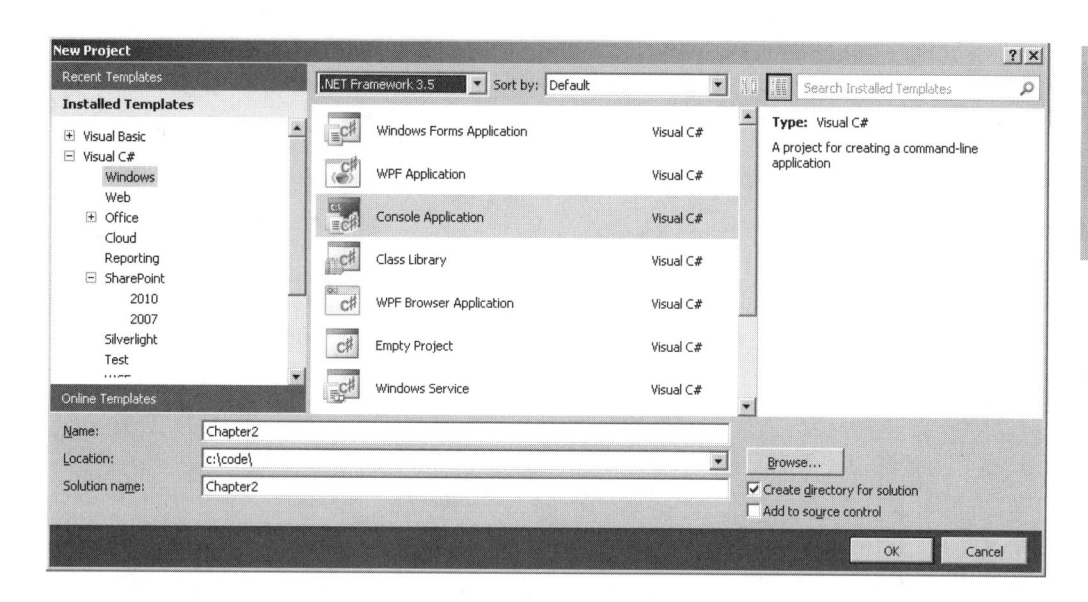

Earlier I discussed the problems that can arise when debugging and unit testing SharePoint applications due to the 64-bit nature of the SharePoint platform. Console Application projects are created with a default build configuration of x86, meaning that they will be built as 32-bit assemblies. Since these will not work when targeting SharePoint, we need to change the default build configuration.

3. In the Solution Configuration drop-down, select Configuration Manager, as shown next:

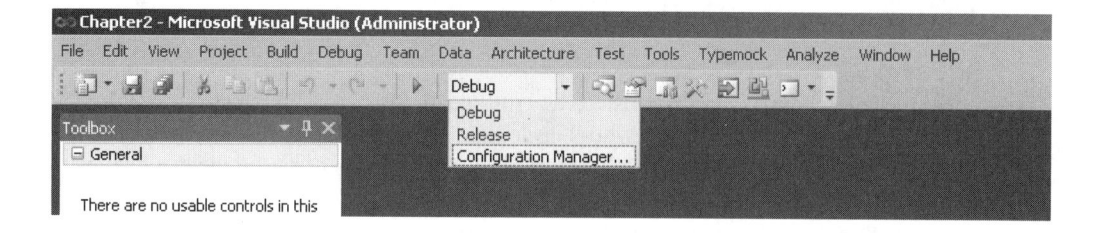

4. From the Active Solution Platform drop-down, select <New..>, and then in the New Solution Platform dialog, select x64 as the new platform, as shown:

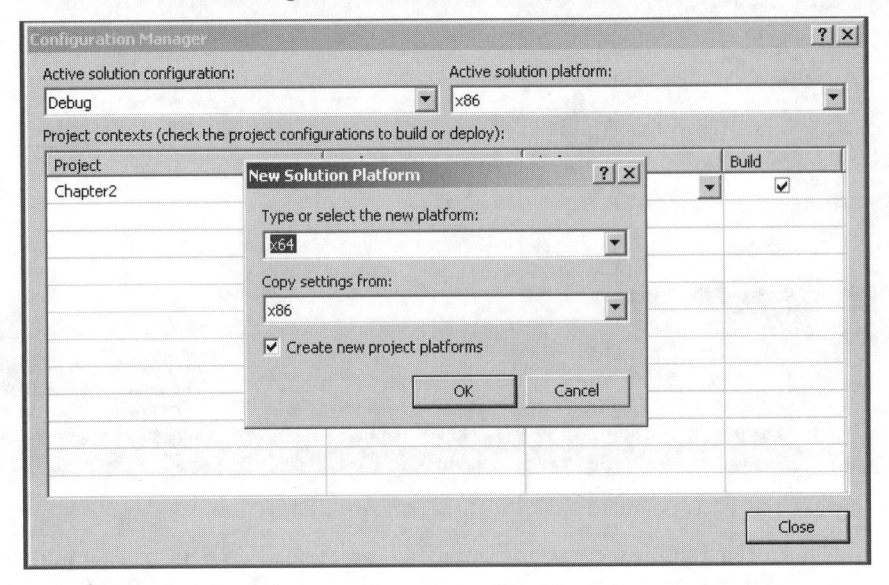

5. Close the Configuration Manager dialog to return to the project.
6. Add a reference to Microsoft.SharePoint by choosing Project | Add Reference, and then select Microsoft.SharePoint from the .NET tab.

## Administration and Configuration Classes

The following classes are generally used for administration and configuration purposes. Many of these are commonly used when implementing service applications, and you'll see this usage in more detail in Chapter 9.

### SPFarm

It will probably come as no surprise to learn that the SPFarm object represents the SharePoint farm. Server Object Model code must be executed on a server that is a member of a SharePoint farm (or on a single stand-alone server, which is effectively a farm with only one server in it), and because of this we can obtain a reference to the SPFarm object that represents the current farm by using code such as this:

```
class Program
  {
    static void Main(string[] args)
    {
      Program p = new Program();
      p.ListServersInFarm();
      Console.WriteLine("Press enter to exit...");
      Console.ReadLine();
    }
```

```
void ListServersInFarm()
{
  Console.WriteLine("Servers in farm:");
  foreach (SPServer server in SPFarm.Local.Servers)
  {
    Console.WriteLine(server.DisplayName);
  }
}
```

## SPServer

The SPServer object represents a specific server within a SharePoint farm. Again, since all Server Object Model code must run on a server within a SharePoint farm, we can pick up a reference to the current SPServer object as follows:

```
void ListServicesOnServer()
{
  Console.WriteLine("Services on local server");
  foreach (SPServiceInstance service in SPServer.Local.ServiceInstances)
  {
    Console.WriteLine(service.TypeName);
  }
}
```

## SPService

At its most fundamental, SharePoint is a platform for running services across a farm of servers. These services can include features such as Web Services, which use IIS to provide web-based content, or Search Services, which provides search functionality to other services within the farm. As you'll learn throughout this book, SharePoint Server 2010 provides many services out of the box. Within the object model, each of these services is represented by an object that derives from the SPService class.

## SPServiceInstance

Since a SharePoint farm may have many servers, each platform server may have more than one instance. The SPServiceInstance object represents an instance of a service that is running on a particular server.

## SPWebService

The SPWebService is the parent service that hosts all front-end web sites within a SharePoint farm.

# Site Provisioning and Content Access Classes

The following classes are used for programmatically provisioning sites as well as for accessing data contained within sites, lists, and libraries. These classes will be commonly used in all SharePoint development.

## SPWebApplication

As you saw earlier when we walked through the creation of a SharePoint site, the web application is the topmost object in the site provisioning hierarchy. Each web application that's configured on a SharePoint farm is represented by an SPWebApplication object in the Server Object Model:

```
void ListWebApplications()
    {
      Console.WriteLine("Web applications in farm:");
      SPWebService webService = SPFarm.Local.Services.
      OfType<SPWebService>().First();
      foreach (SPWebApplication app in webService.WebApplications)
      {
        Console.WriteLine(app.Name);
      }
    }
```

## SPSite

This is where it gets confusing! The next level in the site provisioning hierarchy is the site collection. However, within the SharePoint Object Model, each site collection is represented by an SPSite object. The SPSite object is one of the primary entry points to the Server Object Model and will be used frequently in SharePoint application development.

The following code snippet shows how to create an SPSite object explicitly. Notice that the SPSite object is defined within a using block; for reasons discussed later in this chapter, this is recommended practice whenever an SPSite object is created.

```
void ListSitesInSiteCollection()
    {
      Console.WriteLine("Sites in site collection:");
      using (SPSite site = new SPSite("YourSiteCollectionURL"))
      {
        foreach (SPWeb web in site.AllWebs)
        {
          Console.WriteLine(web.Title);
          web.Dispose();
        }
      }
    }
```

## SPWeb

Continuing with the theme of confusion, within the model, sites are represented by SPWeb objects. Although SPSite objects are the primary entry point to the model, picking up references to objects that we'll likely be writing code against will require a reference to an SPWeb object. The following code snippet shows how to obtain a reference to the root site in a site collection:

```
void ListListsInRootWeb()
    {
      Console.WriteLine("Lists in site collection root site:");
      using (SPSite site = new SPSite("YourSiteCollectionURL "))
      {
```

```
      using (SPWeb root = site.RootWeb)
      {
        foreach (SPList list in root.Lists)
        {
          Console.WriteLine(list.Title);
        }
      }
    }
  }
```

As well as explicitly creating SPWeb objects, references to the current SPWeb object can often be obtained from other sources. For example, when you're writing code that runs in the context of a web page, the static SPContext.Current property provides a reference to the current SPWeb object, as this code snippet shows:

```
SPList list = SPContext.Current.Web.Lists.TryGetList(ListName);
if (list == null)
{
  //do stuff
}
```

We'll explore retrieving SPWeb objects in this manner in some of the examples in this book.

## SPList
Most SharePoint content is stored within lists or document libraries. Within the Server Object Model, both lists and document libraries are represented by an SPList object. Although not included in our diagram, document libraries are also represented by SPDocumentLibrary objects. The SPDocumentLibrary class is derived from the SPList class and provides additional functionality that is appropriate for document libraries. Other classes are derived from SPList and represent specific types of list; for more information, see http://msdn.microsoft.com/en-us/library/microsoft.sharepoint.splist.aspx.

## SPListItem
As mentioned, most content within a SharePoint site is accessed via an SPList object. Each item in a list or library is in turn represented by an SPListItem object that is accessed via the SPList.Items collection. The SPList class and the SPListItem class will feature heavily in practically all development on the SharePoint platform. As you'll see in Chapter 4, these objects also have implementations within the Client Object Model.

## SPFile
Although almost all content is represented by an SPListItem object, where the content in question is a file, the SPListItem object only represents the metadata for the file. For example, if we create a document library and upload a Word document, the SPListItem object that represents the document will contain only the document title as well as a few additional system-generated metadata fields. To perform work on the document, we need to use an SPFile object as shown next.

```
void ListRootWebMasterPages()
    {
        Console.WriteLine("Master Page files in site collection root site:");
        using (SPSite site = new SPSite("YourSiteCollectionURL"))
        {
          using (SPWeb root = site.RootWeb)
          {
            SPList masterPages = root.Lists.TryGetList("Master Page Gallery");
            if (masterPages != null)
            {
              SPListItemCollection items = masterPages.Items;
              foreach (SPListItem fileItem in items)
              {
                SPFile file = fileItem.File;
                Console.WriteLine(file.Name + "\t" +  string.Format("{0:###,### →
bytes}",file.Length));
              }
            }
          }
        }
    }
```

## SPFolder

Most user-generated content within SharePoint sites is stored in lists and document libraries, and these document libraries can also contain folders that operate in the same way as folders in the file system. As well as folders that are used for organizing user content, other folders contain files that are used by the SharePoint platform itself. These files often contain configuration files for platform elements such as content types.

The following code snippet shows how to enumerate folders within a SharePoint site. Folders used for organizational purposes have an attached DocumentLibrary object, whereas system folders do not.

```
void ListRootWebFolders()
{
  Console.WriteLine("Files in site collection root site:");
  using (SPSite site = new SPSite("YourSiteCollectionURL"))
  {
    using (SPWeb root = site.RootWeb)
    {
      listFolders(root.Folders);
    }
  }
}
void listFolders(SPFolderCollection folders)
{
  foreach (SPFolder folder in folders)
  {
    Console.Write(folder.Name + "\t");
    if (folder.DocumentLibrary != null)
    {
      Console.WriteLine("Corresponding library: " + folder.DocumentLibrary.Title);
    }
    else
```

```
    {
      Console.WriteLine(string.Empty);
    }
    listFolders(folder.SubFolders);
  }
}
```

## Saving Changes Using the Server Object Model

Behind the scenes, SharePoint, like many enterprise applications, stores all data within a database. Many of the objects that we've seen are actually an in-memory copy of the state of a particular component, and as a result, changing properties on the object affects only the in-memory copy and not the underlying database. To commit object changes to the database, the **Update** method should be called, as this snippet shows:

```
void UpdateDescription()
    {
      Console.WriteLine("Lists in site collection root site:");
      using (SPSite site = new SPSite("YourSiteColectionURL"))
      {
        using (SPWeb root = site.RootWeb)
        {
          root.Description = "My New Description";
          root.Update();
        }
      }
    }
```

## Best Practice Guidelines

We've covered most of the commonly used objects in the Server Object Model. However, you should bear in mind a few caveats when using these objects. You'll see these practices in most of the examples in this book, so there's no need to dig too deeply into this stuff right now. This section provides a bit of background on the most significant coding practices that you should adopt when working with the SharePoint platform.

### IDisposable

Probably the most important thing to remember is that some of the objects that we've covered here implement the IDisposable interface, as you can see from the hierarchical diagram shown earlier. There is a very good reason for the objects to implement this interface specifically: these objects hold a reference to an SPRequest object, which in turn holds a reference to a COM component. The SharePoint platform uses the COM component to communicate with SQL Server. By implementing IDisposable, these objects can explicitly close the connection to the database and properly clean up the COM component when the .NET Framework objects are no longer required.

So what can we do to ensure that objects are disposed of properly? As a general rule, best practice is to wrap all IDisposable objects in a using block; you can see this technique used in the earlier examples. However, there are exceptions to this rule. On many occasions,

IDisposable objects are passed into a function or are otherwise automatically created by the SharePoint platform. For example, the following code samples use a reference to an IDisposable object that was created by the platform:

```
private void UseSPContext(string myList)
{
  SPList list = SPContext.Current.Web.Lists.TryGetList(myList);
  if (list == null)
  {
    //Do Something
  }
}
```

When creating event handlers (covered in Chapter 8), the **properties** parameter contains a reference to the SPWeb object that has raised the event:

```
public override void ItemUpdating(SPItemEventProperties properties)
{
  string title = properties.Web.Title;
}
```

For situations in which the IDisposable object is created elsewhere, it is not appropriate to dispose of it explicitly since this could cause problems elsewhere.

## Performance

A few common coding practices can lead to performance problems when you're developing SharePoint applications. In addition to the IDisposable issues, which are by far the most common, most other problems relate to the proper use of data access.

You've seen how the SPList and SPListItem classes can be used to retrieve and represent data from a SharePoint content database. However, the SPListItem object is relatively heavyweight and as a result, if we retrieve the contents of a list that contains many items, the resource implications are significant. As you'll see later in this book, the SharePoint platform incorporates throttling to ensure that such resource usage can be managed from an administrative perspective. However, best practice mandates that when retrieving data from a list, we should be specific about how much data we need.

The following code sample shows how we can use the SPQuery object to restrict the number of rows returned and then page through the items in a list. As you'll see in Part IV, we can also make use of a CAML query to restrict even further the size of the dataset returned to include specific fields only or rows that meet specific criteria.

```
SPQuery query = new SPQuery();
query.RowLimit = 20;
do
{
  SPListItemCollection items = myList.GetItems(query);
  //Use the items
  query.ListItemCollectionPosition = items.ListItemCollectionPosition;
} while (query.ListItemCollectionPosition != null);
```

Another common coding pattern that can cause performance issues is demonstrated in this code snippet:

```
SPList masterPages = root.Lists.TryGetList("Master Page Gallery");
if (masterPages != null)
   {
   foreach (SPListItem fileItem in masterPages.Items)
      {
        SPFile file = fileItem.File;
        Console.WriteLine(file.Name);
      }
}
```

Although this code works properly and would probably be our first choice when iterating through a collection of list items, behind the scenes, the implementation to the SPList object makes this a common cause of performance problems. Each time the Items collection is referenced, the underlying SPWeb object makes a call to the SQL database to retrieve the list of items. So if we imagine a list with 2000 items, iterating through the list using this code would generate 2000 database calls with each one returning 2000 rows. If a few users were performing the same actions at the same time, you can see how this quickly would become a major performance drain.

Thankfully, the problem is easy to fix:

```
SPList masterPages = root.Lists.TryGetList("Master Page Gallery");
if (masterPages != null)
   {
   SPListItemCollection items = masterPages.Items;
   foreach (SPListItem fileItem in items)
      {
        SPFile file = fileItem.File;
        Console.WriteLine(file.Name);
      }
}
```

By assigning the Items property to a SPListItemCollection variable and then using that as the target of our iteration, we're generating only a single database query when the SPListItemCollection is assigned.

## Error Handling

In the examples in this book, I've left error handling and boundary checking code out for the sake of brevity. Of course, in real-world code, we'd add these things and create suitable unit tests to validate their functionality. To make it possible for us to filter SharePoint specific errors in try/catch blocks, all SharePoint exceptions are derived from the SPException class.

Earlier we looked at Sysinternals DebugView as a tool to assist in debugging problems in server-side code. Although we could use this as an error logging tool, SharePoint provides a better way to achieve the same result. Using code similar to the following sample, we can write error logging entries to the SharePoint Unified Logging Service (ULS) logs:

```
try
  {
    //some code
  }
  catch (Exception ex)
  {
    SPDiagnosticsCategory myCat=new SPDiagnosticsCategory("A new category",
                                                TraceSeverity.Monitorable,
                                                EventSeverity.Error);
    SPDiagnosticsService.Local.WriteEvent(1, myCat,
                                EventSeverity.Error,
                                "My custom message",
                                ex.StackTrace);
  }
```

## Developer Toolbar

**New in 2010** A new addition to SharePoint 2010 is the Developer Toolbar. The easiest way to understand what the Developer Toolbar does is to see it in action. At the time of writing, the only way to activate the Developer Dashboard is via PowerShell or the STSADM tool. Since STSADM is being phased out as a mechanism for managing SharePoint, we'll use the PowerShell method:

1. From the Start menu, choose SharePoint 2010 Management Shell from the Microsoft SharePoint 2010 Products menu.

2. Type the following PowerShell commands at the prompt:

   ```
   $dash = [Microsoft.SharePoint.Administration.→
   SPWebService]::ContentService.DeveloperDashboardSettings;
   $dash.DisplayLevel = 'OnDemand';
   $dash.TraceEnabled = $true;
   $dash.Update()
   ```

   Using this script, we're setting the Developer Dashboard to OnDemand mode; other possible options are On and Off.

3. Now if we navigate to the demo site that we created earlier, we can see that a new icon has appeared in the upper-right corner, as shown next. Clicking this icon enables or disables the Developer Dashboard.

   — Click this icon to enable or disable the Developer Dashboard.

With the Developer Dashboard enabled, you can see that every page now has additional information appended to the bottom, as shown. You can use this information to track errors that have occurred during page processing as well as resource usage and other important metrics.

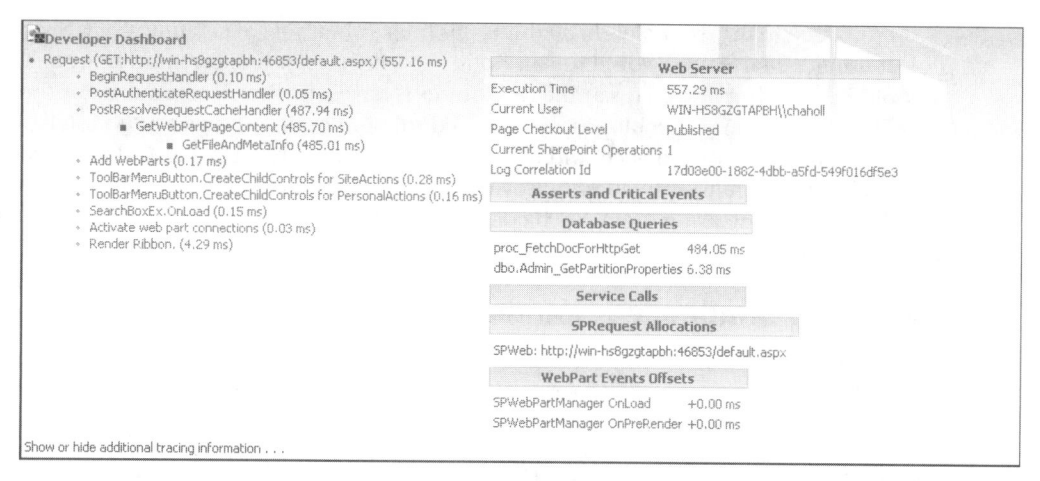

![Developer Dashboard screenshot showing request details, web server info, database queries, service calls, SPRequest allocations, and WebPart events offsets]

Another important feature of the Developer Dashboard is that it allows developers to write custom tracing information to it. Although I mentioned that DebugView is an important tool for debugging complex applications, when it comes to debugging and diagnosing problems at the user-interface level, the Developer Dashboard provides much more information and is therefore a better solution. Where DebugView proves useful is in debugging issues that don't occur in the user interface—for example, issues in workflows or asynchronous event handlers (more on these in later chapters).

Monitoring information from code that is wrapped within a SPMonitoredScope object, as shown, is written to the ULS logs as well as being visible from the Developer Dashboard. As a result, using SPMonitoredScope is a good way to generate tracing information that can be used by administrators to troubleshoot problems on a production system.

```
using (new SPMonitoredScope("My monitored scope"))
{
   //Code to be monitored
}
```

## Sandboxed Solutions

**New in 2010**

One of the most common causes of system instability in SharePoint farms is custom code. As you've seen in a few of the examples in this chapter, it's pretty easy to make coding errors that can quickly destroy the performance of a server. To provide administrators with more control over the custom code that runs on a farm, SharePoint 2010 introduces the concept of a *sandboxed solution*. As the name suggests, a sandboxed solution is a custom code solution that runs in an isolated sandbox. From an administrative perspective, a number of configurable options are available for sandboxed solutions, such as specifying resource quotas and monitoring performance. These options are beyond the scope of this book, but, from our perspective as developers, we need to know a few things about sandboxed solutions.

Sandboxed solutions run in a separate process, whereas other types of solutions run directly within the appropriate SharePoint process. In addition to running in a separate process, sandboxed solutions can utilize only a subset of the SharePoint Object Model. A custom code access security (CAS) policy is applied to prevent sandboxed code from performing actions that could jeopardize system stability.

As you'll see in the examples throughout this book, when you're creating a new SharePoint project using Visual Studio, you'll see an option to select a sandboxed solution or a farm solution. Bearing in mind that sandboxed solutions have access only to a subset of the SharePoint API, when you deploy as a sandboxed solution option, Visual Studio IntelliSense displays assistance only for objects and members that are available. Having said that, there is a catch: although IntelliSense doesn't provide assistance for inaccessible members, it is still possible to write code using them. Such code will compile and deploy fine but will throw an error at runtime.

### Debugging Sandboxed Solutions

As mentioned, sandboxed solutions run under a separate process. To debug such solutions, you need to connect to the SPUCWorkerProcess.exe process manually using the Debug | Attach to Process option in Visual Studio.

### Managing Sandboxed Solutions

Sandboxed solutions are managed from the Solutions Gallery, which is maintained at the site collection level. To access the Solutions Gallery from any site, take the following steps:

1. From the Site Actions menu, select Site Settings.
2. On the Site Settings page, if it's available, select Go To Top Level Site Settings.
3. Click the Solutions link in the Galleries section.

## Summary

This chapter laid a lot of the groundwork for a more in-depth exploration of the SharePoint development platform. As you work through the samples in this book, we'll make use of the techniques and tools that have been briefly described here. Above all else, you should remember two important points in this chapter:

- An SPSite object represents a site collection, and an SPWeb object represents a site.
- Always dispose of SPSite and SPWeb objects properly. If you created it, you need to explicitly dispose of it.

# PART II

# Presentation Layer

**CHAPTER 3**
Presentation Layer Overview

**CHAPTER 4**
Client Object Model

**CHAPTER 5**
InfoPath Forms Services

**CHAPTER 6**
Enterprise Content Management

**CHAPTER 7**
User Interface Customization

# CHAPTER 3

# Presentation Layer Overview

When it comes to software development, it's often the user's experience that makes or breaks an application. The SharePoint platform allows both business and technical users to build bespoke business applications using a range of tools, from Visual Studio, to the web browser. To enable this degree of flexibility, the SharePoint platform offers a highly configurable user interface—from standard ASP.NET development techniques such as master pages and web parts, to more advanced techniques such as page templates, delegate controls, and the rich-client flexibility provided by the Client Object Model.

We'll take a look at all of these technologies in detail. You'll see how and when each should be used to deliver the desired results. This chapter starts by taking a look at the main elements of the SharePoint 2010 user interface. You'll learn how pages are constructed and the different types of pages that are delivered using the SharePoint platform before we move on to examine the architecture of the new ribbon interface.

## Page Types

The SharePoint presentation layer is delivered using a virtual path provider that forwards requests to the SharePoint server object model for processing. As part of the processing pipeline, content is either retrieved from an appropriate database or loaded from disk. Often, the final output is a combination of the two. Bearing this processing model in mind, we can broadly group the content delivered by the SharePoint presentation layer into two groups: application pages and site pages.

### Application Pages

Application pages are loaded from disk and usually provide common user interface functionality such as site administration and configuration tools. Application pages can be found in the file system at %SPRoot%\Template\Layouts. To facilitate the sharing of application pages among sites, this folder is mounted on every web site as http://<web site url>/_layouts.

## Site Pages

Site pages are often loaded from a content database and include all other pages that are not included in the application pages group. All user-generated content is delivered using site pages. Although site pages are often loaded from a content database, when sites are created from a site definition or pages are added to a site by feature activation, the default version of the page is usually loaded from the file system. A common example of this is the default master page that is provisioned for each site. In reality, this page exists in the file system as v4.master, but the provisioning process mounts the file as default.master in the master pages gallery for each site.

Within the site pages group are a few types of site pages: web part pages, standard pages, master pages, and page templates.

### Web Part Pages

The functionality and user interface delivered via web part pages predominantly comprise web part zones that users can populate with web parts. A *web part* is a server control that users can add to a web part page using a browser-based interface. Web parts allow users to customize and configure a page without having to resort to developer tools such as Visual Studio. We'll look at web parts in more detail in Chapter 7.

Keep in mind that although site pages are loaded from a database, web parts and their user interfaces are not. Only the configuration of the web part is stored in the database. Commonly, a web part is installed on each web server and is loaded in much the same way as any server control. Much of the user interface functionality of the SharePoint platform is implemented via web parts, and as a result, most of the pages that are provided out of the box fall into the web part page category.

### Standard Pages

All other types of web pages delivered by the SharePoint platform can be considered standard pages. For all intents and purposes, a standard page is equivalent to a page that could be created using any web design tool. Commonly, standard pages use SharePoint master pages to include common user interface elements such as navigation, but this is not a requirement. We'll look at how pages are constructed in more detail in Chapters 6 and 7.

### Master Pages

We'll look at master pages in more depth in Chapter 7. Essentially, the master pages that are used by SharePoint 2010 are the same as any other ASP.NET master pages—except to support some of the built-in functionality, SharePoint master pages must include a number of specific placeholders.

### Page Templates

Page templates are an essential part of the Enterprise Content Management (ECM) functionality of SharePoint 2010. You construct content pages by using a page template to define the positioning and presentation of data that is retrieved from individual fields in a document library. We'll look at this in more detail in Chapter 6.

## Ghosting/Unghosting

As you've seen, two main page types are featured in SharePoint: application pages that are rendered from the file system, and content pages that are usually rendered from the database. However, pages are often rendered using a number of additional files such as master pages or page templates. Some of these components, while mounted in document libraries, are actually being loaded from the local file system.

When changes are made to these files using SharePoint Designer, the changed page content is stored within the content database. As a result, all future renderings of the page will be retrieved from the content database. Site pages that are loaded from the file system are known as *ghosted* pages, and when these pages have been customized they are known as *unghosted* pages.

With each new version of SharePoint comes another set of terms for this phenomenon. SharePoint 2003 brought us *ghosting/unghosting*; SharePoint 2007 scrapped these terms in favor of the more descriptive *uncustomized/customized*. Now with SharePoint 2010, the terms *attached* and *detached* are used to prevent any ambiguity. In most SharePoint documentation, the terms *ghosted/unghosted* are still in use, however.

In SharePoint 2010, a few new tools enable administrators and developers to better manage ghosted/unghosted pages. When editing pages, SharePoint Designer now loads the page content in safe mode by default. In this mode, parts of the page that are loaded from the file system are highlighted and can't be edited. To make changes to these regions, you must work in Advanced mode. You'll see this in action in the various samples throughout this book. From an administrative point of view, it is now possible to disable the ability for users to enter Advanced mode in SharePoint Designer and therefore prevent pages from being unghosted.

## Executing Server-Side Code

Another difference between site pages and application pages is the way they are parsed by the SharePoint platform. Application pages behave like any other ASP.NET page in that they can contain inline server-side code; however, site pages are rendered using the safe mode parser that prevents inline server-side code from executing. This makes sense when you think about it, because site pages are commonly user-generated, and allowing inline server-side code to execute would present a major system stability risk.

If this were the whole story, SharePoint would be somewhat limited as a development platform. Of course, functionality can be implemented in the form of web parts, and although this is commonly the best approach, in some situations it's vital to be able to handle the various events within the ASP.NET page rendering process—for example, when you want to change the master page dynamically.

Two solutions are possible to this problem: the first solution, which is recommended only in exceptional circumstances, is to add a **PageParserPath** entry to the web.config file, like this:

```
<SharePoint>
   <SafeMode ...>
   <PageParserPaths>
```

```
<PageParserPath VirtualPath="/myFiles/*" CompilationMode="Always"
        AllowServerSideScript="true" IncludeSubFolders="true"/>
</PageParserPaths>
```

Be careful when you're adopting this approach, because it effectively allows users to execute arbitrary code on the server.

A better approach is to create a code-behind class and deploy it to the farm. You can then change the **Page** directive for any page to refer to the code-behind file, as shown:

```
<%@ Page language="C#" MasterPageFile="~masterurl/default.master"
        Inherits="MyAssembly.MyClass,MyAssembly"  %>
```

1. Using SharePoint Designer, create a new blank site at the URL *http://<Your server name>/Chapter3*.

2. From the Site tab, select Document Library | Document Library. Name the new library MyCustomPages.

3. Using Visual Studio, choose File | New | Project. Then select Empty SharePoint Project from the New Project dialog, as shown. Name the project Chapter3.

4. Set the site to use for debugging to the blank site that we set up in step 1. Select the Deploy As Farm Solution option.

5. After the project has been created, choose Project | Add New Item. Add a new Module named MyCustomPages, as shown:

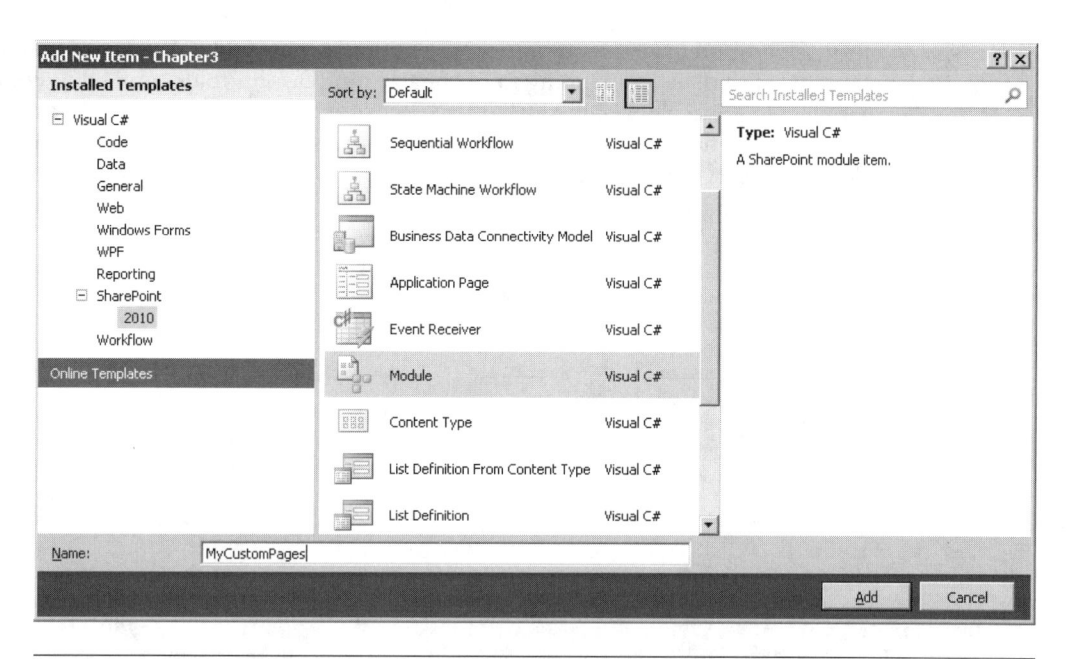

**TIP** Modules can be used to deploy files to SharePoint. This is covered in more detail in Chapter 19.

6. At the time of writing, no template is available for creating site pages with code-behind, and when using a SharePoint project, standard ASP.NET pages are not available in the Add New Item dialog. To get around this limitation, we'll add an application page and then modify it to suit our needs. Choose Project | Add New Item. Select Application Page and name the file MyCustomPage.aspx, as shown:

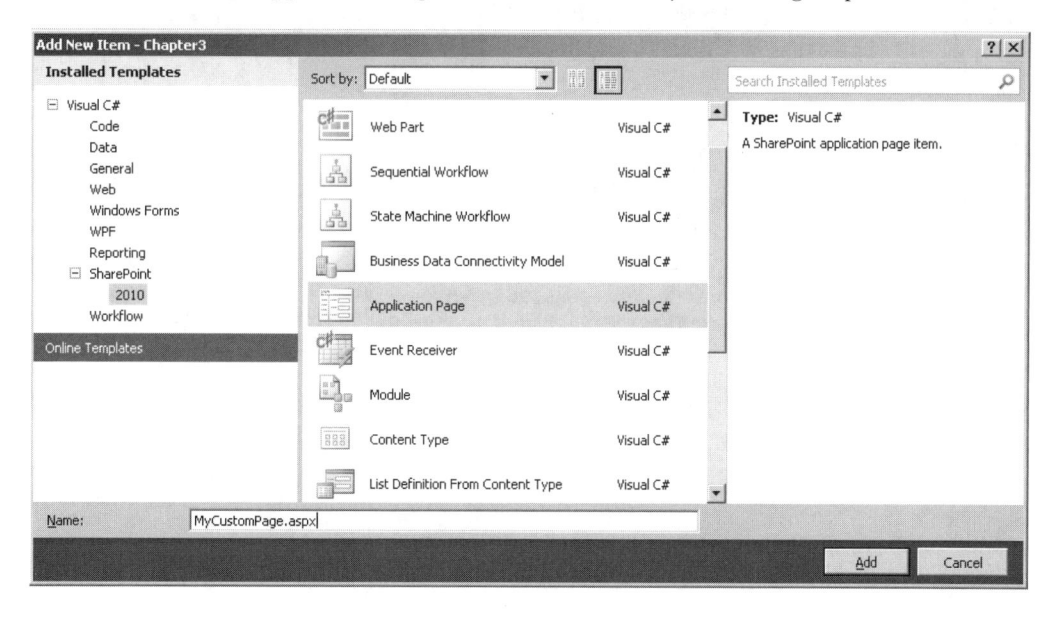

7. Since application pages are always located in the Layouts folder, Visual Studio has automatically created a mapping to the SharePoint Layouts folder and added our new page to a subfolder named Chapter3. Because we're creating a site page rather than an application page, drag the MyCustomPage.aspx file into the MyCustomPages folder, and then delete the Layouts folder since it's no longer required.

8. In the MyCustomPage.aspx file, add the following markup:

```
<%@ Assembly Name="$SharePoint.Project.AssemblyFullName$" %>
<%@ Import Namespace="Microsoft.SharePoint.ApplicationPages" %>
<%@ Register TagPrefix="SharePoint"
    Namespace="Microsoft.SharePoint.WebControls"
    Assembly="Microsoft.SharePoint, Version=14.0.0.0, Culture=neutral,
PublicKeyToken=71e9bce111e9429c" %>
<%@ Register TagPrefix="WebPartPages"
         Namespace="Microsoft.SharePoint.WebPartPages"
         Assembly="Microsoft.SharePoint, Version=14.0.0.0, Culture=neutral, →
PublicKey  Token=71e9bce111e9429c" %>
<%@ Register TagPrefix="Utilities"
         Namespace="Microsoft.SharePoint.Utilities"
         Assembly="Microsoft.SharePoint, Version=14.0.0.0, Culture=neutral, →
PublicKeyToken=71e9bce111e9429c" %>
<%@ Register TagPrefix="asp" Namespace="System.Web.UI"
       Assembly="System.Web.Extensions, Version=3.5.0.0, Culture=neutral, →
PublicKeyToken=31bf3856ad364e35" %>
<%@ Import Namespace="Microsoft.SharePoint" %>
<%@ Assembly Name="Microsoft.Web.CommandUI, Version=14.0.0.0, Culture=neutral, →
PublicKeyToken=71e9bce111e9429c" %>
<%@ Page Language="C#" AutoEventWireup="true"
      CodeBehind="MyCustomPage.aspx.cs" Inherits="Chapter3.MyCustomPage"
      MasterPageFile="~masterurl/default.master" %>
<asp:Content ID="PageHead"
          ContentPlaceHolderID="PlaceHolderAdditionalPageHead"
          runat="server">
</asp:Content>
<asp:Content ID="Main" ContentPlaceHolderID="PlaceHolderMain"
          runat="server">
   <asp:TextBox ID="TitleText" runat="server"/>
<asp:Button ID="Button1" runat="server" Text="Change Title" OnClick="Button1_OnClick"/>
    <table width="100%" cellpadding="0" cellspacing="0" →
         style="padding: 5px 10px 10px 10px;">
       <tr>
          <td valign="top" width="70%">
             <WebPartPages:WebPartZone runat="server"
                   FrameType="TitleBarOnly" ID="Left" Title="loc:Left">
                <ZoneTemplate>
                </ZoneTemplate>
             </WebPartPages:WebPartZone>
              
          </td>
          <td>
              
          </td>
          <td valign="top" width="30%">
```

```xml
            <WebPartPages:WebPartZone runat="server"
                FrameType="TitleBarOnly" ID="Right" Title="loc:Right">
              <ZoneTemplate>
              </ZoneTemplate>
            </WebPartPages:WebPartZone>
             
        </td>
        <td>
             
        </td>
      </tr>
    </table>
</asp:Content>
<asp:Content ID="PageTitle" ContentPlaceHolderID="PlaceHolderPageTitle"
            runat="server">
    My Custom Page
</asp:Content>
<asp:Content ID="PageTitleInTitleArea"
            ContentPlaceHolderID="PlaceHolderPageTitleInTitleArea"
    runat="server">
    <asp:Label ID="MyLabel" runat="server" Text=""></asp:Label>
</asp:Content>
```

9. In the MyCustomPage.aspx.cs file, add the following code:

```csharp
using System;
using Microsoft.SharePoint;
using Microsoft.SharePoint.WebControls;
using Microsoft.SharePoint.WebPartPages;
namespace Chapter3
{
  public partial class MyCustomPage : WebPartPage
  {
    protected void Page_Load(object sender, EventArgs e)
    {
      MyLabel.Text = "Hello World";
    }

    protected void Button1_OnClick(object sender, EventArgs args)
    {
      MyLabel.Text = TitleText.Text;
    }
  }
}
```

10. Since we're deploying our page to a document library, we need to make a few modifications to the Elements.xml file in the MyCustomPages folder. Change the XML as follows:

```xml
<?xml version="1.0" encoding="utf-8"?>
<Elements xmlns="http://schemas.microsoft.com/sharepoint/">
  <Module Name="MyCustomPages"  Url="MyCustomPages">
    <File Path="MyCustomPages\MyCustomPage.aspx" Url="MyCustomPage.aspx"
        Type="GhostableInLibrary" />
  </Module>
</Elements>
```

11. We can now build and deploy the project to SharePoint. Choose Build | Deploy.

12. Using the browser, navigate to http://<your server url>/Chapter3/MyCustomPages/MyCustomPage.aspx to see the results:

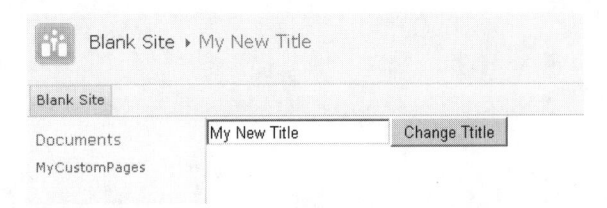

13. Click the Change Title button to modify the title that's displayed on the page, confirming that our code-behind works as expected.

If we select Edit Page from the Page tab, we'll also be able to add web parts to our page. In fact, reviewing the options available on the Page tab, we can see that our custom page effectively behaves in the same way as any other site page, allowing us to set permissions or execute workflows.

# Mobile Pages

**New in 2010**

The ability to render appropriately formatted content for mobile devices is one of the significant improvements in SharePoint 2010. With SharePoint 2007, mobile device users could access mobile versions of a site by appending /_m/ to the page URL. For example, http://mysite/mylist becomes http://mysite/mylist/_m/. With SharePoint 2010, this manual modification of URLs is no longer necessary. Instead, a custom HttpModule component, SPRequestModule, picks up all requests and redirects mobile browsers automatically to an appropriate version of a page. From a development perspective, not much work is involved in providing content for mobile devices.

> **NOTE** While it is possible to implement custom mobile pages, such development is specialist in nature and in-depth coverage is not provided in this chapter. For information on mobile pages, see http://msdn.microsoft.com/en-us/library/ms462572.aspx.

# Ribbon

**New in 2010**

With SharePoint 2010, the biggest single change from a user interface perspective is the introduction of the ribbon. With previous versions, controls and menus were spread between a few components. For example, the ListViewWebPart, which was commonly used to display list data, included its own menu system. However, when it came to managing publishing pages, a separate page editing toolbar was used. With SharePoint 2010, both of these features are delivered via the ribbon, providing a continuity of user experience between SharePoint and other Microsoft Office products.

## Ribbon Architecture

To set the stage for further discussion on how the ribbon can be customized, let's take a look at the underlying architecture and the elements that are involved.

For the most part, the ribbon is defined using XML with client functionality being provided via JavaScript. Most of the functionality for the ribbon as it operates out of the box can be found in a number of files: the client-side script is contained in the file %SPROOT%\TEMPLATE\LAYOUTS\CUI.js, with the majority of the configuration being found in %SPROOT%\TEMPLATE\GLOBAL\XML\CMDUI.XML. An examination of the configuration file reveals the key elements that make up the ribbon:

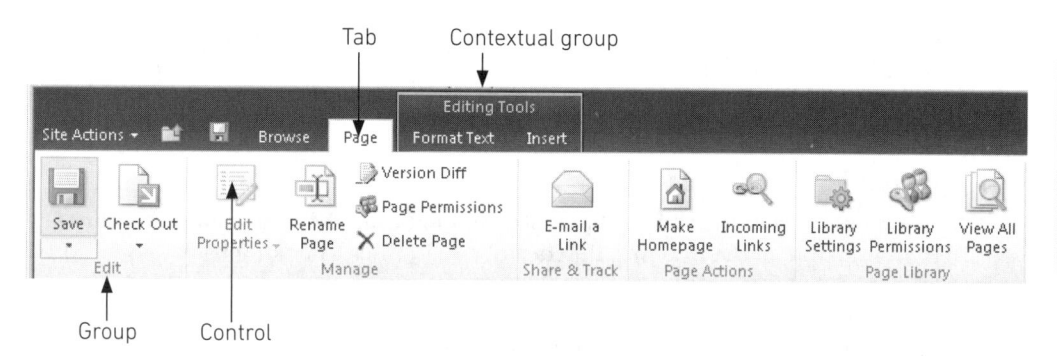

## Tabs
The ribbon uses tabs to show or hide groups of controls. Tabs generally refer to a particular functional area, and their visibility can be programmatically toggled so as to reduce the number of irrelevant options presented to users. Visibility can only be toggled for tabs; you can't hide an individual control or group of controls within a tab. This is a key design element of the ribbon because it helps to reduce user confusion by ensuring that the same controls always appear in the same place.

## Groups
Each tab can contain many controls. So that these controls can be further grouped into logical categories, individual controls must exist within a group.

## Templates
Groups make use of templates to determine the placement of individual controls within a group. These templates can be shared between groups and assist in providing a consistent user experience.

## Controls
Controls are the lowest level of user interface element that can be added to the ribbon. The types of controls are well-defined and cannot be extended; this ensures consistency of user experience. Some of the most commonly used controls include buttons, checkboxes, and drop-downs. A few task-specific controls include a color picker and an insert table control that displays a grid that can be used to specify the dimensions of a table.

## Contextual Tabs
In addition to the preceding components that are the basis of the ribbon user interface, you'll also see contextual elements such as ContextualTabs and ContextualGroup. As mentioned, tabs can be hidden when not required. However, one of the design principles behind the ribbon is that commands should be easily discoverable. As a result, tabs should

not be hidden in real time. For example, if a tab contains controls for editing images, the tab should not be hidden when no images appear on the page.

Although this makes sense from a command discoverability perspective, it also means that sometimes more tabs are available than are absolutely necessary. To get around this problem, the ribbon includes the contextual group, which can contain tabs that should be visible only if a specific action is performed in the user interface. To use our image example, if the user selects an image on the page, the Image Editing Tools contextual group becomes visible, giving access to the required tabs. The difference between using tabs within a contextual group and standard tabs is that a contextual group highlights the fact that the tabs have been added and includes a group name that helps users to establish the context of the tabs.

## Scaling

One other aspect of the ribbon that is also defined using XML is scaling. Another key design principle of the ribbon is the idea of spaciousness. Looking back to older products such as Excel 95, recall that the user interface consisted of many square buttons, each with a different icon. For users familiar with the product, this didn't present an issue because they understood what the icon meant; for new users, these aspects of the user interface meant a steep learning curve. The spaciousness of the ribbon allows as much descriptive information to be added to a control as possible. Rather than using a small button with an icon, a larger button with a more illustrative icon and a text description of the command are used. For new users, this makes life much easier.

To provide user interface designers with control over how commands are represented when the ribbon is resized, each tab must define scaling rules for each group within the tab. This allows user interface designers to prioritize certain commands at the expense of others if space is limited on the page. You can see this at work by navigating to a SharePoint page that contains a number of commands in the ribbon and then resizing the browser window. Generally speaking, the controls on the right side of the page will reduce in size, and the controls in the first group will retain their presentation.

## Extending the Ribbon

You can add controls to the ribbon in a few ways: you can either add the controls declaratively using an elements file, or you can programmatically add controls using custom code. Let's look at how to add a custom tab declaratively.

1. Use the Chapter3 project file that we created earlier. Choose Project | Add New Item. From the Add New Item dialog, select Empty Element. Name the item MyNewTab, as shown:

2. Add the following code to the Elements.xml file in the MyNewTab folder:

```xml
<?xml version="1.0" encoding="utf-8"?>
<Elements xmlns="http://schemas.microsoft.com/sharepoint/">
  <CustomAction Id="Chapter3.CustomTab" Location="CommandUI.Ribbon"
                RegistrationType="List" RegistrationId="101">
  </CustomAction>
</Elements>
```

**CustomAction** elements are used to add command buttons and other elements to the user interface. The **Location** attribute dictates where the commands will be added. Since our custom tab will be added to the ribbon, we've used the location CommandUI.Ribbon.

**TIP** For a complete list of locations, see http://msdn.microsoft.com/en-us/library/bb802730.aspx.

**CustomActions** can optionally be bound to list types; in our example, we're using type 101, which refers to the Document Library list type. You can also bind a custom action to a specific content type. For more information on content types, see Chapter 13.

3. Within the **CustomAction** element, add the following code:

```
<CommandUIExtension>
      <CommandUIDefinitions>
         <CommandUIDefinition Location="Ribbon.Tabs._children">
            <Tab Id="Chapter3.CustomTab" Title="Chapter3"
Description="Demo tab for Chapter 3" Sequence="501">
            </Tab>
         </CommandUIDefinition>
      </CommandUIDefinitions>
   </CommandUIExtension>
```

We're creating a **Tab** element. Because we want to add a new tab to the ribbon, we're setting the **Location** attribute of the parent **CommandUIDefinition** element to **Ribbon.Tabs._children**. If we were adding a group to an existing tab or a control to an existing group, we'd set the **Location** to an appropriate value such as **Ribbon.ListItem.New.Controls._children** to add a control to the New group in the ListItem tab.

4. Within the **Tab** element, add the following code:

```
<Scaling Id="Chapter3.CustomTab.Scaling">
   <MaxSize Id="Chapter3.FirstDemoGroup.MaxSize"
         GroupId="Chapter3.FirstDemoGroup"
         Size="OneLarge"/>
   <Scale Id="Chapter3.FirstDemoGroup.Scaling.CustomTabScaling"
         GroupId="Chapter3.FirstDemoGroup"
         Size="OneMedium" />
</Scaling>
<Groups Id="Chapter3.Groups">
   <Group Id="Chapter3.FirstDemoGroup"
         Description="Contains Demo controls"
         Title="Demo Group"
         Sequence="52"
         Template="Ribbon.Templates.SingleButton">
      <Controls Id="Chapter3.FirstDemoGroup.Controls">
      </Controls>
   </Group>
</Groups>
```

We're performing two actions in this step. First, we're specifying how the groups within our tab should scale. For each group, a **MaxSize** and a **Scale** element should be added to the Scaling group. The **MaxSize** element defines the default template that should be used when there are no space constraints. The **Scale** element defines the template that should be used when there is insufficient space to display the template reference in the **MaxSize** element.

The second action that we're performing is to define the groups that make up the tab. Each **Group** element has a **Template** attribute that is used to specify the template that will be used to lay out the group controls within the ribbon.

5. Within the **Controls** element, add the following code:

```
<Button Id="Chapter3.FirstDemoGroup.HelloWorld"
      Sequence="15"
      Image16by16="/_layouts/images/NoteBoard_16x16.png"
      Image32by32="/_layouts/images/NoteBoard_32x32.png"
```

```
            Description="Displays a Hello World message"
            LabelText="Hello World"
            TemplateAlias="c1"/>
```

This addition is relatively straightforward: we're adding a button control to our group. One thing worth noting is the **TemplateAlias** attribute; as you'll see, this value is used to hook controls up to positions within the template that's specified in the **Group** element.

6. After the **CommandUIDefinition** element, add the following code:

```
<CommandUIDefinition Location="Ribbon.Templates._children">
  <GroupTemplate Id="Ribbon.Templates.SingleButton">
    <Layout Title="OneLarge" LayoutTitle="OneLarge">
      <Section Alignment="Top" Type="OneRow">
        <Row>
          <ControlRef DisplayMode="Large" TemplateAlias="c1" />
        </Row>
      </Section>
    </Layout>
    <Layout Title="OneMedium" LayoutTitle="OneMedium">
      <Section Alignment="Top" Type="OneRow">
        <Row>
          <ControlRef DisplayMode="Medium" TemplateAlias="c1" />
        </Row>
      </Section>
    </Layout>
  </GroupTemplate>
</CommandUIDefinition>
```

In this section, we're defining a template for use by our custom group. Things to notice in this snippet are the **TemplateAlias** attributes, which are used to hook up the **ControlRef** elements in the template to the actual controls in the group. Also notice the two layout elements; each template can contain multiple layout elements. Effectively, a template is a collection of layouts, and groups can be bound to a maximum of two layouts: one layout to use when there are no space restrictions and another to use when space is restricted.

7. We can now deploy our customization. Choose Build | Deploy Chapter3. Using the browser, navigate to the demo site that we created earlier, and from the navigation pane select the MyCustomPages document library. Our new Chapter3 tab will be visible within the ribbon, as shown:

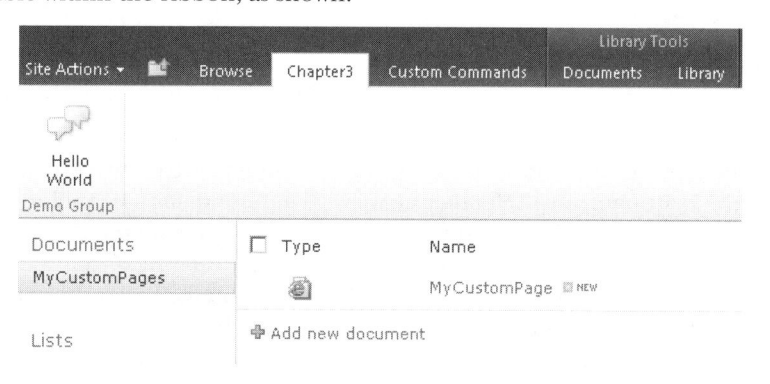

## Handling Events from the Ribbon

You've seen how to add a control to the ribbon declaratively. However, the control we added doesn't do anything useful. Let's look at how we can handle events that are generated from our ribbon customizations. As mentioned, a predefined number of controls can be added to the ribbon. A list of these can be found at http://msdn.microsoft.com/en-us/library/ee537017.aspx.

If we look at the ColorPicker control, we find that the following attributes are defined:

- **Command** This attribute is used to specify a command that should be executed when the control is clicked. This attribute is present on all ribbon controls.
- **CommandPreview** This attribute is used to specify a command that should be executed for previewing a color selection.
- **CommandRevert** This attribute is used to specify a command that should be executed to revert a preview command.
- **QueryCommand** This attribute is used to specify a command that should be executed to retrieve state information. In a sense, these attributes allow us to hook up event handlers for whatever events are defined by the control. Since the ribbon is primarily generated on the client side, handling events must also take place using client-side scripting. In the case of the ribbon, this is commonly done using JavaScript and the Client Object Model (covered in detail in Chapter 4), although it is possible to use other techniques for handling events, as you'll see.

To see how this works in practice, let's add an event handler for our button control.

1. To the Button element in the Elements.xml file, add the following attribute:

```
<Button Id="Chapter3.FirstDemoGroup.HelloWorld"
        Command="Chapter3.HelloWorldCommand"
        Sequence="14"
        Image16by16="/_layouts/images/NoteBoard_16x16.png"
        Image32by32="/_layouts/images/NoteBoard_32x32.png"
        Description="Displays a Hello World message"
        LabelText="Hello World"
        TemplateAlias="c1"/>
```

2. After the closing tag of the **CommandUIDefinitions** element, add the following element:

```
<CommandUIHandlers>
  <CommandUIHandler Command="Chapter3.HelloWorldCommand"
    CommandAction="javascript:
         var notificationId = SP.UI.Notify.addNotification('Hello World');" />
</CommandUIHandlers>
```

The **Command** attribute (and any other event handling attributes on a control) contains a reference to a **CommandUIHandler** element. The **CommandUIHandler** then defines the action that should be taken when the event is raised. In this simple example, we're executing some inline JavaScript to show a notification message using the Client Object Model.

Deploy the revised solution. If all is well, clicking the Hello World button will show a message using the Notifications framework, as shown here:

## Disabling Controls

Earlier you saw that controls on the ribbon can't have their visibility toggled for usability reasons. When a command cannot be used, best practice dictates that it should be disabled. Let's look at how we can add this functionality to our button command.

On our **CommandUIHandler** element, add the following attribute:

```
<CommandUIHandler Command="Chapter3.HelloWorldCommand"
  CommandAction="javascript:
var notificationId = SP.UI.Notify.addNotification('Hello World');"
  EnabledScript="javascript:
function helloWorldEnable()
  {
    return new Date().getMinutes()%2;
  }
helloWorldEnable();"/>
```

This simple example periodically disables the button depending on the current time. The **EnabledScript** attribute should refer to a script that returns a Boolean value. One thing that this example highlights is that the script specified in **EnableScript** is called only when users click controls in the user interface.

## Complex Event Handling

The preceding examples have shown you how to handle events using embedded JavaScript; although this works well, as the JavaScript becomes more complex, it gets increasingly difficult to manage. A common approach to dealing with this problem is to maintain scripts as separate files. Let's look at how we can use external scripts when handling events.

### Adding Script Links Using a Delegate Control

The first thing that we need to do when using external scripts is to find a way to add a link to the script to our page. The best method to achieve this is to use a *delegate control*. Delegates are covered in more detail in Chapter 7—but for now it's enough to know that a delegate can be used to override certain parts of a SharePoint page. The out-of-the-box master page that ships with SharePoint 2010 includes a delegate control named AdditionalPageHead in the page header. By adding our own content to this delegate, we can add references to our external scripts.

1. The easiest way to implement a delegate control is to add a user control to the %SPROOT%/TEMPLATE/CONTROLTEMPLATES folder. This folder is mounted on all SharePoint sites as /_ControlTemplates/, and user controls contained here

can use code-behind in assemblies that are stored in the Global Assembly Cache (GAC). To add a new user control, choose Project | Add New Item. Select User control in the Add New Item dialog and set the name to CustomRibbonHeader.ascx, as shown next:

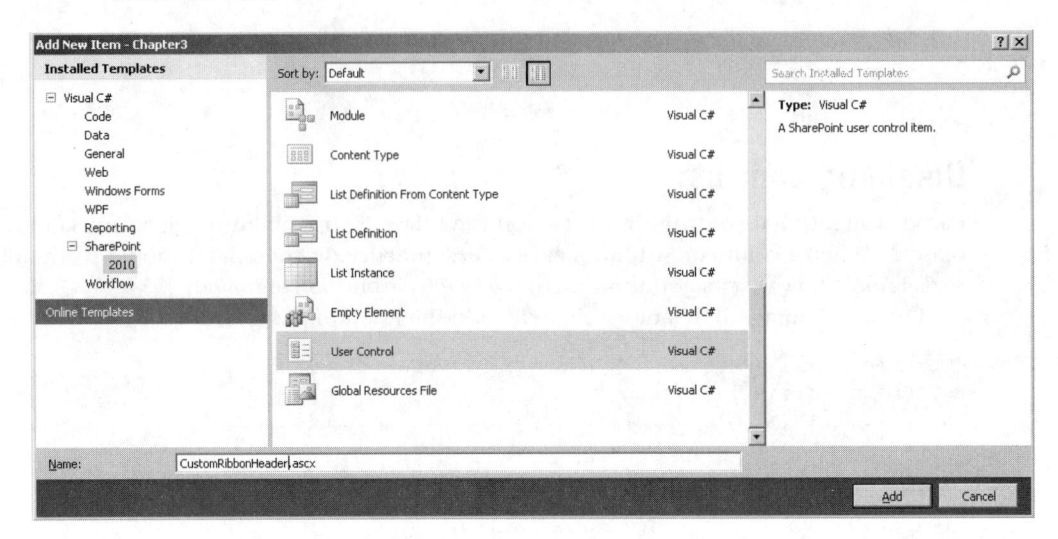

2. The new user control will be placed in the ControlTemplates/Chapter3 folder by default. In the CustomRibbonHeader.ascx file, add the following markup:

```
<SharePoint:ScriptLink Name="SP.js" LoadAfterUI="true"
    OnDemand="false" Localizable="false" runat="server" ID="ScriptLink1" />
<SharePoint:ScriptLink Name="CUI.js" LoadAfterUI="true"
    OnDemand="false" Localizable="false" runat="server" ID="ScriptLink2" />
<SharePoint:ScriptLink Name="/_layouts/Chapter3/Chapter3.PageComponent.js"
                LoadAfterUI="true" OnDemand="false" Localizable="false"
                runat="server" ID="ScriptLink3" />
```

This code snippet uses **ScriptLink** controls to ensure that all required scripts are loaded. SP.js contains core functions for the JavaScript Client Object Model, whereas CUI.js contains functions necessary for the operation of the ribbon.

3. In the Elements.xml file containing our **CustomAction** element, add the following element after the closing tag of the **CustomAction** element:

```
<Control Id="AdditionalPageHead"
    Sequence="49"
    ControlSrc="~/_controltemplates/Chapter3/CustomRibbonHeader.ascx"/>
```

This code hooks up our delegate control to the AdditionalPageHead delegate.

4. Since the whole purpose of adding a delegate control is to include a link to our custom external script file, our next step is to create the file. Select the Chapter3 project node in the Solution Explorer pane, and then choose Project | Add SharePoint Layouts Mapped Folder.

5. Add a new JavaScript file into the Layouts\Chapter3\ folder named Chapter3.PageComponent.js. The final ScriptLink control in the preceding code snippet will ensure that a reference to this file appears on the page.

## Creating a Page Component

A page component is effectively a JavaScript code-behind file for our ribbon customization. Page components are derived from the CUI.Page.PageComponent class that can be found in cui.js, the out-of-the-box JavaScript file that is concerned with delivering the core functionality of the ribbon.

> **TIP** Many script files used in SharePoint have a debug version that is easier to read. These files commonly have a .debug.js extension, such as CUI.debug.js.

By creating a custom page component and overriding the appropriate methods, we can encapsulate the event handlers for our tab in a separate file. Follow these steps to create a simple page component to support the demo tab that we added earlier.

1. In the Chapter3.PageComponent.Js file that we created earlier, add the following code:

```
Type.registerNamespace('Chapter3.PageComponent');
Chapter3.PageComponent = function () {
    Chapter3.PageComponent.initializeBase(this);
}
Chapter3.PageComponent.initialize = function () {
    ExecuteOrDelayUntilScriptLoaded(Function.createDelegate(null, →
Chapter3.PageComponent.initializePageComponent), 'SP.Ribbon.js');
}
Chapter3.PageComponent.initializePageComponent = function () {
    var ribbonPageManager = SP.Ribbon.PageManager.get_instance();
    if (null !== ribbonPageManager) {
        ribbonPageManager.addPageComponent(Chapter3.PageComponent.instance);
    }
}
Chapter3.PageComponent.prototype = {
    init: function () { },
    getFocusedCommands: function () {
        return [''];
    },
    getGlobalCommands: function () {
        return ['Chapter3.HelloWorldCommand']
    },
    canHandleCommand: function (commandId) {
        if (commandId == 'Chapter3.HelloWorldCommand') {
            return true;
        }
        else {
            return false;
        }
    },
    handleCommand: function (commandId, properties, sequence) {
        if (commandId === 'Chapter3.HelloWorldCommand') {
```

```
            var notificationId =
        SP.UI.Notify.addNotification('Hello World from page component');
        }
    },
    isFocusable: function () { return true; },
    receiveFocus: function () { return true; },
    yieldFocus: function () { return true; }
}
Chapter3.PageComponent.registerClass('Chapter3.PageComponent',
                                    CUI.Page.PageComponent);
Chapter3.PageComponent.instance = new Chapter3.PageComponent();
NotifyScriptLoadedAndExecuteWaitingJobs("Chapter3.PageComponent.js");
```

This script defines a new class, **Chapter3.PageComponent**, which inherits from **CUI.Page.PageComponent**. By using this object, we can add all of our event handling code within a separate file rather than having everything contained within the **CommandAction** attribute of **CommandUIHandler** elements.

The **getGlobalCommands** method returns a list of the commands that are supported by the page component—in our case, we're supporting only one command. The **canHandleCommand** method is used to specify whether an item should be disabled or not, and the **handleCommand** method is where we can add the actual implementations for our event handlers. Commonly, these will take the form of method calls.

2. Since we're no longer using the inline script in our **CommandUIHandler** element, replace the attribute as follows:

```
<CommandUIHandlers>
    <CommandUIHandler Command="Chapter3.HelloWorldCommand" CommandAction=""/>
</CommandUIHandlers>
```

3. To initialize our custom page component, add the following JavaScript to the CustomRibbonHeader.ascx file after the **ScriptLink** controls:

```
<script type="text/javascript">
//<![CDATA[
    function initChapter3Ribbon() {
        Chapter3.PageComponent.initialize();
    }
ExecuteOrDelayUntilScriptLoaded(initChapter3Ribbon, 'Chapter3.PageComponent.js');
//]]></script>
```

We're now ready to deploy the revised solution. This time, clicking the Hello World button will return the message specified in the Chapter3.PageComponent.js file.

### Server-Side Event Handling

So far, you've seen how to add ribbon customizations and handle events using inline JavaScript as well as via a custom page component. While this is very much the recommended approach, for some functionality, access to the Server Object Model may be a requirement.

As well as creating page component files and manually writing JavaScript to handle our events, SharePoint 2010 also provides server-side objects that can be used to add commands to an existing custom page component. We'll add a new button for the purposes of this demonstration.

1. In the Elements.xml file, add the following Group element after the closing tag for the existing Group element:

   ```xml
   <Group Id="Chapter3.SecondDemoGroup"
       Description="Contains Demo controls"
       Title="Demo Group 2"
       Sequence="51"
       Template="Ribbon.Templates.SingleButton">
   <Controls Id="Chapter3.SecondDemoGroup.Controls">
     <Button
       Id="Chapter3.SecondDemoGroup.HelloWorld"
       Command="Chapter3.HelloWorldServerCommand"
       Sequence="15"
       Image16by16="/_layouts/images/NoteBoard_16x16.png"
       Image32by32="/_layouts/images/NoteBoard_32x32.png"
       Description="Displays a Hello World message"
       LabelText="Hello World"
       TemplateAlias="c1"/>
   </Controls>
   </Group>
   ```

2. So that the new group will display properly, we need to add a **Scaling/MaxSize** element. Between the existing **MaxSize** and **Scale** elements, add the following element:

   ```xml
   <MaxSize Id="Chapter3.SecondDemoGroup.MaxSize"
            GroupId="Chapter3.SecondDemoGroup" Size="OneLarge"/>
   ```

3. Add the following code to the CustomRibbonHeader.ascx.cs file:

```csharp
public partial class CustomRibbonHeader : UserControl, IPostBackEventHandler
{
   public void RaisePostBackEvent(string eventArgument)
   {
     SPRibbonPostBackEvent pbEvent =
       SPRibbonPostBackCommand.DeserializePostBackEvent(eventArgument);
     SPContext.Current.List.Title = "Updated " + DateTime.Now;
     SPContext.Current.List.Update();
   }
   protected override void OnPreRender(EventArgs e)
   {
     List<IRibbonCommand> commands = new List<IRibbonCommand>();
     commands.Add(new SPRibbonPostBackCommand("Chapter3.HelloWorldServerCommand",
                                     this, "true"));

     SPRibbonScriptManager sm = new SPRibbonScriptManager();
     sm.RegisterGetCommandsFunction(this.Page, "getGlobalCommands", commands);
     sm.RegisterCommandEnabledFunction(this.Page, "canHandleCommand", commands);
     sm.RegisterHandleCommandFunction(this.Page, "handleCommand", commands);
   }
}
```

4. Make the following modification to the Chapter3.PageComponent.js file:

```
Chapter3.PageComponent.prototype = {
    init: function () { },
    getFocusedCommands: function () {return [''];},
    isFocusable: function () { return true; },
    receiveFocus: function () { return true; },
    yieldFocus: function () { return true; },
    getGlobalCommands: function () {
        var commands = getGlobalCommands();
        return commands.concat(['Chapter3.HelloWorldCommand']);
    },
    canHandleCommand: function (commandId) {
        if (commandId == 'Chapter3.HelloWorldCommand') {
            return true;
        }
        else {
            return commandEnabled(commandId);
        }
    },
    handleCommand: function (commandId, properties, sequence) {
        if (commandId === 'Chapter3.HelloWorldCommand') {
            var notificationId =
            SP.UI.Notify.addNotification('Hello World from page component');
        }
        else {
            return handleCommand(commandId, properties, sequence);
        }
    }
}
```

5. Deploy the revised solution. The Chapter 3 tab will now contain two buttons: When the first button is clicked, a notification will be displayed as before. When the second button is clicked, the name of the current list will be updated to include a time stamp, confirming that our server-side code is being executed.

In this sample, we've used the **SPRibbonPostBackCommand** to create a command programmatically that emits the JavaScript code necessary to perform a server post back. When using this technique, bear in mind that a custom page component is required. The page component must make calls into the base class for **getGlobalCommands**, **commandEnabled**, and **handleCommand** to hook up the server side event handler properly.

# Summary

In this chapter, we looked at the main user interface components in SharePoint 2010 and covered how pages are composed using a combination of local file system resources and database content. We also looked at how the ribbon is constructed and covered how customizations can be applied declaratively.

It's fair to say that there's something of a learning curve when it comes to ribbon customizations and particularly in handling events. We covered the three key methods of handling ribbon events; using these techniques, you can implement practically any custom code. As you work through the remaining chapters in Part II, you'll learn more about some of the concepts discussed in this chapter.

# CHAPTER 4

# Client Object Model

**New in 2010**

Although the primary user interface for the SharePoint platform is the web browser, as the capabilities of the platform have matured over time, more integration points in the form of web services have been added to enable client applications to make better use of the platform. With SharePoint 2010, Microsoft has taken this process to the next evolutionary level by including a comprehensive Client Object Model. By using the Client Object Model, you can integrate the functionality of SharePoint with traditional desktop applications, or create a rich web-based user experience by using client-side technologies such as JavaScript and Silverlight.

This chapter looks at the capabilities of the Client Object Model and digs a little deeper into how the object model interacts with the traditional Server Object Model that's also covered in this book.

## Architecture

The client object model has three variants:

- **JavaScript Client Object Model**   This version is implemented in %SPRoot%\Template\Layouts\SP.js. A lot of the new functionality in the SharePoint 2010 user interface is implemented using the JavaScript Object Model, and you saw some examples of this in Chapter 3's discussion of the ribbon. The JavaScript Object Model is useful for enhancing the user experience without requiring additional plug-ins.

- **Silverlight Client Object Model**   This version was designed for use by Silverlight client applications and is implemented in %SPRoot%\Template\Layouts\ClientBin\Microsoft.SharePoint.Client.Silverlight.dll and Microsoft.SharePoint.Client.Silverlight.Runtime.dll. The Silverlight object model is useful when you're developing a more visually appealing and interactive user experience. While JavaScript is useful for improving the interactivity of the user interface by minimizing server-side post backs and page redrawing, at the end of the day, the visual presentation is still constrained by the limitations of HTML. Silverlight has no such limitations, and when you're using the Silverlight Object Model, creating user interface components that reference SharePoint data is relatively straightforward.

- **Managed Client Object Model**   This version has been designed for use by .NET-managed applications and is implemented in %SPRoot%\ISAPI\Microsoft.SharePoint.Client.dll and Microsoft.SharePoint.Client.Runtime.dll. As you've already seen, Silverlight and JavaScript are great tools for developing a rich web-based user interface. However, the services available on the SharePoint platform are not only useful to web clients, but they have myriad uses in rich-client applications as well. For example, using a SharePoint document library as the data store for a purchasing application would allow users to store created purchase orders in a web-based system that could be used as an extranet tool by suppliers.

Although each of these variants has a slightly different implementation, in terms of the capabilities exposed and the way that the object model works, they are all practically identical. Each Client Object Model variant exposes a number of client-side representations of server-side objects. Communication from the client-side object to the server-side counterpart is accomplished via a new Windows Communication Foundation (WCF) service called Client.svc, as the following illustration shows:

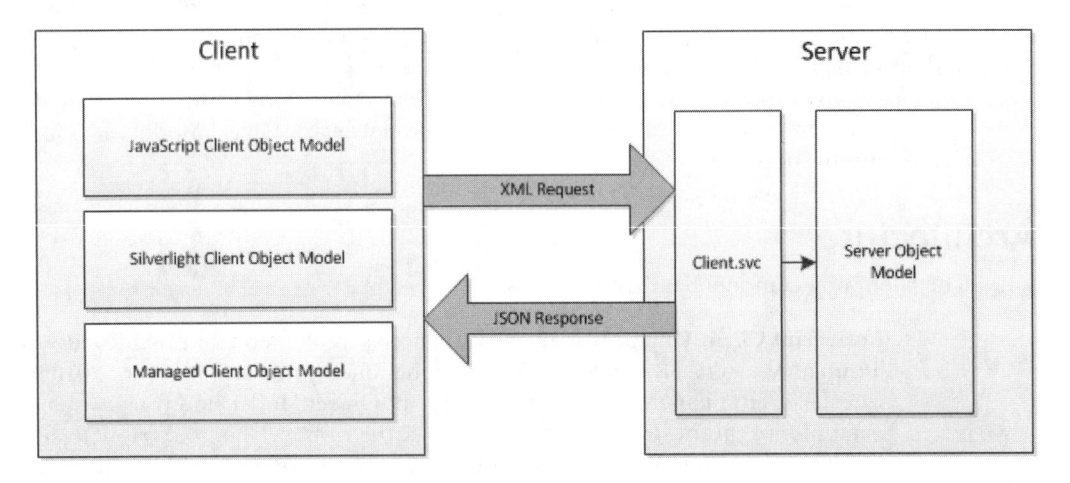

Effectively, Client.svc acts as a proxy for the actions performed on the client. It performs the appropriate actions using the Server Object Model and returns the results to the client using the lightweight JavaScript Object Notation (JSON) data exchange format.

> **NOTE** From an implementation perspective, to ensure that the classes exposed by the Client Object Model exactly matched the classes within the Server Object Model, the client classes were created using a code-generation tool that examined the Server Object Model for classes that were decorated with the ClientCallableType attribute.

## Demonstration Environment Setup

To show some of the code snippets in this chapter in action, we'll start by setting up a demonstration environment and add some test data.

1. Using a web browser, navigate to an appropriate root site within your SharePoint farm—for example, http://<Your Server Name>. From the Site Actions menu, choose New Site.
2. In the Create dialog, select Team Site. Type the title for the new site, **Chapter 4**, and the URL Name, **Chapter4**.
3. After the site has been created, click the Lists link and select the Announcements list.
4. Add a few rows of sample data; we'll use this for our demo code.

## Host Silverlight in SharePoint

To demonstrate the Silverlight Client Object Model, we'll create a basic application and host it in a page on our SharePoint test site. Take the following steps:

1. Using Visual Studio, choose File | New Project.
2. In the New Project dialog, select Empty SharePoint Project and name the new project **Chapter4**, as shown:

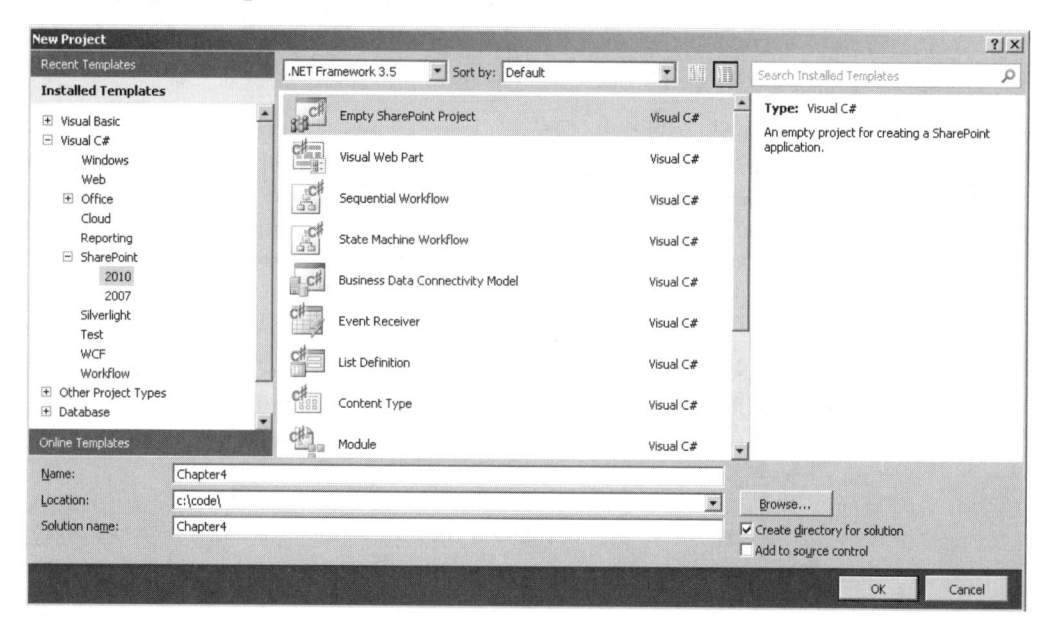

3. In the SharePoint Customization Wizard dialog, set the debugging site to the demo site that we created earlier. Select Deploy As A Farm Solution, and then click Finish.
4. Choose File | Add | New Project.

5. In the Add New Project dialog, select Silverlight in the Installed Templates list and Silverlight Application in the middle pane, and then type the project name, **SilverlightCOMDemo**, as shown:

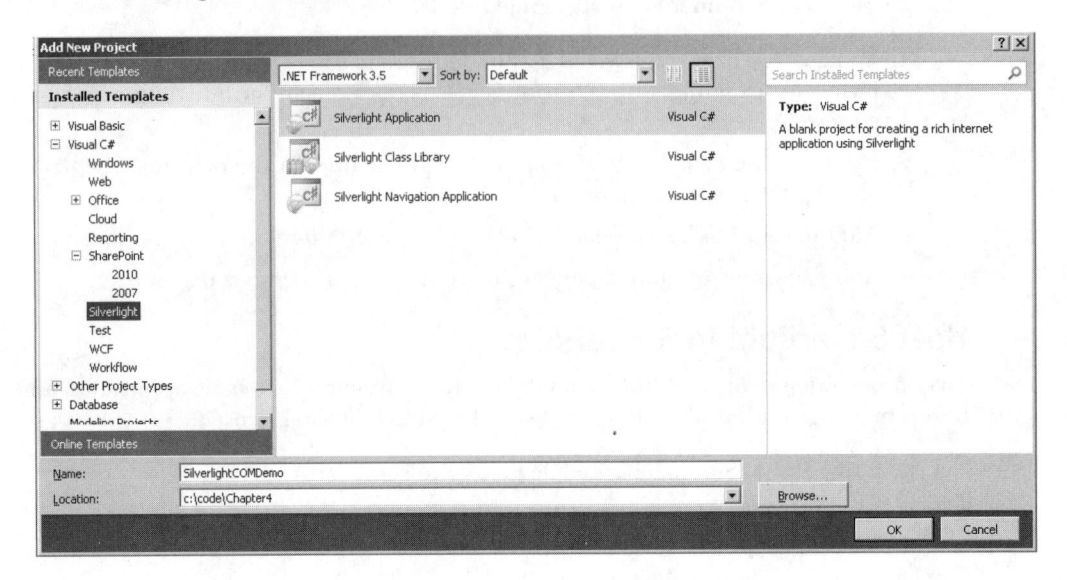

6. In the New Silverlight Application dialog, uncheck the Host The Silverlight Application In A New Web Site checkbox, and then click OK.
7. Choose Project | Add Reference.
8. Select the Browse tab and navigate to %SPRoot%\Template\Layouts\ClientBin and add references to Microsoft.SharePoint.Client.Silverlight.dll and Microsoft .SharePoint.Client.Silverlight.runtime.dll. Be aware that the SPRoot environment variable isn't resolved in the Add Reference dialog, so you'll need to enter the complete path: **C:\Program Files\Common Files\Microsoft Shared\Web Server Extensions\14\Template\Layouts\ClientBin**.

To ensure that our Silverlight project is automatically deployed as part of our SharePoint project, let's create a new document library in SharePoint and add the compiled output of our Silverlight project to it as part of the build process:

1. Right-click the Chapter4 project and select Add | New Item.
2. Select List Instance from the list, and type the name **SilverlightControls** as shown:

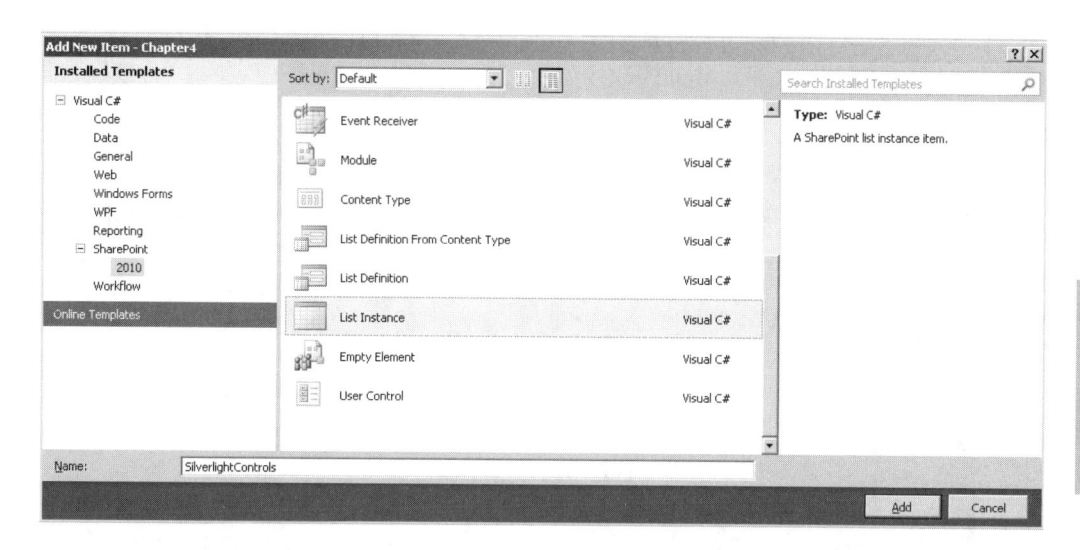

3. Type the display name for the list as **SilverlightControls** and then, from the Which List Do You Want To Instantiate drop-down, select Document Library.
4. Set the relative URL to **SilverlightControls** and click Finish.
5. A new SilverlightControls folder will be added to the Chapter4 project. If it's not already open, open the Elements.xml file from the SilverlightControls folder and add the following XML after the closing ListInstance tag:

```
<Module Name="SilverlightControls" Url="SilverlightControls">
    <File Path="SilverlightControls\SilverlightCOMDemo.xap"
          Url="SilverlightCOMDemo.xap" Type="GhostableInLibrary" />
    <File Path="SilverlightControls\JScriptTest.js"
          Url="JScriptTest.js" Type="GhostableInLibrary" />
</Module>
```

Element files are covered in more detail in Chapter 19. These files are used by the deployment mechanism to determine configuration settings and files that should be deployed to SharePoint when the package is installed. The additional XML that we've added will load SilverlightCOMDemo.xap and JScriptTest.js into our SilverlightControls document library. Of course, before we can load these files into the library we need to create them.

6. In the SilverlightControls folder, add a new JScript file named JScriptTest.js.
7. Right-click the SilverlightCOMDemo project node and select Properties.

8. Select the Build Events tab, and in the Post-build event command line, enter the following (on a single line):

```
xcopy "$(TargetDir)$(TargetName).xap"
      "$(SolutionDir)Chapter4\SilverlightControls" /Y
```

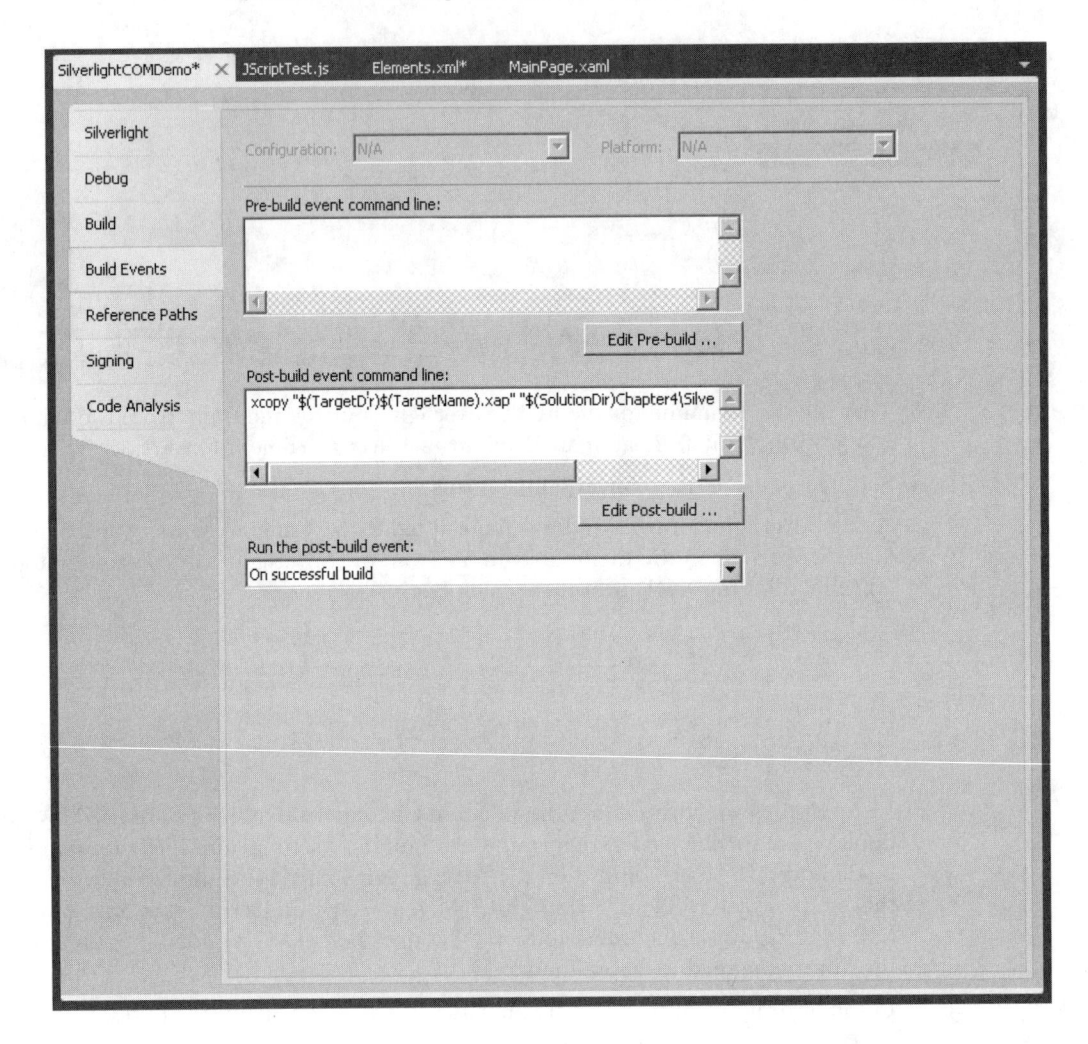

This command line statement will copy the .xap file that's built by the Silverlight project into the SilverlightControls folder in our SharePoint project.

9. To be sure that all is working correctly, build the Silverlight project by right-clicking the SilverlightCOMDemo node and selecting Build.

10. Click the Show All Files icon at the top of the Solution Explorer pane, as shown, and then right-click the SilverlightCOMDemo.xap file in the SilverlightControls folder and select Include In Project.

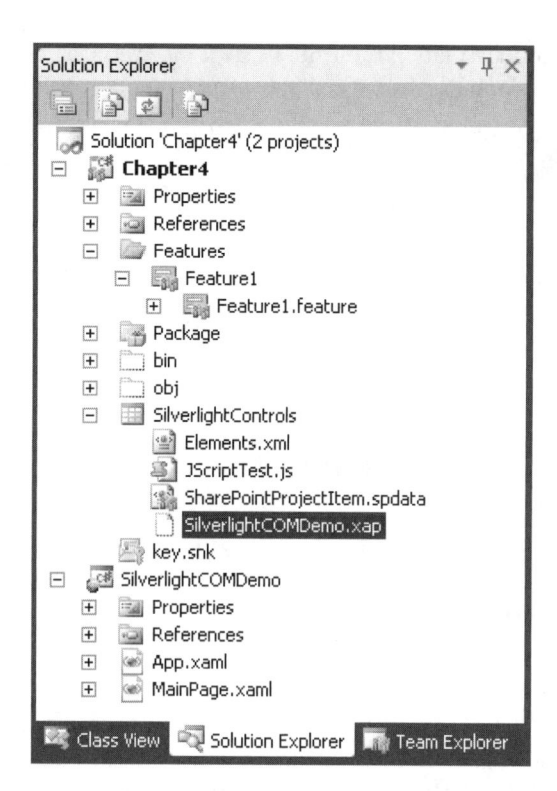

11. Click the Show All files icon again to hide extraneous files. Select the JScriptTest.js file, and then in the Properties pane, set the Deployment Type to ElementFile. Repeat this process for the SilverlightCOMDemo.xap file.
12. To ensure that the Silverlight project is always updated, right-click the Chapter 4 node and select Project Build Order.
13. In the Dependencies tab, select Chapter4 from the Projects drop-down, and then check the SilverlightCOMDemo dependency.
14. We're now ready to deploy our solution to our SharePoint site. Choose Build | Deploy Chapter4.

## Using the Silverlight Web Part

**New in 2010**

Our solution will create a new document library named SilverlightControls on our test site. So that we can see our demo control, we need to host it within a SharePoint page. The easiest way to do this is to use the new Silverlight web part that's included out-of-the-box with SharePoint 2010.

1. Using a web browser, navigate to the Chapter4 demo site that we set up earlier. Notice that a new SilverlightControls document library has been added, which contains our Silverlight package and test JavaScript file.
2. From the Site Actions menu, choose New Page. Name the new page **SilverlightTest**.

3. From the Insert tab in the ribbon, click the Web Part button. Then select the Silverlight Web Part from the Media And Content category, as shown. Then click Add.

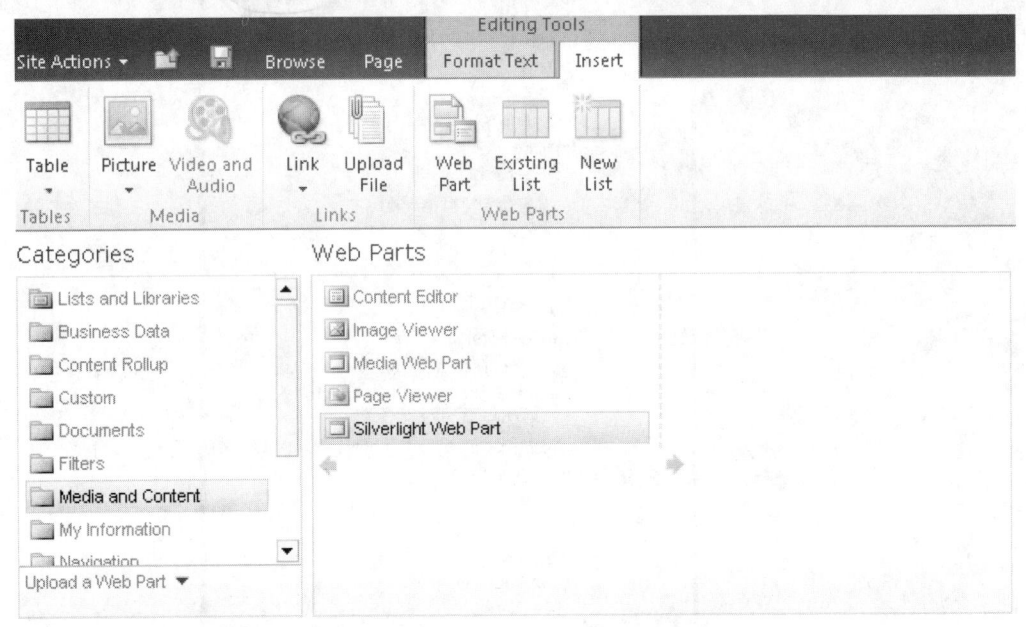

4. In the Silverlight Web Part dialog, set the URL to **&lt;Demo SiteUrl&gt;/ SilverlightControls/SilverlightCOMDemo.xap**.

5. From the Page tab in the ribbon, select Save.

## Referencing the JavaScript Client Object Model

We'll adopt a similar technique to test our JavaScript code. However, in this case, we don't have the luxury of a web part that hooks everything up for us, so we'll need to edit the page template to add the appropriate references.

1. From the Site Actions menu, choose New Page. Name the new page **JavaScriptTest**.

2. From the Page tab in the ribbon, click Save.

3. Also from the Page tab, click the arrow under the Edit button and select Edit In SharePoint Designer.

4. In SharePoint Designer, from the Home tab on the ribbon, select Advanced Mode.

5. In the Content control with the ID PlaceHolderAdditionalPageHead, add the following markup after the SharePoint:RssLink tag (on one line):

    ```
    <SharePoint:ScriptLink runat="server" Name="sp.js"
                Localizable="false" LoadAfterUI="true"/>
    ```

6. Scroll to the bottom of the page, and before the WebPartPage:WebPartZone tag, add the following markup (on one line):

    ```
    <script type="text/javascript"
            src="../SilverlightControls/JScriptTest.js" ></script>
    <div id="DemoConsole"></div>
    ```

7. Click the Save icon in the upper-left corner of the window to save the changes to SharePoint. Click Yes in the Site Definition Page Warning.

We're now good to go. Our Chapter4 demo site has a Site Pages library containing a JavaScript test page and a Silverlight test page. At the moment, neither of these pages will display anything interesting, but as we progress through the examples in this chapter, they'll start to show how the Client Object Model works.

## Available Client-side Objects

Not all server-side objects are available within the Client Object Model. Generally speaking, all objects from SPSite downward are included. No representations of administrative classes, such as those found in the Microsoft.SharePoint.Administration namespace, are included.

The Client Object Model is encapsulated in four namespaces:

- **Microsoft.SharePoint.Client**  This namespace contains representations of many commonly used server objects such as SPSite, SPWeb, SPList, SPListItem, and SPField. These objects are implemented in the Client Object Model without the *SP* prefix—so, for example, SPSite in the Server Object Model maps to Site in the Client Object Model. This is the same for all variants of the Client Object Model. The exception to this rule is the SPContext object, which is represented as ClientContext in the Client Object Model. The ClientContext object is a key component in the Client Object Model and exposes functionality that has no direct counterpart in the SPContext server-side object. We'll cover ClientContext in greater detail in the next section.

- **Microsoft.SharePoint.Client.Utilities**  This namespace contains representations of a few commonly used server-side utility classes. Those included are HttpUtility, which maps to SPHttpUtility on the server side; PrincipalInfo, which maps to SPPrincipalInfo on the server side; and Utility, which maps to SPUtility on the server side.

- **Microsoft.SharePoint.Client.WebParts**  This namespace contains representations of server-side objects that are commonly used in the management of web parts. Using the classes in this namespace, you can access and modify web parts and web part pages.

- **Microsoft.Sharepoint.Client.Workflow**  This namespace contains representations of a number of server-side classes concerned with the operation of workflows. Using the classes in this namespace, you can manage workflow associations and templates.

## ClientContext

When writing code that uses the Server Object Model, you generally start with something like this:

```
string GetWebName(string url)
    {
      using (SPSite site = new SPSite(url))
      {
        using (SPWeb web=site.OpenWeb(url))
        {
```

```
        return "Title:" + web.Title + ", Description:" + web.Description;
    }
  }
}
```

Or, if you're writing code for a web part, you can use the following:

```
string GetWebName(string url)
    {
        return "Title:" + SPContext.Current.Web.Title
            + ", Description:" + SPContext.Current.Web.Description;
    }
```

Let's take a look at how to achieve a similar result by using the Silverlight Client Object Model:

1. Using the SilverlightCOMDemo project that we added earlier, in MainPage.xaml, add a button control and a label control.
2. Select the button control and then, using the Properties pane, set the Content to Get Web Details.
3. Switch to the Events tab in the Properties pane and add Button_Click as the hander for the Click event, as shown:

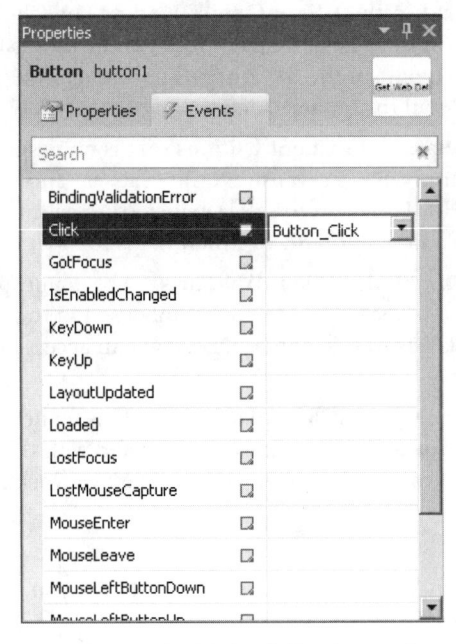

4. Switch to MainPage.xaml.cs and add the following code:

```
private void Button_Click(object sender, RoutedEventArgs e)
    {
       ClientContext ctx=new ClientContext("Your Site URL Here");
```

```
Web web = ctx.Web;
ctx.Load(web);
ctx.ExecuteQueryAsync((s, args) =>
{
  Dispatcher.BeginInvoke(() => {
                  label1.Content = "Title:" + web.Title
                          + ", Description:" + web.Description; });
}, null);
}
```

5. Build the SilverlightCOMDemo project and then deploy the solution. If a Deployment Conflict dialog is presented indicating a conflict in the SilverlightControls project item, check the Do Not Prompt Me Again For These Items checkbox and click Resolve Automatically. The conflict occurs because list instances are not automatically removed when a solution is retracted. (For more on this, see Chapter 19.)

6. Navigate to the Silverlight Test page that we created earlier: http://<your Server Url>/Chapter4/SitePages/SilverlightTest.aspx.

If we're using the JavaScript version of the object model, we could take the following steps:

1. Using SharePoint Designer, edit the JavascriptTest.aspx page that we created earlier.

2. Above the WebPartPages:WebPartZone at the bottom of the page, insert the following HTML:

```
<script type="text/javascript"
        src="../SilverlightControls/JScriptTest.js" ></script>
<input name="Button1" type="button" value="Get Web Details"
        onclick="Button_Click()"></input>
<div id="DemoConsole"></div>
```

3. In the JScriptTest.js file that we added earlier, add the following code:

```
/// <reference path="C:\Program Files\Common Files\Microsoft Shared\ →
Web Server Extensions\14\TEMPLATE\LAYOUTS\MicrosoftAjax.js" />
/// <reference path="C:\Program Files\Common Files\Microsoft Shared\Web →
Server Extensions\14\TEMPLATE\LAYOUTS\SP.debug.js" />

function Button_Click() {
    var ctx = new SP.ClientContext.get_current();
    var web = ctx.get_web();
    ctx.load(web);
    ctx.executeQueryAsync(function(s,args) {
        var console = document.getElementById('DemoConsole');
        console.innerHTML = "Title:" + web.get_title()
                     + ", Description:" + web.get_description();
    },
    null);
}
```

4. Deploy the solution, and then navigate to the JavaScript Test page that we created earlier: http://<your Server Url>/Chapter4/SitePages/JavaScriptTest.aspx.

The important thing to notice in these samples is the use of the ClientContext object as the entry point to the Client Object Model. When called by the Silverlight sample, a URL is required, but the JavaScript sample doesn't need a URL because the URL is derived from the current page. Also notice the use of the reference elements. These allow Visual Studio 2010 to provide IntelliSense support for the Client Object Model.

> **NOTE** Slight naming differences exist between the JavaScript and .NET versions of the object model. Rather than explicitly state the various names for each object, I'll use the .NET names here. As a general rule, names in the JavaScript object model begin with lowercase characters and properties are prefixed with get_.

## Operation Batching

The ClientContext class includes a few methods that are essential to the workings of the Client Object Model. The first of these methods is the ClientContext.ExecuteQueryAsync method.

Earlier, in our architecture diagram, we saw that the Client Object Model makes use of a WCF service as a proxy to perform operations on the server. To reduce network load, what actually happens is that all requests are queued by the ClientContext object and are sent to the server only when the ExecuteQueryAsync method is called. Conceptually, this is easy to understand, but it makes for some interesting caveats when it comes to developing against the Client Object Model.

To see how this works, consider our earlier Silverlight code sample:

```
private void Button_Click(object sender, RoutedEventArgs e)
  {
    ClientContext ctx=new ClientContext("Your Site URL Here");
    Web web = ctx.Web;
    ctx.Load(web);
    ctx.ExecuteQueryAsync((s, args) =>
    {
      Dispatcher.BeginInvoke(() => {
        label1.Content = "Title:" + web.Title +
          ", Description:" + web.Description; });
    }, null);
  }
```

In this snippet, we're creating a ClientContext object and then picking up a reference to its Web property. However, before we can read the values of the web object, we need to call the ClientContext.Load method to queue the object for loading and then call ExecuteQueryAsync to execute the queued operations.

As its name suggests, ExecuteQueryAsync is an asynchronous operation. It accepts as parameters two delegates: one to be called if the operation fails and another to be called when the operation is successful. For simplicity, we've used lambda expressions in this sample. When writing code that uses the Silverlight Client Object Model or the JavaScript Client Object Model, ExecuteQueryAsync must be used to make an asynchronous call to Client.svc. However, if using the Managed Client Object Model, which is generally the case when integrating rich client applications, it's possible to call Client.svc synchronously by using the ClientContext.ExecuteQuery method.

## Retrieving Data

As you saw in the preceding code snippets, although the Client Object Model defines client-side representations of server objects and we can create instances of those objects in our code, the objects are not populated with a copy of the server-side data until it is explicitly loaded.

### In-place Load

This Silverlight code snippet shows how to execute a Collaborative Application Markup Language (CAML) query against a list:

```
private void CAMLQUery_Click(object sender, RoutedEventArgs e)
    {
        ClientContext ctx = new ClientContext("Your site here");
        CamlQuery query = new CamlQuery();
        query.ViewXml = "<View><Query><OrderBy>
                        <FieldRef Name=\"Editor\" Ascending=\"False\" />
                        </OrderBy></Query></View>";
        List announcements = ctx.Web.Lists.GetByTitle("Announcements");
        FieldCollection fields = announcements.Fields;
        ctx.Load(fields);
        ListItemCollection listItems = announcements.GetItems(query);
        ctx.Load(listItems);
        ctx.ExecuteQueryAsync((s, args) =>
        {
            Dispatcher.BeginInvoke(() =>
            {
                BuildTable(fields, listItems);
            });
        }, (s, args) =>
        {
            Dispatcher.BeginInvoke(() =>
            {
                label1.Content = args.Message;
            });
        });
    }
```

To perform the same function using JavaScript, you can use this:

```
function CAMLQuery_Click() {
    var ctx = new SP.ClientContext.get_current();
    var query = new SP.CamlQuery();
    query.viewXml = "<View><Query><OrderBy>
                    <FieldRef Name=\"Editor\" Ascending=\"False\" />
                    </OrderBy></Query></View>";
    var announcements = ctx.get_web().get_lists().getByTitle("Announcements");
    var listItems = announcements.getItems(query);
    ctx.load(listItems);
    var fields = announcements.get_fields();
    ctx.load(fields);
    ctx.executeQueryAsync(function (s, args) {
```

```
        var console = document.getElementById('DemoConsole');
        console.innerHTML = buildTable(fields,listItems);
    }, null);
}
```

The important thing to note about these code samples is the use of the ClientContext.Load method. This method flags the passed in object to be populated the next time ExecuteQueryAsync is called, so in the preceding example, **ctx.Load(listItems)** will flag the listItems object for population.

To use these code snippets with the demo project that we set up earlier, take the following steps—first, for the Silverlight sample:

1. Add a new button labeled Execute CAML Query to MainPage.xaml, and set the Click event handler to CAMLQuery_Click.
2. Add the Silverlight code snippet listed above into MainPage.xaml.cs.
3. Add a ScrollViewer control to MainPage.xaml and then, inside the ScrollViewer, add a Grid control named grid1.
4. Add the following code into MainPage.xaml.cs:

```
void BuildTable(FieldCollection fields, ListItemCollection listItems)
    {
        grid1.RowDefinitions.Clear();
        grid1.ColumnDefinitions.Clear();
        grid1.ShowGridLines = false;
        grid1.RowDefinitions.Add(new RowDefinition {
                    Height=new GridLength(0,GridUnitType.Auto)});
        int i = 0;
        foreach (var field in fields)
        {
            if (!field.Hidden)
            {
                grid1.ColumnDefinitions.Add(new ColumnDefinition {
                    Width=new GridLength(0,GridUnitType.Auto)
                });
                TextBlock label = new TextBlock
                {
                    Text = field.Title,
                    HorizontalAlignment = HorizontalAlignment.Center,
                    FontWeight = FontWeights.Bold,
                    Margin = new Thickness(10, 0, 10, 0),
                };
                label.SetValue(Grid.RowProperty, 0);
                label.SetValue(Grid.ColumnProperty, i);
                grid1.Children.Add(label);
                i++;
            }
        }
        int row = 1;
        foreach (var item in listItems)
        {
            i = 0;
            grid1.RowDefinitions.Add(new RowDefinition {
```

```
                    Height=new GridLength(0,GridUnitType.Auto)});
            foreach (var field in fields)
            {
                if (!field.Hidden)
                {
                    TextBlock label = new TextBlock {
                        HorizontalAlignment = HorizontalAlignment.Center,
                        Margin = new Thickness(10, 0, 10, 0),
                    };
                    try
                    {
                        label.Text = item[field.StaticName].ToString();
                    }
                    catch (Exception)
                    {
                        label.Text = "--";
                    }
                    label.SetValue(Grid.RowProperty, row);
                    label.SetValue(Grid.ColumnProperty,i);
                    i++;
                    grid1.Children.Add(label);
                }
            }
            row++;
        }
    }
```

5. Build the SilverlightCOMDemo project.

   Now, for the JavaScript sample, do the following:

   1. Using SharePoint Designer, modify JavascriptTest.aspx to include an additional button.

   2. Above the DemoConsole **div** tag that we added earlier, insert the following markup:

      ```
      <input name="Button2" type="button" value="Execute CAML Query"
            onclick="CAMLQuery_Click()"></input>
      ```

6. Within the JScriptTest.js file in our SharePoint project, add the CAMLQuery_Click JavaScript sample method listed above and then add the following function:

```
function buildTable(fields,listItems) {
    var output = "";
    output = "<table><thead style=\"font-weight:bold\"><tr>";
    var fieldEnum = fields.getEnumerator();
    while (fieldEnum.moveNext()) {
        var field = fieldEnum.get_current();
        if (field.get_hidden() != true) {
            output += "<td>" + field.get_title() + "</td>";
        }
    }
    output += "</tr></thead>";
    var enumerator = listItems.getEnumerator();
    while (enumerator.moveNext()) {
```

```
        var item = enumerator.get_current();
        fieldEnum.reset();
        output += "<tr>";
        while (fieldEnum.moveNext()) {
            var field = fieldEnum.get_current();
            if (field.get_hidden() != true) {
              try {
                output += "<td>" + item.get_item(field.get_staticName()) + "</td>";
              } catch (e) {
                  output += "<td>--</td>";
              }
            }
        }
        output += "</tr>";
    }
    output += "</table>"
    return output;
}
```

With these changes in place, by deploying the solution, we can view the results of our CAML query as a table using either the Silverlight test page or the JavaScript test page that we added earlier in the chapter.

## Object Identity

Although property values are not populated until they are explicitly loaded, it is still possible to make use of the properties in expressions, as long as the expressions themselves are not enumerated until after the properties are loaded. In our code sample, we can see an example of this in the following line:

```
List announcements = ctx.Web.Lists.GetByTitle("Announcements");
```

If we were to attempt to enumerate any of the properties of the announcements object, an error would be thrown since the value has not been initialized. The same is also true of the properties of the object referred to by the ctx.Web property. We can use the property in an expression because an expression uses a reference to the property rather than its actual value.

You can see that our code sample makes use of the announcements object in various places, but we never explicitly populate it. Loading an object is necessary only if its properties will be converted to a value.

One easy way to look at it is to consider that each object is a proxy for an appropriate server-side object. Using the proxy, we can perform many of the same actions, but until we explicitly load data from the real object into the proxy, we can't use the data on the client side because it exists only on the server.

## Filtering Returned Data

When we execute the preceding code samples, a table is generated containing the field values that are returned for each list item, as shown:

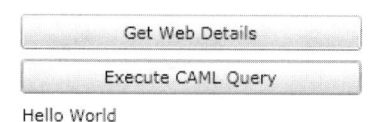

| ID | Content Type | Title | Modified | |
|----|--------------|-------|----------|---|
| 1 | -- | Get Started with Microsoft SharePoint Foundation! | 24/05/2010 15:55:57 | 24/0! |
| 2 | -- | A New Announcement 1 | 25/05/2010 15:04:45 | 25/0! |
| 3 | -- | A New Announcement 2 | 25/05/2010 15:04:56 | 25/0! |
| 4 | -- | A New Announcement 3 | 25/05/2010 15:05:03 | 25/0! |

This works well and doesn't present much of a problem when only a few items are included in the list or library. But what happens if tens of thousands of items are included and we need only one or two columns? Transferring all this redundant data to the client would have a major performance impact.

Thankfully, we can eliminate redundant data by filtering the properties that are populated by the Load method, as the following snippets show. To see the results of these samples, create a new button and hook up the Click event to the sample code, as we've done in the past few samples.

Here's the snippet in Silverlight:

```
private void FilterQuery_Click(object sender, RoutedEventArgs e)
{
    ClientContext ctx = new ClientContext("Your site here");
    CamlQuery query = new CamlQuery();
    query.ViewXml = "<View><Query><OrderBy>
                    <FieldRef Name=\"Editor\" Ascending=\"False\" />
                    </OrderBy></Query></View>";
    List announcements = ctx.Web.Lists.GetByTitle("Announcements");

    FieldCollection fields = announcements.Fields;
    ctx.Load(fields,
        fs => fs.Include(
            f => f.Hidden,
            f => f.Title,
            f => f.StaticName).Where(f => f.Hidden == false)
        );
    ListItemCollection listItems = announcements.GetItems(query);
    ctx.Load(listItems,
        items => items.Include(
          item => item["Title"]
        ));
```

```
            ctx.ExecuteQueryAsync((s, args) =>
            {
                Dispatcher.BeginInvoke(() =>
                {
                    BuildTable(fields, listItems);
                });
            }, (s, args) =>
            {
                Dispatcher.BeginInvoke(() =>
                {
                    label1.Content = args.Message;
                });
            });
}
```

And here's the JavaScript:

```
function FilteredQuery_Click() {
    var ctx = new SP.ClientContext.get_current();
    var query = new SP.CamlQuery();
    query.viewXml = "<View><Query><OrderBy>
                    <FieldRef Name=\"Editor\" Ascending=\"False\" />
                    </OrderBy></Query></View>";
 var announcements = ctx.get_web().get_lists().getByTitle("Announcements");
    var listItems = announcements.getItems(query);
    ctx.load(listItems,"Include(Title)");
    var fields = announcements.get_fields();
    ctx.load(fields,"Include(Hidden,Title,StaticName)");
    ctx.executeQueryAsync(function (s, args) {
        var console = document.getElementById('DemoConsole');
        console.innerHTML = buildTable(fields, listItems);
    }, null);
}
```

In the Silverlight sample, we're making use of lambda expressions and Language Integrated Query (LINQ) to filter the returned data. (If you're unfamiliar with LINQ or lambda expressions, see Chapter 14 for more information.) Because LINQ syntax isn't supported by JavaScript, we're using a string containing a filter expression. When creating JavaScript filter strings, LINQ operations such as Where are not supported.

You can see that by running these samples, the resulting table contains only the Title column. Although you can't see it from the output, the population of the fields collection has been filtered to include only the properties that are required for the logic. The result of these changes is that the data exchanged between client and server is greatly reduced.

**NOTE** When querying lists or libraries, you need to be aware of how filtering is applied behind the scenes. First, the CAML query object passed into the GetItems method is used to retrieve a list of items into memory. With the item list in memory, LINQ to Objects is used to apply the filters that we're defining with the Load method. This is significant, because when you're querying large lists, item-level filtering should always be done using CAML to reduce the memory usage on the server. As you'll see in Chapter 13, restrictions are imposed on the number of items that can be retrieved from a list in a single query.

## Queryable Load

In addition to the ClientContext.Load method used in the preceding examples, the Client Object Model also provides a ClientContext.LoadQuery method. The difference between these two methods is in the object that receives the results of the method. When calling Load, we'll pass in a reference to the object that we want to load along with any filtering expression; when the method has executed, that object that we passed in is loaded with the appropriate data. With LoadQuery, when the method has executed, an IEnumerable(T) collection is returned.

You may be wondering about the benefits of such a subtle difference between these methods. The main benefit is that LoadQuery can accept a LINQ query as a parameter; also, the results returned can be further processed using LINQ.

In the preceding Silverlight example, we could replace this

```
FieldCollection fields = announcements.Fields;
    ctx.Load(fields,
        fs => fs.Include(
            f => f.Hidden,
            f => f.Title,
            f => f.StaticName).Where(f => f.Hidden == false)
        );
```

with this:

```
var filteredFields = announcements.Fields.Include(
                f => f.Hidden,
                f => f.Title,
                f => f.StaticName);
var fields = ctx.LoadQuery(from f in filteredFields
                        where f.Hidden == false
                        select f);
```

In the second example, the fields variable contains an IEnumerable<Field> object as opposed to the FieldCollection object that would be populated with the first example.

Although the JavaScript object model also includes the loadQuery method, since JavaScript doesn't support LINQ, its primary function is to return the results as a separate variable rather than populating the appropriate ClientContext property. Other than that, there is no real benefit to using loadQuery in JavaScript.

## Adding Data

Adding data using the Client Object Model is a relatively straightforward process, as these snippets show. However, the ListItemCreationInformation object can also be used to set a few system properties when creating a new list item. For example, when you're creating a list item within a folder, you can use the FolderUrl property to specify the location of the folder.

The following code sample shows how a new list item can be added using the Silverlight Client Object Model:

```
private void Add_Click(object sender, RoutedEventArgs e)
{
    ClientContext ctx = new ClientContext("Your Server Here");
    List announcements = ctx.Web.Lists.GetByTitle("Announcements");
    ListItemCreationInformation createInfo = new ListItemCreationInformation();
    ListItem newItem = announcements.AddItem(createInfo);
    newItem["Title"] = "A new item";
    newItem.Update();
    ctx.ExecuteQueryAsync((s, args) =>
    {
        Dispatcher.BeginInvoke(() =>
        {
            label1.Content = "Item Added";
        });
    }, (s, args) =>
    {
        Dispatcher.BeginInvoke(() =>
        {
            label1.Content = args.Message;
        });
    });
}
```

When using the JavaScript object model, the code is similar:

```
function Add_Click() {
    var ctx = new SP.ClientContext.get_current();
    var announcements = ctx.get_web().get_lists().
getByTitle("Announcements");
    var createInfo = new SP.ListItemCreationInformation();
    var newItem = announcements.addItem(createInfo);
    newItem.set_item("Title", "A new javascript item");
    newItem.update();
    ctx.executeQueryAsync(function (s, args) {
        var console = document.getElementById('DemoConsole');
        console.innerHTML = "Add Completed";
    }, null);
}
```

## Updating Data

So far, you've seen a few ways to retrieve data using the Client Object Model, as well as how to add new items to SharePoint lists and libraries. Our next logical step is to look at how we can update the data that we've retrieved and submit the changes back to SharePoint.

Here's how to do this in Silverlight:

```
private void Update_Click(object sender, RoutedEventArgs e)
{
    ClientContext ctx = new ClientContext(Your Server Here");
```

```csharp
        CamlQuery query = new CamlQuery();
        query.ViewXml = "<View><Query><OrderBy>" +
                    "<FieldRef Name=\"Editor\" Ascending=\"False\" />" +
                    "</OrderBy></Query></View>";
        List announcements = ctx.Web.Lists.GetByTitle("Announcements");
        ListItemCollection listItems = announcements.GetItems(query);
        ctx.Load(listItems);
        ctx.ExecuteQueryAsync((s, args) =>
        {
            foreach (var item in listItems)
            {
                item["Title"] = "Updated";
                item.Update();
            }
            ctx.ExecuteQueryAsync((s1, args1) =>
                {
                    Dispatcher.BeginInvoke(() =>
                        {
                            label1.Content = "Records Updated";
                        });
                }, null);
        }, (s, args) =>
        {
            Dispatcher.BeginInvoke(() =>
            {
                label1.Content = args.Message;
            });
        });
    }
```

And here it is in JavaScript:

```javascript
function Update_Click() {
    var ctx = new SP.ClientContext.get_current();
    var query = new SP.CamlQuery();
    query.viewXml = "<View><Query><OrderBy>" +
                "<FieldRef Name=\"Editor\" Ascending=\"False\" />" +
                "</OrderBy></Query></View>";
    var announcements = ctx.get_web().get_lists().getByTitle("Announcements");
    var listItems = announcements.getItems(query);
    ctx.load(listItems, "Include(Title)");
    ctx.executeQueryAsync(function (s, args) {
        var itemEnum = listItems.getEnumerator();
        while (itemEnum.moveNext()) {
            var item = itemEnum.get_current();
            item.set_item("Title","JavaScript Update");
            item.update();
        }
        ctx.executeQueryAsync(function (s, args) {
            var console = document.getElementById('DemoConsole');
            console.innerHTML =" JavaScript Update Completed";
        }, null);
    }, null);
}
```

As you can see from these code samples, updating values from the Client Object Model works in a similar way to updating objects on the server, in that the Update method must be called to commit the changes.

## Deleting Data

Deleting data is relatively straightforward and follows a pattern similar to how it's done using the Server Object Model.

To delete an item using the Silverlight Client Object Model, we could use code such as this:

```
private void Delete_Click(object sender, RoutedEventArgs e)
{
    ClientContext ctx = new ClientContext("Your Server Here");
    CamlQuery query = new CamlQuery();
    query.ViewXml = "<View><Query>" +
                "<OrderBy><FieldRef Name=\"Editor\" Ascending=\"False\" />" +
                "</OrderBy></Query></View>";
    List announcements = ctx.Web.Lists.GetByTitle("Announcements");

    ListItemCollection listItems = announcements.GetItems(query);
    ctx.Load(listItems);
    ctx.ExecuteQueryAsync((s, args) =>
    {
        ListItem lastItem = listItems[listItems.Count - 1];
        lastItem.DeleteObject();
        announcements.Update();

        ctx.ExecuteQueryAsync((s1, args1) =>
            {
                Dispatcher.BeginInvoke(() =>
                {
                    label1.Content = "Last record deleted";
                });
            }, null);
    }, (s, args) =>
    {
        Dispatcher.BeginInvoke(() =>
        {
            label1.Content = args.Message;
        });
    });
}
```

If using JavaScript, our code would look like this:

```
function Delete_Click() {
    var ctx = new SP.ClientContext.get_current();
    var query = new SP.CamlQuery();
    query.viewXml = "<View><Query><OrderBy>" +
                "<FieldRef Name=\"Editor\" Ascending=\"False\" />" +
                "</OrderBy></Query></View>";
    var announcements = ctx.get_web().get_lists().getByTitle("Announcements");
```

```
    var listItems = announcements.getItems(query);
    ctx.load(listItems, "Include(Title)");
    ctx.executeQueryAsync(function (s, args) {
        var lastItem=listItems.get_item(listItems.get_count()-1);
        lastItem.deleteObject();
        announcements.update();
        ctx.executeQueryAsync(function (s, args) {
            var console = document.getElementById('DemoConsole');
            console.innerHTML = " Last Item Deleted";
        }, null);
    }, null);
}
```

## Using the Status Bar, Notifications, and the Dialog Framework

Along with using the JavaScript Client Object Model to read and write to SharePoint data structures, SharePoint 2010 also introduces a few of new APIs for providing user feedback. All these new APIs are accessed via the SP.UI namespace and the JavaScript Client Object Model.

### The Status Bar

The status bar is a permanent fixture on the page. Messages added here remain on the page until they are specifically removed programmatically. We can see an example of a status bar message on the JavaScriptTest.aspx page. Since we've customized the page using SharePoint Designer, a message informing us that "The current page as been customized from its template" is automatically shown.

Using the SP.UI.Status object, we can add our own status messages as follows:

```
function StatusBarUpdate_Click() {

    SP.UI.Status.removeAllStatus(true);

    var sid = SP.UI.Status.addStatus("My New Status:",
                            "Information Message", true);

    window.setTimeout(function () {
                UpdateStatusBar("D", "red", sid) }, 1000);
    window.setTimeout(function () {
                UpdateStatusBar("D I", "green", sid) }, 2000);
    window.setTimeout(function () {
                UpdateStatusBar("D I S", "blue", sid) }, 3000);
    window.setTimeout(function () {
                UpdateStatusBar("D I S C", "yellow", sid) }, 4000);
    window.setTimeout(function () {
                UpdateStatusBar("D I S C O", "green", sid) }, 5000);
    window.setTimeout(function () {
                SP.UI.Status.removeStatus(sid) }, 6000);
}

function UpdateStatusBar(message, color, sid) {
```

```
        SP.UI.Status.updateStatus(sid, message);
        SP.UI.Status.setStatusPriColor(sid, color);
}
```

The call to Status.addStatus returns an identifier that can be used subsequently to change the settings of the status bar. Notice that only one status bar exists, but it can contain many status messages. The status bar always uses the color of the highest priority message. For example, the color red is used for very important messages and the color blue is used for information messages. If a very important message is displayed on the status bar and an information message is added, the status bar will be rendered in red. For more details on the mapping of color to priority, see http://msdn.microsoft.com/en-us/library/ff408240.aspx.

## Notifications

Although the status bar is great for showing permanent messages to the user, sometimes we simply need to display a transient notification message. Using the SP.UI.Notify object, we can show such messages:

```
function SendNotification_Click() {
      var nid=SP.UI.Notify.addNotification("My New notification", false);
}
```

By default, notification messages are displayed for 5 seconds, which is generally sufficient for most throwaway notification messages. However, if we need the user to perform some action, such as clicking a link, we can use code similar to this:

```
var nid;

function SendNotification_Click() {

    if (nid == null) {
        nid = SP.UI.Notify.addNotification(
"My New notification <a href='Javascript:hideNote_Click();'>Click Me</a>", true);
    }
}

function hideNote_Click() {
    SP.UI.Notify.removeNotification(nid);
    nid = null;
}
```

## Dialogs

Another addition in SharePoint 2010 is the Dialog framework. For the most part, this is encapsulated in the functionality exposed by the SP.UI.Dialog and SP.UI.ModalDialog classes. Although the notifications and status bar functionality is included in the SP.js file, the dialog framework code is included in the SP.UI.Dialog.js file. To get IntelliSense support in Visual Studio when writing JavaScript that targets the dialog framework, add the following reference element to the JavaScript file:

```
/// <reference path="C:\Program Files\Common Files\Microsoft Shared\Web →
Server Extensions\14\TEMPLATE\LAYOUTS\SP.UI.Dialog.debug.js" />
```

Showing a modal dialog is a relatively straightforward affair. First, we create a DialogOptions object, and then we call the showModalDialog method of the SP.UI.ModalDialog object, as this sample shows:

```
function ShowDialog_Click() {

 var options = {url: 'http://www.chaholl.com',tite: 'My Dialog',
             allowMaximize: false,showClose: true,
             width: 150,height: 150,
             dialogReturnValueCallback: SendNotification_Click};
         var did = SP.UI.ModalDialog.showModalDialog(options);
}
```

In this sample, we're redirecting to an Internet page for the sake of simplicity. In a real-world application, we'd create a custom page that implemented the required functionality. In Chapter 9, you'll see examples of custom dialogs when we build setting pages for service applications.

The important thing to note about the DialogOptions object is the dialogReturnValueCallback property. This contains details of a callback method that will be called when the dialog is closed. In this callback, we can write code to pick up the dialog result and perform any necessary actions. In this simple example, we've generated a notification using our notification sample code.

## Summary

This chapter has shown how the Client Object Model can be used to create, update, and delete SharePoint data. With three variants, the Managed Client Object Model, the Silverlight Client Object Model, and the JavaScript Client Object Model, the SharePoint platform provides a great deal of flexibility when it comes to creating rich user interfaces. We also looked at how JavaScript can be used to create and manage a number of useful user interface elements such as dialogs and status notifications. As you get to know the SharePoint 2010 user interface, you'll see these techniques being used frequently by the platform itself.

# CHAPTER 5

# InfoPath Forms Services

SharePoint is a tool that's been designed to be usable by nontechnical users. One of the key design tenets is the notion that nontechnical users should be able to create basic web-based solutions using the web user interface and applications from the Microsoft Office suite. Although Microsoft Word and Excel undoubtedly have their place in SharePoint application design, when it comes to creating data capture forms, a more tailored tool is available.

The primary goal of InfoPath 2010 is to make it easy for nontechnical users to create forms that can be used to capture user input. Forms can be completed offline using the InfoPath client application, or, by using InfoPath Forms Services in SharePoint 2010, InfoPath forms can be rendered as web pages. In effect, coupling InfoPath 2010 with InfoPath Forms Services in SharePoint 2010 allows nontechnical users to create web-based data capture applications using a user interface that is familiar to users of other Office suite applications such as Word and Excel.

In this chapter, we'll look at how and where you can use InfoPath forms as well as covering the key features of the product.

## InfoPath Overview

From a technical perspective, InfoPath is an XML-based editor. Ultimately, an InfoPath form is an XML style sheet that makes use of XML-based data both for populating the form and for retrieving data from external data sources. For the most part, the bare bones XML functionality is hidden from the end user. However, as we take a closer look at the features available, you'll begin to see a few telltale signs. When we move on to look at creating code behind our InfoPath forms, you'll see how the application hangs together.

### InfoPath Forms Services

Introduced in MOSS 2007, InfoPath Forms Services allows forms created using the InfoPath client application to be rendered as HTML, allowing users to complete forms without having the client application installed.

Most services in SharePoint 2010 are implemented as service applications and are configured via the Manage Service Applications option in Central Administration. InfoPath Forms Services works a bit differently and can be configured as follows:

1. Open SharePoint Central Administration.
2. Select General Application Settings from the Central Administration pane on the left:

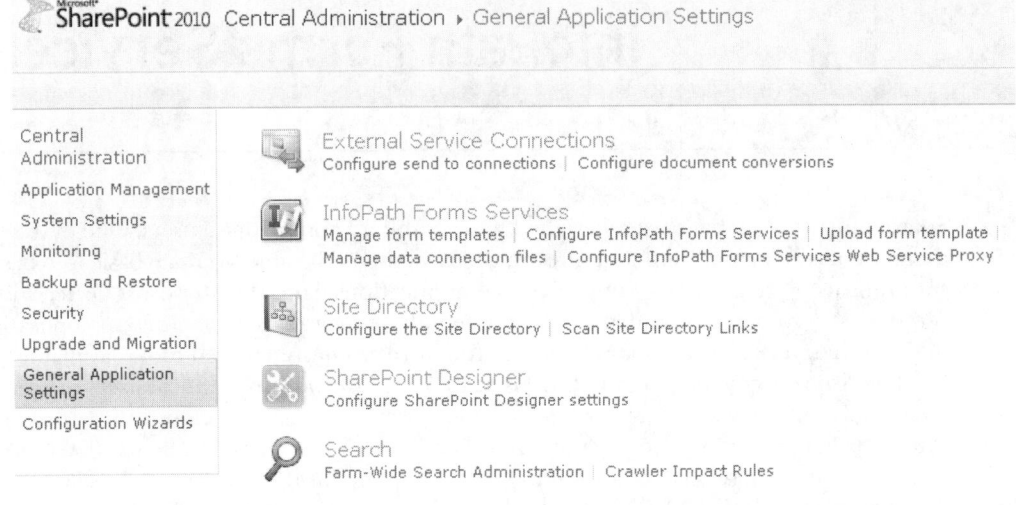

**SharePoint 2010** Central Administration ▸ General Application Settings

Central Administration
Application Management
System Settings
Monitoring
Backup and Restore
Security
Upgrade and Migration
General Application Settings
Configuration Wizards

External Service Connections
Configure send to connections | Configure document conversions

InfoPath Forms Services
Manage form templates | Configure InfoPath Forms Services | Upload form template | Manage data connection files | Configure InfoPath Forms Services Web Service Proxy

Site Directory
Configure the Site Directory | Scan Site Directory Links

SharePoint Designer
Configure SharePoint Designer settings

Search
Farm-Wide Search Administration | Crawler Impact Rules

In the InfoPath Forms Services section, you'll see various configuration links. (In-depth coverage of each of these options is outside the scope of this chapter; for more information, see http://technet.microsoft.com.) Generally speaking, the default configuration is appropriate for most situations. The Manage Form Templates and the Manage Data Connection Files options are useful for allowing you to manage form templates and connections.

To enable InfoPath Forms Services within a web site, you must enable the SharePoint Server Enterprise Site Collection features at the site-collection level. To add these features, take the following steps:

3. From the Site Actions menu, select Site Settings.
4. In the Site Collection Administration section, click Go To Top Level Site Settings.

Look and Feel
Title, description, and icon
Quick launch
Top link bar
Tree view
Site theme

Site Actions
Manage site features
Save site as template
Reset to site definition
Delete this site
Site Web Analytics reports
Site Collection Web Analytics reports

Site Collection Administration
Go to top level site settings

5. In Site Collection Administration, choose Site Collection Features. If it's not already activated, click the Activate button next to SharePoint Server Enterprise Site Collection Features.

## BrowserForm Web Part

Rendering of InfoPath forms in the web browser is carried out by the new BrowserForm web part. So that we can see this in action, we'll create a basic Hello World InfoPath form.

1. Using SharePoint Designer, create a new blank web site named Chapter5.
2. Follow the preceding steps to ensure that InfoPath Forms Services is enabled at the Site Collection level.
3. From the Site Objects pane, select Lists and Libraries, and then select Document Library from the New section of the Lists and Libraries tab on the ribbon. Create a new Form Library named MyForms, as shown:

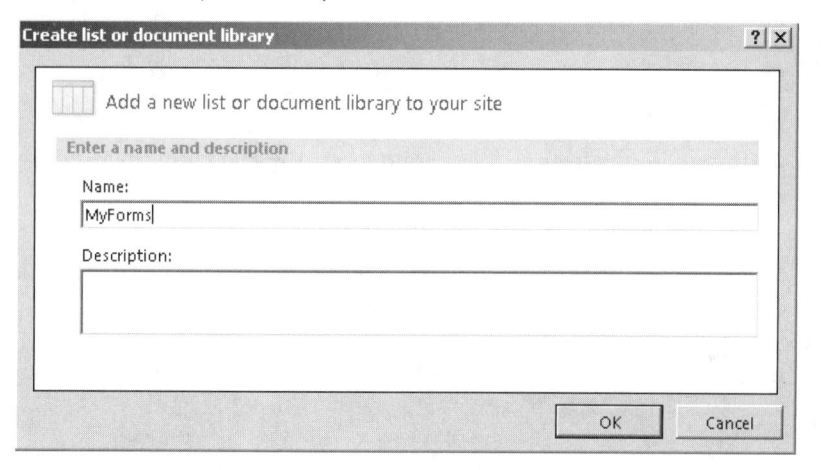

4. Open InfoPath Designer 2010, click on the File menu to see the backstage area, choose New, and then click the Blank form icon, as shown:

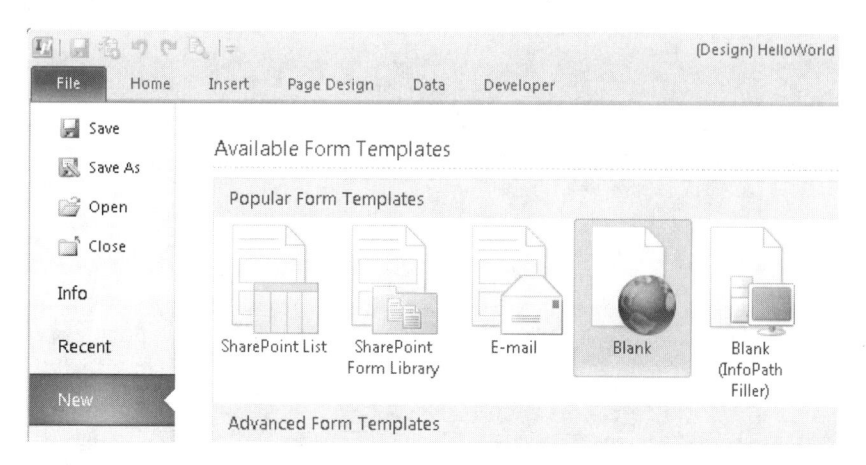

5. Click Design This Form to create a new form template.
6. Change the title to Hello World:

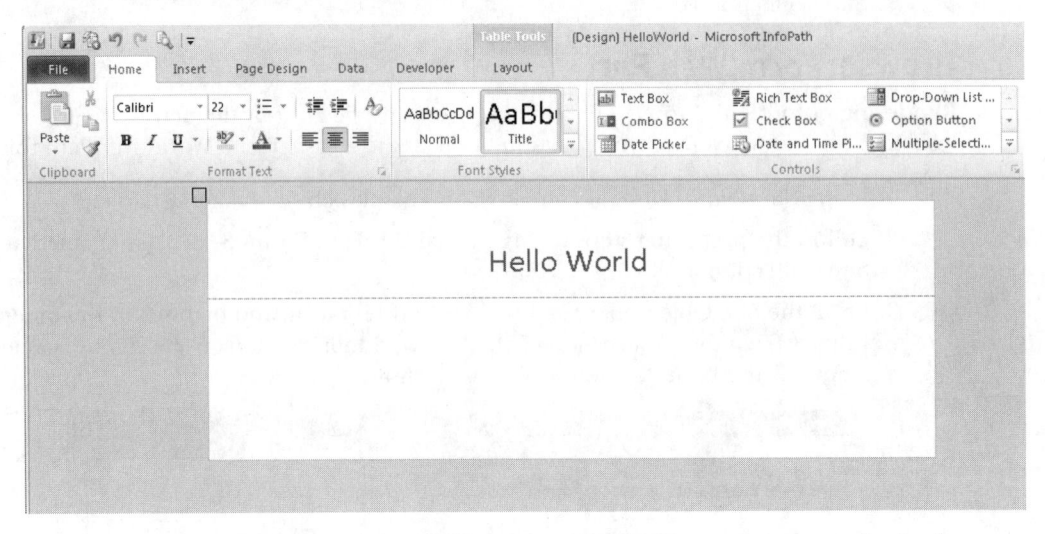

7. To publish the form to SharePoint, open the File menu to return to the backstage area. Click Publish Your Form to view the publishing options.
8. Select Publish Form to a SharePoint Library.
9. When prompted to save the form, save a copy to a location on the local file system.
10. In the Publishing Wizard dialog, enter the URL of the blank SharePoint site that we created earlier, as shown. Click Next to move to the next step.

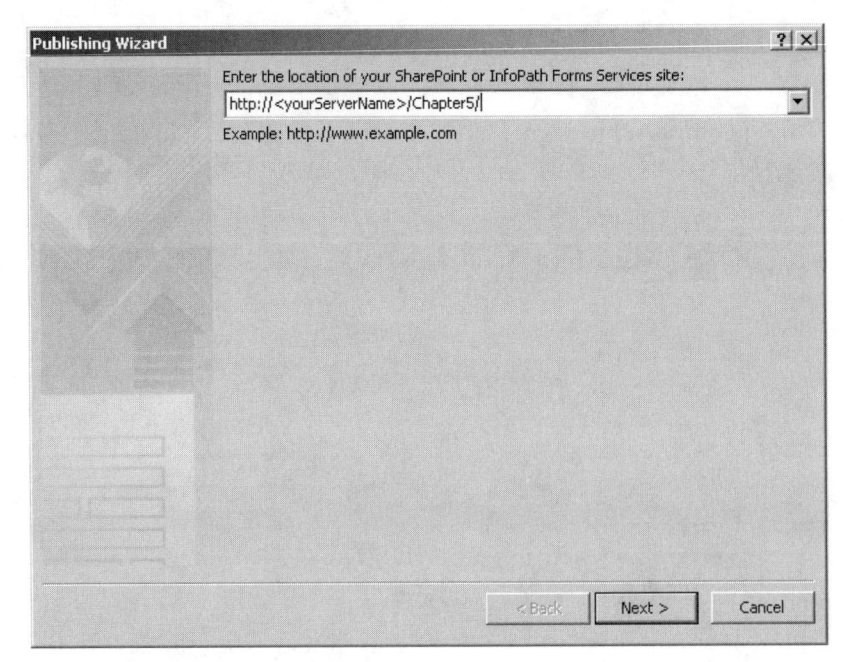

11. For the purposes of this simple demonstration, we'll publish the form as a template for the form library that we created earlier. Select Form Library from the list of options and ensure that the Enable This Form To Be Filled Out By Using A Browser Checkbox is checked. Click Next to move to the next step.

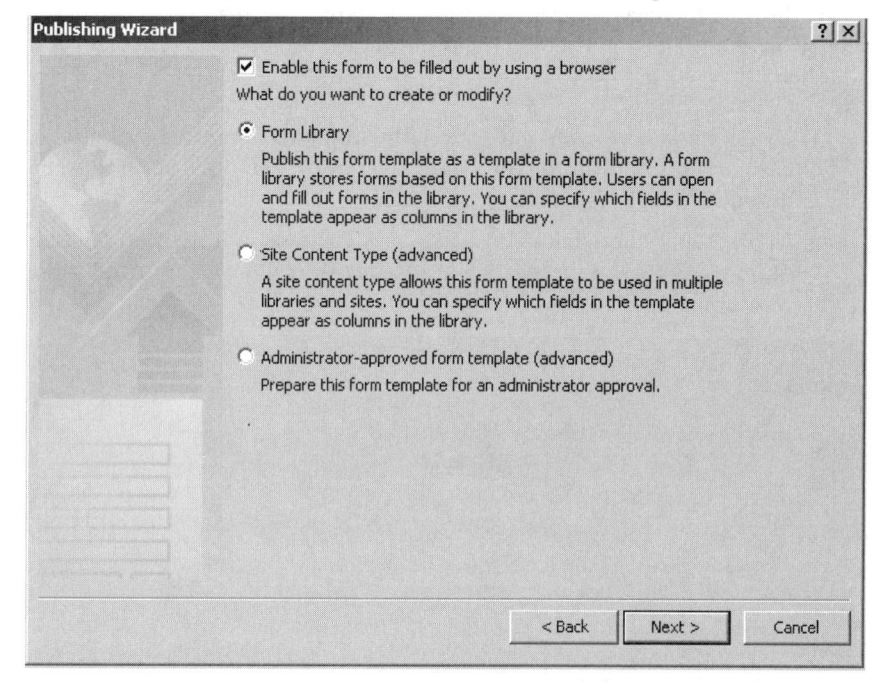

12. Select Update The Form Template In An Existing Form Library and then select the MyForms library from the list. Click Next to move to the next step.

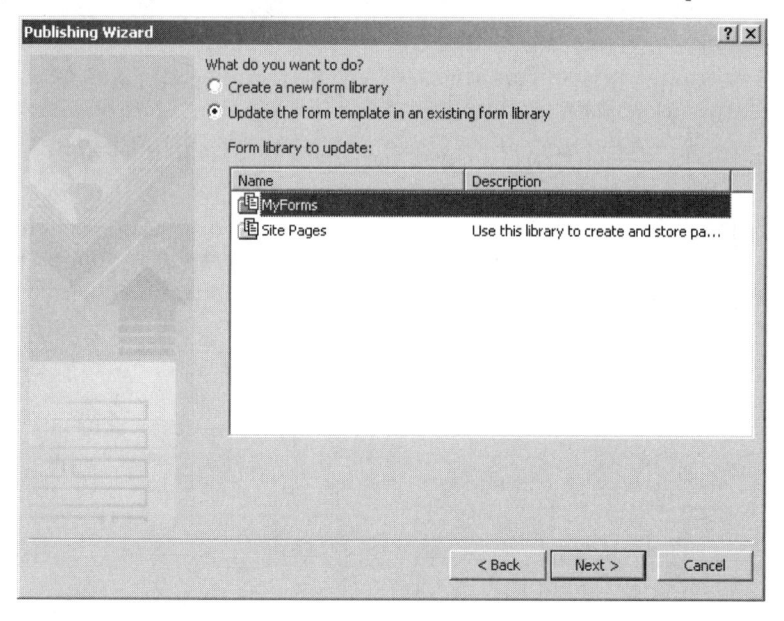

13. In this simple demo, we're not collecting any data or using any parameters. Click Next to move to the final step of the wizard, and then click Publish to publish the form to SharePoint.

**New in 2010**

To illustrate the use of the BrowserForm web part, we'll add the web part to the home page of our blank site and then configure it to pick up the Hello Word form that we've published.

1. Using the web browser, navigate to the home page of the blank site that we created earlier (http://<YourServerName>/chapter5/default.aspx). From the Site Actions menu on the ribbon, choose Edit Page.

2. In the Left section, click the Add a Web Part link and then, in the web part selector that appears at the top of the page, select the Office Client Applications category, as shown:

3. Select the InfoPath Form Web Part, and then click Add at the far right of the window to add it into the left zone of the page.

4. Click the Click Here To Open The Tool Pane link in the InfoPath Form Web Part section of the page.

5. From the List or Library drop-down, select MyForms. The Content Type and Views drop-downs will be populated automatically. Click OK to commit the changes.

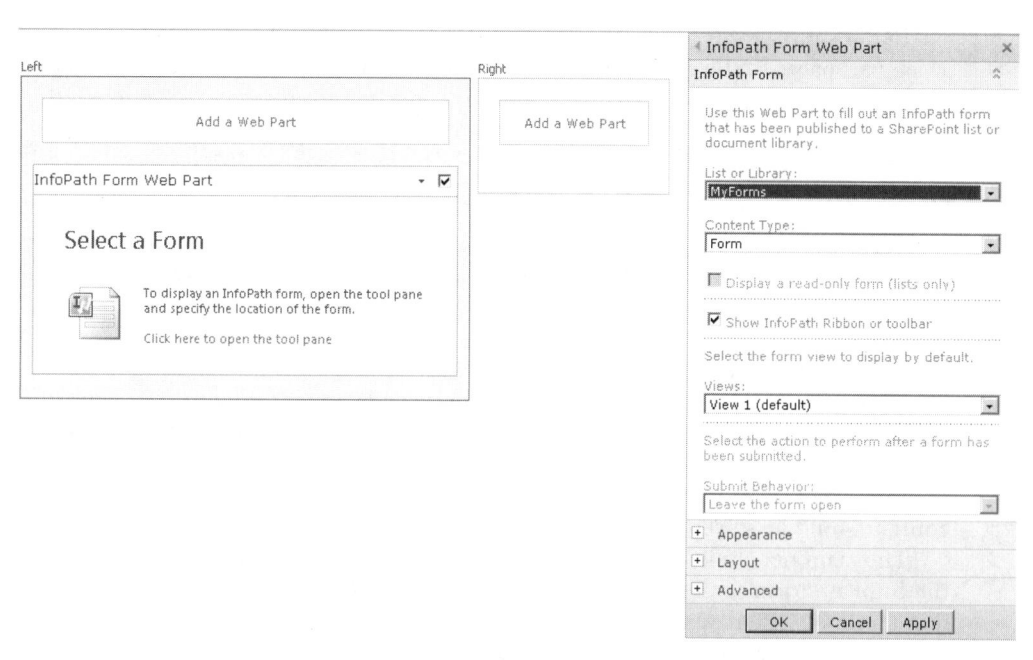

6. The demonstration InfoPath form will now be displayed on the page, as shown next. Click Stop Editing from the ribbon to exit design mode.

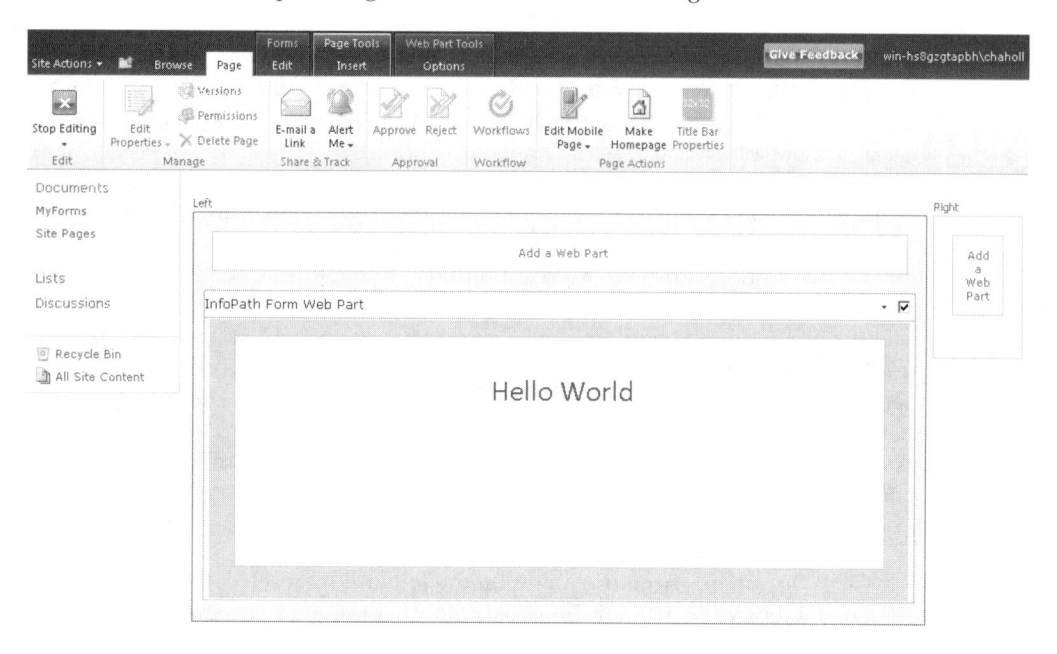

In this simple example, you've seen how to create an InfoPath form and use it within a web part page. In the examples that follow, we'll delve further into the functionality of InfoPath. However, as you'll see, the publishing mechanism remains pretty much the same regardless of the type of form you're creating.

## Using InfoPath Forms in SharePoint

In SharePoint applications, InfoPath forms are used in four main ways: to create form templates, custom forms for SharePoint lists, document information panels, and workflow forms.

### Creating Form Templates

SharePoint form templates are similar to forms used by other Office applications such as Word and Excel. Using the InfoPath client, you create form templates that are used for a SharePoint document library. As users complete the form and submit the data to SharePoint, the form is stored in the document library in the same way a Word document or any other content would be stored.

The main benefit in using InfoPath in this context as opposed to Word is that, although the InfoPath form can be completed using the InfoPath client application, for users who don't have the client application installed, the form will be automatically rendered for completion in the browser. Another key benefit is that the individual data items captured in an InfoPath form can be bound to columns in the document library. Although this is also possible using other Office applications, with InfoPath it's a bit more transparent.

**NOTE** In SharePoint 2010, you can install Office web applications so that a web-based version of applications such as Word and Excel will be available for use via the web browser if a user doesn't have the client application installed. In this case, using a Word template would also allow users to complete forms within the browser.

In the preceding example, you learned how to create a basic form and publish it to a form library. In effect, we created a form template that SharePoint can use to create new documents for storage within the MyForms library. To see this working, navigate to the MyForms library, open the Documents tab in the ribbon, and select New Document. You can see that our InfoPath template is displayed in a new page. Click Save and then enter **MyTestFile** as the filename. Click Close to return to the MyForms document library. You can see that a new document named MyTestFile has been added to the library.

Let's take a look at a more in-depth example of this type of form to see how you can capture data in InfoPath and save it within specific columns in SharePoint. In this example, we'll create a custom form that can be used by employees to request demonstration equipment. We'll create a new form library for this example.

1. Click Documents from the menu on the left and then select Create. Add a new Form Library and name it **Demonstration Equipment Requests**.

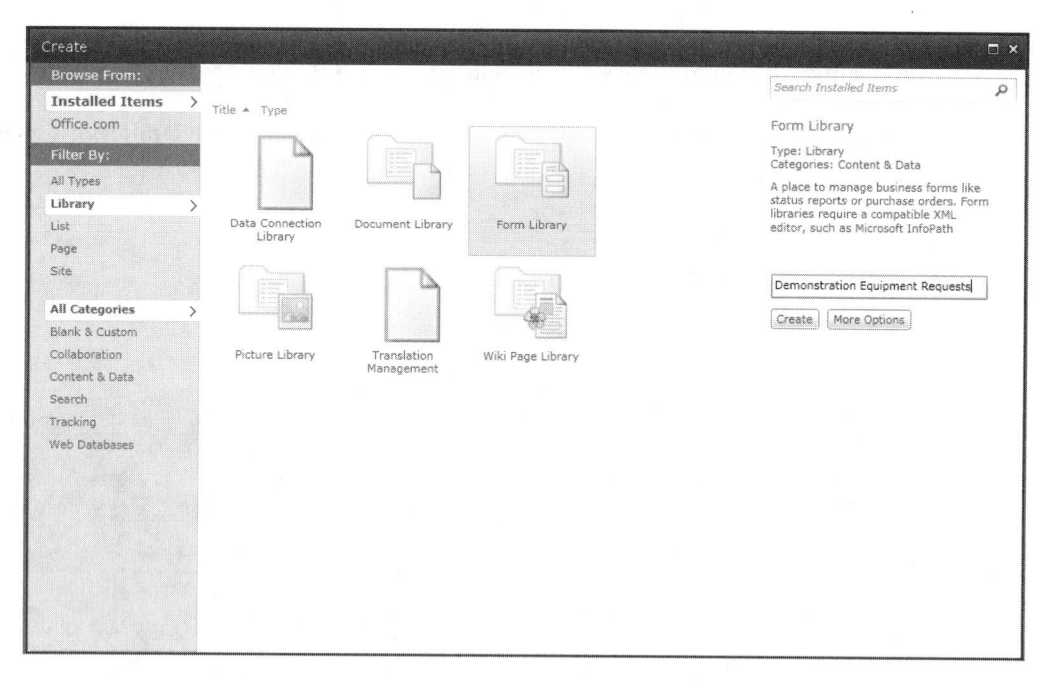

2. Open InfoPath Designer. In the New section of the backstage area, select SharePoint Form Library and then click Design This Form.
3. Change the form title to Demonstration Equipment Request, the top section title to Customer Details, and the bottom section title to Equipment Details, as shown here:

4. Before we add data entry controls to the page, we'll define the data structure for our form. Behind the scenes, the data structure is defined as an XML schema. In the Fields pane on the left side of the page, right-click the myFields node and then select Properties from the context menu. Change the Name to **EquipmentRequest**.

5. In the Actions section, click Add Field. Create a new field of type Group and type the Name as **Customer**. Repeat this step to create another group named **Equipment**.

6. Select the Equipment node and then click Add Field. Add a group node and type the Name **Item**; however, this time check the Repeating checkbox, as shown:

7. Now we can begin to add nodes for our individual fields. Within the Customer group, add the following fields:

| Name | Type | Data Type |
|---|---|---|
| CustomerId | Field (element) | Whole Number (integer) |
| CompanyName | Field (element) | Text (string) |
| AddressLine1 | Field (element) | Text (string) |
| AddressLine2 | Field (element) | Text (string) |
| City | Field (element) | Text (string) |
| StateProvince | Field (element) | Text (string) |
| PostalCode | Field (element) | Text (string) |

8. Within the Item repeating group, add the following fields:

| Name | Type | Data Type |
|---|---|---|
| ProductNumber | Field (element) | Text (string) |
| ProductName | Field (element) | Text (string) |
| StandardCost | Field (element) | Decimal (double) |
| ListPrice | Field (element) | Decimal (double) |
| Quantity | Field (element) | Whole Number (integer) |
| LineTotalCost | Field (element) | Decimal (double) |
| LineTotalValue | Field (element) | Decimal (double) |

9. In the Equipment group, add the following fields:

| Name | Type | Data Type |
|---|---|---|
| TotalCost | Field (element) | Decimal (double) |
| TotalValue | Field (element) | Decimal (double) |

10. After all fields have been added, the data structure should look as shown next. If any fields are not in the correct location, right-click the wayward field and select Move from the context menu to relocate the field within the data structure.

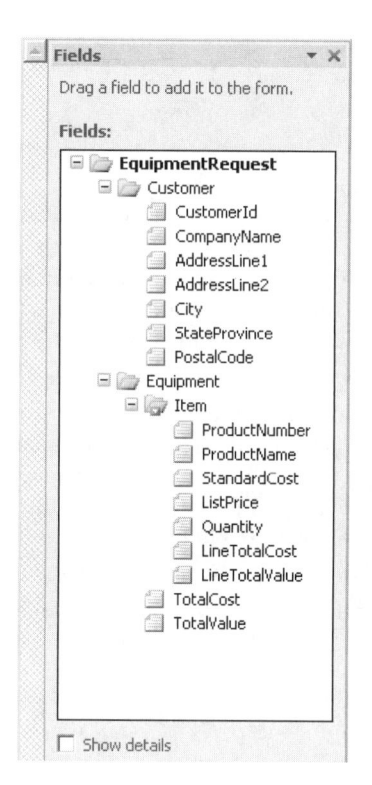

```
Fields

Drag a field to add it to the form.

Fields:
  EquipmentRequest
    Customer
      CustomerId
      CompanyName
      AddressLine1
      AddressLine2
      City
      StateProvince
      PostalCode
    Equipment
      Item
        ProductNumber
        ProductName
        StandardCost
        ListPrice
        Quantity
        LineTotalCost
        LineTotalValue
      TotalCost
      TotalValue

☐ Show details
```

We can now start adding controls to capture data for our fields. The design experience in InfoPath is very much data-led. When we define the data source first, creating a user interface is often a case of simply dragging the appropriate data elements onto the page. InfoPath Designer automatically inserts an appropriate input control that is bound to the correct field.

11. In the Customer Details section, select the cells that are underneath the title, and then, from the Layout tab of the ribbon, select Merge Cells. Repeat this step for the Equipment Details section. The revised form should look as follows:

12. Drag the Customer group element into the Customer Details section of the form. InfoPath Designer will automatically add text boxes for each field together with labels for the field name. Rather than having the controls laid out sequentially on the page, we can reformat them into a table by converting the section control into a Controls in Layout Table control. Select the Section control, and from the Properties menu in the ribbon, select Change Control | Controls in Layout Table.

13. Although our layout table looks much tidier than the standard section control layout, we no longer have field labels. We can add these in by selecting a control within the layout table and then choosing Insert Left from the Layout tab in the ribbon. To get the name of the field, place the cursor over the adjacent text box control; this will show the field element to which the control is bound. Using this technique, add in appropriate labels for each field.

14. Tables in InfoPath can be resized in much the same way as they are changed in Word and Excel: simply drag the edges of the columns to the appropriate size. Using this method, resize the table so that all data can be clearly seen as shown:

Now that we've added controls to capture details of the customer that's requesting demonstration equipment, the next section of our form allows users to enter details of the equipment required. Since more than one piece of equipment may be required by a customer, we've added a repeating Item section to our data set. We can allow users to add as many items as they need by creating a repeating table on the form.

1. Drag the Item repeating Group onto the Equipment Details section of the form.
2. Select Repeating Table from the pop-up list of options.

**Adding Formulae to Fields**   Our Item data element contains two columns, LineTotalCost and LineTotalValue, that should be calculated based on the values entered in other columns in the row. To add formulae for these fields, take the following steps:

1. Select the Line Total Cost text box in the repeating table control. From the Properties tab in the ribbon, select Default Value.
2. In the Field Or Group Properties dialog, click the fx button next to the Default Value text box.
3. Using the Insert Field or Group button to select the appropriate fields, add this formula, as shown next: **Quantity * StandardCost**.

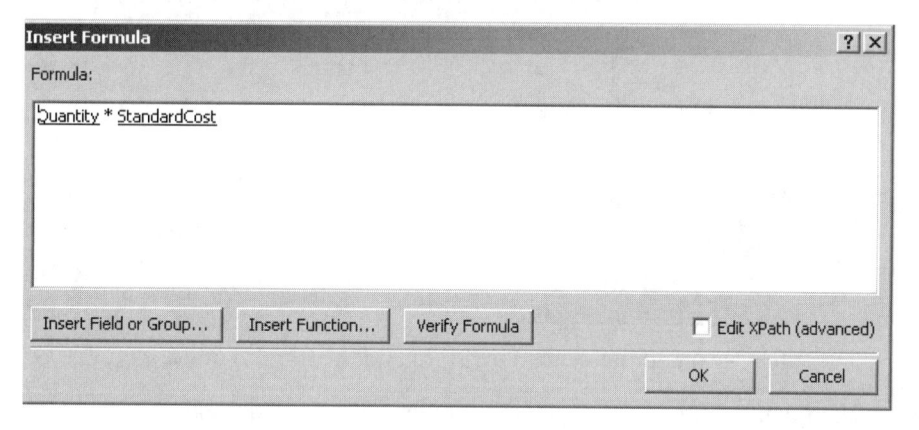

4. Repeat the process for the Line Total Value text box. This time add this formula: **Quantity * ListPrice**.
5. To prevent users from entering values in these calculated fields, we need to change them from text boxes to labels. Click the Change Control option from the Properties tab on the ribbon, and then select CalculatedValue.

**Publishing a Form Template to SharePoint**   Our basic Demonstration Equipment Request form is now complete. To publish it to SharePoint and use it for capturing data for our Demonstration Equipment Request library, take the following steps:

1. As we did earlier, from the backstage area, click Publish Form To A SharePoint Library. Type the server URL as **http://<YourServerName>/Chapter5**. When prompted, save a copy of the form named EquipmentRequest.xsn to the local file system.

2. Select Form Library from the list of options, and then select the Demonstration Equipment Requests library. Click Next to move to the next step of the wizard.

3. When we published our simple form earlier, we skipped this section. Since we want to capture data from our equipment request form, we need to specify which fields we want to include as columns in our document library. By clicking the Add button in the upper section of the form, add all fields within the Customer group to the library, as shown:

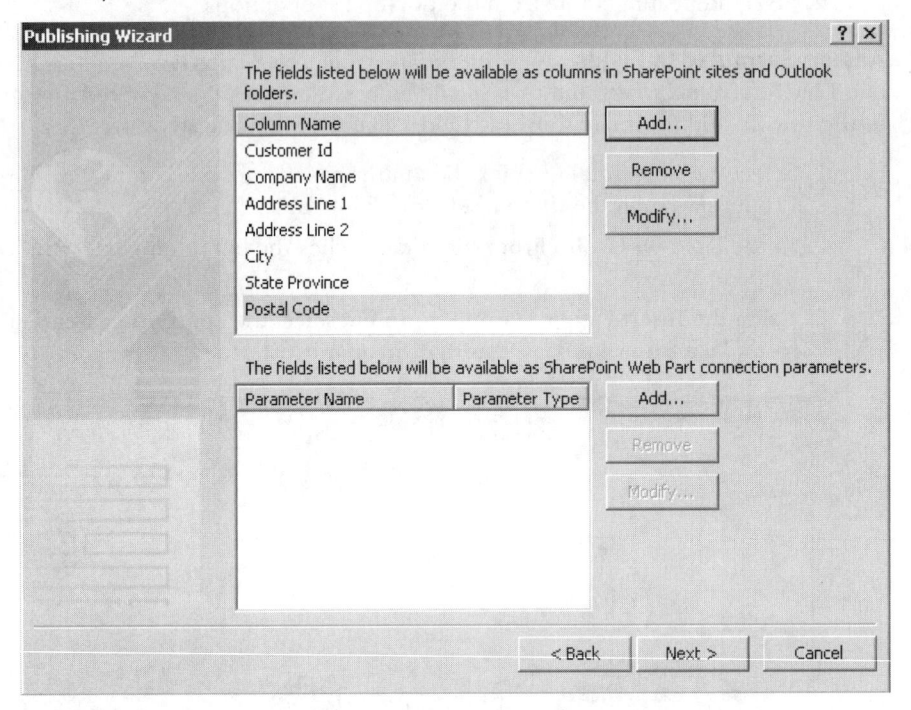

[Publishing Wizard dialog showing fields: Customer Id, Company Name, Address Line 1, Address Line 2, City, State Province, Postal Code]

4. Click Next and then click Publish to add the form to our library.

Using the browser to navigate to the Demonstration Equipment Requests library, you can see that by clicking the New Document button on the Documents ribbon, our InfoPath form is displayed, allowing us to enter details as expected. To store the form in the document library, we must use the Save option and name the form. By performing this step, we're saving a copy of the form in the document library and at the same time copying the field values that we specified earlier into columns.

## Creating Custom Forms for SharePoint Lists

Another use of InfoPath forms, and one that's become more prevalent with SharePoint 2010, is in the creation of custom new and edit forms for SharePoint lists. Custom forms differ from the form templates that we saw earlier: the form itself is not stored in the library. Since custom forms can be used only with lists, only the field data that we elect to include is copied to columns in the list as opposed to the entire completed form. Let's create a custom form for a SharePoint list:

1. Using SharePoint Designer, create a new custom list named MyCustomList. From the Lists and Libraries navigator, double-click the MyCustomList icon to manage the settings for the list.
2. In the List Settings tab of the ribbon, select Design Forms in InfoPath | Item. InfoPath Designer will then open, displaying a basic template for capturing list item data.
3. Additional fields can be added using the Add Field link in the Fields pane. When you add a field to the form, a column is also added to the underlying list to store the captured data. For example, we could add a field named Description. Once the form is published, a new column named Description will be added to our custom list.
4. To publish the customized form, click Info in the left pane and then click the Quick Publish button in the backstage area:

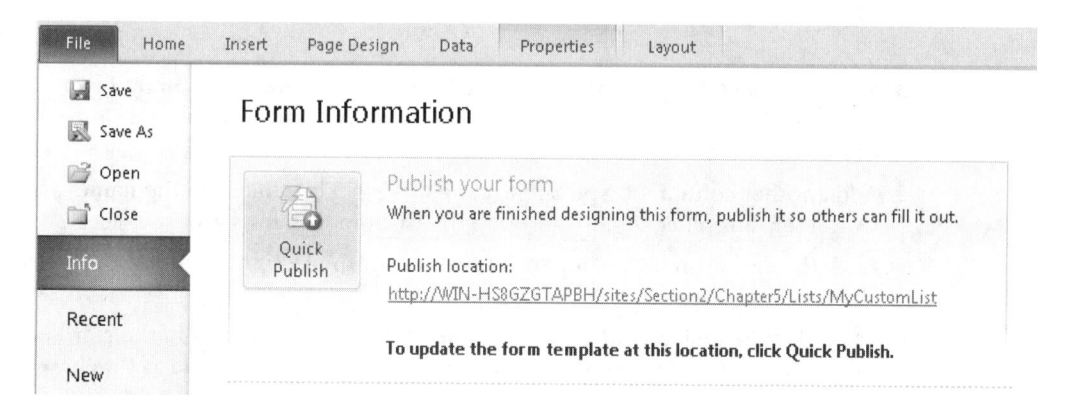

## Creating Document Information Panels

When creating Office documents for use with SharePoint, certain metadata is required by default, such as a title for the document and any relevant tags. Along with the default metadata that's required by the Document content type, you can add additional metadata that will be stored as specific columns in the document library. This data is captured using a Document Information Panel, and customization of such a panel is another important use of InfoPath.

1. From the Site Objects pane in SharePoint Designer, select Lists And Libraries. Add a new Document Library and name it **Purchase Orders**.

2. Double-click the Purchase Orders icon to manage the settings for the document library. In the Settings section, check the Allow Management Of Content Types checkbox, as shown. Click the Save icon in the upper-right corner of the Designer window to persist the changes.

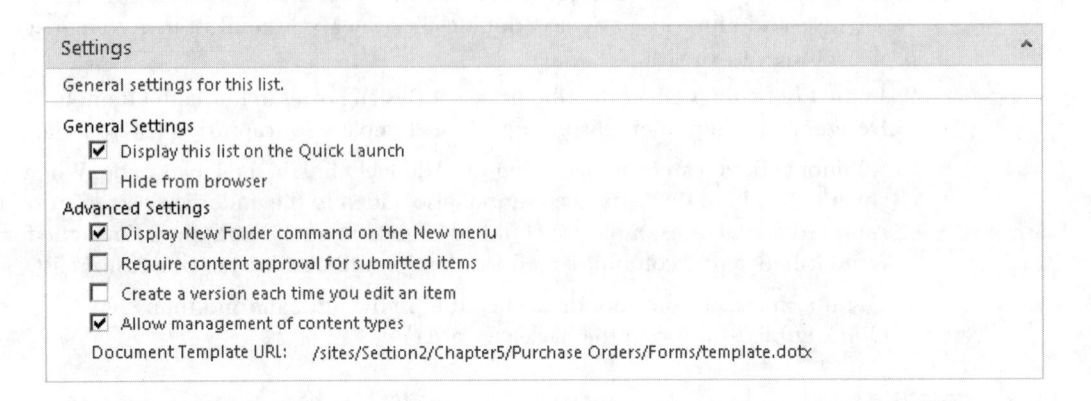

```
Settings
General settings for this list.
General Settings
    ☑ Display this list on the Quick Launch
    ☐ Hide from browser
Advanced Settings
    ☑ Display New Folder command on the New menu
    ☐ Require content approval for submitted items
    ☐ Create a version each time you edit an item
    ☑ Allow management of content types
Document Template URL:    /sites/Section2/Chapter5/Purchase Orders/Forms/template.dotx
```

3. From the Site Objects pane, select Site Columns. Add a new column of type Currency. Type the Name of the column as **Amount** and add it to the Custom Columns group.

4. Add another column of type Single Line of Text. This time type the name **Customer Reference**. Again, add it to the Custom Columns group.

5. Click the Save icon in the upper-right corner of the Designer window to persist the changes.

6. From the Site Objects pane, select Content Types, and then, from the New section of the Content Types ribbon, click Content Type. Type the Name as **Purchase Order** and the parent content type to Document, as shown next. Add the content type to the Document Content Types group.

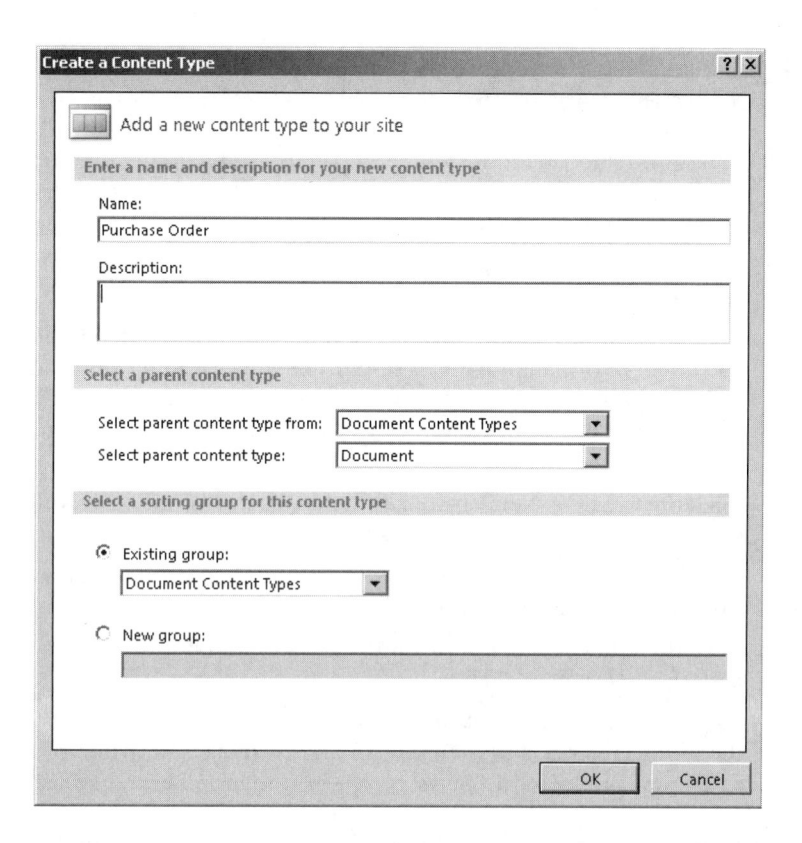

7. Double-click the Purchase Order content type to manage its settings, and then click the Edit Columns button in the ribbon.
8. Click the Add Existing Site Column button to add the Amount and Customer Reference columns that we created earlier. Click the Save icon to persist the changes.
9. With the Purchase Order content type selected, from the Actions section of the Content Types ribbon, select Apply to List. Select the Purchase Orders document library from the Lists and Libraries picker.

> **NOTE** We've touched on a few key concepts of the SharePoint data structure in the course of setting up this example. For more details on content types and site columns, see Chapter 13.

10. Configuring document information panels can be done only from a browser-based user interface. Using the browser, navigate to the Purchase Orders document library. From the Library tab of the ribbon, select Library Settings.
11. In the Content Types section, click the Purchase Order content type and then select the Document Information Panel settings link.

    Document Information panels are configured at the content type level. In effect, a document information panel is responsible for providing a user interface to capture and display data that is stored in the columns that are referenced by the content type. In the case of our example, we added two additional columns: Amount and Customer Reference.
12. Click the Create A New Custom Template link. This will open InfoPath Designer, where we can customize the system generated Document Information panel.
13. Select the Customer Reference text box, and then from the Properties tab of the ribbon, select Change Control | Combo Box.
14. Click the Edit Choices button, and using the Add button, enter a few sample customer reference values.
15. To publish the Document Information panel to SharePoint, click File to enter the backstage area, and then select Publish Your Form. When prompted, enter a filename on the local file system to save the form before publishing.

If you navigate to the Purchase Orders document library, you can now select New Document | Purchase Order from the Documents tab to see the fruits of our labor. A blank Word document is shown with our custom information panel at the top of the page.

### Creating Workflow Forms

The final use, and one that I'll cover in more detail in Chapter 11, is the creation of workflow forms. Often, as part of a workflow process, you'll need to capture additional user input. InfoPath, and particularly the ability of SharePoint Designer to create appropriate InfoPath forms automatically, makes it easy to capture this additional information.

## Accessing Data in InfoPath Forms

One of the powerful features of InfoPath, especially when it comes to generating browser-based forms, is the ability to connect to additional data sources. We can reuse our earlier Demonstration Equipment Request form to see this in action.

1. Open the EquipmentRequest.xsn file from the local file system. Our form has two sections: the top section captures customer details and the bottom section captures a list of products. Rather than manually keying in customer details, we'll make use of a SQL Server database to look up the required information and automatically populate the fields.

**TIP** For demonstration purposes, SQL connections are easiest to use. However, their usefulness within InfoPath forms is pretty limited. Passing parameters generally requires custom code, as you'll see later. As a general rule, the best way to communicate with external data sources is to create a custom web service interface. InfoPath can then parse the Web Service Definition Language (WSDL) and create fields for any parameters that may be required.

To provide some sample data to work within our various examples, we need to download and install the SQL Server 2008 sample databases, which can be found at www.codeplex.com/MSFTDBProdSamples. Our examples make use of the AdventureWorksLT database installed on the local instance of SQL Server 2008.

2. At the bottom of the Customer Details section, add a button. Buttons and other controls can be found in the Controls section of the Home ribbon. Type the button label as **Find Customer**.

3. To add a data connection, switch to the Data tab on the ribbon, and then click From Other Sources | From Database, as shown:

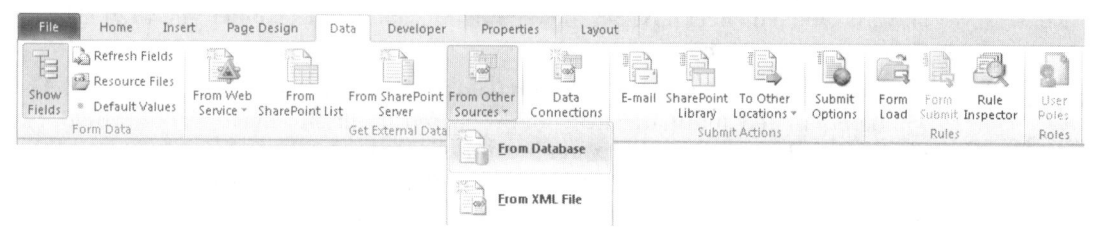

4. Click Select Database to select from the data sources that are available on the current machine. If one is not available for the AdventureWorksLT database, click New Source to add one. Select the Customer table when prompted. Once the data connection has been made, the columns will be listed, as shown next:

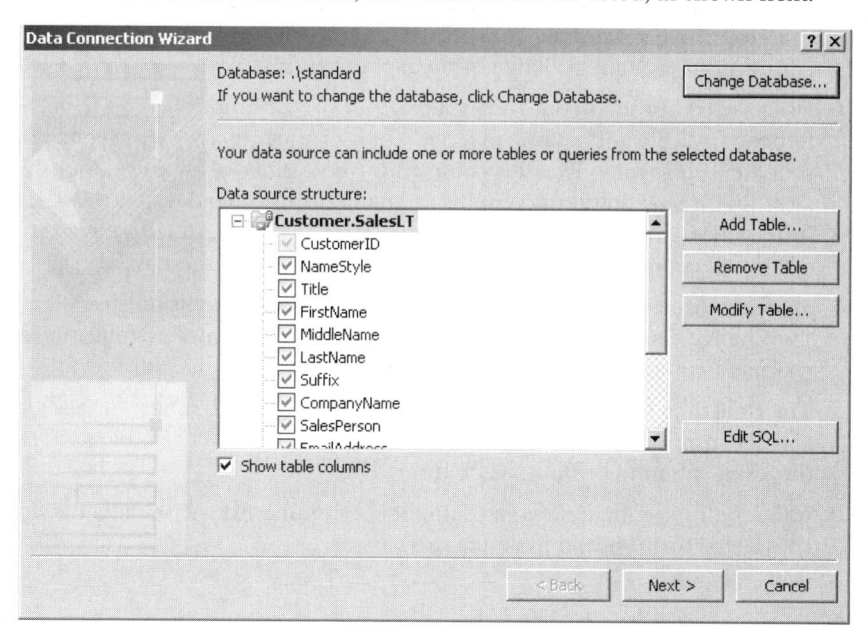

5. Since we want to use a query to extract data from more than one table, click Edit SQL and enter the following SQL statement:

```
Select          C.CustomerID,
                C.CompanyName,
                A.AddressLine1,
                A.AddressLine2,
                A.City,
                A.StateProvince,
                A.PostalCode
From            SalesLT.Customer as C
Inner Join      SalesLT.CustomerAddress as CA
On              CA.CustomerID=C.CustomerID
Inner Join      SalesLT.Address as A
On              A.AddressID=CA.AddressID
```

6. Click Next. Leave the Store A Copy Of The Data In The Form Template checkbox unchecked. Click Next and then uncheck the Automatically Retrieve Data When Form Is Opened checkbox. Set the connection name to **Customer** and then click Finish to create the connection.

7. We'll make use of the Company Name field to search for customers. All other fields will be populated automatically from the search results. To make all other fields read-only, select the field and then from the Properties tab of the ribbon, check the Read-Only option in the Modify section. Repeat this process for all fields in the Customer Details section other than the Company Name field.

8. We'll display our search results on a separate page. From the Page Design tab's Views section, select New. Name the new view **Customer Search Results**.

9. Type the title of the new view as **Customer Search** and then, from the Fields pane, in the Fields drop-down, select Customer (Secondary). (The Fields drop-down is something of a misnomer. In reality, the drop-down contains a list of the data connections that are available to the current form.)

10. Drag the d:Customer repeating group onto the Customer Search form. Select Repeating Table as the control type. When producing a schema from a SQL statement, InfoPath also adds columns for both sides of a join relationship. As a result, three redundant columns are named CustomerID1, AddressID, and AddressID1. To remove these from our repeating table, simply select the offending columns and choose Delete | Columns from the Layout tab.

11. Since we don't want the user to be able to edit the contents of these fields, using the Change Control button on the Properties menu that we demonstrated earlier, change the controls to Calculated Values.

12. The final item that we need to add to our search form is a button to select the correct customer. Place the cursor in the first column of the table and then, from the Table tab in the ribbon, click Insert Left.

13. Add a button in the data area of the new column and type the label as **Select**. The completed form should look like this:

## Data Connection Libraries

When we added our data connection, the connection details were stored along with the InfoPath form. This technique is known as "embedding connection details." In simple cases, this approach works well; however, in larger developments, such a technique may not be appropriate. Often multiple environments exist for testing, staging, and production. Embedding connection details within a form template would require the template to be changed for each environment. Also, if an embedded connection contains user credentials, these are stored as plain text within the file.

To get around problems like this and to promote the reuse of administrator controlled data connections, InfoPath can save data connections to a data connection library. To create a new data connection library, take the following steps:

1. Browse to the home page of the sample site that we created earlier: (http://<YourServerName>/Chapter5).
2. From the Site Actions menu, select More Options, and then, from the Create dialog, select Data Connection Library. Name the new library **MyConnections**.

We can now publish the data connection from our Demonstration Equipment Request form by taking the following steps:

1. In InfoPath Designer Fields pane, click the Manage Data Connections link.
2. Select the Customer data connection and then click Convert To Connection File.
3. Using the Browse button on the Convert To Data Connection dialog, select the MyConnections Document Library and save the file as Customer.udcx.
4. Click OK to save the Universal Data Connection (UDC) file.

## Modifying UDC Files

By default, our data connection is configured to use Integrated Windows Authentication. This means that connections to the data store are made using the credentials of the user viewing the form. There are, however, a few problems with this approach. Probably the most obvious is that all users accessing the form must have permissions to the underlying data store. Another problem that isn't so apparent is what's known as the "double-hop issue." NT LAN Manager (NTLM) doesn't allow credentials to be delegated by an intermediary system. This is a problem when using InfoPath Forms Services, because the credentials are captured on the user interface tier, but it is the middle tier, the InfoPath

Forms Services layer, that actually connects to the data source. Since the middle tier can't impersonate the user connected to the user interface tier, it's not possible to connect to a data source on a separate server using Integrated Windows Authentication.

You can, however, deal with this problem in a few ways: One way is to make use of the Secure Store Service (see Chapters 12 and 15). The other way is to embed a username and password in the connection details. Although using the Secure Store Service is the most secure option, for the purposes of this demonstration, we'll use embedded credentials.

1. Create a login on the SQL server that contains the AdventureWorksLT database. Create a SQL login named InfoPathDemo with a password of password. Make sure that the server is configured to use Windows and SQL authentication.

2. With the login created, grant it read permissions on the AdventureWorksLT database. Check that it can connect by using the Connect option in SQL Server Management Studio.

3. UDC files are stored as plain text files containing XML in the SharePoint document library. However, by opening a file with Visual Studio 2010, the XML Designer makes it easier to see what's going on. Navigate to the MyConnections document library, and then click the Check Out button on the Documents tab to check out the Customer data connection file.

4. From the Library tab, click the Open With Explorer button as shown:

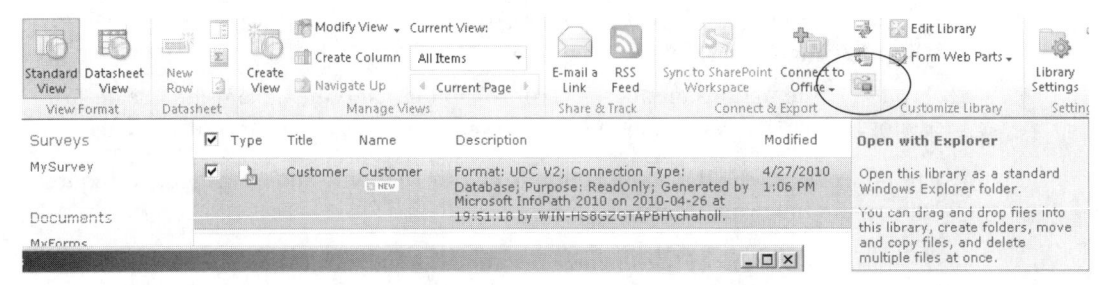

5. The document library will be opened in Windows Explorer. Open the Customer.udcx file with Visual Studio and find the udc:ConnectionString element.

6. Change the connection string to include the following:

```
Provider=SQLOLEDB.1;
Persist Security Info=True;
Initial Catalog=AdventureWorksLT;
User Id=InfoPathDemo;Password=password;
Data Source=<YourServerName>;
```

7. Save the file and then switch back to the MyConnections document library and check in the updated document.

8. Before the connection string can be used, a system administrator must explicitly approve embedded credentials in connection files. Navigate to Central Administration | General Application Settings | Configure InfoPath Forms Services. Check the Embedded SQL Authentication checkbox.

Our connection file is now set up to use embedded connection credentials and will work properly for all users accessing it.

> **NOTE** Within the UDC file is a udc:Authentication element that's commented out by default. To configure the connection to use Secure Store Service for authentication, uncomment this section. The AppId is the Target Application Id and the CredentialType will either be *NTLM* for Windows authentication or *SQL* for SQL Authentication. For more details on configuring this element, see http://msdn.microsoft.com.

# Responding to Events in InfoPath Forms

Carrying on with our Equipment Request form, let's look at how we can hook up the buttons on the form using a few methods that follow.

## Using the Rules Engine

The easiest way to handle events in an InfoPath form is to use the built-in rules engine. Three different types of Rules can be applied to a control or field:

- **Validation** Allows users to add a validation formula to a field or control. Where the validation formula does not return true, a user-defined message is displayed.

- **Formatting** Formatting works a bit like conditional formatting in Excel. The user can define a condition or formula that must evaluate to true or false. If the formula evaluates to true, the format is applied.

- **Action** Within InfoPath most event handling is done using Action rules. By using Action rules, a user can perform a series of actions when a specified condition occurs. Some examples of a condition that can trigger an action rule are Field Changed and Button Clicked.

We'll make use of an Action rule to switch to our Customer Search view when the Find Customer button is clicked on our form:

1. If you haven't already done so, switch back to the default view: in the Page Design tab of the ribbon, select View 1 (default) from the View drop-down. Then click the Find Customer button.

2. From the Properties tab's Button section of the ribbon, select Rules. You'll see the Rules pane on the right side of the page.

3. Select New | Action from the Rules pane, and then type the rule name as **Do Customer Search**.

4. In the Run These Actions section, click Add | Switch Views, and then select Customer Search Results from the list of views.

5. As well as showing our search results page, we need to perform the actual query. This time select Add | Query For Data, and then select the Customer data connection from the list.

We can now publish this form and see the results using the browser. When the user clicks the Find Customer button, a list of customers is displayed, allowing the user to select an appropriate record. The next step is to copy the selected customer details into our main form and then switch back.

1. In the Page Design tab of the ribbon, switch to the Customer Search Results view, and then highlight the Select button.
2. From the Properties tab on the ribbon, click Add Rule | When This Button is Clicked | Set A Field's Value.
3. In the Rule Details dialog, set the Field to the CompanyName field on the Main data source, as shown. The selector can be accessed by clicking the down-arrow button at the right of the Fields text box.

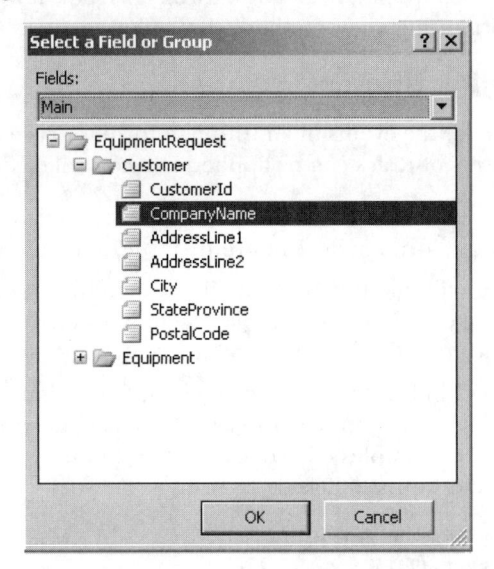

4. Set the Value to the CompanyName field of the Customer data source. Again this can be done by clicking the down-arrow button to the right of the text box. Click Insert Field Or Group on the Insert Formula dialog that appears to show the selector.
5. Repeat this process to copy all fields from the d:Customer group into the Customer group of the main data source. Rather than using the Add Rule button in the ribbon, which will create a new rule, you can add an additional action to the current rule by choosing Add | Set A Field's Value from the Rules pane.

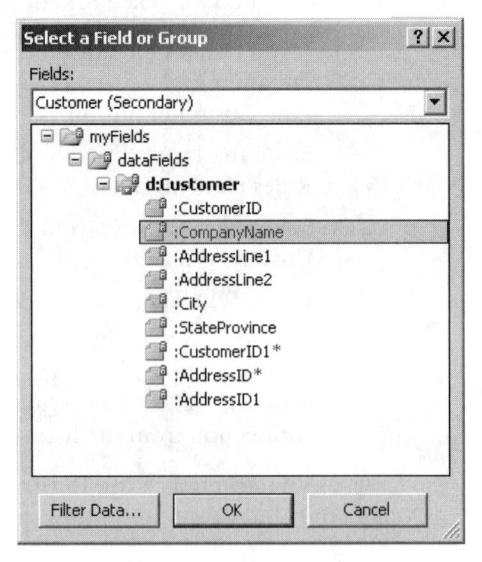

6. After all the field values are copied, switch back to default view. From the Rules pane, click Add | Switch Views and set the view to View 1.

We can now publish the updated form and navigate to the document library to see the fruits of our labor. This time, when you click Find Customer and select a customer from the list, the details are copied into our main form and the search view is hidden from view.

## Adding Code-Behind

You may have noticed in our demonstration form that no matter what is entered in the Company Name field, all companies are returned each time the Find Customer button is clicked. Because we're using a database connection to retrieve our customer details, we don't have the facility to pass in a parameter using the data connection interface in InfoPath. However, behind the scenes, InfoPath exposes a full object model that allows us to control practically all aspects of the data connection using managed code.

By adding a managed code event handler to our Find Customer button, we'll dynamically modify the SQL query that's used to generate our search results.

**NOTE** Using managed code with InfoPath 2010 requires Visual Studio Tools for Applications. This feature can be installed using the Office 2010 setup program. Under Microsoft Office InfoPath, select Visual Studio Tools for Applications in the .NET Programmability Support group.

Before we start writing our custom event handler, we'll modify the rules that we added earlier to prevent the database from being queried twice.

1. Click the Find Customer button and then in the Rules pane, delete the Query using a data connection action: click the arrow to the right of the action and choose Delete.

2. From the Developer tab in the ribbon, click the Language button. Make sure the Form template Code language is set to C#. (You can use VB, but the code in this sample is written in C#.)

3. Switch to the Properties tab, and then click the Custom Code button in the Button section of the ribbon. The Visual Studio Tools for Applications interface will be loaded and a stub method will be created to handle the click event for our button.

4. Type the following code in the body of the stub method:

```
string xpath=@"/my:EquipmentRequest/my:Customer/my:CompanyName";
XPathNavigator nav = this.MainDataSource.CreateNavigator();
string companyName = nav.SelectSingleNode(xpath,this.NamespaceManager).Value;
DataSource customer = this.DataSources["Customer"];
AdoQueryConnection cnn = customer.QueryConnection as AdoQueryConnection;
string allItemsQuery = cnn.Command;
cnn.Command =allItemsQuery + " Where C.CompanyName like '%" + companyName + "%'";
cnn.Execute();
cnn.Command = allItemsQuery;
```

A few items in this code sample require some explanation—first, the **xpath** variable: As mentioned earlier, InfoPath is an XML-based form designer. On the surface, this may seem trivial, since all developers are familiar with XML and the various objects in the .NET Framework that can be used to work with XML. However, because InfoPath is completely XML-based, things work a bit differently and it can take time to fully understand the difference.

In traditional WinForms or ASP.NET programming, the presentation user interface is separate from the data. Often, most of the code that we write involves either reading data from or writing data to controls. Since the presentation layer in InfoPath is simply a transformation of the data (that is, an XSLT transform of XML data), there is no presentation layer to manipulate programmatically. Data is automatically bound to the appropriate controls. If we were writing an ASP.NET application, we may retrieve the value of the CompanyName text box by examining the Text property of the appropriate control; in InfoPath, there is no such control and we retrieve the value of the CompanyName field by querying the data model directly. The most common way to perform this query is to use XPath, and the **xpath** variable stores the XPath expression that refers to the appropriate field.

> **TIP** InfoPath Designer makes it easy to determine the XPath expression for a particular field. In the Fields pane, right-click the required field and select Copy XPath from the context menu. The XPath expression will be placed on the clipboard ready for use in custom code.

The next item that warrants some explanation is the DataSource object. The following class diagram shows how data sources are defined by the InfoPath object model:

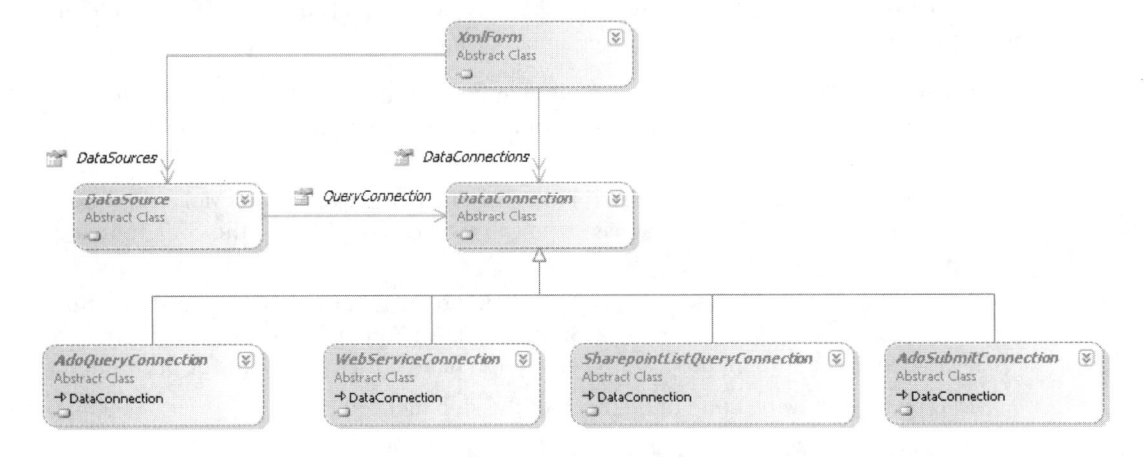

You'll notice that all of the classes in this diagram are abstract. All data connections are ultimately defined using XML schemas and other XML-based configuration data. At runtime, InfoPath creates objects from these files that derive from the appropriate base class. For example, in our code sample, we declare an object of type AdoQueryConnection to allow us to modify the query for our database connection. In reality, the actual type of this object is AdoQueryConnectionHost, which is an internal type that is created when the connection details are deserialized.

> **NOTE** Not all InfoPath forms can make use of managed code due to security restrictions in SharePoint. Custom list template forms and workflow forms that are automatically generated using SharePoint Designer can't use managed code. When managed code is not available for a particular form type, the Developer tab will not appear in the ribbon.

Now that our customer search function works properly, we can publish the form to SharePoint and check out the results.

## Summary

This chapter covered the main uses of InfoPath forms within SharePoint. You've seen how nontechnical users can create custom forms using a user interface that's similar to that of other applications in the Microsoft Office suite. You've also seen how we, as developers, can extend this basic functionality with managed code where required. By using advanced functionality such as data connections, InfoPath can be used to build a complex user interface for practically any data-driven business application. Furthermore, the user interface can be customized easily by nontechnical users. From a development perspective, this is a very powerful feature. Traditional development approaches mean that developers are often called upon to make trivial changes to user interface elements such as field validation or control layouts. By building a solution that leverages InfoPath, users are free to make these changes themselves, freeing developers to focus on more in-depth customizations.

# CHAPTER 6

# Enterprise Content Management

One of the greatest strengths of the Internet may also be its greatest weakness: Anybody can create and publish new content. Without content, there would be no Internet; however, without quality standards, there are no guarantees that content is accurate. Indeed, one of the biggest problems facing Internet users is relevance. With so much to choose from, how do we know which sources are reliable and relevant to us? A few answers to this problem are discussed in Chapters 16 and 17, which deal with search and social computing. The point is this: Creating content is easy, but because it's so easy, maintaining quality standards is a bit difficult.

We've touched on the Internet as an example of a global content free-for-all. However, in many organizations, a similar effect is experienced when it comes to internal content. With myriad Word documents and Excel spreadsheets scattered far and wide, it becomes impossible to know which information is accurate and reliable. "Content management" refers to managing web content, but when it comes to SharePoint, Enterprise Content Management (ECM) is all about managing the creation of content and maintaining quality standards throughout an organization. ECM relates to the management of all content within an organization, from document management, to more traditional web content management.

## Managed Metadata

**New in 2010**

If only a few files are stored in a folder, it's probably relatively easy for you to find what you need—and this may be the case for a few thousand files in a hierarchical file system as well. But if you're talking about tens of thousands of files, or even millions of files, with many more being added each day, then storing a file in the wrong place in the hierarchy can make information practically impossible to find. The answer to such a problem is *metadata*, which literally means data about data. SharePoint 2010's new Managed Metadata service is the core of many of the ECM improvements. By attaching metadata to content, you can use the metadata to organize, index, and navigate to content automatically.

Chapter 17 covers the creation of metadata and its wider implications in more detail. For now, it's enough to know that metadata is an essential part of content management.

## Configuring the Managed Metadata Service

The Managed Metadata Service can be configured as follows:

1. From Central Administration, select Manage Service applications in the Application Management section.

2. Select the Managed Metadata Service, and from the Operations section of the Service Applications ribbon, select Manage. This will open the Term Store Management Tool. Notice that the Taxonomy Term Store pane on the left side of the page, and shown in the following illustration, displays the terms and term stores that have been defined for the selected Managed Metadata Service application. The root node—Managed Metadata Service—represents the service application.

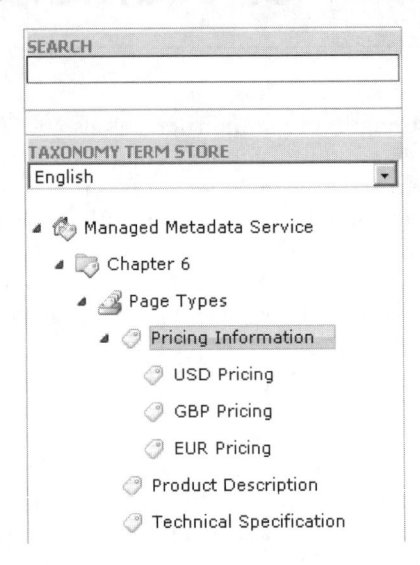

The lowest level of metadata definition is the *term*, which is a tag for all intents and purposes. Terms can be hierarchically organized, as illustrated. Moving up from the term is the *term set*, which groups terms into a logical set. One common use for a term set is to provide a list of possible options; as shown in the illustration, the Page Types term set lists possible terms for page types.

Term sets come in two types: *open*, in which users can add terms, and *closed*, in which all terms are predefined by a user with appropriate permissions. By using these different types, you can create taxonomies or folksonomies (and a discussion on the merits of each is presented in Chapter 17).

3. Since we'll make use of the demonstration terms shown in the illustration, we'll add them to the term store. Right-click the Managed Metadata Service node and select New Group from the context menu. Enter **Chapter 6** as the name for the group.

4. Right-click Chapter 6, and then select New Term Set. Name the Term Set Page **Types**.

5. Right-click Page Types, and then add new terms as shown in the illustration. Notice how new blank terms are added automatically while you're inserting terms, making it easier to enter several terms at the same time.

## Managed Metadata Field

**New in 2010**

Taxonomies and folksonomies are covered in detail in Chapter 17; for now, however, you should know that a *taxonomy* is a well-defined categorization scheme that can usually be changed only by administrative users, whereas a *folksonomy* is a loosely defined scheme that can be changed by users of the system.

Let's look at how this data can be captured as part of our content creation process. The primary user interface for capturing metadata published using the Managed Metadata Service is the Managed Metadata field. By default, all content types that are derived from the Page content type include a Managed Keywords field that makes use of the Managed Metadata field type.

**NOTE** The Managed Keywords field is actually provisioned by a hidden taxonomy feature, which should be enabled by default. However, at the time of writing, on SharePoint 2010 Beta 2, in certain circumstances the feature isn't enabled and therefore the column isn't available. To remedy this problem, you can manually enable the feature using PowerShell. (See Chapter 20 for details.)

To illustrate the use of the Managed Metadata field, we'll create a new blank site.

1. Using SharePoint Designer, create a new blank web site at http://<ServerName>/Chapter6.
2. From the Site tab of the ribbon, select Document Library | Document Library. Name the new document library **MyTaggedDocs**.
3. In the List Settings tab of the ribbon, click Administration Web Page from the Manage section. (At the time of writing, Managed Metadata columns can't be added using SharePoint Designer.)
4. In the Columns section of the Document Library Settings page, select Create Column.
5. Add a new column named Document Type of type Managed Metadata.
6. Scroll down the page to the use a managed term set option. Using the navigator, select the Page Types term set, as shown. Notice that you can select any term within the term set hierarchy as the starting point for the field. Only the subset of terms that are found below the selected term will be available for selection.

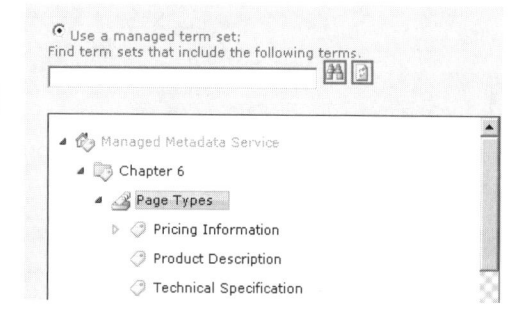

7. Click OK to create the new column.

In addition to being able to define metadata manually for content, you can configure default metadata based on the location to which content is saved. For example, a document library may contain folders for a number of customers. When a document is stored in a particular folder, it may be desirable to attach a customer reference by default.

1. Navigate to the MyTaggedDocs document library using the browser. From the Documents tab, select New Document to add a new document to the library.

2. Enter some sample text in the document, and then in the Document Properties panel add the title **MyTechnicalSpec**.

3. In Document type column, type **Tech**. Notice that as you type a list of suggestions appear. In this case, the only suggestion is Technical Specification, which is selected by default if you press RETURN.

4. Try to enter an invalid value, such as foo; notice that the invalid term is highlighted as an error.

5. Click the icon to the right of the Document Type text box. From the Select: Document Type dialog, select the Technical Specification term, as shown. Click OK to use the selected term.

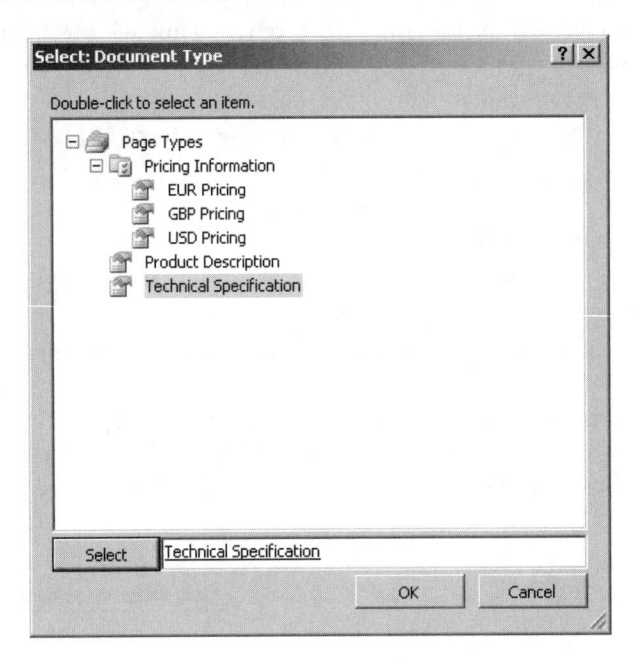

6. Click the Save icon in the upper-left corner of the screen to save the new document to our MyTaggedDocs document library. Save the document as MyTechnicalSpec.docx, and then close Word after the document has been saved.

To illustrate how default terms can be applied when documents are created, we'll add a few folders to our MyTaggedDocs library and then specify default terms for each folder.

1. From the Documents tab, select New Folder. Create a new folder and name it **Pricing Docs**.
2. Repeat the process to create another new folder named **Product Descriptions**, as shown:

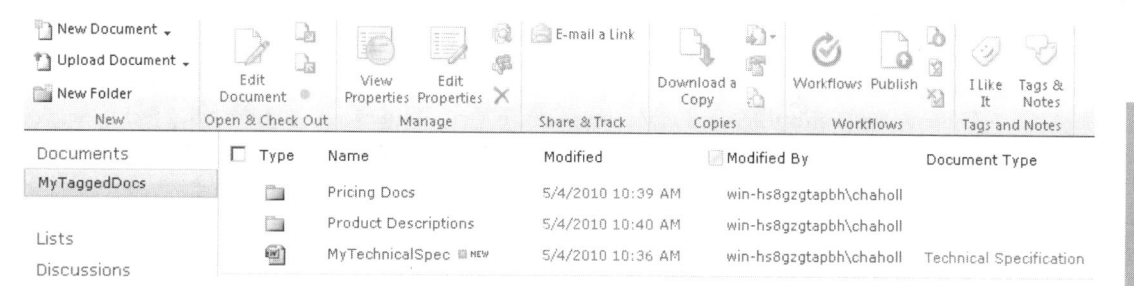

| | Type | Name | Modified | Modified By | Document Type |
|---|---|---|---|---|---|
| | 📁 | Pricing Docs | 5/4/2010 10:39 AM | win-hs8gzgtapbh\chaholl | |
| | 📁 | Product Descriptions | 5/4/2010 10:40 AM | win-hs8gzgtapbh\chaholl | |
| | 📄 | MyTechnicalSpec NEW | 5/4/2010 10:36 AM | win-hs8gzgtapbh\chaholl | Technical Specification |

3. From the Library tab on the ribbon, select Library Settings, and then select Column Default Value Settings from the General Settings section.
4. Select the Pricing Docs node from the Location To Configure tree on the left side. Click the Document Type column, and then select the Use The Default Value option.
5. In the Default Value text box, type **Pricing**. Again, notice how suggestions are automatically generated as you type. Select Pricing Information, and then click OK to store the default.
6. Repeat this process to set a default value for Product Description.

Now navigate to the Pricing Docs folder in the MyTaggedDocs library. Add a new document. This time, save the document without setting the Document Type value and then close Word. Notice that the default value that we specified earlier has been applied.

---

**CAUTION** Default metadata is applied by attaching an event receiver to the appropriate document library. Be careful not to remove the system-specified event receiver by accident when working with custom receivers. For more information on event receivers, see Chapter 8.

## Metadata Navigation

**New in 2010**

Filing hierarchies are great if you're dealing with only a few items, but they're not so good as the number of items increases. Unfortunately, the hierarchy has to get more and more complicated to enable things to be found. For example, you could start off with a folder named Customers, with subfolders for each customer. In each customer subfolder, you could store all correspondence for a given customer. This works well if you need to store only a few documents, but what happens over time when the aggregate volume of correspondence increases? The typical answer is to create date folders within the customer folder. But what if the volume within a particular time period is still too high to make it easy to find what you need? You could again subdivide the time period or maybe create subfolders for each type of correspondence.

The point is this: over time, hierarchies must continually get more complicated to make it possible to find content. As they get more complicated, they become more targeted to a particular search approach. In our example, what would happen if we wanted to retrieve all the sales invoices created on a particular day for all customers? With the current folder structure, this would be possible, but not exactly the most efficient content management mechanism. At this point, the answer may be to create a new hierarchy that is easier to understand, which is no mean feat by any measure, and is still targeted to a particular search approach.

The answer to this dilemma is to create many virtual hierarchies, each targeted to a particular search context. By using the Metadata Navigation functionality in SharePoint 2010, creating virtual hierarchies is a straightforward affair. Before Metadata Navigation can be used, it must be enabled for a site.

1. From the Site Actions menu, select Site Settings.
2. In the Site Settings page, select Site Features and then click the Activate button for the Metadata Navigation and Filtering feature, as shown:

> **Metadata Navigation and Filtering**
> Provides each list in the site with a settings pages for configuring that list to use metadata tree view hierarchies and filter controls to improve navigation and filtering of the contained items.
> [Deactivate] **Active**

3. Navigate to the MyTaggedDocs library that we created earlier. From the Library tab, select Library Settings. Notice that the General Settings section now contains two additional options: Metadata Navigation Settings and Per-location View Settings.
4. Click the Metadata Navigation Settings link, and then from the list of Available Hierarchy Fields, add the Document Type field to the list of Selected Hierarchy Fields.
5. From the Available Key Filter Fields list, add the Created By field to the Selected Key Filter Fields list.
6. Click OK to apply the changes, and then navigate to the MyTaggedDocs library.

By configuring Metadata Navigation for our document library, a hierarchy browser is now visible on the left side of the page. From the hierarchy, we can select from the list of folders or the Managed Metadata terms that we specified for the Document type field. Also, by adding Created By as a Filter Field, we can enter a username to show only the documents that were created by a particular user. Combining these two techniques makes it easier to find data using a combination of virtual hierarchies and filtering.

## Content Organizer

**New in 2010**

Another use for metadata is to organize content automatically. One of the problems of a hierarchical filing system is that documents must be placed in the correct place for the system to work. By defining rules that determine where a document should be saved, the Content Organizer feature in SharePoint 2010 allows users to save all content to a drop-off location; SharePoint will automatically route it to the correct place.

To configure the Content Organizer feature, take the following steps:

1. From the Site Actions menu, select Site Settings and then click the Manage Site Features link. Activate the Content Organizer feature, as shown:

**Content Organizer**
Create metadata based rules that move content submitted to this site to the correct library or folder.

2. Using the Navigate Up button that appears next to the Site Actions menu, navigate back to the Site Settings page. The Site Administration section now shows two additional options: Content Organizer Settings and Content Organizer Rules. Also, a Drop-Off Library has been automatically created within the site. The first option, Content Organizer Settings, allows you to configure the settings for the Content Organizer feature. For this simple demonstration, the default settings will be sufficient. (You can find out more about the configuration settings at http://technet.microsoft.com.)

3. Click the Content Organizer Rules link to display the list of configured rules. One thing that may not be immediately apparent is that a Content Organizer Rule is implemented as a Content Type and the collection of rules are stored in a custom list defined at the site level named RoutingRules. To add a new rule, click the Add New Item icon.

4. Name the new rule **Move Product Specs**. In the Submission's Content Type section, choose Document as the content type, as shown. When it comes to defining rules, bear in mind that each rule is bound to a specific content type. In the preceding samples, we added a column to our MyTaggedDocs library but didn't create a specific content type; as a result, we can't use our custom Managed Metadata field to create a rule. Instead, we've selected the Document content type, allowing the rule to execute against all content that inherits from the Document content type.

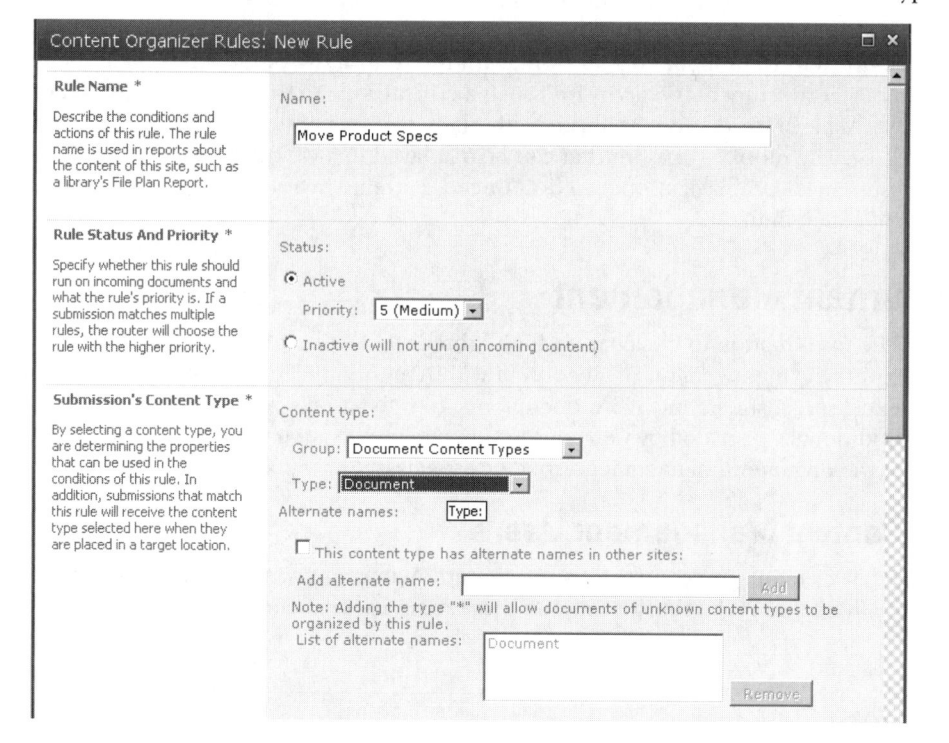

5. In the Conditions section, select the Managed Keywords property; then, in the Value box, enter **Product**. Select the Product Description term when it is suggested.

6. Set the Target Location to the Product Descriptions folder in the MyTaggedDocs document library that we created earlier. Click OK to save the new rule.

To see our rule in action, navigate to the automatically created Drop-Off Library, and then create a new document by selecting New Document from the Document tab on the ribbon. Enter some sample text and a Title for the document, and then, in the Managed Keywords text box, enter the **Product Description** term. Save the document to the library. Notice that as each document is being saved, the status messages in Word indicate that the Content Organizer is processing. Once the save process has completed, the final location of the document will be shown in the Location text box at the upper-right corner of the Document Information panel:

```
Location: Chapter6/MyTaggedDocs/Product%20Descriptions/This%20document  * Required field  X
```

## Large Libraries

In SharePoint 2007, the recommended maximum number of items in a single folder was 2000, and while the recommended maximum number of documents in a single library was 5 million, achieving this limit could really be done only by having multiple nested folders of around 2000 documents each. With SharePoint 2010, some practical limitations still exist regarding what can be done in lists and libraries, but these limits have been increased significantly. For example, the maximum number of items that can be shown in a single view is now 5000 instead of 2000, and the maximum number of documents in a library has doubled to 10 million. Furthermore, with thoughtful use of metadata, your focus on creating a perfect document hierarchy isn't such a critical issue to the design of a SharePoint solution.

Achieving a document library with many millions of items is much easier in SharePoint 2010. The number of items that can be displayed in a view has increased to 5000, and by using metadata navigation, you don't need to create myriad folders just to stay within the 5000-item limit.

# Document Management

The introduction to this chapter highlighted the fact that SharePoint's ECM functionality covers the management of all content within an organization, from documents such as Excel spreadsheets and Word documents, to web-based content and the functionality traditionally provided by web content management systems. In this section, we'll look at the document management–specific aspects of SharePoint ECM.

## Content Management Users

A few elements are common to any content management system, and these can be more easily explained by considering the three main users of content management systems:

**Content Creators** Content creators are users who create the content that is stored within the system. In an organization, these users typically cover a wide range of disciplines and use a variety of tools to create the content they will publish. Typically, content creators are nontechnical users who are experts in their own specific fields.

**Readers** Readers are users that consume the content published by the content management system. These readers may be anonymous or identified and may be subdivided into particular groups or audiences for content targeting purposes.

**Editors/Administrators** Editors and administrators are responsible for the management of content within the system. Typically, they will set publishing guidelines and define processes to ensure that content meets these guidelines.

## Multi-user Editing

*New in 2010*

When a content creator is working on a particular piece of content, it's important that no other user can make changes at the same time without the creator's knowledge. This is managed via a check-in/check-out function, whereby a content creator must check out a document before he or she can make any changes to it. While a document is checked out, only the user who has checked out the document can see the changes that are in progress; all other users will continue to see the last checked-in version. When an updated document is checked in and versioning is enabled, a new version is created. SharePoint 2010 takes this functionality a step further when managing Office 2010 content: now it is possible for multiple content users to collaborate on the same document at the same time, with all users seeing an indication of the changes made by others in real time.

## Item-Level Permissions

Although documents are commonly stored in folders and permissions are applied to those folders to determine who has access to their contents, if this was the lowest level of security granularity available within a system, folders would quickly become security containers rather than navigational aids and this would greatly complicate any folder hierarchy. A more flexible approach is to allow permissions to be defined at the individual item level. Of course, forcing all permissions to be defined at this level would be an administrative nightmare, since any changes would have to be made to each and every document. To get around this problem, in SharePoint 2010 permissions are inherited from containing folders, document libraries, and ultimately web sites. More often than not, folder or document library–level permissions are appropriate. However, on the rare occasions that a specific file requires different permissions, inherited folder permissions can be easily overridden.

## Workflows

We've looked at a few of the tools that make life easier for content creators, but what about editors and administrators? How can they ensure that content is created in accordance with appropriate procedures? The answer to this problem is workflow. As content is created, edited, or deleted, editors have the facility to specify business process that should be followed. These processes, when encapsulated in a workflow, are automatically enforced by the SharePoint platform to ensure that editors and administrators achieve the level of control that is the raison d'être of any content management system.

> **NOTE** Workflow is a large subject touching on more than just content management business processes. More comprehensive coverage can be found in Chapter 11.

## Document Sets

**New in 2010**

Another new feature introduced in SharePoint 2010 is the ability to create document sets. Often when you're creating complex work products such as an annual report or a sales presentation, many elements are required to make up the final product. For example, a report may contain multiple Word documents, Excel spreadsheets, and Adobe Acrobat documents. In previous versions of SharePoint, each of these documents could be managed only in isolation, which meant that facilities such as versioning and check-in/check-out functionality had to be manually enforced on all documents in the set to ensure that they remain consistent. With SharePoint 2010, the document set allows all documents to be managed as a group while still retaining the ability to manage individual documents in isolation if required.

To use document sets within a site collection, take the following steps:

1. From the Site Actions menu, select Site Settings.
2. In the Site Collection Administration section, click the Site Collection Features link. If the link is not available, click the Go To Top Level Site Settings link to go to the root site of the site collection.
3. If it's not already activated, Activate the Document Set feature by clicking the Activate button to the right of the feature name.

The Document Set feature makes a new Document Set content type available for use within the site collection. Before we can create content using this new content type, we need to attach it to a document library. Note that although we're manually attaching the document set content type to a document library in this example, certain site templates have this behavior enabled by default—for example, the Document Center template.

1. Using SharePoint Designer, Connect to the sample site that we created earlier in the chapter (http://<ServerName>/Chapter6).
2. Add a new document library named DocumentSets using the methods described earlier in the chapter.
3. Before we can add a new content type to the DocumentSets document library, we need to allow management of content types. In the Settings section of the DocumentSets settings page, check the Allow Management Of Content Types option, as shown:

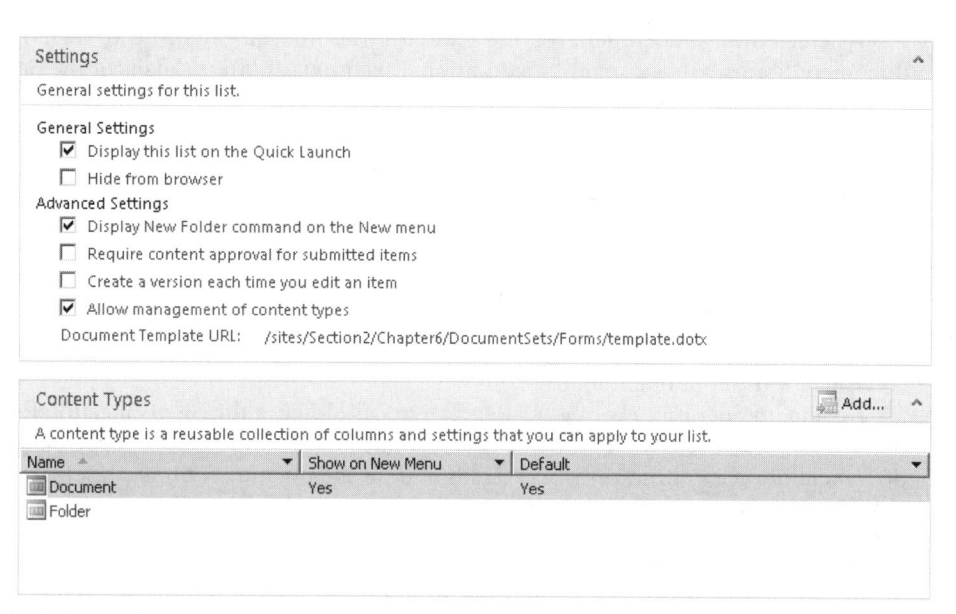

4. Using the Add button in the Content Types section, add the Document Set content type.

5. Click the Save icon in the upper-left corner of the Designer window to commit the changes.

6. We can now navigate to the DocumentSets document library and create a new document set: from the Documents tab of the ribbon, select New Document | Document Set. Type the name the new document set, **My First Document Set**, as shown:

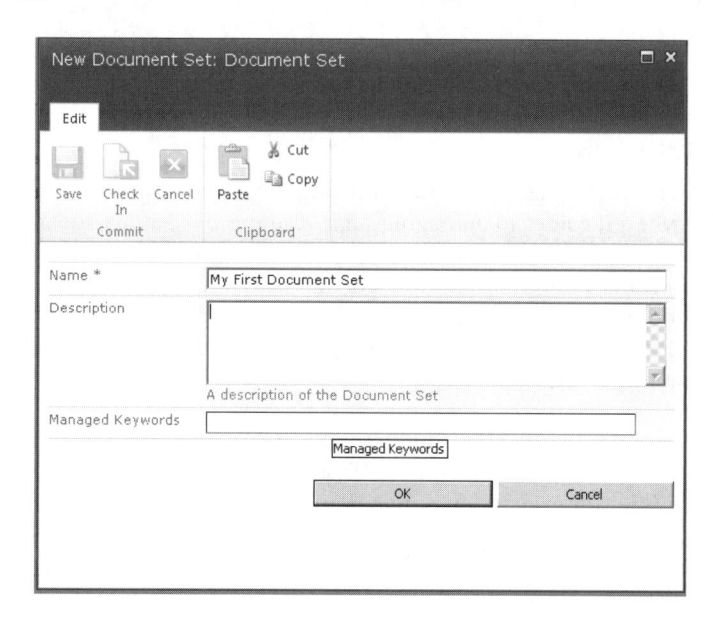

When creating a document set, the standard user interface that you've seen in other document libraries now contains an additional section that offers details of the document set and links to additional properties. By selecting Edit Page from the Site Actions menu, you can see that this user interface contains a few additional web parts, most notably the Document Set Properties web part. If you make changes to the layout of this page, the welcome page for all document sets based on the same content type will also be changed for the current document library.

Document sets are based on the new Document Set content type. However, this is only the beginning of the story; we can create our own custom content types that derive from the Document Set and configure them better to meet our requirements. For example, we can add columns or add default content. We can also specify which content types can be contained within our document set.

Document Set option configurations can occur either at the Site Collection level, making it possible to cascade the changes to all instances of the content type on all document libraries within the site collection, or at the document library level. To configure at site collection level, do the following:

1. From the Site Actions menu, select Site Settings. Click Go To Top Level Site Settings from the Site Collection Administration section if the site is not the current root of the site collection.

2. From the root site, select Site Content Types from the Galleries section, and then scroll to and click the Document Set content type link.

3. In the Settings section, the Document Set settings link will allow configuration of the document set.

To configure at the Document Library level, do the following:

1. From the Library tab, select Library Settings.

2. Click the Document Set content type from the Content Types section.

3. Click the Document Set settings link.

## Document IDs

**New in 2010**

This chapter has extolled the virtues of metadata at every opportunity; hopefully, you'll agree that when it comes to managing high volumes of content, metadata is the way to go. However, as a consequence of the more flexible approach to document storage that metadata permits, often the URL to a document is not as predictable as it might be if a well-designed hierarchical structure were in place. Furthermore, when saving a document to a drop-off location using the Content Organizer functionality, the final location of the document may change, making it difficult to determine the ultimate URL for the document.

To get around this problem, and to make documents easier to find generally, SharePoint 2010 includes a Document ID service. The Document ID service generates a unique identifier for every document and allows documents to be retrieved using a single static URL in this format: *http://myserver/mysite/DocIdRedir.aspx?ID=documented.*

To configure the Document ID service, take the following steps:

1. From the Site Actions menu, select Site Settings. Navigate to the top level site settings page if appropriate.
2. In the Site Collection Administration section, select Site Collection Features. Activate the Document ID service if it's not already activated. Return to the Site Settings page.
3. An additional menu option has been added to the Site Collection Administration section, named Document ID settings. Click this link to configure the service.
4. To begin assigning document IDs, click the Assign Document IDs checkbox. Enter a unique prefix for document IDs originating from the current site collection, as shown:

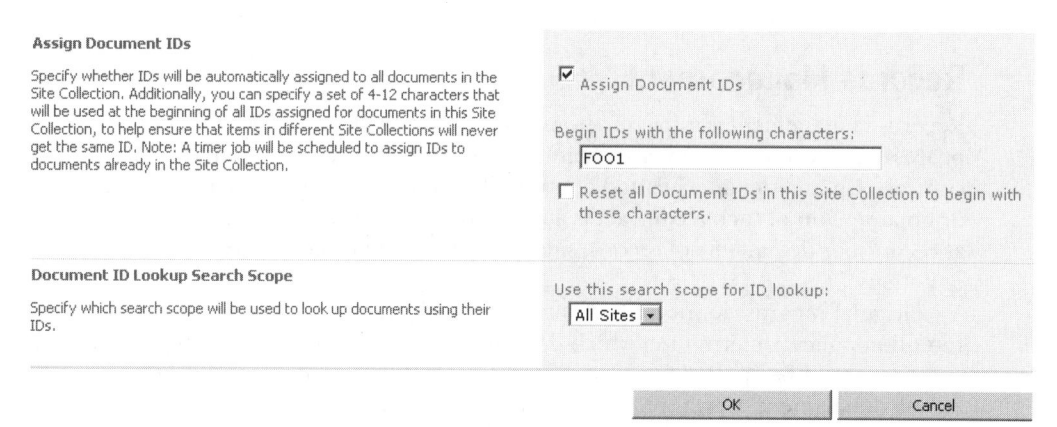

**Assign Document IDs**

Specify whether IDs will be automatically assigned to all documents in the Site Collection. Additionally, you can specify a set of 4-12 characters that will be used at the beginning of all IDs assigned for documents in this Site Collection, to help ensure that items in different Site Collections will never get the same ID. Note: A timer job will be scheduled to assign IDs to documents already in the Site Collection.

☑ Assign Document IDs

Begin IDs with the following characters:
FOO1

☐ Reset all Document IDs in this Site Collection to begin with these characters.

**Document ID Lookup Search Scope**

Specify which search scope will be used to look up documents using their IDs.

Use this search scope for ID lookup:
All Sites

Although we've configured the document ID service, behind the scenes SharePoint uses timer jobs to activate the service and make the necessary changes to document libraries within the site collection. As a result of this, the changes that we've made may take some time to be implemented. To check on the progress of these timer jobs or to run them manually, take the following steps:

1. Navigate to Central Administration.
2. From the Monitoring section, click Check Job Status. The Schedules, Running, and History sections will report the current status of any timer jobs.
3. To kick off the jobs manually, select the Job Definitions link from the Timer Links menu. Run the Document ID enable/disable job first and then the Document ID assignment job.

**NOTE** As an alternative to using the built-in Document ID generator, you can create a custom ID generator if identifiers must meet a specific format or must be synchronized with an external system. Full coverage of this subject is outside the scope of this chapter, but for information see http://msdn.microsoft.com.

## Document Metadata

You've seen how metadata is used for content management and how, by using the Managed Metadata field, metadata can be captured within the SharePoint user interface. However, when it comes to document management, things work a bit differently. More often than not, the content creator user interface for a document management system will be a document creation tool such as Word or Excel. I'm sure it'll come as no surprise to learn that all products in the Microsoft Office suite offer tight integration with SharePoint via the use of the backstage area that you've seen in various examples throughout this book. As well as providing the high level of integration that allows us to save and open documents directly from SharePoint, products such as Word also provide a document information panel that can be customized by developers to capture appropriate metadata in the content-creation interface. Creating document information panels is covered in more detail in Chapter 5.

## Records Management

Records management is a specific branch of document management that deals with the processing of critical documents. One example of a critical document may be a sales contract. Changes to an executed contract should follow a rigid process, and retaining an original version of such a contract is absolutely critical. Documents such as these are known as records, or documents of record, since they are often electronic records of specific events or actions.

Original records can never be changed after the fact and are usually subject to some retention policy. Determining which documents should be considered records and what policies should be applied for each record is often the task of an organization's compliance or risk department. Certain businesses are subject to a greater degree of statutory compliance regulation, and as a result records management may form a significant part of any document management strategy. For other businesses, records management may be a much simpler affair.

# Digital Asset Management

**New in 2010** The digital assets managed by an organization commonly include such items as product images, corporate logos, video presentations, podcasts, and other types of rich content. Managing assets such as product descriptions can be accomplished using a similar approach to managing other documents. However, when it comes to managing other content, such as images or video and audio files, a few specific requirements are necessary.

## Media Content Types

I've mentioned the idea of content types in various places throughout this book, and a full discussion can be found in Chapter 13. In essence, on the SharePoint platform, a content type can be used to attach specific attributes and behaviors to a particular type of information. When it comes to managing digital assets in SharePoint 2010, three new Media Content types are available, Audio, Image, and Video, as shown here:

| Digital Asset Content Types | |
|---|---|
| Asset | Document |
| Audio | Asset |
| Image | Asset |
| Video | Asset |

## Rich Media Content

Image files are relatively straightforward in terms of their storage and presentation. Appropriate metadata such as the image size and details of the creator are captured by way of additional fields on the Image content type.

Video and audio files are a different story, however. Although specific metadata is also captured via additional fields attached to the appropriate content type, a number of challenges need to be overcome in the storage and presentation of video and audio data.

One of the first challenges involves the sheer size of the files required to store such content. Even relatively low-definition video files can easily run into hundreds of megabytes. From a user experience perspective, downloading such files to play them is not an ideal situation. Even with a very fast network connection, such downloads would take a considerable length of time. A better approach is to stream content on demand, effectively allowing the user to download the content in real time as it's being viewed. To facilitate this type of functionality, SharePoint 2010 includes a Silverlight-based media player that can be easily accessed via a custom pop-up dialog that's automatically attached to media items.

To see this in action, take the following steps:

1. From the Site Actions menu, select More Options.
2. Use the Asset Library template to create a new document library named MyMediaAssets.
3. After the library has been created, upload a Windows Media Video file (.wmv).
4. By default, the Asset Library template defines two views: Thumbnails and All Assets. When the Thumbnails view is used (which it is by default), you can click the thumbnail for a particular asset to display a dialog that features a Play button. Click the Play button to launch the Silverlight media player control, allowing you to view the content directly from the document library without the need for downloading.

## Disk-based Caching

As well as the challenges involved in providing a respectable user interface for video and audio content, physically storing such data within SharePoint can also present a problem. This is especially the case where the aggregate data volume is very high. By default, SharePoint stores all content in a SQL database. Video and audio data is stored as a binary large object (BLOB). Of course, some overhead is inherent in retrieving this content from the database as opposed to from the local file system—more so in a farm deployment where the database exists in a separate physical server and must be accessed over a network connection.

To reduce the latency involved in retrieving BLOB data from the database, SharePoint includes a disk-based cache for BLOB data. Effectively, data is stored in the local file system, allowing it to be easily pushed out to the client browser on demand without a database round trip. For more information on disk-based caching, see http://msdn.microsoft.com/en-gb/library/aa604896(office.14).aspx.

### Remote BLOB Storage

Another problem that occurs when a high volume of binary data is stored involves content database performance. Because all SharePoint content for a given site is stored in the same content database, extensive use of large video and audio files will degrade performance for other types of data. Furthermore, a recommended size limitation of 200GB exists for SharePoint 2010 content databases.

> **TIP** If a site content database is greater than 4GB and contains a large amount of binary data such as documents or audio and video files, consider using Remote BLOB Storage as part of your overall data storage solution.

*Remote BLOB Storage (RBS)* is an add-on application programming interface (API) for Microsoft SQL Server 2008 and 2008 R2. In a nutshell, RBS transparently stores BLOB data externally rather than within SQL Server. Data is still accessed in the same manner from an end user perspective; however, the RBS API uses a provider model to connect physically to the external BLOB data store behind the scenes.

A number of third-party vendors supply RBS providers for SQL Server 2008. However, Microsoft provides a free out-of-the-box FILESTREAM provider that effectively makes use of the file system for the storage and retrieval of BLOB data.

## Web Content Management

SharePoint is predominantly a web-based development platform. Of course, as you'll see in later chapters, much more is going on behind the scenes than simply generating and publishing web pages; fundamentally, the fact remains that the main user interface for SharePoint is rendered via HTML. Web content management, therefore, touches upon a number of fundamental aspects of the SharePoint platform itself. In this section, we'll look at how web content is generated by the SharePoint platform and then move on to look at how the generation of such content can be managed using the techniques that you saw earlier in this chapter in relation to managing other types of content.

### Page Model

Although SharePoint is based on ASP.NET, the mechanism by which pages are generated is a bit different from the traditional ASP.NET page rendering model.

**TIP** In practically every SharePoint book you'll ever read, somewhere you'll find an assertion to the effect of "SharePoint is based on ASP.NET; therefore, SharePoint pages can be customized using the same tools and technologies that you'd use to generate standard ASP.NET pages." Although this is undoubtedly true, it is not quite as simple as it seems. At a fundamental level, SharePoint is based on ASP.NET, but in practice, building web applications using SharePoint is probably 20 percent ASP.NET programming and 80 percent SharePoint-specific programming. This is a critical consideration if you're new to SharePoint.

## Master Pages

SharePoint makes use of master pages, an ASP.NET concept, but with a slight twist: SharePoint master pages must have certain placeholders defined. While we can add custom placeholders, as we might if we were creating an ASP.NET site from scratch, the mandatory placeholders that are defined by SharePoint host all of the content that is generated by the SharePoint platform. As a result, master pages are of limited value when it comes to customizing specific pages. More often than not, an entire site or even site collection will make use of a single master page.

## Page Layouts and Content Types

A more effective way to control the layout of SharePoint-managed content is through the use of page layouts. Page layouts are a SharePoint-specific concept and are used in conjunction with master pages to compose a complete web page.

If we were creating a standard ASP.NET application, we may define a master page with common elements such as a header and footer. We would then create an ASP.NET page that referenced the master page and replaced the content of any placeholders defined on the master page. To a certain extent, page layouts in SharePoint work in the same way. However, the key difference is that if we were using ASP.NET, we'd enter content directly onto the page; when using SharePoint, the content for the page is retrieved from the SharePoint content database and is added to the page using field controls. In effect, a page layout acts as a template for pages that are created from a specific SharePoint content type. It is the content type that determines which fields are available to be included in the page layout.

Each SharePoint site contains a Master Page gallery containing both master pages and page layouts. Only master pages and page layouts that are stored in the root site of a site collection can be used to create new pages. Although most content in SharePoint can be accessed by selecting Site Actions | View All Site Content, the Master Page gallery can be accessed by selecting Site Actions | Site Settings and then selecting Master Pages under Galleries. If the site is not the root site, select Go To Top Level Site Settings under Site Collection Administration, and then select Master Pages under Galleries.

## Field Controls and Columns

Chapter 13 takes a deeper look at how the SharePoint data structure is built up. From a page-rendering perspective, you need to know that a content type specifies the fields that are present for a particular piece of content. For example, a sales invoice may contain a customer reference, an invoice date, and an invoice amount. To a certain extent, a content type is also a template, with the difference being that a content type defines a template for the storage of data, whereas a page layout is a template for the presentation of data. Each page layout is bound to a single content type, although more than one page layout can use the same content type.

You've seen how a page layout is analogous to a content type from a presentation perspective. When it comes down to showing actual data on the page, each column or field also has a default field control, and this control provides the default user interface used to display or capture data for a specific field. For example, our sales invoice content type defines a Customer Reference field. The Customer Reference field may be of type Customer Lookup. When the page is displayed in read mode, a Customer Lookup field might render the name, address, and reference number of the customer. However, when the page is in edit mode, the Customer Lookup field type may provide customer search facilities, allowing the user to find the appropriate customer. Behind the scenes, the data required by the Customer Reference field is stored within the SharePoint content database in the same way as data entered in a SharePoint list. For an example of how to create custom fields and field controls, see Chapter 13.

## Publishing

Now that you have a good understanding of how a SharePoint page is composed, let's move on to look at how these capabilities come together to deliver web content management in SharePoint 2010. One of the first requirements of any web content management system is the ability to publish content and, more importantly, to allow editors and administrators to control the publishing process. As described, by using custom workflows, you can implement practically any business process that may be required.

The main difference between creating web content and other document managed content is in the primary user interface. Other types of managed content commonly make use of a specific tool such as Microsoft Word, which has rich functionality for the creation and layout of word processing documents. However, generating web content is a different story. With rich client applications such as Word, the content creator is free to use all the features of the product without having to consider how the finished result will be rendered to the reader, since the reader will be using the same client application. Web content, on the other hand, must accommodate a much wider audience, and limitations must be in place regarding how the content is presented and, therefore, on the functionality exposed to content creators. Defining these limitations and enforcing them is an important difference for a web content management system.

To see how SharePoint 2010 addresses these issues, let's work through a demonstration.

### Create Page Content Type

We start by creating a page content type:

1. Using SharePoint Designer, navigate to the root site of the site collection that contains the sample site that we created earlier (http://<ServerName>/). Then, from the Site Objects pane, select Content Types.

2. Create a new content type name Product Page with a parent content type of Page, as shown.

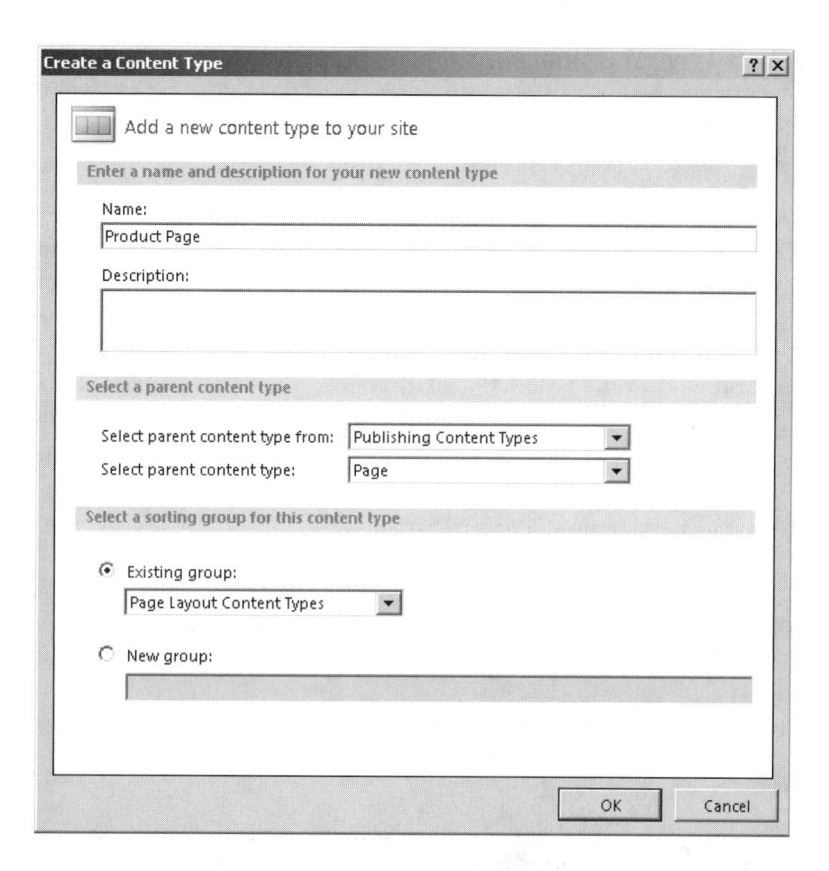

3. From the Content Type menu, select Administration Web Page. This will display the Site Content Type Information page for the Product Page content type. Click the Add From New Site Column link, and then add a new column named Product Description with a type of Full HTML content with formatting and constraints for publishing.

## Create Page Layout Using Content Type

Now that we have a custom content type with an additional column for product information, we can create a page layout that uses this data structure.

1. Choose Site Actions | Site Settings, and then select Master Pages from the Galleries section.
2. From the Documents tab on the ribbon, select New Document | Page Layout.
3. Configure the Associated Content Type to use the Product Page content type that we created earlier. Type the URL Name as **ProductPageLayout.aspx** and the Title as **Product Page Layout**. Click OK to save the changes.

## Edit Page Layout Using SharePoint Designer

Although we've created a page layout based on our content type, by default no fields other than the page title will be displayed. We can edit the page using SharePoint Designer to show how pages are constructed.

1. Open SharePoint Designer and connect to the root site that we used earlier.
2. From the Site Objects pane, select All Files | _catalogs | masterpage. The All Files option allows us to browse all files within a SharePoint site in a hierarchical manner. The _catalogs folder contains the gallery folders that we would normally access via Site Settings.
3. Double-click the ProductPageLayout.aspx file that we added earlier to open its property page, and then click the Edit File link in the Customization section, as shown next:

Use this page to view and manage settings for this file.

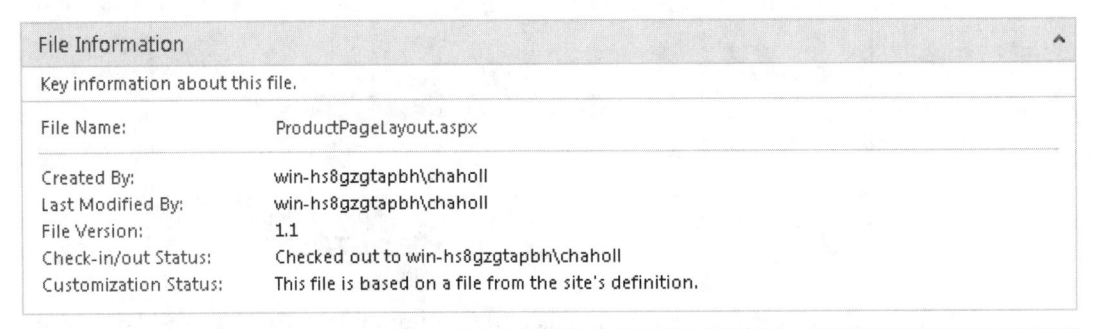

### File Information
Key information about this file.

| | |
|---|---|
| File Name: | ProductPageLayout.aspx |
| Created By: | win-hs8gzgtapbh\chaholl |
| Last Modified By: | win-hs8gzgtapbh\chaholl |
| File Version: | 1.1 |
| Check-in/out Status: | Checked out to win-hs8gzgtapbh\chaholl |
| Customization Status: | This file is based on a file from the site's definition. |

### Customization
Links to file customization tools.

- Edit file
- Manage all file properties in the browser

4. In the Safe Mode dialog that appears, select Yes to use Advanced Mode. By default, the page will be displayed using the Code view. If it's not already visible, show the Toolbox by selecting Task Panes | Toolbox from the View tab in the ribbon. See the sidebar "SharePoint Controls" for information about what you'll find in the toolbox.

### SharePoint Controls

The toolbox includes many controls, most of which will be familiar to ASP.NET developers. However, an additional section, SharePoint Controls, contains the items that we're interested in for the purposes of this demonstration. Within SharePoint Controls are a few sections that warrant some further explanation.

**Data View Controls**   As you'll see throughout this book, for the most part, document libraries and lists are rendered on the page using a Data View web part. Effectively, the Data View web part makes use of an Extensible Stylesheet Language Transformations (XSLT) template to transform XML-based data from an SPDataSource control. SharePoint Designer makes it easy to create XSLT templates by providing a full WYSIWYG interface, and as part of this, Data View controls can be dragged onto the Data View web part design surface to include specific fields in the template. (For an example of this functionality, check out http://www.chaholl.com/.)

**Server Controls (SharePoint)**   Server controls are SharePoint-specific custom controls. These controls inherit from the Microsoft.SharePoint.WebControls.SPControl and are registered as safe for the web application to which SharePoint Designer is connected.

**Page Fields (from <ContentType Name>)**   Page fields are derived from the columns that are bound to the content type on which the page is based. In our example, we created a custom content type named Product Page. The page fields that are shown in the toolbox are the default field controls that are bound to that content type. Chapter 13 takes a deeper look at the relationships among fields, field controls, and content types.

**Content Fields (from <ContentType Name>)**   Content fields work similarly to page fields and are grouped separately for convenience rather than because they are fundamentally different. The main difference is that content fields are generally based on field types that are enabled by the SharePoint Publishing feature.

5. SharePoint Designer is ultimately a web design tool, and many features are available to help us design and build aesthetically pleasing page layouts. However, in the interests of keeping these examples simple, we'll ignore all that good stuff here and create a very basic page. From the Page Fields section, drag the Title control into the PlaceHolderMain content placeholder. Repeat this process to include the Product Description control from the Content Fields section.

6. In a minor concession to proper formatting, add highlighted labels for each control and lay them out using the following HTML:

```
<asp:Content ContentPlaceholderID="PlaceHolderMain" runat="server">
<h3><label>Product Name:</label></h3>
<SharePointWebControls:TextField FieldName="fa564e0f-0c70-4ab9-b863-
0177e6ddd247" runat="server" DisableInputFieldLabel="true"/>
<h3><label>Product Information:</label></h3>
<PublishingWebControls:RichHtmlField FieldName="683ecabb-52d9-4f11-ace8-
8bb3375a049e" runat="server" DisableInputFieldLabel="true"/>
</asp:Content>
```

7. After the page layout has been saved, we need to check in the file and create a published version. Although we could create a page from this layout without checking it in and publishing it, the layout would be visible only to us (that is, the document creator). Save the page and then navigate to the Site Settings page of the root site using the browser. Select the Master Pages gallery.

8. Select the ProductPageLayout.aspx file, and then from the Documents tab of the ribbon click the Check In button. In the pop-up dialog, select a Major Version and then click OK.

9. Again select the ProductPageLayout.aspx file and click the Approve icon in the Workflow section of the ribbon, as shown:

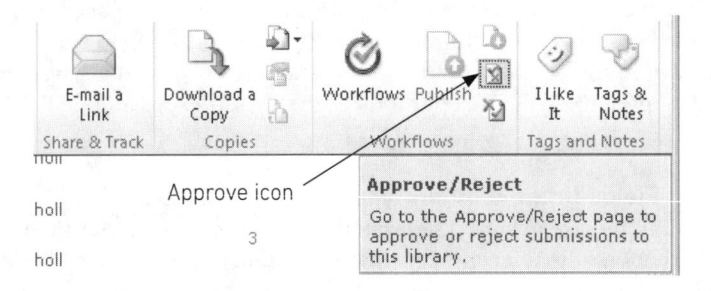

10. Click Approved to approve the checked-in version for publishing.

## Create a Web Page Using Layout

With our layout page in place, we can now create new web pages based on the layout. You'll see how page creation works from a content creator's perspective. Before we can allow users to create pages on our site, we need to enable the SharePoint Server Publishing feature.

1. Navigate to the http://<ServerName>/Chapter6 sample site that we created earlier. Choose Site Actions | Site Settings, and then click the Manage Site Features link.

2. Activate the SharePoint Server Publishing feature.

When the Publishing feature is enabled, a Pages document library is automatically added to the site. All new pages that are created are stored in the Pages library by default. Since we've created a custom content type that we'll use for our pages, we need to add this content type to the Pages document library before we can create pages using it. Take the following steps:

1. Choose Site Actions | View All Site Content. Click the hyperlink for the Pages document library.
2. From the Library tab of the ribbon, select Library Settings; then, in the Content Types section, click the Add From Existing Content Types link.
3. Add the Product Page content type, as shown:

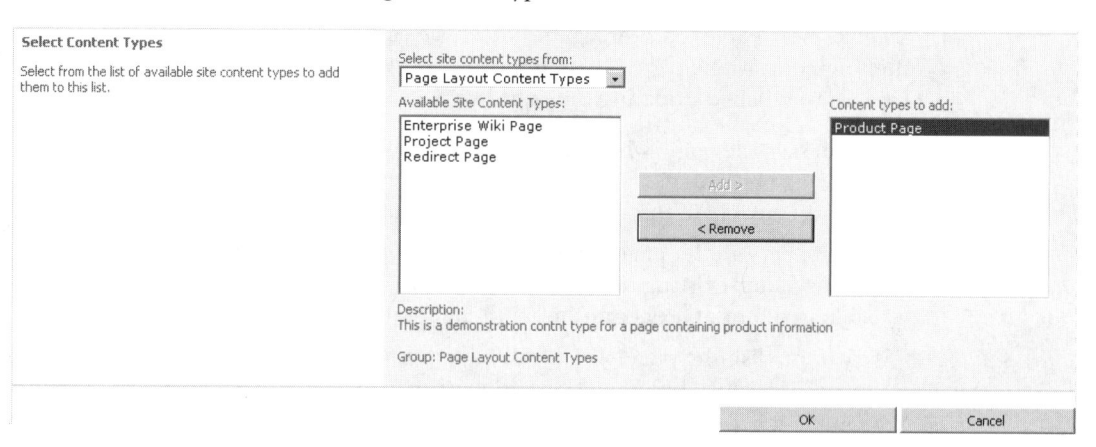

We can now create new pages using our custom layout and content type.

1. Choose Site Actions | New Page. Name the new page **MyFirstProduct**.
2. By default, the page will be created using the Body Only layout since Article is set as the default content type for the Pages library and Body Only is the first layout that's bound to the Article content type. We can change this to use our Product Page layout and our underlying Product content type by clicking the Page Layout button in the Page tab of the ribbon, as shown here:

3. Once the layout has been changed, a text box appears where we can enter the page title, and a flashing cursor appears under the Product Information heading. We can add content to the page by typing at the cursor or by entering text in the Title text box. Both of these input controls are rendered automatically when the page is in edit mode; the type of control that's rendered is determined by the underlying field type in our content type.

4. As well as being able to enter arbitrary text, we can also format and add images and other elements to the page by using the Format Text and Insert tabs on the ribbon. Once we've finished updating the page, we have a few options:

   - We can save the page, which will create a minor version and allow us to continue editing at a later date. The page will remain checked out to us and no other users will be able to update it.
   - We can check in the page, which will automatically check for spelling errors, warn us of any existing draft version, and allow us to add a comment that will be visible to editorial users or other content creators.
   - We can publish the page, which will have a similar effect to checking in the page, the key difference being that a major version will be created rather than a draft version.

### Customize the Page Editing Experience

You've seen how easy it is to create pages using page layouts and also how custom page layouts can be used to control the formatting and layout of pages within a site. However, one of the key administrative and editorial requirements of a web content management system is the ability to restrict the type of functionality that is available to content creators to ensure that any created content properly adheres to organizational standards.

When we created our page layout and dragged our Product Description field onto the page, a RichHtmlField control was added automatically. The various properties of the RichHtmlField control are the key to customizing the editing functionality for content creators. (For more information, see http://msdn.microsoft.com/en-us/library/microsoft.sharepoint.publishing.webcontrols.richhtmlfield_members(office.14).aspx.)

## Content Deployment

For security reasons, it's considered best practice not to make an internal SharePoint farm accessible via the Internet. Of course, this does not mean that SharePoint is not suitable for Internet usage; indeed, the opposite is true. It simply means that you need to take care to ensure proper segregation between public Internet content and private internal content. One common approach to this segregation is to create a public SharePoint farm that is responsible for displaying Internet-facing content only while also having an internal farm that is responsible for the generation and management of content. Effectively, the public farm is a read-only copy of specific elements on the internal farm. SharePoint facilitates such segregation by including a comprehensive Content Publishing API.

## Web Parts and Fields

Earlier you saw how field types and page layouts are used to render web-based content in SharePoint. However, these are not the only ways to add functionality to a page. Another tool, the web part, can also be used. A web part is a user-configurable control that can be added to most pages within SharePoint. The key difference between a web part and the field types that you saw earlier is that a web part is not bound to the underlying content type of the page—that is, the web part is not used to capture or display the value of a specific field. Instead, each web part has a number of properties, and the configuration of these properties determine its behavior. Web part development is a big part of SharePoint and is covered in more detail in Chapter 7.

## Content Query Web Part

When it comes to generating content management solutions, one of the most useful web parts is the Content Query web part. It can be used to extract specific data from various lists and libraries within a SharePoint farm and display them within a page. This functionality allows for the dynamic generation of web pages. For example, a company may require a list of the top five most popular products on a particular page. While it would be possible to create a content type and page layout to store this information and then manually update the page each day, a much better approach is to create a basic page that uses the Content Query web part to execute a query that returns the top five products and then formats the results for display on the page.

# Summary

This chapter discussed how SharePoint can be used to manage many different types of electronic content, from word processing documents, to user-generated web content. Designing and building enterprise content management systems is very much a discipline in its own right, and this chapter serves as an introduction to the key concepts so that as developers we can see where they may be used to augment or eliminate the need for custom development.

# CHAPTER 7

# User Interface Customization

You've seen how the SharePoint user interface is built up, and you've seen some of the technologies that allow you to enhance the user experience such as the Client Object Model and InfoPath forms services. Chapter 6 looked at how the content rendered in the user interface is created and managed. This chapter moves on to look at how we can shape the presentation of content to suit our requirements. We'll also take a look at how we can use custom web parts to implement custom user interface functionality.

## Working with Pages

Before we get into the nuts and bolts of customizing pages and applying branding to sites, let's take a step back and quickly look at how branding and page rendering work in SharePoint.

### Master Pages

The SharePoint page model is based on the ASP.NET model—that is, each page refers to a master page that defines a number of placeholder controls that can be overridden with custom content. By using master pages, you can apply a lot of global branding by customizing the appropriate master page. All pages that make use of the master page will automatically incorporate the changes.

This might seem like all you need to know in order to brand SharePoint—you can simply make the changes you need in the master page and the job's pretty much done. Unfortunately, however, it's not quite that simple. Although master pages are undoubtedly a good thing when it comes to maintaining consistent site design, one of their drawbacks is that as more and more placeholders are added, the pages become more and more difficult to customize. Placeholders may contain content for some pages and not for others, or, some pages may hold a little content while others hold a lot. Creating a design that can accommodate all these variables is challenging, and as the number of placeholders increases, so do the challenges.

Within SharePoint 2010 are two main master pages: v4.master, which is used by most of the pages generated by SharePoint and is found at %SPRoot%/Template/Global, and Simplev4.master, which is used as a failsafe for a few pages such as Login.aspx, Error.aspx, and AccessDenied.aspx. As you can imagine, given the extensive functionality of the platform, v4.master contains many placeholders. Along with these main master pages are also a few others such as Applicationv4.master, mwsdefault4.master, and dialog.master, which are used to support specific aspects of functionality.

> **CAUTION** Do not change the V4.master page in the Global folder. Doing so could seriously damage your SharePoint installation and may require a reinstall to fix.

Generally speaking, you shouldn't need to customize any of the built-in master pages. Each site can make use of a custom master page for both application pages and user-generated pages.

## Creating a Custom Master Page

Although every site has a master pages gallery, and master pages stored there can be bound to a site using code or manually via SharePoint Designer, only the master pages that are stored in the root site of the site collection can be bound to sites using the SharePoint user interface. This allows site collection administrators to retain control of the master pages that are available throughout a site collection. Bearing this in mind, let's create a new site collection for the purposes of this demonstration:

1. Using SharePoint Central Administration, select Create Site Collections from the Application Management section.

2. Name the new site collection **Section1** and use the Blank site template. Set an appropriate administrator account and then click OK.

3. Navigate to the newly created site. Then, from the Site Actions menu, select Site Settings. The ability to change the site master page via the user interface is available as part of the SharePoint Server Publishing Infrastructure feature, which is only available on SharePoint Server 2010. To enable this feature, select Site Collection Features from the Site Collection Administration section, and then click the Activate button next to the SharePoint Server Publishing Infrastructure feature.

4. We also need to activate the publishing feature at the site level. Navigate back to the Site Settings page using the navigate up icon next to the Site Actions menu. In the Site Actions section, select Manage Site Features; then activate the SharePoint Server Publishing feature.

5. From the Site Actions menu, select Edit Site in SharePoint Designer.

6. From the Site Objects pane, select Master Pages. Then, from the Master Pages tab on the ribbon, select From Content Type | Publishing Master Page. Name the new master page **Chapter7.master**.

7. Select Edit File from the Master Pages tab of the ribbon to open the page for editing.

    We can now make whatever changes that we want to the master page. Remember that the placeholders that are included in this Publishing Master Page template are required for the page to function correctly. Rather than deleting placeholders, a better practice is to place them within a hidden ASP:Panel control.

8. Save the new master page by clicking the Save icon in the upper-left corner.
9. Switch back to the browser and navigate to the Site Settings page. Select Master Pages and Page Layouts from the Galleries section, and then select the Chapter7.master file.
10. From the Documents tab in the ribbon, select Check In, and then in the Check-in dialog, select 1.0 Major Version (publish).
11. Before the master page will be visible to all users, it must be approved. Click the Approve/Reject button in the Workflows section of the Document ribbon as shown, and then select Approved.

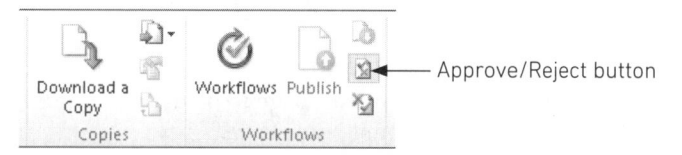

12. To set the page as the default publishing master page for the site, navigate back to the Site Settings page and select Master Page in the Look and Feel section. In the Site Master Page section, select Chapter7.master from the drop-down list. Then click OK to continue.

    We've specified that our custom master page should be used for all publishing pages within our demo site. Before we can see our master page in action, we need to add a new publishing page.

13. Navigate back to the site home page and then, from the Site Actions menu, select New Page. Type the page name as **My New Page** and then click OK.

A new publishing page that uses our custom master page will be added to the site. If no changes were made to the master page, we'll see a basic rendering of the page contents.

In this example, you've seen how to create a custom master page for use with publishing pages. If you want to create a master page that can be used to replace the system master page, you can follow the same process. However, rather than creating a page using the From Content Type button, you can copy the v4.master page and rename it before making customizations. The Publishing Master Page template does not contain all the placeholders that are required by a system master page.

## Using Master Page Tokens

You've seen the process for creating master pages using SharePoint Designer as well as how to specify the default publishing master page for a site. But what happens if you're not using a publishing page, or if you want to use a specific master page for a particular page on your site?

Using SharePoint Designer, you can specify the master page to use on a page-by-page basis. While it's perfectly acceptable to use a standard path for a master page reference, such as this,

```
<%@ Page language="C#" MasterPageFile="~ /MyMasterPages/default.master %>
```

the SharePoint page rendering engine also includes two dynamic tokens that can be used to refer to master pages. By using dynamic tokens, you can change the value of the token and therefore change the master page that is applied to all pages using the token. Pages with a hard-coded master page path would each have to be updated any time the master page changed.

The following dynamic tokens are available:

```
<%@ Page language="C#" MasterPageFile="~masterurl/default.master %>

<%@ Page language="C#" MasterPageFile="~masterurl/custom.master %>
```

By default, both of these tokens refer to /_catalogs/masterpage/default.master. Their values can be changed programmatically using the SPWeb object or by using SharePoint Designer as follows:

1. In the Site Object pane, select Master Pages.
2. Right-click the master page to be used, and then select Set As Default Master Page or Set As Custom Master Page.

In addition to the dynamic tokens ~masterurl/default.master and ~masterurl/custom.master, SharePoint also provides two static tokens, ~site/<your master page name> and ~sitecollection/<Your master page name>. These tokens refer to the master page gallery at the site level and site collection level, respectively.

## Delegate Controls

Take a look at the v4.master page, and you can see that the page comprises a number of different controls, such as SharePoint:SPRibbon and SharePoint:SPLinkButton. To a certain extent, truly mastering SharePoint branding and user interface design comes down to knowing what all of these controls are and how each one can be customized. However, before we start thinking about how to master UI customization, we need to pay particular attention to one other control: SharePoint:DelegateControl.

A delegate control is a SharePoint-controlled placeholder. All master pages make use of ContentPlaceHolder controls to dictate the areas of the page that can be populated with content that's defined in the content page. The delegate control does the same thing, except the content is determined by the configuration of the SharePoint site that is hosting the page. One example of this is the search box functionality that appears on most pages. This is defined on the v4.master page as a delegate control with the ID SmallSearchInputBox. Depending on which features are enabled on the site, this delegate control may be implemented using a Microsoft.SharePoint.WebControls.SearchArea control or a Microsoft.SharePoint.Portal.WebControls.SearchBoxEx control.

The configuration of a delegate control is done via an Elements.xml file that is usually deployed as part of a feature. If we wanted to replace the search box on all pages of our site, we could create an elements file with XML similar to the following:

```
<Elements xmlns="http://schemas.microsoft.com/sharepoint/">
  <Control Id="SmallSearchInputBox" Sequence="50"
ControlClass="My.Control.Class"
```

```
ControlAssembly="My.Assembly, Version=…, Culture=neutral, PublicKeyToken=…">
    <Property Name="aProperty">foo</Property>
    <Property Name="anotherProperty">bar</Property>
  </Control>
</Elements>
```

The creation and deployment of elements files is covered in more detail in Chapter 19. In this chapter, the main point that you need to know is that delegates are configurable placeholders and can be used to swap out page markup or controls. In this sample, we've created a delegate that loads an assembly; you can also create a delegate that refers to a user control by setting the ControlSrc attribute of the Control element rather than the ControlClass and ControlAssembly attributes. One other important attribute of the Control element is the Sequence attribute. Because it's possible that a given site may have more than one definition for a single delegate, the Sequence attribute is used to determine which one takes priority. The delegate with the lowest number will be displayed.

## Cascading Style Sheets

Although master pages do the job of determining how the markup for the completed page fits together, best practice dictates that the styling of the completed markup is the job of *Cascading Style Sheets (CSS)*. In much the same way that master pages can be configured at the site level, so can style sheets. Using the Master Page option in the Look and Feel section of the Site Settings menu, you can specify an alternative style sheet for all pages on a site.

## Themes

*Themes* have been around for a while as an option to customize the visual appearance of SharePoint. Introduced in SharePoint 2003, the themes that were available in SharePoint consisted of a custom style sheet that could be applied to a site by a site owner. Although this approach worked well, it did have a drawback in that style sheets could be created only by web designers with some experience of styling the SharePoint platform. Given the complexity of the built-in style sheets, this was no easy feat.

With SharePoint 2010, things have moved on considerably. It's no longer solely the domain of a developer to create custom styles; nontechnical users can now create and modify styles easily by using the SharePoint user interface.

### Themes from a User's Perspective

An important consideration when it comes to themes is that they are now packaged using an OpenXML file format. As a result, themes can be created in and shared among many Office applications. For example, you can create a theme in Microsoft Word and export that theme for use in SharePoint.

To see how themes work from a user's perspective, navigate to the demo site that we created earlier. From the Site Actions menu, select Site Settings. Then, from the Look and Feel section, select Site Theme.

**NOTE** Customizing themes using the user interface requires the SharePoint Server Publishing Infrastructure to be activated at the site-collection level.

Using the controls in the Customize Theme section of the page, shown next, you can specify colors and fonts for a number of standard text types and preview your custom theme.

### Themes from a Developer's Perspective

**New in 2010**

Users can customize themes by overriding a number of standard elements such as Accent 1 or Hyperlink. Let's look at how the new SharePoint theming engine takes this information and converts it to CSS for use by the user interface.

Out of the box, themes are stored in the %SPRoot%\Template\Global\Lists\Themes folder, and, as you can see by examining the contents of this folder, they are packaged with a .thmx extension using the OpenXML format. (We'll look at OpenXML in a bit more detail in Chapter 10.) Effectively, an OpenXML file is a ZIP archive containing a number of XML files and other content such as images.

It is generally considered best practice to refer to style sheets within the SharePoint platform using a **CssLink** control and a **CssRegistration** control. You can see examples of these controls in the v4.master page. The **CssLink** control acts as a placeholder for the output of CSS links for a page and is generally placed in the header, whereas a **CssRegistration** control can be used anywhere within a page or in the child objects that make up a page, such as user controls and web parts. The **CssRegistration** control contains details of a particular style sheet that should be linked to the page.

At runtime, before the page is output, the style sheets referred to by all of the **CssRegistration** controls within the consolidated control hierarchy of a page are collated and output by the **CssLink** control. You can see this in action if you look at the output for any SharePoint page without a theme applied; in the header of the page, you'll see tags such as these:

```
<link rel="stylesheet" type="text/css" href="/_layouts/1033/styles/Themable/→
search.css?rev=<snipped>"/>
<link rel="stylesheet" type="text/css" href="/_layouts/1033/styles/Themable/→
corev4.css?rev=<snipped>"/>
```

However, if you look at the default v4.master page, you'll find only this:

```
<SharePoint:CssLink runat="server" Version="4"/>
```

This dynamic generation of CSS links is leveraged by the SharePoint 2010 theming engine. If you apply a theme to a site and then look at the output HTML, you'll see that the CSS links have changed to these:

```
<link rel="stylesheet" type="text/css" href="/sites/Section1/_themes/3/→
layouts-9C6B8173.css?ctag=4"/>
<link rel="stylesheet" type="text/css" href="/sites/Section1/_themes/3/→
corev4-8A0ABD2F.css?ctag=4"/>
```

Notice that the style sheet links have changed and now refer to the _themes folder for the current site. When a theme is applied using the user interface, the SharePoint platform automatically generates style sheets and image files based on the theme and stores these files within the _themes folder. You can see the generated output by browsing to the referenced folder using SharePoint Designer.

### Supporting Themes in Custom Style Sheets

One of the properties of the **CssRegistration** control is **EnableTheming**. As its name suggests, this is a Boolean value that dictates whether the referenced style sheet should be replaced with a themed alternative if a theme is applied to a site. When creating custom style sheets, you're not required to support themes—after all, maintaining a consistent style may be the aim of a custom style sheet. However, to use themes in a custom style sheet, you will need to create some additional markup. Looking at Core.Css (%SPRoot%/Layouts/1033/Styles/Core.Css), you can see a few interesting comments, such as these:

```
.ms-dlgTitle
{
/* [RecolorImage(themeColor:"Light2",includeRectangle:{x:0,y:51,width:1,height:→
21})] */ background:url("/_layouts/images/bgximg.png") repeat-x -0px -51px;→
/* [ReplaceColor(themeColor:"Dark2",themeShade:"0.90")] */ background-color:→
#21374c;
height:32px;
white-space:nowrap;
cursor:default;
overflow:hidden;
}
```

These comments are used by the theming engine to generate style sheets and images dynamically that make use of the various attributes of the theme. Notice that by using the **RecolorImage** tag, you can recolor images based on theme colors. You have to admit, that's pretty clever!

## Adding Custom Functionality

Now that you've got a good understanding of how a SharePoint page is constructed and what factors are important in determining the overall look and feel of a site, let's move on to look at how you can add additional functionality to a page.

### Web Parts

You've seen how you can use tools such as InfoPath forms services to customize input forms. But what if you want to add functionality that goes beyond the capabilities of InfoPath? Let's look at a few options—the first is to create a custom web part.

Two types of web parts can be used within SharePoint: legacy web parts that are derived from the Microsoft.SharePoint.WebPartPages.WebPart base class, and standard ASP.NET web parts that are derived from the System.Web.UI.WebControl.Webparts.WebPart base class. The recommended approach for creating new web parts is to use the ASP.NET model.

#### Web Part Infrastructure

Before we delve into a discussion on how to create web parts for use with SharePoint, let's recap how the ASP.NET web part infrastructure works and what it does. A web part is a server control that exposes functionality that allows it to be configured or personalized by nontechnical users. In a sense, web parts are like building blocks: we can choose the web parts that we need to build something and stick them on the page wherever we want them.

To provide this functionality, the web part infrastructure has a few additional elements that should be included on a page. One of the first is the WebPartManager control, which is used to manage the configuration information for each web part on a page. As well as a WebPartManager, to allow designers some control over where web parts can be placed, the web part infrastructure makes use of WebPartZone controls that represent zones within a page where web parts can be added.

The SharePoint platform defines custom WebPartManager and WebPartZone controls that are derived from their ASP.NET counterparts. This allows web part settings to be persisted and controlled in a way that better suits the SharePoint page rendering mechanism. For example, one of the new features in SharePoint 2010 is the ability to version web part configuration along with other elements on a page. This functionality makes use of the custom SPWebPartManager class.

Earlier we looked at the default v4.master page that provides the basis for rendering all SharePoint pages. It's worthwhile to note that this master page contains a SPWebPartManager control, so all pages that are derived from this master page can make use of web parts.

#### Web Part Security

Web parts are a bit like building blocks; users can build whatever they like with them. However, left unchecked, users can potentially build resource-hogging monstrosities that can kill a site for all other users. To prevent this and to give administrators some control over the web parts that can be included on a page, SharePoint requires that all controls be registered as safe before they are allowed to be included. Safe controls are specified using a series of SafeControl elements within the site's web.config file.

In addition to requiring controls to be explicitly specified as safe for a given site, web parts can also make use of code access security to restrict the actions of web part code even more.

## Creating a Web Part

To demonstrate how web parts can be created and used within a SharePoint page, let's work through an example. We'll create a simple web part that accepts two property values: a color and the name of a SharePoint list. The web part will display a list of items in the list using the selected colors. Although this is a trivial example, it will illustrate the key elements that are used when building more useful web parts.

1. In Visual Studio, choose File | New | Project. In the New Project dialog, select Empty SharePoint Project. Name the project **Chapter7WebPart**, as shown:

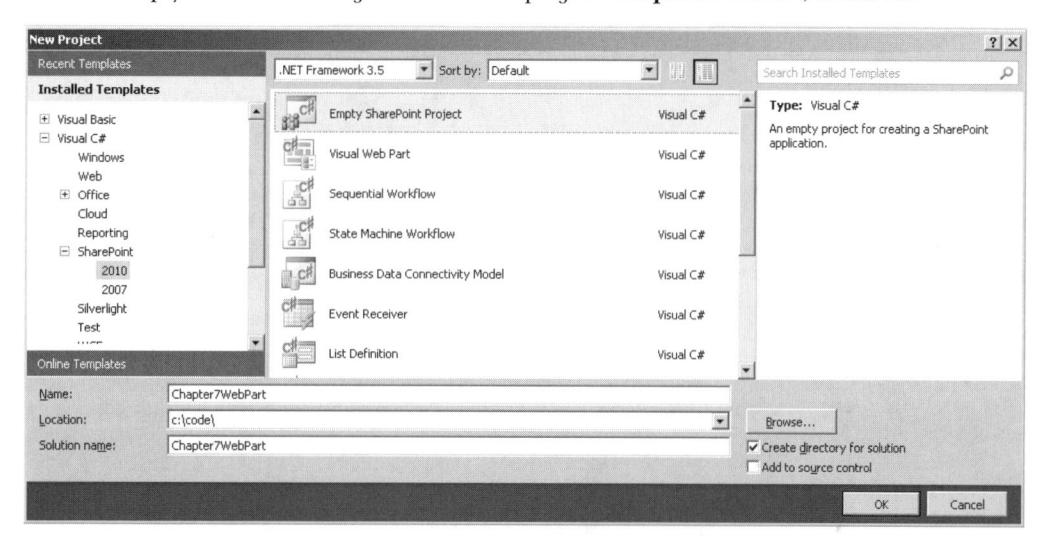

2. Set the local site to use for debugging to the demo site that we created earlier (http://<server name>/sites/Section1) and select the Deploy As Farm Solution option.

3. Choose Project | Add New Item. In the Add New Item dialog, select Web Part. Name the web part **DemoWebPart**.

4. In the file DemoWebPart.cs, add the following code:

```
[ToolboxItemAttribute(false)]
public class DemoWebPart : System.Web.UI.WebControls.WebParts.WebPart
{
    private ColorEnum _textColor = ColorEnum.Black;
    private string _listName = string.Empty;

    public enum ColorEnum
    {
        Red,
        Green,
        Blue,
        Black,
        White
    }
```

```csharp
[Personalizable(true),
WebBrowsable(true),
WebDescription("Select the font color used to display text"),
WebDisplayName("Text Color") ,
SPWebCategoryName("Color")]
public ColorEnum TextColor {
    get
    {
        return _textColor;
    }
    set
    {
        _textColor = value;
    }
}

[Personalizable(true),
WebBrowsable(true),
WebDescription("Select the list name from which text will be retrieved"),
WebDisplayName("List Name")]
public string ListName {
    get
    {
        return _listName;
    }
    set
    {
        _listName = value;
    }
}

protected override void CreateChildControls()
{
    HtmlGenericControl div = new HtmlGenericControl("div");
    SPList list=SPContext.Current.Web.Lists.TryGetList(ListName);

    if (list != null)
    {
        SPQuery query = new SPQuery();
        query.RowLimit = 50;
        SPListItemCollection items = list.GetItems(query);
        StringBuilder sb = new StringBuilder();
        sb.Append("<ul style=\"color:" +
                System.Enum.GetName(typeof(ColorEnum), TextColor)
                + "\";>");

        foreach (SPListItem item in items)
        {
            sb.Append("<li>" + item.Title + "</li>");
        }
        sb.Append("</ul>");

        div.InnerHtml = sb.ToString();
    }
```

```
    else
    {
        div.InnerHtml = "List not found";
    }

    this.Controls.Add(div);
    }
}
```

We're querying the configured list and creating an unordered list of the title of the top 50 items. Notice that the attributes that are applied to the TextColor and ListName properties. For the property to be visible in the Property Editor pane, WebBrowsable must be set to true.

5. To see how the web part works on a page, select Deploy Chapter7WebPart from the Build menu.

6. In the browser, navigate to the home page of the demo site that we set up earlier, and then choose Site Actions | Edit Page. From the Insert tab on the ribbon, select Web Part.

7. From the Custom category, select DemoWebPart, and then click Add:

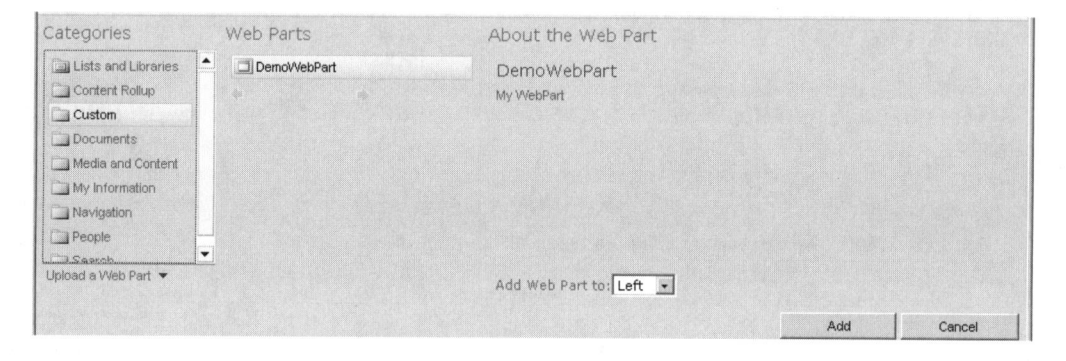

8. Since we haven't configured a list, the web part will display "List not found." To edit the web part properties, right-click the arrow to the right of the web part and select Edit Web Part from the context menu, as shown:

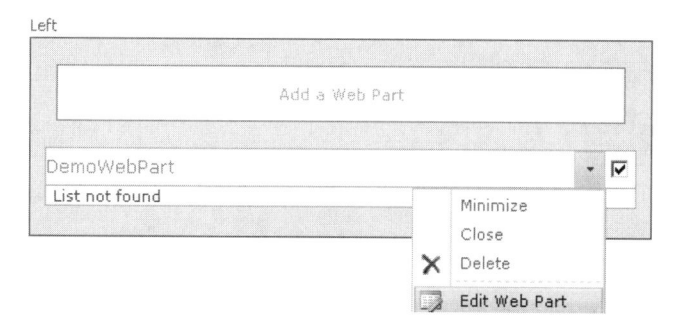

9. Our custom properties appear in the Color section and the Miscellaneous section, as configured by the attributes that we applied to the properties. By placing the cursor over the property name, you'll see the description text that we added as a tooltip. In the List Name text box, enter **Web Part Gallery** as the name of the list, and then click OK.

## Improving the Property Editing Experience: Editor Parts

For our sample web part, we've used a text box to allow users to enter the name of a list. While this works as we expected, it's not exactly an ideal interface. A better approach would be to show a drop-down list of available lists and allow the user to select one. To implement this functionality, we'll use an editor part. Editor parts are also server controls and work in a similar fashion to web parts. However, editor parts are rendered within the Property Editor pane, and their primary function is to enhance the design-time experience for users.

To add a new editor part, take the following steps:

1. Within the DemoWebPart folder in Visual Studio, add a new class file named ListPickerEditor.cs. Add the following code:

```
class ListPickerEditor : EditorPart
{
    private HtmlSelect _listsDropdown;
    private string _selectedValue = "";

    [Personalizable(true), WebBrowsable(false)]
    public string selectedValue
    {
        get { return _selectedValue; }
        set { _selectedValue = value; }
    }
    public ListPickerEditor(string webPartId)
    {
        this.ID = "ListPickerEditor" + webPartId;
        this.Title = "List Picker";
    }

    protected override void CreateChildControls()
    {
        _listsDropdown = new HtmlSelect();
        Controls.Add(_listsDropdown);
    }

    public override bool ApplyChanges()
    {
        EnsureChildControls();
        DemoWebPart _part = WebPartToEdit as DemoWebPart;
        _part.ListName = _listsDropdown.Items[_listsDropdown.SelectedIndex].Value.➔
ToString();
        return true;
    }

    public override void SyncChanges()
    {
        DemoWebPart _part = WebPartToEdit as DemoWebPart;
```

```
        EnsureChildControls();
        selectedValue = _part.ListName;

        PopulateDropDown();

        if (_listsDropdown.Items.FindByValue(_selectedValue)!=null)
        {
            _listsDropdown.Value = selectedValue;
        }

    }

    private void PopulateDropDown()
    {
        SPListCollection lists = SPContext.Current.Web.Lists;
        _listsDropdown.Items.Clear();
        foreach (SPList list in lists)
        {
            if (list.Fields.ContainsField("Title"))
            {
                _listsDropdown.Items.Add(list.Title);
            }
        }
    }
}
```

2. To hook up this editor part to our web part, we need to implement the IWebEditable interface. In DemoWebPart.cs, change the class definition to this:

   ```
   public class DemoWebPart : WebPart, IWebEditable
   ```

3. Add the following overrides to the DemoWebPart.cs file:

   ```
   EditorPartCollection IWebEditable.CreateEditorParts()
   {
     List<EditorPart> editors = new List<EditorPart>();
     editors.Add(new ListPickerEditor(this.ID));
     return new EditorPartCollection(editors);
   }
   object IWebEditable.WebBrowsableObject
   {
     get { return this; }
   }
   ```

4. Finally, since we have an editor for our ListName property, we don't need to display the text box default implementation. So that our ListName property is not shown in the Editor pane, change the WebBrowsable attribute to false.

We can now deploy this revised web part and use a drop-down list to configure the list to be displayed rather than having to type it manually.

## Visual Web Parts

**New in 2010** In our examples so far, we've adopted the standard ASP.NET approach to building web parts. Because a web part is a server control, the user interface needs to be manually constructed. In our simple examples, this didn't cause too much trouble; however, as the user interface gets more complicated, this approach becomes a problem due to the lack of a design-time interface and the extra code required to hook up controls to their events. Once again, the folks at Microsoft realized that this was a major pain for SharePoint developers, and in SharePoint 2010 introduced the Visual Web Part. A Visual Web Part is a web part that loads an embedded user control. Since user controls have a design-time interface in Visual Studio, creating complex web parts becomes much simpler.

To create a Visual Web Part, take the following steps:

1. In the Chapter7WebPart project that we created earlier, choose Project | Add New Item.

2. In the Add New Item dialog, create a new Visual Web Part named DemoVisualWebPart, as shown:

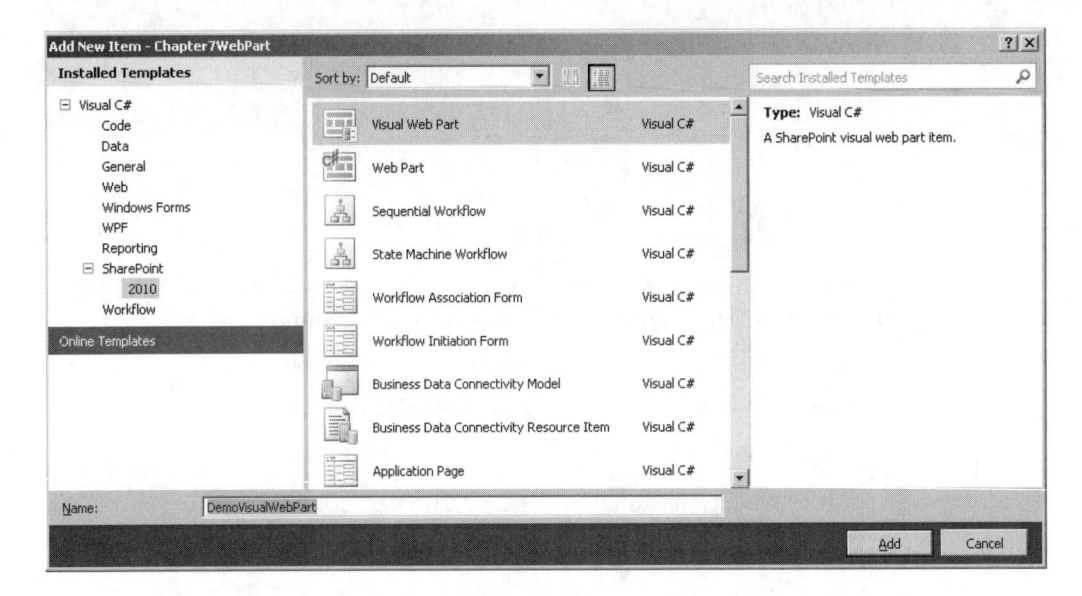

3. In the DemoVisualWebPartUserControl.ascx, drag an UpdatePanel control from the toolbox. Drag a Label control into the UpdatePanel. From the AJAX Extensions category in the toolbox, drag a Timer control. Set the timer interval to 5000.

4. Set the Triggers property of the UpdatePanel control to use the Tick event of the timer, as shown:

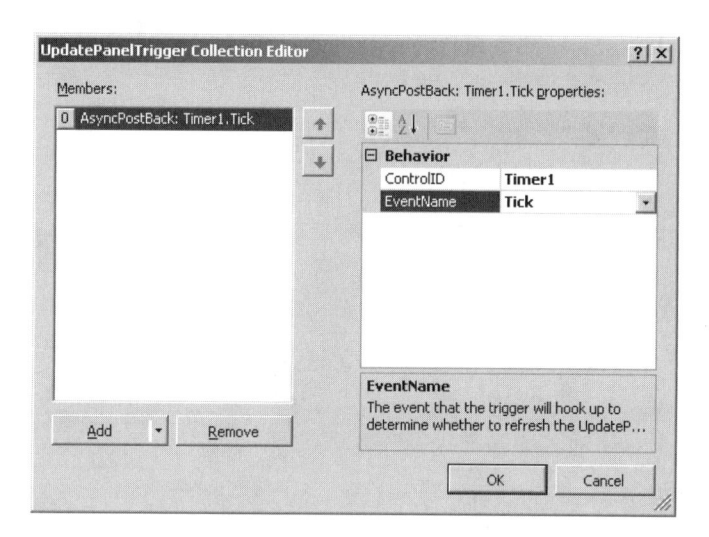

5. In the DemoVisualWebPart.cs file, add the following code:

```
public class DemoVisualWebPart : WebPart
{
    private const string _ascxPath = @"~/_CONTROLTEMPLATES/Chapter7WebPart→
.DemoWebPart/DemoVisualWebPart/DemoVisualWebPartUserControl.ascx";

    protected override void CreateChildControls()
    {
        DemoVisualWebPartUserControl control = Page.LoadControl(_ascxPath) →
as DemoVisualWebPartUserControl;
        control.ListName = this._listName;
        Controls.Add(control);
    }

    private string _listName = string.Empty;

    [Personalizable(true),
    WebBrowsable(true),
    WebDescription("Select the list name from which text will be retrieved"),
    WebDisplayName("List Name")]
    public string ListName
    {
        get
        {
            return _listName;
        }
        set
        {
            _listName = value;
        }
    }
}
```

6. In the code-behind file from the user control (DemoVisualWebPartUserControl.ascx.cs), add the following code:

```csharp
public partial class DemoVisualWebPartUserControl : UserControl
{
    public string ListName { get; set; }

    protected void Page_Load(object sender, EventArgs e)
    {
        GetNextListName();
    }

    private void GetNextListName()
    {
        SPList list = SPContext.Current.Web.Lists.TryGetList(ListName);
        if (list == null)
        {
            Label1.Text = "List not found";
            ViewState.Remove("ItemId");
            Timer1.Enabled = false;
            return;
        }
        SPQuery query = new SPQuery();
        query.RowLimit = 50;
        SPListItemCollection items = list.GetItems(query);

        if (items.Count > 0)
        {
            int nextIndex = 0;
            if (ViewState["ItemId"] != null)
            {
                int currentValue = (int)ViewState["ItemId"];

                if (currentValue >= items.Count - 1)
                {
                    nextIndex = 0;
                }
                else
                {
                    nextIndex = currentValue + 1;
                }

            }
            Label1.Text = items[nextIndex].Title;
            ViewState["ItemId"] = nextIndex;
        }
        else
        {
            Label1.Text = "No Items found";
            ViewState.Remove("ItemId");
        }
        Timer1.Enabled = true;
    }
}
```

When this web part is deployed and then added to a page, it performs a function similar to that in our earlier example. The difference is that this web part makes use of Asynchronous JavaScript and XML (AJAX) to cycle periodically through the items in the configured list. Of course, we could have created a similar web part without the benefit of a visual designer, but I'm sure you'll agree that using a Visual Web Part makes the job much simpler.

## Summary

This chapter looked at the key elements of the SharePoint platform with regard to user interface development. You've seen that by using the underlying master page model of ASP.NET, SharePoint sites can implement common user interface elements in a single location. You've also see how themes created in any Microsoft Office application can be easily applied to SharePoint, allowing nontechnical users to create custom themes without having to resort to any development tools. Finally, you saw how web parts can be used to add functionality in a modular fashion that can be configured by nontechnical users as and when required.

# PART III
# Application Services

**CHAPTER 8**
Application Services Overview

**CHAPTER 9**
Service Application Framework

**CHAPTER 10**
Word Automation Services

**CHAPTER 11**
Workflow

**CHAPTER 12**
Excel Services

# CHAPTER 8

# Application Services Overview

When it comes to evaluating software applications, many organizations often pay too much attention to the eye candy and not enough to the clever stuff that goes on behind the scenes. With SharePoint, this is easy to do, and in my experience, many organizations have invested in a SharePoint implementation without fully appreciating the potential of the platform. SharePoint is more than a platform that allows users to create web sites or collaborate on content creation. In Part II, you saw a lot of clever SharePoint user interface features, but the real meat of the SharePoint platform is in the application services layer.

In this part of the book, we'll take a look at the service application architecture and dig into a few application services in more detail. Before we get into that stuff, though, this chapter spends a bit of time covering one of the fundamental tools for implementing application layer processing on the SharePoint platform: event handling.

## Handling Events

Most software applications are event driven—that is, the order in which code executes is determined by a sequence of events. Events can be raised by many different sources, such as a user clicking a button or the contents of a file changing. To support an event-driven software development approach, the SharePoint platform also raises many different events that can be programmatically handled.

A few different levels of event handling apply to applications developed using the SharePoint platform. One of the most obvious is the events that are raised and handled by the underlying ASP.NET framework. Some of these events, also known as post-back events, are raised when users interact with controls on a web page. Along with these user-initiated events are system-generated events such as the PreInit, Load, and Render events that form part of the ASP.NET page processing lifecycle. Handling events such as these are run-of-the-mill tasks for developers familiar with the ASP.NET platform, so I won't spend much time covering them other than to acknowledge that they are an important part of any SharePoint application design.

In addition to the event handling model provided by the ASP.NET framework and the various user controls that SharePoint provides that directly use this mode, SharePoint also provides an additional level of event handling that is tied more directly to the operations in the SharePoint platform.

## Event Hosts

As you've seen in many of the examples in this book, a few core objects provide most of the functionality that we commonly use when developing SharePoint applications: SPSite, SPWeb, SPList, and SPContentType. Each of these objects is capable of hosting events and as such is known as an event host. To compare this to the Windows forms event model, an example of an event host might be a button on a form.

## Event Receivers

Events raised by any of the event host classes are handled by event receivers, which work in a similar fashion to an event handler in traditional ASP.NET programming. Each event receiver is implemented in a class that's derived from a base class that defines methods for each event that can occur. The primary difference between SharePoint events and traditional ASP.NET events is that the event receiver is decoupled from the event host—that is, the event receiver exists in an assembly that's completely separate from the event host and the connection between the two is dynamically made via configuration as opposed to being established within code. A direct comparison with the Windows forms event model isn't possible, since Windows forms events make use of delegates, which allow events to be handled in any class. Each SharePoint event receiver is a class in its own right; in a sense, each method defined within an event receiver serves the same purpose as a delegate in the Windows forms model.

## Receiver Base Classes

As mentioned, each event receiver must be based on an appropriate receiver base class. The base class dictates which events can be handled by the event receiver as well as which event hosts can call the event receiver. Naturally, not all event hosts are capable of raising the same events, so it makes sense that not all event hosts support each receiver base class.

Within the SharePoint platform are four receiver base classes that are derived from SPEventReceiverBase. Event receivers can be derived from these classes to handle events from the SPSite, SPWeb, SPList, and SPContentType event hosts.

### SPItemEventReceiver

This base class defines methods that can be used to trap events that are raised by items. As you've seen, an item can be either a document or a list item. For a complete list of the events that can be handled using this base class, see http://msdn.microsoft.com/en-gb/library/microsoft.sharepoint.spitemeventreceiver_members.aspx.

### SPListEventReceiver

This base class defines methods that can be used to trap events that are raised by lists. As you've seen, an SPList object can represent either a list or a document library. For a complete list of the events that can be handled using this base class, see http://msdn.microsoft.com/en-gb/library/microsoft.sharepoint.splisteventreceiver_members.aspx.

### SPWebEventReceiver

This base class defines methods that can be used to trap events that are raised by web sites. Each web site is represented by a SPWeb object. For a complete list of the events that can be handled using this base class, see http://msdn.microsoft.com/en-gb/library/microsoft.sharepoint.spwebeventreceiver_members.aspx.

### SPWorkflowEventReceiver

**New in 2010**

The SPWorkflowEventReceiver class is a new addition in SharePoint 2010. In previous versions, it was not possible to create event receivers to handle workflow events such as Starting or Completed. This presented a problem when further validation of processing was required before a workflow could be started. With SharePoint 2010, four new workflow events have been added: WorkflowCompleted, WorkflowPostponed, WorkflowStarted, and WorkflowStarting.

## Synchronous and Asynchronous Events

If we look at a few of the events that can be handled by the SPItemEventReceiver class, we see that usually two events occur for each action—for example, ItemAdded and ItemAdding. This duplicity can exist because these events occur at different points in the process of adding an item.

If a new SPItem is created and added via the object model, when the Update method is called on the appropriate object, the ItemAdding event is fired. This event runs in the same thread as the code that added the item; as a result, this type of event is known as a *synchronous* event.

After the Update method has been called and any synchronous event receivers have been called, processing returns to the code that added the item. However, behind the scenes, the SharePoint Object Model commits the changes to the content database. After this has completed, the ItemAdded event is fired and runs in a separate thread; it is known as an *asynchronous* event handler.

The main reason for handling a synchronous event as opposed to an asynchronous event is to perform some validation before the results of an action are committed to the content database. For example, before an item is added to a list, some managed code can be executed to check that all required fields are populated. If this check fails, the action can be canceled and return an error message to the user. With an asynchronous event handler, any problems would need to be resolved by rolling back already committed changes, and since the event occurs in a separate thread, no mechanism is in place to alert the user of any problem.

In previous versions of SharePoint, events that were fired after changes were committed to the content database and were always asynchronous. With SharePoint 2010, it's now possible to dictate that these events should be fired either synchronously or asynchronously. As we saw earlier, one way to add an event receiver to a particular event host was to create a new object of type SPEventReceiverDefinition. One of the properties of the SPEventReceiverDefinition object, Synchronization, allows us to specify which mode should be used when firing the event.

## Security Context

When event receivers are called, generally speaking, they run in the security context of the user who initiated the changes that caused the event to be fired. If the events have been raised as the result of changes made by a workflow process, the events run in the context of the user who either started the workflow or made the change that caused the workflow to be started automatically. This behavior differs from previous versions of SharePoint, in which events that were initiated by workflow changes always executed under the SharePoint\System security context.

> **NOTE** SharePoint\System is a virtual account that's mapped to a physical account by the SharePoint platform when a web application is created. Each web application can potentially have a different application pool account. So that developers and the SharePoint platform itself have a single, well-defined way to refer to this account, regardless of the underlying physical account that's used, "SharePoint\System" is used as a pseudonym throughout the platform. Since all system processes are started by the SharePoint\System account, this account has full control over all aspects of a web application.

In some situations, the default security context may not be appropriate. If an event receiver is executing under the security context of a particular user and a higher level of system privilege is required, using **SPSecurity.RunWithElevatedPrivileges** allows code to be executed as SharePoint\System:

```
public override void ItemAdded(SPItemEventProperties properties)
{
    SPSecurity.RunWithElevatedPrivileges(() =>
        {
            using (SPSite site = new SPSite(properties.SiteId))
            {
              using (SPWeb web = site.OpenWeb(properties.Web.ID))
              {
                SPListItem item = web.Lists[properties.ListId].Items[properties.➜
ListItem.UniqueId];
                item["Title"] = "Updated as System Account";
                item.Update();
              }
            }
        }
    );
}
```

Although this works well for elevating system privileges, it doesn't do much to help us when the receiver is running as SharePoint\System and we want to revert to the security context of the user who originated the event. For example, in this code snippet, because the **Update** method is being called with a section of code that is being run with elevated privileges, any **ItemUpdated** or **ItemUpdating** event receivers that are defined will run under the SharePoint\System security context.

To get around this problem, SharePoint 2010 adds a new property that allows us to pick up the security token of the originating user and make use of it to switch security context manually, as this example shows:

```
public override void ItemUpdating(SPItemEventProperties properties)
    {
```

```
   Trace.Write("Updating receiver running as : " + properties.Web.CurrentUser.Name);
   using (SPSite site = new SPSite(properties.SiteId, properties.OriginatingUserToken))
   {
     using (SPWeb web = site.OpenWeb(properties.Web.ID))
     {
       Trace.Write("originating user was : " + web.CurrentUser.Name);
     }
   }
}
```

## Event Properties

Four different receiver base classes can be used to create event receivers for the event hosts described earlier. Since each of these hosts represents a different object within the SharePoint platform, the properties that are available to each event receiver are also different. Each receiver base class makes use of a specific event properties class that is derived from **SPEventPropertiesBase** to communicate with the respective event receiver. These base classes are **SPItemEventProperties**, **SPListEventProperties**, **SPWebEventProperties**, and **SPWorkflowEventProperties**.

### SPItemEventProperties

The **SPItemEventProperties** class is used to communicate details of the item on which an event was raised to the appropriate event receiver. Two important properties of the class that warrant further explanation are **AfterProperties** and **BeforeProperties**. Earlier we looked at synchronous events and asynchronous events, and we discovered that in SharePoint 2010, it is possible to specify that events that would normally occur asynchronously can instead be called synchronously. For the sake of clarity, let's consider events that are synchronous by default as *before* events, and events that are asynchronous by default as *after* events.

When a before event is raised, **AfterProperties** contains the item properties that will be stored in the content database if the event is processed successfully. **BeforeProperties** contains the item properties that are currently stored in the content database.

When an after event is raised, either synchronously or asynchronously, **BeforeProperties** contains the values that were previously stored in the content database, whereas **AfterProperties** contains the values that are currently stored in the content database.

**CAUTION** **BeforeProperties** works only for document items. For all other items, **BeforeProperties** will always be null.

### SPListEventProperties

The **SPListEventProperties** class is used to communicate the details of the list or field on which an event was raised to the appropriate event receiver.

### SPWebEventProperties

The **SPWebEventProperties** class is used to communicate the details of the web or site on which an event was raised to the appropriate event receiver. The **SPWebEventProperties** class contains both a **ServerRelativeUrl** and a **NewServerRelativeUrl** property. When the event being handled is a before event (as defined above), the **ServerRelativeUrl** property will contain the current URL of a site or web, and the **NewServerRelativeUrl** will contain the URL that the site or web will have if the event is processed successfully.

When the event being handled is an after event, the **ServerRelativeUrl** property will contain the previous URL of the site or web, whereas the **NewServerRelativeUrl** will contain the current URL.

If the event is a Delete or Deleting event, the **NewServerRelativeUrl** will throw an InvalidOperationException.

### SPWorkflowEventProperties

The **SPWorkflowEventProperties** class is used to communicate the details of the workflow instance on which an event was raised to the appropriate event receiver.

### Shared Properties

The base **SPEventPropertiesBase** class defines a few interesting properties that are inherited by all event properties classes.

First, the **Status** property allows code within an event receiver to specify the outcome of an event. Possible outcomes are defined by the **SPEventReceiverStatus** enumeration and include the following:

- **Continue**  All is well; carry on as normal.
- **CancelNoError**  Cancel the request but don't present a notification to the caller.
- **CancelWithError**  Cancel the request and raise an error message as specified by the **ErrorMessage** property.
- **CancelWithRedirectUrl**  Cancel the request and redirect the caller to the URL specified in the **RedirectUrl** property.

> **NOTE** **CancelWithRedirectUrl** doesn't work when events are raised by clients using Microsoft Office applications, since these applications do not provide a web browser. Effectively, the redirect is ignored.

Second, the **EventUserToken** and **OriginatingUserToken** properties, as discussed earlier, can be used to switch between security contexts.

## Packaging and Deployment Events

Along with the event hosts that we looked at earlier, the SharePoint platform also includes an additional host, the SPFeatureDefinition class, which is used for packaging and deployment purposes. Events in the packaging and deployment framework are hooked up a bit differently, and more in-depth coverage of this subject will be provided in Chapter 19. For now, it's enough to know that these events exist and also make use of event receivers in a similar manner.

## Creating Event Receivers

Now that you understand how event receivers let us implement custom business logic for our SharePoint applications, let's take a look at how we can create them and hook them up with the platform.

1. Create a new blank site named Chapter 8. Add a custom list named Test List.
2. Using Visual Studio, create a new Empty SharePoint Project named DemoEventReceivers, as shown next. Set the debugging site to the new site created in step 1, and then select the Deploy As A Farm Solution option.

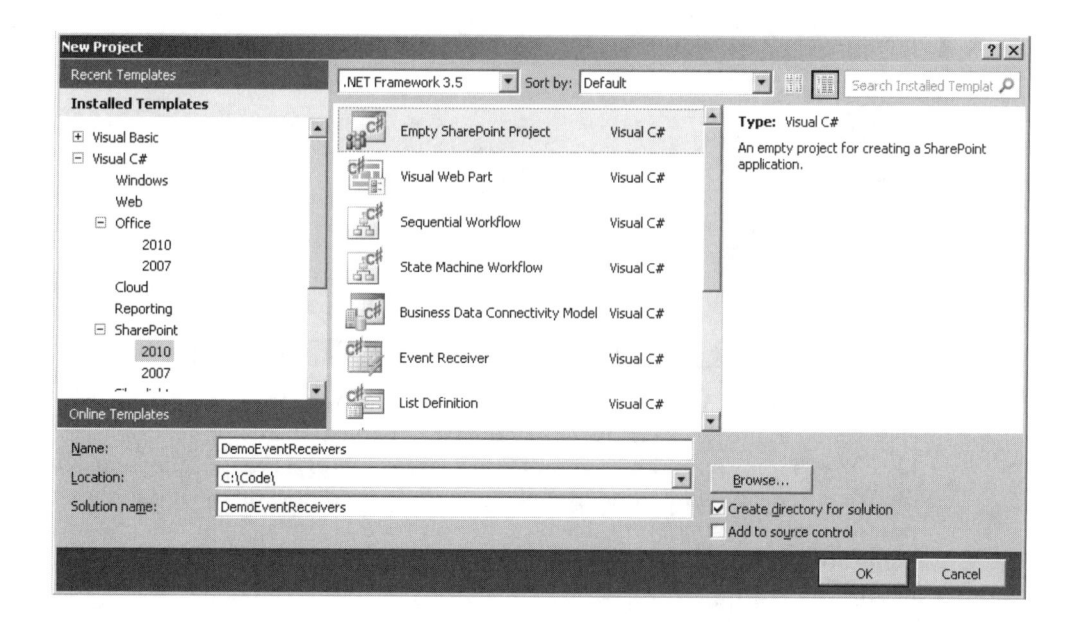

3. Choose Project | Add New Item. From the Add New Item dialog, select Event Receiver and type the name as **ListEventReceiver**.

   The SharePoint Customization Wizard will prompt for additional settings before creating an event receiver class in the project, as shown next. Let's take a look at the settings so that we can understand how they relate to the concepts that we discussed earlier.

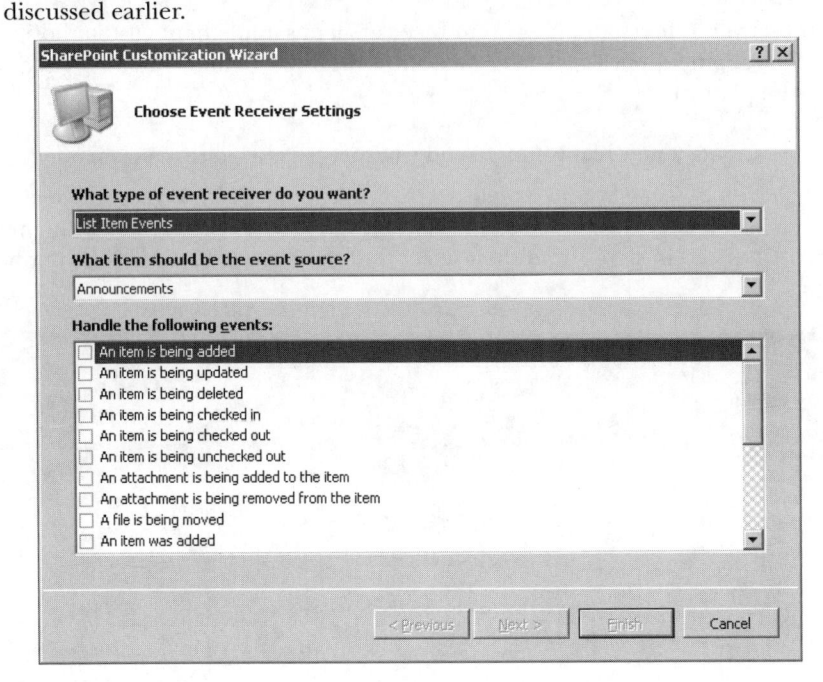

*[Screenshot: SharePoint Customization Wizard – Choose Event Receiver Settings. What type of event receiver do you want? List Item Events. What item should be the event source? Announcements. Handle the following events: An item is being added, An item is being updated, An item is being deleted, An item is being checked in, An item is being checked out, An item is being unchecked out, An attachment is being added to the item, An attachment is being removed from the item, A file is being moved, An item was added.]*

The options in the What Type Of Event Receiver Do You Want? drop-down list correspond to the receiver base classes discussed earlier. The exception to this is the List Email Events option, which we'll look at later in this chapter. The items in the What Item Should Be The Event Source? drop-down list correspond to the event host that will raise the event. Each option represents a specific instance of an event host.

4. For this demonstration, set the type of event receiver to List Item Events and then select Custom List from the event source drop-down. We're creating an event receiver that will be called by all SPList objects that use the Custom List template.

5. The Handle The Following Events checkbox list lets us select which events we want to handle in our event receiver. For our demonstration, choose An Item Is Being Added and An Item Was Added.

6. Click Finish to create the event receiver.

The SharePoint customization Wizard will add a file named ListEventReceiver.cs to the solution containing the following code (comments removed for brevity):

```
public class ListEventReceiver : SPItemEventReceiver
{
    public override void ItemAdding(SPItemEventProperties properties)
    {
        base.ItemAdding(properties);
    }
    public override void ItemAdded(SPItemEventProperties properties)
    {
```

```
      base.ItemAdded(properties);
   }
}
```

From this code snippet, we can see that our event receiver is derived from the **SPItemEventReceiver** base class, and both of the defined methods accept **SPItemEventProperties** objects as parameters.

7. Update the **ItemAdding** method with the following code:

```
public override void ItemAdding(SPItemEventProperties properties)
  {
    switch (properties.AfterProperties["Title"].ToString())
    {
      case "Cancel Me":
        properties.Status = SPEventReceiverStatus.CancelNoError;
        break;
      case "Update Me":
        properties.AfterProperties["Title"] = "Updated title";
        break;
      case "Throw Error":
        properties.ErrorMessage = "An error occurred";
        properties.Status = SPEventReceiverStatus.CancelWithError;
        break;
      case "Redirect":
        properties.RedirectUrl = "/_layouts/gear.aspx";
        properties.Status = SPEventReceiverStatus.CancelWithRedirectUrl;
        break;
      default:
        break;
    }
  }
```

8. Deploy the event receiver by choosing Build | Deploy DemoEventReceivers.

This simple example demonstrates a few of the key features of synchronous event handlers. By adding a new item to the Test List that we created earlier with the title set to Cancel Me, the page will be refreshed and no item will be stored in the list. This illustrates how we can cancel an action by setting the **SPItemEventProperties.Status** property appropriately.

By creating a new item with the title set to Update Me, the event handler updates the title value before the item is stored in the content database.

Setting the title to Throw Error or Redirect illustrates the capability to return a custom error message to the user and to redirect to a custom page. In both of these cases, the item is not added to the list.

1. Now update the **ItemAdded** method with the following code:

```
        public override void ItemAdded(SPItemEventProperties properties)
        {
           Thread.Sleep(5000);
           properties.ListItem.Delete();
        }
```

2. Deploy the updated event receiver by choosing Build | Deploy DemoEventReceivers.

With our revised ItemAdded event receiver, we can see the difference between a synchronous event and an asynchronous event. In the code snippet, the calling thread is put to sleep for a few seconds before execution continues. During this time, the page will continue to refresh and will show the added item in the list. This demonstrates that the ItemAdded event receiver is running on a separate thread. Once the thread resumes execution, it will delete the added item. Since this action occurs on a separate thread, the results are not immediately visible to the user. This highlights one of the drawbacks of asynchronous event receivers.

As mentioned earlier, we can configure whether an after event handler runs synchronously or asynchronously. One easy way to do this is as follows:

1. In the Elements.xml file, edit the XML as follows:

```xml
<Elements xmlns="http://schemas.microsoft.com/sharepoint/">
  <Receivers ListTemplateId="100">
    <Receiver>
      <Name>ListEventReceiverItemAdding</Name>
      <Type>ItemAdding</Type>
      <Assembly>$SharePoint.Project.AssemblyFullName$</Assembly>
      <Class>DemoEventReceivers.ListEventReceiver.ListEventReceiver</Class>
      <SequenceNumber>10000</SequenceNumber>
    </Receiver>
    <Receiver>
      <Name>ListEventReceiverItemAdded</Name>
      <Type>ItemAdded</Type>
      <Assembly>$SharePoint.Project.AssemblyFullName$</Assembly>
      <Class>DemoEventReceivers.ListEventReceiver.ListEventReceiver</Class>
      <SequenceNumber>10000</SequenceNumber>
      <Synchronization>Synchronous</Synchronization>
    </Receiver>
  </Receivers>
</Elements>
```

Note the addition of the Synchronization element for the ListEventReceiverItemAdded receiver.

2. So that we can confirm that our event receiver is being called, update the code in the ItemAdded method like so:

```
public override void ItemAdded(SPItemEventProperties properties)
{
    Thread.Sleep(5000);
    properties.ListItem.Recycle();
}
```

3. Deploy the updated event receiver by choosing Build | Deploy DemoEventReceivers.

We can check that our ItemAdded event handler is now running synchronously by creating a new item. The first thing to note is that when you click the Save button, the page will take a bit longer to refresh than previously, because the Thread.Sleep(5000) instruction is now running synchronously. When the page is refreshed, the new item will not appear in the list; by clicking the Recycle Bin link, we can confirm that the item was created and then moved to the recycle bin by the ItemAdded event receiver.

## Enabling or Disabling Event Firing

You've seen how to create event handlers using the SharePoint Customization Wizard in Visual Studio. Let's look at how we can handle additional events in an existing event receiver.

1. In Visual Studio, select the ListEventReceiver item, as shown:

2. In the Properties pane, set the values for Handle ItemUpdated and Handle ItemUpdating to True.

3. In the ListEventReceiver.cs file, the following additional methods have been added to handle the ItemUpdated and ItemUpdating events:

```
public override void ItemUpdated(SPItemEventProperties properties)
{
  base.ItemUpdated(properties);
}

public override void ItemUpdating(SPItemEventProperties properties)
{
  base.ItemUpdating(properties);
}
```

As we did earlier, we can now add whatever custom code we need to these method stubs.

4. For demonstration purposes, update the **ItemUpdated** method as follows:

```
public override void ItemUpdated(SPItemEventProperties properties)
{
  int count = 0;
  string title = properties.AfterProperties["Title"].ToString();
  if (title.Contains("Updated Title"))
  {
    count = int.Parse(title.Replace("Updated Title", string.Empty));
    count++;
  }
  properties.ListItem["Title"] = "Updated Title" + count;
  properties.ListItem.Update();
}
```

5. Comment the body of the **ItemAdded** method to allow new items to be added.

6. Deploy the updated event receiver, and then edit an existing list item.

   From the preceding code, we might reasonably expect our edited item to have its title changed to Updated Title0. Another reasonable expectation is that the title will be continually updated since updating an item within an **ItemUpdated** event handler effectively sets up an infinite loop.

   In reality, however, neither of these two possibilities occurs. Instead, the item is updated ten times and the title remains at Updated Title9.

   This highlights an interesting feature of SharePoint 2010: In previous versions, code such as this would indeed cause an infinite loop and cause major performance problems with a server. With SharePoint 2010, protection is built in for this type of issue.

   Nonetheless, prevention is always better than a cure. Rather than relying on the platform to handle such coding errors gracefully, you should explicitly prevent them.

7. Revise the **ItemUpdated** method as follows:

```
public override void ItemUpdated(SPItemEventProperties properties)
{
  this.EventFiringEnabled = false;
  int count = 0;
```

```
    string title = properties.AfterProperties["Title"].ToString();
    if (title.Contains("Updated Title"))
    {
      count = int.Parse(title.Replace("Updated Title", string.Empty));
      count++;
    }
    properties.ListItem["Title"] = "Updated Title" + count;
    properties.ListItem.Update();
    this.EventFiringEnabled = true;
}
```

After deploying and repeating the test, we can see that our code now behaves as expected: it updates the item title to Updated Title0.

## Binding Events

Fundamentally, you can bind event receivers to event hosts in two ways. The first method, which is used by the SharePoint Customization Wizard in Visual Studio, is via Collaborative Application Markup Language (CAML). When an event receiver is added to a SharePoint project, two files are added to the solution: An Elements.xml file and a code file to contain the implementation of the event receiver. The Elements.xml file contains XML similar to this snippet:

```
<Elements xmlns="http://schemas.microsoft.com/sharepoint/">
  <Receivers ListTemplateId="100">
    <Receiver>
      <Name>ListEventReceiverItemAdding</Name>
      <Type>ItemAdding</Type>
      <Assembly>$SharePoint.Project.AssemblyFullName$</Assembly>
      <Class>DemoEventReceivers.ListEventReceiver.ListEventReceiver</Class>
      <SequenceNumber>10000</SequenceNumber>
    </Receiver>
  </Receivers>
</Elements>
```

Element files and CAML are covered in more detail in Chapter 19. For the purposes of binding event receivers, the key thing that you need to know is that each **Receivers** element can contain one or more **Receiver** elements, where a **Receiver** element defines an event receiver class.

The second method, which offers a much greater degree of granularity, is to bind event receivers programmatically. While the CAML method is definitely the easiest to use, it has a major drawback in that the lowest level of granularity is the list template. To bind an event receiver to a particular list would require a new list template specific to that list. In our example, we bound our event receivers to the custom list template (ListTemplateID 100). In our simple test site, only one list used this template, so this didn't present a problem. Let's see what happens if we add another custom list.

1. In the test site that we created earlier, add a new custom list named Another Test List.

2. Add a new item to the list with the title Throw Error.

When clicking the Save button, an error page is shown. From this, we can see that our new list is also calling the event handlers that we configured for our test list. To resolve this problem, we need to programmatically attach our event receiver to our test list only.

Take the following steps to make this change:

1. Choose Build | Retract. This will retract our solution from the site, effectively detaching all event handlers that were attached by our CAML file previously.
2. In the Solution Explorer pane, right-click the Feature1 node, and then select Add Event Receiver.
3. Uncomment the **FeatureActivated** method and insert the following code:

```
public override void FeatureActivated(SPFeatureReceiverProperties properties)
    {
      using (SPWeb web = properties.Feature.Parent as SPWeb)
      {
        SPList testList = web.Lists.TryGetList("Test List");
        if (testList != null)
        {
          AssemblyName currentAssembly = Assembly.GetExecutingAssembly().GetName();

          SPEventReceiverDefinitionCollection eventReceivers=testList.EventReceivers;

          SPEventReceiverDefinition itemAdding = eventReceivers.Add();
          itemAdding.Name = "ListEventReceiverItemAdding";
          itemAdding.Type = SPEventReceiverType.ItemAdding;
          itemAdding.SequenceNumber = 10000;
          itemAdding.Assembly = currentAssembly.FullName;
          itemAdding.Class = "DemoEventReceivers.ListEventReceiver.ListEventReceiver";
          itemAdding.Update();
        }
      }
    }
```

4. So that the event receiver is removed again when the solution is retracted, uncomment the **FeatureDeactivating** method and add the following code:

```
public override void FeatureDeactivating(SPFeatureReceiverProperties properties)
    {
      using (SPWeb web = properties.Feature.Parent as SPWeb)
      {
        SPList testList = web.Lists.TryGetList("Test List");

        if (testList != null)
        {
          foreach (SPEventReceiverDefinition def in testList.EventReceivers)
          {
            if (def.Name == "ListEventReceiverItemAdding")
            {
              def.Delete();
            }
          }
        }
      }
    }
```

5. In the Elements.xml file, comment out or delete the **Receivers** element and its contents.

6. Deploy the revised solution.

### E-mail Events

One other type of event receiver base class that we haven't looked at is the SPEmailEventReceiver. This receiver can be used to handle the EmailReceived event for a particular document library or list. The first thing to note about e-mail events is that not all lists and libraries can accept incoming e-mail, and those that can accept it include document libraries, announcement lists, calendars, and discussion lists. Also, before e-mail can be sent to a list or library, it must first be configured in Central Administration and within an organization's network. This is a relatively in-depth process; for more information, see http://technet.microsoft.com/en-us/library/cc262947.aspx.

## Summary

When it comes to developing custom applications in SharePoint, it's practically impossible to get anywhere without having to write a few custom event receivers. As you've seen in this chapter, the event handling functionality of the platform is powerful enough to meet practically any requirement. Having both synchronous and asynchronous handlers for many events makes it possible to carry out long-running processes if required while still having the ability to intercept user actions. With a good understanding of how the overall event framework hangs together, you can work through the additional chapters in this section and understand how the event framework is the glue that hooks our behind-the-scenes application services with the eye candy of our presentation layer.

# CHAPTER 9

# Service Application Framework

Previous chapters looked at how web sites and applications are represented within the SharePoint architecture. We've made use of various services such as the Managed Metadata Service but one thing we haven't looked at in depth is how these services fit into the overall architecture of the SharePoint platform. As with most things in SharePoint, a standard framework is in place for provisioning and using services within a farm: the Service Application Framework. This chapter examines how the framework hangs together. We'll create a simple custom service to illustrate the implications for us as software developers.

## Implementation

The Service Application Framework is commonly represented as a new addition in SharePoint 2010. So that you can fully understand how services are provisioned and managed within a SharePoint farm, we need to look at the overall services architecture. Although new additions are included in SharePoint 2010, a lot of the underlying framework will be familiar to users of previous versions of the product.

### Server-side Implementation

If you've read the preceding chapters, you will be familiar with the notion of a *farm* within the SharePoint platform. A farm represents one or more servers that are logically grouped together for the purposes of administration, scalability, and reliability. Within the SharePoint object model, the farm is represented by the SPFarm object.

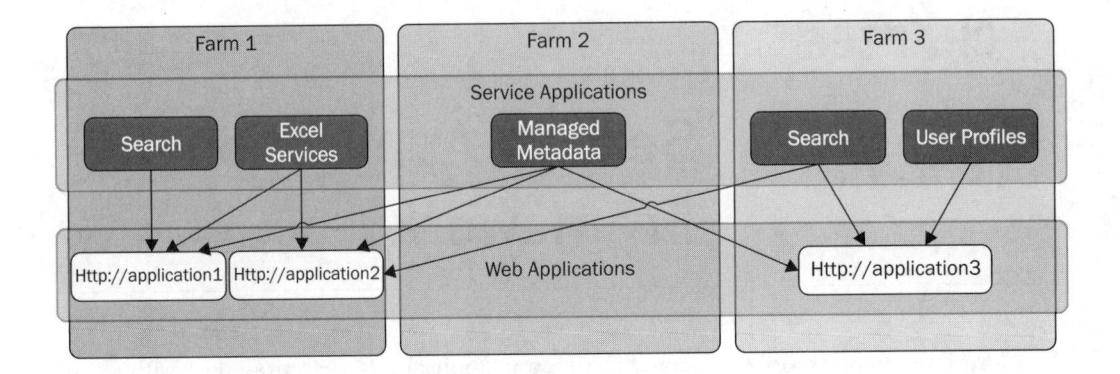

```
┌─────────────────┬─────────────────────────┬─────────────────┐
│     Farm 1      │         Farm 2          │     Farm 3      │
│                 │   Service Applications  │                 │
│  ┌──────┐ ┌─────┴──┐  ┌─────────┐         │ ┌──────┐ ┌────────────┐ │
│  │Search│ │ Excel  │  │ Managed │         │ │Search│ │User Profiles│ │
│  │      │ │Services│  │Metadata │         │ │      │ │            │ │
│  └──────┘ └────────┘  └─────────┘         │ └──────┘ └────────────┘ │
│                                           │                         │
│ ┌──────────────┐┌──────────────┐          │        ┌──────────────┐ │
│ │Http://app…1  ││Http://app…2  │ Web Apps │        │Http://app…3  │ │
│ └──────────────┘└──────────────┘          │        └──────────────┘ │
└─────────────────┴─────────────────────────┴─────────────────┘
```

Clearly, there's more to SharePoint than just hosting web sites; much of the additional functionality, such as the ability to service search queries or functionality for sending and receiving e-mail, is provided by a range of discrete platform services. Each of these services is managed at the farm level and is represented within the SharePoint object model as an object derived from SPService.

In a simple environment with one server, it may be sufficient to have a single object that allows configuration and management of a single service; however, the SharePoint platform has been designed to be scalable across many servers, with each server potentially running one or more instances of a service. As a result, the SharePoint Object Model makes use of two additional objects to manage services: The SPServiceInstance object represents a single instance of a service that is installed on a particular server (represented in the object model by the SPServer object). The SPServiceApplication object represents a single farm-level instance of a particular service.

For example, within a farm it is possible to run more than one instance of the Managed Metadata Service. Each instance will have its own configuration, and this configuration, defined at farm level, is represented by an SPServiceApplication-derived object. Although we've got an object to configure and manage the service at the form level, we need another object so that we can control the service on individual servers within the farm, and that's where the SPServiceInstance-derived object comes in. The SPServiceApplication object is a new addition in SharePoint 2010, and as you'll see later, it provides a much greater degree of flexibility than was available in earlier versions.

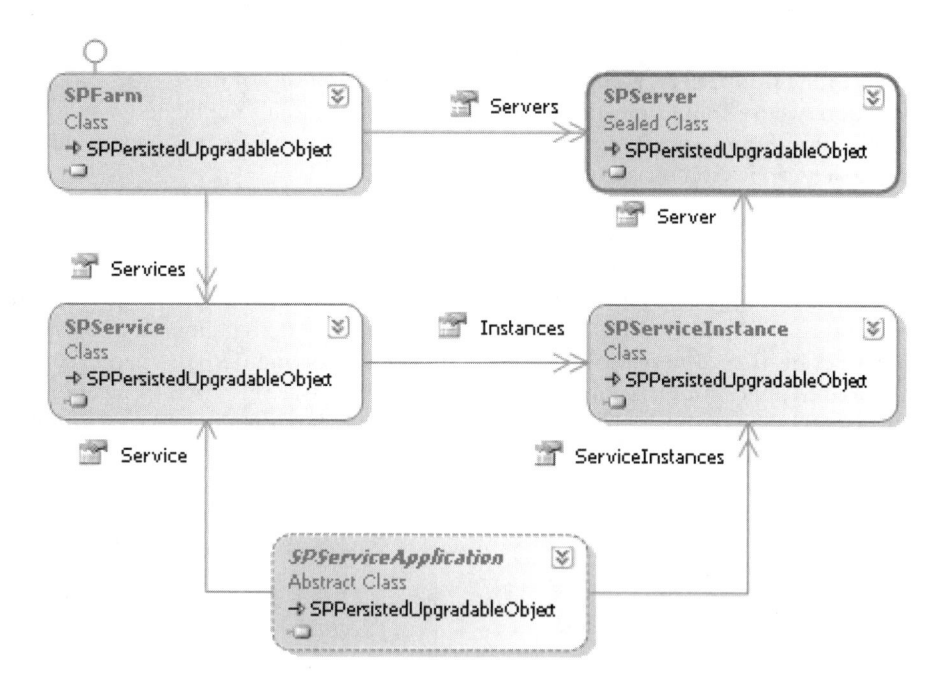

```
                            ┌──────────────┐
                            │   SPFarm     │──── Servers ────┐
                            │   Class      │                 ▼
                            │ SPPersistedUpgradableObject │  ┌──────────────┐
                            └──────┬───────┘                 │   SPServer   │
                                   │                         │ Sealed Class │
                                   │ Services                │ SPPersistedUpgradableObject │
                                   ▼                         └──────┬───────┘
                            ┌──────────────┐                        │ Server
                            │  SPService   │──── Instances ───┐     │
                            │   Class      │                  ▼     │
                            │ SPPersistedUpgradableObject │   ┌──────────────┐
                            └──────┬───────┘                  │SPServiceInstance│
                                   │ Service                  │   Class      │
                                   │                          │ SPPersistedUpgradableObject │
                                   │                          └──────┬───────┘
                                   │                                 │ ServiceInstances
                                   │   ┌──────────────────────┐      │
                                   └───│  SPServiceApplication │─────┘
                                       │   Abstract Class     │
                                       │ SPPersistedUpgradableObject │
                                       └──────────────────────┘
```

The services architecture within SharePoint is very clever and provides a lot of functionality out of the box. The SPServiceApplication object (I'll use this term to also include any object that's derived from SPServiceApplication), acts as an endpoint for potentially many server-level instances of a service. As a result, by making use of the SPServiceApplication object for all calls into the service, you can easily implement advanced functionality such as load balancing and fault tolerance. Furthermore, since the configuration of the service is also done at the SPServiceApplication level, providing backup and restore functionality is also relatively straightforward.

## Client-side Implementation

You've seen how services are configured and managed on the server side within a SharePoint farm. The primary focus of the service object model is on the configuration and management of services as opposed to the actual implementation. When it comes to physically doing whatever the service needs to do many implementations are possible, each appropriate in different situations. For example, the SharePoint Server Search Service makes use of a Windows Service that can be installed on various servers throughout the farm, whereas the

Secure Store Service uses a central database to store its data and instead handles requests in real time on the server where they are received. In both of these cases, and for all situations where communication is made with a service that's managed using the Service Application Framework, communication between client and server occurs via the SPServiceApplication server object.

From a client perspective, because the SPServiceApplication object is well-defined, you can create an appropriate matching proxy object. This is represented in the object model by the SPServiceApplicationProxy object, as shown next. This client/server proxy pattern makes it easy to develop code that uses a particular service, since a strongly typed proxy object is readily available that exposes the appropriate functionality. We don't need to worry about where the service is running, how it's implemented, or even how the SPServiceApplicationProxy object communicates with the SPServiceApplication object; all we need to know is which methods to call and which parameters to pass in. I'm sure you'll agree that this is pretty powerful stuff.

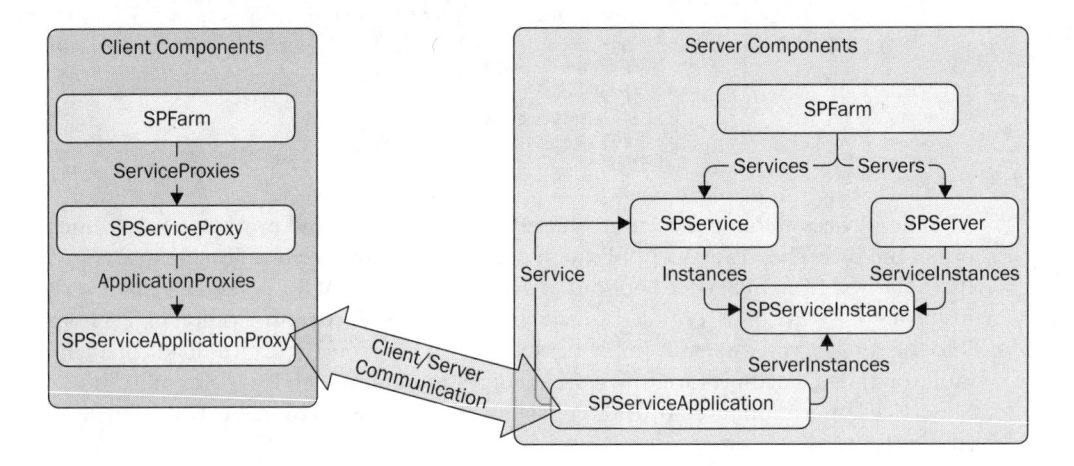

```
Client Components                           Server Components

    SPFarm                                      SPFarm
      |                                        /      \
ServiceProxies                            Services    Servers
      ↓                                      ↓           ↓
  SPServiceProxy                          SPService    SPServer
      |                                      |            |
ApplicationProxies          Service      Instances    ServiceInstances
      ↓                                      ↓            ↓
SPServiceApplicationProxy ←→           SPServiceInstance
         Client/Server                        ↑
         Communication                    ServerInstances
                                   SPServiceApplication
```

So the SPServiceApplicationProxy is our entry point into a service application on the SharePoint platform. This raises the question, How do we pick up a reference to the appropriate proxy object? More than one instance of a service may be running on a farm, so how can we be sure that we have the correct one? The answer is the SPServiceProxy object. As you saw in the discussion of server objects, each service is represented by an SPService object that in turn provides a collection of SPServiceApplication objects that each represent a single instance of a service. The same is also true on the client side: the SPServiceProxy object provides a collection of SPServiceApplicationProxy objects, each representing a proxy for a single instance of a service.

**NOTE** I've done a lot of talking here about client and server components. It's important for you to recognize that on many occasions, both client and server are essentially different aspects of the same server farm. Both SPServiceProxy objects and SPService objects can be referenced via the Service and ServiceProxies properties of the SPFarm object.

## Client/Server Communication

You've seen that the communication mechanism between client and server is abstracted by means of the strongly typed SPServiceApplication and SPServiceApplicationProxy classes. In fact, the SPServiceApplication and SPServiceApplicationProxy classes are *abstract classes*—to use these objects, a concrete implementation must first be created. Out of the box, we can use two default concrete implementations in our custom applications: SPUsageApplicationProxy, which is used to communicate with services such as the Web Analytics Data Processing Service and the SPIisWebServiceApplicationProxy, which is used for all other services. The main difference between these implementations is the underlying communications mechanism used between client and server. The SPIisWebServiceApplicationProxy makes use of the Windows Communication Foundation (WCF) for all communications and therefore offers a high level of built-in flexibility. This is why it's used by almost all of the services available on the SharePoint platform.

> **NOTE** You can create custom implementations of the SPServiceApplicationProxy and SPServiceApplication. This may be appropriate when communication is being made to a legacy system. In-depth discussion of this is outside the scope of this chapter, but you can find information at http://msdn.microsoft.com.

## Configuring Service Applications

Now that you understand the architecture behind the service application framework, let's take a look at how services are configured using the SharePoint user interface. We'll start by configuring a service application.

1. Open SharePoint Central Administration and select Manage Service Applications from the Application Management group, as shown next:

    On the Service Applications page, notice that in the list of services, most services have an entry for the service application followed by a second entry for the service application proxy. For example, at the top of the list you may see a service of type Access Service Web Service Application, followed by a proxy of type Access Service Web Service Application Proxy. These two entries are represented in the object model by an SPServiceApplication object and a SPServiceApplicationProxy object, respectively.

2. From the Service Applications tab in the ribbon, select New | Managed Metadata Service. You'll see a number of services listed in the New menu. Each service is represented in the object model by an object of type SPService. By selecting a particular SPService from the list, we're creating a new SPServiceApplication instance within the farm.

3. Type the name of the new Managed Metadata Service: **Demo Managed Metadata Service**. Then type the database name as **DemoManagedMetadata**.

4. Create a new application pool named **DemoAppPool** and register a new managed account if required.

A new service of type Managed Metadata Service will be added to the list as well as a proxy of type Managed Metadata Service Connection. Although the farm contains only one service of type Managed Metadata Service, you can create many instances, each with a different configuration, or, in the case of the Managed Metadata Service, a different datastore.

## Connecting to Remote Applications

As you've seen, both client and server elements of a service are commonly configured within a single farm. However, you can connect to services hosted on another farm and also to make services hosted on a farm available for consumption by other farms. Here's how to connect to a remote application:

1. From the list of services, select the Demo Metadata Service that we created earlier. Don't click the hyperlink; instead, click the row to select the item.

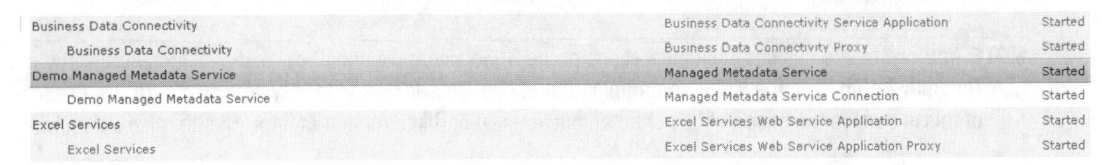

| Business Data Connectivity | Business Data Connectivity Service Application | Started |
| Business Data Connectivity | Business Data Connectivity Proxy | Started |
| Demo Managed Metadata Service | Managed Metadata Service | Started |
| Demo Managed Metadata Service | Managed Metadata Service Connection | Started |
| Excel Services | Excel Services Web Service Application | Started |
| Excel Services | Excel Services Web Service Application Proxy | Started |

2. From the Service Applications tab of the ribbon, click the Publish button, as shown:

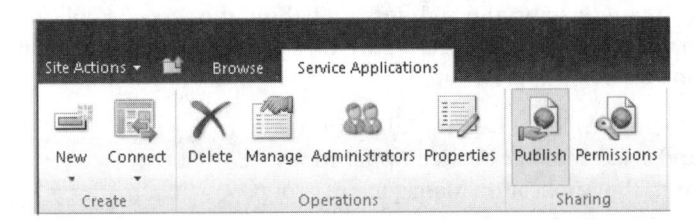

3. By completing the Publish Service Application form, we can make the Demo Metadata Service available to other trusted farms. The Published URL that's automatically generated is required to make a connection. If you have another farm available, complete the form and click OK; otherwise, click Cancel to return the Manage Service Applications page.

4. To connect to a Managed Metadata service that's hosted on another farm, choose Connect | Managed Metadata Service Connection from the Service Applications tab of the ribbon. In the Connect To A Remote Service Application dialog, enter the Published URL that was automatically generated when publishing the service to which you want to connect, if appropriate. The items that are listed when the Connect button is clicked are defined in the object model as objects of type SPServiceProxy.

## Topology Service

One of the things you may have noticed in the preceding example is that when connecting to or publishing a remote service, the Published URL references a service named Topology.svc. Although I won't cover the service in depth, I will briefly explain what it does and why.

Although the WCF service name is Topology.svc, within the SharePoint user interface, the service is referred to as the Application Discovery and Load Balancer Service Application and can be found in the list of service applications. For brevity, I'll continue to refer to it as the "topology service."

When a service application is published on a farm, the topology service maintains a list of the service applications that have been published and are available for consumption; in this respect, it provides application discovery functionality. As well as maintaining a list of the SPServiceApplications that are available, the service also maintains a list of the individual SPServiceInstances that are available for each SPServiceApplication. Using this information, the service is able to load balance incoming requests between available servers in the farm. For load balancing to work effectively, information on which servers are available must be passed to the client so that a connection can be made to the next available service instance. On the consuming farm side, the topology service periodically receives this information from the publishing farm and makes use of it when creating SPServiceApplicationProxy objects for the published services.

# Demonstration Scenario

Understanding the Service Application Framework, in terms of its function and architecture, is relatively straightforward. However, taking this information and making use of it in a real world situation is a bit more involved. Conceptually, the purpose of the Service Application Framework is to make scalable, enterprise-ready services easy to maintain and consume. Although the architecture lays out how this will be done, at a nuts-and-bolts level, implementing this in a practical way introduces a fair amount of complexity.

So that you can properly understand the workings of the framework and make use of it when creating your own service applications, let's create a basic translation service. The service will be configured using the Manage Service Applications section of Central Administration and will be capable of being used by custom web parts within a site.

## Prerequisite: Generating a New AppId

Our scenario makes use of the Microsoft Translation service that's accessed via Bing.com. To make use of the Bing.com web service API, we first need to generate a unique AppId that can be used within our code. To generate a new AppId, follow the process detailed at www.bing.com/developer.

## Creating a New SharePoint Project

So that we can easily deploy our custom service to our SharePoint farm, we'll make use of the deployment capabilities of Visual Studio 2010.

1. In Visual Studio, choose File | New | Project. Select Empty SharePoint Project, and then type **TranslatorDemo** as the project name, as shown:

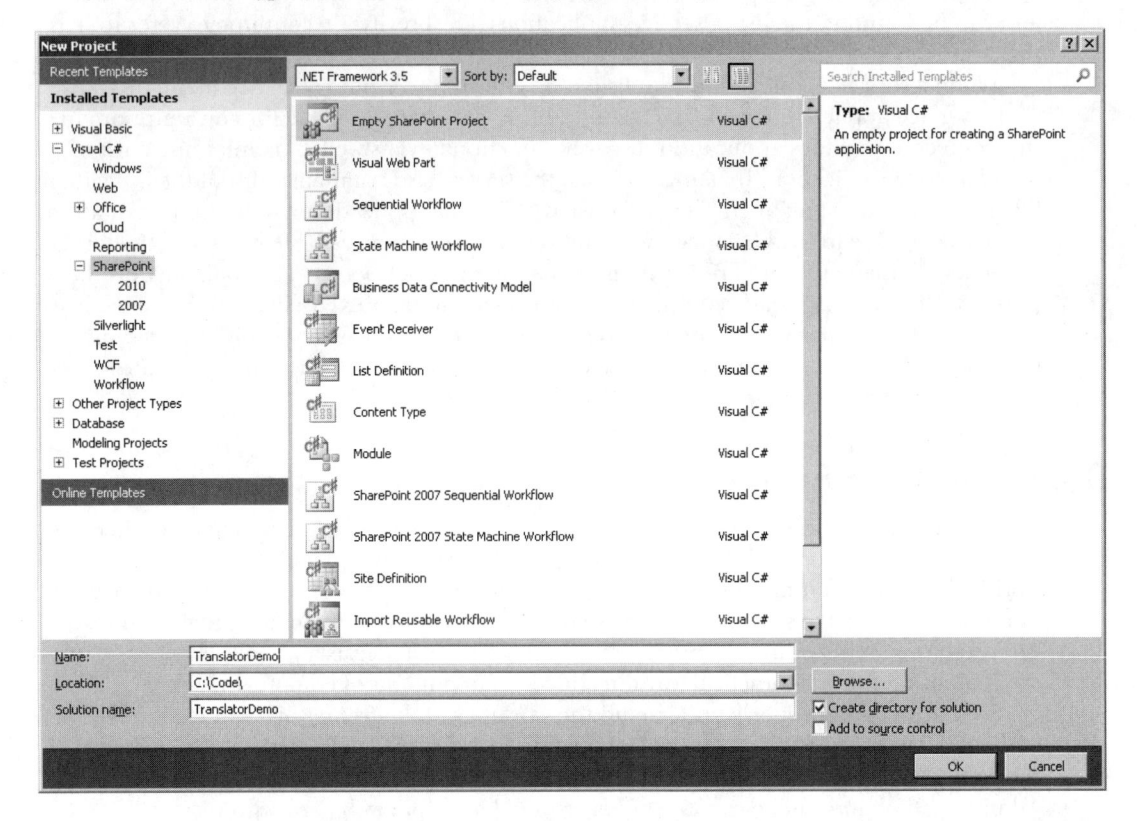

2. In the SharePoint Customization Wizard dialog, enter the URL of the Central Administration site as the local site to be used for debugging.
3. Select the Deploy As Farm Solution option, and then click Finish to complete the wizard.

## Adding Server-side Configuration Classes

With our empty project up and running, our next step is to add server-side configuration classes for our custom service. Earlier I discussed these classes as being derived from SPService, SPServiceInstance, and SPServiceApplication. Since our service application will be deployed as a WCF service, we'll make use of the inherited classes: SPIisWebService, SPIisWebServiceInstance, and SPIisWebServiceApplication. These classes provide WCF specific functionality, as you'll see later.

Chapter 9  Service Application Framework  **177**

1. Add a new folder named Server to the project. Within the Server folder, create a new class named TranslationService.cs. Add the following code:

```
[System.Runtime.InteropServices.Guid("C9DD4A67-47FB-11D2-83E7-00C04F9902C1")]
public sealed class TranslationService : SPIisWebService
{
    private static TranslationService _local = null;

    public TranslationService()
    { }

    public TranslationService(SPFarm farm) : base(farm)
    {
      this.Name = "TranslationService";
    }

    public static TranslationService Local
    {
      get
      {
        if (TranslationService._local == null)
        {
           TranslationService._local = SPFarm.Local.Services.GetValue➔
<TranslationService>("TranslationService");
        }

        return TranslationService._local;
      }
    }
        public override void Delete()
        {
        base.Delete();
        _local = null;
        }
    }
}
```

A few things are worth mentioning in this code snippet. First, notice the use of the Guid attribute and the default public constructor. Many of the classes that are used for storing and managing configuration data within the SharePoint platform are derived from SPPersistedObject. SPPersistedObject makes use of serialization to persist the object to the SharePoint configuration database and therefore requires a unique Guid for each type and a default constructor. Also notice that the TranslationService implements a singleton pattern. Each service is defined only once per farm, so using a singleton makes sense because the object will be retrieved from the farm's services collection.

2. Within the Server folder, add a new class named TranslationServiceApplication.cs. Add the following code:

```
[System.Runtime.InteropServices.Guid("0B42E5CF-B5BC-438C-997F-996E61CE572B")]
  class TranslationServiceApplication : SPIisWebServiceApplication
  {

    public TranslationServiceApplication()
```

```csharp
    {
    }

    internal TranslationServiceApplication(string name,
TranslationService service, SPIisWebServiceApplicationPool applicationPool)
        : base(name, service, applicationPool)
    {
    }

    protected override string InstallPath
    {
      get
      {
        return Path.GetFullPath(SPUtility.GetGenericSetupPath(@"WebServices\
TranslatorDemo"));
      }
    }

    protected override string VirtualPath
    {
      get
      {
        return "TranslatorService.svc";
      }
    }

    public override string TypeName
    {
      get
      {
        return "Translation Service Application";
      }
    }
}
```

In this code snippet, notice the overridden InstallPath and VirtualPath properties. As mentioned, our service will make use of WCF as a communications protocol. These properties must be overridden to provision correctly the WCF service that supports our custom service.

3. Within the Server folder, add a new class named TranslationServiceInstance.cs. Add the following code:

```csharp
[System.Runtime.InteropServices.Guid("0B42E5CF-B5BC-438C-997F-996E61CE572D")]
  class TranslationServiceInstance : SPIisWebServiceInstance
  {
    public TranslationServiceInstance()
    {
    }

    internal TranslationServiceInstance(SPServer server,
        TranslationService service)         : base(server, service)
    {
    }

    internal TranslationServiceInstance(string name,
```

```
                      SPServer server, TranslationService service)
      : base(server, service)
    {
    }

    public override string TypeName
    {
      get { return "Demo Translation Service"; }
    }
  }
```

We now have the basics of our server-side configuration object model. TranslationService represents our service at the farm level, TranslationServiceApplication represents a configured instance of our service at the farm level, and TranslationServiceInstance represents an instance of our service running on a particular server within the farm.

## Adding Client-side Configuration Classes

Now that we have the basis of our server-side configuration object model, our next logical step is to add in our client objects.

> **NOTE** For the purposes of this demonstration, we'll add both client and server within the same SharePoint project. If the server and client were designed to run on separate farms, a more appropriate deployment strategy might be to create two separate projects, allowing client and server binaries to be installed independently.

1. Add a new folder named Client to the project. Within the Client folder, create a new class named TranslationServiceApplicationProxy.cs. Add the following code:

```
[System.Runtime.InteropServices.Guid("0B42E5CF-B5BC-438C-997F-996E61CE572C")]
  class TranslationServiceApplicationProxy : SPIisWebServiceApplicationProxy
  {
    public TranslationServiceApplicationProxy()
    {
    }

    public TranslationServiceApplicationProxy(string name,
            SPIisWebServiceProxy serviceProxy, Uri serviceEndpointUri)
      : base(name, serviceProxy, serviceEndpointUri)
    {
    }

    internal TranslationServiceApplicationProxy(string name,
                 SPIisWebServiceProxy serviceProxy,
                 TranslationServiceApplication serviceApplication)
      : base(name, serviceProxy, serviceApplication.Uri)
    {
    }

    public override string TypeName
    {
      get
      {
```

```
      return "Translation Service Application Proxy";
    }
  }
}
```

2. Add another class to the Client folder named TranslationServiceProxy.cs. Add the following code:

```
[System.Runtime.InteropServices.Guid("0B42E5CF-B5BC-438C-997F-996E61CE572E")]
class TranslationServiceProxy : SPIisWebServiceProxy,
                                IServiceProxyAdministration
{
  private static TranslationServiceProxy _local;

  public TranslationServiceProxy()
  {
  }

  internal TranslationServiceProxy(SPFarm farm)
    : base(farm)
  {
    this.Name = "TranslationServiceProxy";
  }

  public static TranslationServiceProxy Local
  {
    get
    {
      if (TranslationServiceProxy._local == null)
      {
        TranslationServiceProxy._local =
    SPFarm.Local.ServiceProxies.GetValue<TranslationServiceProxy>(
                               "TranslationServiceProxy");
      }
      return TranslationServiceProxy._local;
    }
  }

  public override void Delete()
  {
    base.Delete();
    _local = null;
  }
  public SPServiceApplicationProxy CreateProxy(Type serviceApplication →
ProxyType, string name, Uri serviceApplicationUri, SPServiceProvisioningContext →
provisioningContext)
  {
      return new TranslationServiceApplicationProxy(name, this, service →
ApplicationUri);
  }

    public SPPersistedTypeDescription GetProxyTypeDescription(Type →
serviceApplicationProxyType)
    {
        return new SPPersistedTypeDescription(
```

```
            "Translation Web Service Proxy",
            "Connects to the Translation Web Service.");
    }

    public Type[] GetProxyTypes()
    {
      return new Type[] { typeof(TranslationServiceApplicationProxy) };
    }
}
```

## Adding Windows Communication Foundation Components

With our client- and server-side components up and running, we can move on to look at how to deploy a WCF endpoint that can be used to communicate between client and server.

1. Generally speaking, WCF endpoints should be installed within the %SPRoot%\WebServices folder. (See Chapter 2 for details on configuring the %SPRoot% variable.) So that we can have our Visual Studio project automatically deploy to the WebServices folder, we first need to add a SharePoint Mapped folder. Choose Project | Add SharePoint Mapped Folder. Then select WebServices from the dialog.

2. In the WebServices mapped folder that's been added to the Visual Studio project, create a new folder named TranslatorDemo. This new folder will ensure that our deployed files don't conflict with files already installed on the server.

3. Right-click the new TranslatorDemo folder and choose Add | New Item. Select WCF Service from the Visual C# category, as shown. Name the new service TranslatorService.cs.

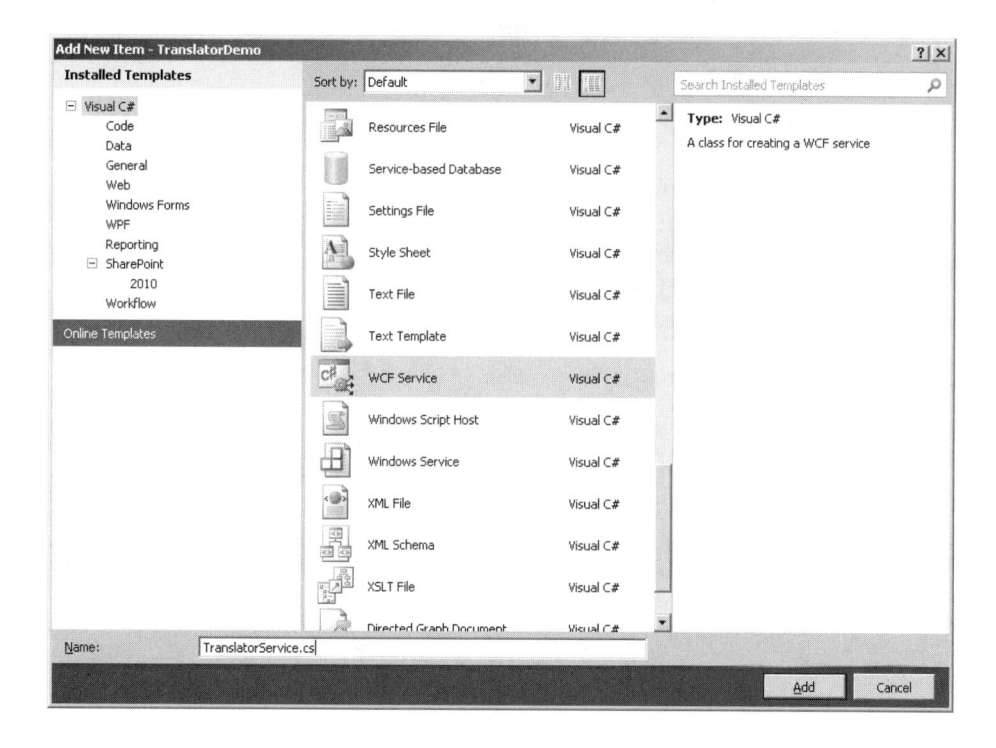

4. Delete the app.config file that's automatically added to the project, and then create a new web.config file in the TranslatorDemo folder. Add the following XML to the web.config file:

```xml
<?xml version="1.0" encoding="utf-8" ?>
<configuration>
  <system.serviceModel>
    <services>
      <service
        name="TranslatorDemo.WebServices.TranslatorDemo.TranslatorService">
        <endpoint
            address=""
            binding="basicHttpBinding"
            bindingConfiguration="TranslatorServiceHttpBinding"
contract="TranslatorDemo.WebServices.TranslatorDemo.ITranslatorService" />
      </service>
    </services>
    <bindings>
      <basicHttpBinding>
        <binding
            name="TranslatorServiceHttpBinding">
        </binding>
      </basicHttpBinding>
    </bindings>
  </system.serviceModel>
  <system.webServer>
    <security>
      <authentication>
        <anonymousAuthentication enabled="true" />
        <windowsAuthentication enabled="true" />
      </authentication>
    </security>
  </system.webServer>
</configuration>
```

At the time of writing, Visual Studio RC doesn't automatically create a .svc file. This may be resolved in the final version of the product. If not, you'll need to create a text file named TranslatorService.svc manually and add the following code:

```
<%@ Assembly Name="$SharePoint.Project.AssemblyFullName$"%>
<% @ServiceHost
Service="TranslatorDemo.WebServices.TranslatorDemo.TranslatorService"
Factory="TranslatorDemo.ApplicationHostFactory" %>
```

5. We're using token replacement to insert the details of our assembly automatically into the WCF service file when the project is built. At the time of writing, token replacement in SharePoint projects doesn't replace tokens in files with an .svc extension. To remedy this, we can manually modify the project file. Open the project file TranslatorDemo.cspoj using Notepad. Before the closing **Project** tag at the end of the file, add the following XML element:

```xml
<PropertyGroup>
<TokenReplacementFileExtensions>$(TokenReplacementFileExtensions);svc; →
</TokenReplacementFileExtensions>
</PropertyGroup>
```

6. From our .svc file, we can see that our WCF service makes use of a ServiceHostFactory class. In the WebServices folder, add a new class named ApplicationHostFactory.cs. Add the following code:

```
namespace TranslatorDemo
{
  internal sealed class ApplicationHostFactory : ServiceHostFactory
  {
    public override ServiceHostBase CreateServiceHost(string →
constructorString, Uri[] baseAddresses)
    {
      return new ApplicationHost(baseAddresses);
    }
  }
}
```

7. As well as a host factory, we also need to add a host class. Create a new class file named ApplicationHost.cs in the TranslatorDemo folder. Add the following code:

```
namespace TranslatorDemo.WebServices.TranslatorDemo
{
  class ApplicationHost:ServiceHost
  {
      internal ApplicationHost(params Uri[] baseAddressess)
          : base(typeof(TranslatorService), baseAddressess)
      {
      }
  }
}
```

## Implementing Translation Functionality

Now that we have set up most of the plumbing for our service, we can do a bit of work to implement our translation functionality. For the purposes of this demonstration, our service will simply accept an input string in English and will make use of Microsoft Translator to convert the text to French before returning the converted string to the caller.

1. We need to modify the contract for our WCF server to accept the correct parameters. In the ITranslatorService.cs class, change the source code like so:

```
[ServiceContract]
public interface ITranslatorService
{
  [OperationContract]
  string Translate (string input);
}
```

2. With the contract changed, we can now update the implementation. Update the code in TranslatorService.cs as follows:

```
public class TranslatorService : ITranslatorService
{
  public string Translate (string input)
```

```
        {
            throw new NotImplementedException();
        }
    }
```

3. Before we can add an implementation, we need a service reference to the Microsoft Translator service. Choose Project | Add Service Reference. In the Address box, type **http://api.microsofttranslator.com/V2/Soap.svc**, and then click Go. Type the Namespace **Microsoft.Translator**, and then click OK to create the reference:

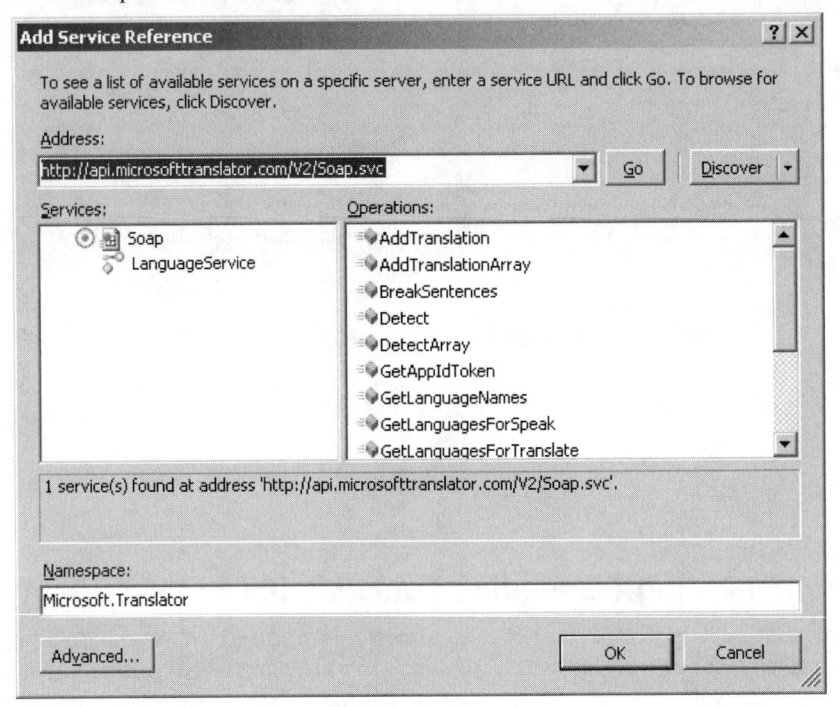

4. With the reference in place, update the implementation as shown next. Note the **apiKey** variable, which should contain a valid Bing API key discussed in the section "Prerequisite: Generating a New AppId."

```
public string Translate (string input)
{
    BasicHttpBinding binding = new BasicHttpBinding();

    EndpointAddress address = new EndpointAddress("http:// →
api.microsofttranslator.com/v2/Soap.svc");
    Microsoft.Translator.LanguageServiceClient client = new →
Microsoft.Translator.LanguageServiceClient(binding, address);

    string apiKey = "Enter Your Bing API Key here";
    string output = string.Empty;
    output=client.Translate(apiKey, input, "en", "fr");
    return output;
    }
}
```

**NOTE** Since we've adopted the namespace Microsoft.Translator for our service reference, it may be necessary to add **using Microsoft.Translator** to the code file. Visual Studio can do this automatically if you press SHIFT-ALT-F10 when the cursor is on a reference to the Microsoft.Translator object.

## Installing Service Application Components

Service Application components can be installed in several different ways. The simplest method is to create a feature that will programmatically install the server and client components for the application when activated.

**NOTE** For more information on features, see Chapter 19.

1. In the Solution Explorer pane, right-click the Features node and select Add Feature. Set the scope of the feature to Farm and type the title **Demo Translation Service**, as shown here:

2. So that we can add custom code that will execute when the feature is activated, right-click the Feature1 node and select Add Event Receiver. Uncomment the FeatureActivated override and add the following code:

```
public override void FeatureActivated(SPFeatureReceiverProperties properties)
    {
       TranslationService svc = TranslationService.Local;

       if (svc == null)
       {
         svc = new TranslationService(SPFarm.Local);
         svc.Update();
         svc.Provision();
       }

       TranslationServiceProxy proxy = TranslationServiceProxy.Local;

       if (proxy == null)
       {
         proxy = new TranslationServiceProxy(SPFarm.Local);
         proxy.Update(true);
         proxy.Provision();
       }
    }
```

3. Although it's not strictly necessary, we'll also add some code to clean up our service application when the feature is deactivated. When developing services, having clean-up code is a good idea because it removes orphaned configuration information from the SharePoint configuration database that would be difficult to clean up otherwise. Uncomment the FeatureDeactivating override and add the following code:

```
public override void FeatureDeactivating(SPFeatureReceiverProperties properties)
    {
       TranslationService svc = TranslationService.Local;

       if (svc != null)
       {
         svc.Unprovision();

         foreach (var instance in svc.Instances)
         {
           instance.Unprovision();
           instance.Delete();
         }

         foreach (var application in svc.Applications)
         {
           application.Unprovision();
           application.Delete();
         }
         svc.Delete();
       }
       TranslationServiceProxy proxy = TranslationServiceProxy.Local;
```

```
        if (proxy != null)
        {
          foreach (var appProxy in proxy.ApplicationProxies)
          {
            appProxy.Unprovision();
            appProxy.Delete();
          }
          proxy.Delete();
        }
      }
```

4. Our project is now in a state where it can be built and deployed to SharePoint. To create and deploy the package, choose Build | Deploy TranslatorDemo. If all is well, the package will be built and deployed to the farm. You can confirm that the package has deployed successfully by opening Central Administration and then selecting Manage Farm Features from the System Settings section. Our Demo Translation Service feature will appear in the list and should be activated.

## Provisioning Service Application Instances

You've seen how to install both client and server components for our service. Before we can actually use the service, however, we need to provision a new instance of our service. As discussed earlier in the chapter, this instance will be represented by an object of type SPServiceApplication—in our case, this will be the server-side TranslationServiceApplication object.

To configure our TranslationServiceApplication, we need details of the application pool under which the service will run. In this section, we'll work through the steps necessary to create a user interface that will allow us to capture this information and make use of it to provision the application.

As you saw earlier, service applications are usually provisioned by clicking the New button on the Manage Service Applications page. Integration with the functionality available on the Manage Service Applications page is done by implementing the IServiceAdministration interface on the service class.

1. Open the TranslationService.cs file and amend the class definition to implement the IServiceAdministration interface, as this code snippet shows:

```
[System.Runtime.InteropServices.Guid("C9DD4A67-47FB-11D2-83E7-00C04F9902C1")]
    public sealed class TranslationService : SPIisWebService,
                                              IServiceAdministration
```

2. Add the following additional code to the TranslationService.cs file to implement the methods required by the IServiceAdminstration interface:

```
#region IServiceAdministration Implementation

public SPServiceApplication CreateApplication(string name,
             Type serviceApplicationType,
             SPServiceProvisioningContext provisioningContext)
{
```

```
        throw new NotImplementedException();
    }

    public SPServiceApplicationProxy CreateProxy(string name,
                 SPServiceApplication serviceApplication,
                 SPServiceProvisioningContext provisioningContext)
    {
        return new TranslationServiceApplicationProxy(name,
                TranslationServiceProxy.Local,
                (TranslationServiceApplication)serviceApplication);
    }

    public SPPersistedTypeDescription GetApplicationTypeDescription(
                                     Type serviceApplicationType)
    {
        return new SPPersistedTypeDescription(
          "Translation Service Application",
          "Demonstration Translation Service application.");
    }

    public Type[] GetApplicationTypes()
    {
        return new Type[] { typeof(TranslationServiceApplication) };
    }

    #endregion
```

## Adding a Create Application Dialog

Although we've added the code required to provision a service application, we still need to capture parameters required for the configuration of the application. So that we can present a user interface for this, we can override the GetCreateApplicationLink method of the base SPService class, allowing us to return a custom URL to which users will be directed when creating an instance of our service.

    1. Add the following method to the TranslationService.cs class:

```
public override SPAdministrationLink GetCreateApplicationLink →
(Type serviceApplicationType)
    {
    return new SPAdministrationLink("/_admin/TranslatorDemo/ →
CreateService.aspx");
    }
```

    2. So that we can create a page that will be automatically deployed to the %SPRoot%/Template/Admin folder, we need to add another SharePoint-mapped folder to our project. Choose Project | Add SharePoint Mapped Folder, and then select Template/Admin from the dialog.

    3. In the Admin folder, add a new folder named TranslatorDemo.

    4. In the TranslatorDemo folder, add a new Application Page named CreateService.aspx, as shown:

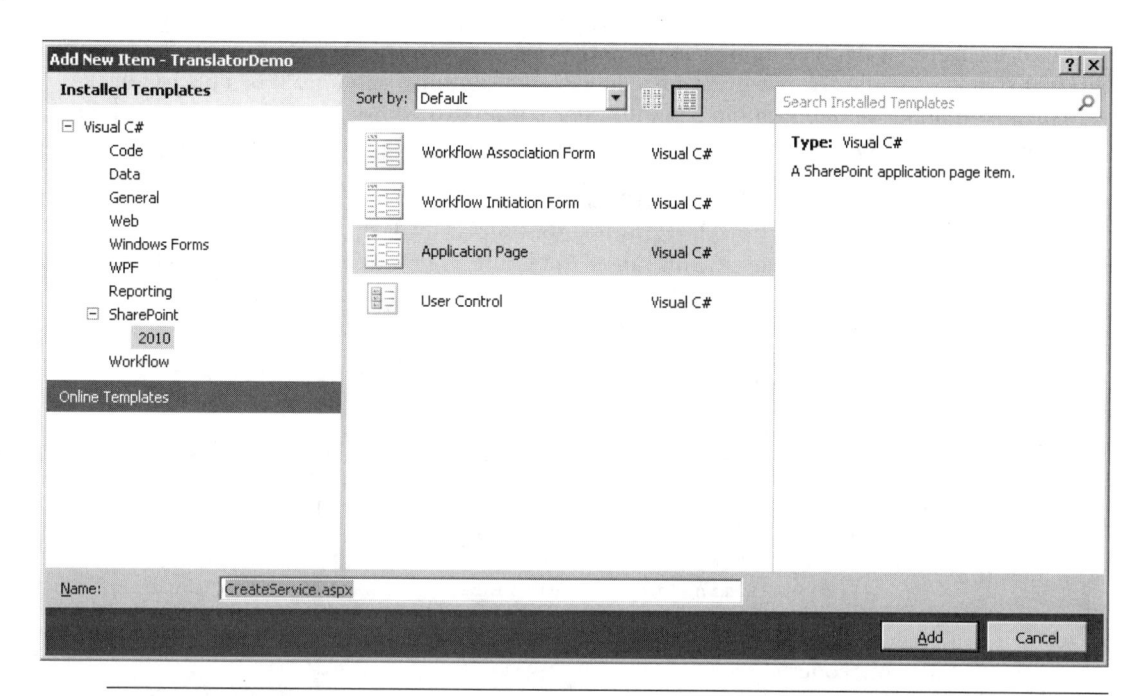

**CAUTION** Application Pages are automatically added to the Layouts folder. After the Admin/TranslatorDemo folder has been created, drag the page into the folder.

Because we want our CreateService page to appear as a dialog rather than a standard page, we need to make a few changes to the generated HTML, since dialog pages use a different master page and therefore have different placeholders.

5. Edit the **Page** tag by deleting the DynamicMasterPageFile attribute and replacing it with this:

```
MasterPageFile="~/_layouts/dialog.master"
```

6. Delete the auto-generated content tags and replace them with this:

```
<asp:Content ID="Content1" ContentPlaceHolderID="PlaceHolderDialogHeaderPageTitle"
    runat="server">
    <asp:Literal ID="CreateAppTitle"
        Text="Translation Service Application" runat="server" />
</asp:Content>
<asp:Content ID="Content2"
        ContentPlaceHolderID="PlaceHolderDialogDescription"
        runat="server">
    <asp:Literal ID="CreateAppDesc"
            Text="Create a new Translation service application"
            runat="server" />
</asp:Content>
<asp:Content ID="Content3" ContentPlaceHolderID="PlaceHolderDialogBodyMainSection"
    runat="server">
    Hello World!
    <SharePoint:FormDigest ID="FormDigest1" runat="server" />
</asp:Content>
```

We can now deploy our project to see the effects of our changes. If we navigate to the Manage Service Applications page in Central Administration, we'll be able to select Translation Service Application from the New button drop-down in the Service Applications tab. Our new CreateService page will be shown in a dialog ready to receive user input.

## Capturing Application Pool Details

The SharePoint platform provides a number of user controls that can be used for capturing user input. If you use these controls rather than building input forms from scratch, it's much easier to maintain a uniform user experience throughout the application. For our CreateService page, we'll use three such user controls.

1. Directly following the **Page** element in the CreateService.aspx page, add the following tags:

```
<%@ Register TagPrefix="wssuc" TagName="InputFormSection"
        Src="/_controltemplates/InputFormSection.ascx" %>
<%@ Register TagPrefix="wssuc" TagName="InputFormControl"
        Src="/_controltemplates/InputFormControl.ascx" %>
<%@ Register TagPrefix="wssuc" TagName="IisWebServiceApplicationPoolSection"
        Src="~/_admin/IisWebServiceApplicationPoolSection.ascx" %>
```

2. Replace the *Hello World* text that we added to the Content3 content control with the following code:

```
<table class=propertysheet border="0" width="100%"
        cellspacing="0" cellpadding="0" id="diidProjectPageOverview">
    <wssuc:InputFormSection Title="Name"
 Description="Specify the name for this service application instance."
        runat="server">
        <template_inputformcontrols>
            <wssuc:InputFormControl LabelText=""
LabelAssociatedControlID="m_asAppName" runat="server">
                <Template_control>
                    <SharePoint:InputFormTextBox
title="Name" class="ms-input" ID="m_asAppName" Columns="35"
Runat="server" MaxLength=256 />
                    <SharePoint: →
InputFormRequiredFieldValidator ID="m_asAppNameValidator"
                        ControlToValidate="m_asAppName"
                        ErrorMessage="Required field"
                        width='300px'
                        Runat="server"/>
    <SharePoint:InputFormCustomValidator ID="m_uniqueNameValidator"
        ControlToValidate="m_asAppName"
                        OnServerValidate="ValidateUniqueName"
                        runat="server" />
                </Template_control>
            </wssuc:InputFormControl>
        </template_inputformcontrols>
    </wssuc:InputFormSection>
    <wssuc:IisWebServiceApplicationPoolSection →
id="m_applicationPoolSection" runat="server" />
```

```
        <wssuc:InputFormSection Title="Set as Default" →
Description="" runat="server">
          <template_inputformcontrols>
            <wssuc:InputFormControl LabelText=""
              LabelAssociatedControlID="m_default"
             runat="server">
                        <Template_control>
                          <asp:CheckBox ID="m_default" Runat="server"
Text="Set this instance as the default Translation service application."
                          Title="Set as Default" checked="true" />
                        </Template_control>
            </wssuc:InputFormControl>
          </template_inputformcontrols>
        </wssuc:InputFormSection>
    </table>
```

3. With our controls in place, we can move on to work on the code-behind. In the CreateService.aspx.cs file, add the following code:

```
public partial class CreateService : LayoutsPageBase
{
  protected void CancelButtonClick(object sender, EventArgs e)
  {
    this.SendResponseForPopUI();
  }

  protected void OkButton_Click(object sender, EventArgs e)
  {
    if (this.Page.IsValid)
    {
      this.CreateNewServiceApp();
      this.SendResponseForPopUI();
    }
  }

  protected override void OnInit(EventArgs e)
  {
    base.OnInit(e);
    ((DialogMaster)this.Page.Master).OkButton.Click +=
                new EventHandler(this.OkButton_Click);
  }

  private void CreateNewServiceApp()
  {
    using (SPLongOperation operation = new SPLongOperation(this))
    {
      operation.Begin();
      try
      {
        string name = this.m_asAppName.Text.Trim();

        TranslationServiceApplication serviceApplication =
                    CreateServiceApplication(name);
```

```csharp
            TranslationServiceApplicationProxy proxy = 
            CreateServiceApplicationProxy(name, serviceApplication);

            if (this.m_default.Checked)
            {
                SPServiceApplicationProxyGroup group = 
                            SPServiceApplicationProxyGroup.Default;
                group.Add(proxy);
                group.Update(true);
            }
        }
        catch (Exception ex)
        {
            throw new SPException("Failed to create service application", ex);
        }
    }

    private TranslationServiceApplicationProxy CreateServiceApplicationProxy →
(string name, 
                    TranslationServiceApplication serviceApplication)
    {
        SPServiceApplicationProxy proxy = 
TranslationService.Local.CreateProxy(name, serviceApplication, null);
        proxy.Update(true);
        proxy.Provision();
        return proxy as TranslationServiceApplicationProxy;
    }

    private TranslationServiceApplication CreateServiceApplication(string name)
    {
        SPIisWebServiceApplicationPool appPool = null;

        if (this.m_applicationPoolSection != null)
        {
            appPool = (this.m_applicationPoolSection as →
IisWebServiceApplicationPoolSection).GetOrCreateApplicationPool();
        }
        TranslationServiceApplication serviceApplication = 
new TranslationServiceApplication(name, TranslationService.Local, appPool);
        serviceApplication.Update();
        serviceApplication.AddServiceEndpoint(string.Empty, 
                                SPIisWebServiceBindingType.Http);
        serviceApplication.Update(true);
        serviceApplication.Provision();
        return serviceApplication;
    }

    protected void ValidateUniqueName(object sender, ServerValidateEventArgs e)
    {
        string name = this.m_asAppName.Text.Trim();
        TranslationServiceApplication applicationByName = TranslationService. →
Local.Applications.GetValue<TranslationServiceApplication>(name);
        bool flag = true;
        if (applicationByName != null)
```

```
      {
         flag = false;
      }
      e.IsValid = flag;
      this.m_uniqueNameValidator.ErrorMessage =
            "The specified service application name is already in use.";
   }
}
```

You should notice a few things in this code snippet. First, the use of SPLongOperation in CreateNewServiceApp. When lengthy operations are performed on page post backs, wrapping the code to be executed with a SPLongOperation object provides the user with an "In Progress" display and prevents timeouts from occurring. Using this approach is considered good practice for all configuration changes. The second thing to notice is the provisioning of the WCF service endpoint in the CreateServiceApplication method. The SPIisWebServiceApplication base class defines the AddServiceEndpoint method, which can be used to store endpoint configuration at the application level. When service instances are created, the endpoint configuration is replicated to each instance automatically.

## Provisioning Service Instances

Although we now have enough code to capture the parameters required for our application and provision both the application and an appropriate proxy, we still need to do some work to ensure that service instances are created for our application. We can do this by overriding the Provision and Unprovision methods in our TranslationServiceApplication class.

1. In the TranslationServiceApplication.cs file, add the following code:

```
#region Service Instance Provisioning

   public override void Provision()
   {
     base.Provision();
     TranslationServiceInstance inst = SPServer.Local.ServiceInstances. →
OfType<TranslationServiceInstance>().FirstOrDefault();
     if (inst == null)
     {
       inst = new TranslationServiceInstance(SPServer.Local,
                            this.Service as TranslationService);
       inst.Name = "TranslationServiceInstance";
       inst.Update();
       inst.Provision();
     }
     this.Update();
   }

   public override void Unprovision(bool deleteData)
   {
     base.Status = SPObjectStatus.Unprovisioning;
     this.Update();
     if (this.Service.Applications.Count == 1)
     {
       SPServiceInstance inst = this.ServiceInstances.FirstOrDefault();
       if (inst != null)
       {
```

```
        inst.Unprovision();
        inst.Delete();
      }
  }
  base.Unprovision(deleteData);
  base.Status = SPObjectStatus.Disabled;
  this.Update();
}
#endregion
```

> **NOTE** In this code snippet, we're provisioning a single service instance for all service applications. In effect, the service instance is used to start and stop the service on individual servers. In some circumstances, it may be appropriate to create a separate service instance for each service application allowing more granular control. By overriding the Provision and Unprovision methods, we can implement service instances in a manner that exactly meets our specific requirements.

2. We've now got everything we need to deploy and configure our custom service application. Choose Build | Deploy TranslatorDemo. As before, we can now create a new Translation Service Application from the Manage Service Application page. Our CreateService page contains the required controls to capture a unique name and an appropriate application pool, as shown:

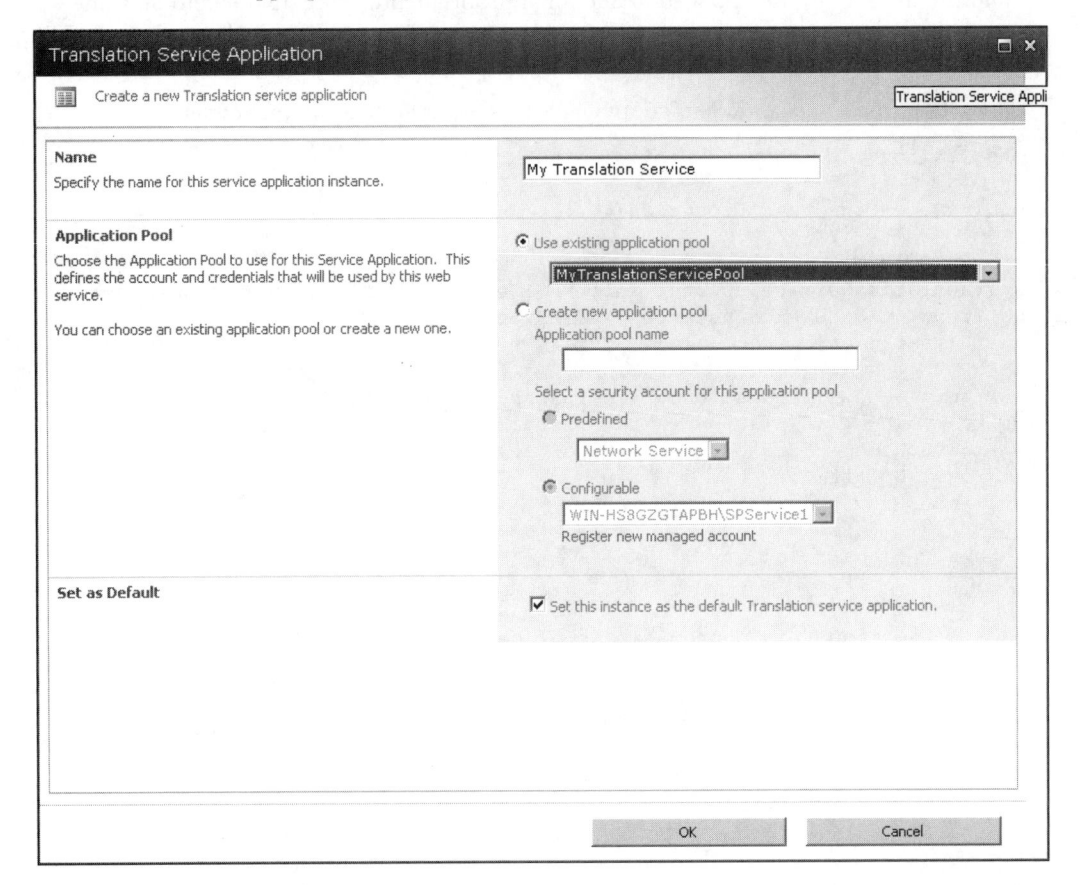

3. Navigate to the Manage Services On Server page in Central Administration, and notice that a new service named Demo Translation Service has been added, as shown next, allowing us to start and stop the service on a particular server.

**Complete all steps below**

⊞ Server: **WIN-HS8GZGTAPBH** ▾

⊞ Start services in the table below:

View: **Configurable** ▾

| Service | Status | Action |
|---|---|---|
| Access Database Service | Started | Stop |
| Application Registry Service | Started | Stop |
| Business Data Connectivity | Started | Stop |
| Central Administration | Started | Stop |
| Demo Translation Service | Started | Stop |
| Document Conversions Launcher Service | Started | Stop |
| Document Conversions Load Balancer Service | Started | Stop |
| Excel Calculation Services | Started | Stop |
| Lotus Notes Connector | Stopped | Start |

To see how the service has actually been implemented, use IIS Manager. Choose Start | Administrative Tools | Internet Information Services (IIS) Manager. Expand the SharePoint Web Services site to see a number of applications, which are the various service endpoints used by the Service Application Framework. Click through the list of endpoints, to find one containing our TranslatorService.svc endpoint, as shown here:

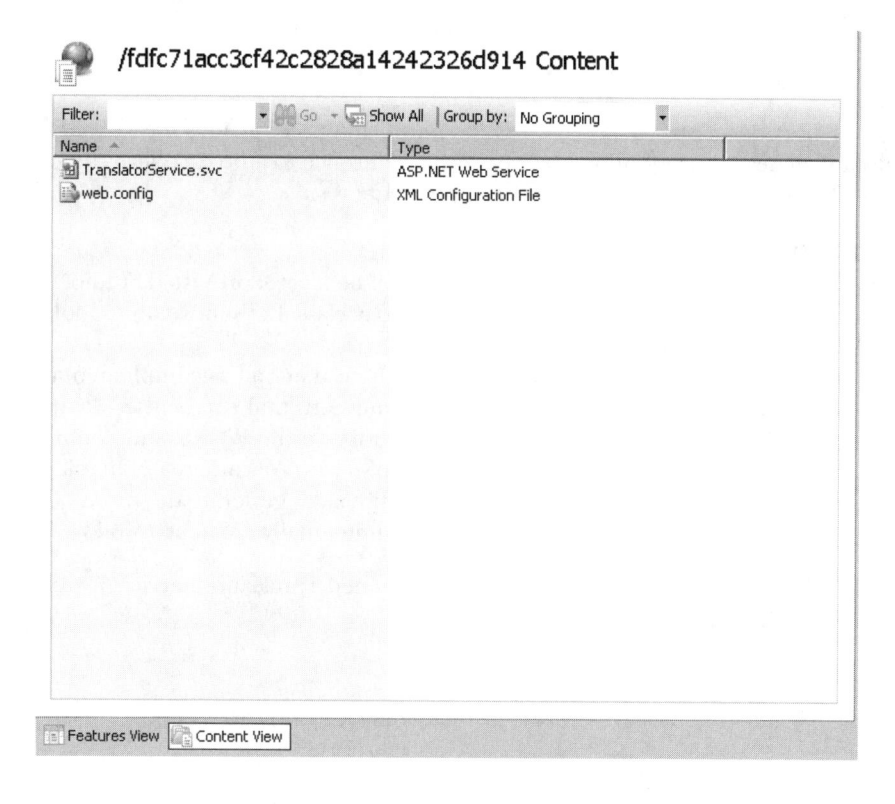

/fdfc71acc3cf42c2828a14242326d914 **Content**

Filter: ▾ Go ▾ Show All | Group by: No Grouping ▾

| Name ▲ | Type |
|---|---|
| TranslatorService.svc | ASP.NET Web Service |
| web.config | XML Configuration File |

Features View | Content View

## Using Service Application in Front-end Components

We've done most of the work to build and deploy a custom service application. To see the fruits of our labor in action, our next step is to create a simple web part that will make use of our service.

1. Add a new Visual Web Part to our SharePoint project by choosing Project | Add New Item. Select Visual Web Part from the dialog and name of the web part **TranslationWebPart**.

2. A user control file named TranslationWebPartUserControl.ascx will be added to the project automatically. Add the following code to the user control file:

   ```
   <asp:TextBox ID="OriginalText" runat="server"></asp:TextBox>
   <asp:Button ID="Translate" runat="server" Text="Translate"
               OnClick="Translate_Click" />
   <asp:TextBox ID="TranslatedText" runat="server"></asp:TextBox>
   ```

3. In the code-behind file for the user control (TranslationWebPartUserControl.ascx.cs), add the following code:

```
public partial class TranslationWebPartUserControl : UserControl
{
  protected void Translate_Click(object sender, EventArgs e)
  {
    TranslationServiceApplicationProxy proxy =
SPServiceContext.Current.GetDefaultProxy(typeof(TranslationServiceApplicationProxy)) →
as TranslationServiceApplicationProxy;
    TranslatedText.Text=proxy.Translate(OriginalText.Text);
  }
}
```

This code snippet makes use of SPServiceContext to retrieve the default service proxy that matches our translation service. With a reference to a proxy object, the code then calls the Translate method to retrieve the appropriate results.

## Calling Service Applications

As the code stands at the moment, an error will be flagged in Visual Studio, because the Translate method does not yet exist on the proxy class. Let's move on to look at how that can be implemented.

Our TranslationServiceProxy class currently contains a basic implementation of a proxy class. However, it doesn't contain any custom methods that can be used to invoke the functionality of our custom application. Since we're using WCF as our communications mechanism, we first need to create a WCF proxy class. We can create this class by creating an instance of the service and then using svcutil.exe to generate the proxy automatically. However, for the purposes of this demo, we can manually create it as follows:

1. In the Client folder, add a new class named TranslationServiceClient.cs. Add the following code:

```
using System.ServiceModel;

[ServiceContractAttribute(ConfigurationName="ITranslatorService")]
```

```
public interface ITranslatorService
{
    [OperationContractAttribute(
Action="http://tempuri.org/ITranslatorService/Translate",
ReplyAction="http://tempuri.org/ITranslatorService/TranslateResponse")]
    string Translate(string input);
}
public interface ITranslatorServiceChannel : ITranslatorService, →
IClientChannel
{
}
internal class TranslatorServiceClient : ClientBase<ITranslatorService>,
                                         ITranslatorService
{
    public TranslatorServiceClient()
    { }
    public TranslatorServiceClient(string endpointConfigurationName) :
            base(endpointConfigurationName)
    { }
    public TranslatorServiceClient(string endpointConfigurationName,
                                   string remoteAddress) :
            base(endpointConfigurationName, remoteAddress)
    { }
    public TranslatorServiceClient(string endpointConfigurationName,
                System.ServiceModel.EndpointAddress remoteAddress) :
            base(endpointConfigurationName, remoteAddress)
    { }
    public TranslatorServiceClient(System.ServiceModel.Channels.Binding →
binding, System.ServiceModel.EndpointAddress remoteAddress) :
            base(binding, remoteAddress)
    { }
    public string Translate(string input)
    {
        return base.Channel.Translate(input);
    }
}
```

2. In the TranslationServiceApplicationProxy.cs file, add the following code:

```
    private SPRoundRobinServiceLoadBalancer _balancer;

    ~TranslationServiceApplicationProxy()
    {
      if (_balancer != null)
      {
        _balancer.Unprovision();
      }
    }

    internal SPRoundRobinServiceLoadBalancer LoadBalancer
    {
      get
      {
        if (_balancer == null)
```

```
            {
                _balancer = new SPRoundRobinServiceLoadBalancer(this. →
ServiceEndpointUri);
                _balancer.Provision();
            }
            return _balancer;
        }
    }

    public string Translate(string input)
    {

        BasicHttpBinding binding = new BasicHttpBinding();
        SPRoundRobinServiceLoadBalancerContext ctx = LoadBalancer →
.BeginOperation() as SPRoundRobinServiceLoadBalancerContext;
        EndpointAddress address = new EndpointAddress(ctx.EndpointAddress);
        TranslatorServiceClient client =
                        new TranslatorServiceClient(binding, address);

        string output= client.Translate(input);
        ctx.EndOperation();
        return output;
    }
```

This code snippet makes use of the SPRoundRobinServiceLoadBalancer. Earlier in the chapter, the workings of the topology service were covered, along with how a proxy service could query the topology service for a list of endpoints for a particular service and then make use of the list to provide load-balancing capabilities. The SPIisWebServiceApplicationProxy class on which our proxy is based requires that this type of functionality be implemented. Although the class exposes a ServiceEndpointUri property, the value returned is not the URI of a particular endpoint, but is the URI for the service application—only by using the topology service can a list of real endpoints be retrieved. The SPRoundRobinServiceLoadBalancer handles this automatically, and as you can see from the code, it will provide an appropriate endpoint address for each operation.

We're now ready to build and deploy our sample application. As before, choose Build | Deploy TranslatorDemo in Visual Studio. After the project has been deployed, navigate to the Manage Service Applications page in Central Administration and create a new instance of the Translation Service Application. With the service up and running, we can add our custom web part to a page and check that things are working as expected.

**NOTE** Because we set up our project to target the Central Administration site for debugging, the web part will not be installed on other site collections. In a real-world situation, our web part would be created in a separate project and deployed to front-end servers.

If all is well, our web part will be displayed and will translate text as shown:

## Managing Service Applications

So far, we've created, installed, and provisioned service applications. One important area that hasn't been covered is how to manage existing applications. In this section, we'll look at how we can add a management page for our translation service and how we can pick up properties gathered from our management page and make use of them in the implementation of our service.

In much the same way that we added our CreateService page earlier, adding a management page is also a case of overriding a method. This time it's the ManageLink method on the SPServiceApplication class.

> **TIP** You can also add a configuration page for the SPServiceApplicationProxy class if required by overriding the ManageLink method on the SPServiceApplicationProxy class.

1. In the TranslationServiceApplication.cs class, add the following code:

```
public override SPAdministrationLink ManageLink
  {
    get
    {
      string linkWithQuerystring =
          string.Concat("/_admin/TranslatorDemo/ManageService.aspx?appid=",
          this.Id.ToString());
      return new SPAdministrationLink(linkWithQuerystring);
    }
  }

  public string AlternativeLanguage { get; set; }
```

2. Add a new Application Page to the Admin/TranslatorDemo folder. Name the page ManageService.aspx.

3. This time, we'll use the default master page rather than showing the page as a pop-up dialog. Add the following code to the page:

```
<%@ Register TagPrefix="wssuc" TagName="InputFormSection"
         Src="/_controltemplates/InputFormSection.ascx" %>
<%@ Register TagPrefix="wssuc" TagName="InputFormControl"
         Src="/_controltemplates/InputFormControl.ascx" %>
<%@ Register TagPrefix="wssuc" TagName="ButtonSection"
         Src="/_controltemplates/ButtonSection.ascx" %>
```

```
<asp:Content ID="PageHead"
            ContentPlaceHolderID="PlaceHolderAdditionalPageHead"
            runat="server">
</asp:Content>
<asp:Content ID="Main" ContentPlaceHolderID="PlaceHolderMain"
            runat="server">
    <table class="propertysheet" border="0" width="100%"
         cellspacing="0" cellpadding="0"
        id="diidProjectPageOverview">
        <wssuc:InputFormSection Title="Alternative Language"
Description="Enter an alternative language code for this service. →
Examples include: fr,no,pl,en,it"
            runat="server">
            <template_inputformcontrols>
<wssuc:InputFormControl LabelText="" LabelAssociatedControlID="LanguageCode" →
runat="server">
<Template_control>
<SharePoint:InputFormTextBox title="Language Code" class="ms-input" →
ID="LanguageCode" Columns="35" Runat="server" MaxLength=256 />
</Template_control>
</wssuc:InputFormControl>
</template_inputformcontrols>
        </wssuc:InputFormSection>
        <wssuc:ButtonSection runat="server">
            <template_buttons>
<asp:Button runat="server" class="ms-ButtonHeightWidth"
OnClick="UpdateButton_Click" Text="<%$Resources:wss,multipages_okbutton_text%>"
id="updateButton" accesskey="<%$Resources:wss,okbutton_accesskey%>"/>
</template_buttons>
        </wssuc:ButtonSection>
    </table>
</asp:Content>
<asp:Content ID="PageTitle"
ContentPlaceHolderID="PlaceHolderPageTitle" runat="server">
    Manage Translation Service
</asp:Content>
<asp:Content ID="PageTitleInTitleArea"
ContentPlaceHolderID="PlaceHolderPageTitleInTitleArea"
    runat="server">
    Manage Translation Service
</asp:Content>
```

4. Add the following code to the code-behind file (ManageService.aspx.cs):

```
public partial class ManageService : LayoutsPageBase
  {
    private Guid _appId;
    protected void Page_Load(object sender, EventArgs e)
    {
      string appId=this.Request.QueryString["appId"];
      if (!string.IsNullOrEmpty(appId))
      {
        _appId = new Guid(appId);
        updateButton.Enabled = true;
      }
```

```
    else
    {
      updateButton.Enabled = false;
    }
  }

  protected void UpdateButton_Click(object sender, EventArgs e)
  {
    TranslationServiceApplication app=TranslationService.Local.Applications→
.GetValue<TranslationServiceApplication>(this.AppId);
    app.AlternativeLanguage = LanguageCode.Text;
    app.Update();
  }

  public Guid AppId
  {
    get
    {
      return _appId;
    }
  }
}
```

We've now implemented our ManageService page. By deploying the application and creating a new instance of the Translation Service Application, we can see that our application name now appears as a hyperlink in the Manage Service Application page in Central Administration and the Manage button is enabled in the ribbon when our application is selected. By navigating to the Manage Translation Service page, we have the option to configure an alternative language, as shown here:

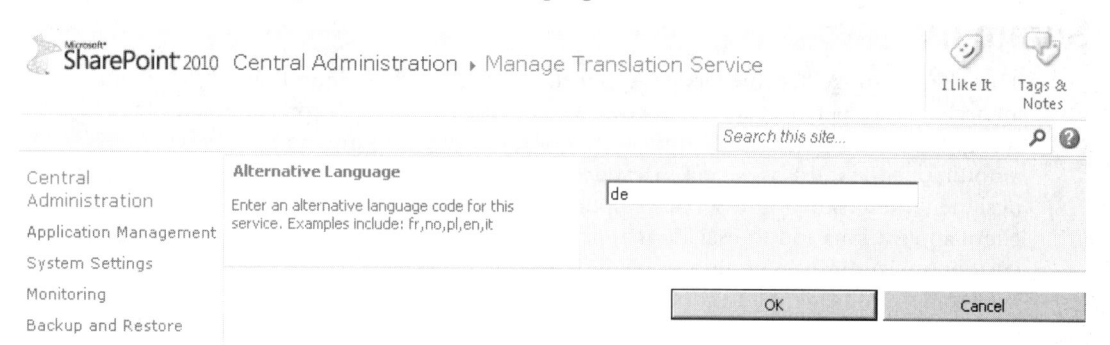

## Reading Service Application Properties

Although we've implemented a user interface to capture properties for our custom application, our service implementation needs to be modified to make use of these properties.

In the TranslatorService.cs file, update the Translate method as follows:

```
public string Translate(string input)
{
```

```
        BasicHttpBinding binding = new BasicHttpBinding();

        EndpointAddress address =
new EndpointAddress("http://api.microsofttranslator.com/v2/Soap.svc");
        Microsoft.Translator.LanguageServiceClient client =
new Microsoft.Translator.LanguageServiceClient(binding, address);

        string apiKey = "Your Bing API key goes here";
        string output = string.Empty;
        string language = "fr";

        TranslationServiceApplication app=
TranslationServiceApplication.Current as TranslationServiceApplication;

        if (!string.IsNullOrEmpty(app.AlternativeLanguage))
        {
          language = app.AlternativeLanguage;
        }

        output=client.Translate(apiKey, input, "en", language);

        return output;
    }
```

With this final code change in place, we can deploy our application and confirm that everything works as expected. By changing the alternative language value in our ManageService page, we can control which language is used for translations for all users of our service.

## Summary

This chapter looked at the Service Application Framework in SharePoint 2010. From an architecture perspective, the Service Application Framework appears relatively straightforward. However, when it comes down to using it to implement services, a fair amount of code must be written. Despite the overhead in terms of coding for the service designer, the upside of the Service Application Framework is that it's easy to use to create client applications and tools. Client applications can make use of scalable, enterprise-ready custom services by using only a single line of code.

From a deployment and configuration perspective, the Service Application Framework offers a number of hooks into the SharePoint Central Administration interface. This makes our custom services much easier to use by SharePoint administrators because of the commonality with other services.

It can take awhile to master service applications, but given the benefits of this highly flexible architecture, it's well worth your efforts.

# CHAPTER 10

# Word Automation Services

In Office 2007, Microsoft introduced a new file format called OpenXML. As an ECMA (European Computer Manufacturers Association) standard, OpenXML is well documented and open to all developers to use as they see fit on all platforms.

One of the immediate benefits of this innovation is that it allows the programmatic creation and modification of Microsoft Office files such as Word documents and Excel spreadsheets. Before OpenXML, the only way to create or modify these documents was to automate the appropriate client application. Although this works well in a client scenario, performing such automation on a server is prone to problems. Using OpenXML, particularly with SharePoint, allows developers to create composite Office documents easily using server-side code and return the finished results to users in a format that can be used by most common Office applications. Having said that, however, certain actions can't be performed using OpenXML. Because OpenXML is simply an XML-based file format, none of the capabilities of the client application are available. Performing actions such as repagination or updating dynamic content isn't possible via OpenXML. As a result, developers requiring this type of functionality are required to go down the client application automation route with its attendant issues.

With SharePoint 2010, Microsoft picked up on this shortfall and introduced a new application service known as *Word Automation Services*. This chapter takes a look at this new service and discusses how you can leverage OpenXML to create custom line-of-business applications.

## Word Automation Services

Word Automation Services is available as a service application in SharePoint Server 2010. Three components make up the overall architecture:

- **Front-end object model**   In Chapter 9, you saw how the architecture of the framework allows for the generation of proxy classes that can be used on the front end to access the underlying service. The Word Automation Services object model is an example of such proxy classes.

- **Document queue**   The Word Automation Services application makes use of a central database to maintain a queue of jobs being processed. Each job may contain one or more documents. The primary function of the service application is to write items to the queue and to retrieve details of the status of current jobs.

- **Word Automation Services engine**   The real work behind Word Automation Services occurs in a separate rendering engine that is capable of rendering Word documents and providing a range of features such as file format conversions, dynamic data updates, and repagination. The output of the rendering engine is then stored in the SharePoint content database as a new document.

## Creating Conversion Jobs

From a front-end object model perspective, the primary interface to Word Automation Services is the ConversionJob class. The following code snippet shows how to create a job to convert a document to a PDF format:

```
SPFile temp = folder.Files.Add("temp.docx", mem, true);
SPServiceApplicationProxy proxy=SPServiceContext.Current.GetDefaultProxy(
                     typeof(WordServiceApplicationProxy));
ConversionJob convJob = new ConversionJob(proxy.Id);
convJob.Name = "Document Assembly";
convJob.UserToken = SPContext.Current.Web.CurrentUser.UserToken;
convJob.Settings.UpdateFields = true;
convJob.Settings.OutputFormat = SaveFormat.PDF;
convJob.Settings.OutputSaveBehavior = SaveBehavior.AlwaysOverwrite;
string siteUrl = SPContext.Current.Site.Url + "/";
string outputUrl = siteUrl + temp.Url.Replace(".docx", ".pdf");
convJob.AddFile(siteUrl + temp.Url, outputUrl);
convJob.Start();
```

Determining which action should be performed on all documents within a job is a job for the ConversionJobSettings class. The following class view shows the main properties:

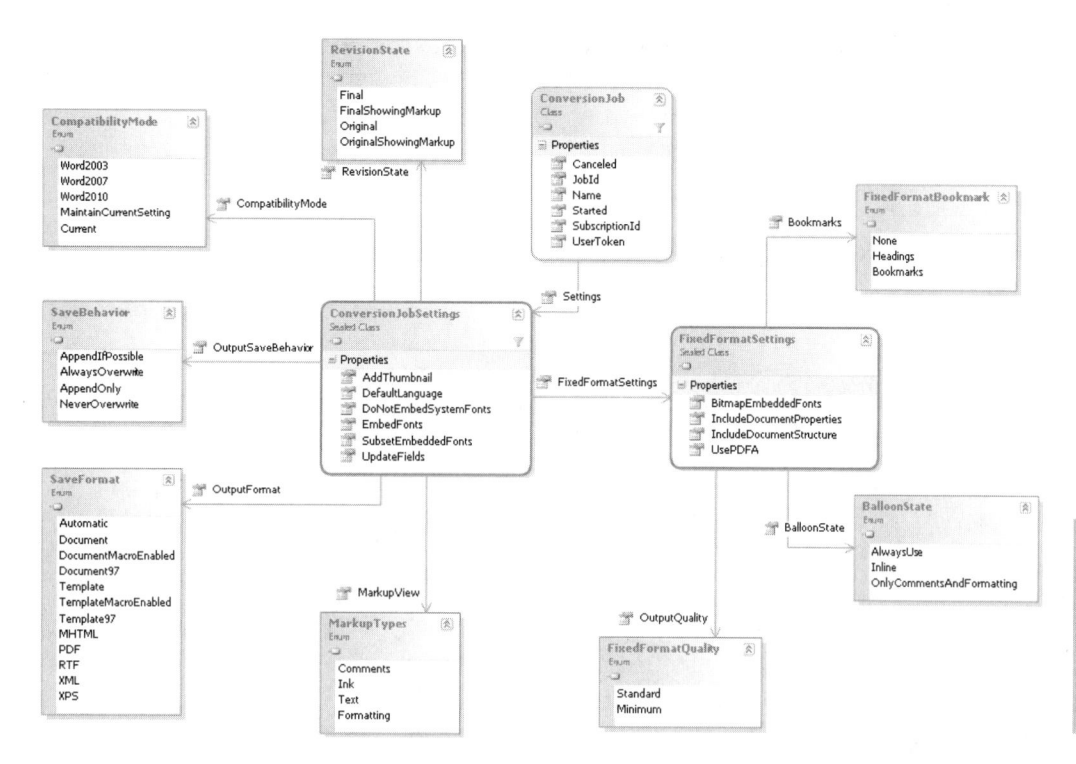

## Checking Status of Conversion Jobs

In Word Automation Services, document processing actually occurs in a separate process, and all jobs are queued for processing. As a result of this, determining the status of a submitted job is an important requirement when it comes to designing an application that makes use of the service.

We can retrieve the status of a submitted job by querying the ConversionJob object that we used to create the job. Effectively, a ConversionJob object is passed as a Windows Communication Foundation (WCF) message from client to server; on the server side, after the job has been written to the document queue database, a job identifier is returned to the client. The identifier can be obtained by querying the ConversionJob.JobId property.

Because conversion jobs can take a long time to complete, common practice is to store the job identifier for later use. A separate process can then periodically check on the status of the job, as the following snippet shows:

```
string ConversionJobId = SPContext.Current.ListItem.GetFormattedValue(
                                                "ConversionJobId");

    if (!string.IsNullOrEmpty(ConversionJobId))
    {
WordServiceApplicationProxy proxy = SPServiceContext.Current.GetDefaultProxy(
typeof(WordServiceApplicationProxy)) as WordServiceApplicationProxy;

        ConversionJobStatus status = new ConversionJobStatus(
                        proxy, new Guid(ConversionJobId), null);

        if (status.Count == status.Succeeded + status.Failed)
        {
            //Job Completed
        }
        else
        {
            //Job in progress
        }
    }
```

## OpenXML

As described at the beginning of this chapter, OpenXML is an XML-based file format that's supported by applications in the Microsoft Office 2007 suite and later. Although an in-depth discussion on all aspects of OpenXML is beyond the scope of this chapter, we'll take a look at a few of the key objects and work through an example showing how the technology can be used when building SharePoint applications.

> **NOTE** Although OpenXML files are XML-based and can therefore be created and modified by using the various XML manipulation classes that are present in the .NET Framework, Microsoft provides an OpenXML SDK to make it easier to deal with the complex document structure in managed code. It can be downloaded from www.microsoft.com/downloads/details.aspx?FamilyId=C6E744E5-36E9-45F5-8D8C-331DF206E0D0&displaylang=en.

### Getting Started with OpenXML

OpenXML documents are in fact ZIP files. Each ZIP archive contains a collection of XML files and other elements. Relationships exist among the different XML files stored within the archive, and these relationships are defined in XML format in files with a .rels file extension.

> **TIP** To see how an OpenXML archive is structured, try renaming a .docx file to .zip and then open it with Windows Explorer.

Many of the files in the archive serve a particular function. For example, the fontTable.xml file contains details of the fonts that are in use within a document. Word documents store an XML file named document.xml; if you examine this file, you'll see most of the user-generated content.

Dealing with each of the individual files and maintaining references between them by using standard XML processing components such as XmlDocument and XPathNavigator is certainly possible. However, it should be apparent from looking at the number of files involved that such an approach is no trivial undertaking. With that in mind, we'll continue our discussion with a focus on the object model provided by the OpenXML SDK.

Within the OpenXML object model, a document is represented by a class derived from the OpenXmlPackage class. A document is actually a ZIP archive containing many files, and each of these files is defined as an object derived from OpenXmlPart. For example, the main document element in a Word file can be referenced by examining the MainDocumentPart property of a WordProcessingDocument object. WordProcessingDocument inherits from OpenXmlPackage and MainDocumentPart inherits from OpenXmlPart.

Each OpenXmlPart is made up of one or more OpenXmlElement objects, which in turn can contain OpenXmlAttribute objects. Naturally, these are abstract objects and specific implementations will often be used when processing a document. For example, when adding a Caption to a WordProcessingDocument object, an instance of the WordProcessing.Caption class will be used.

## Demonstration Scenario

To give you an idea of how OpenXML and Word Automation Services can be used together to build useful line-of-business applications, consider the following demonstration scenario:

> You've been engaged by AdventureWorks to design and build a document creation and collaboration tool. The tool will be used by the company's sales department for producing sales proposals. Each proposal is made up of a number of different documents contributed by various users from different departments. The tool to be built should combine these documents into a single read-only document that can be sent to the customer for consideration.
>
> The input documents will be saved in Microsoft Word OpenXML format. The output document should be in Adobe Acrobat (PDF) format.

### Architecture

You need to consider the following points to create an architecture that fits this scenario:

- Multiple documents will logically make up a single set. Bearing this in mind, we can use the Document Set functionality discussed in Chapter 6.
- By using OpenXML, we can combine a number of different types of documents into a single OpenXML document.
- Word Automation Services can be used to convert the output OpenXML document into an Adobe Acrobat–compatible file.

- Because the process of combining documents is likely to be long-running, we have two possibilities: we could use the SPLongOperation object, which will present the user with the familiar spinning disc image while the process runs. Or we could use a custom job on the server, which will free up the user to perform other activities while the process completes. For the purposes of our demonstration, we'll use the custom job approach since it illustrates functionality that is useful in many development situations.

Bearing these points in mind, we can create a custom content type that derives from the Document Set content type. We'll then develop a custom web part control that will provide a user interface for combining the contents of our custom content set. To do the actual combination, we'll create a custom job that uses OpenXML and Word Automation Services to put the finished document together and convert the output to PDF.

## Creating a Custom Content Type

First we'll create a new bank site and then provision the Document Set content type before we add a custom content type and define our user interface.

1. From the Site Actions menu, create a new Blank Site named Chapter 10, as shown:

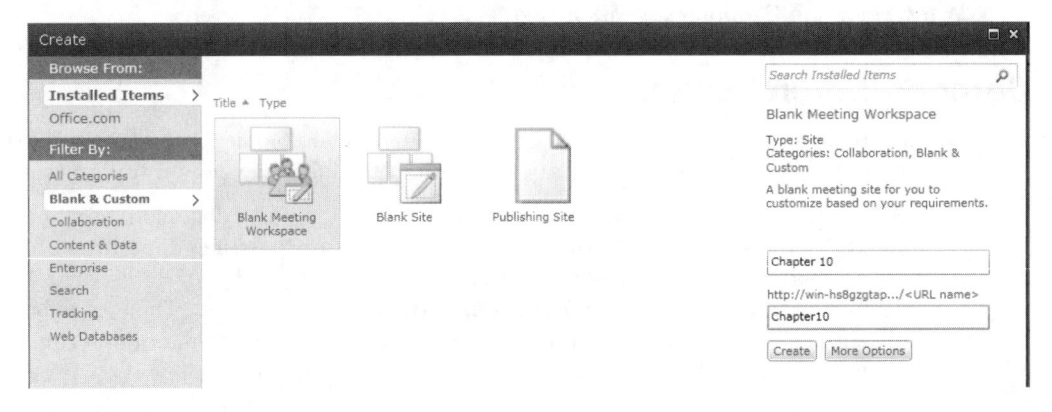

2. As described in detail in Chapter 6, enable the Document Sets feature. From the Site Actions menu, select Site Settings | Go To Top Level Site Settings | Site Collection Features. Activate the Document Sets feature.

3. We'll next add a custom content type for our Sales Proposal. Navigate back to the blank site that we created earlier (http://<ServerName>/Chapter10). From the Site Actions menu, select Site Settings. In the Galleries section, select Site Columns, as shown.

4. Create a new column named **JobId** of type Single Line Of Text. Save the column in the Custom Columns group.

5. Create a new column named **TemplateUrl** of type Single Line Of Text. Save the column in the Custom Columns group.

6. Navigate back to the Site Settings page, and then select Site Content Types from the Galleries section.

7. Create a new content type named **Sales Proposal**. Set the Parent Content Type field to Document Set and save it within the Custom Content Types group, as shown:

8. With our new content type created, we can add in the site columns that we created earlier. In the Columns section, click Add From Existing Site Columns. From the Custom Columns group, add the JobId and the TemplateUrl columns. Click OK to commit the changes.

**NOTE** We've largely skipped over content types and site columns here. For a more in-depth look, see Chapter 13.

## Customizing the DocumentSetProperties Web Part

Before we can customize the welcome page for our custom document set, we need to build a web part with the following additional features:

- A Build Sales Proposal button that creates and starts the compilation job
- A status indicator that shows the progress of the compilation job
- A link to the compiled output file

Although we could create a separate web part that could be used in conjunction with the built-in DocumentPropertiesWebPart, it wouldn't be overly useful as a stand-alone component elsewhere. Instead, we'll create a web part that inherits from the DocumentPropertiesWebPart and adds our required additional functionality.

1. Using Visual Studio 2010, create a new Empty SharePoint Project named SalesProposalApplication, as shown:

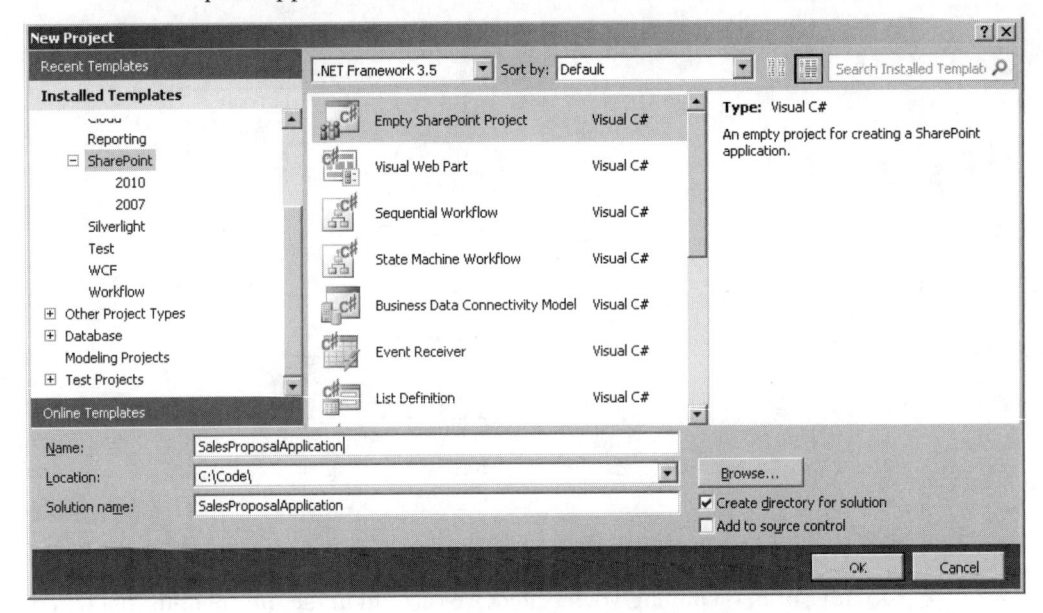

2. Set the debugging site to be the blank site that we created in the preceding section, and select the Deploy As Farm Solution option. Click Finish to create the project.

3. After the project has been created, add a new Visual Web Part named SalesProposalPropertiesWebPart.

As you saw in Chapter 7, Visual Web Parts provide a design surface when we're creating web parts. However, since we're planning to override a built-in web part that already has its own rendering logic, we need to change some of the generated code for the Visual Web Part.

1. Add a reference to the Microsoft.Office.DocumentManagement assembly, located in the %SPROOT%isapi folder, to the project.

2. In the SalesProposalPropertiesWebPart.cs file, add the following code:

```
using System.ComponentModel;
using System.Web.UI;
using Microsoft.Office.Server.WebControls;

namespace SalesProposalApplication.SalesProposalPropertiesWebPart
{
  [ToolboxItemAttribute(false)]
  public class SalesProposalPropertiesWebPart : DocumentSetPropertiesWebPart
  {
    // Visual Studio might automatically update
    //this path when you change the Visual Web Part project item.
    private const string _ascxPath =
@"~/_CONTROLTEMPLATES/SalesProposalApplication/SalesProposalPropertiesWebPart/→
SalesProposalPropertiesWebPartUserControl.ascx";

    protected override void CreateChildControls()
    {
      Control control = this.Page.LoadControl(_ascxPath);
      this.Controls.Add(control);
      base.CreateChildControls();
    }

    protected override void RenderWebPart(HtmlTextWriter writer)
    {
      base.RenderWebPart(writer);
      this.Controls[0].RenderControl(writer);
    }
  }
}
```

**TIP** When overriding any built-in SharePoint classes, it can be challenging to work out exactly what you need to do to get the behavior that you expect. In the code snippet, to get our web part to render properly, we explicitly need to render our custom user control by overriding RenderWebPart method. Uncovering details such as this from the documentation is often impossible, and this is where Reflector Pro, discussed in Chapter 2, is invaluable.

With our custom user control properly hooked up to our web part, we can implement the rest of our custom logic via the user control.

1. We'll make use of Asynchronous JavaScript and XML (AJAX) so that the web part can periodically check on the status of the timer job and redraw the controls. Add an UpdatePanel control to the SalesProposalPropertiesWebPartUserControl.ascx file.

2. We'll use an AJAX Timer so that we can automatically refresh the status indicator on our control. Drag the Timer control from the toolbox onto the user control design surface. Name the Timer RefreshTimer and set its Enabled property to False.

3. From the toolbox, add a Label control, a Hyperlink control, and a Button control to the SalesProposalPropertiesWebPartUserControl.ascx file. Within the UpdatePanel control markup, lay out and rename the controls as follows:

```
<asp:UpdatePanel runat="server">
    <ContentTemplate>
        <div width="100%">
            <br />
            <asp:Label ID="StatusLabel" runat="server" Text=""></asp:Label>
            <br />
            <asp:HyperLink ID="OutputHyperlink" runat="server">
                Click here to download a compiled copy</asp:HyperLink>
            <br />
            <asp:Button ID="StartCompilation" OnClick="StartCompilation_Click"
                    runat="server" Text="Start Compilation" />
        </div>
    </ContentTemplate>
    <Triggers>
      <asp:AsyncPostBackTrigger ControlID="RefreshTimer" EventName="Tick" />
    </Triggers>
</asp:UpdatePanel>
<asp:Timer runat="server" ID="RefreshTimer" Enabled="False">
</asp:Timer>
```

4. In the code-behind file (SalesProposalPropertiesWebPartUserControl.aspx.cs), add the following code:

```
public partial class SalesProposalPropertiesWebPartUserControl : UserControl
{
  protected void Page_Load(object sender, EventArgs e)
  {
    RedrawUI();
  }

  private void RedrawUI()
  {
    if (SPContext.Current.ListItem != null)
    {
      string ConversionJobId =
            SPContext.Current.ListItem.GetFormattedValue("JobId");

      if (!string.IsNullOrEmpty(ConversionJobId))
      {

        OutputHyperlink.NavigateUrl =
                SPContext.Current.RootFolderUrl + "/temp.pdf";

        SPJobHistory history = (from j in
                        SPFarm.Local.TimerService.JobHistoryEntries
                    where j.JobDefinitionId.ToString() == ConversionJobId
                        orderby j.StartTime descending
                        select j
```

```csharp
                       ).FirstOrDefault();
      if (history != null)
      {
        StatusLabel.Text = history.Status.ToString();
        if (history.Status == SPRunningJobStatus.Succeeded)
        {
          OutputHyperlink.Visible = true;
          StartCompilation.Enabled = true;
          RefreshTimer.Enabled = false;
        }
        else if (history.Status == SPRunningJobStatus.Failed |
                 history.Status == SPRunningJobStatus.Aborted)
        {
          OutputHyperlink.Visible = false;
          StartCompilation.Enabled = true;
          RefreshTimer.Enabled = false;
        }
        else
        {
          OutputHyperlink.Visible = false;
          StartCompilation.Enabled = false;
          RefreshTimer.Enabled = true;
        }
      }
      else
      {
        StatusLabel.Text = "Processing";
        OutputHyperlink.Visible = false;
        StartCompilation.Enabled = false;
        RefreshTimer.Enabled = true;
      }
    }
  }
  else
  {
    OutputHyperlink.NavigateUrl = "#";
    OutputHyperlink.Visible = true;
    StatusLabel.Text = "My Status";
    StartCompilation.Enabled = false;
  }
}
protected void StartCompilation_Click(object sender, EventArgs e)
{
  throw new NotImplementedException();
}
```

Before our customized web part can be deployed, we need to make a few changes to the solution. The default packaging mechanisms that are set up in Visual Studio work well for creating web parts that are derived directly from System.Web.UI.WebControls.Webparts. Webpart. However, when creating a web part that's derived from another base class, we'll occasionally see an "Incompatible Web Part Markup" error message when we're trying to use the deployed web part on a page. To resolve this error, we need to use an alternative packaging format.

1. Rename the SalesProposalPropertiesWebPart.webpart file to SalesProposalPropertiesWebPart.dwp.
2. Replace the contents with the following XML:

```xml
<WebPart xmlns="http://schemas.microsoft.com/WebPart/v2">
<Assembly>
$SharePoint.Project.AssemblyFullName$
</Assembly>
  <TypeName>
SalesProposalApplication.SalesProposalPropertiesWebPart.SalesProposalPropertiesWebPart➔
</TypeName>
  <Title>SalesProposalPropertiesWebPart</Title>
  <Description>Web Part Description</Description>
</WebPart>
```

3. So that the renamed file is installed properly, edit the Elements.xml file in the SalesProposalPropertiesWebPart folder as follows:

```xml
<?xml version="1.0" encoding="utf-8"?>
<Elements xmlns="http://schemas.microsoft.com/sharepoint/" >
  <Module Name="SalesProposalPropertiesWebPart" List="113"
        Url="_catalogs/wp">
    <File Path="SalesProposalPropertiesWebPart\SalesProposalPropertiesWebPart.dwp"
        Url="SalesProposalPropertiesWebPart.dwp"
        Type="GhostableInLibrary" >
      <Property Name="Group" Value="Custom" />
    </File>
  </Module>
</Elements>
```

## Creating a Custom Job Definition

With our user interface largely complete, our next step is to define a custom job that will compile all documents in our document set and send the compiled output to Word Automation Services for conversion to PDF.

In Visual Studio, add a new class named DocumentCombinerJob.cs. Add the following code to the file:

```csharp
public class DocumentCombinerJob : SPJobDefinition
{
  [Persisted]
  private Guid _siteId;
  [Persisted]
  private Guid _webId;
  [Persisted]
  private Guid _folderId;
  [Persisted]
  private Guid _proxyId;

  public DocumentCombinerJob()
```

```
      : base()
    {
    }

    public DocumentCombinerJob(SPListItem documentSet)
      : base("Combine Documents" + Guid.NewGuid().ToString(),
              SPFarm.Local.TimerService, null, SPJobLockType.None)
    {
      _siteId = documentSet.Web.Site.ID;
      _webId = documentSet.Web.ID;
      _folderId = documentSet.Folder.UniqueId;
      _proxyId = SPServiceContext.Current.GetDefaultProxy(
                          typeof(WordServiceApplicationProxy)).Id;
      Title = "Combine Documents - " + documentSet.Folder.Url;
    }

    protected override bool HasAdditionalUpdateAccess()
    {
      return true;
    }
  }
}
```

Developers familiar with SharePoint 2007 should notice a few interesting elements in this code snippet. First, check out the HasAdditionalUpdateAccess override. In previous versions of SharePoint, only farm administrators could create jobs. This greatly restricted their usefulness for offloading ad hoc tasks. With SharePoint 2010, where the HasAdditionalUpdateAccess method returns true, any user can create a job.

Also notice that when we're creating a job, the job can be associated with either a service or an application pool. These associations are primarily for administrative purposes since most jobs run via the SPTimerV4 service. In our example, we're associating our custom job with the TimerService.

The final thing to notice is that job definitions are serialized when a job is created. As a result, not all types of objects can be defined as properties. For example, the SPListItem isn't serializable and therefore can't be stored as a property. To get around this problem, we're storing a number of identifiers that can be used to recover a reference to the appropriate SPListItem object when the job is deserialized.

## Combine Documents Using OpenXML

Before we can make use of OpenXML, we need to add a reference to the OpenXML SDK binaries:

1. Download and install the OpenXML SDK; then, in Visual Studio, add a reference to the DocumentFormat.OpenXML assembly.

2. Add a reference to the WindowsBase assembly.

3. To prevent any confusion between similarly named objects within the OpenXML SDK, add the following Using statement to the DocumentCombinerJob.cs file:

   ```
   using Word = DocumentFormat.OpenXml.Wordprocessing;
   ```

4. In the DocumentCombinerJob.cs file, add the following code:

```csharp
public override void Execute(Guid targetInstanceId)
    {
      using (SPSite site = new SPSite(_siteId))
      {
        using (SPWeb web = site.OpenWeb(_webId))
        {
          SPFolder folder = web.GetFolder(_folderId);

          SPListItem documentSet = folder.Item;

          SPFile output = CombineDocuments(web, folder, documentSet);

          ConvertOutput(site, web, output);
        }
      }
    }

    private SPFile CombineDocuments(SPWeb web, SPFolder folder,
                                    SPListItem documentSet)
    {
      char[] splitter = { '/' };
      string[] folderName = folder.Name.Split(splitter);
      string templateUrl = documentSet.GetFormattedValue("TemplateUrl1");
      SPFile template = web.GetFile(templateUrl);
      byte[] byteArray = template.OpenBinary();
      using (MemoryStream mem = new MemoryStream())
      {
        mem.Write(byteArray, 0, (int)byteArray.Length);
        using (WordprocessingDocument myDoc =
                          WordprocessingDocument.Open(mem, true))
        {
          MainDocumentPart mainPart = myDoc.MainDocumentPart;
          foreach (Word.SdtElement sdt in
             mainPart.Document.Descendants<Word.SdtElement>().ToList())
          {
            Word.SdtAlias alias =
                   sdt.Descendants<Word.SdtAlias>().FirstOrDefault();
            if (alias != null)
            {
              string sdtTitle = alias.Val.Value;
              if (sdtTitle == "MergePlaceholder")
              {
                foreach (SPFile docFile in folder.Files)
                {
                  if (docFile.Name.EndsWith(".docx"))
                  {
                    if (docFile.Name != "temp.docx")
                    {
                      InsertDocument(mainPart, sdt, docFile);
                      Word.PageBreakBefore pb = new Word.PageBreakBefore();
                      sdt.Parent.InsertAfter(pb, sdt);
                    }
                  }
                }
                sdt.Remove();
```

```
          }
        }
      }
    }
    SPFile temp = folder.Files.Add("temp.docx", mem, true);
    return temp;
  }
}

protected int id = 1;

void InsertDocument(MainDocumentPart mainPart, Word.SdtElement sdt,
                    SPFile filename)
{
  string altChunkId = "AIFId" + id;
  id++;
  byte[] byteArray = filename.OpenBinary();

  AlternativeFormatImportPart chunk = mainPart.AddAlternativeFormatImportPart(
  AlternativeFormatImportPartType.WordprocessingML, altChunkId);
  using (MemoryStream mem = new MemoryStream())
  {
    mem.Write(byteArray, 0, (int)byteArray.Length);
    mem.Seek(0, SeekOrigin.Begin);
    chunk.FeedData(mem);
  }
  Word.AltChunk altChunk = new Word.AltChunk();
  altChunk.Id = altChunkId;
  OpenXmlElement parent = sdt.Parent.Parent;
  parent.InsertAfter(altChunk, sdt.Parent);
}

private void ConvertOutput(SPSite site, SPWeb web, SPFile output)
{
  throw new NotImplementedException();
}
```

In this code snippet, the CombineDocuments method loads a Microsoft Word format template. The code then searches for all content controls within the document, and where the content control has a title of MergePlaceholder, the contents of all files with a .docx extension within the document set are merged into the template. The merge process makes use of the AlternativeFormatImportPart control to merge contents. This control inserts a binary copy of data into the template at a specific position. When the completed document is rendered in a client application, the merge is performed dynamically each time the document is opened.

## Converting an OpenXML Document to an Alternative Format

Before we can make use of Word Automation Services in our application, we need to add a reference to the appropriate assembly:

1. In Visual Studio, add a reference to Microsoft.Office.Word.Server.dll. At the time of writing, this appears in the Add Reference dialog as one of two components named Microsoft Office 2010 component; this problem may be resolved in the final release.

2. Update the ConvertOutput method in DocumentTimerJob.cs as follows:

```
private void ConvertOutput(SPSite site, SPWeb web, SPFile output)
{
  ConversionJob convJob = new ConversionJob(_proxyId);
  convJob.Name = "Document Assembly";
  convJob.UserToken = web.CurrentUser.UserToken;
  convJob.Settings.UpdateFields = true;
  convJob.Settings.OutputFormat = SaveFormat.PDF;
  convJob.Settings.OutputSaveBehavior = SaveBehavior.AlwaysOverwrite;
  string webUrl = web.Url + "/";
  convJob.AddFile(webUrl + output.Url, webUrl + output.Url.Replace(".docx", ".pdf"));
  convJob.Start();
  Guid jobId = convJob.JobId;
  ConversionJobStatus status = new ConversionJobStatus(_proxyId, jobId, null);
  while (status.Count != (status.Succeeded + status.Failed))
  {
    Thread.Sleep(3000);
    status.Refresh();
  }
  if (status.Failed == status.Count)
  {
    throw new InvalidOperationException();
  }
}
```

With our custom job definition completed, we can change the implementation in our user interface to create a new instance of the job.

3. In SalesProposalWebPartUserControl.ascx.cs, change the StartCompilation_Click method as follows:

```
protected void StartCompilation_Click(object sender, EventArgs e)
{
    SPListItem current = SPContext.Current.ListItem;

    current["JobId"] = string.Empty;
    current.Update();

    DocumentCombinerJob job = new DocumentCombinerJob(current);

    job.Update();
    job.RunNow();

    current["JobId"] = job.Id;
    current.Update();

    RedrawUI();
}
```

We've now completed the code required to implement our demonstration scenario. Deploy the project by selecting Deploy SalesProposalApplication from the Build menu.

## Customizing Document Set Welcome Page

As you saw in Chapter 6, each document set has a welcome page that contains a list of the documents within the set as well as information about the set itself. The web part that we created earlier will be used to customize the welcome page for our Sales Proposal document set so that whenever the content type is used, our custom control will be displayed instead of the built-in DocumentSetProperties control.

1. Navigate to the Chapter 10 site that we created earlier. Select Site Settings from the Site Actions menu.
2. Select Site Content Types from the Galleries section and then click the Sales Proposal content type.
3. Select the Document Set settings link in the Settings section and then, in the Welcome Page section, click the Customize the Welcome Page link, as shown here:

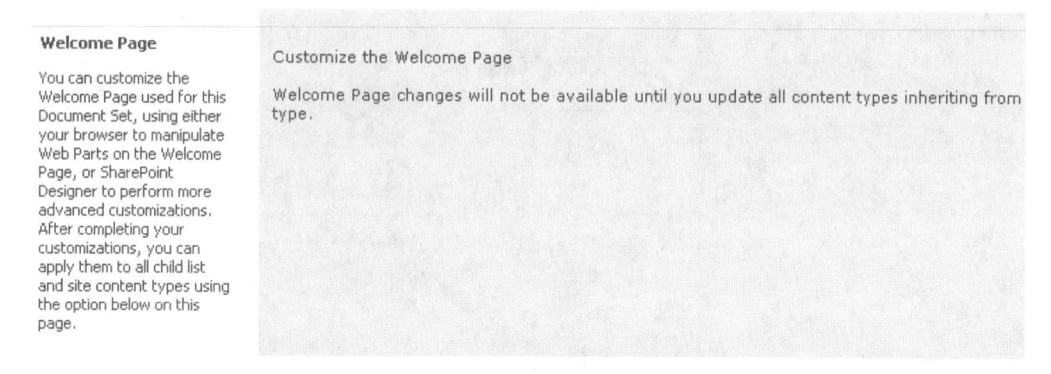

**Welcome Page**

You can customize the Welcome Page used for this Document Set, using either your browser to manipulate Web Parts on the Welcome Page, or SharePoint Designer to perform more advanced customizations. After completing your customizations, you can apply them to all child list and site content types using the option below on this page.

Customize the Welcome Page

Welcome Page changes will not be available until you update all content types inheriting from type.

4. From the Page tab in the ribbon, select Edit Page.
5. Delete the Document Set Properties web part, and then click the Add a Web Part link in Zone 2 to show the web part selector.
6. Add the SalesProposalPropertiesWebPart from the Custom category, as shown:

| Categories | Web Parts | About the Web Part |
|---|---|---|
| Recommended Items | SalesProposalPropertiesWebPart | SalesProposalPropertiesWebPart |
| Lists and Libraries | | Web Part Description |
| Business Data | | |
| Content Rollup | | |
| **Custom** | | |
| Documents | | |
| Filters | | |
| Media and Content | | |
| Meetings | | |
| Upload a Web Part ▼ | | Add Web Part to: Zone 2 |

7. Click Stop Editing to commit the changes to the welcome page.

## Create a Document Library

Before we can begin creating sales proposals, we need to create a new document library that is bound to our Sales Proposal content type.

1. From the Site Actions menu, select New Document Library. Name the new library **Sales Proposals**.
2. After the new library has been created, select Library Settings from the Library tab of the ribbon.
3. In the Document Library Settings page, select Advanced Settings, and then select the Allow Management Of Content Types option. Click OK to save the changes.
4. From the Content Types section, click Add From Existing Site Content Types, and then select the Sales Proposal content type, as shown. Click OK to save the changes.

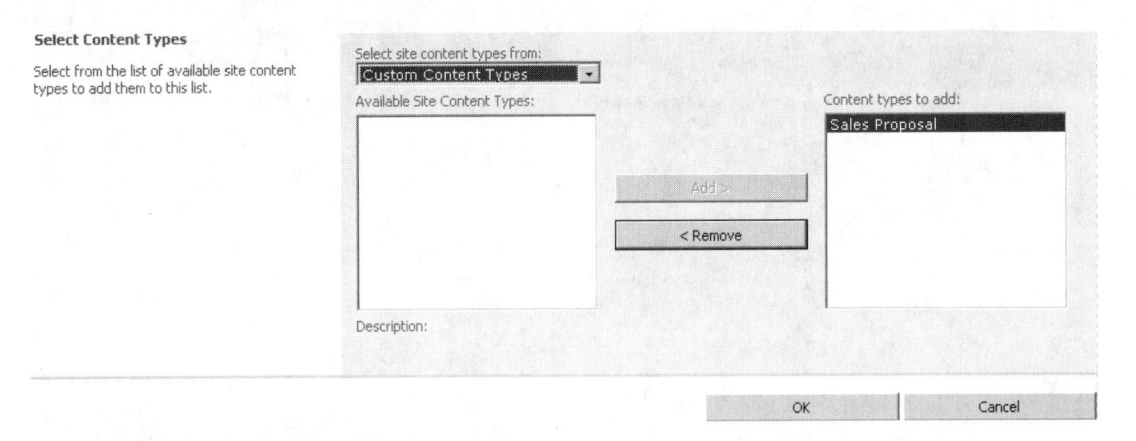

## Create a Document Template

Our final step before we can see our document set functionality in action is to create a template for our compilation process. Since we need to add Content Controls to our template document, we can create the document using Visual Studio.

1. To our SalesProposalApplication solution, add a new project of type Word 2010 Document, as shown. Name the project **SampleTemplate**.

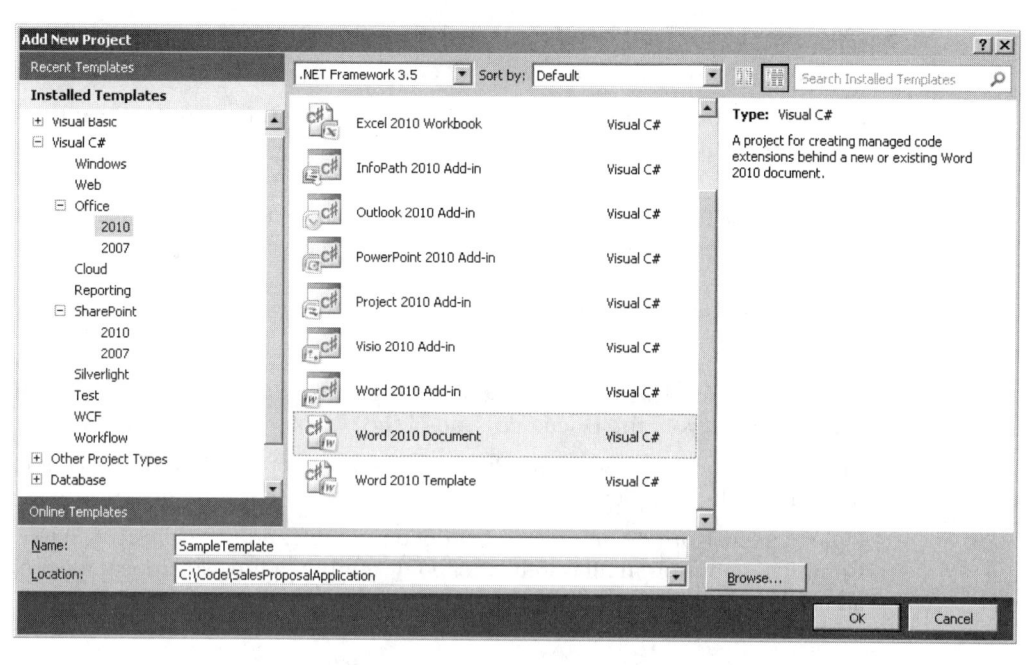

2. Drag a RichTextContentControl onto the SampleTemplate.docx file. Type the Title property as **MergePlaceholder**, as shown:

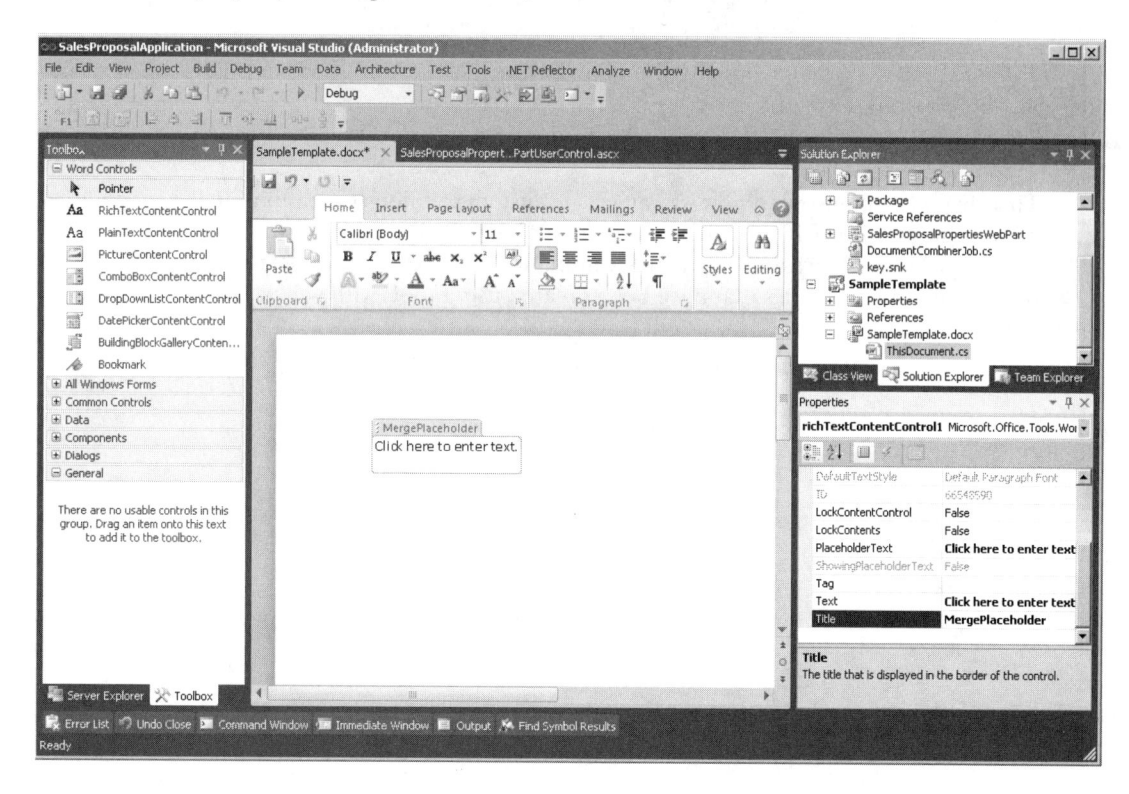

3. Close the SampleTemplate.docx pane in Visual Studio, and then save the project.
4. Right-click the project node and select Open Folder in Windows Explorer.
5. Create a new document library named Document Templates and upload the SampleTemplate.docx file.

**TIP** When you select the Upload Document | Upload Multiple Documents option from the Documents tab, the file can be uploaded by dragging and dropping it onto the dialog box.

We can now make use of our Sales Proposals document set to create a composite document.

1. Navigate to the Sales Proposals document library, and then select New Document | Sales Proposal from the Documents tab of the ribbon.
2. In the New Document Set: Sales Proposal dialog, enter the URL of the sample template in the TemplateUrl box.
3. Upload a few Word documents to the document set, and then click the Start Compilation button. If all is well, after a few minutes a link will appear as shown, allowing us to download a PDF copy of the compiled sales proposal:

My Sales Proposal

View All Properties
Edit Properties

Succeeded
Click here to download a compiled copy
Start Compilation

## Summary

This chapter demonstrated how we can create custom solutions by combining the capabilities of Microsoft Office 2010 and SharePoint Server 2010. By leveraging tools such as OpenXML and application services such as Word Automation Services, we can perform extensive processing on documents that have been created using tools with which users are already familiar.

# CHAPTER 11

# Workflow

Although Windows Workflow Foundation (WF) is one of the most important technologies included in the .NET Framework, it hasn't quite hit the prime time in terms of developer adoption, because it requires a whole load of plumbing before it can be used effectively. It's possible to use the default runtime WF implementation out of the box, but a fair bit of work is required to incorporate that into a real-world application.

This is where SharePoint comes into its own as an application development platform. It provides a runtime engine for WF as well as seamless communication between the SharePoint Object Model and the actual workflow itself. One of MOSS 2007's biggest drawbacks was its inability to communicate with external processes using Workflow. In SharePoint 2010, this limitation no longer exists, and as you'll see in this chapter, creating and hosting workflows using SharePoint lets you build powerful and scalable business applications easily.

## Workflow Foundation Fundamentals

Before delving into how workflows can be used in SharePoint, you should get familiar with WF and the key concepts and structures involved.

What is a workflow? Perhaps the easiest way to answer this question is to illustrate how a workflow differs from the traditional applications on which we developers spend most of our time.

Workflows are *declarative*—that is, they focus on what should be done rather than how to do it. This has a significant implication: Determining what should be done within an organization is a role performed by business users as opposed to developers, and exactly what should be done often changes as business priorities change. As developers, we're very aware of this problem since it often leads to a constant shifting of deliverables when it comes to developing line-of-business applications. By adopting a workflow-based approach, organizations can change business processes simply by amending the workflows that define them.

Secondly, workflows are long running and stateful. You may be thinking that most business applications are long running and stateful, but there is an important difference with workflows: The management of state and the processing of interactions with running workflows is handled automatically by the runtime engine. Although building business applications that maintain state is common practice, such an implementation will usually involve a lot of custom code. The same is also true for managing interactions with long-running processes. There is a fundamental difference between using workflows and traditional application development, and it all comes down to perspective. When building traditional applications, we focus on handling events and managing data; with workflows, the focus is on the actual process logic with event handling and data management handled automatically.

## Types of Workflow

You can host two types of workflow using SharePoint: sequential workflows and state machine workflows. A sequential workflow is probably the most common type of workflow. State machine workflows are not widely used within organizations.

### Sequential Workflow

This type of workflow commonly manifests itself as a business process and is the muse of many a Visio artist the world over. Sequential workflows generally have a single starting point and follow a series of sequential steps before reaching a discrete stopping point.

Consider the expenses approval workflow, for example. An employee completes an expenses claim document. Completing the document starts an approvals workflow that sees the document being sent to a manager for approval. Once the manager has approved the document, it is automatically passed to the accounts department for payment. When the claim has finally been paid, the workflow is concluded. This business process follows a series of steps toward a final conclusion and is therefore typical of a sequential workflow.

### State Machine Workflow

A common perception, possibly arising from the assumptions of the various process improvement methodologies, assumes that everything can be reduced to a series of well-defined sequential processes. However, the core assumption of the sequential workflow is that a process will progress in a predictable manner toward a well-defined conclusion. In reality, however, this is not always the case.

Consider, for example, the processing of a customer order. A customer places an order for a particular item. The item is not currently in stock and is ordered from a supplier. At the time of ordering, the supplier provides an estimated delivery date, and from this date an expected delivery date for the customer is provided. The supplier ships the goods as expected, which are ultimately forwarded to the final customer. On the surface, this may seem like a perfect candidate for a sequential workflow, but what happens if the customer decides to cancel the order? Or if the supplier can't deliver the goods? Or if the price of the goods changes between the time the customer places the order and the order being fulfilled? Of course, we could create complex sequential workflows to handle these exceptions, but the point is this: Many exceptions can occur; trying to capture all of them and define processes for handling all of them in a model intended to represent a core business process can result in a process that is fraught with minute detail. We've moved from defining what should be done to defining *how* it should be done.

The state machine workflow is a far more powerful tool when it comes to mapping business processes within a software application. It allows us to focus on the key steps while still allowing flexibility in handling unexpected events. In the processing of a customer order example, using a state machine approach, we could use four states:

- **Order Placed**   The customer has placed an order.
- **Order Fulfilled**   The items ordered are in stock and have been allocated to the customer order.
- **Order Received**   The order has been dispatched and the customer has confirmed receipt.
- **Order Cancelled**   The customer has cancelled the order.

Of course, several other business processes are involved in the transitions between these four states, but the important difference is that the actual logic of those business processes does not necessarily need to be well defined. For example, when the customer places an order, if the ordered item is out of stock, most likely a business process would be in place to order it from a supplier. However, the details of that process don't matter to our workflow, because we're simply waiting for the state of the order to be updated to Order Fulfilled after the ordered item becomes available.

As you can see, not all processes are predictable, and sometimes modeling every eventuality simply muddies the waters and creates a rigidity that defeats the objective of workflow. State machine workflows allow you to focus on the goal of declaratively defining business processes while still maintaining operational fidelity.

## Making Workflows Work

Let's move on to consider how workflows are defined and the nuts and bolts of performing useful functions. As you'll see in our demonstration scenario, SharePoint allows you to create workflows in a number of ways. The end result is the same: an eXtensible Application Markup Language (XAML) file containing an XML representation of the steps to be performed and the rules governing their execution. Although the file format used by WF is XAML, workflow files use the extension *.xoml*, allowing design time tools to differentiate between other uses of XAML syntax such as Windows Presentation Framework artifacts. Workflow XAML defines two key elements: workflow rules and workflow activities.

## Workflow Rules

Let's consider an example of a simple workflow that might make use of workflow rules: An employee completes a purchase requisition form, starting a sequential workflow. The workflow rules determine that if the amount specified is less than $5000, the requisition can be approved by any manager within the organization. However, if the amount is greater than $5000, the requisition must be approved by the purchasing manager.

Since the amount is a significant factor in determining what should be done, it's important that it can be changed as part of the workflow definition. To make this possible, workflows can contain rules and define variables for use by these rules. We'll see a practical example of this in our demonstration scenario a bit later in the chapter.

## Workflow Activities

When it comes down to performing actual work, workflows use a series of activities. Each activity effectively defines a method call, and within the method is code that performs a particular function. So, for example, if a requisition is sent to the purchasing manager for approval, a workflow activity creates an e-mail message containing the details of the requisition and then sends it to the manager for approval. When the manager clicks the approval button in the e-mail, the workflow activity completes processing and returns the results to the workflow runtime. The results of workflow activities can be assigned to variables and can therefore be used by workflow rules.

Out of the box, SharePoint 2010 includes many workflow activities. Confusingly, within SharePoint, workflow activities are sometimes known as *actions*, which include the following:

- **CreateItemActivity**   Used to create an item in a SharePoint list.
- **CreateTask**   Used to create a task with specified properties.
- **EmailActivity**   Used to send an e-mail to specified users.
- **SetStateActivity**   Used in state machine workflows to transition between states.

## Custom Workflow Activities

Although more than 80 workflow activities are available in SharePoint 2010, when it comes to building custom applications, you will invariably have to create new activities that are specific to your problem domain.

Custom workflow activities can be used in exactly the same way built-in workflow activities are used; although it's fair to say that a bit more effort is involved in creating a custom workflow activity than in writing a standard function. Workflow activities have to satisfy the needs of two distinct audiences. First, workflow activities need to do something useful at runtime. As developers, we're completely comfortable with writing the code to make our custom activity do something useful. In addition to performing some function, a workflow activity must also provide a useful design-time interface. Business users must be able to configure our custom activity easily within a workflow design tool if its runtime functionality is to be used.

### Runtime Behavior

From a runtime perspective, creating a custom activity is simply a case of creating a new class that is derived from **System.Workflow.ComponentModel.Activity**. Custom code can then be executed simply by overriding the virtual **Execute** method from the **Activity** base class.

### Design-time Behavior

As well as the runtime behavior, you need to consider the design-time experience. The WF framework allows you to define the design time experience in three distinct areas, which are discussed in the sections that follow.

**Adding Validation**   By adding validation to an activity, you can catch configuration errors at design time. To implement this functionality, you create a new class that derives from **System.Workflow.ComponentModel.Compiler.Validator**. As before, by overriding the virtual **Validate** method from the **Validator** base class, you can add your custom validation code.

**Customizing Toolbox Behavior** When you create workflows using Visual Studio, you can add activities to the design surface by dragging them from the toolbox, as you're accustomed to doing with other design-time elements. WF lets you customize the behavior of your activity when it's dragged onto the design surface by implementing a custom **ActivityToolboxItem** class and attaching it to your activity.

**Creating a Custom Designer** As well as validating the configuration of our activity using a validator and automatically setting up default values using a custom toolbox item class, you can also extend the visual representation of your activity by implementing a custom designer. In much the same way as other WF objects, a custom designer can be implemented by deriving a new class from **System.Workflow.ComponentModel.Design.ActivityDesigner**.

By implementing a custom designer, you can not only alter the visual appearance of an activity at design time, but you can also implement logic that determines how your activity behaves on the design surface. For example, you can determine whether child activities can be added to your activity or how many connection points your activity exposes.

## External Activities via Pluggable Workflow Services

A new addition to SharePoint 2010 is the ability to use external activities. Connecting to external systems has always been available as part of the WF framework. However, creating a practical implementation required a few additions to the workflow runtime. In MOSS 2007, extending the workflow runtime was not possible, and therefore implementing the extensions required to support external activities was not possible. Now with SharePoint 2010, communicating with external systems is simply a matter of creating a new class that inherits from the **SPWorkflowExternalDataExchangeService** base class.

The addition of external activities to the SharePoint workflow runtime greatly expands the scope of SharePoint as a workflow host. To pick up on the order fulfillment example used earlier, if a product is out of stock and requires an order to be placed with a supplier, it's now possible for the order to be placed directly from the workflow. Furthermore, any response from the supplier can also be picked up within the workflow and acted upon automatically. Bearing in mind the declarative nature of workflow and the aim of easily allowing business users to model business requirements, this is a very powerful enhancement to the platform.

## Creating Workflows

When it comes to creating workflows for use with SharePoint, you have a choice of a few methods, each targeted to a particular audience and set of requirements.

### Using SharePoint Designer

Creating workflows using SharePoint Designer provides a complete no-code design experience. As you'll see in the upcoming demonstration scenario, workflows can be created by using a series of simple wizard-based steps. In previous versions of SharePoint, workflows created using SharePoint Designer were not portable—that is, if you wanted to use the same workflow on more than one list, you had to re-create it again for each list. With SharePoint 2010, that's no longer the case; workflows can be easily used across multiple lists and can also be exported for further enhancement using Visual Studio 2010.

## Using Visio 2010

**New in 2010**

The ability to use Visio 2010 to create workflows is a new feature in SharePoint 2010. Visio is undoubtedly the tool of choice when it comes to documenting business processes, and now, by adopting the Microsoft SharePoint Workflow template, workflows created in Visio can be imported into SharePoint Designer for implementation. Furthermore, by using Visio Services, imported workflows can make use of the Visio model to provide a runtime status indicator.

As well as importing workflows from Visio, you can also export workflows from SharePoint Designer in a format that can be modified in Visio and then re-imported.

## Using Visual Studio 2010

Using SharePoint Designer and Visio 2010 to create workflows is undoubtedly the easiest way to go for the majority of cases. But what happens when you need a bit more flexibility? You can use Visual Studio 2010 to take advantage of the entire range of functionality exposed by the WF framework.

Some features aren't available outside of Visual Studio, such as the ability to use pluggable workflow services or the ability to use the **CodeActivity** which allows developers to execute arbitrary code easily without having to create a custom activity. Another important feature that is available only to Visual Studio users is the ability to create state machine workflows.

# Demonstration Scenario

There's a lot to demonstrate when it comes to workflows. Consider this demonstration scenario:

> You've been asked to design and build an online ordering system for an electronic component manufacturer. To comply with international regulations relating to environmental protection, each product available for order must have achieved compliance with the appropriate standards for the country into which it will be sold. Determining compliance involves performing a series of calculations to determine the level of specific substances within the finished product. Since the calculation is relatively complex, it will be performed by a separate system. Once the calculation has been performed, the results should be sent to an environmental control officer for verification.
>
> In addition to the environmental control procedure, products being offered for sale must also follow a specific publishing process before being included in the site. New products will be added by the sales department. So that relevant technical information is available, details of the product will be passed to the engineering department, which will update the product record with appropriate details. With these details in place, the marketing department will then be responsible for collating and attaching the appropriate artwork before the product is sent for final approval by the online sales manager.
>
> From this scenario, an appropriate design might involve three sequential workflows:
>
> - The first workflow will implement the environmental control procedure.
> - The second will implement the publishing procedure.
> - The third will do the work of physically making the product available for sale once the environmental procedure and the publishing procedure have completed successfully.

**TIP** All three processes could be implemented using a single workflow. However, in my experience, there's only one constant when it comes to business processes and that's change. In the interests of reuse and maintainability, three separate workflows are being created, since each addresses a discrete business process. This means that if the environmental control process changes, for example, only that workflow needs to be changed regardless of where it's used across the organization. Had the process been incorporated into many separate workflows, making changes would be time-consuming and could lead to inconsistent results. It's always a good idea to limit the scope of a workflow to a particular business process when possible.

## Prerequisites

Before we can demonstrate workflows in SharePoint 2010, let's create a sample site collection to hold the appropriate data.

1. In SharePoint Designer, choose File | Sites | New Blank Web Site.
2. Type this location for the new web site: **http://localhost/chapter11**.
3. With our new blank web site in place, we can start defining the data structures that are required by our application. From the Site Objects pane, select Site Columns:
4. From the Columns ribbon, choose New Column | Currency. In the Create a Site Column dialog that appears, type the name **Unit Price**. Choose the New Group radio button and type the name **Online Sales Columns** in the text box. The completed dialog should look like this:
5. Now we'll create a few new columns. Choose New Column | Hyperlink Or Picture from the Columns ribbon. In the Create a Site Column dialog that appears, type the name **Product Image**. Then choose New Column | Yes/No (checkbox) and type the name **Environmental Compliance**. Then choose New Column | Multiple Lines Of Text and type the name **Technical Details**. Then choose New Column | Single Line Of Text and type the name **Product Name**.

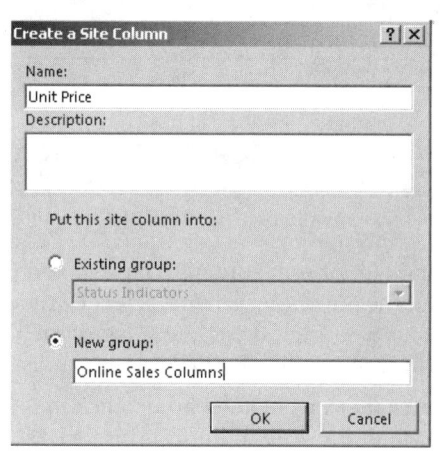

6. Now we'll make use of these site columns to define a new Product content type to hold details of our product catalog. From the Site Objects pane, select Content Types. From the Content Types ribbon, in the New section, click the Content Type button to define a new content type. In the Create a Content Type dialog that appears, type **Product** in the Name field. In the Select A Parent Content Type section, from the Select Parent Content Type drop-down, choose List Content Types. In the Select Parent Content Type drop-down, choose Item. Select the New Group radio button, and in the text box, enter the name **Online Shopping Content Types**. The completed dialog should look as illustrated:

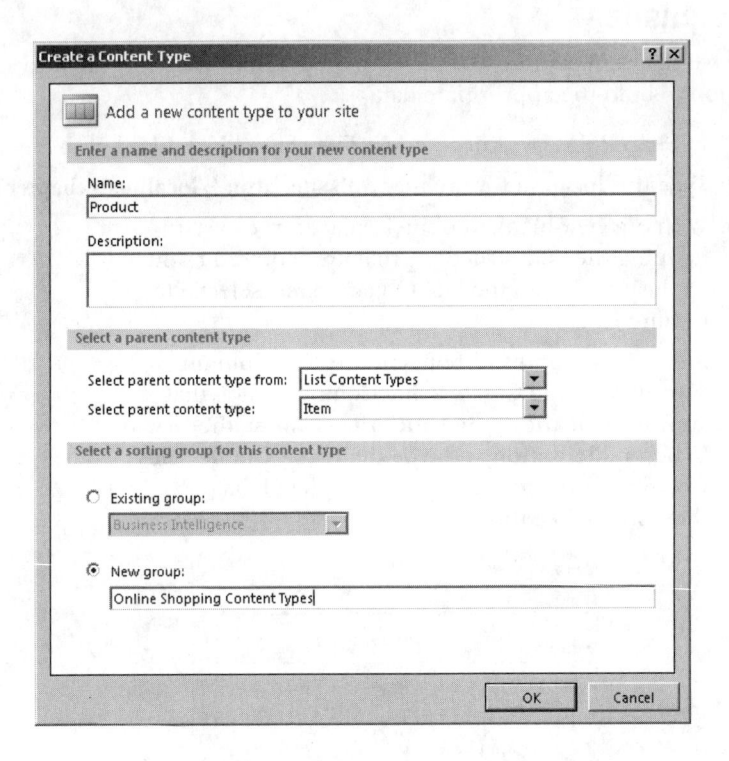

7. The next step in creating our custom content type is to add the site columns that we defined earlier. From the Site Objects pane, select Content Types and then select the Product content type from the content types list. Then, on the Content Types ribbon, in the Edit section, click Edit Columns.

8. To attach the site columns that we created earlier, click the Add Existing Site Column button on the Columns ribbon. Repeat this process to include all the columns in the Online Sales Columns group that you added in steps 4 and 5. Once all columns have been added, the completed list should look as follows:

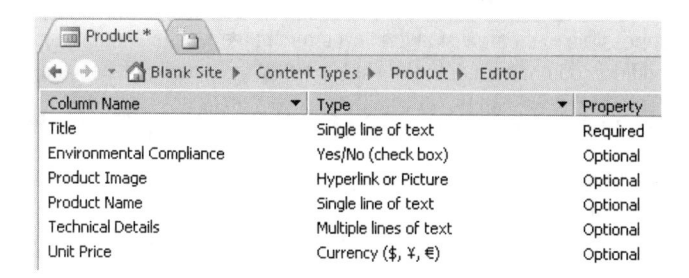

| Column Name | Type | Property |
|---|---|---|
| Title | Single line of text | Required |
| Environmental Compliance | Yes/No (check box) | Optional |
| Product Image | Hyperlink or Picture | Optional |
| Product Name | Single line of text | Optional |
| Technical Details | Multiple lines of text | Optional |
| Unit Price | Currency ($, ¥, €) | Optional |

9. Click the Save icon in the upper-left corner of the SharePoint Designer window to commit the changes to the Product content type.

10. Our next step is to create a list using our custom content type. The list will be used to store our product data. From the Site Objects pane, select Lists and Libraries. From the Lists and Libraries ribbon, select SharePoint List | Custom List, as shown:

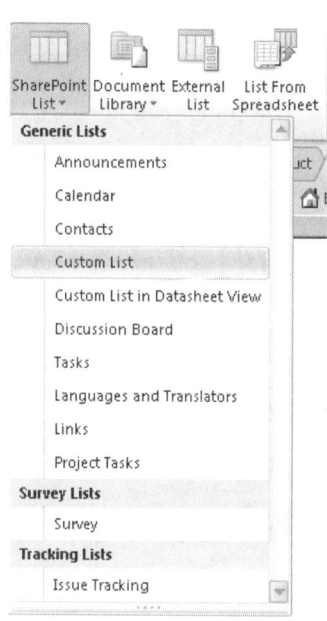

11. In the Create List Or Document Library dialog, enter **Products** as the name and then click OK to create the list.

12. The final step in preparing our demonstration site is to attach our Product content type to our Products list. Double-click the Products list to manage the list settings. In the Settings section, check the Allow Management Of Content Types checkbox.

13. In the Content Types section, click the Add button, and then select the Product content type from the list. Highlight the Item content type and then click Show on New Menu from the ribbon. Removing the content type from the new menu will prevent content of type Item from being created using the user interface.

14. Click the Save icon to commit our changes to the Products list.

## Designing a Workflow Using Visio 2010

Visio 2010 includes a new template for creating SharePoint workflows. By using the Microsoft SharePoint Workflow template, designed workflows can be exported from Visio into SharePoint Designer for further configuration. Furthermore, regardless of whether a workflow was created using Visio originally, SharePoint Designer provides the facility to export the workflow in a format that can be imported into Visio for refinement.

> **NOTE** It's not possible to create Visio Workflow Interchange files for Visual Studio generated workflows. These workflows do not appear in the Workflows list in SharePoint Designer.

## Using the Microsoft SharePoint Workflow Template

Our scenario calls for three workflows: an environmental control procedure, a publishing procedure, and an advert promotion procedure. To demonstrate the creation of workflows using Visio 2010, we'll implement the publishing procedure.

To recap the procedure:

New products will be added by the sales department. So that relevant technical information is available, details of the product will be passed to the engineering department, which will update the product record with appropriate details. With these details in place, the marketing department will then be responsible for collating and attaching the appropriate artwork before the product is sent for final approval by the online sales manager.

Let's look at how this can be modeled using Visio:

1. Open Visio 2010. From the Flowchart template category, select the Microsoft SharePoint Workflow template. Click Create to create a new document based on the template.

2. The first thing we need to add are terminators that denote the start and endpoints for our workflow. Drag Start and Terminate shapes onto the page, as shown next:

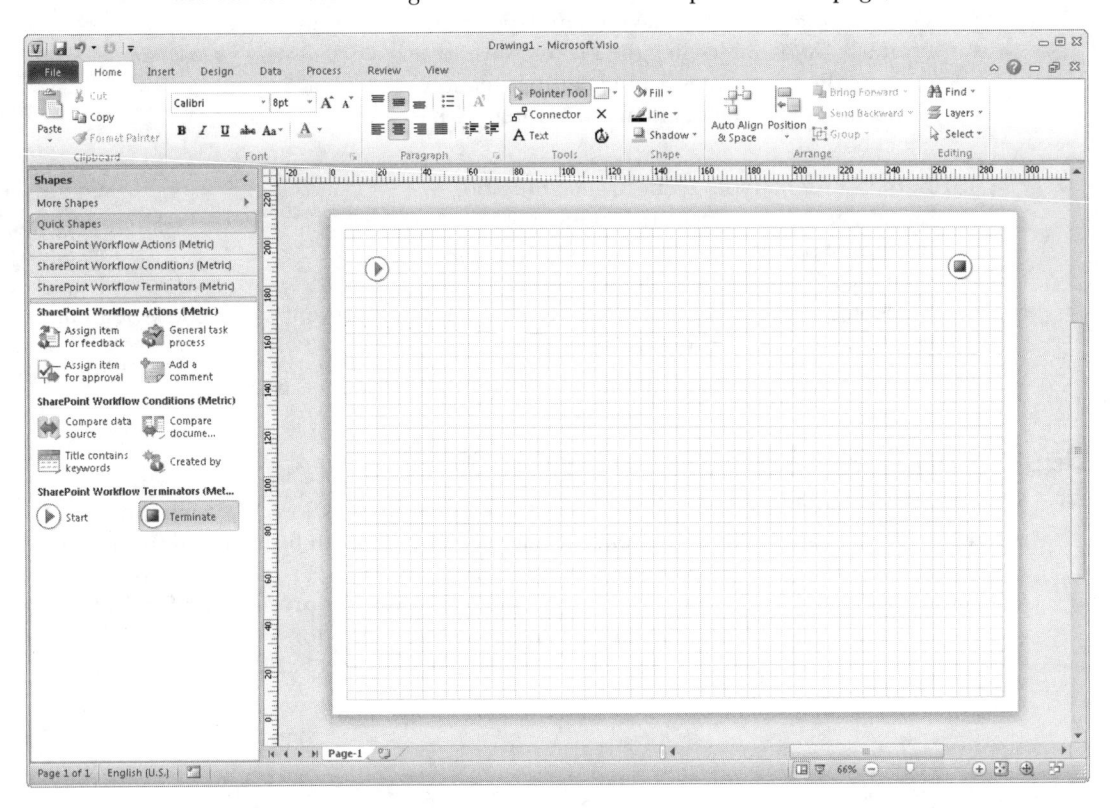

3. Our scenario specifies that the engineering department will provide appropriate technical details for our product record. We want to create a task requesting further information and assign that task to the engineering department for completion. To model this, we can use the Collect Data From A User shape. Click the SharePoint Workflow Actions header, and then drag a Collect Data From A User shape onto the page. Double-click the shape and type the description **Collect Technical Details from Engineering Department**.

4. The next step in our process is to have the marketing department provide artwork for our product record. Again we can model this using the Collect Data From A User shape. This time type the description **Collect Product Image from Marketing Department**.

5. The final step in our process is to assign the completed product record to the online sales manager for approval. Since we don't require any content to be added this time, a more appropriate shape to model this interaction is the Assign Item For Approval shape in the SharePoint Workflow Actions stencil. Drop the shape on the page and type the description **Assign to Online Sales Manager for Approval**.

6. Now that we have the steps of our workflow laid out, our next step is to connect them using the standard Visio Connector tool on the Home ribbon in the Tools section. Use the connector tool to join up the steps of the process. The completed workflow will look like this:

7. With our Visio model complete, we can create a Visio Workflow Interchange (.vwi) file that can be imported into SharePoint Designer. Select the Process ribbon. Before exporting a workflow, we should check for any errors. Click the Check Diagram button to validate our model. All being well, a dialog will confirm that "No issues were found in the current document." We can then move on to create the interchange file by clicking the Export button. Name the file by typing **PublishingProcedure.vwi**.

8. We're done with Visio for now. Click the Save icon in the upper-left corner and save the document as **PublishingProcedure.vsd**.

## Implementing a Visio Workflow Using SharePoint Designer

In the preceding section, you saw how to model a workflow using Visio and create an interchange file that can be imported into SharePoint Designer. In this section, we'll move on to flesh out the logic defined in Visio using the built-in workflow activities available via SharePoint Designer.

1. In SharePoint Designer, select Workflows from the Site Objects pane.
2. In the Workflows ribbon's Manage section, click the Import From Visio button.
3. Browse to the PublishingProcedure.vwi file that we created in the preceding section. Click Next to import the file.

4. In the Import Workflow From Visio Drawing dialog, type the Workflow name as **Product Publishing**. Two different workflow types are available: List Workflow and Reusable Workflow. The main difference between these workflows is that the List Workflow is attached to a particular list and cannot be used by multiple lists, whereas a reusable workflow can be bound to any number of lists or content types. List workflows provide comparable functionality to SharePoint Designer workflows in MOSS 2007. Choose Reusable Workflow as the type, and then from the content types drop-down, select Product. The completed dialog will look like the following illustration. Click Finish to complete the import process.

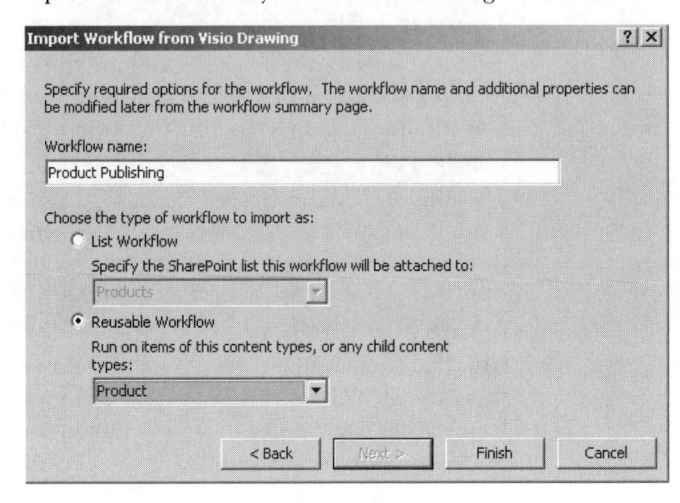

Once our Visio model has been imported, SharePoint Designer will create a new workflow named Product Publishing and will automatically open the workflow editor, shown next, where we can complete the configuration of the workflow.

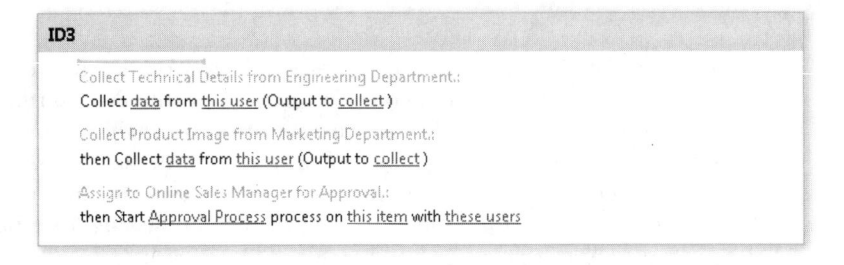

5. The logic steps from our Visio model have been automatically inserted into our SharePoint workflow, and hyperlinked terms in each step allow us to finalize the configuration. In the Collect Technical Details from Engineering Department step, click the *data* hyperlink so that we can define exactly what data should be collected. In the Custom Task Wizard that appears, click Next to begin creating a new task.

6. Name the new task **Collect Technical Details**. Click Next to add fields for the data in which we're interested.

7. Add a field and name it **Technical Data**. Set the Information Type to Multiple lines of text. Click Next, accept the default columns settings, and then click Finish to add the field.

8. Click Finish to complete the Custom Task Wizard.

## Using Workflow Variables

Now that we've created a custom task to capture data, we need a way to retrieve the data that we've captured so that we can do something useful with it. As its name suggests, the Custom Task Wizard creates a task with a custom form. When a user completes the form, any data captured is stored in the associated task. The output of this step is an identifier for the task item that was created. As you'll see later, we can use this to pick up a reference to the task and from there access any data that was captured in our custom form.

You'll remember reading about workflow rules and variables. Since we need to use our task identifier in another step of our workflow, we must create a variable and assign the output to it.

1. To add a new variable, click the Local Variables button from the Workflow ribbon. Add a new variable named TechnicalDetailsTaskId with a type of List Item Id, as shown next. Click OK.

2. To assign the output of our Collect Technical Details task to our new variable, click the *(Output to collect)* hyperlink and then select Variable:TechnicalDetailsTaskId.

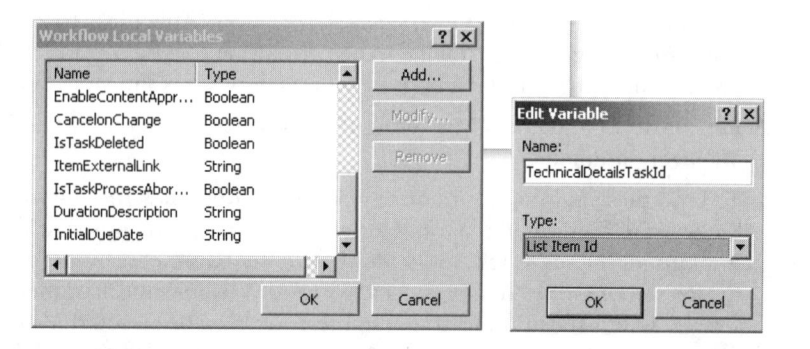

3. Use the Custom Task Wizard to add a Collect Product Image from Marketing Department step. This time, add a field and name it **Product Image** of type Hyperlink or Picture and uncheck the Allow Blank Values option in Column settings. Add a variable named **ProductImageTaskId** to store the output of the task.

4. Now that we've configured our data capture tasks, the only item remaining is the approval action. Click the *this item* hyperlink to select the items that should be the subject of the approval process. In our case, it should be the *Current Item*.

5. With these configuration changes in place, our revised workflow should look like this:

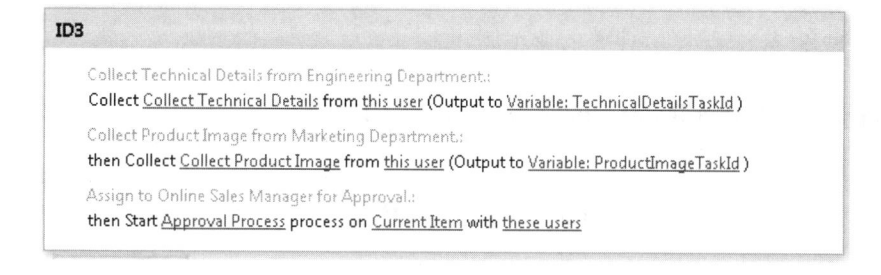

**ID3**

Collect Technical Details from Engineering Department.:
Collect <u>Collect Technical Details</u> from <u>this user</u> (Output to <u>Variable: TechnicalDetailsTaskId</u> )

Collect Product Image from Marketing Department.:
then Collect <u>Collect Product Image</u> from <u>this user</u> (Output to <u>Variable: ProductImageTaskId</u> )

Assign to Online Sales Manager for Approval.:
then Start <u>Approval Process</u> process on <u>Current Item</u> with <u>these users</u>

## Using Initiation and Association Forms

You'll notice that a few properties still need to be configured. These properties contain details of the users to which each task should be assigned. Generally speaking, properties such as these, which are likely to change over time, should be user-configurable—that is, the user should be able to change them without having to edit the underlying workflow. SharePoint workflows provide two forms for user configuration: the Association form, which is presented when a workflow is attached to a list, and the Initiation form, which is presented when a workflow is manually started.

There's one thing to bear in mind when using the initiation form: it's not shown if the workflow is started automatically. So, for example, if we created a workflow that was set to start every time an item changed, the initiation form would never be shown.

In the case of our workflow, an association form is a more appropriate choice, because it allows us to define parameters that can be set at the list level.

1. To define a parameter that appears on an association form, click the Initiation Form Parameters button in the ribbon. Add a new field named **Engineering Department** with an Information type of Person or Group. In the Collect From Parameter During drop-down, select Association (Attaching To A List). In the Column Settings dialog, uncheck the Allow Blank Values option and select the All Users radio button in the Choose From section. Click Finish to add the parameter.

2. Repeat step 1 and add a **Marketing Department** parameter and an **Online Sales Manager** parameter.

3. To bind these parameters to our workflow actions, click the *this user* hyperlink. Since we're binding to a parameter rather than an actual user, select Workflow Lookup for a User. Click Add to configure the parameter binding. In the Lookup for Person or Group dialog, select Workflow Variable and Parameters as the Data source. Our association form parameters can now be selected from the Field From Source drop-down. Select the appropriate parameter and then click OK to complete the binding.

4. Repeat step 3 to bind all association form parameters to our workflow actions. The completed workflow should look as illustrated:

```
ID3
    Collect Technical Details from Engineering Department.:
    Collect Collect Technical Details from Parameter: Engineering Department (Output to Variable: TechnicalDetailsTaskId )

    Collect Product Image from Marketing Department.:
    then Collect Collect Product Image from Parameter: Marketing Department (Output to Variable: ProductImageTaskId )

    Assign to Online Sales Manager for Approval.:
    then Start Approval Process process on Current Item with Parameter: Online Sales Manager
```

## Using the SharePoint Designer Lookup Dialog

Although we've configured the actions that were imported from Visio, the end result of our workflow in its current state won't be quite as we expected. Although we're collecting data from engineering and marketing, we're not actually attaching that data to our product, it's stored in the custom tasks only. To fix this problem and achieve the desired result, we need to add a few more actions.

Moving the mouse to the end of the list of workflow steps will show an orange cursor. Click the cursor to open a text box that can be used to search for the action that we want to add next. (This cursor appears between each workflow action and before the first action, so we can add actions wherever we need them.)

1. Type **Set f** and then press the ENTER key to insert a Set Field in Current Item action. Configure the field as Technical Details and then click the *value* hyperlink. Click the fx button to display the Lookup dialog.

2. You'll remember that the data entered in our custom task forms is stored in the task. Using the Lookup dialog, we can extract this data using the ID of the task in which we're interested. Set the data source to Tasks. When a workflow is associated with a list, one of the mandatory parameters is the name of a task list to be used by the workflow for creating tasks. This task list can be referenced using the Tasks data source.

3. In the Field From Source drop-down, select Technical Data. The column contains the details that a user enters in the custom Collect Technical Details form.

    Since the data source to which we're binding contains potentially more than one item, we need to filter it to return only the specific task in which we're interested. We created variables to store the output of our custom task actions earlier in this chapter, and we can use these variables here to pick up references to the appropriate tasks.

4. In the Find the List Item section, set the Field to ID and then click the fx button to show the Lookup dialog. In that dialog, set the Data Source to Workflow Variables and Parameters and the Field From Source to Variable: TechnicalDetailsTaskId. Since we intend to use this to look up an item, set the Return Field As to Item Id, as illustrated:

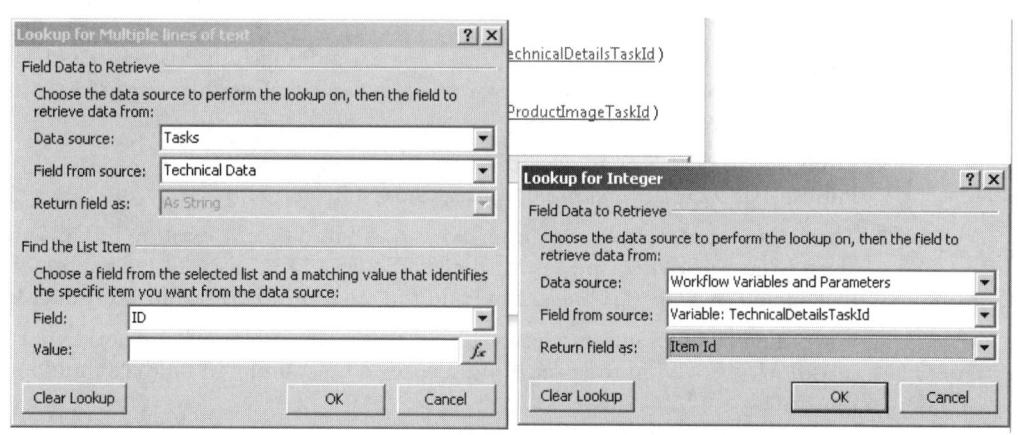

5. We've added this action at the end of the workflow when really it makes more sense to attach this data before sending the product record for approval. To move the action up, highlight it and then click the Move Up button on the Workflow ribbon.

6. Add a new Set Field in Current Item action directly underneath the action. Use the Lookup dialog to attach our Product Image data.
7. Click Save to commit these configuration changes.

We've now completed our first workflow using SharePoint Designer and Visio. The finished workflow should look as shown:

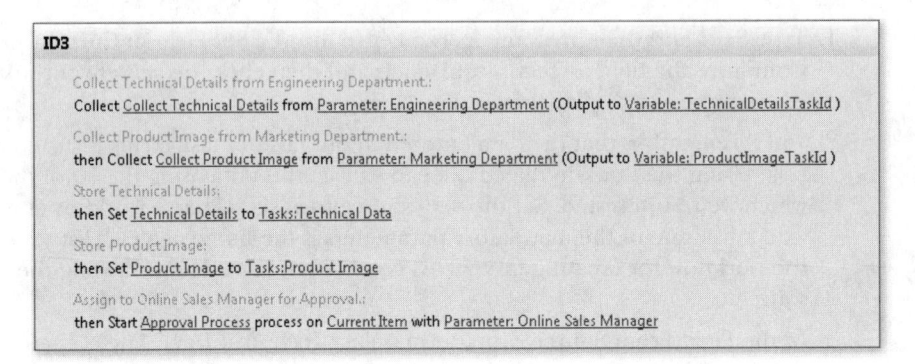

```
ID3
    Collect Technical Details from Engineering Department.:
    Collect Collect Technical Details from Parameter: Engineering Department (Output to Variable: TechnicalDetailsTaskId )
    Collect Product Image from Marketing Department.:
    then Collect Collect Product Image from Parameter: Marketing Department (Output to Variable: ProductImageTaskId )
    Store Technical Details:
    then Set Technical Details to Tasks:Technical Data
    Store Product Image:
    then Set Product Image to Tasks:Product Image
    Assign to Online Sales Manager for Approval.:
    then Start Approval Process process on Current Item with Parameter: Online Sales Manager
```

## Using Visio Services to Visualize Workflow State

In addition to the actions that we defined in our original Visio model, we've also included a few new actions to attach the captured data to our product item. We can export our updated workflow to Visio so that we can update our diagram with appropriate descriptions for these new actions. Once our model is updated, we can use it to provide status visualization for our workflow.

1. In SharePoint Designer, select Workflows from the Site Objects pane. Select the Product Publishing workflow from the list.
2. From the Workflows ribbon, click the Export To Visio button. Save the interchange file as **PublishingProcedure.vwi**.
3. Open Visio 2010, and then either open the saved PublishingProcedure.vsd document that we created earlier or create a new document from the Microsoft SharePoint Workflow template.
4. From the Process ribbon, click the Import button. Browse to the PublishingProcedure.vwi file that we exported in step 2.
5. The revised workflow will be imported and will update our existing model where appropriate. Add descriptions for the two Set Field In Current Item actions. The first should be **Store Technical Data** and the second should be **Store Product Image**.
6. With these changes made, we can tidy up the layout if appropriate and export our workflow as we did in the preceding section. The completed model should look as illustrated:

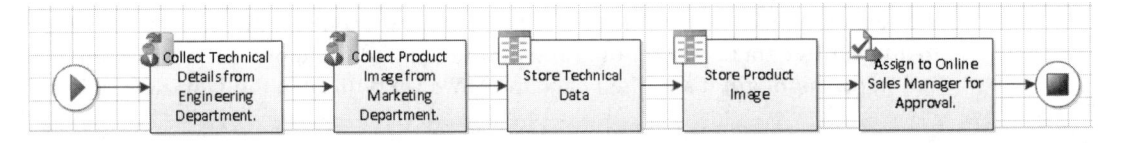

```
▶ → [Collect Technical Details from Engineering Department.] → [Collect Product Image from Marketing Department.] → [Store Technical Data] → [Store Product Image] → [Assign to Online Sales Manager for Approval.] → ■
```

7. Switch back to SharePoint Designer to import the changes. Select the Product Publishing workflow and then click the Import From Visio button in the Workflows ribbon to import the changes. You'll notice that, this time, SharePoint Designer recognizes that the interchange file relates to an existing workflow, and rather than prompt you for details to create a new workflow, it automatically upgrades the existing workflow with the changes.

8. To use our Visio diagram to provide status visualization for our workflow, we need to check the Show Workflow Visualization On Status Page checkbox in the Settings section, as illustrated. Click the Save icon in the upper-left corner to save the changes to the Product Publishing workflow.

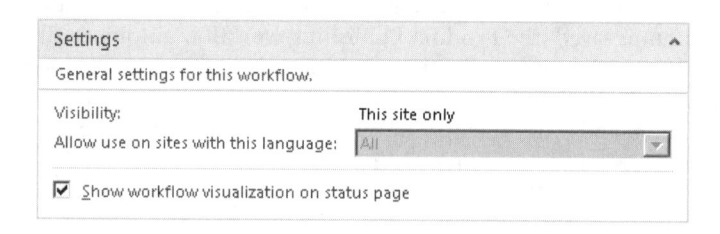

```
Settings                                                              ▲
General settings for this workflow.
Visibility:                              This site only
Allow use on sites with this language:   All
☑ Show workflow visualization on status page
```

9. Before we can use the workflow, we need to publish it. After you publish the workflow, SharePoint Designer will automatically generate any required InfoPath forms. If the workflow being published is already attached to a list or content type, all new instances of the workflow will use the new published version, while currently running instances will continue to use the previous version. To publish our Product Publishing workflow, click the Publish button in the Workflow ribbon.

## Associating Reusable Workflows

With our new workflow published, we can now associate it with our Product content type. You'll remember that when we created our workflow, we specified that it should target the Product content type. Even though we specified this targeting, the workflow isn't bound to any content type until we specifically bind it. When creating a workflow, the main reason for setting a content type target is to ensure that the fields of that content type are available as values within the workflow logic. For example, we specified Product so that we could make use of the Product Image and Technical Data fields.

1. To associate our workflow with the Product content type, click the Associate To Content Type button in the ribbon. You'll notice that the only option available in the drop-down list is Product. Since our workflow targets the Product content type, only content types that are derived from Product or the Product content type itself are valid selections. Select Product to begin the association process.

2. The association process is performed using the SharePoint user interface. Since we want our workflow to start automatically when a new item is created, check the appropriate start option and then click Next to continue.

3. SharePoint Designer automatically generates a custom association form based on the parameters that we specified in our workflow. Since we're using a blank site, we don't have specific user accounts for each of the three departments. We can use

the built-in Approvers group for the purposes of this demo. Complete the form as illustrated, and then click Save to complete the association.

To see our new workflow in action, browse to the Products list and add a new item. Once the item is saved, the Product Publishing workflow automatically starts. By clicking the In Progress link in the Product Publishing column, we can see more detail on the workflow progress, including our Visio visualization, as illustrated. We can click the tasks that are created and enter the appropriate information to complete our workflow. Notice that the progress is indicated on our Visio visualization.

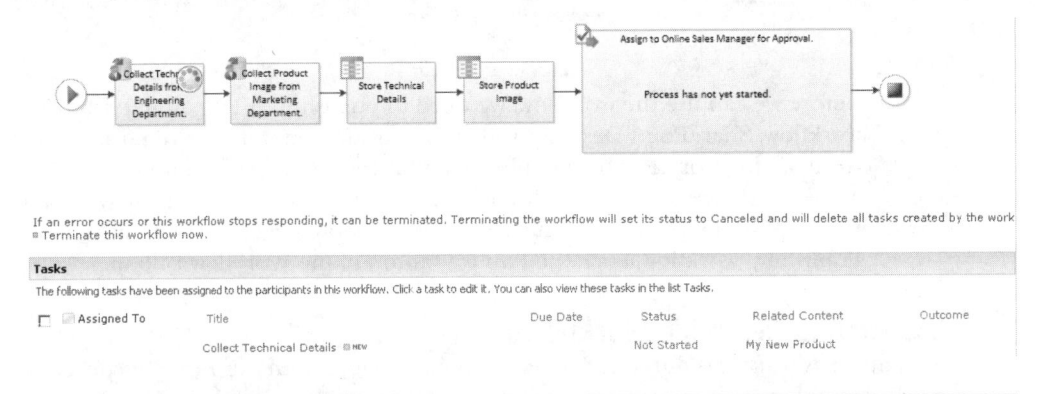

**NOTE** You'll notice that the New Item form contains text boxes for each of the fields in our content type. Of course, this is perfectly reasonable in most situations, but in our case, we don't want the Product Image and Technical Details fields to be populated, because these are completed by the appropriate department. As described in more detail in Chapter 5, we can easily customize this form to suit our requirements using InfoPath.

# Creating a Pluggable Workflow Service

In this section, we'll build the environmental control procedure as defined in our demonstration scenario. Here's a recap:

> To comply with international regulations relating to environmental protection, each product available for order must have achieved compliance with the appropriate standards for the country into which it will be sold. Determining compliance involves performing a series of calculations to determine the level of specific substances within the finished product. Since the calculation is relatively complex, it will be performed by a separate system. Once the calculation has been performed, the results should be sent to an environmental control officer for verification.

We can see that our workflow should make use of calculation facilities provided by an external system. Since the calculation process is long running, an asynchronous pattern will be used—that is, a request will be sent to the external system, the system will acknowledge the request, and it will then begin performing the relevant work in a separate asynchronous process. Once the system has completed the prescribed work, it will communicate the results to the original caller.

## Creating a Sample WCF Calculation Service

We'll implement our demo calculation service using Windows Communication Foundation (WCF). WCF itself is a separate topic and in-depth coverage is out of scope of this chapter, but I'll use it for this example since it is one of the primary mechanisms used for communicating with external systems.

Since we don't actually need to perform any calculations, we'll create a Windows Forms client application that receives incoming requests and writes them to a list. We'll then be able to select requests from the list and manually submit a response to the workflow.

To make this work, we need two WCF services—one in the Windows Forms client to receive the calculation request, and another within SharePoint to receive the response from the calculation service. We'll create the Windows Forms client first.

### Create a Windows Forms Client Hosting a WCF Service

1. In Visual Studio 2010, choose File | New | Project. From the New Project dialog, select Visual C# | Windows | Windows Forms Application, as shown. Name the project **DemoCalculationEngine**.

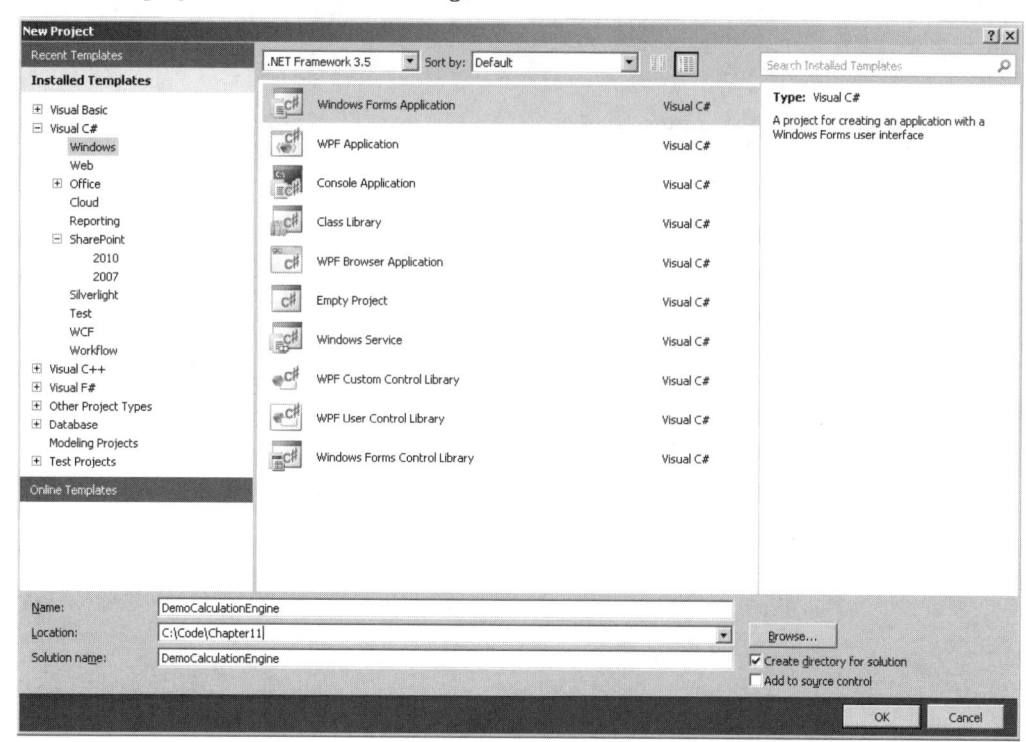

2. Our user interface will be very simple. Add a DataGridView control and a Button. Anchor them appropriately so that they resize with the form. Set the Text property of the Button control to Send Result.

3. With our user interface complete, the next step is to add a WCF service to receive the calculation requests. To add a new item to the project, press CTRL-SHIFT-A (alternatively, choose Project | Add New Item). In the Add New Item dialog, select Visual C# Items | WCF Service. Name the new service class **CalculationRequestService.cs**.

4. Since we're creating a WCF service, Visual Studio will add two new files to the solution. The first file, CalculationRequestService.cs, contains the implementation of the service. The second file, ICalculationRequestService.cs, contains the service contract definition for the service. We'll start by defining the contract since we can easily use Visual Studio to create a default implementation. In the ICalculationRequestService.cs file, add the following code:

```
using System;
using System.Collections.Generic;
using System.Linq;
using System.Runtime.Serialization;
using System.ServiceModel;
using System.Text;

namespace DemoCalculationEngine
{

    [ServiceContract]
    public interface ICalculationRequestService
    {
       [OperationContract]
        bool SubmitCalculation(CalculationRequest request);
    }

    [DataContract]
    public class CalculationRequest
    {
        [DataMember(IsRequired = true)]
        public Guid SiteId { get; set; }

        [DataMember(IsRequired = true)]
        public Guid WebId { get; set; }

        [DataMember(IsRequired = true)]
        public Guid InstanceId { get; set; }
```

```
            [DataMember(IsRequired = true)]
            public string ProductName { get; set; }
        }
    }
```

5. With our service contract and data contract defined, we can move on to focus on the implementation of the service. In the CalculationRequestService.cs file, add the following code:

```
namespace DemoCalculationEngine
{
    public class CalculationRequestService : ICalculationRequestService
    {
        public bool SubmitCalculation(CalculationRequest request)
        {
            Program.theForm.SaveRequest(request);
            return true;
        }
    }
}
```

**TIP** To create a default implementation of an interface automatically using Visual Studio, right-click the name of the interface and then select Implement Interface | Implement Interface from the context menu.

Our service implementation probably warrants some explanation. Since we're going to write incoming requests to the data grid that we added to our user interface, we need to do this using the same thread that's running the user interface to avoid cross-threading issues. In effect, our service does nothing more than write the requests to the user interface.

6. You may notice that the code in our SubmitCalculation method contains a "Form has not yet been defined" error. To fix this, add the following code to Program.cs:

```
using System;
using System.ServiceModel;
using System.Windows.Forms;

namespace DemoCalculationEngine
{
    static class Program
    {
        public static Form1 theForm;

        [STAThread]
        static void Main()
```

```
                    {
                        using (ServiceHost host = newServiceHost
                                (typeof(CalculationRequestService)))
                        {
                            host.Open();
                            Application.EnableVisualStyles();
                            Application.SetCompatibleTextRenderingDefault(false);
                            theForm = new Form1();
                            Application.Run(theForm);
                        }
                    }
                }
            }
```

7. As is too often the case, with that error fixed, you'll notice that we now have a different problem. SaveRequest is not defined on Form1. So add the following code to form1.cs to complete our implementation:

```
using System.ComponentModel;
using System.Windows.Forms;

namespace DemoCalculationEngine
{
  public partial class Form1 : Form
  {
    private delegate void SaveRequestMethod(CalculationRequest request);
    private BindingList<CalculationRequest> _calculationList;

    public Form1()
    {
      InitializeComponent();
      _calculationList = new BindingList<CalculationRequest>();
      dataGridView1.DataSource = _calculationList;
      dataGridView1.SelectionMode = DataGridViewSelectionMode.FullRowSelect;
      dataGridView1.MultiSelect = false;
      dataGridView1.AllowUserToAddRows = false;
    }

    internal void SaveRequest(CalculationRequest request)
    {
      if (this.InvokeRequired)
      {
        SaveRequestMethod theDelegate = new SaveRequestMethod(this.SaveRequest);
        this.Invoke(theDelegate, new object[] { request });
      }
```

```
      else
      {
        _calculationList.Add(request);
      }
    }
  }
}
```

We can make use of the WCF test tools that are provided with Visual Studio to check that everything is working properly. Open up a Visual Studio command prompt and type the following:

```
C:\Program Files (x86)\Microsoft Visual Studio 10.0\VC>WCFTestClient
```

This will start the WCFTestClient.exe application that we can use to submit requests to our calculation engine.

Before we can connect, we need to know the endpoint URI for our service. This can be found in the app.config file for our client application under system.serviceModel | Services | service | host | baseAddress. The URI will be similar to this: http://localhost:8732/Design_Time_Addresses/DemoCalculationEngine/CalculationRequestService/. Now, if we run the client application, we can choose File | Add Service in the WCFTestClient tool to generate a proxy that will allow us to send a test request. If all is well, we'll see the requests being queued in our client app, as shown next:

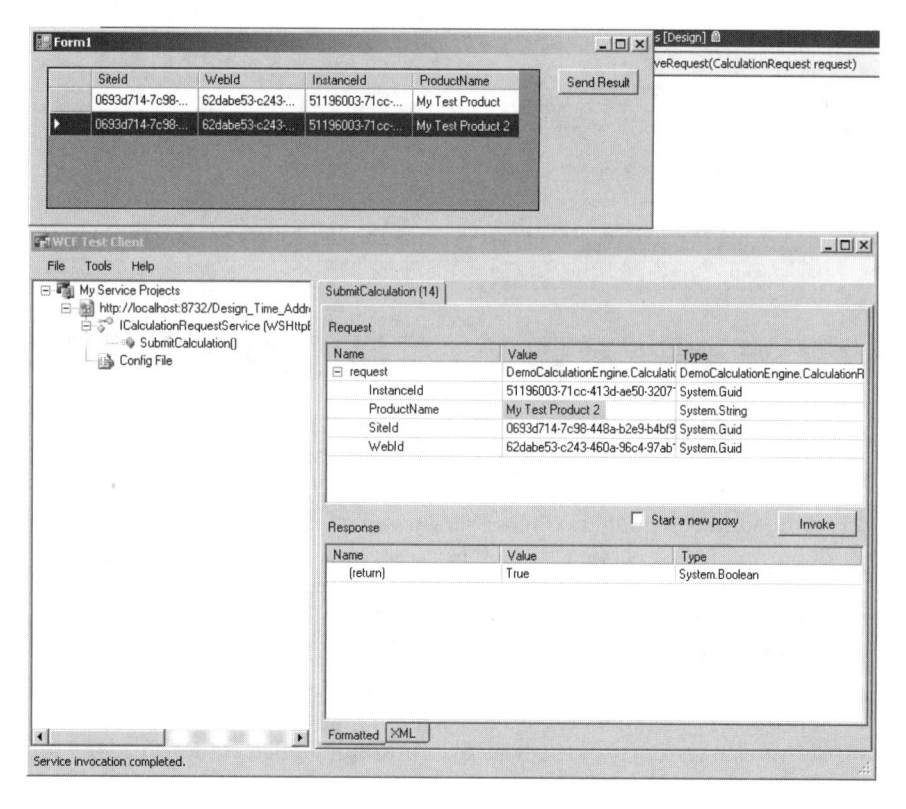

## Add a SharePoint-Hosted WCF Service

Now that our client WCF service is up and running, our next logical step is to implement a WCF service that can be hosted within SharePoint to receive calculation results from our client application.

1. We'll make use of the packaging and deployment capabilities of Visual Studio to set up our WCF service on SharePoint. In Visual Studio, choose File | New | Project and then from the New Project dialog, choose SharePoint | 2010 | Empty SharePoint Project. Name the new project **WorkflowDemonstration** as illustrated.

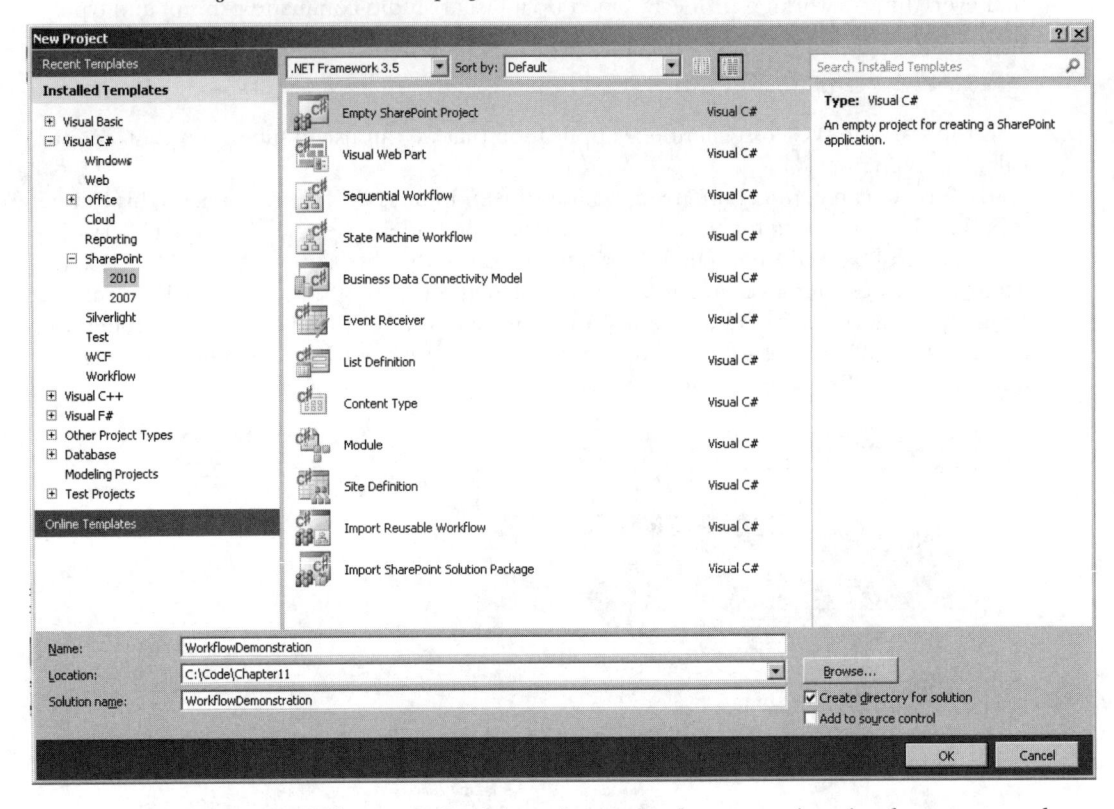

2. Set the local site to use for debugging to the demonstration site that we created earlier: http://localhost/chapter11. We need to deploy as a farm solution since the components that we're about to add are not supported in a sandbox.

3. At the time of writing, no SharePoint specific template item is available for deploying a WCF service, so we have to set up the solution file manually. The first thing we need to do is to add a new WCF Service item. Press CTRL-SHIFT-A to show the Add New Item dialog. Select Visual C# | WCF Service. Name the new class **CalculationResultService.cs**.

4. As before, Visual Studio will add two new files to our solution together with the appropriate references required to support WCF. Again, we'll start off by defining our service contract. In the ICalculationResultService.cs file, enter the following:

```
using System;
using System.Runtime.Serialization;
using System.ServiceModel;

namespace WorkflowDemonstration
{
  [ServiceContract]
  public interface ICalculationResultService
  {
    [OperationContract]
    bool ProcessCalculationResult(CalculationResult result);
  }

  [DataContract]
  public class CalculationResult
  {
    [DataMember(IsRequired = true)]
    public string Result { get; set; }
    [DataMember(IsRequired = true)]
    public Guid SiteId { get; set; }
    [DataMember(IsRequired = true)]
    public Guid WebId { get; set; }
    [DataMember(IsRequired = true)]
    public Guid InstanceId { get; set; }
  }
}
```

5. Since our service will ultimately send events to workflows hosted on the SharePoint workflow runtime, we have a few things to do before we can fully implement the required functionality. For now, we'll create a stub method based on our interface. In the CalculationResultService.cs file, enter the following:

```
using System;
using System.Collections.Generic;
using System.Linq;
using System.Runtime.Serialization;
using System.ServiceModel;
using System.Text;

namespace WorkflowDemonstration
{
 [AspNetCompatibilityRequirements(RequirementsMode = AspNetCompatibilityRequirements-
Mode.Allowed)]
  public class CalculationResultService : ICalculationResultService
  {
    public bool ProcessCalculationResult(CalculationResult result)
```

```
    {
      return true;
    }
  }
}
```

**Hosting an .svc File in SharePoint**   To make our service available for our client application, we need to host it somewhere. Since SharePoint runs on Internet Information Server (IIS), we need to create a .svc file with details of our service implementation. Of course, before we create the file, we need somewhere to put it; for the purposes of this demonstration, we'll use a custom subfolder within the %SPROOT%\TEMPLATE\Layouts folder. We can set up this folder automatically using our Visual Studio project.

1. Choose Project | Add SharePoint "Layouts" Mapped Folder. You'll notice that a new Layouts folder is added to the solution:

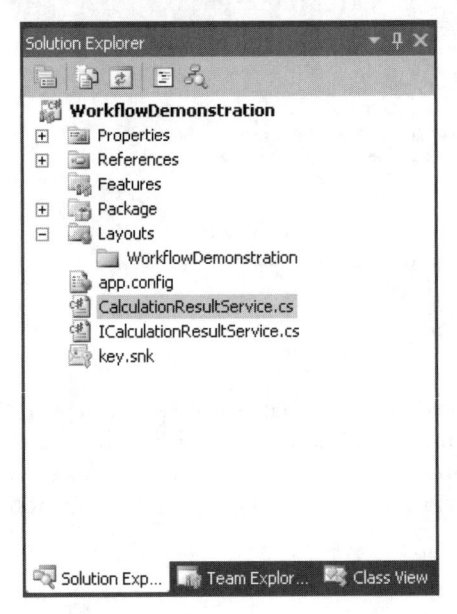

2. We can now go ahead and add our CalculationResultService.svc file. In the Layouts\WorkflowDemonstration folder, add a new XML file named CalculationResultService.svc. Replace the contents of the file with the following:

```
<%@ Assembly Name="$SharePoint.Project.AssemblyFullName$"%>
<% @ServiceHost Service="WorkflowDemonstration.CalculationResultService" %>
```

**Token Replacement in Visual Studio**   Visual Studio 2010 allows the use of replaceable tokens when creating SharePoint solution packages. Our code sample makes use of the token $SharePoint.Project.AssemblyFullName$ that will be replaced when the package is built, by the four-part assembly name for the associated assembly. However, at the time of writing, no WCF template is available for SharePoint. Therefore, tokens are not automatically replaced in files with an .svc extension.

Thankfully, this is a simple problem to resolve. Navigate to C:\Program Files (x86)\MSBuild\Microsoft\VisualStudio\v10.0\SharePointTools and then open the Microsoft.VisualStudio.SharePoint.targets file. This is an XML format file that defines various configuration settings for building SharePoint projects. Find the TokenReplacementFileExtensions element and append svc to the list of file extensions as shown:

```
<TokenReplacementFileExtensions>$(TokenReplacementFileExtensions);xml;aspx;ascx;
webpart;dwp;svc </TokenReplacementFileExtensions>
```

**Adding WCF Service Configuration to SharePoint**   As well as an .svc file, IIS also needs to read the configuration of the WCF service from the web.config file. For the purposes of our demonstration, we'll make the necessary changes manually.

1. Open the web.config file for our application (at C:\inetpub\wwwroot\wss\VirtualDirectories\80\web.config if the application is the first application running on port 80). In the **system.serviceModel** element, add the following configuration details:

```
<serviceHostingEnvironment aspNetCompatibilityEnabled="true" />
<bindings>
    <basicHttpBinding>
        <binding name="WfDemoBinding">
            <security mode="TransportCredentialOnly">
                <transport clientCredentialType="Ntlm" />
            </security>
        </binding>
    </basicHttpBinding>
</bindings>
<behaviors>
    <serviceBehaviors>
        <behavior name="WfDemoBehavior">
            <serviceMetadata httpGetEnabled="true" />
            <serviceDebug includeExceptionDetailInFaults="false" />
        </behavior>
    </serviceBehaviors>
</behaviors>
<services>
    <service behaviorConfiguration="WfDemoBehavior"
          name="WorkflowDemonstration.CalculationResultService">
        <endpoint address="" binding="basicHttpBinding"
         bindingConfiguration="WfDemoBinding"
         contract="WorkflowDemonstration.ICalculationResultService">
            <identity>
                <dns value="localhost" />
            </identity>
        </endpoint>
```

```xml
      <host>
        <baseAddresses>
          <add baseAddress="http://localhost/_layouts/WorkflowDemonstration" />
        </baseAddresses>
      </host>
    </service>
</services>
```

We're now ready to deploy the service to SharePoint. From the Build menu select Deploy WorkflowDemonstration. Visual Studio will now build the solution, create a WSP package, and then deploy the package to our SharePoint server.

As we did for our client application, we can now make use of WCFTestClient to send a test call to our WCF service. This time the endpoint address will be http://localhost/_layouts/WorkflowDemonstration/CalculationResultService.svc. If all is well, our service will return True when invoked as per our stub implementation.

## Creating a Pluggable Workflow Service

Having set up the communications mechanism between the calculation engine and SharePoint, our next step is to create a pluggable workflow service that can be hooked up to our SharePoint service to broker requests between the WCF service and SharePoint's workflow engine. Before we get into the code, I'll show you how pluggable workflow services work.

As mentioned, pluggable workflow services can be created by inheriting from **SPWorkflowExternalDataExchangeService**. External data exchange services, also known as local services, are a key component of the WF framework. Without local services, a workflow runtime has no means of communicating with the external environment, and in fact SharePoint defines two local services that allow the workflow runtime to communicate with the SharePoint platform itself: **SPWinOEWSSService** and **SPWinOETaskService**. For the most part, the SharePoint workflow activities that are available out of the box make use of these services for communication.

Generally speaking, WF can be configured using a configuration file. The configuration can specify which services should be available to the runtime and how certain functions are performed. Since allowing changes to the configuration at this level could cause major support issues, Microsoft chose to disallow workflow configuration in SharePoint via the normal channels. In previous versions of SharePoint, this meant that no additional local services could be added. However, with SharePoint 2010, an additional configuration handler has been implemented that allows objects of type **SPWorkflowExternalDataExchangeService** to be added to the workflow runtime.

External data exchange services are created in a similar fashion to WCF services. An interface is defined that determines the methods and events that should be available to the workflow runtime. Once the interface is completed, a local service class based on **SPWorkflowExternalDataExchangeService** and implementing the interface is created. Finally, the local service class is added to the configuration for the workflow runtime.

### Using the ExternalDataExchange Attribute

Now that you understand how pluggable services work, let's move on to our implementation.

We first add an interface for our service. Add a new interface file to the WorkflowDemonstration solution named IExternalCalculationService.cs. Add the following code:

```
using System;
using System.Workflow.Activities;

namespace WorkflowDemonstration
{
  [ExternalDataExchange]
  public interface IExternalCalculationService
  {
      event EventHandler<CalculationResultArgs> CalculationComplete;
      void SubmitCalculation(string product);
  }

  [Serializable]
  public class CalculationResultArgs : ExternalDataEventArgs
    {
      public CalculationResultArgs(Guid id) : base(id) { }
      public string Result;
    }
}
```

**NOTE** Creating workflow services requires references to System.Workflow.Activities and System.Workflow.Runtime.

Notice a few things about this code sample. Firstly, the **ExternalDataExchange** attribute is used to let the workflow runtime know that the interface should be accessible to workflow activities. We'll build up a workflow later to see this in action. Secondly, any events that are raised must be derived from the **ExternalDataEventArgs** class and must be serializable. The **ExternalDataEventArgs** class defines the base parameters that are required to route the event to the correct workflow instance. Because the workflow will most likely be running in a different application domain, events must be serializable in order to be passed to the runtime.

### Deriving from SPWorkflowExternalDataExchangeService

With the interface in place, we can move on to creating an implementation of the service.

Add a new class named **CalculationWorkflowService** and then add the following code to the CalculationWorkflowService.cs file:

```
using System;
using System.Collections.Generic;
using System.Linq;
using System.Text;
using System.Workflow.Activities;
```

```csharp
using System.ServiceModel.Activation;
using Microsoft.SharePoint.Workflow;
using System.Workflow.Runtime;

namespace WorkflowDemonstration
{
  [AspNetCompatibilityRequirements(RequirementsMode = AspNetCompatibilityRequirements-
Mode.Allowed)]
  class CalculationWorkflowService: SPWorkflowExternalDataExchangeService, IExternal-
CalculationService
    {
      public event EventHandler<CalculationResultArgs> CalculationComplete;

      public void SubmitCalculation(string product)
      {
        //Call WCF Service
      }

      public override void CallEventHandler(Type eventType,
                                            string eventName,
                                            object[] eventData,
                                            SPWorkflow workflow,
                                            string identity,
                                            IPendingWork workHandler,
                                            object workItem)
      {
        //raise event
      }
    public override void CreateSubscription(MessageEventSubscription subscription)
      {
        throw new NotImplementedException();
      }

      public override void DeleteSubscription(Guid subscriptionId)
      {
        throw new NotImplementedException();
      }
    }
 }
```

The main thing worth mentioning with regard to this code sample is the override of **CallEventHandler**. **CallEventHandler** is defined on the **SPWorkflowExternalDataExchangeService** base class and is used to relay events back to the workflow runtime with sufficient information to recover the relevant SharePoint context. **CreateSubscription** and **DeleteSubscription** are marked as **MustInherit** in the base class but are not required by our service and therefore have default implementations.

## Calling a WCF Service

The next step is to flesh out the implementation of the **SubmitCalculation** method. Since this is where we'll make a call out to our external calculation service, we need to add a service reference to generate the appropriate proxy.

1. So that our service endpoint is available, start up the DemoCalculationEngine application that we created earlier.
2. In the WorkflowDemonstration solution, select Project | Add Service Reference. Add the address of the client WCF service and then click Go to retrieve the service metadata. Set the Namespace to **CalculationEngine** as illustrated.

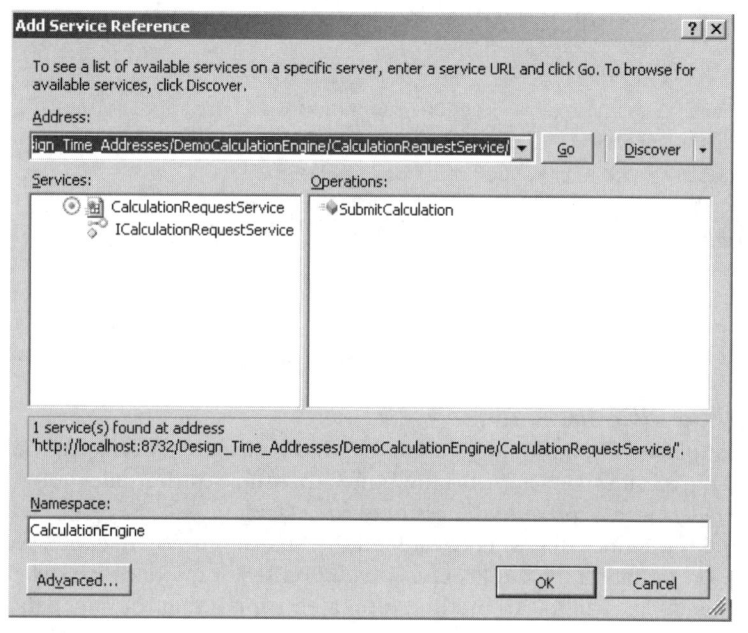

When a service reference is added to a project, Visual Studio automatically stores the binding and endpoint configuration in either app.config or web.config, depending on the type of project. In our case, the configuration has been added to app.config even though this file is not utilized by the SharePoint deployment mechanism.

Since SharePoint runs on IIS, any configuration information has to be included in the appropriate web.config file. However, when it comes to workflow, storing information in web.config doesn't work as expected. Depending on the state of the workflow, it will be running either within IIS or within a separate server process. The problem here is that configuration information that will be available when running under IIS will not be available when running under the server process.

To avoid problems locating configuration data, it's generally good practice to capture such information as part of the workflow association process. For the purposes of our demonstration, we'll hard code the configuration information for now.

In the SubmitCalculation method, add the following code:

```
public void SubmitCalculation(string product)
{
```

```
    //Call WCF Service
    CalculationEngine.CalculationRequest request = new
                    CalculationEngine.CalculationRequest();
    WSHttpBinding binding = new WSHttpBinding();

    EndpointAddress address = new EndpointAddress("ClientServiceURI");

    //So that we can pick up the correct workflow
    //we need WorkflowInstanceId & a reference to web
    CalculationEngine.CalculationRequestServiceClient client = new
            CalculationEngine.CalculationRequestServiceClient(binding,address);
    request.ProductName = product;

    request.InstanceId = this.CurrentWorkflow.InstanceId;
    request.SiteId = this.CurrentWorkflow.SiteId;
    request.WebId = this.CurrentWorkflow.WebId;

    client.SubmitCalculation(request);
}
```

One important thing to note about this code is the **EndpointAddress**. This should be the URI for the DemoCalculationEngine WCF service to which we added a reference.

### Receiving WCF Messages

The next piece of functionality that we need to consider is raising the **CalculationComplete** event. This event will let our workflow know that the external calculation process has completed as well as provide the result of the calculation.

You'll remember that when we added the SharePoint WCF service, we added a basic stub implementation for the **ProcessCalculationResult** method. We can now go back and revisit this since a call to this method ultimately signals that the calculation process has completed.

Rather than have two separate objects, one for handling the **ProcessCalculationResult** message and another for passing that message onto the workflow, we can perform both tasks in a single method on the CalculationWorkflowService.

1. Add the following code to CalculationWorkflowService.cs:

```
public bool ProcessCalculationResult(CalculationResult result)
{
  using (SPSite site = new SPSite(result.SiteId))
  {
    using (SPWeb web = site.OpenWeb(result.WebId))
    {
      RaiseEvent(web,
```

```
                              result.InstanceId,
                              typeof(IExternalCalculationService),
                          "CalculationComplete",
                          new object[] { result.Result });

            return true;
        }
    }
}
```

2. So that we can direct WCF calls for **ProcessCalculationResult** to this method, we need to make a few additional changes. First, delete the CalculationResultService.cs file containing our stub method. Then add **ICalculationResult** to the list of implemented interfaces on **CalculationWebService**, like so:

```
class CalculationWorkflowService:SPWorkflowExternalDataExchangeService,
IExternalCalculationService, ICalculationResultService
```

3. Since we'll no longer be using the **CalculationResultService** class to handle method calls for our WCF service, we need to modify the service configuration in web.config. Within the **system.serviceModel** element, change the service element named **WorkflowDemonstration.CalculationResultService** to **WorkflowDemonstration.CalculationWorkflowService** as shown:

```
<services>
<service behaviorConfiguration="WfDemoBehavior"
name="WorkflowDemonstration.CalculationWorkflowService">
```

4. The final change we need to make is to the **ServiceHost** entry in the CalculationResultService.svc file. Change this to **WorkflowDemonstration.CalculationWorkflowService** as shown:

```
<%@ Assembly Name="$SharePoint.Project.AssemblyFullName$"%>
<% @ServiceHost Service="WorkflowDemonstration.CalculationWorkflowService" %>
```

**Raising Events in a Workflow Service**   We can see that the ProcessCalculationResult makes use of the parameters received to create a reference to an SPWeb object. It then passes this reference together with a workflow instance identifier to the RaiseEvent method. As its name suggests, RaiseEvent is responsible for raising an event within the appropriate workflow instance. Before the event is queued for the appropriate workflow instance, the CallEventHandler method is called to populate an appropriate ExternalDataEventArgs-derived object.

Add the following code to the **CallEventHandler** override to populate our **CalculationResultArgs** structure before the event is passed to the workflow:

```
public override void CallEventHandler(Type eventType,
                                      string eventName,
                                      object[] eventData,
```

```
                                       SPWorkflow workflow,
                                       string identity,
                                       IPendingWork workHandler,
                                       object workItem)
{
  CalculationResultArgs args = new CalculationResultArgs(workflow
.InstanceId);

  args.Result = eventData[0].ToString();
  args.WorkHandler = workHandler;
  args.WorkItem = workItem;
  args.Identity = identity;
  this.CalculationComplete(null, args);
}
```

### Configuring Pluggable Workflow Services

You'll remember that SharePoint 2010 introduces a new configuration handler for pluggable workflow services. The final step that we need to take to enable our service is to add a configuration entry in web.config.

In web.config, navigate to the configuration | SharePoint | WorkflowServices section and then insert the following element:

```
<WorkflowService Assembly="WorkflowDemonstration, Version=1.0.0.0,
Culture=neutral, PublicKeyToken=YourPublicKey"
Class="WorkflowDemonstration.CalculationWorkflowService">
             </WorkflowService>
```

Unfortunately, on this occasion, we don't have the luxury of Visual Studio token replacement so we have to find the PublicKeyToken by examining the properties of the WorkflowDemonstration assembly within the Global Assembly Cache (GAC). With this done, we can deploy the project to SharePoint.

We've now completed the implementation of our pluggable workflow service as well as our SharePoint-hosted WCF service. Although we could test the service using WCFTestClient, we'll receive errors since no genuine workflow instances are awaiting a calculation response.

### Calling a SharePoint-Hosted WCF Service

To complete our calculation engine implementation, we need to add some code to our DemoCalculationEngine project. We need a method that can make a call into our SharePoint WCF service to notify the workflow that calculation is complete. With the SharePoint project deployed, we first need to add a service reference to the SharePoint WCF service.

1. In the DemoCalculationEngine project, choose Project | Add Service Reference. Set the Address to **http://localhost/_layouts/WorkflowDemonstration/ CalculationResultService.svc**.

2. Since the service is hosted within SharePoint, requests must be authenticated; as a result, we need to enter credentials for a user account with permissions to connect to the SharePoint site.

3. Once the service metadata has been retrieved, set the Namespace to CalculationResultService and the click OK to complete the process.

**NOTE** When adding a service reference for a SharePoint, you'll sometimes see multiple prompts to enter credentials. Usually, after entering valid credentials once, clicking Cancel on subsequent prompts will allow the process to continue.

4. With our service reference in place, we can move on to add the following code to handle the button click event in Form1.cs:

```
private void button1_Click(object sender, System.EventArgs e)
   {
     foreach (DataGridViewRow row in dataGridView1.SelectedRows)
     {
       CalculationResultService.CalculationResultServiceClient client = new
                 CalculationResultService.CalculationResultServiceClient();
       client.ClientCredentials.Windows.AllowedImpersonationLevel =
             System.Security.Principal.TokenImpersonationLevel.Impersonation;
       CalculationResultService.CalculationResult result = new
                         CalculationResultService.CalculationResult();

       CalculationRequest selected = row.DataBoundItem as CalculationRequest;

       result.Result = selected.ProductName + " Complete";
       result.InstanceId = selected.InstanceId;
       result.SiteId = selected.SiteId;
       result.WebId = selected.WebId;

       if (client.ProcessCalculationResult(result))
       {
         row.Selected = false;
         _calculationList.Remove(selected);
       }
     }
   }
```

We can now manually trigger calculation results by selecting an item from the data grid and then clicking the Send Result button.

**TIP** When hosting WCF services in SharePoint, it's important that the client proxy allows impersonation; otherwise, some weird and wonderful COM errors may be thrown by SharePoint. To allow impersonation, set the **AllowedImpersonationLevel** to **Impersonation**, as shown in the preceding code sample.

## Creating a Workflow Using Visual Studio 2010

With our pluggable workflow service and external calculation engine up and running, we can create a basic workflow in Visual Studio that will send messages to the calculation engine. Our test workflow will be very simple; when a new item is added to a list, its title will be sent to the calculation engine. We will then be able to trigger a response manually from the calculation engine, which will be passed to the workflow. The workflow will log the response and complete.

1. We can add our workflow to the WorkflowDemonstration solution that we created earlier. In Visual Studio, select Project | Add New Item. From the Add New Item dialog, select SharePoint | 2010 | Sequential Workflow. Name the new workflow **External Calculation**, as shown:

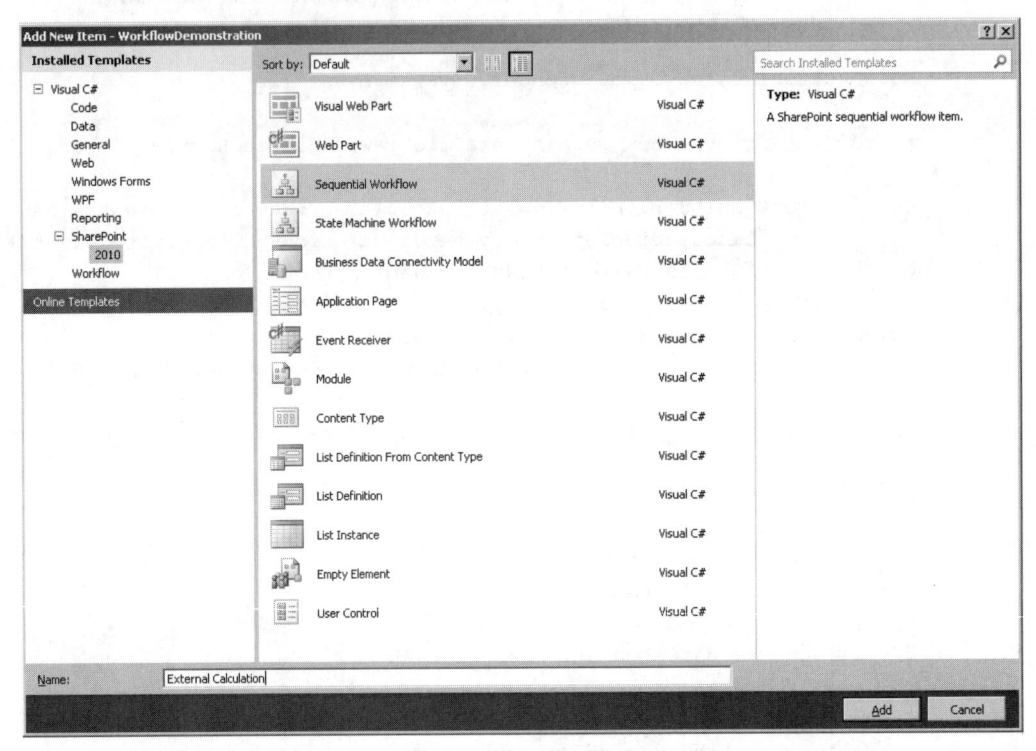

2. In the SharePoint Customization Wizard dialog, leave the default name as WorkflowDemonstration - External Calculation. We can see that the same types of workflow that are available in SharePoint Designer are also available for Visual Studio workflows: List Workflow and Site Workflow. Since we're planning to use data in a list to trigger our workflow, set the type to List Workflow.

3. Accept the default association settings. This will associate our workflow with the Products list that we created earlier. Click Finish to complete the process.

## Using the Visual Studio Workflow Designer

When the workflow has been added to the project, the workflow designer tool will be displayed. You can see that its user interface is similar to the one we created earlier using Visio 2010. You can drag workflow activities from the toolbox on to the design surface to build up the workflow logic.

Our workflow needs five additional steps: **CallExternalMethod**, which can be found in the Windows Workflow v3.0 group in the toolbox; **SetState**, which can be found in the SharePoint Workflow group; **HandleExternalEvent**, which can be found in the Windows Workflow v3.0 group; **LogToHistoryListActivity**, which can be found in the SharePoint Workflow group; and **CodeActivity**, which can be found in the Windows Workflow v3.0 group.

Drag the required activities onto the designer surface, as illustrated:

## Configuring Workflow Activities

You can see from the designer that a few of our activities have not been configured properly. This is indicated by the icon in the upper-right corner of the activity control. Let's work through them in sequence to set the appropriate configuration details.

**CallExternalMethodActivity**   Starting with callExternalMethodActivity1, when we select the activity we can see in the Properties pane that the values for InterfaceType and MethodName are invalid as shown. This activity is used to communicate with a pluggable workflow service and in our case will be used to invoke the SubmitCalculation method on our CalculationWorkflowService.

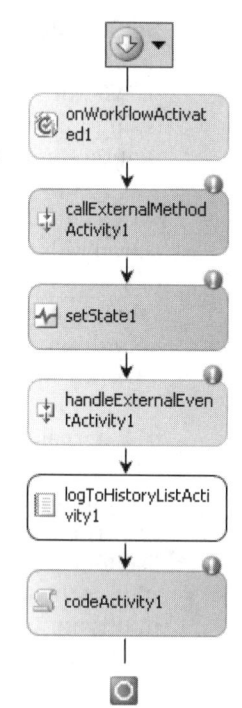

1. The first property to configure is InterfaceType. This is the interface that we tagged earlier with the **ExternalDataExchange** attribute. Click the ellipsis to show the Browse and Select a .NET Type dialog. The IExternalCalculationService is already selected since it's the only interface in our solution with the appropriate attribute. Click OK to use this.

2. Now the MethodName property needs to be configured. From the drop-down list, select SubmitCalculation. The values in the drop-down list are populated from the InterfaceType by using reflection. Since SubmitCalculation is the only method on our interface, it is the only item in the list.

3. Once SubmitCalculation has been selected, a new property appears: product. The property is added automatically since it appears in the list of arguments for the SubmitCalculation method. For out test workflow, we'll set this to the title of the list items on which the workflow has been started. Click the ellipsis to show the Bind dialog, an important part of the workflow designer because it allows us to bind properties to local variables or other properties. We can add new variables by selecting the Bind To A New Member tab if required. For our purposes, we need to bind the product property to the Title property of the current workflow item. Expand workflowProperties | Item | Title, and then click OK to store the binding.

**SetStateActivity and CorrelationTokens** Moving onto the setState1 activity, we can see that the CorrelationToken property is invalid. CorrelationTokens are an important aspect of WF workflows and are used to determine the scope of the activity. A CorrelationToken is simply a text value that is used to group activities and, more importantly, the properties that they use. If a workflow has a property named foo, for example, when a workflow activity with a correlation token of token A writes to the foo property, other workflow actions with a correlation token of token A will be able to read the value. However, if a workflow action with a correlation token of token B writes to the property, the actions with a token of token A will still see the original value, whereas actions with token B will see the new value. In effect, every property is actually an array with the correlation token being used as an indexer. When it comes to SharePoint workflows, this is particularly relevant when using Task activities.

Set the CorrelationToken for setState1 to workflowToken with an OwnerActivityName of External_Calculation.

**Adding Custom Status Values to SharePoint** Although the configuration of the setState activity is now valid, it doesn't quite do what we want it to. When a workflow is added to a list item in SharePoint, a new column is added to the appropriate list that shows the current state of the workflow. The setState activity allows us to specify the value that should appear in this list. In our case, we want to show the text *Awaiting Calculation Result*.

Before we can display a custom value for workflow status, we need to let SharePoint know what our new value is. Workflow states are stored in SharePoint in a similar format to lookup values, so each state needs an ID and a text value. To add new states, we need only the text value, since SharePoint will automatically generate a new ID.

We can add the text for the new state in the Elements.xml file that exists under our External Calculation workflow in the Solution Explorer pane. Add an ExtendedStatusColumnValues element to the MetaData element, as shown:

```
<MetaData>
  <AssociationCategories>List</AssociationCategories>
  <StatusPageUrl>_layouts/WrkStat.aspx</StatusPageUrl>
  <ExtendedStatusColumnValues>
    <StatusColumnValue>Awaiting Calculation Result</StatusColumnValue>
  </ExtendedStatusColumnValues>
</MetaData>
```

With the text value for our new status added, we can now configure our setState activity to use it. Unfortunately, it's not quite as simple as that though. SetState expects the ID of our new state, and since this will be generated by SharePoint when our workflow is installed, we don't currently have a reference to the ID value. We can calculate the ID for our new state simply by adding one to the ID of the last state that SharePoint defines internally.

1. Right-click the workflow designer and then select View Code to see the code behind for our workflow. Add the following field:

    ```
    public int AwaitingCalculationState = ((int) SPWorkflowStatus.Max);
    ```

**SPWorkflowStatus** is an enumeration of the workflow states that SharePoint provides by default. Our new extended status column value will be assigned the next ID in the sequence, which we can retrieve using the **SPWorkflowStatus.Max** value. If we wanted to add more than one additional state, we could use **SPWorkflowStatus.Max +1**, **SPWorkflowStatus.Max+2**, and so on, to determine the IDs for subsequent states.

2. We can now bind the State property of our **SetState** activity to our new AwaitingCalculationState field.

**HandleExternalActivity** The next activity to configure is handleExternalEventActivity1. This activity listens for an event from a pluggable workflow service. It's configured in much the same way as callExternalMethodActivity1.

1. Set the InterfaceType to IExternalCalculationService, and then select CalculationComplete from the EventName drop-down.

2. Since this is an event, we don't need to specify any parameters. Although, since we're interested in the **CalculationResultArgs** parameter that is passed with the event, we can bind this value to a local variable using the **e** property. Click the ellipsis to show the Bind dialog. This time, select the Bind To New Member tab and then add a new property with the name **CalculationCompleteArgs**, as shown. This binding will store the values passed with the event in a local variable called **CalculationCompleteArgs** that we'll be able to use in subsequent workflow activities.

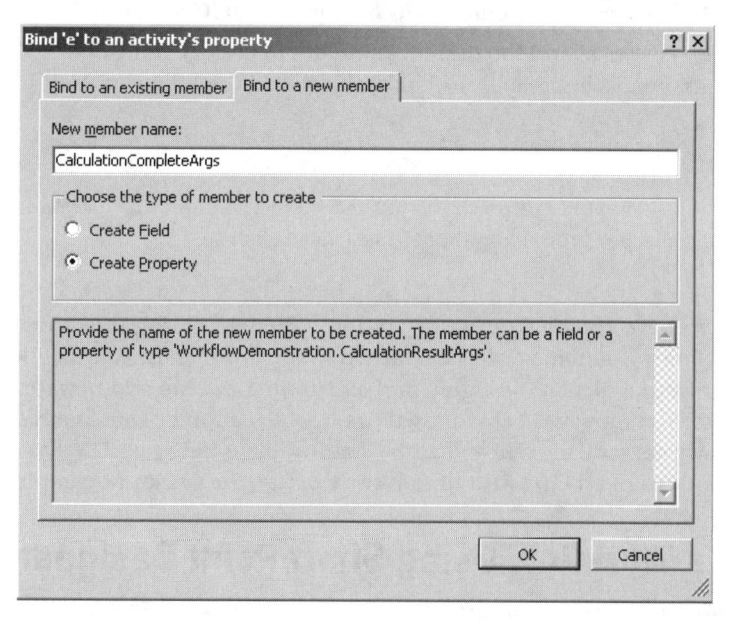

**LogToHistoryListActivity** We've now configured all the mandatory properties for our workflow. Before we deploy, we need to make one additional change. The logToHistoryListActivity1 action is not set up to log anything useful to the workflow history list. Since we want it to pick up the calculation result, we need to set a few properties.

1. For HistoryOutcome, type **Calculation Result**.
2. Using the Bind dialog, bind the HistoryDescription property to CalculationCompleteArgs.Result, as shown:

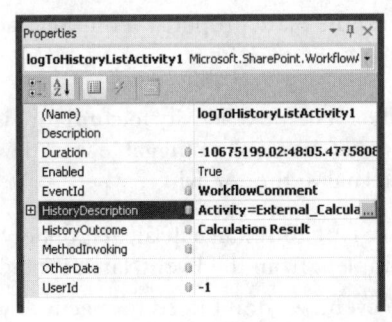

```
Properties                                              ▼ ╬ ×
logToHistoryListActivity1  Microsoft.SharePoint.Workflow▼
    ₂↓  ▣  ✔
    (Name)                        logToHistoryListActivity1
    Description
    Duration                    0  -10675199.02:48:05.4775806
    Enabled                        True
    EventId                     0  WorkflowComment
 ⊞  HistoryDescription          0  Activity=External_Calcula...
    HistoryOutcome              0  Calculation Result
    MethodInvoking              0
    OtherData                   0
    UserId                      0  -1
```

**CodeActivity**  The CodeActivity can be used to execute arbitrary code within the workflow engine. Our workflow requires that, as a result of the external calculation process, the Environmental Compliance flag is set to true or false. For the purposes of our demonstration, we'll assume that our organization manufactures only environmentally friendly products and that the result of the calculation always indicates compliance.

1. To configure the CodeActivity for the ExecuteCode property, enter **UpdateFlag**.
2. Press ENTER, and the designer switches to code-behind view and a new method is automatically created for **UpdateFlag**. Add the following code:

```
private void UpdateFlag(object sender, EventArgs e)
{
    workflowProperties.Item["Environmental Compliance"] = true;
    workflowProperties.Item.Update();
}
```

We've now completed our test workflow. When deploying the solution to SharePoint, our workflow will automatically be attached to the Product list at http://localhost/chapter11. With our DemoCalculationEngine project running, we can add new items to the Product list and see the messages being passed to our calculation engine as expected. Viewing the workflow history will also show that the status value is being updated as expected and the calculation result is being written to history before the workflow completes.

# Creating a Workflow Using SharePoint Designer

In the preceding sections, we've implemented two of the three workflows that are required for our demonstration scenario. The final workflow simply waits for the other two workflows to complete successfully before allowing the product to be advertised.

We've covered creating workflows using Visio 2010 with SharePoint Designer and Visual Studio 2010. For this simple workflow, we'll make use of SharePoint Designer on its own and then export the workflow to Visual Studio to add some custom code.

1. In SharePoint Designer, select Workflows from the Site Objects pane.
2. From the Workflows ribbon, select Reusable Workflow.
3. Name the new workflow **Product Advertising** and limit the workflow to the Product content type.
4. Add three Wait for Field Change in Current Item actions to the workflow. Configure them as illustrated:

```
Step 1

    Wait for Technical Details to be not empty

    then Wait for Product Image to be not empty

    then Wait for Environmental Compliance to equal Yes
```

5. Since these activities can be completed in parallel, we can add them to a parallel block. From the Workflow ribbon, in the Insert section, select Parallel Block.
6. Using the Move Up and Move Down buttons in the Workflow ribbon, move the three actions into the Parallel Block.
7. Set the status to Available for Advertising. Add a Set Workflow Status action after the Parallel Block.
8. In the status combo box, type **Available for Advertising**, as illustrated:

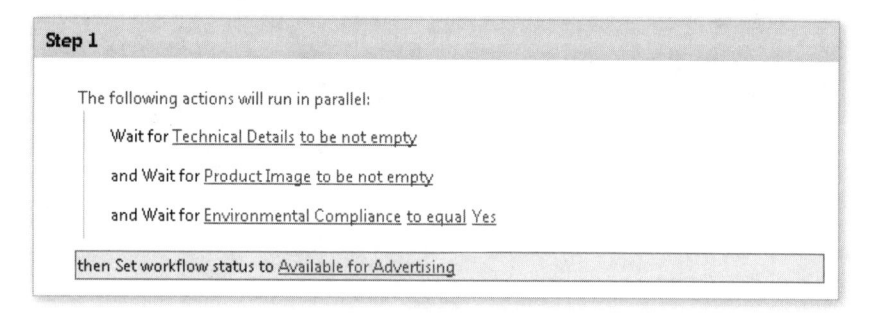

```
Step 1

    The following actions will run in parallel:

        Wait for Technical Details to be not empty

        and Wait for Product Image to be not empty

        and Wait for Environmental Compliance to equal Yes

    then Set workflow status to Available for Advertising
```

9. Publish the workflow using the Publish button in the Save section of the Workflow ribbon.
10. To attach the workflow to the Product content type, select Workflow Settings from the Workflow ribbon. This will close the workflow editor and display the Workflow Settings page instead.
11. From the Workflow Settings ribbon, select Associate to Content Type | Product.
12. On the Add a Workflow page, set the Start Options to Start This Workflow When A New Item Is Created. Click OK to complete the process.

We can now create a new product and, using the workflows that we've implemented, complete the process defined in our demonstration scenario. When a new item is added to the Products list, our workflows are started automatically. The Product Publishing workflow creates tasks for the capture of additional information, while the Environmental Compliance workflow submits a calculation request to our sample calculation engine. When both of these workflows are complete, the Product Advertising workflow completes with a status of Available for Advertising.

## Summary

We've covered a lot of ground in this chapter. Windows Workflow Foundation is more than a feature of SharePoint; it's an alternative way of developing software. One of the things you'll have noticed as we worked through this chapter was that we spent absolutely no time on workflow "plumbing." We didn't worry about how the workflow state was persisted or how the events that we raised got routed to the correct workflow instance. The workflow runtime that's hosted within SharePoint took care of all this stuff for us. Using SharePoint 2010 as a platform, building workflow-enabled applications is now easier than ever before.

# CHAPTER 12

# Excel Services

SharePoint started life as a collaboration tool that allowed teams to create basic web sites and use them for sharing documents. Building on this idea, the good folks at Microsoft added some integration between Microsoft Office applications and SharePoint, allowing documents to be opened and edited from a SharePoint site in the same way as a network file share. Given that the aim of the game was to make collaboration easier, this worked very well. Users had a central location for all documents relating to a particular project and could seamlessly access them.

There was a drawback, however: This system was great for static documents, such as Microsoft Word docs, that can easily be displayed on a web site without losing any of their original functionality. But what about interactive documents such as Microsoft Excel? A spreadsheet's purpose is to allow users to perform calculations and analyze the results; doing this effectively requires some interactivity. A static spreadsheet is no more useful than a list of numbers in a Word document. Realizing this, the SharePoint team at Microsoft introduced Excel Services in MOSS 2007. In effect, Excel services provide the calculation and display engine of Microsoft Excel as a server-side component. It allows documents created using the Excel client application to be stored on a SharePoint site and used via a web browser, all without the need to install the Excel client application.

SharePoint 2010 extends this concept. Although the inclusion of Excel data and visualizations within SharePoint pages was possible with MOSS 2007, using SharePoint 2010, a new REST API makes this easier than ever before. Furthermore, the addition of a JavaScript object model means that the calculation and visualization capabilities of Excel can now easily be used to deliver richer browser-based applications.

In addition to the functionality of Excel Services, Microsoft also provides Office Web Applications, web-based versions of Microsoft Office tools that can be deployed as a feature on SharePoint Foundation Server 2010. Using the Excel web application also allows real-time sharing of web-based Excel documents: more than one user can be working on the same document at the same time, and changes made by all parties are simultaneously applied to all open documents.

Excel is very much the tool of choice when it comes to analyzing numerical data. As we progress through this chapter, you'll see how you can leverage this tool to add a new dimension to your business applications that would previously have been impossible without a huge amount of development work.

# Excel Capabilities on SharePoint 2010

As mentioned, MOSS 2007 introduced Excel Services as a mechanism for using Excel-based models and data on the server. With SharePoint 2010, Microsoft has extended this offering to Excel Services 2010, an updated version of the existing Excel Services functionality, and the Excel Web Application, a browser-based version of the Excel client application.

Let's take a look at the features available in Excel Services 2010.

## Excel Application Services

**New in 2010**

The Excel Services application service can be configured on SharePoint Server 2010. Comprising Excel Calculation Services and potentially a collection of user-defined functions, Excel Services is responsible for loading workbooks and performing appropriate calculations. Where workbooks contain links to external data or user-defined functions, Excel Calculation Services is responsible for making the appropriate connections and loading any required external assemblies. Excel Calculation Services maintains a session for each open workbook user, and the session remains open until it is either explicitly closed by the user or it times out. Furthermore, when loading workbooks into memory, Excel Services maintains a cache of workbooks as well as any associated external datasets.

Excel Calculation Services does not support the complete range of features offered by the Excel client application. In the previous version of Excel Services, if a workbook contained a feature that was unsupported, it was impossible to load it using Excel Services. With Excel Services 2010, a more pragmatic approach has been taken; it's now possible to load any workbook, and if the workbook contains unsupported features, a warning is generated. This allows users to continue using supported features within Excel Services without having to modify the spreadsheet.

### User-Defined Functions

As mentioned, Excel Calculation Services has the responsibility of calling external functions as required by a workbook. User-defined functions (UDFs) make it easy to extend the capabilities of Excel Services to include interactions with external systems as well as custom calculation logic. In fact, anything that can be defined using a .NET assembly can be referenced as a UDF provided the appropriate interfaces are implemented.

## Excel Client Service

As you've seen, Excel Calculation Services is responsible for loading workbooks and performing the necessary calculations. However, when it comes to accessing the results of those calculations both programmatically and for display purposes, the Excel Client Service provides a number of different mechanisms.

### UDF Real-World Example

Here's an example of where all of this could be useful: I was involved in the redesign of a hydrocarbon accounting system. Hydrocarbon accounting, for those uninitiated in the art, is a consequence of the fact that most oil extraction companies do not operate refineries or their own dedicated pipelines. Generally speaking, a refinery operator provides a pipeline that connects up all oil extraction companies to the refinery. In an ideal world where oil was just oil, this would be a straightforward affair; oil extraction companies would simply meter how many barrels of oil they sent down the pipeline and receive payment from the refinery based on the number of barrels. Unfortunately, oil isn't just oil. In fact, oil is a generic name for a collection of hydrocarbons, each with different relative values—for example, lighter hydrocarbons that make up petroleum tend to have higher values than the heavier components of bitumen. As a consequence of the different hydrocarbon blends that are pumped into the pipeline by each extractor, each blend must be periodically sampled to determine exactly which hydrocarbons are present, and these samples are used to determine which portion of the consolidated mix that reaches the refinery belongs to which extractor. Considering that a pipeline may have 40 to 50 different extractors and each extractor may have several different wells all producing a different blend, you can see that determining the relative value of the product being pumped is no easy feat.

The system that I worked on made extensive use of Microsoft Excel and Visual Basic for Applications (VBA) in performing these complex calculations. Samples were stored in a database and were extracted into a complex series of spreadsheets that were ultimately used to produce statements for the connected extraction companies. Since the application worked its magic on the client, all calculations had to be performed in real-time whenever a statement was required. As you can imagine, this was a time-consuming process. However, given the technologies of the day, Excel as a calculation engine was unsurpassed and the system worked well for a number of years.

Now to get back to UDFs and Excel Services—had I been rebuilding this system today, Excel Services would have allowed the calculations to be performed on the server. Furthermore, the calculation results would be automatically cached and available to multiple users effectively instantly. UDFs could be easily used to replace the complex calculation functions that were previously coded using VBA and sample data; in my example, this was stored in an Oracle database and entered via a PowerBuilder user interface, and this could easily be captured using an InfoPath form and stored in a SharePoint list. The key thing to note in all of this is that the exact same spreadsheets that we were using in the original system could be reused with Excel Services with practically no major modifications.

## Excel Web Access

So that workbooks calculated using Excel Calculation Services can be rendered in the browser, Excel Services provides the Excel Web Access web part. This web part effectively creates HTML based on the output of Excel Calculation Services that mirrors the output we would expect to see if we were using the Excel client application. As well as rendering output, the web part also provides a similar level of interactivity to the Excel client application as well as a few custom features that have been designed for use in web applications. For example, an Excel Web Access web part can be placed on a page and configured to display only a particular chart. If the chart is generated based on a table of data within the spreadsheet, the data that makes up that table can be filtered by hooking up a filter web part to the Excel Web Access web part. By using techniques such as this, you can create highly interactive data visualization tools simply by leveraging the functionality of Excel.

### Excel Web Services

Sometimes we don't really need to see an entire spreadsheet; sometime we're just interested in the bottom line and we want to use that value in our application. Using Excel Web Services allows us to interact with a workbook in much the same way as we can interact with the Excel object model when building complex client applications. For example, using Web Services, we can set values within a spreadsheet or extract values from particular cells. We can even generate a snapshot of a spreadsheet that can be downloaded.

If, for example, we apply this to the hydrocarbon accounting story (in the sidebar "UDF Real-World Example") using Excel Web Services, we could produce a simple application that accepted a range of dates and use those to provide production statistics for a particular extraction company.

### JavaScript Object Model

*New in 2010*

Using Web Services is all fine and well when it comes to interacting with Excel services from a client application, but what happens if we simply want to display a particular value of a web page? Or perform a calculation based on user input? Of course, we can still use Web Services, but calling Web Services from JavaScript is not for the faint of heart and imposes restrictions on the implementation of the Web Service itself. One of the new features of Excel Services 2010 is the JavaScript Object Model. (Strictly speaking, it's called the ECMAScript object model, but that term's always had a hint of Ghostbusters for me so I'm going to stick with the JavaScript Object Model.) The JavaScript Object Model (JSOM) can be used by inserting JavaScript onto a page containing the Excel Web Access web part. In effect, the web part emits the client-side objects necessary to interact with its contents via JavaScript.

### REST API

*New in 2010*

One technology that's gained a lot of momentum in recent years is Representational State Transfer (REST). I say it's gained a lot of momentum because REST, like XML, is a description of an aspect of something that we already know and love and have been using successfully for many years: the World Wide Web. REST describes the architecture of the Web, and one of its key principals is that each resource should have a unique global identifier. Resources can be accessed using a standardized interface, and representation of the resource can be exchanged using a well-known format. Sound familiar? In web terms, this means that each resource should have a uniform resource indicator (URI), and the URI can be accessed using the ubiquitous Hypertext Transport Protocol (HTTP), and a representation of the resource generally in the form of HTML can be retrieved.

The reason REST has gained a lot of attention in recent years is due to the extension of these principles into other areas. What if a resource is not just a web page? What if a resource is a record in a dataset? And, what if, rather than an HTML representation, a JSON representation is returned? You can see that we're stepping into the world of Web Services without the formality that comes with Simple Object Access Protocol (SOAP). For a lot of purposes, this is a more attractive proposition.

The key difference between a REST-ful web service and a SOAP web service is the existence of a message. SOAP is all about sending a well-defined message to a particular endpoint (or *resource* in REST parlance), whereas REST is about communicating with the endpoint only. There is no message, just a simple request for a specific resource. We could, of course, make the case that SOAP is an implementation of a REST-ful service, but that's a whole different story.

The introduction of REST to Excel Services is an immensely useful feature, especially when you consider that one of the main uses of Excel Services is to create and use server-based calculation models. The thing with models is that they exist only to provide results. More often than not, the model itself is not of interest, only the conclusions that can be reached by using it. By applying REST principles to a model, we can retrieve only the conclusions. More importantly, we can do so by using a human-readable uniform resource locator (URL), and this exponentially increases the potential for reusing that data.

For example, if an Excel workbook contains a chart of sales figures that is generated using data in the workbook, using REST we can pick up the URL for the chart itself and use it within our web site in the same way that we'd use any other image. The difference between using a normal image and a REST URL is that the chart will be updated automatically as the data in the underlying workbook changes. To give some contrast, consider what would be involved if we had to do this using SOAP.

## Excel Web App

**New in 2010**

With the announcement of Office 2010, Microsoft introduced a new product version: the Office Web Apps. Office Web Apps consists of new web-based versions of Excel, Word, PowerPoint, and OneNote, which are available via Windows Live, Microsoft Online, or as an add-on service for SharePoint 2010.

The key aim of the Excel Web App is to mirror the user experience of the client application within the browser, allowing users to access their spreadsheets from anywhere using only a web browser. Beyond this, the web-based nature of the product delivers a few additional features that are not available in the client version. Probably the most significant of these is the ability to co-author documents. Consider the current situation when using Excel client, where each user editing a file must apply a lock, and a locked file cannot be edited by any other user. As developers, we experience this type of problem regularly when using source code control systems. There's no more heinous a crime than a developer locking a file and then going off on vacation for two weeks. The Excel Web App prevents this problem by allowing all users with the appropriate permissions to edit a document simultaneously. Changes are pushed down in real time to all user sessions.

Using Excel Services, this collaboration can be further enhanced by using Excel Web Services or the REST API. It's possible for an external application to update a spreadsheet using a web service call or the REST API. Just as with other changes, these will be automatically pushed down to open user sessions.

## PowerPivot

**New in 2010**

I read a paper recently that suggested that the average cost of a single reusable business report could be as high as $20,000. At first, this seemed like an astronomical figure, but the more I thought about it, when you factor in the infrastructure costs and the to and fro between business users and developers, it's not an unrealistic cost.

Of course, the bigger question that this raises is whether the information provided by the report is sufficiently valuable to justify the cost incurred in obtaining it, and this highlights one of the big conflicts of business intelligence. To achieve the goal of business intelligence is to make up-to-the-minute, relevant information available to the right people at the right time. The problem is that determining what information is relevant and how it should be collected and presented is usually filtered through business analysts and IT project staff. Even when report definitions remain true to their original purpose, the world has changed by the time the reports are delivered. True business intelligence must incorporate a large self-service element, not just in terms of retrieving data from a selection of predefined reports but in using this data together with data from many heterogeneous sources in a manner that best fits the problem at hand.

PowerPivot is an add-in for SQL Server 2008 R2 and Excel 2010 that aims to address this issue directly. In effect, PowerPivot allows users to create unique data models from a range of data sources and embed the completed model within an Excel workbook. After the data is embedded within Excel, it can be easily analyzed using PivotTables, charts, or any of the myriad analysis features available within Excel.

You might be thinking, what's different between PowerPivot and simply using external data sources? Excel is a versatile tool, but it's fair to say that it has two main functions: to create numerical models and to analyze numerical data. When it comes down to creating models, using external data sources is a great way to import raw data into a model; however, when we're using Excel as an analysis tool, there are a few issues with imported data. The first issue is volume: Excel has a limit of 1 million rows. The next issue is performance: If you've tried to run a PivotTable on a sheet with a huge number of rows, you know it's not a pretty picture! PowerPivot addresses both of these issues by using an in-memory version of Analysis Services to process queries and store the underlying data. This means that it's possible to analyze data sets containing tens or even hundreds of millions of rows, and, furthermore, it's fast. As the old adage goes, "Always use the right tool for the job," and the right tool for analyzing high volumes of data is Analysis Services. PowerPivot is all about making the right tool available to the right audience at the right time.

Impressive as PowerPivot is, this chapter doesn't cover it in full; see Chapter 18 for more.

## Configuring Excel Services

Developing solutions using Excel Services is pretty straightforward. We're all familiar with Excel and what it can do, so all we really need to do is save our spreadsheet onto our SharePoint server and our mission is accomplished. (Maybe it's not quite as simple as that, but the point I'm making is that we're not facing a near vertical learning curve here.)

Where we do need to pay a bit more attention is in the configuration of Excel Services. Left unchecked, users could upload server-crushing calculation mayhem. They could easily create a spreadsheet that dragged in the entire contents of the company customer relationship management (CRM) database and performed string matches on description fields before extracting the top ten customers and the value of their sales during the past two weeks. We could, of course, argue that this is a job for the IT pros and it's probably fair to say that as a day-to-day task it is, but what we'll find as we start developing solutions using Excel Services is that practically all the problems we'll encounter come down to configuration issues.

## Service Application Settings

Chapter 9 covered the Service Application Framework and how it's used by SharePoint to provide services that can be shared among web applications. It will probably come as no surprise to learn that Excel Services is implemented using the Service Application Framework.

To configure Excel Services, we use the SharePoint 2010 Central Administration tool. From the Central Administration home page, the Excel Services configuration settings can be reached by clicking Application Management | Manage Service applications | Excel Services. Of course, if more than one instance of Excel Services is running, you'll be able to configure that using whatever name you assigned when you set it up.

When you're configuring and using Excel Services, keep in mind the notion of trust. System administrators determine what is trusted and what isn't, and users are allowed to create and use workbooks that make use of trusted resources only. So, for example, a system administrator may decide that data from a particular source—such as a data warehouse—is trusted, whereas data from a second source—such as a CRM application—isn't trusted. Making this distinction doesn't mean that the CRM system data is any less accurate than the data warehousing data; of course, the opposite is likely true. What it means is that the system administrator has determined that the schema and data volumes within the CRM system are likely to cause issues if they are used freely within Excel. By choosing not to trust this data source, users will be unable to reference it when creating workbooks. So the notion of trust is actually about trusting the resource to play nicely within Excel Services.

The configuration settings for Excel Services involve five sections, as shown next. I'll quickly run through these, calling out any settings that are relevant to developers.

**SharePoint 2010** Central Administration ▸ Manage Excel Services
Use this page to change settings for Excel Services

Central Administration
Application Management
System Settings
Monitoring
Backup and Restore
Security
Upgrade and Migration
General Application Settings
Configuration Wizards

**Global Settings**
Define load balancing, memory, and throttling thresholds. Set the unattended service account and data connection timeouts.

**Trusted File Locations**
Define places where spreadsheets can be loaded from.

**Trusted Data Providers**
Add or remove data providers that can be used when refreshing data connections.

**Trusted Data Connection Libraries**
Define a SharePoint Document Library where data connections can be loaded from.

**User Defined Function Assemblies**
Register managed code assemblies that can be used by spreadsheets.

## Global Settings
As you might expect, this section covers most of the high-level configuration options such as load balancing and memory utilization. For the most part, these settings are unlikely to cause developers problems and are best left to the IT pros as part of maintaining and configuring the farm overall—with one exception: the external data settings. When a spreadsheet is created that connects to an external data source, you need to consider a few options for authentication. These are covered in more detail later in the section "Using Data Connection Libraries," but for now you should know that if the authentication type is set to None, connections are made using the unattended service account. Since the unattended service account may be used to connect to many different types of data source, the Secure Store Service is used to map appropriate credentials to the account. This allows non-Windows credentials to be used where appropriate. The configuration of this is covered in the "Demonstration Scenario" section later in the chapter.

## Trusted File Locations
The Trusted File Locations section is probably not going to cause you too many problems. In previous versions of SharePoint, this was not configured by default, so no Excel Service workbooks would load properly. Thankfully, with SharePoint 2010, the default setting is to allow all workbooks stored within SharePoint to be accessed using Excel Services.

You can use workbooks that are not stored within SharePoint within Excel Services. Trusted file locations can be created for Universal Naming Convention (UNC) paths or other web sites. A few things worthy of mention include the User-Defined Functions setting and the settings in the External Data section. Although User-Defined Functions have a separate configuration heading, they can be disabled or enabled at the trusted file location level. By default, UDFs are allowed. In the External Data section, external data can be disabled at the trusted file location, and the ability to refresh external data when using the REST API is determined by a setting in this section.

## Trusted Data Providers
Trusted Data Providers defines the lists of drivers that can be used when connecting to external data sources. If a driver isn't listed, it can't be used to create a connection. Having said that, even if a driver is listed, there's no guarantee that it *can* be used.

## Trusted Data Connection Libraries
Data Connection libraries serve a few functions: They allow a system administrator to create a library with a series of preconfigured connections that can be easily used by business users for various tasks. In addition, data connection information is stored in a central location, and any changes that may be required can be made globally without having to update myriad documents throughout an organization. At the Trusted File Location level, you can restrict data connections to trusted data connection libraries only. Unless this option is selected, users are free to create their own data connections using any of the trusted providers and embed those connection details within a workbook.

## UserDefined Function Assemblies
In this section, you can configure any assemblies containing user-defined functions. UDF assemblies can either be loaded from a file location or from the Global Assembly Cache

(GAC). Note that the assembly must be available on all machines running Excel Services. For ease of administration, an assembly can be disabled, meaning that it remains configured but can't be used by Excel Services.

## Demonstration Scenario

To demonstrate the capabilities of Excel Services, consider the following scenario:

> AdventureWorks, one of your clients, has implemented SharePoint 2010 as its corporate intranet platform. To increase awareness of company performance within the organization, you've been asked to add an indicator of global sales to the front page of the intranet site. Since AdventureWorks is a global organization, it should be possible to filter the sales figures by geographic region, and the amounts shown should be visible in a range of currencies, selectable by the user.

It probably comes as no surprise to learn that we can implement this solution using Excel Services. We can render an interactive chart using the Excel Web Access web part, and if we base the chart on a pivot table, data will be automatically refreshed. To filter the sales figures by geographic region, we can incorporate a slicer into the design, which will allow users to select from a graphical list of available regions.

Displaying the results in various currencies is a bit more involved, since the data in the underlying database is stored in a single currency only. To achieve this, we'll create a custom UDF that will retrieve current exchange rates via a web service call. We'll then make use of that data to recalculate the workbook in the appropriate currency. Because we want to allow the user to select from a list of currencies, we'll make use of the JavaScript API to pass in a currency code selected from a drop-down list. When the currency code is passed into the workbook via the API, the workbook will be refreshed using the appropriate currency.

### Set Up Adventure Works Sample Database

To provide some sample data to work with in our various examples, we need to download and install the SQL Server 2008 sample databases from www.codeplex.com/MSFTDBProdSamples. Our examples make use of the AdventureWorks OLTP database installed on the local instance of SQL Server 2008.

### Create a Sample Site

Now we'll create a new blank site to use for development. Note that if we were creating a complete Business Intelligence (BI) solution or intended to use the site mainly for hosting dashboards, the Business Intelligence Center site template would be a more appropriate place to start. Since we're using only a single Excel workbook, we'll make use of a basic blank site.

1. In SharePoint Designer, choose File | Sites, and then click the New Blank Web Site button. Type the name of the new site as **http://localhost/Chapter12**.
2. We'll add a new document library to host our Excel Workbook. From the Site Objects pane, select Lists and Libraries.

3. From the ribbon, select Document Library | Document Library. Name the new library **Excel Workbooks**:

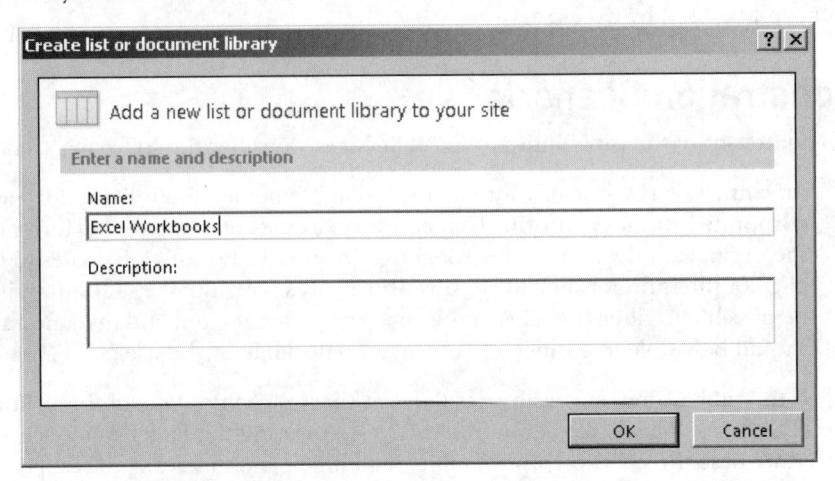

## Create a Workbook for Use with Excel Services

Before we can make use of an Excel workbook in SharePoint 2010, we need to create it using the Excel client application. For our demonstration scenario, we need a simple workbook that contains a pivot table and a pivot chart. The pivot table should be generated from data stored in the organization's ERP system.

1. Open Excel 2010. A new blank workbook will be automatically created, and we can make use of this workbook for our demonstration. First, we need to add a data connection so that we can retrieve appropriate sales data. On the Data tab, in the Get External Data section of the ribbon, select From Other Sources | From Data Connection Wizard, as illustrated:

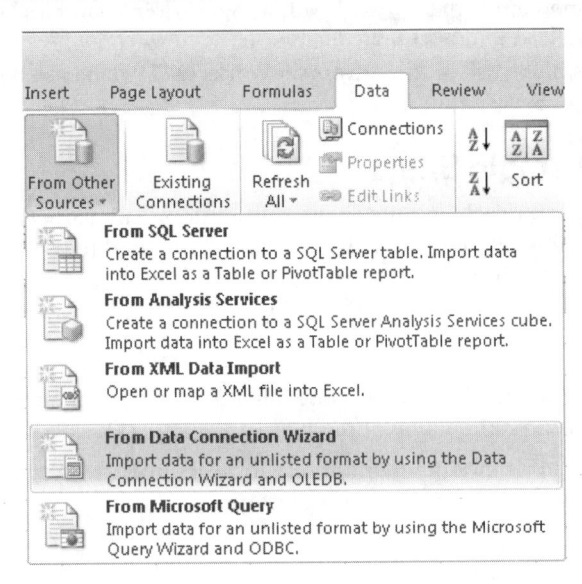

2. In the Data Connection Wizard dialog, accept the default selection of Microsoft SQL Server by clicking Next to proceed.

3. In the Server Name text box, enter **.\SQLExpress**. For the Log On Credentials, select Use Windows Authentication. Click Next.

4. In the Select Database and Table step, change the selected database to AdventureWorks, and uncheck the Connect To A Specific Table checkbox as shown. Click Finish to complete the wizard.

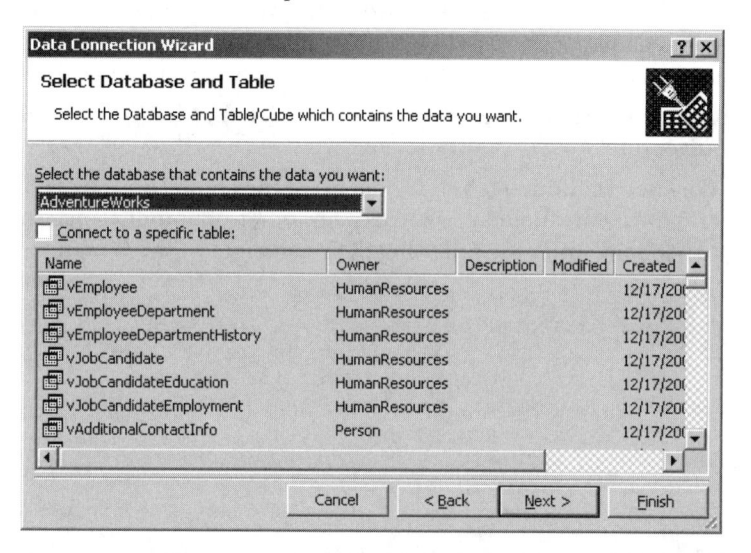

5. After the wizard has completed, the Select Table dialog is displayed. Although the data that we require comes from more than one table, we need to select a table to create a connection in our workbook. Select the SalesOrderHeader table, as shown, and then click OK.

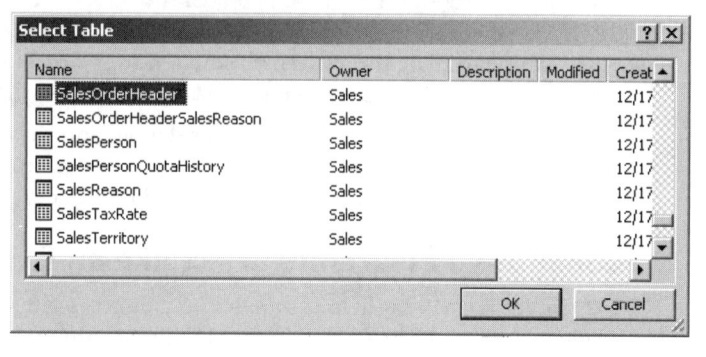

6. The Import Data dialog allows us to select what we want to do with the connected data and includes a few options, such as Table and PivotTable as well as a range selector that we can use to specify where the data should appear in the workbook. When using Excel Services, you should be aware that only PivotTables can be refreshed on the server. Although it is possible to add a table and use the data within the table in Excel Services, the only way to refresh the table data will be to open the spreadsheet in Excel and refresh manually. Bearing this in mind, select PivotTable Report and put the data at the default location of $A$1 in the current worksheet.

## Configure a Data Connection

A new PivotTable is inserted on the page at the specified location. Before we start configuring the PivotTable, we need to review our connection settings. Recall that we selected the SalesOrderHeader table as the source of our data; before we can set up our pivot table, we need to change this to use a SQL query instead.

1. From the Data tab, select the Connections option. In the Workbook Connections dialog, select the ._sqlexpress AdventureWorks connection. Notice that your connection may have a slightly different name, depending on your database server and whether an existing connection with that name already exists.

2. Click Properties to view the connection details. Change the connection name to AdventureWorksLast30DaysSales.

3. Click the Definition tab to see details of the connection string, the command type, and the command text as well as a few other options. Change the Command type to SQL and enter the following SQL statement in the Command Text text box:

   ```
   SELECT      H.OrderDate,
               T.Name as Territory,
               T.CountryRegionCode as CountryCode,
               sum(TotalDue) as TotalSales
   FROM        [Sales].[SalesOrderHeader] as H
   INNER JOIN  [Sales].[SalesTerritory] as T
   ON          H.TerritoryID=T.TerritoryID
   WHERE       H.OrderDate>'2004-07-01'
   GROUP BY    H.OrderDate, T.Name, T.CountryRegionCode
   ```

4. When a data connection is used by Excel, a copy of the connection information is stored in the workbook. In the Properties dialog, we're effectively editing the properties of this cached copy of the data connection. To update our locally saved connection file, click Export Connection File and then, in the file dialog that appears, type the filename as **AdventureWorksLast30DaysSales.odc**. Click Save to create the new Office Database Connection file.

5. Click OK to close the Properties dialog, and then click Close to close the Workbook Connections dialog. Notice that the fields listed in the PivotTable Field List have changed to match those in our amended query.

## Configure a PivotTable to Act like an External Data List

PivotTables are a great help for analyzing a data set interactively. We can easily add in row headers or columns headers or formulas and grouping to the data. Sometimes we don't need to do any of that clever stuff, though; we might want a simple list of the data as it looks in the database. In Excel client, we could of course achieve such a result by creating an External Data List as opposed to a PivotTable. However, External Data Tables aren't supported in Excel Services, so we're stuck trying to reign in the analytical faculties of the PivotTable to produce a more sedate output.

To create a PivotTable that behaves in a similar manner to an External Data List, take the following steps:

1. From the PivotTable Field List, drag OrderDate, CountryCode, and Territory into the Row Labels section. Drag Sum of TotalSales into the Values section, as illustrated:

2. From the PivotTable Tools tab, select the Design menu. In the Layout section of the ribbon, select Report Layout | Show In Tabular Form. Again from the Layout section, select Report Layout | Repeat All Item Labels.

3. The resulting PivotTable is starting to look a bit like a data list. We can now remove the total rows by selecting Subtotals | Do Not Show Subtotals from the Layouts section of the ribbon.

4. To remove the +/− buttons, open the Options menu from the PivotTable Tools tab. Click the +/− button on the Show section of the ribbon to toggle the buttons off.

## Using Named Ranges in Excel Services

You may be wondering why we had to go to the trouble of changing our PivotTable to a flat data list. It's fair to say that, generally speaking, we wouldn't normally need to take this step when using data in Excel Services, but this case is a bit different. The TotalSales value retrieved from the database represents the sales value in US dollars (USD). However, our demonstration scenario requires us to be able to present this data using a variety of currencies. So that we can convert this value to a different currency, we need to use a formula, and formulas within PivotTables are limited to include only data from within the PivotTable. In our case, the exchange rate value that will be used by our formula will be stored elsewhere in the workbook, so using a PivotTable formula isn't an option. We can achieve our desired outcome by flattening our PivotTable and then adding appropriate formulae in adjacent cells.

Let's move on to add a few named ranges that will be used on our calculation logic:

1. Navigate to Sheet2 in the Excel workbook. We'll use this sheet to store the values required by our exchange rate calculation.
2. In cell A1, type **Exchange Rate**. In the adjacent cell (B1), type the number **1**. We'll come back to this later when we create a UDF. With the cell B1 selected, in the Name box, enter **ExchangeRate**, as illustrated:

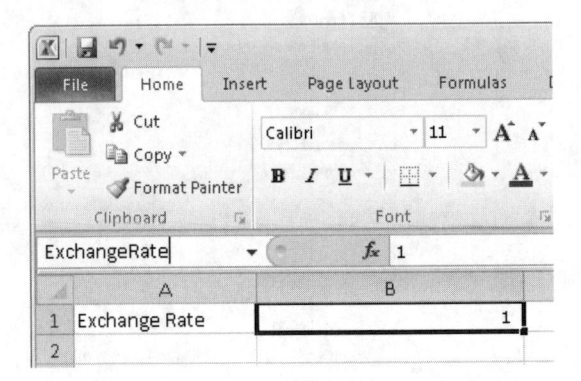

3. In cell A2, type **Currency Code**. In the adjacent cell (B2), type **USD**. With cell B2 selected, in the Name box, type **CurrencyCode**.
4. In cell A3, type **Chart Title**. In the adjacent cell (B3), add the following formula:

   ```
   ="Last 30 Days Sales in " & CurrencyCode
   ```

   When completed, the first few cells of Sheet2 should look like this:

| | A | B | C |
|---|---|---|---|
| 1 | Exchange Rate | | 1 |
| 2 | Currency Code | USD | |
| 3 | Chart Title | Last 30 Days Sales in USD | |
| 4 | | | |
| 5 | | | |
| 6 | | | |
| 7 | | | |
| 8 | | | |

## Perform Calculations Using PivotTable Values

Now that we've defined the parameters for our exchange rate calculation, we can add the necessary formulae to Sheet1.

1. Switch back to Sheet1. In column E, cell E1, add header text **SelectedCurrencyValue**.
2. In cell E2, add this formula:

```
=GETPIVOTDATA("TotalSales",$A$1,"OrderDate",A2,"Territory",C2,"CountryCode",B2)*ExchangeRate
```

This formula extracts the value of the TotalSales column from the PivotTable, where the OrderDate, Territory, and CountryCode columns match the values contained in cells A2, C2, and B2. In plain English, the formula returns the TotalSales value for the current row.

3. Since we want to perform this calculation for each row in the table, we need to use this formula in every cell down to the bottom of the table. To do this, type **E2:E206** in the Name box, and then press CTRL-D. Alternatively, we can manually select the cells in question and then click Fill | Down from the Editing section of the Home ribbon.

---

**NOTE** Using formulae in this manner requires special consideration when the PivotTable referenced will be periodically refreshed. If, during a subsequent refresh, the PivotTable ends up with a different number of rows, the formulae will not automatically be filled down to accommodate the growth of the table. It is important that you ensure that the size of the returned dataset remains constant, and generally this can be done using Transact-SQL (T-SQL) or by calling a stored procedure to produce the required data.

---

4. Since we'll use the data contained in the PivotTable and our calculated column later, we'll give it a name for ease of reference. Either manually highlight the cells in the range A1:E206 or enter the range in the Names box. Once the range is highlighted, type **SourceDataTable**. Sheet1 should now look like this:

|    | A | B | C | D | E |
|----|---|---|---|---|---|
| 1  | OrderDate | CountryCode | Territory | Sum of TotalSales | SelectedCurrencyValue |
| 2  | 02/07/2004 | AU | Australia | 313.4222 | 313.4222 |
| 3  | 02/07/2004 | CA | Canada | 348.5063 | 348.5063 |
| 4  | 02/07/2004 | DE | Germany | 99.7153 | 99.7153 |
| 5  | 02/07/2004 | FR | France | 52.9958 | 52.9958 |
| 6  | 02/07/2004 | GB | United Kingdom | 181.0432 | 181.0432 |
| 7  | 02/07/2004 | US | Northwest | 224.4367 | 224.4367 |
| 8  | 02/07/2004 | US | Southeast | 43.0729 | 43.0729 |
| 9  | 02/07/2004 | US | Southwest | 410.0989 | 410.0989 |
| 10 | 03/07/2004 | AU | Australia | 244.3599 | 244.3599 |
| 11 | 03/07/2004 | CA | Canada | 672.437 | 672.437 |
| 12 | 03/07/2004 | DE | Germany | 96.7207 | 96.7207 |
| 13 | 03/07/2004 | FR | France | 77.339 | 77.339 |
| 14 | 03/07/2004 | GB | United Kingdom | 323.1795 | 323.1795 |
| 15 | 03/07/2004 | US | Northwest | 394.6951 | 394.6951 |
| 16 | 03/07/2004 | US | Southwest | 176.7669 | 176.7669 |
| 17 | 04/07/2004 | AU | Australia | 393.8554 | 393.8554 |
| 18 | 04/07/2004 | CA | Canada | 153.8492 | 153.8492 |
| 19 | 04/07/2004 | FR | France | 233.0336 | 233.0336 |
| 20 | 04/07/2004 | GB | United Kingdom | 169.5733 | 169.5733 |

## Add a PivotChart

Now that we've created a data source that can be automatically refreshed by Excel Services, we can move on to create a chart based on the source data. We'll render the chart on our web page to provide a graphical representation of the sales data.

1. Select Sheet3. We'll use this sheet to contain the elements of our workbook that will be rendered on our sample site. Choose Insert | PivotTable | PivotChart.

2. In the Create PivotTable with PivotChart dialog, type **SourceDataTable** as the Table/Range:

3. From the PivotTable Field List, drag OrderDate into the Axis Fields section, CountryCode into the Legend Fields section, and SelectedCurrencyValue into the Values section. The field lists should look as shown:

4. Our chart is automatically generated based on our PivotTable data. However, the default clustered bar chart type doesn't make it easy to visualize our data set, so let's change this to something more appropriate. From the Design menu, select the Change Chart Type button. In the Change Chart Type dialog, select the Stacked Area chart type.

5. To add a title to our chart, select the Chart Title button from the Layout menu. Since we want our chart title to be automatically generated based on the currency code selected, we can add the following formula:

   ```
   =Sheet2!$B$3
   ```

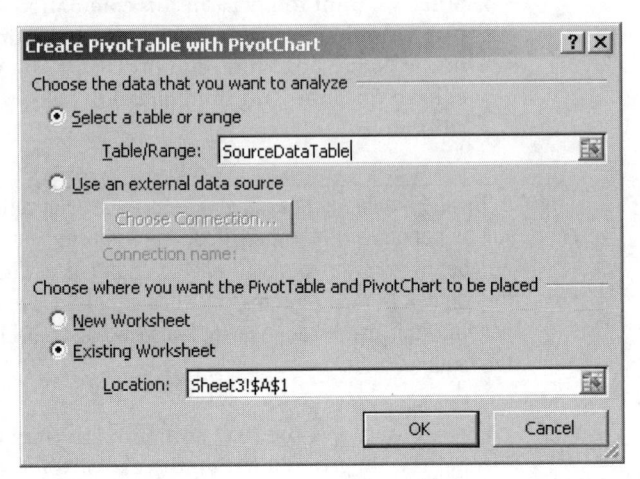

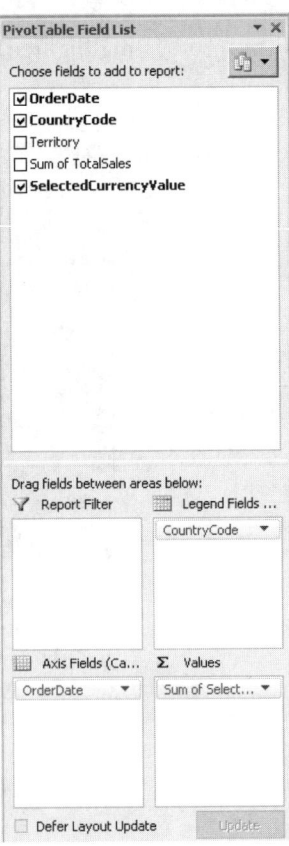

The PivotChart should look like this:

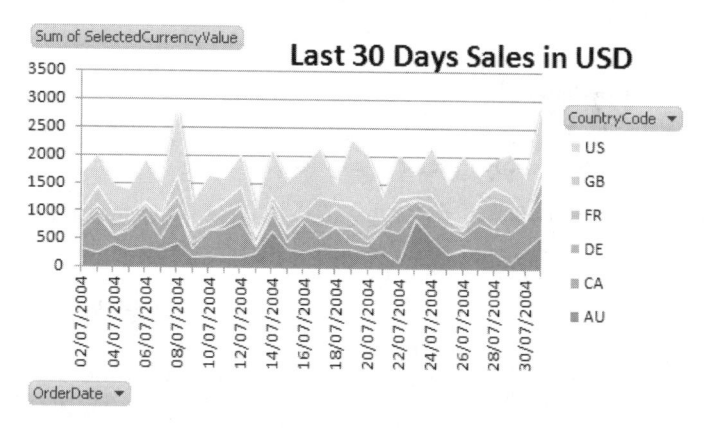

## Publish to Excel Services

The first version of our workbook is now complete and ready to be published to our SharePoint site:

1. In Excel, click the File menu to enter the backstage area. Select Share from the list of options and then select Publish to Excel Services.
2. Set the path to **http://localhost/Chapter12/Excel Workbooks** and the filename to **Last30DaysSales.xlsx**.
3. Click to save the file to SharePoint.

**TIP** When using Excel 2010 on Windows 2008 server, trying to save files to SharePoint doesn't quite work as it should. This is because the WebClient service that maps the SharePoint URL to a UNC path behind the scenes, isn't configured by default since it has no purpose on a server operating system. To fix this problem, install the Desktop Experience feature using Server Manager. See Chapter 2 for a step-by-step guide on configuring Windows 2008 Server as a development machine.

## Create a User Interface Using the Excel Web Access Web Part

Now that we have our workbook published to SharePoint, we can move on to make use of it when generating a user interface for our sample application. We'll customize the homepage of our site to include our sales chart.

1. Navigate to http://localhost/Chapter12/Default.aspx. From the Site Actions menu, choose Edit Page.
2. In the Left Web part zone, click Add A Web Part.
3. Select the Excel Web Access (EWA) web part from the Office Client Applications category. Click Add to include the web part on the page.

**NOTE** If this web part is missing from the web part gallery, ensure that the SharePoint Server Enterprise Site Features and SharePoint Server Enterprise Site Collection Features are enabled for the current site and site collection.

4. To set the properties of the web part, click the Click Here To Open The Tool Pane link.

5. In the Workbook Display section, type the workbook as **/Chapter12/Excel Workbooks/Last30DaysSales.xlsx**.

6. Since we're interested only in the chart for now, in the Named Item field type **Chart 1**. Click **Apply** to see the results.

We've now got our PivotChart on the page ready for use. Let's tidy up a few of the remaining web part settings to give the page a more integrated look:

1. Set the Type of Toolbar to None. This will hide the toolbar that appears above the chart.

2. In the Appearance section, set the Chrome type to None.

3. Click OK to commit the changes and stop editing the web part.

4. From the Page ribbon, click the Stop Editing button to switch back to View mode.

## Adding Interactivity Using a Slicer

*New in 2010*

You've seen how easy it is to make use of Excel data on a page when using the Excel Web Access web part. Let's move on to look at an example of the interactive features available via the web part. Our demonstration scenario requires that the data displayed in our chart be filterable using geographical locations. Although we have listed multiple series, one for each country code, at the moment we don't have any way to select which series should be displayed on the chart.

This section introduces the Slicer, one of the new features available in Excel 2010 that works very well with Excel Services. Before we can use a Slicer, we need to add it to our Excel workbook.

1. Navigate to the Excel Workbooks document library at http://localhost/Chapter12. Open the Last30DaysSales.xlsx file using Microsoft Excel by right-clicking the file and selecting Edit in Microsoft Excel from the context menu.

2. Note that the workbook opens in Protected View mode. This happens because the workbook is opened from a web site as opposed to a local folder. Click Enable Editing to proceed.

3. The next warning we receive says that "Data Connections have been disabled." This is a standard security feature of Excel that prevents active content from running until it is explicitly allowed. Click Enable Content to refresh the connected data.

4. We have the option to make the document trusted. Click Yes, and the workbook won't open in Protected View mode each time. This is OK since we'll be doing a bit of work with it.

5. Adding a Slicer is simple. Select the PivotChart and then, from the Analyze menu, click the Insert Slicer button.

6. From the Insert Slicers dialog, check the Territory checkbox and then click OK to add the Slicer to our worksheet.

7. To see the Slicer in action, try selecting one or more (by holding down the CTRL key while clicking) of the listed Territory values. We can see that the PivotTable data is filtered based on our selection and the PivotChart is redrawn accordingly.

## Grouping Excel Items for Display Purposes

Since we want to display only the Slicer and chart on our web page, we need to lay them out in a specific manner. You'll remember that when we configured the EWA web part earlier in the chapter, we entered a specific named item to display—Chart 1. We now need to display the chart and the Slicer, and since we can enter only one named item, we need to group these into a single item.

As you've seen earlier, named ranges can be defined by selecting a range of cells and then adding a name. We'll use a named range to refer to our chart and Slicer control.

1. Place the chart and the Slicer next to each other on the sheet.
2. Resize the chart and the Slicer so that they fill entire cells as much as possible. This will reduce unnecessary white space when the control is rendered in the web page. The zoom function is very useful for this purpose.
3. Select the underlying range using one of the methods described earlier and type the name **ChartAndSlicer** in the Name box.
4. Click the Save icon in the upper-left corner to save the changes to SharePoint. We'll keep the workbook open for now since we'll be making additional changes later.

If we now open the home page of our sample site using Internet Explorer, unsurprisingly we'll find that our chart is still there just as before, without our new Slicer control. One thing that may be apparent is that the chart now shows only the territories that we selected earlier when we were messing around with the Slicer in Excel client. Note that slicer selections are published along with the workbook, so it's important to make sure that an appropriate default is set before saving.

Let's move on to change our Excel Web Access web part to display our Slicer as well as our chart.

1. From the SiteActions menu, select Edit Page.
2. Highlight the Excel Web Access web part by clicking the header; then, from the Web Part Tools tab, select Web Part Properties from the Options menu.
3. Change the Named Item to **ChartAndSlicer**. Click Apply to view the change.

Our recently defined named item should be displayed on the page, but, instead, we're presented with the following error message stating that the named item cannot be displayed:

4. Click OK to acknowledge the error message. Then from the Page menu, select Stop Editing. The page will now be blank except for the error message.

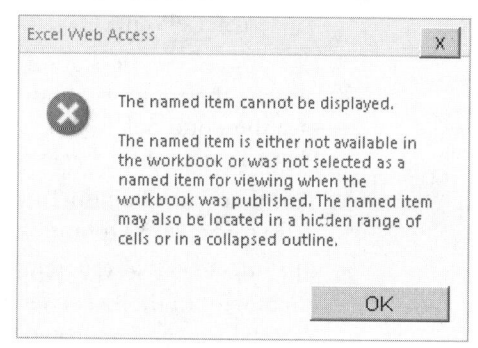

## Change Published Items Within a Workbook

When we initially published our workbook to Excel Services, we simply gave it a name and accepted the default values. Whenever we click the Save icon, rather than re-publishing the workbook, we're merely saving the data back to the document library. The significance here is that when publishing a workbook to Excel Services, we have the option of specifying additional metadata, but when saving, the metadata is not changed. We received the error because the metadata did not contain details of our new named item.

1. Switch back to Excel client. Click the File menu to enter the backstage area. Select the Share option, as shown:

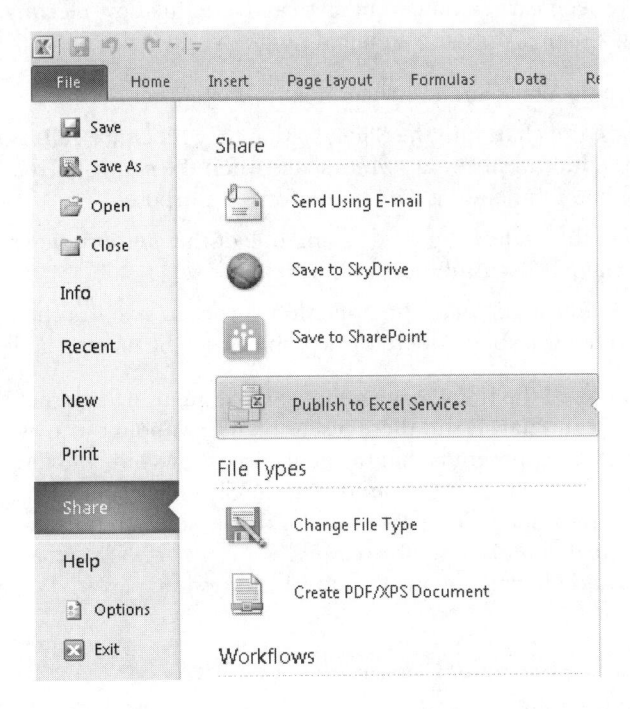

2. The Share section offers two options: Save to SharePoint and Publish to Excel Services. As described, the difference between these two options is the ability to add metadata that's useful to Excel Services. Let's see what that means in practice. Click Save to SharePoint.

3. Click the Current Location icon to open the Save As dialog, which automatically displays the contents of our Excel Workbooks document library and allows us to save the workbook in the normal manner. Click Cancel and then return to the Share section of the backstage area.

4. This time, click Publish To Excel Services to open the Save As dialog, but notice that an Excel Services Options button now appears in the bottom section of the dialog.

5. Click the Excel Service Options button to define or overwrite metadata for the document. In the Excel Services Options dialog's Show tab, select Items In The Workbook from the drop-down list.

6. Check the All Named Ranges and the All Charts options to ensure that they will be available for use by the EWA web part.

> **NOTE** At the time of writing, a bug (or feature, depending on your point of view) exists within Excel 2010. Named ranges that are blank are not detected by the Excel Services publishing process and therefore don't appear in the list of Items in the workbook. To resolve this issue, select the ChartAndSlicer named range and press the SPACEBAR. This will ensure that the range appears in the list of metadata.

7. Click Save to complete the publishing process.

With our metadata updated appropriately, if we return to the sample site home page, we can see that our EWA web part now displays our chart and Slicer as expected. The Slicer behaves in much the same manner as we saw earlier when we used it within the Excel client application.

# Using the Excel Services REST API

Although we could add another EWA web part to our page to display the underlying data for our chart, doing so would introduce unnecessary overhead since we don't need any level of interactivity with the data. Notwithstanding our unquestioned dedication to ensuring optimum performance at all times, another really good reason for not adding a second EWA web part is to give us an opportunity to explore the new REST API that ships with Excel Services 2010.

## Excel Services REST API Syntax

The REST API, as discussed earlier, provides a lightweight mechanism for accessing content within Excel workbooks that have been published using Excel Services. In effect, accessing data using a REST-ful service comes down to using the correct URL, and for the Excel Services REST API, the URL format is http://<*RootUrl*>/_vti_bin/ExcelRest.aspx/<*Filename*>/model/<*Selector*>?<*Parameters*>.

### RootUrl

The *RootUrl* value contains the URL of the SharePoint site containing the workbook. In our case, this will be http://localhost/Chapter12.

### Filename

The *Filename* value contains the relative path to the Excel workbook. In our case, this will be Excel Workbooks/Last30DaysSales.xlsx. However, since we're creating a URL, we need to encode the space in Excel Workbooks. This value then becomes Excel%20Workbooks/Last30DaysSales.xslx.

### Selector

The *Selector* value is where the fun begins in the REST URL. Let's run through a quick demonstration of how it works.

If you enter the following URL into a web browser, you'll see a page listing the types of data available within the model:

http://localhost/Chapter12/_vti_bin/ExcelRest.aspx/Excel%20Workbooks/Last30DaysSales.xlsx/model

As you can see, in the case of Excel, the types available are Ranges, Charts, Tables, and PivotTables.

You can build up the selector value by first deciding in which type of data you're interested. In our case, it's Charts. Enter the following URL into a web browser to see a list of available charts:

http://localhost/Chapter12/_vti_bin/ExcelRest.aspx/Excel%20Workbooks/Last30DaysSales.xlsx/model/Charts

From the returned data, you can see that our workbook contains only one chart, Chart 1. Let's create a selector for the Chart 1 object. In the browser, enter the following URL:

http://localhost/Chapter12/_vti_bin/ExcelRest.aspx/Excel%20Workbooks/Last30DaysSales.xlsx/model/Charts('Chart%201')

Notice that this simply specifies that you want Chart 1 from the Charts collection. Again the space is encoded in the name *Chart 1* since we're building a URL. This time the browser will display a Portable Network Graphics (PNG) image representing our chart.

## Parameters

The *Parameters* value allows us to pass values into Excel Services as part of our request. For example, our workbook defines a named range called CurrencyCode. The value of CurrencyCode is used to produce the chart title, so by changing CurrencyCode as part of our REST URL, our chart title will change as well. To see this in action, in the browser, enter the following URL:

http://localhost/Chapter12/_vti_bin/ExcelRest.aspx/Excel%20Workbooks/Last30DaysSales.xlsx/model/Charts('chart%201')?Ranges('CurrencyCode')=MyCurrencyCode

You can see that the chart has been produced with a label that reads Last 30 Days Sales in MyCurrencyCode.

## Retrieving a PivotTable Using REST

Now that you understand how a REST URL can be generated, let's put this knowledge to good use by creating a URL that we can use to include data from our PivotTable on our sample site home page.

If we enter the following URL in the browser, we'll get a 404 error:

http://localhost/Chapter12/_vti_bin/ExcelRest.aspx/Excel%20Workbooks/Last30DaysSales.xlsx/model/PivotTables('PivotTable1')

Before we can access items using the REST API, we need to make sure that we've published the appropriate metadata from the Excel client. You'll remember earlier that we didn't select any of the PivotTables in our list of items, and that's why we're seeing a 404 error now.

1. Switch back to the Excel client application. Before we publish our PivotTables, let's give them useful names. Switch to Sheet3 and then click anywhere within the PivotTable.

2. From the PivotTable Tools tab, select the Options menu. In the PivotTable section, in the PivotTable Name box, type **ChartData**, as illustrated:

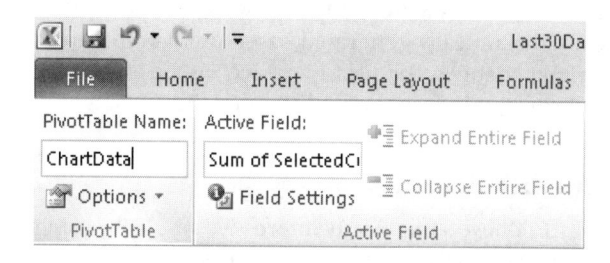

3. Switch to Sheet1 and type the name of the PivotTable as **SourceData**.
4. We'll add an additional PivotTable to summarize our sales figures. Add a new worksheet named Sheet4. Insert a new PivotTable that makes use of SourceDataTable as its data source.
5. Add OrderDate as a RowLabel and SelectedCurrencyValue as a Value.
6. Right-click the Sum of SelectedCurrencyValue column header, and then select Value Field Settings. In the Custom Name text box, type **Total Sales**.
7. Name the new PivotTable **TotalSalesData**.
8. Click the File menu to enter the backstage area, and then click the Publish To Excel Services button in the Share section.
9. Click the Excel Services Options button, and then select All Pivot Tables in the Items In The Workbook section.
10. Save the workbook to update the metadata.

We can now enter the following URL in the browser and see an HTML representation of our chart data:

http://localhost/Chapter12/_vti_bin/ExcelRest.aspx/Excel%20Workbooks/Last30DaysSales.xlsx/model/PivotTables('TotalSalesData')

## Using REST-Generated Content Within a Web Part Page

Now that we have a URL, the next step is to make use of that on our home page. The easiest way to include additional content on the page is to use a PageViewer web part.

1. From the SiteActions menu, select Edit Page.
2. Click Add a Web Part in the Right web part zone, and then select the Page Viewer web part from the Media and Content category.
3. Set the Link property of the Page Viewer web part to the REST API URL for our TotalSalesData PivotTable.
4. Click OK to commit the changes, and then click Stop Editing from the Page ribbon to return to view mode.

We've now created a user interface for our sales data that allows users to filter data by territory. As well as using the EWA web part, we've also included content generated using the REST API on our page via a Page Viewer web part. All of the items presented in the user interface are dynamically generated based on data from an external data source. As the underlying data changes, the user interface will be automatically updated to reflect those changes. Bear in mind, so far, we haven't written a single line of code.

# User-Defined Functions

We've managed to achieve some pretty impressive results by using the tools that are available out of the box with Excel 2010 and Excel Services. However, one of the areas from our demonstration scenario that we haven't properly addressed is the requirement to dynamically convert the sales data to a range of currencies. We've designed our workbook to allow for such a calculation; we just haven't done the actual calculation part yet, and there's a good reason for that: Excel doesn't have a function for automatically retrieving exchange rates for a stated currency.

In this section, we'll create a UDF that accepts a currency code as an input parameter. The function will then connect to a web service to retrieve a current exchange rate for the selected currency and will pass the resulting value back to Excel for use by the calculations within our workbook.

## Attributes Used when Creating UDFs

UDFs are simply managed code assemblies that have been marked up using specific attributes that denote methods and classes that are callable from Excel Services. The attributes in question can be found in the Microsoft.Office.Excel.Server.Udf namespace, which is defined in the Microsoft.Office.Excel.Server.Udf.dll assembly. The following attributes are available.

### UdfClassAttribute

This attribute is applied to a public class and is used to denote that the class may contain UDFs that can be used by Excel Services.

### UdfMethodAttribute

This attribute can be applied to public methods and is used to indicate that the method is a UDF and can be used by Excel Services. The **UdfMethodAttribute** accepts a couple of properties:

**IsVolatile**  This Boolean value specifies whether or not the UDF should be considered volatile. When referring to Excel functions, specifying that a function is volatile indicates that the function should be reevaluated whenever any value in the workbook changes. The default behavior is non-volatile, which means that the function is reevaluated only when any of the parameters that are passed into it change. Generally, the default behavior is appropriate unless the UDF is reading other related data behind the scenes that may have changed as a result of activities elsewhere in the workbook.

**ReturnsPersonalInformation**  This Boolean value determines whether the identity of the calling user can be accessed via the executing thread's current principal. This means that where this value is set to true, details of the calling user can be retrieved as follows:

```
[UdfMethod(ReturnsPersonalInformation = true)]
public string GetCallersUsername()
{
  if (Thread.CurrentPrincipal.Identity != null)
  {
    return Thread.CurrentPrincipal.Identity.Name;
  }
  else
  {
    return string.Empty;
  }
}
```

## Usable Data Types Within UDFs

The .NET Framework contains many different data types, and any of these types can be used as a parameter or return value for a method. However, as you may imagine, Excel doesn't necessarily know how to process each and every data type and can therefore use only a small subset of the types available. General speaking, only types defined in the System namespace are supported, such as String, Boolean, DateTime, and Object. Exceptions to this rule are Int64 and UInt64, which are not supported.

As well as passing simple values, contiguous ranges can also be passed into a UDF as one- or two-dimensional object arrays. For example, the following two functions accept a single row and a range of cells, respectively:

```
[UdfMethod]
public int ProcessSingleRow(object[] row)
{
  return row.Length;
}

[UdfMethod]
public int ProcessRange(object[,] range)
{
  return range.Length;
}
```

## Creating a UDF Using Visual Studio 2010

For most of our code samples throughout this book, we've made use of the SharePoint 2010 templates that are available in Visual Studio. Since a UDF is simply a managed assembly, we can create it using a basic class library project. We can then configure SharePoint to pick up the assembly from the file system whenever it is required by a workbook.

1. Open Visual Studio 2010. Choose File | New | Project.

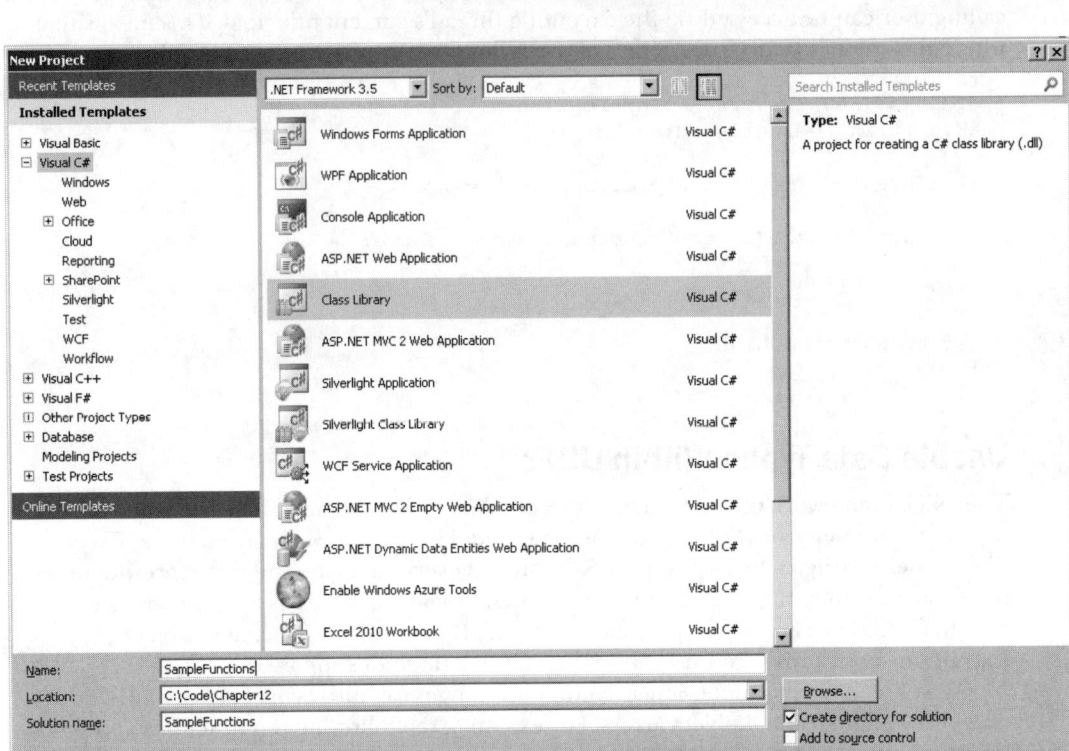

2. Create a new Class Library project and name it SampleFunctions, as illustrated:

3. Rename Class1.cs to CurrencyConvertor.cs.
4. As mentioned, this UDF will make a web service call to obtain a current exchange rate. Before we add the code for the UDF function, we need to add a reference to the web service. Choose Project | Add Service Reference.
5. The Add Service Reference wizard is used to create WCF service references. Generally speaking, this wouldn't cause any problems. However, the web service to which we're connecting makes use of the ISO-8859-1 encoding standard, and unfortunately the binding types provided with WCF don't support this standard. Rather than writing a load of code to support the standard in WCF, we'll work around the problem by creating a .NET 2.0 Web Reference instead. Click the Advanced button in the Add Service Reference dialog and then in the Service Reference Settings page, click the Add Web Reference button.
6. In the Add Web Reference dialog's URL text box, enter **http://xurrency.com/api.wsdl**.
7. Type **XurrencySoap** in the Web Reference Name text box, as shown, and then click Add Reference to generate a proxy for the web service.

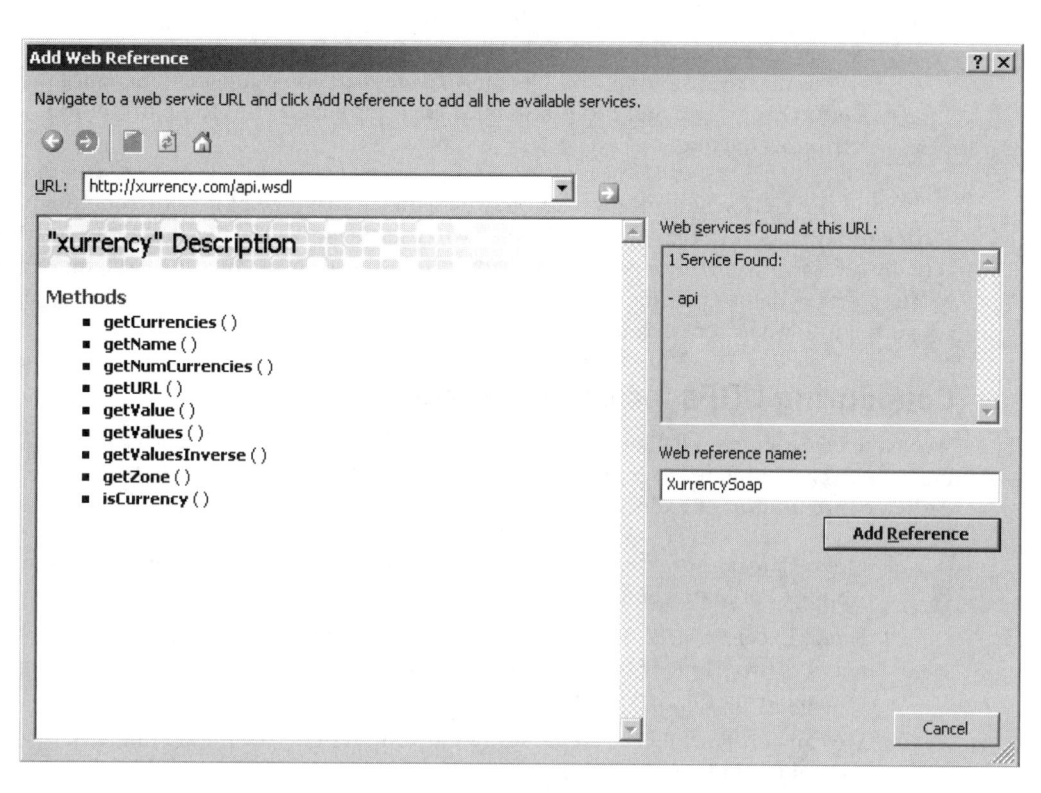

![Add Web Reference dialog showing xurrency Description with methods: getCurrencies(), getName(), getNumCurrencies(), getURL(), getValue(), getValues(), getValuesInverse(), getZone(), isCurrency(). URL: http://xurrency.com/api.wsdl. Web reference name: XurrencySoap.]

8. Before we can add our UDF method, we need to add a reference to the Excel Services UDF Framework. Choose Project | Add Reference. In the .NET tab, select Excel Services UDF Framework. Click OK to add the reference.

9. We're now ready to add some code to our CurrencyConvertor class. In the CurrencyConvertor.cs file, add the following code:

```
using System;
using Microsoft.Office.Excel.Server.Udf;

namespace SampleFunctions
{
  [UdfClass]
  public class CurrencyConvertor
  {

    [UdfMethod(IsVolatile = false, ReturnsPersonalInformation = true)]
    public double GetExchangeRate(string currencyCode)
    {
      XurrencySoap.xurrency client = new XurrencySoap.xurrency();
      client.Url = "http://xurrency.com/servidor_soap.php";
      return client.getValue(1, "usd", currencyCode.ToLower());
    }
  }
}
```

Notice a few things about this short code sample. First, the **CurrencyConvertor** class is marked as public and has the **UdfClass** attribute attached. Second, the **GetExchangeRate** method is also marked as public and has the **UdfMethod** attribute attached.

Within the **GetExchangeRate** method, we create an instance of the **XurrencySoap** web service proxy class, and then we use the proxy to call the **getValue** method. Since **getValue** actually performs a currency conversion rather than simply providing the exchange rate, we've specified via our parameters that the method should return the value of $1 when converted into whatever currency code is passed into the function.

## Configuring UDFs for Development

We've created a simple UDF using Visual Studio. We can now build the project and then move on to make the necessary configuration changes within SharePoint. As discussed earlier, configuration of Excel Services is done via the Central Administration tool.

1. Open Central Administration and then select Manage Service Applications in the Application Management section.
2. Select Excel Services from the list of application either by clicking the Excel Services hyperlink or by highlighting the Excel Services row and then clicking Manage from the Service Applications menu.
3. We can configure UDF assemblies by clicking the User Defined Function Assemblies link on the Manage Excel Services page.

When it comes to adding UDF assemblies, we have two options. We can either place the assembly in the GAC or we can access it directly from the file system. For development purposes, reading the assembly from the file system is easiest since we can simply build the project on our development machine and the new assembly will be immediately available to SharePoint without us having to take any additional steps. However, bear in mind that reading assemblies directly from the file system represents a significant security risk. It's a trivial task to tamper with the assembly and have it perform all kinds of nefarious acts under the security context of any unfortunate Excel user who happens to open a workbook that references the function. It is therefore best practice to sign all UDFs on production servers and deploy them to the GAC.

Let's look at how we'd configure an assembly to be picked up from the file system and how we can debug UDFs.

1. Click the Add User-Defined Function Assembly link.
2. Select File Path as the Assembly Location.
3. In the Assembly text box, enter the path to the assembly. In our case, we'll enter **C:\Code\Chapter12\SampleFunctions\SampleFunctions\bin\Debug\SampleFunctions.dll**.
4. Click OK to add the assembly. The User-Defined Functions page will look as illustrated:

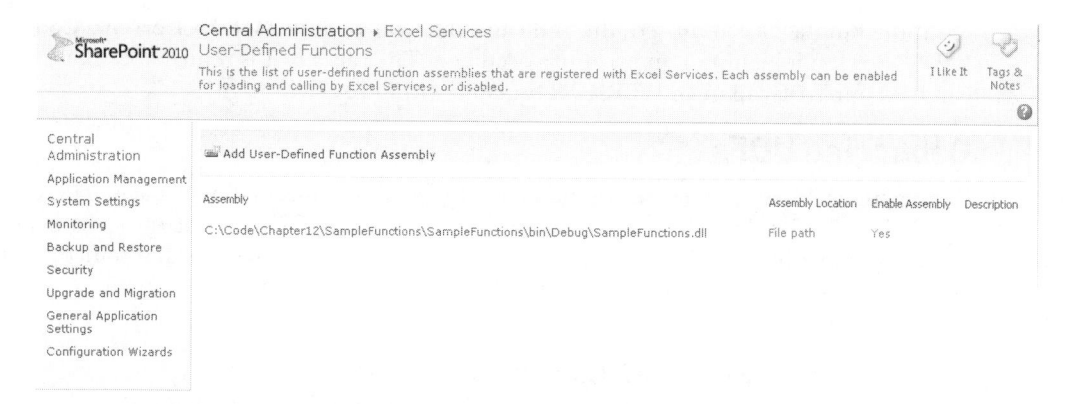

## Using UDFs Within Excel

We can now make use of our custom function in our Excel workbook.

1. If it's not already open, in our sample site, navigate to the Excel Workbooks document library and open the Last30DaysSales workbook using the Excel client application.

2. Switch to Sheet2, and in the cell B1, enter the following formula:

   `=IFERROR(GetExchangeRate(CurrencyCode),1)`

   This formula simply calls our UDF **GetExchangeRate** and passes in the value of the **CurrencyCode** named range. The call to our UDF is wrapped in an **IFERROR** function so that data is still rendered on the client if an error occurs. Where an error occurs, we've used an exchange rate of 1, which will effectively generate charts and PivotTables based on the raw data as opposed to a pile of #NAME? or #VALUE? errors. Note that UDFs are not accessible within Excel client and will always display a #NAME? error.

3. Commit the changes to SharePoint by clicking the Save button in the upper-left corner. We can use the Save button in this instance because the underlying metadata hasn't changed. We don't need to use the Publish to Excel Services function that we used previously.

## Using the REST API to Test a UDF

As it stands, we don't have a user interface to switch between currency codes, but we can check that our UDF is working properly by using the REST API. In a web browser, enter the following URL:

http://localhost/Chapter12/_vti_bin/ExcelRest.aspx/Excel%20Workbooks/Last30DaysSales.xlsx/model/Ranges('ExchangeRate')?Ranges('CurrencyCode')=AUD

This URL is using the REST API to return the contents of the **ExchangeRate** named range when the **CurrencyCode** named range contains the value **AUD**. In other words, we're using the REST API to display the exchange rate between **USD** and **AUD**. The resulting output should be a number similar to 1.15, depending on the actual exchange rate at the time you call the API.

If the number 1 is returned, this indicates that you've either set the **CurrencyCode** to USD (or left it blank) or an error has occurred. The value of 1 is returned because we wrapped our UDF call in an **IFERROR** function within Excel.

## Debugging UDFs

Debugging UDFs is not quite as simple as debugging other SharePoint artifacts. The UDF is called by the Excel Services service application, which runs as a separate process. Bearing this in mind, we have two options: we can either attach our debugger to all instances of the w3wp.exe process, or we can find out which process is being used to run service applications on our server.

### Discovering the ProcessID Used to Run a UDF

Even though most of us will take the lazy option of attaching to all worker processes, here's how we can find out the correct Process ID.

As mentioned, Excel Services runs under a separate process. All service applications running on a server are published under the SharePoint Web Services application in Internet Information Server 7.0 (IIS7) and run within a specific application pool. Knowing the name of this application pool is important when we're working with UDFs since we may need to recycle it to free up locked assemblies.

1. In IIS Manager, navigate to the SharePoint Web Services site, expand the root node, and select the first service application.

2. From the Actions pane, select Advanced Settings. In the General section, the name of the Application Pool appears:

3. Armed with the name of the application pool, we can now do a bit of digging to discover the Process ID. Open a command prompt and navigate to the C:\Windows\System32\inetsrv folder.

4. Enter the following command to list all the worker processes that are being used by IIS:

    ```
    appcmd list wp
    ```

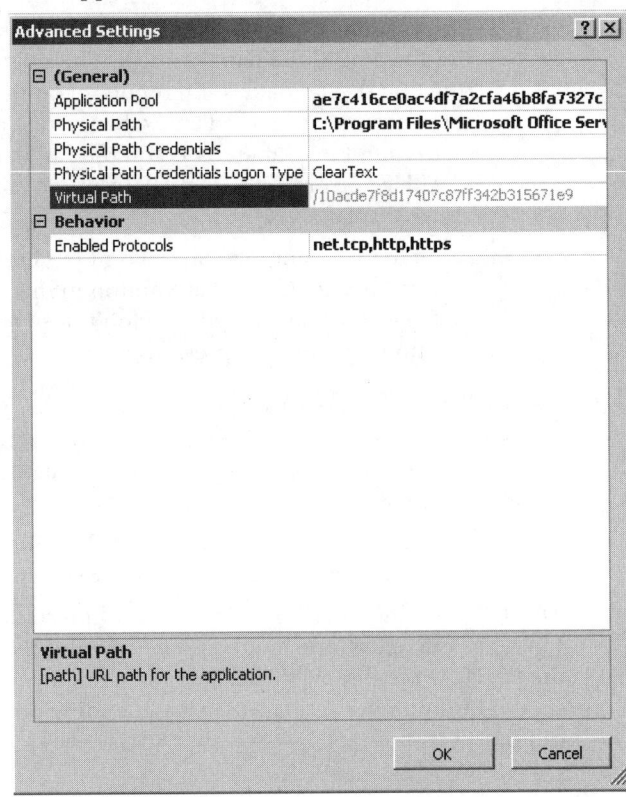

The returned list will be formatted as follows:

```
WP "7260" (applicationPool:SharePoint - 80)
WP "7444" (applicationPool:SharePoint Central Administration v4)
WP "4556" (applicationPool:1c549b9ed5ad4dac8e977df6da3c733b)
WP "4428" (applicationPool:ae7c416ce0ac4df7a2cfa46b8fa7327c)
```

The first column, **WP**, identifies the type of record—in our case worker process. The second column contains the process ID, and the last column contains the application pool that is using the process. By finding the process that corresponds to our SharePoint Web Services application pool, we can determine the process ID.

Note that the process ID may change between debugging sessions, but the application pool name will remain constant unless SharePoint is reinstalled.

### Manually Attaching the Visual Studio 2010 Debugger

Now let's manually attach the Visual Studio Debugger and recycle the SharePoint Web Services application pool.

1. In Visual Studio 2010, choose Debug | Attach to Process.
2. Select the w3wp.exe process with the correct ID value, and then click **Attach**.
3. Add a breakpoint within the UDF function. Execution will stop on the breakpoint, allowing debugging to take place.

You've seen how to debug UDFs using Visual Studio; now let's step into our UDF code. What happens if we need to make changes to our code and recompile our assembly? You'd think it would simply be a case of clicking the Build button, but unfortunately it's not quite that straightforward if we've configured SharePoint to pick up the UDF from our bin folder. The Excel Services service application will maintain a lock on the file while it's in use, making it impossible for Visual Studio to overwrite when compiling a new version. Thankfully, this is an easy problem to fix. All we need to do is recycle the SharePoint Web Services application pool and the lock will be released. This can be done using IIS or using the command line by entering the following:

```
appcmd recycle apppool /apppool.name:<the name of the app pool>
```

### Configuring UDFs for Production

You've already learned the two ways for SharePoint to reference UDF assemblies: either directly via file path or indirectly via the Global Assembly Cache. I covered the steps required to reference an assembly via a file path in a development environment and the steps required to debug UDF assemblies.

Now that development of our UDF is complete, let's take a look at the steps required to reference our assembly via the GAC:

1. Within Visual Studio, right-click the SampleFunctions node in the SolutionExplorer pane. Select Properties from the context menu.
2. In the Solution Properties Designer, click the Signing tab and check the Sign The Assembly checkbox.

3. From the Choose A Strong Name Key File drop-down, select <New…> to create a new Strong Name Key.
4. Now that we've specified that the assembly should be signed, we must recompile it before the signature is applied. Choose Build | Build SampleFunctions.
5. Now copy our assembly to the C:\Windows\Assembly folder to register it with the Global Assembly Cache.
6. Switch over to the SharePoint 2010 Central Admin site, where we'll change the UDF configuration within the Manage Excel Services page. Delete the previous development entry for SampleFunctions.dll.
7. Click Add User-Defined Function Assembly. Set the Assembly Location to Global Assembly Cache.
8. To find the strong name for our assembly, switch back to Visual Studio 2010. Either press CTRL-ALT-A or choose View | Other Windows | Command Window to display the Visual Studio Command Window.
9. In the command window, enter the following command:

   ``` 
   ? typeof(SampleFunctions.CurrencyConvertor).Assembly.FullName
   ```

   The resulting output will be the strong name for our assembly:

   ```
   SampleFunctions, Version=1.0.0.0, Culture=neutral,
   PublicKeyToken=your-token-here
   ```

10. Copy this value into the Assembly text box on our Add User-Defined Function Assembly page, as shown:

**Assembly details**
Settings for a .NET assembly that contains User-Defined Functions.

**Assembly**
Strong name or full path of an assembly that contains user-defined functions, which Excel Calculation Services can call.
Examples: SampleCompany.SampleApplication.SampleUdf, C:\UDFs\SampleUdf.dll, \\MyNetworkServer\UDFs\SampleUdf.dll.

SampleFunctions, Version=1.0.0.0, Cult

**Assembly Location**
Location of the assembly:
○ Global assembly cache
○ File path

**Enable Assembly**
Allow this user-defined function assembly to be loaded and used by Excel Calculation Services. Turning off this option disables the assembly without having to completely remove the entry from the list.
☑ Assembly enabled

11. Click OK to register the assembly and then recycle the SharePoint Web Services application pool to pick up the new reference.

We can now test using the REST API URL that we created earlier to confirm that our assembly is being correctly picked up from the GAC.

## Using the JavaScript Object Model

We've almost met the requirements of our demonstration scenario. The only item missing is a user-interface element that can be used to switch currencies. Let's move on and take a look at how we can implement this functionality using the JavaScript Object Model (JSOM).

### A Whirlwind Tour of Excel JSOM

Before we jump into adding script to the page, let's look at the objects that are exposed via JSOM and the mechanism for connecting to EWA web parts.

#### EwaControl

The **EwaControl** is the entry point to the object model and represents an EWA web part. As well as representing a specific instance of an EWA web part, the **EwaControl** has a static **getInstances** method that can be used to retrieve a collection of the EWA web parts on a page. For example, the following code snippet returns an **EwaControl** object that represents the first EWA web part on a page:

```
var myEwa = Ewa.EwaControl.getInstances().getItem(0);
```

As well as the methods mentioned, all events exposed by JSOM are defined on the **EwaControl** object. These include events such as **activeCellChanged**, **gridSynchronized**, and **workbookChanged**.

Event-handling delegates can be hooked up using JavaScript code similar to this snippet:

```
var myEwa;
_spBodyOnLoadFunctionNames.push("EwaPageLoad");
function EwaPageLoad() {
    Ewa.EwaControl.add_applicationReady(GetEwa);
}
function GetEwa(){
    myEwa = Ewa.EwaControl.getInstances().getItem(0);
    if(myEwa)
    {
        myEwa.add_activeSelectionChanged(activeSelectionChangedHandler);
    }
}
```

#### Workbook

The **Workbook** object represents an Excel workbook. A reference to the workbook used by a particular **EwaControl** can be retrieved using the following code:

```
var myWorkbook = myEwa.getActiveWorkbook();
```

The **Workbook** object provides a number of methods that can be used to retrieve particular ranges, worksheets, or named ranges. As well as these methods, refreshing the underlying data of a workbook can be performed by calling the **refreshAllAsync** method. Note that to refresh a workbook, the referenced EWA web part must have the Refresh Selected Connection, Refresh All Connections option checked.

### Range

The **Range** object represents one or more cells. The most common use of the **Range** object is to get or set particular values within a workbook. The following code snippet sets the value of the first cell in a workbook:

```
var theRange = myWorkbook.getRange("A1", 1, 1, 1, 1);
theRange.setValuesAsync(values, myCallBack, null);
```

Notice a few things about this snippet. First, when calling **setValuesAsync**, the values property must contain a two-dimensional array of cell values. Second, all interactions with the Excel workbook are performed asynchronously. This makes sense when you think about it, since the workbook is actually being processed on the server and is being accessed via Asynchronous JavaScript and XML (AJAX).

### Sheet

The **Sheet** object represents a single worksheet within a workbook. References to specific sheets can be obtained using the **getSheets** method of the **Workbook** object, which will return a **SheetCollection** object, or using the **getActiveSheet** method of the **Workbook** object, which will return a reference to the currently active sheet.

### NamedItem

The **NamedItem** object represents a named range. For all practical purposes, the **NamedItem** object is useful only for selecting a particular named range via the **activateAsync** method. When it comes down to reading data from a named range or writing data to a named range, both of these actions must be performed using a **Range** object. For example, this code snippet reads values from a named range:

```
function someFunction()
{
  var myEwa = Ewa.EwaControl.getInstances().getItem(0);
  var myWorkbook = myEwa.getActiveWorkbook();
  var theRange = myWorkbook.getRange("MyNamedRange", 1, 1, 1, 1);
  var values = theRange.getValuesAsync(Ewa.ValuesFormat.Formatted, getCallBack, null);
}
function getCallBack(returnValues) {
    window.status = returnValues.getReturnValue();
}
```

## Adding a Content Editor Web Part Containing JavaScript

To make our demonstration focus on the specifics of communicating with Excel via JSOM, our user interface will consist of a simple drop-down list of currencies. We can include JavaScript on a web part page in a few ways. One is to modify the page using SharePoint Designer and physically insert the script into the page. Another method, and the one that we'll use for our demonstration, is to add a Content Editor web part that uses a link to a text file containing the appropriate script.

When I covered the JSOM earlier, I mentioned that it works by leveraging a collection of JavaScript objects provided by one or more Excel Web Access web parts. As a result of this, we can access the Excel JavaScript API only on pages containing at least on EWA web part. We'll make use of this functionality on the home page of our sample site.

1. Navigate to http://localhost/Chapter12/Default.aspx, and choose Site Actions | Edit Page.
2. In the Left web part zone, click Add a Web Part and then select the Content Editor web part from the Media and Content category.
3. Select the Content Editor web part by clicking the header; then, from the Options menu, select Web Part Properties. In the Content Link text box, enter this: **http://localhost/Chapter12/Excel%20Workbooks/JSOM.content.txt**.
4. Click OK to save the changes to the web part properties. Then click Stop Editing from the Page menu to return to View mode.

## Creating JSOM Content in an External File

We've configured our content editor web part to read its contents from an external file; we'll now move on to create a file containing the appropriate JSOM content. Note that we could enter the JavaScript directly into the Content Editor web part, but using an external file makes debugging and editing easier.

1. Open Notepad.exe and enter the following text in a new document:

```
<select id="Select1" onchange="UpdateChart(this)">
   <option value="ARS">Argentine Peso</option>
   <option value="AUD">Australian Dollar</option>
   <option value="GBP">British Pound</option>
   <option value=vJPY">Japanese Yen</option>
   <option value="EUR">Euro</option>
   <option value="USD" selected="selected">US Dollar</option>
</select>
<script type="text/javascript">
    var myEwa;
    _spBodyOnLoadFunctionNames.push("EwaPageLoad");

    function EwaPageLoad()
    {
        Ewa.EwaControl.add_applicationReady(GetEwa);
    }

    function GetEwa()
    {
        myEwa = Ewa.EwaControl.getInstances().getItem(0);
    }

    function UpdateChart(sender)
    {
        if (myEwa) {
            var values = new Array();
            values[0] = sender.value;

            var values2 = new Array();
            values2[0] = values;

            var currencyCode=myEwa.getActiveWorkbook().getRange("CurrencyCode", 1, 1, values.length, 1);
            currencyCode.setValuesAsync(values2, setCallBack, null);
        }
```

```
    else
    {
        window.status = 'Excel Web Access not ready';
    }
}

function setCallBack(returnValues) {
    myEwa.getActiveWorkbook().refreshAllAsync(refreshCallback,null);
}

function refreshCallback(returnValues) {
    window.status = 'Sales chart has been refreshed';
}
```

`</script>`

    2. Save the file as **JSOM.Content.txt** to \\localhost\Chapter12\Excel Workbooks.

We can now refresh our home page to see the fruits of our labor. We can select a currency from the drop-down list and our chart will be recalculated using that currency, as shown next:

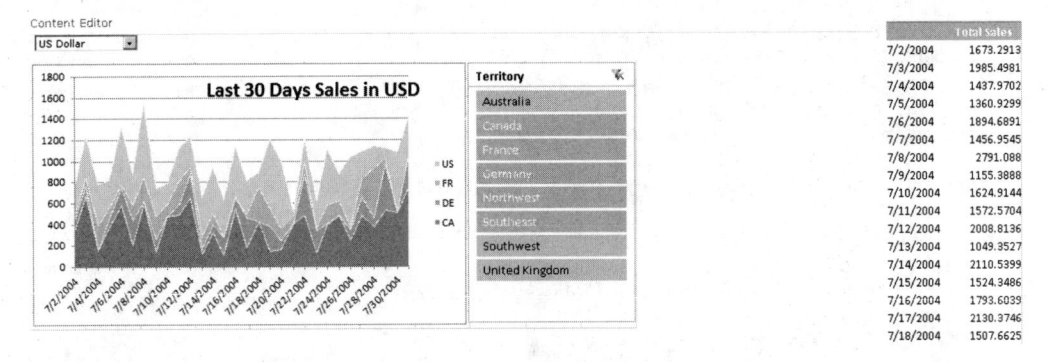

As you can see, when we try to select a new currency, however, things are not quite as simple as we'd hoped. For example, if we switch the currency to Japanese Yen, we see an Excel Web Access error telling us "A Setting on Excel Services does not allow the requested operation to be performed." Errors of this type can happen quite often when using JSOM, and the reason comes back to what I said at the beginning of this section: JSOM works by using a set of objects that are exposed by an Excel Web Access web part. Although the error suggests that an Excel Services setting is responsible for our problem, more often than not it's a property setting on the EWA web part that we're referencing in script. In our case, the problem is that we're trying to set the value of the CurrencyCode named range but the Interactivity Settings for the EWA web part don't allow Typing and Formula Entry. Switch to Edit mode and modify the properties of the EWA web part to resolve this issue. Our home page will now behave as expected.

## Using Data Connection Libraries

We've managed to meet the requirements of our demonstration scenario and conveniently in the process have touched upon all the major features of Excel Services. Although our demonstration site works as required, in a real-world environment, we'd need to consider a few other aspects, particularly those with regard to how data connection information is stored and used.

Our sample workbook includes an embedded data connection that has been configured to use the credentials of the currently logged-in user. This approach has a few drawbacks, however. First, all users of the web site must also be granted permissions to access the data source referred to by the workbook. Second, anybody with permissions to edit the workbook can make changes to the data connection, possibly creating a connection to a server that's not generally accessible. In such a case, the generated workbook would display just fine for users with appropriate permissions on the data source but would display an error message for other users. As well as creating connections to restricted servers, a user might also be able to create a connection that returned an unnecessarily large volume of data. For example, a user could read every single sales transaction record from an ERP system into a pivot table and then summarize the total sales data by quarter. While this would deliver the required end result, the performance implications of using such a Workbook in Excel Services are considerable.

To resolve these issues, you can restrict data connection availability to specific data connection libraries. Permissions can be set on the libraries so that only authorized users can create connections. This provides a much higher degree of control over what data sources can be used, how authentication is handled, and how queries are written. Furthermore, it allows users who are not familiar with the nuances of connecting to database servers and retrieving data to create useful Excel workbooks simply by selecting the appropriate data source from a list.

## Restricting Data Connection Types

Let's start by denying our embedded connection the rights to run under Excel Services:

1. Using SharePoint 2010 Central Administration, select Manage Service Applications from the Application Management section.

2. Select the appropriate Excel Web Service Application instance from the list of available services.

3. In the Trusted File Locations section, add a new location specifically for our sample site. This will allow us to override the default settings for our sample site without affecting the settings for other sites that use our Excel Services instance. Click the Add Trusted File Location link.

4. In the Location section, type the Address as **http://<your server name>/Chapter12** and then check the Children Trusted checkbox. Notice that we're using the physical server name rather than localhost because Excel Services configuration uses the URL that was assigned to an application when it was first created. Although we've accessed our sample site using the URL http://localhost/Chapter12, this URL isn't configured within SharePoint and therefore can't be used as a SharePoint trusted file location.

5. In the External Data section, select the Trusted Data Connection Libraries Only option for Allow External Data.

6. Currently our workbook is set up to refresh external data content manually. As it happens, the first time we select a currency from the drop-down list, the workbook

is refreshed, causing the underlying external data to be reloaded. The caching settings within the External Data section determine how often external data is reloaded, and the default values mean that external data is cached for a period of 5 minutes. When we reconfigure our data connection to use a Data Connection library, we'll set it up to refresh automatically when the workbook is loaded. To prevent the user from having to confirm this refresh every time the workbook is opened, uncheck the Refresh Warning Enabled checkbox.

7. In the User-Defined Functions section. check the User-Defined Functions Allowed checkbox.

8. Click OK to apply the settings.

We can now revisit our sample site home page to see the damage that we've done to our application. Bearing in mind that external data is refreshed only whenever the currency code is changed, select an alternative currency from the drop-down list to trigger a refresh. If our configuration changes have been properly applied, we should see an error, as shown:

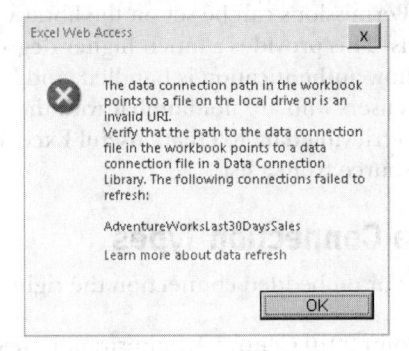

Excel services makes extensive use of caching, both in terms of the workbooks and the external data that's used within them. If the expected error is not shown, it's most likely because the workbook has been cached on the server. To force the configuration changes to take immediate effect, you can recycle the SharePoint Web Services application pool using the methods described earlier.

## Adding Connections to Data Connection Libraries

Now that we've broken our sample application, we need to fix it again. We can do this by adding a new data connection library and then creating an Office Data Connection (.odc) file containing our connection settings. We'll then tweak our workbook to use our new connection file instead of an embedded connection.

1. Create a new Data Connection library. From our sample site home page, click the Documents link to view the list of document libraries. Click the Create link to show the Create dialog.

2. From the Content & Data category, select Data Connection Library. Type the name of the new library as **Sample Data Connections**, and then click the Create button.

3. With our new library available, we need to let Excel Services know that all data connections stored there can be trusted. Switch back to the Manage Excel Services page in Central Administration and click the Trusted Data Connection Libraries link.

4. Click the Add Trusted Data Connection Library to add a new library. Type the address **http://<your server name>/Chapter12/Sample%20Data%20Connections**, and then click OK to save the changes.

---

**TIP** In the real world, where trusted connection libraries are used, it makes sense to have a single central connection library at a well-known location. Given that the purpose of the connection library is to allow all users to access trusted business data freely, making connections to the data as easy to find as possible is a worthwhile aim.

---

5. Now we'll create a data connection in the library and reconfigure our Excel workbook to use that instead. Navigate to the Excel Workbooks document library in our sample site and then edit our Last30DaysSales workbook using Excel client.

6. From the Data menu, select the Connection button.

7. In the Workbook Connection dialog, make sure the AdventureWorksList30DaysSales connection is selected and then click the Properties button.

8. While we're changing stuff, we'll configure our data connection to reload external data when the file is opened. In the Usage tab, check the Refresh Data When Opening The File checkbox.

9. Switch to the Definition tab. Click the Export Connection File button and then in the File Save dialog, save the connection to http://<your server name>/chapter12/Sample Data Connections.

10. Since we're uploading the file to SharePoint, we'll be prompted for some additional metadata. Make sure that the Content Type is set to Office Data Connection File, and then click OK to complete the upload.

11. We can see in the Connection Properties dialog that the Connection file path has changed to our data connection library. Even though we've saved the connection details to our SharePoint server, Excel still uses an embedded copy of the connection details. To force a reload every time the connection is used, check the Always Use Connection File checkbox.

12. Click OK to close the Connection Properties dialog, and then click Close to return to Excel. We can now save our revised workbook back to SharePoint by clicking the Save icon in the upper-left corner.

When we return to the home page of our sample site, we'll find that our chart now functions properly. If an error is still being displayed, try recycling the application pool to clear out any cached copies of the workbook.

## Connecting to Data Using Alternative Credentials

One of the reasons for creating a central library of trusted data connections is to allow administrators to identify specific user credentials for each connection rather than using the Windows credentials of the calling user. So far, our connection is still set up to use Windows authentication, so let's take a quick look at how we can change this to use specific credentials.

1. Before we can change our connection to use specific credentials, we need to set up the credentials in question. Create a new local user account named testuser, and give this account read-only access to our sample database.

2. Within SQL Server Management Studio, add a new Login for our testuser account. This can be achieved by expanding the Security node, right-clicking the Logins node, and then selecting New Login from the context menu.

3. In the Login - New dialog, enter details of our testuser account in the Login Name textbox. Type the default database as **AdventureWorks**.

4. Switch to the User Mapping page and map our account to the db_datareader role for the AdventureWorks database, as shown:

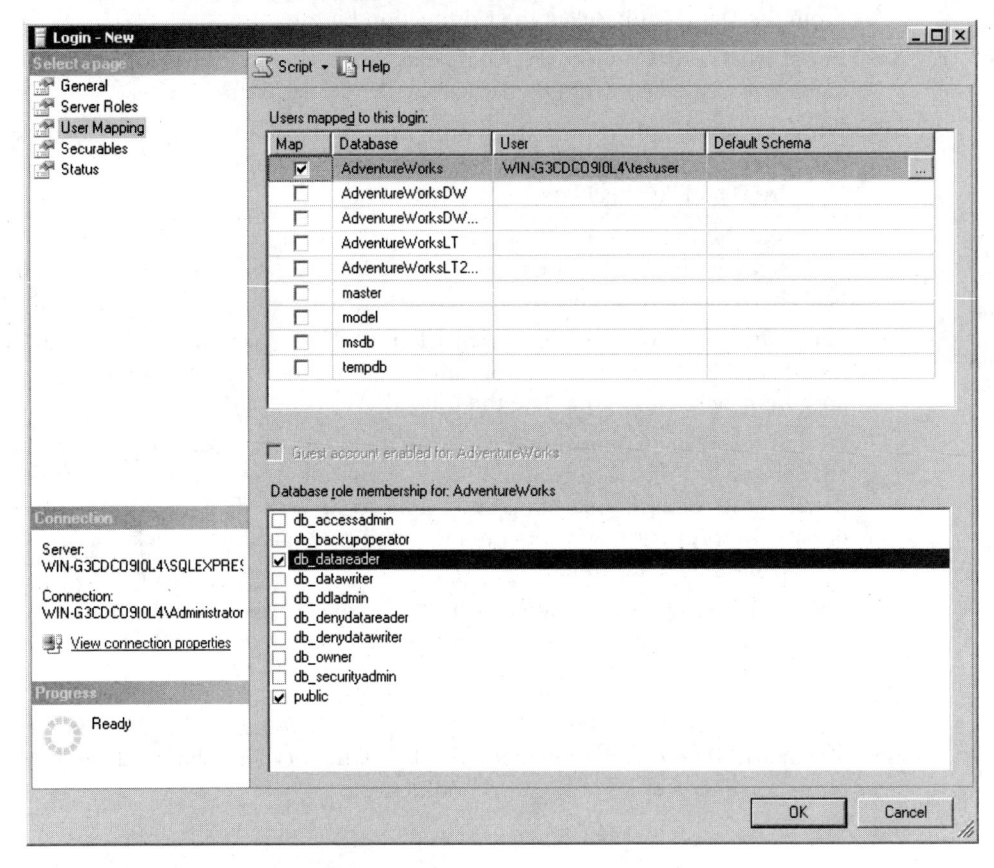

5. Click OK to complete the process.

Now that we have a created specific user account with the appropriate permissions to our database, we can look at how these permissions can be used within Excel Services. Three possibilities exist for using specific credentials within Excel Services:

**Embedded in Connection String**   We could embed credentials in the connection string that we used when creating the data connection. This has an obvious drawback in that the username and password are freely visible to anybody with access to view the data connection. Furthermore, this won't allow us to use a specific Windows user account.

**No Credentials**   This option isn't as crazy as it sounds. When a data connection is created and the authentication type is set to None, Excel Services uses default credentials to connect. This account is known as an "unattended service account" and is configured using the Secure Store Service.

**Secure Store Service Account**   The Secure Store Service provides a secure mapping of user credentials between systems. We can make use of this service within Excel Services to retrieve securely stored connection credentials. The difference between explicitly using the Secure Store Service and using it indirectly via the Unattended Service account is that the Unattended Service account is configured globally for the entire Excel Services application. However, when we're explicitly using the Secure Store Service, we can specify which application ID should be used for each connection.

## Configuring the Secure Store Service

Since two of our three options make use of the Secure Store Service, let's look at how to set it up:

1. Within SharePoint Central Administration, select Manage Service Applications from the Application Management section.
2. From the List of Service Applications, select the Secure Store Service Application and then, from the Service Applications menu, click Manage.
3. If this is the first time the Secure Store Service has been used, we need to initialize it by clicking the Generate New Key button in the Key Management section of the Edit menu.

Once the service has been initialized with a key, we can add a new application for use with our Excel Services external data store. Before we move on to take this step, however, I'll clarify what an application is and how it works within the Secure Store Service. An application is similar to an Excel worksheet: along the top of the worksheet are columns that relate to the properties that are defined by the application. These might include things like Username and Password but can include practically any content. Each row represents a mapping for a particular user account or group of users. For each mapping, values are stored in the respective columns. When a request is made to the Secure Store Service, the request will contain details of the application, and using this together with the SharePoint user credentials, the appropriate row will be selected and returned.

Now let's add a new application for Excel Services:

1. In the Manage Target Applications section, click the New button.

2. In the Target Application Settings page, enter the Target Application ID as **ExcelServicesUnattendedAccount**.

3. Set the Display Name to the same name as the Target Application ID, and add an appropriate e-mail address in the Contact E-Mail text box.

4. Various Target Applications Types are available when we're creating applications, but these can be split into two broad categories: Individual and Group. Individual types create a one-to-one mapping between a SharePoint user and a set of properties, or to refer back to our earlier analogy, each row in our workbook represents only one SharePoint user. Group types, on the other hand, create a many-to-one mapping. Effectively, our workbook has only one row, which can be mapped to any number of SharePoint user accounts or groups.

5. For our Excel Services application, we'll create a Group application, and this will allow us to map all users to a single set of credentials. Click Next to proceed to the next step of the process.

6. Specify which field will be used by our application. To refer to our earlier analogy, each field is a column in our worksheet. For our purposes, the default fields—Windows User Name and Windows Password—are sufficient. Click Next to move on.

7. Now specify which accounts have administrative permissions for this application. Enter an appropriate username in the Target Application Administrators picker. As well as specifying administrative users, we also need to specify which users and groups will use the credentials that are mapped to our application. In this case, we want everybody to use the same credentials, so we'll specify All Users (windows). Click OK to finish creating our application.

8. To set credentials for our application, we must select the application by clicking the checkbox next to it and then click the Set button in the Credentials section of the ribbon, as shown:

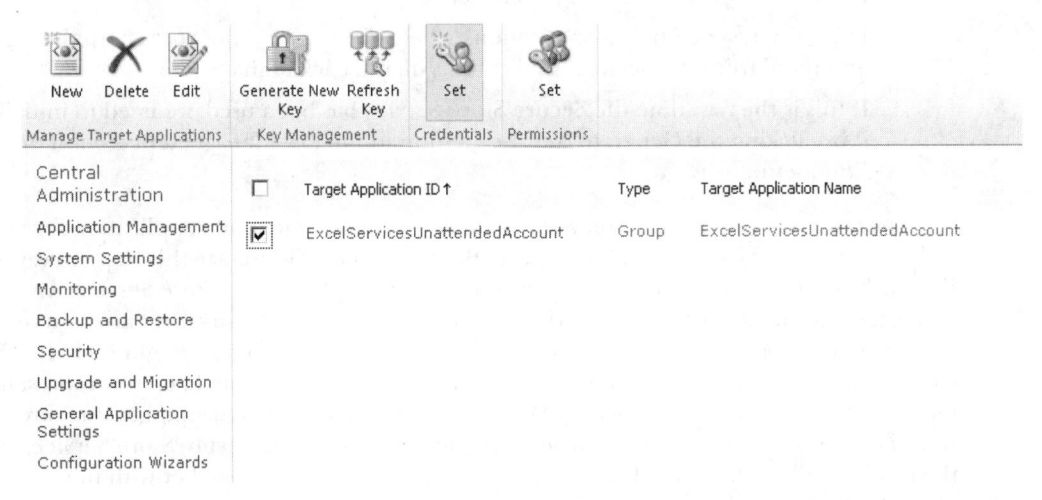

9. Enter details of the testuser account that we created earlier, remembering to prefix the username with the local computer name (that is, *yourcomputer\testuser*). Click OK to store the credentials.

**NOTE** Although we've created a group application for use with our Unattended Service account, we could also have created an Individual application and mapped the Windows username of the Excel Services service account to our testuser account. The drawback in doing this, however, is that if the service account changes, somebody must remember to add the new service account manually to the application. However, this approach does benefit from being more secure since only an appropriately configured account can use our testuser credentials. Our Group application allows our testuser account to be used by any Windows account.

Now that we've set up our Secure Store Service application, we can take the final step necessary to use it as our Unattended Service Account within Excel Services.

1. Navigate to the Manage Excel Services page within Central Administration. Click the Global Settings link.
2. Scroll down to the External Data section, and in the Application ID text box, enter the ID for our Secure Store Service application—in our case, type **ExcelServicesUnattendedAccount**. Click OK to commit the configuration changes.

Before we can see our unattended service account in action, we need to reconfigure our data connection to use no authentication:

1. Browse to the Sample Data Connections library of our sample site and then, from the context menu, edit the AdventureWorksList30DaysSales connection file using Excel.
2. The Excel client application is opened automatically. In the Security Notice dialog, click Enable to allow our data connection to execute. A table of data from our external data source will be displayed. This data is just for reference purposes; it effectively allows us to see what our data connection will return when executed.
3. To modify the data connection properties, from the Data menu click Properties, and then in the External Data Properties dialog, select the icon to the right of the Name text box, as shown:

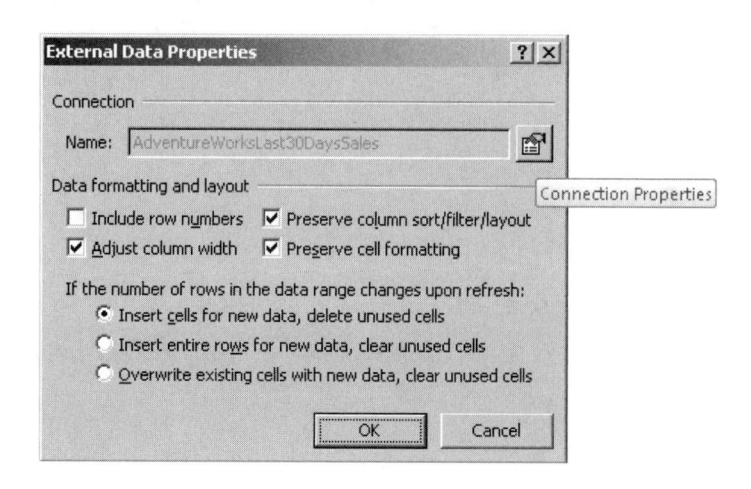

4. We'll be presented with the familiar Connection Properties dialog that we used earlier when creating our workbook. Switch to the Definition tab, and then click the Authentication Settings button.
5. Set the authentication type to None, and then click OK to close the dialog.
6. As we did when we modified the connection, click Export Connection File to save the changes back to our data connection library.
7. After the connection has been exported, click OK to close the dialog, and then close Excel. Discard the workbook that was automatically created.

We're now ready to return to our sample site home page to confirm that our data is still being refreshed properly. We can use SQL Server Profiler to confirm that connections to the database are now being made using our testuser account.

You've learned how to set up an Unattended Service account using the Secure Store Service. To use a specific application ID, the process is practically identical. The only difference is that in the Connection Properties dialog, rather than specifying the authentication type as None, the type is set to SSS and the application ID is entered.

## Summary

In this chapter, you've seen how Excel Services allows you to leverage the power of Excel within a web-based environment. Creating powerful data visualization solutions is now achievable for users who have little or no development skills. Furthermore, the powerful calculation engine that is Excel can be used by skilled developers to address practically any business specific problem. The key to bear in mind as application developers is this: If we need even basic data visualization or calculation facilities, the amount of work involved in creating a tool with even 10 percent of the flexibility of Excel Services is considerable. By leveraging Excel Services on SharePoint Server 2010, we give our users a lot more bang for their buck, and we can focus on the aspects of our application that are completely custom made.

# PART IV

# Data Access Layer

**CHAPTER 13**
Data Access Overview

**CHAPTER 14**
LINQ to SharePoint and SPMetal

**CHAPTER 15**
Business Connectivity Services

**CHAPTER 16**
Enterprise Search

**CHAPTER 17**
User Profiles and Social Data

**CHAPTER 18**
Business Intelligence

# CHAPTER 13

# Data Access Overview

More often than not, when it comes to designing a data access layer for a custom application, your only consideration is how the layer can be accessed and used programmatically. You don't usually need to consider how a nontechnical user might configure and amend the data structure. Naturally, this makes life much simpler for the designer, because the data structure can be designed with only the application goals in mind. The exception to this rule occurs, of course, when the application itself is a configurable data store; in that case, the primary aim is to create a user-configurable data access layer. SharePoint is such an application, as a web-based platform for storing and sharing data and applications that allows nontechnical users to create data structures that meet their unique requirements.

This part of the book covers the various data access features available in SharePoint 2010. However, before we delve into these advanced features in detail, we'll look at how data is stored and managed in the underlying platform. Given that the target audience for the data access platform is the nontechnical end user, from a development perspective, we have something of a learning curve to undergo before we can effectively make use of the platform to implement the structures required by our custom applications.

This chapter aims to cover the fundamental building blocks of the data access features available on the SharePoint platform, to help create a strong foundation for the advanced features that are discussed later in the book.

## Content Types

The aim of the SharePoint data access platform, and indeed of SharePoint itself, is to provide a web-based tool that can be easily customized by end users to store any business data, either in raw database-style by using custom lists or embedded in documents by using document libraries and features such as Excel Services. At the fundamental level, both of these approaches have a common implementation in the form of *content types*. Basically, a content type is a metadata definition of a particular type of content.

## Content Type Inheritance

One important feature of content types is *inheritance*. In SharePoint, all content types inherit properties from the System content type, and when users create new content types, they must select an appropriate parent content type from which to inherit.

You can see from the hierarchy shown in Figure 13-1 that custom list data can be stored by creating a content type that inherits from the Item content type whereas documents can be stored by using the appropriate Document content type or by creating a new content type that inherits from Document.

## Content Type Identifiers

One thing that may be apparent from Figure 13-1 is the use of concatenated unique identifiers for each content type. For example, the identifier for the Master Page content is type is 0x010105, which is shown in Figure 13-2.

Although from a development perspective, the use of concatenated identifiers may seem a bit archaic and prone to data entry errors, there is a very good reason for taking this approach as opposed to the more traditional technique of assigning automatically generated sequential identifiers. Practically all of the functionality of the SharePoint platform is defined at the content type level. For example, a web page containing web parts is based on the Web Part Page content type. It is the use of this content type that provides the necessary data structure required to store the properties of the web parts that are stored on the page. However, the Web Part Page content type is also based on the Basic Page content type, and it is via this inheritance that a physical representation of the page can be rendered from the database.

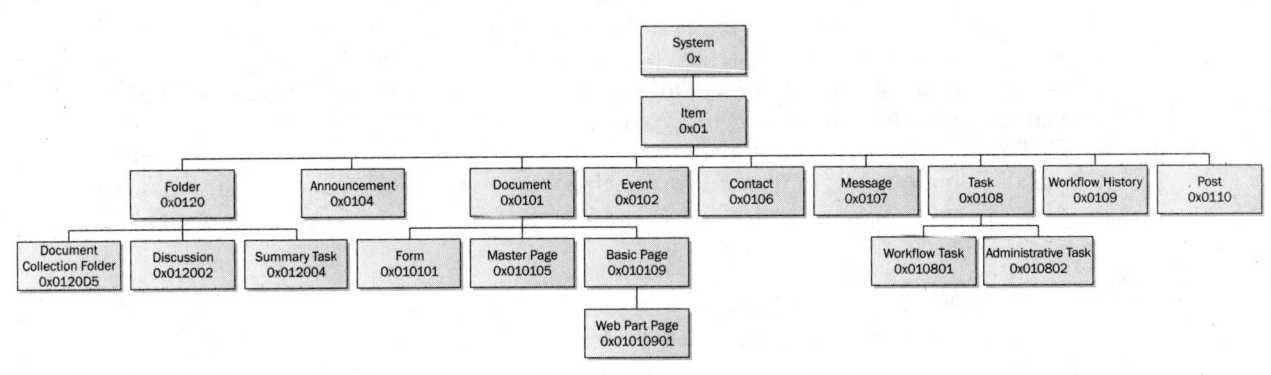

**Figure 13-1**  The System content type hierarchy in SharePoint 2010

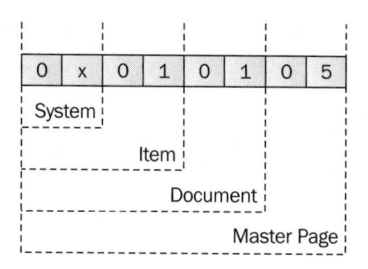

```
0 x 0 1 0 1 0 5
```
- System: `01`
- Item: `0101`
- Document: `010105`
- Master Page: `0x010105`

**Figure 13-2** Breakdown of content type identifier for Master Page content type

Since functionality is effectively layered based on the content type hierarchy, being able to navigate up and down the structure efficiently is key to the overall performance of the system. By using concatenated identifiers, system code can easily derive the hierarchy without having to resort to database lookups or other methods.

## Generating Content Type Identifiers

When programmatically creating content types, you can use two approaches to generating content type identifiers. The first approach, which is used by out-of-the-box content types, is to use this:

*Parent content type ID + 2 hexadecimal digits* (other than 00, because this is reserved for use by the second method)

For example, if we wanted to create a new content type derived from Master Page, we could use the following identifier:

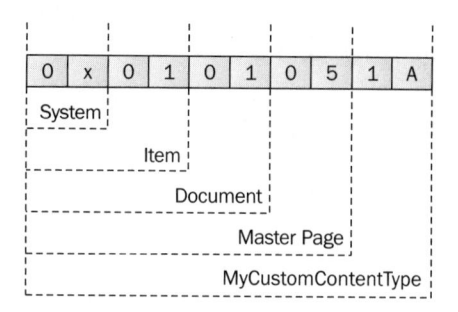

```
0 x 0 1 0 1 0 5 1 A
```
- System: `01`
- Item: `0101`
- Document: `010105`
- Master Page: `0x010105`
- MyCustomContentType: `0x0101051A`

The second approach, which is recommended when creating a content type that inherits from a parent that you didn't create, is to use this:

*Parent content type ID + 00 + hexadecimal GUID*

Using the preceding example of a content type derived from Master Page, we could use the following identifier:

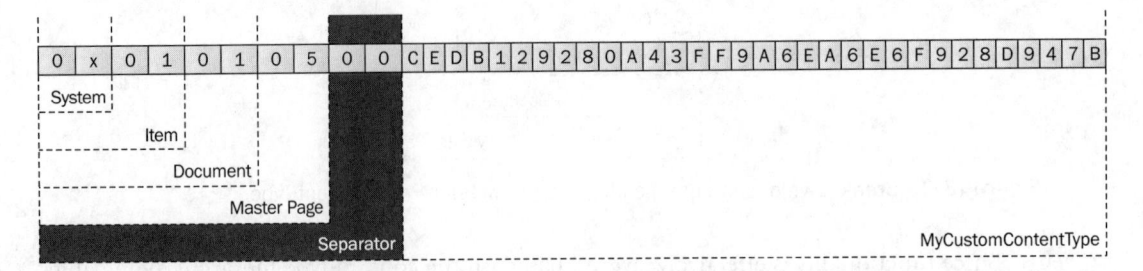

```
0x 01 01 05 00 CEDB129280A43FF9A6EA6E6F928D947B
   System
      Item
         Document
            Master Page
               Separator                         MyCustomContentType
```

## The SPContentTypeId Object

To make parsing of content type identifiers easier in code, the SharePoint object model includes the SPContentTypeId class. The SPContentTypeId class makes it easy to perform various actions against content types, such as determining the parent content type identifier or finding a common parent of two identifiers.

The following code listing shows how to create a content type programmatically with a user-defined identifier as well as with a system-defined identifier. You can see that system-defined identifiers always adopt the lengthier GUID concatenation approach.

```
static void Main(string[] args)
{
  string siteUrl = "http://localhost";
  Program p = new Program();
  using (SPSite site = new SPSite(siteUrl))
  {
    using (SPWeb web = site.OpenWeb())
    {
      Console.WriteLine("{0} | {1} | {2}","Name".PadRight(20),
                                    "ContentTypeId".PadRight(40),
                                    "Parent Name".PadRight(10));
      Console.WriteLine(new string('-', 78));
      SPContentType newContentType;
      newContentType=p.CreateContentType(web, "MyFirstContentType", "Item");

      Console.WriteLine("{0} | {1} | {2}", newContentType.Name.PadRight(20),
                            newContentType.Id.ToString().PadRight(40),
                            newContentType.Parent.Name.PadRight(10));

      SPContentTypeId newId = new SPContentTypeId("0x01AB");
      newContentType=p.CreateContentType(web, newId, "MySecondContentType");

      Console.WriteLine("{0} | {1} | {2}", newContentType.Name.PadRight(20),
                            newContentType.Id.ToString().PadRight(40),
                            newContentType.Parent.Name.PadRight(10));
    }
  }
  Console.ReadLine();
}
```

```
SPContentType CreateContentType(SPWeb web, string name, string parentName)
{
  if (web.AvailableContentTypes[name] == null)
  {
    SPContentType parent = web.AvailableContentTypes[parentName];
    SPContentType contentType = new SPContentType(parent,
                                                  web.ContentTypes,
                                                  name);

    //To save this new content type, update must be called
    //contentType.Update();

    return contentType;
  }
  else
  {
    return web.AvailableContentTypes[name];
  }
}

SPContentType CreateContentType(SPWeb web, SPContentTypeId newId,string name)
{
  if (web.AvailableContentTypes[newId] == null)
  {
    SPContentType contentType = new SPContentType(newId,
                                                  web.ContentTypes,
                                                  name);
    //To save this new content type, update must be called
    //contentType.Update();
    return contentType;
  }
  else
  {
    return web.AvailableContentTypes[newId];
  }
}
```

Generally speaking, performing such actions using code would be required only as part of the initial setup of a site or site collection. We'll look at this in more detail in Chapter 19.

## Content Type Groups

Although all content types are fundamentally derived from the System content type and exist as part of a well-defined hierarchy, for ease of reference, content types can also be grouped. Grouping is purely a metadata activity and has no bearing on content type inheritance. That said, some groups serve specific purposes within the SharePoint platform, and one example is the _Hidden group. Content types belonging to this group are not displayed in the user interface.

Another thing to bear in mind when using content types is the way in which folders and content hierarchy are implemented. When creating a document library, you cannot add content types that are not derived from Document. By the same token, when you're creating a custom list, you cannot add content types that are derived from Document.

Notwithstanding these rules, lists and document libraries can contain content conforming to many different content types. For example, a document library can contain Master Pages and Web Part Pages.

## Content Type Metadata

You've seen how content types are organized into a hierarchy and how inheritance determines the functionality that is enabled by a given content type. Now let's take a look at the type of metadata, and therefore the types of functionality, that can be exposed by content types.

### Workflow Associations

Workflows can be associated with content types and set to run in response to certain events. By attaching workflows to content types rather than individual lists, you can define business processes for specific types of data regardless of where the data is stored within a SharePoint site.

### Document Template

For some types of content, particularly those based on Microsoft Office documents such as Word or Excel docs, custom templates can be specified that users can populate with relevant details. Details of such a template can be specified as content type metadata, allowing the template to be used wherever the content type is added to a document library.

### Display, Edit, and New Forms

Each content type can define custom display, edit, and new forms allowing customization of the user interface presented at these stages. Various options are available for customizing these forms; however, from a content type perspective, it's important to note that two properties exist for each form. For example, to set the Display form, you can use a DisplayFormTemplateName property and a DisplayFormUrl property. Which property you use depends on the level of customization that's required. By setting the DisplayFormTemplateName property, you can specify a template that will be used by the DataForm Web part to render the appropriate view. However, if a greater level of customization is required, the DisplayFormUrl can be set to the URL for a custom Active Server Page Framework (ASPX) page, allowing a much greater degree of flexibility with the drawback that none of the usual SharePoint user interface elements will be present on the page by default.

### Mobile Display, Edit, New Pages

**New in 2010**
SharePoint 2010 provides a number of new features for rendering content for mobile browsers. One example of this new functionality is the ability to specify custom forms for creating and editing content using mobile browsers at the content type level.

### XML Documents

The ability to add practically any XML-based metadata to a content type is an incredibly powerful feature. Interestingly, some of the metadata already described, although accessible through the object model via dedicated properties, is actually attached to a content type via additional XML documents.

The following code sample shows how metadata can be added by creating a custom class that supports XML serialization and then setting properties on the class to contain the appropriate values. Using this technique, you can attach practically any additional data to a content type.

```
static void Main(string[] args)
{
  string siteUrl = "http://localhost";
  Program p = new Program();
  using (SPSite site = new SPSite(siteUrl))
  {
    using (SPWeb web = site.OpenWeb())
    {
      SPContentType newContentType;
      newContentType = p.CreateContentType(web, "MyFirstContentType", "Item");
      CustomMetadata metaData = new CustomMetadata();
      metaData.MyIntegerProperty = 46;
      metaData.MyTextProperty = "Data stored as custom metadata";
      p.AddCustomMetadata(metaData, newContentType);
      metaData = null;
      metaData = p.ReadCustomMetaData(newContentType);
      Console.WriteLine(metaData.MyTextProperty);
    }
  }
  Console.ReadLine();
}

void AddCustomMetadata(CustomMetadata data, SPContentType contentType)
{
  XmlSerializer s = new XmlSerializer(typeof(CustomMetadata));
  StringBuilder sb = new StringBuilder();
  using (XmlWriter writer = XmlWriter.Create(sb))
  {
    s.Serialize(writer, data);
  }
  XmlDocument doc = new XmlDocument();
  doc.LoadXml(sb.ToString());
  contentType.XmlDocuments.Add(doc);
}

CustomMetadata ReadCustomMetaData(SPContentType contentType)
{
  CustomMetadata data;
  Type t = typeof(CustomMetadata);
  var attrib = (XmlRootAttribute)t.GetCustomAttributes(
                      typeof(XmlRootAttribute), false).FirstOrDefault();
  if (contentType.XmlDocuments[attrib.Namespace] != null)
  {
    XmlDocument doc = new XmlDocument();
    doc.LoadXml(contentType.XmlDocuments[attrib.Namespace]);
    using (StringReader sr = new StringReader(
                      contentType.XmlDocuments[attrib.Namespace]))
    {
```

```csharp
            using (XmlReader rdr = XmlReader.Create(sr))
            {
                XmlSerializer s = new XmlSerializer(t);
                data = (CustomMetadata)s.Deserialize(rdr);
            }
        }
        return data;
    }
    else
    {
        throw new KeyNotFoundException();
    }
}

[XmlRoot(Namespace="Http://www.chaholl.com/SP2010Apps/ContentTypesDemo")]
public class CustomMetadata
{
    [XmlElement()]
    public int MyIntegerProperty { get; set; }
    [XmlElement()]
    public string MyTextProperty { get; set; }
}
```

## Enterprise Content Types

**New in 2010**

Earlier in this book, site collections and sites and the hierarchical nature of these structures were discussed. This hierarchy also has implications for content types, because content types are also inherited by child sites. For example, if an organization creates a site collection named HR with a root site of Benefits, a content type named Employee defined on the Benefits site would be available to all child sites, no matter where they sat within the hierarchy, as shown next:

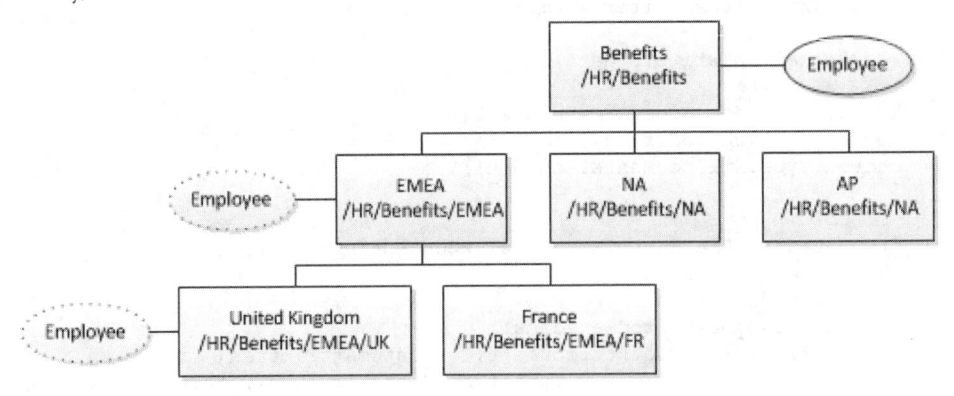

This cross-site scoping is an important feature in SharePoint, because it facilitates the creation of centrally managed data structures. However, while this inheritance works well *within* site collections, it doesn't work *across* site collections. From the preceding illustration, if another site collection named Training existed with a root site of LearningCenter that also wanted to make use of a common Employee content type, using previous versions of SharePoint it would be necessary to create a new content type on the LearningCenter site.

SharePoint Server 2010 introduces a new feature known as *enterprise content types*, and it's aimed at providing an answer to this problem. To enable content type publishing, take the following steps:

1. Either create a new site collection that's going to be the content type repository or use an existing site collection.

2. In the Site Settings page, select Site Collection Features and then activate the Content Type Syndication Hub feature.

3. Content Type syndication makes use of the Managed Metadata service application to distribute content types between connected applications. To specify that our newly created Content Type Hub should be used by a particular Managed Metadata Service application, select the appropriate service from the Manage Service Applications page in Central Administration. Click the Properties button in the ribbon, as shown next:

4. In the Create New Managed Metadata Service dialog, set the Content Type Hub URL to the appropriate site collection, as shown:

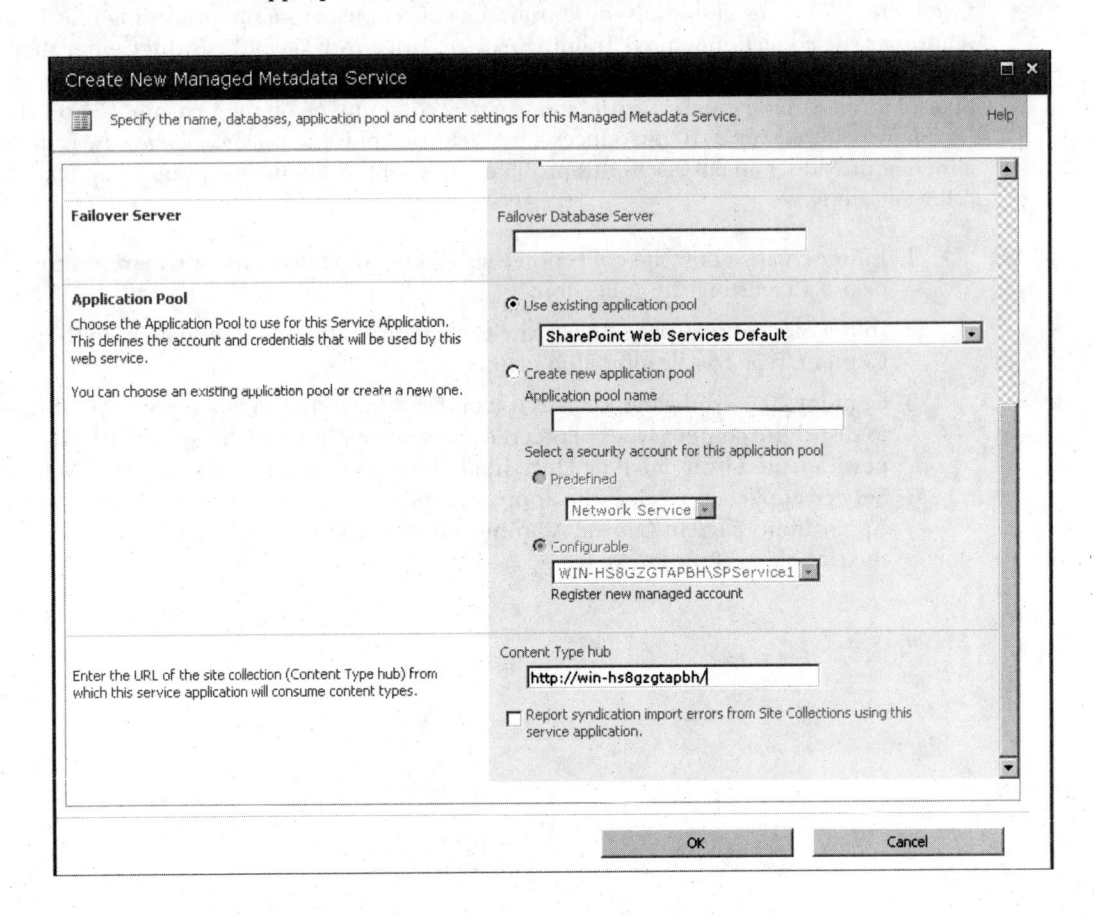

5. The final step in configuring content type publishing is to enable it on the appropriate Managed Metadata Service Connection. Select the appropriate connection, and then click the Properties button on the ribbon. Check the Consumes Content Types From The Content Type Gallery option, as shown next:

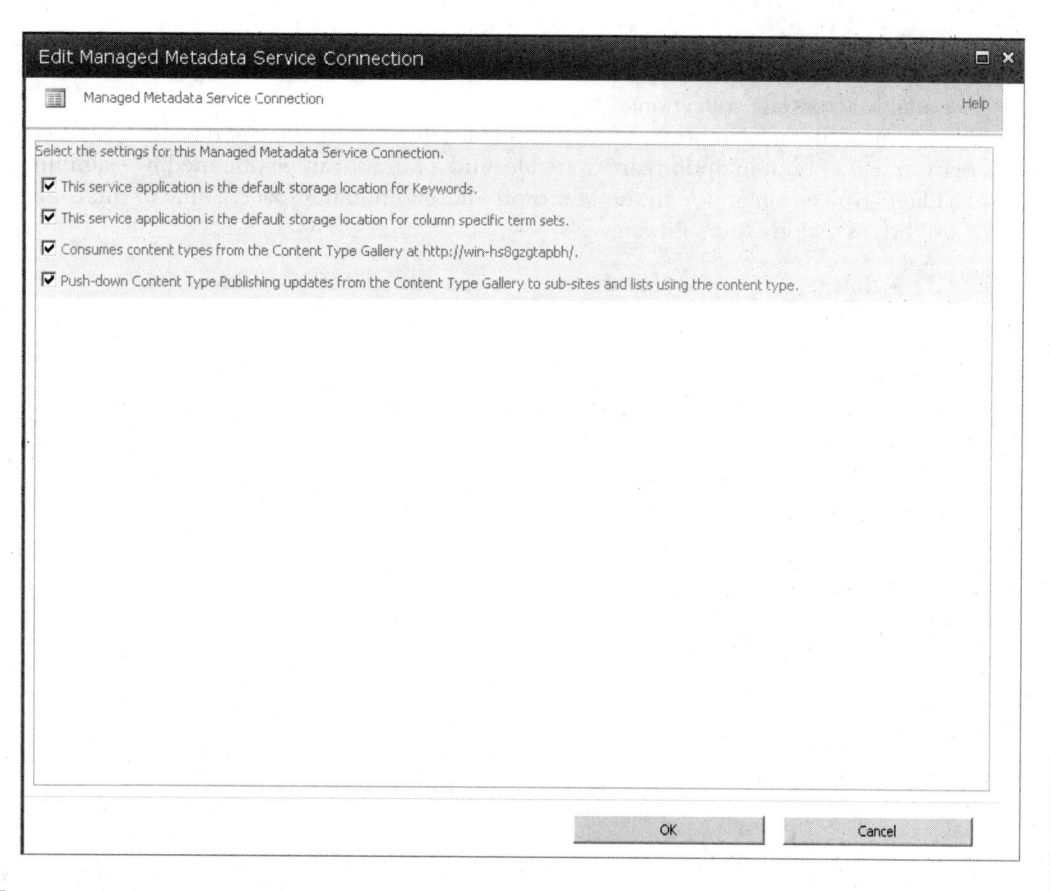

## Columns

You've seen how content types are used throughout SharePoint to determine how specific types of data should be handled. We've looked at the types of metadata that can be stored within a content type. One of the areas that we haven't discussed so far is how individual items of data are defined, and that's where *columns* come in. Every content type contains a reference to one or more column objects, where a column defines a specific data element together with any appropriate metadata required to capture, process, and render it. Columns can be reused in multiple content types, and in fact this reuse is central to the way content type inheritance is implemented. For example, suppose the Item content type references a column named Title. As a result, all content types that inherit from Item also contain a reference to this Title column.

Columns, like content types, are available across child sites. Where the columns are used in a content type that is published using content type publishing, the columns are available across site collections.

One of the most important properties of a column is the type of data that it can contain. A number of built-in options are available, and a full list can be obtained by examining the SPFieldType enumeration in the Microsoft.SharePoint namespace. Some of the commonly used types include the following:

- **Integer**   Specifies that the column contains an Integer value
- **Text**   Specifies that the column contains a single line of text
- **Note**   Specifies that the column contains multiple lines of text
- **Number**   Specifies that the column contains a floating point number
- **Lookup**   Specifies that the column contains a reference to a value in another list

The following code sample shows how to create columns and associate them with content types:

```
static void Main(string[] args)
{
    string siteUrl = "http://localhost";
    List<string> fieldNames = new List<string>();
    Program p = new Program();

    using (SPSite site = new SPSite(siteUrl))
    {
      using (SPWeb web = site.OpenWeb())
      {
        SPContentType newContentType;
        newContentType = p.CreateContentType(web,
                            "MyFirstContentType",
                            "Item");

        p.CreateSiteColumn(web, "MyColumn",
                            SPFieldType.Text,
                            false);

        fieldNames.Add("MyColumn");

        p.CreateSiteColumn(web, "MyColumn2",
                            SPFieldType.Text,
                            false);

        fieldNames.Add("MyColumn2");
```

```
            p.AddFields(web, fieldNames.ToArray(), newContentType);

            Console.WriteLine("{0} | {1} | {2}", "Title".PadRight(20),
                                                 "Type".PadRight(20),
                                                 "Group".PadRight(20));
            Console.WriteLine(new string('-', 70));

            foreach (SPField fld in newContentType.Fields)
            {
               Console.WriteLine("{0} | {1} | {2}", fld.StaticName.PadRight(20),
                                                    fld.TypeDisplayName.PadRight(20),
                                                    fld.Group.PadRight(20));
            }
         }
      }
      Console.ReadLine();
}


void CreateSiteColumn(SPWeb web, string name, SPFieldType fieldType,
                                              bool isRequired)
{
   if (!web.AvailableFields.ContainsField(name))
   {
      web.Fields.Add(name, fieldType, isRequired);
   }
}

void AddFields(SPWeb web, string[] fieldNames, SPContentType contentType)
{
   foreach (string fieldname in fieldNames)
   {
      if (web.Fields.ContainsField(fieldname))
      {
         SPFieldLink fieldLink = new SPFieldLink(web.Fields[fieldname]);
         contentType.FieldLinks.Add(fieldLink);
      }
   }
   //Update should be called to persist these changes
   //contentType.Update();
}
```

## Field Types

As you've seen, the SPFieldType enumeration can be used to determine the type of data that a column can contain. However, it's possible to create custom field types that inherit from these base types and in turn use those custom field types to create columns.

There's more to field types than simply specifying the type of data that a field can contain. Let's take a look at the objects involved before we delve into how they interact to provide data access services for SharePoint. The following diagram shows the key objects involved in creating custom field types.

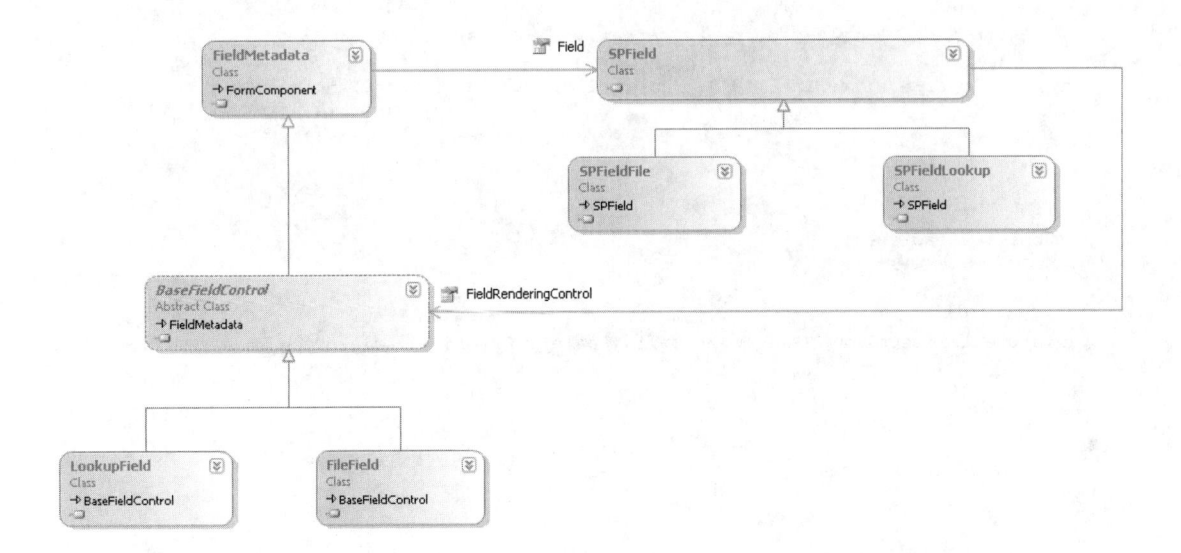

## Inheriting from SPField

The SPField class is the base class for all field types. Some examples of these field types include SPFieldFile, which contains file data, and SPFieldLookup, which contains details of a lookup to a column in another list or library. All field types must ultimately derive from SPField either directly or indirectly. From a data access perspective, the SPField class is the lowest level at which we can implement custom data access code, since behind the scenes of the SPField class, the SharePoint platform handles the appropriate database interactions to persist the value of the object.

As of this writing, Visual Studio 2010 does not provide a template for creating custom field controls, so let's take a look at how this can be done manually.

1. Create a new Empty SharePoint project using Visual Studio 2010, as shown next.

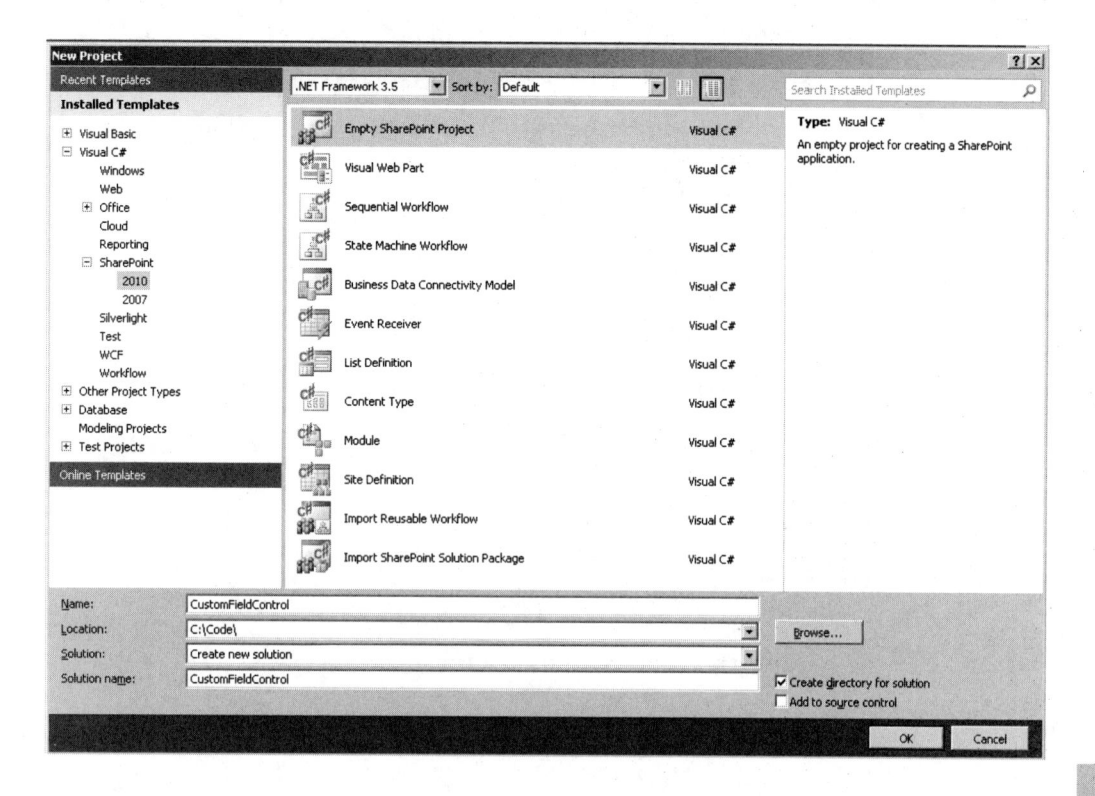

2. In the SharePoint Customization Wizard, be sure to select the Deploy As A Farm Solution option.

3. Add a new class file to project named SPFieldAddress.cs. This class will be our implementation of SPField. Add the following code:

```
using Microsoft.SharePoint;

namespace CustomField
{
  public class SPFieldAddress : SPFieldMultiColumn
  {
    public SPFieldAddress(SPFieldCollection fields, string fieldName)
      : base(fields, fieldName) { }
```

```csharp
    public SPFieldAddress(SPFieldCollection fields, string typeName,
        string displayName): base(fields, typeName, displayName) { }

    public override object GetFieldValue(string value)
    {
      if (!string.IsNullOrEmpty(value))
      {
        return new SPAddressValue(value);
      }
      else
      {
        return null;
      }
    }

    public override string GetFieldValueAsHtml(object value)
    {
      if (value!=null)
      {
        return base.GetFieldValueAsHtml(value);
      }
      else
      {
        return "<strong>--No Address Present--</strong>";
      }
    }
  }
}
```

Our sample field will store multiple values in a single field. Rather than write a lot of the code to implement this functionality from scratch, we've based our field on SPFieldMultiColumn as opposed to SPField. SPFieldMultiColumn stores values of type SPFieldMultiColumnValue, and by inheriting from this class, we can create a custom data structure for our field.

4. Add a new class named SPAddressValue.cs. Add the following code:

```csharp
using Microsoft.SharePoint;

namespace CustomField
{
  public class SPAddressValue : SPFieldMultiColumnValue
  {
    public SPAddressValue() : base(5) { }
    public SPAddressValue(string value) : base(value) { }

    public string StreetAddress
    {
      get { return this[0];}
      set { this[0] = value;}
    }

    public string ApartmentNumber
    {
      get { return this[1];}
```

```
        set { this[1] = value;}
      }

      public string City
      {
        get { return this[2];}
        set { this[2] = value;}
      }

      public string State
      {
        get { return this[3];}
        set { this[3] = value;}
      }

      public string Zip
      {
        get { return this[4];}
        set { this[4] = value;}
      }
    }
  }
```

5. So that the SharePoint platform knows about our new field, we need to create a file containing some definition XML. The file should be deployed to %SPROOT%Template\xml. Choose Project | Add SharePoint Mapped Folder.

6. Map Template\Xml and then create a new XML file in the mapped folder named fldtypes_FieldDemo.xml. When creating field definition files, it is important that they be named appropriately. SharePoint loads files with names in the format *fldtypes_<whatever>.xml*

7. Add the following XML:

```
<?xml version="1.0" encoding="utf-8" ?>
<FieldTypes>
  <FieldType>
    <Field Name="TypeName">AddressField</Field>
    <Field Name="ParentType">MultiColumn</Field>
    <Field Name="TypeDisplayName">Demo Address Field</Field>
    <Field Name="TypeShortDescription">
Demonstration custom field for entering addresses</Field>
    <Field Name="UserCreatable">TRUE</Field>
    <Field Name="FieldTypeClass">
CustomField.SPFieldAddress, $SharePoint.Project.AssemblyFullName$</Field>
    <RenderPattern Name="HeaderPattern">
      <Property Select="DisplayName" HTMLEncode="TRUE"/>
    </RenderPattern>
    <RenderPattern Name="DisplayPattern">
      <Switch>
        <Expr>
          <Column/>
        </Expr>
        <Case Value="">
```

```
          <HTML>
            <![CDATA[--No Address Present--]]>
          </HTML>
        </Case>
        <Default>
          <Column SubColumnNumber="0" HTMLEncode="TRUE"/>
          <HTML><![CDATA[,]]></HTML>
          <Column SubColumnNumber="1" HTMLEncode="TRUE"/>
          <HTML><![CDATA[,]]></HTML>
          <Column SubColumnNumber="2" HTMLEncode="TRUE"/>
          <HTML><![CDATA[,]]></HTML>
          <Column SubColumnNumber="3" HTMLEncode="TRUE"/>
          <HTML><![CDATA[,]]></HTML>
          <Column SubColumnNumber="4" HTMLEncode="TRUE"/>
        </Default>
      </Switch>
    </RenderPattern>
  </FieldType>
</FieldTypes>
```

## Inheriting from BaseFieldControl

The SPField class has many properties that define how a column based on the field type will behave. One of these properties, FieldRenderingControl leads us onto the BaseFieldControl class.

Each SPField-derived class must implement the FieldRenderingControl property, which will return an object of type BaseFieldControl. Notice, however, that BaseFieldControl is an abstract class. This means that in practice, each SPField derived class must return a concrete implementation of the BaseFieldControl. Some examples of these implementations include LookupField and FileField. These FieldRenderingControls are responsible for defining and implementing the user interface for each field type. For example, in the case of the LookupField control, when the page is in edit mode, the user interface may consist of a drop down control containing values from the configured lookup list. In the same way as the SPField object represents the lowest level of data access code, the BaseFieldControl represents the lowest level of user interface code that can be written against the SharePoint platform.

Continuing with our earlier SPField example, we'll add a custom field control to provide us with a user interface for capturing data.

1. Add a new class file named AddressField.cs. Insert the following code:

```
using System.Web.UI.WebControls;
using Microsoft.SharePoint.WebControls;

namespace CustomField
{
  class AddressField : BaseFieldControl
  {
    private TextBox _address;
    private TextBox _apartmentNumber;
    private TextBox _city;
    private TextBox _state;
    private TextBox _zip;
    protected override void CreateChildControls()
    {
```

```csharp
      if (this.Field == null || this.ControlMode == SPControlMode.Display
                             || this.ControlMode == SPControlMode.Invalid)
      {
        return;
      }
      else
      {
        base.CreateChildControls();
        _address = new TextBox();
        _apartmentNumber = new TextBox();
        _city = new TextBox();
        _state = new TextBox();
        _zip = new TextBox();
        Table tab = new Table();
        tab.Controls.Add(BuildRow("Street Address", _address));
        tab.Controls.Add(BuildRow("Apartment Number", _apartmentNumber));
        tab.Controls.Add(BuildRow("City", _city));
        tab.Controls.Add(BuildRow("State", _state));
        tab.Controls.Add(BuildRow("ZIP Code", _zip));
        this.Controls.Add(tab);
      }
    }

    private TableRow BuildRow(string labelText, WebControl valueControl)
    {
      TableRow row = new TableRow();
      TableCell label = new TableCell();
      TableCell value = new TableCell();
      label.Text = labelText;
      value.Controls.Add(valueControl);
      row.Controls.Add(label);
      row.Controls.Add(value);
      return row;
    }

    public override object Value
    {
      get
      {
        EnsureChildControls();
        SPAddressValue field = new SPAddressValue();
        field.StreetAddress = _address.Text;
        field.ApartmentNumber = _apartmentNumber.Text;
        field.City = _city.Text;
        field.State = _state.Text;
        field.Zip = _zip.Text;
        return field;
      }
      set
      {
        if (value != null && !string.IsNullOrEmpty(value.ToString()))
        {
          SPAddressValue field = new SPAddressValue(value.ToString());
          _address.Text = field.StreetAddress;
          _apartmentNumber.Text = field.ApartmentNumber;
```

```
                _city.Text = field.City;
                _state.Text = field.State;
                _zip.Text = field.Zip;
            }
        }
    }
}
```

2. To hook up our custom BaseFieldControl to our SPField implementation, add the following code to the SPFieldAddress.cs class:

```
public override BaseFieldControl FieldRenderingControl
{
    get
    {
        BaseFieldControl control = new AddressField();
        control.FieldName = this.InternalName;
        return control;
    }
}
```

## Validation

**New in 2010**

In SharePoint 2007, adding validation to fields was one of the main reasons for creating a custom field control. As you've seen, creating field controls is a time-consuming task. The good people at Microsoft realized that, from a development perspective, this wasn't a good use of resources and as a result, in SharePoint 2010, column validation has been added to the SPField class. In effect, column validation eliminates the need for a lot of custom field development by making it possible to enter validation formulae via the user interface.

When you're adding a new column, you'll see a new Column Validation section at the bottom of the page, as shown next. Validation formulae use the same syntax as calculated columns and as such can include pretty complex logic.

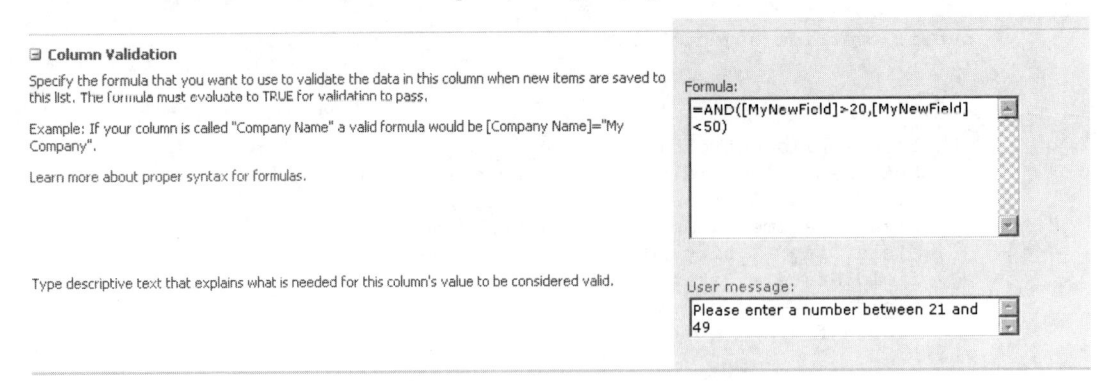

One thing that isn't apparent from the user interface is that behind the scenes, SharePoint creates a JavaScript representation of the validation formula. This allows for values to be validated in the user interface without the need for a post back.

The values for these properties are stored in the ValidationEcmaScript, ValidationFormula, and ValidationMessage properties of the SPField object.

## Lists and Document Libraries

We've looked at how content within SharePoint is defined using content types, columns, and field types. The next element to consider is how the content is stored within the SharePoint data store. That brings us to lists and document libraries.

Lists and document libraries don't physically exist. There is a perception that data stored in lists and libraries is slow to use because it exists in a file structure as opposed to a relational database, but this is not the case. All content managed by SharePoint lives in a relational database. Having said that, the highly abstracted nature of the data structure doesn't lend itself to high performance data access, and as you'll see later, there are other means of achieving this goal if it's critical to your application design. Behind the scenes, all user data is actually stored in a single table in the content database.

SharePoint offers two types of content containers: lists and document libraries. The difference between these two is in the types of content that they can contain. Lists can contain only content that is not derived from the document content type, and document libraries can contain only content that is derived from the document content type.

From an object model perspective, a document library is a specialized form of a list. This is an important point, because the SPList object and its properties are the starting point for much of the custom code that we'll write for the SharePoint platform. The following class diagram shows the SPList object and how it corresponds to the objects discussed earlier in this chapter:

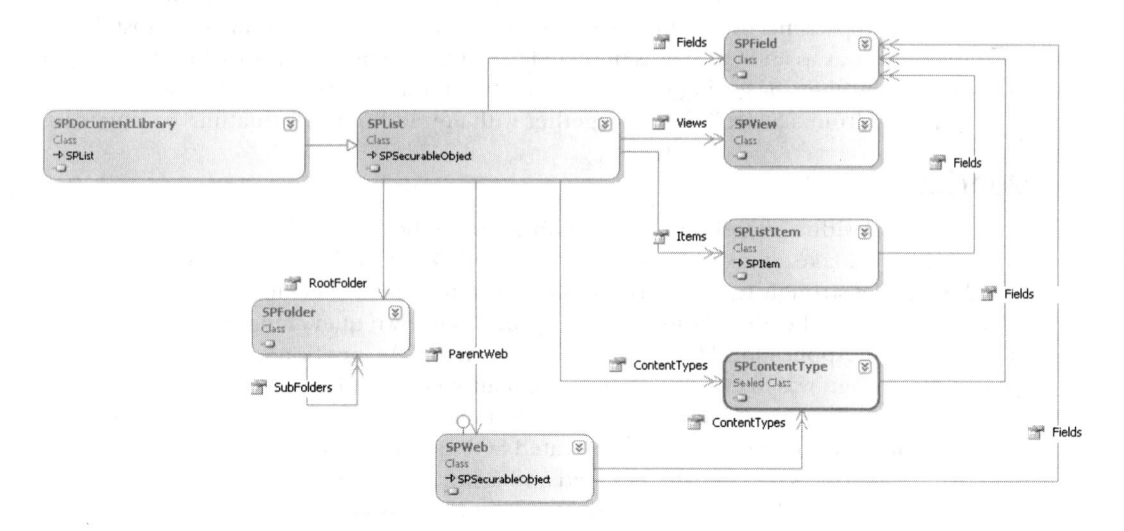

This class diagram highlights an interesting point that we haven't discussed so far: how columns and content types are related to lists and document libraries. You've seen how a content type can contain references to reusable columns, and you should understand how these content types can be used by lists and libraries to define the types of content that may be stored. However, from the class diagram, you can see that the SPList class has a Fields collection as well as a ContentTypes collection. From the diagram, you can also see that the SPWeb object has a Fields collection and a ContentTypes collection.

When we create content types or add new columns using the user interface, these columns are defined at the site level (which the object model confusingly represents using the SPWeb object). These columns are known as *site columns* and we can see this terminology used in the user interface and throughout the documentation. The same is also true for content types: when we create them using the user interface, they are known as *site content types*.

If we assign a content type to a list or library, SharePoint behind the scenes creates a new content type that inherits from our Site content type. This new content type is known as a *List content type*. Generally speaking, the ContentTypes collection of the SPList object will contain List content types. List content types and list columns can be freely changed at the list or document library level without affecting other instances of the associated site content type or column that are in use elsewhere.

As mentioned, columns exist independently of content types. A content type simply references the columns that it uses. As a result of this, when multiple content types are added to a list or library, the Fields collection of the associated SPList object contains an amalgamation of all the fields that are required. However, as well as the fields that are required by associated list content types, you can also add arbitrary fields to a list that are not associated with any content type.

## Views

As we've seen from the class diagram, the SPList object has a collection of SPView objects. This raises the question, What is an SPView and how does it relate to lists and libraries? An SPView object represents the definition of a view on data contained within an SPList. In much the same way as an SQL view is ultimately an SQL statement that specifies the columns to select and any filters or sorting conditions, an SPView represents a query that selects values to be displayed from a SharePoint list together with any additional formatting parameters.

## Queries

Data contained within SharePoint lists and libraries can be queried in a few ways. In Chapter 14, we'll take a look at Language Integrated Query (LINQ) to SharePoint and how this enables strongly typed queries while providing syntax checking at design time.

Fundamentally, the SharePoint platform provides its own query language in the form of Collaborative Application Markup Language (CAML). As mentioned, one of the design goals of SharePoint was to create a platform that allowed nontechnical users to define data structures easily. As a consequence of this requirement, the underlying database schema does not lend itself to executing user-generated SQL queries. In fact, direct access to the underlying database is strongly discouraged and is not supported by Microsoft. Since executing standard SQL statements is not an option, Microsoft introduced CAML as a SharePoint-specific query language. Behind the scenes, the SharePoint platform converts CAML queries into valid SQL that extracts the required data from the underlying database schema, hiding the complexity of the schema from users.

Here's an example of a CAML query:

```
<Query>
   <Where>
      <And>
         <Contains>
            <FieldRef Name='Title' />
```

```
            <Value Type='Text'>abc</Value>
        </Contains>
        <Lt>
            <FieldRef Name='FileSizeDisplay' />
            <Value Type='Computed'>50</Value>
        </Lt>
    </And>
    </Where>
    <OrderBy>
        <FieldRef Name='Created' Ascending='False' />
    </OrderBy>
</Query>
```

## Performance

Extracting data using CAML is a pretty efficient operation. There is, of course, the overhead of converting the CAML query into a SQL statement and the performance implications of the highly abstracted database schema, but all in all, the process works well and the minor performance hit is a reasonable price to pay for the flexibility available. There's a problem when the data access pattern gets a bit more complicated. For example, using SQL, we can easily write a complex statement such as this:

```
Update      Person.Contact
Set         EmailPromotion=1
from        HumanResources.Employee
Inner Join  Person.Contact
on          Person.Contact.ContactID=HumanResources.Employee.ContactID
Where       Where HumanResources.Employee.Title like '%manager%'
```

This statement will execute a query and use the rows returned by the query to select other rows in a second table that will then be updated. However, CAML does not support updates, and as a consequence, in order to perform a similar action on SharePoint, an appropriate CAML query will be executed and the resulting list will be loaded in memory. The SharePoint runtime will then iterate through the list, making the necessary updates one row at a time.

This presents a few problems, and the first is memory usage. If the query returns a huge amount of data, either because the rows contain a lot of content or because there are a large number of rows, the memory requirements will be considerable. To make this problem worse, remember that SharePoint is a web-based platform. Many users could be performing similar operations at the same time, exponentially increasing the memory requirements. The second problem is timeouts and perceived application performance; if such an operation is performed during a page post-back, the user will need to wait for the operation to complete before the page is refreshed. For very large operations, the process may take so long that the page request times out and the user subsequently refreshes the page, compounding the performance problem.

Of course, complicated data access operations such as this are not very common, and with some careful programming, you can work around them. But what about simpler operations that can be performed using the user interface? You've seen how nontechnical users can create custom views of a list or library. What if a user creates a view that returns 10,000 rows on a single page? All of that data needs to be loaded into memory to render the page, and worse still, the resultant page then needs to be downloaded to the browser, causing network performance issues.

## List Throttling

**New in 2010**

To prevent rogue database operations from bringing down a SharePoint server, SharePoint 2010 introduces the concept of *list throttling*. List throttling allows an administrator to specify the maximum number of items that can be retrieved in a single request. So in our example, if a user created a view with a page size of 10,000 but the administrator had specified a List View Threshold of 2000 items, no rows would be returned and instead the user would receive an error message indicating that the query exceeded the specified threshold.

Here's how to configure list throttling:

1. From SharePoint Central Administration, select Manage Web Applications.
2. Select the appropriate application from the list, and then in the ribbon select Resource Throttling under General Settings, as shown next:

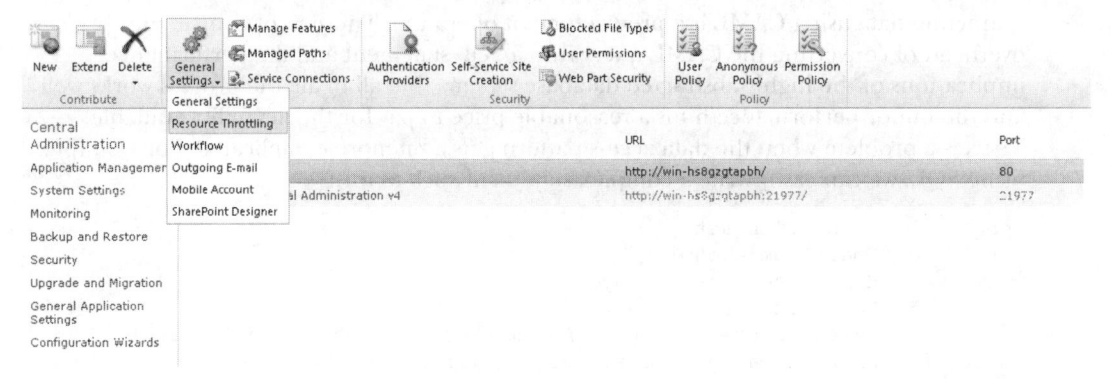

The Resource Throttling dialog has a number of options that warrant explanation:

- **List View Threshold**   This value determines the maximum number of items that can be returned by a single query. For our example, we could set this to 2000 (which is the minimum value).

- **Object Model Override**   In some situations, it is necessary to execute larger queries, and a few options are available regarding how to tackle this problem. Object Model Override allows developers to override the List View Threshold on a per-query basis using code similar to this:

    ```
    private void DoQuery(SPList list, string theCaml)
    {
      SPQuery query = new SPQuery();

      query.Query = theCaml;
      query.QueryThrottleMode = SPQueryThrottleOption.Override;

      SPListItemCollection results=list.GetItems(query);
    }
    ```

- **List View Threshold for Auditors and Administrators**   This value is the upper limit for auditors and administrators. Note that when using the Object Model Overrides the limit is not removed; this value is used instead of the List View Threshold.

- **Daily Time Windows for Large Queries**   This is the preferred solution for dealing with large queries. Administrators can define a time window when usage is low and allow large queries to execute. During this window of time, no limits are applied.

## Column Indexes

When a list or library contains a large number of rows, executing a CAML query to return a selection of data can take some time. To improve the performance of such operations, you can apply indexes to columns in a list, although this approach has a few caveats.

Bearing in mind that the SharePoint database schema mandates the storage of all user data in a single table, the indexes that we're creating using the SharePoint object model or user interface are not *indexes* in the SQL sense of the word. Such an index is not possible, because in the underlying database schema, a single column may contain values for different fields and different lists in subsequent rows. Applying an index to the column would have unintended consequences. Without going into technical minutiae, to get around this limitation of the database schema, when an index is created on a column, the value being indexed is copied to a separate table. As a consequence, if a list has 10,000 rows, for each column being indexed, a further 10,000 rows are created in the separate index table. For example, if 5 columns were indexed, 50,000 rows would be added to the index table. The drawback with this is that the table has to be kept in sync with the main data table, and as the number of rows in the table increases, it creates an element of diminishing returns. Here's how to add an index to a column using the user interface:

1. Open the list containing the column to be indexed. In the ribbon, select List Settings from the List Tools tab, as shown:

2. Select Indexed columns in the Columns section of the page, and then click Create A New Index.

Here's how to add an index using code:

```
private void AddIndex(SPList list, string primaryFieldName,
                                   string secondaryFieldName)
    {
      SPField primary;
      SPField secondary;
      if (list.Fields.ContainsField(primaryFieldName))
      {
        primary = list.Fields[primaryFieldName];
        if (!string.IsNullOrEmpty(secondaryFieldName))
        {
          if (list.Fields.ContainsField(secondaryFieldName))
          {
            secondary = list.Fields[secondaryFieldName];
```

```
            list.FieldIndexes.Add(primary, secondary);
        }
      }
      else
      {
        list.FieldIndexes.Add(primary);
      }
    }
    list.Update();
}
```

## Summary

This short whirlwind tour of the SharePoint data access model has demonstrated the flexibility and extensibility built into the fundamentals of the platform. In the remainder of this part of the book, you'll see how other features of SharePoint build on this flexibility to address a host of other, more specific business requirements such as Enterprise Search, Business Intelligence, and Social Computing.

Having said that, it's only fair to point out that the built-in data access model is not suitable for every scenario. When the ability to access the database schema using SQL is a key factor in determining performance, it makes more sense to implement a standard relational database than try to fit a square peg into a round hole. However, as we've seen throughout this book, there's so much more to SharePoint than data access.

Even with a separate data store, it's still perfectly possible to leverage the many other features of SharePoint—and in a sense that's one of the key strengths of the platform. If one component doesn't work quite the way you need it to, more often than not you can easily swap it out with some custom code that exactly meets your requirements.

# CHAPTER 14

# LINQ to SharePoint and SPMetal

In previous versions of SharePoint, you could query lists and document libraries using Collaborative Application Markup Language (CAML). As an XML dialect, CAML syntax is relatively easy to pick up—you simply need to know which elements perform which functions, and then combine them to form a query. For example, a CAML query to return all items in a list named *Products,* where the product name begins with the letter *A,* might look something like this:

```
<Query>
   <Where>
      <BeginsWith>
         <FieldRef Name='Title' />
         <Value Type='Text'>A</Value>
      </BeginsWith>
   </Where>
</Query>
```

The CAML syntax covers a number of standard functions, including logic operations such as *AND* and *OR* as well as comparison operations such as *greater than, less than, equal to,* and *between.* The drawback of the CAML syntax, however, is that it's not parsed by the compiler at compile time. Only when the statement is processed at runtime will an error be detected. To make matters worse, it's often possible to parse an erroneous statement and have the query return no results without returning an error. Take the following code snippet as an example:

```
SPList theList = SPContext.Current.Web.Lists["Products"];
SPQuery query=new SPQuery();
query.Query="<Query><Where><BeginsWith><FieldRef Name=\"Title\" />"+
         "<Value Type=\"Text\">A</Value></BeginsWith></Where></Query>";
SPListItemCollection results = theList.GetItems(query);
```

At first glance, this query looks correct; however, the enclosing **<Query>** element is unnecessary. As a result, this query will not return any results. As you can imagine, debugging problems like this can be difficult and time consuming.

One of the major drawbacks of the default SharePoint data access model is the use of indexed properties to store data. Since it isn't possible for the compiler to determine whether an index value or key is valid at compile time, bugs often go undetected until runtime, when they are much more expensive to fix. Furthermore, even small changes to field names or identifiers can wreak havoc in an application, making refactoring a minefield.

Since the introduction of SharePoint 2007, a number of solutions to this problem have been proposed. Ultimately, all such proposals have one common thread: the creation of a strongly typed data access layer. Index-based fields are wrapped with a strongly typed interface, which is in turn presented to the rest of the application as the single method of accessing data stored in indexed fields. Of course, this solution does not resolve the problem of a lack of compile time validation for indexed fields, but it does isolate runtime errors within a single layer, making resolving bugs much easier.

So, instead of program logic that looks like this,

```
SPListItem myItem=properties.ListItem;
String myField=myItem["TestField"].ToString();
```

and we mistakenly enter this,

```
String myField=myItem["testField"].ToString();
```

we'll get an object not found error, since the fields collection does not contain an item with the index **testField**.

We end up with something that looks like this:

```
MyDataObject d=new MyDataObject(properties.ListItem);
String myField=d.TestField;
```

With this code, a compilation error will occur if we mistype the field name. Furthermore, IntelliSense support will allow us to enter code much faster and more accurately.

Of course, some overhead is incurred in implementing an additional data access layer. The programmer must create additional wrapper objects for each list, document library, or content type. In addition, the actual code involved in creating these objects is pretty mundane. As a result, a number of utilities have been written over the years that automatically generate data access objects from SharePoint lists and libraries. One such utility started life as SPMetal, part of a CodePlex project to deliver Language Integrated Query (LINQ) to SharePoint, created by Bart De Smet in 2007. Now, with SharePoint 2010, the SharePoint development team has picked up where Bart left off and have added complete LINQ functionality, including a new version of SPMetal as part of the standard toolset.

# Overview of LINQ

Before we delve into the workings of SPMetal, let's spend some time looking at LINQ. We'll examine what it is, where it came from, and why it's an essential tool for developing applications using SharePoint 2010.

I have to confess that I'm a relatively late convert to LINQ. I've been aware of the technology for some time but had always assumed it to be some kind of framework for generating Structured Query Language (SQL). As a developer who has spent many years avoiding dynamically generating SQL statements in favor of well-written and much more secure stored procedures, I'd always considered the technology to be somewhat contradictory to established best practice. What I'd failed to see was the power of LINQ outside the SQL world.

LINQ is not just about SQL—fair enough, the syntax is deliberately similar to SQL—but as a technology, it's about working with collections of data, not specifically relational database type data, but in fact practically any collection of data that you're ever likely to use in the .NET world.

To illustrate the implications of such a tool, think about the last application you wrote. How many for loops did you use to locate specific items within collections of data? How many lines of code did you write to handle situations in which the item you expected wasn't found within the collection? What about multiple collections with related items? Did you use nested for loops to extract common data into a new collection for use within your logic? If you've written any application of more than a few lines long, you've likely used one or more of these techniques.

The true power of LINQ is that it provides a much more effective way to find and process exactly the data that you need. No longer do you need to knock on every door in the street to find out who lives at number 15; you can simply ask the question, "I'd like to know the occupant name where the house number is 15," and voila, the magic that is LINQ will return the correct answer. But what if you live in a town with many streets, each one with a "Number 15"? What if you want to know who lives at number 15 Main Street specifically? You don't need to walk up and down every street knocking on every door; you can simply ask the question, "I'd like to know the occupant name where the house number is 15 and the street name is Main Street," and, again, LINQ will return the correct answer. This truly is powerful stuff. When it comes to working with collections of data, LINQ is the tool we've been waiting for.

Of course, LINQ isn't really magic. There's a certain amount of smoke and mirrors involved, particularly with regard to the SQL-like syntax. But behind the scenes it's actually quite simple. Let's take a look at a few examples to illustrate how it works.

## Locating Data Using an Iterator

One of the built-in implementations of LINQ is LINQ to Objects, which is installed as part of the .NET Framework 3.5. Take a look at this code snippet to get an idea of how it works:

```
List<string> members = new List<string> { "John", "Paul", "George", "Ringo" };
List<string> results = new List<string>();
        foreach (string m in members)
            {
                if (m.Contains("n")) results.Add(m);
            }
```

As you can see, this piece of code iterates through a list of strings, returning a new list containing only those items from the original list where the character *n* was found. Nothing groundbreaking here. However, if you include the **System.Linq** namespace in your class file, you'll notice that the IntelliSense members' list for the results object now includes a whole host of new methods. Interestingly, however, if you look up the documentation for a **List<T>** object, you'll find that none of the new methods are listed. There's a perfectly good explanation for this: these new methods are implemented as *extension methods*, an essential new feature in .NET 3.5 for supporting LINQ. Extension methods allow developers to attach methods to a class by defining additional static methods in a referenced assembly. Here's an example:

```
public static class MyExtensions
{
    public static string MyExtension(this List<string> list, string message)
    {
        return "MyExtension says " + message;
    }
}
```

Notice the use of the **this** modifier in the function signature. The modifier specifies the type to which the extension methods should be attached. This example specifies that the extension method should be available to objects of type **List<string>**. Extension methods work only when their containing namespace is explicitly imported—hence, the necessity to import the **System.Linq** namespace to see the additional methods for this generic list. Strictly speaking, the extension methods that we see are actually added to the generic **IEnumerable<TSource>** interface and as such are available to any object that implements this interface.

## Locating Data Using an Anonymous Delegate

One of the extension methods that we can make use of is the **Where()** method that we could use to rewrite our code as follows:

```
List<string> members = new List<string> { "John", "Paul", "George", "Ringo" };
var results = members.Where(delegate(string m) { return m.Contains("n"); });
```

The **Where** method accepts an anonymous delegate as a parameter, and behind the scenes the method is actually calling the delegate for every item in the list. Whenever the delegate returns *true*, the item is added to a new results list. The results list is then returned when the **Where** method has iterated through each item in the collection. From this explanation, you can see that we're actually performing much the same work as our original function; we're simply writing less code to do it.

## Locating Data Using a Lambda Expression

We used an anonymous delegate in the preceding example, but .NET 3.5 introduces another new feature known as the *lambda expression*. Using a lambda in place of the anonymous delegate, we can rewrite our code as follows:

```
List<string> members = new List<string> { "John", "Paul", "George", "Ringo" };
var results = members.Where((string m) => { return m.Contains("n"); });
```

Lambda expressions make use of the => operator to separate the expression parameters from the expression body. This example defines an expression that accepts a **string** parameter named **m**. You'll notice that we don't need to define the return type; just as with an anonymous delegate, the compiler does this automatically for us.

Hopefully, you'll see that using lambda expressions offer a more concise way of writing an anonymous method.

## Locating Data Using LINQ

With more than a little sleight of hand and a healthy dose of compiler voodoo, LINQ takes this expression syntax a step further. Instead of hammering out several different styles of brackets, we can simply rewrite our code as follows:

```
List<string> members = new List<string> { "John", "Paul", "George", "Ringo" };
var results = from m in members
              where m.Contains("n")
              select m;
```

As you've seen by working through these simple examples, behind the scenes, LINQ to Objects is doing much the same work that we would have done using an iterator; the new syntax simply provides a much cleaner way of presenting the logic. However, consider this example, which we'll revisit later in this chapter:

```
var changes = (from c in dxWrite.ChangeConflicts
               from m in c.MemberConflicts
               where m.CurrentValue.Contains(m.OriginalValue)
               && m.CurrentValue is string
               select m).ToList();
```

I'm sure you can realize the benefit of the LINQ syntax when compared to the complicated logic that you'd have to implement to produce this result set using iterators.

## LINQ to SharePoint

In the preceding few examples, we used LINQ to Objects to illustrate the query syntax of LINQ—in fact, the syntax is pretty similar regardless of which provider you're using. For example, to retrieve a list of records from a table using LINQ to SQL, you'd write something like this:

```
NorthwindDataContext context = new NorthwindDataContext());
var customers = from c in context.Customers
                where c.Name.Contains("n")
                select c;
```

Or to get a list of nodes from an XML document using LINQ to XML, you'd use something like this:

```
XDocument loaded = XDocument.Load(@"C:\users.xml");
var q = from u in loaded.Descendants("user")
        where u.Name.Contains("n")
        select u;
```

As you'll see, the only major difference is in the way that the "table" is referenced. When we used LINQ to Objects, the "table" was simply the collection variable, whereas when using LINQ to SQL the "table" is actually a database table. To make this less confusing, this "table" object is commonly referred to as a *gateway object*, since technically it doesn't necessarily represent a table—the way it's used in the SQL-like syntax makes it seem like a table.

## Microsoft.SharePoint.Linq.DataContext

The gateway object for LINQ to SharePoint is **Microsoft.SharePoint.Linq.DataContext**. The **DataContext** object exposes a number of methods and properties, of which the following are most significant for the purposes of this discussion:

- **GetList(T)**   This method returns a generic **EntityList** object that represents that specified list. Here's an example:

```
EntityList<Customer> customers=dataContext.GetList<Customer>("Customers");
```

- **Refresh**   This method can be used to refresh one or more entities with the latest data from the content database. It has three overloads:
  - **Refresh(RefreshMode, IEnumerable)**   Refreshes the collection of entities that are defined by the **IEnumerable** parameter
  - **Refresh (RefreshMode, Object)**   Refreshes a single entity as defined by the object parameter
  - **Refresh(RefreshMode, Object[])**   Refreshes an array of entities as defined by the object array parameter

Each of the overloads for the **Refresh** method accepts a **RefreshMode** parameter. This enumeration is used to specify how concurrency conflicts should be handled. Here are the possible values:

- **KeepChanges**   Accept every user's changes with prejudice for the current user
- **KeepCurrentValue**   Rolls back all other users' changes
- **OverwriteCurrentValues**   Gives absolute prejudice to the database version

These descriptions are pretty vague, and I'll cover how LINQ to SharePoint handles concurrency conflicts in more detail a bit later. For now, it's enough to know that the **Refresh** methods of the **DataContext** object require one of these three values.

- **RegisterList**   This method enables continued reading and writing to an **EntityList** object after it's been renamed or moved. Since the **EntityList** object is effectively a snapshot of a list at time of creation, if the list is subsequently moved or renamed, the **EntityList** object will become invalid. The **RegisterList** method allows you to re-point the **EntityList** object to the new destination rather than having you dispose and re-create the **EntityList** object. This method has two overloads:
  - **RegisterList<T>(String,String)**   Used if the list is renamed within the same site

- **RegisterList<T>(string *newListName*, string *newWebUrl*, string *oldListName*)**   Used if the list is moved to another web site
- **SubmitChanges()**   As with the **Refresh** method, this method has three overloads that are used to specify how concurrency conflicts are handled:
  - **SubmitChanges()**   Persists changes to the content database. If a concurrency conflict occurs, a **ChangeConflictException** will be thrown and the **ChangeConflicts** property will be populated with one or more **ChangeConflict** objects. This method assumes a failure mode of **FailOnFirstConflict**. When items are updated using this method, the version number is automatically incremented if versioning is enabled.
  - **SubmitChanges(ConflictMode)**   Used when you don't want to use the default conflict handling behavior. Two possible values can be used for **ConflictMode**: **ContinueOnConflict**, which attempts all changes, throws an exception if any concurrency errors occurred, and then rolls back all changes; or the default of **FailOnFirstConflict**, which throws an error when the first concurrency error occurs, and then rolls back all changes made up to that point. When items are updated using this method, the version number is automatically incremented if versioning is enabled.
  - **SubmitChanges(ConflictMode, bool *systemUpdate*)**   Used for the same reason as the preceding overload, with one significant difference: if the *systemUpdate* flag is set to *true*, updates are performed using the **SystemUpdate()** method rather than the **Update()** method. This is significant because updating an item using **SystemUpdate** does not increment the version number. Setting the *systemUpdate* flag to *false* would have the same effect as using the preceding overload with the same **ConflictMode**.

In addition to these methods are a number of properties that are worth covering briefly:

- **ObjectTrackingEnabled**   This **Boolean** property is used to determine whether the **DataContext** object should track changes for each entity that's associated with it. If this value is set to *false*, calling **SubmitChanges** will have no effect. This property exists for performance reasons; by setting the value to *true*, the **DataContext** object has a lot of extra work to do to track any changes to its associated objects. As a rule of thumb, you should set this value to *false* unless you specifically need to add, edit, update, or delete data. By default, object tracking is enabled.
- **ChangeConflicts**   This **ChangeConflictCollection** property, as its type suggests, is a read-only collection of **ObjectChangeConflict** objects. Each **ObjectChangeConflict** object represents a set of one or more discrepancies between the in-memory version of a list item and the current persisted version. The **ObjectChangeConflict** object has a **MemberConflicts** collection that contains a collection of **MemberChangeConflict** objects, with each object representing the discrepancy in a single field. It's possible to have an **ObjectChangeConflict** object without any associated **MemberChangeConflict** objects. In this case, the **ObjectChangeConflict** object exists because the original item has been deleted. This condition can be verified by checking the **IsDeleted** property of the **ObjectChangeConflict** object.

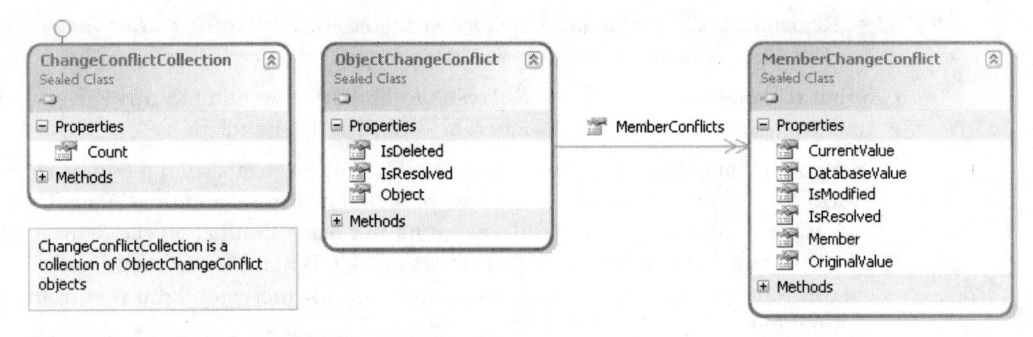

**Figure 14-1** Conflict resolution object relationships

**TIP** Depending on the profile of your application, you may find that you use LINQ most often for querying data as opposed to making changes. Furthermore, you'll generally be making changes to a very small dataset, whereas you may be querying much larger datasets. In this situation, maintaining a separate **DataContext** object for updates is usually the most efficient approach. In effect, you'll have one **DataContext** with object-tracking enabled that you can use for updates, and another with object-tracking disabled that you can use for queries.

Figure 14-1 shows the relationship between the conflict resolution objects. Conflict resolution is covered in more detail later in this chapter in the section "Record Level Conflict Resolution."

I've covered the main functional elements of the gateway class for LINQ to SharePoint, and a few other objects are significant as well, such as **EntityList**, **EntityRef**, and **EntitySet**. I won't cover these in detail since their operation is practically identical to similar objects used on other variants of LINQ; their usage will become apparent in the code samples that follow. The **DataContext** object has special significance since it provides the gateway to using standard LINQ syntax, although, as you'll see when we look at SPMetal, generally the **DataContext** object isn't used directly; instead, common practice is to create a number of derived classes that represent each list in the data structure.

## Demonstration Scenario

Hopefully, you now have a clear understanding of what LINQ is and how it works. We need to use entity objects that represent the data in our application if we want to use LINQ syntax. To illustrate the use of LINQ to SharePoint and the tools for generating entity classes, consider the following scenario:

Your company is involved in renting industrial machinery. You're working on a web-based application that allows customers to view a list of the items that the company currently rents, together with details of the individual rental contracts. Customers come from a number of geographical locations and sometimes relocate equipment from one location to another. To make it easier for customers to track the location of the rented equipment, your application allows the customer to add multiple notes for each item, and these notes should also be visible in your web application.

**NOTE** You might appreciate a bit of clarification regarding some of the terminology used here. You non-British readers *rent* equipment, and equipment is said to be *rented* from the company. In the United Kingdom, we *hire* equipment, and equipment is said to be *on hire* when it is rented. So an "on-hire asset" refers to an asset that can be rented and is subject to a rental contract (or hire contract).

Since your company has a relatively small number of large customers, you've opted for an extranet solution. Each customer has a private site within your SharePoint farm that they can use to assist with managing their account with your company. Since *Hire Contracts* are standard documents used by all customers, you've defined a *Hire Contract* content type in your farm. Each customer site has a *Contracts* document library that contains *Hire Contract* documents. Additionally, you've defined an *On-Hire Asset* content type that represents the individual item of machinery that is subject to the rental contract. Each asset has a unique asset tag, and you allow customers to add notes against each asset tag in a separate list called *Asset Notes*. If implemented using a relational database, your data structure would look similar to Figure 14-2.

A common misconception is to equate a list or document library in SharePoint with a logical entity in your data structure. However, this isn't necessarily the best approach and often making such an assumption makes you miss out on a lot of the real power of the SharePoint platform. A more useful parallel is to equate a logical entity with a content type. Since lists and document libraries can contain items of more than one content type, and sites can contain more than one list with the same content type, using lists and documents libraries to store items is mainly useful for setting security on a subset of items or for grouping items based on their status or some other business-specific reason. Bearing this in mind, when we translate our data structure into a SharePoint model, we end up with something similar to Figure 14-3. Logically, we still end up with the same collections of entities, but our use of content types allows us to create an unlimited number of web sites, each with the same structure and permissions to view only the customer-specific subset of data.

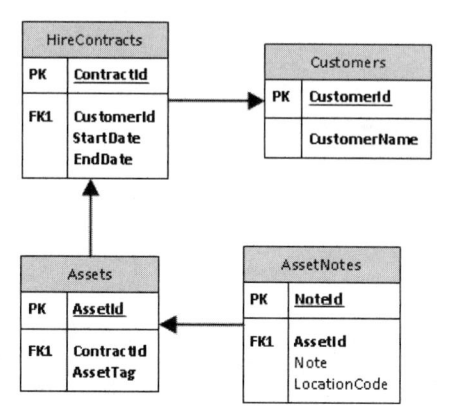

**Figure 14-2** Logical data structure for extranet application

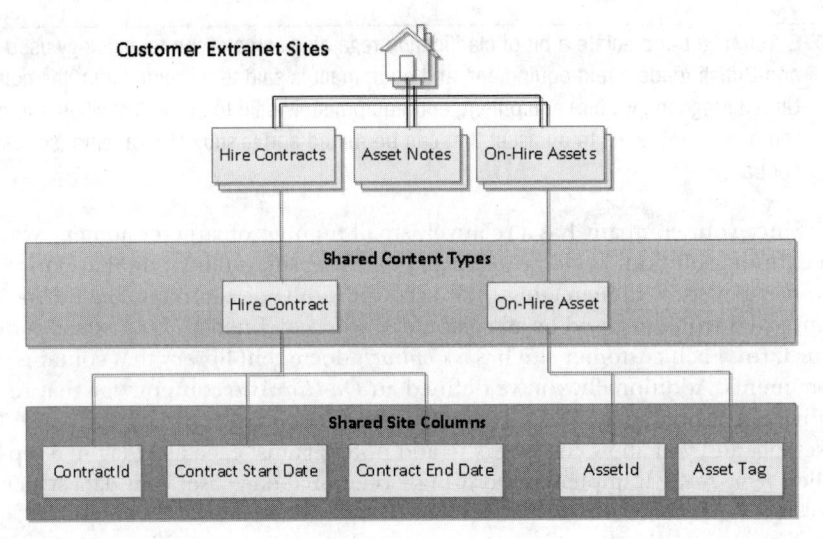

**Figure 14-3** SharePoint implementation of logical data structure

If you compare this model to a standard ASP.NET application using a relational database to implement our original logical data structure, you can see that implementing security and filtering for each customer would incur significant overhead.

## Create a Data Structure Using SharePoint 2010

To create the demonstration scenario data structure, take the following steps:

### Create Site Columns

1. Open SharePoint Designer 2010. Click New Blank Web Site.

2. In the dialog box that appears, type the site name as **Chapter14**.
3. Once your new site has been created, you'll see a Site Objects menu, as shown next. Click Site Columns.

4. From the ribbon menu at the top of the window, click New Column, and then choose Single Line of Text from the menu.

5. In the dialog that appears, enter the name **ContractId**, and then, in the Put This Site Column Into area, select New Group and enter **Hire Sample Columns**. The completed dialog should look like this:

6. Repeat steps 4 and 5 to create the following columns:

| Column Type | Name | Group |
|---|---|---|
| AssetId | Single Line of Text | Hire Sample Columns |
| AssetTag | Single Line of Text | Hire Sample Columns |
| Contract Start Date | Date & Time | Hire Sample Columns |
| Contract End Date | Date & Time | Hire Sample Columns |
| Location Code | Single Line of Text | Hire Sample Columns |

7. Since each of these fields is mandatory, it's necessary to disallow blank values. To do this, select the column from the Site Columns list, and then select Column Settings from the ribbon. In the dialog that appears, uncheck the Allow Blank Values checkbox. Perform this action on each created field.

**TIP** To make it easier to find specific columns, the column headers in the site columns list can be used to filter the view. For example, clicking the down arrow on the far right of the Group header allows you to select Hire Sample Columns as a filter. Only items that match the filter are shown in the list.

## Create Content Types

1. From the Site Objects menu, select Content Types, and then select New Content Type from the ribbon. In the dialog that appears, enter **Hire Contract** as the content type name. Then, in the Select a Parent Content Type From drop-down, select Document Content Types. In the Select Parent Content Type drop-down, select Document.

2. Create a new group to hold your custom content types. Click the New Group checkbox, and then, in text field, type **Hire Sample Content Types**.

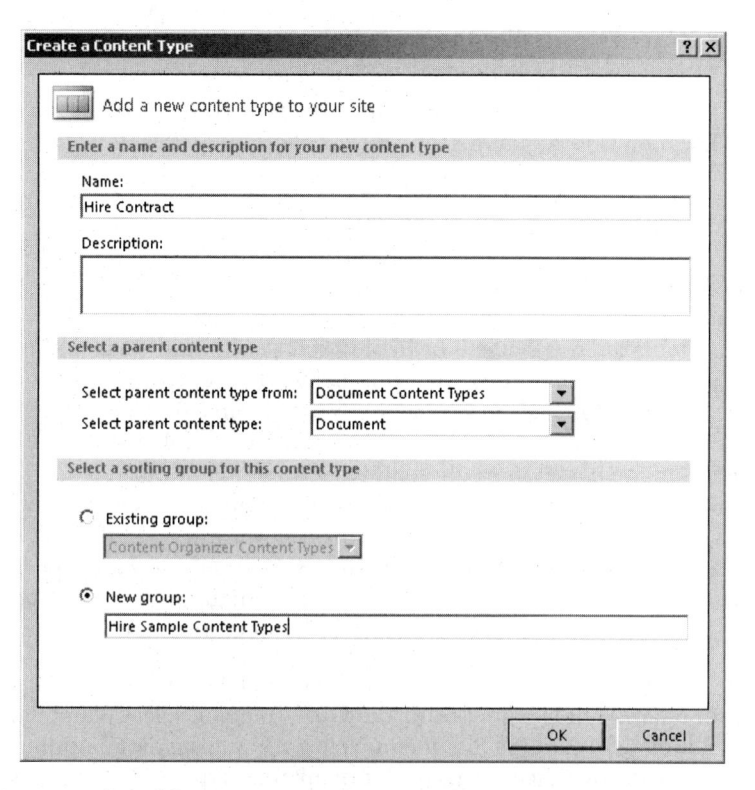

3. Repeat steps 1 and 2 to create another content type named *On-Hire Asset*, also in the Hire Sample Content Types group. This time, set the Parent Content Type drop-downs to List Content Types and Item.
4. You now have two new, blank content types. The next step is to associate your site columns with these content types. To do this, highlight the Hire Contract content type and select Edit Columns from the ribbon. A list of the columns associated with the content type will appear. You'll notice that a number of columns are already defined. These columns are inherited from the parent content type that you selected when creating this new content type. To add in your precreated site columns, select Add Existing Site Column from the ribbon, and then use the dialog that appears to find and add the ContractId column, the Contract Start Date column, and the Contract End Date column. Once you've added the required columns, click the Save icon in the title bar.

5. Repeat step 4 for the On-Hire Asset content type. This time add the AssetId column and the AssetTag column.

6. Repeat steps 3 and 4 to create an Asset Note content type. This time add the Location Code column.

You should now have three content types within the Hire Sample Content Types group: Asset Note, Hire Contract, and On-Hire Asset.

## Create Customer Template Site

Now that we've defined the content types that make up our data structure, our next step is to create a template site that can be deployed for each individual customer. You might have noticed a Customer content type was not included to represent our customer. By using multiple sites, one for each customer, the site itself effectively becomes the Customer data container. This may seem a bit bizarre when thinking in relational database design terms, but when you give it a bit more thought it makes sense: In our relational data structure, the Customer table existed only as a means of identifying which customer corresponded to which contract. In effect, it provided a means of segmenting the contract data (and therefore any data that was related to contracts). By using content types within multiple sites, we achieve similar segmentation. Each site contains only data that should be visible to a particular customer. To see data for a different customer, we look at a different site.

1. The first thing that we need to do is generate a new subsite to act as our template. In SharePoint Designer 2010 Site Objects menu, select Blank Site to change the ribbon to display the Site menu. Select the Subsite menu option from the ribbon. In the dialog that appears, select Blank Site. Type in the location of the new site: **http://<your_Server_Name>/Chapter14/CustomerTemplate**. Then click OK.

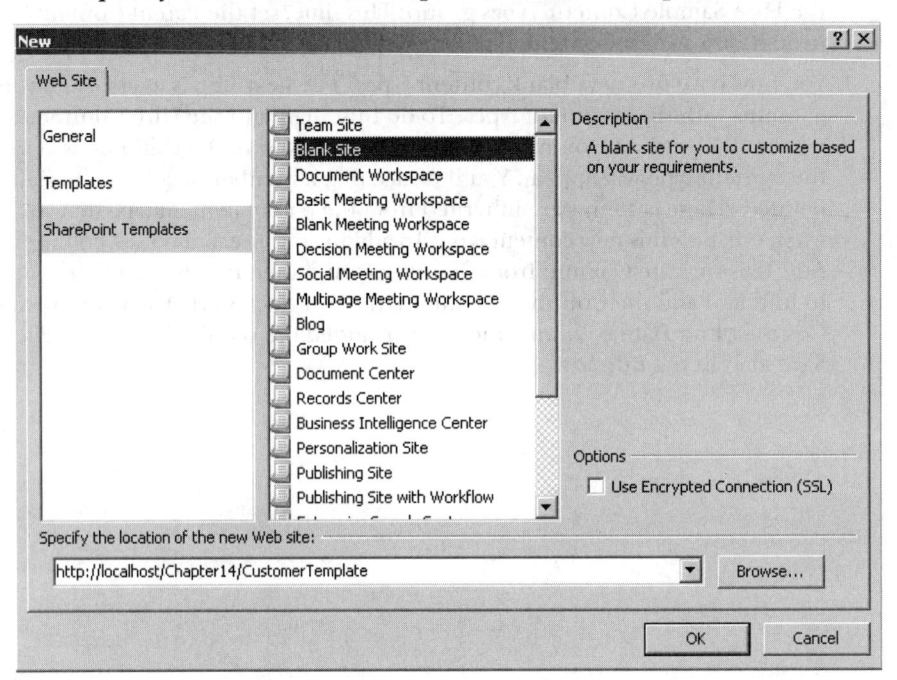

After the subsite has been created, a new instance of SharePoint Designer 2010 will open automatically. You'll see from the title bar that it's pointing to the new subsite. If you select Content Types or Site Columns from the Site Objects menu, you'll notice that the content types and columns that were created in the preceding steps are available to this new site. By default, content types are inherited by all subsites within a site collection; as a result, our content types will be available to any sites that are created as subsites of our *http://localhost/Chapter14/* site.

2. Now that we have a new blank site, we need to add lists to hold our data. To do this, select Lists and Libraries from the Site Objects menu. Then, from the ribbon, select Custom List. Type **On-Hire Assets** as the name of the list.

3. Repeat step 2 to create another custom list named *Asset Notes*.

4. Since hire contracts are documents rather than simple collections of data, we'll create a document library instead of a list. To do this, select Document Library from the ribbon, and then choose Document Library from the list of options. Type **Hire Contracts** for the name in the dialog that appears.

## Associate Content Types

The next step is to associate our content types with the lists that we've created. Do this:

1. Highlight the Asset Notes list, and then select List Settings from the ribbon. The list configuration page for the Asset Notes list will appear. You'll notice a section named Settings with a series of checkboxes, as illustrated. Check the Allow Management Of Content Types checkbox. By default, SharePoint creates simple lists and libraries that are bound to basic system content types, such as Item and Document. Since we want to bind the list to a specific content type, we must configure the list to allow such binding. With this option selected, we are free to add and delete content types as appropriate.

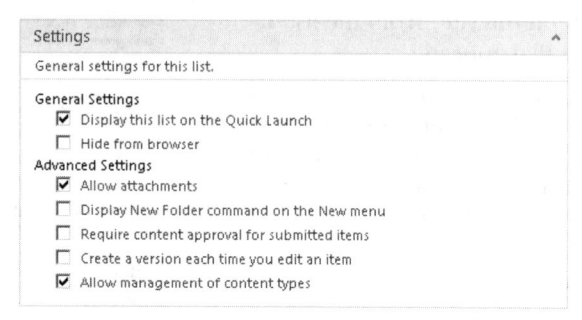

2. In the Site Objects menu, select Content Types. Then click the Add button. Select and add the Asset Note content type. Then highlight the Item content type select Delete from the ribbon.

3. Click the Save icon in the title bar to save the changes.

4. Repeat steps 1–3 for the On-Hire Assets list. This time, add the On-Hire Asset content type instead of the Asset Note content type.

5. Repeat steps 1–3 for the Hire Contracts document library. This time add the Hire Contract content type.

## Defining Relationships

We now have a template site with each of our three content types bound to a list or library. We could start entering data into these lists. However, one thing that we haven't considered is the relationships between the various content types. In SharePoint, relationships are defined by using lookup fields. Each lookup field is bound to a particular column in a particular list (although other columns can also be carried through if required). In relational database terms, the lookup field works like a foreign key, holding a value that uniquely identifies a record on the source list.

**NOTE** It is possible to create lookups that can accept multiple values, but for the purposes of defining this data structure, we're interested only in single value lookups.

Lookup columns target a specific list. While it is possible to include lookup fields in content types, each time the content type is used the lookup field is bound to the list that was set when the content type was created, potentially causing security issues if the list is in a separate site. For that reason, when using lookups to define data structures, you should view them as a constraint to be added on the list, as opposed to a field to contain data within the content type. Adding lookups in a content type greatly reduces the portability of the content type.

Our data structure requires two relationships:

- On-Hire Asset is related to Hire Contract via ContractId.
- Asset Note is related to On-Hire Asset via AssetId.

To create these relationships, take the following steps:

1. In the Site Objects menu, select Lists and Libraries. Highlight the Asset Notes list. Select Edit Columns from the ribbon.

2. Select Add New Column from the ribbon and then choose Lookup (information already on this site) from the list of options that appears.

3. In the dialog that appears (shown next), select On-Hire Assets from the List Or Document Library drop-down. In the Field drop-down, select the AssetId. Uncheck the Allow Blank Values checkbox. Click OK to create the new column.

4. Once the column has been created, right-click the column name and select Rename. Change the column name by typing **Asset Reference**.

5. Click the Save button in the title bar to save the changes.
6. Repeat steps 1–5 for the On-Hire Assets list. This time, bind the lookup column to the Hire Contracts document library and set the field to ContractId. Rename the new field *Contract Reference*.

### Create a Site Template

We've now created a template web site for use by our customers, complete with a data structure that's logically identical to the relational schema that we defined in Figure 14-2. The final step that we need to take is to save this site as a template so that we can easily create a new site for each customer as required. To do this, do the following:

1. From the Site Objects menu, select Blank Site. In the ribbon, select Save as Template.
2. In the browser window that appears, enter **Hire Sample Template** in the File Name text box, and then in the Template Name text box, enter **Hire Sample Template**. Then click OK to create the template.

The new template will be stored in the User Solutions Gallery, where it can be activated and used to create additional sites as required. The solutions gallery is accessible from the root site on any web application. So, for example, if your server is named *MyServer* and you have a web application running on *http://MyServer*, then the solutions gallery can be found at http://MyServer/_catalogs/solutions/Forms/AllItems.aspx. Using solutions for deployment is covered in more detail in Chapters 2 and 19, but for the purposes of demonstrating the use of LINQ, we can simply use our template site as our data source.

## Creating Entities Using SPMetal

Now that we've created a basic data structure, let's make use of SPMetal to generate some entity classes. At the time of writing, SPMetal is implemented as a command line only tool. It's installed by default at %SPROOT%\Bin\SPMetal.exe and can be called using the command line arguments in Table 14-1.

The tool will produce a .cs or .vb file containing class definitions for each entity available within the site referenced by the **/web:** argument. Additionally, it will also create a strongly typed **DataContext** object with properties for each list and document library within the data structure.

### Create a Windows Forms Sample Application

First things first: if we're going to make use of LINQ, we'll need a Visual Studio 2010 project. Create a new Windows Forms Application project. It's important to make sure that the project is set to use .NET Framework 3.5 and not version 4.0. For ease of narrative, save the project in C:\Code\Chapter14 and call it LinqSampleApplication.

| Option | Value Definition | Example |
|---|---|---|
| web | The complete, absolute URL of the web site whose data is modeled by the entity classes | /web:http://localhost/Chapter14 |
| code | The relative or absolute path and filename of the output file | /code:Chapter14.cs |
| language | The programming language of the generated code | /language:csharp |
| namespace | The namespace that contains the entity class declarations | /namespace:Chapter14.HireSample |
| useremoteapi | No value | /useremoteapi |
| user | The user in whose context SPMetal executes | /user:mydomain\bob |
| password | The password for the user specified in the user option | /password:Pa$$w0rd |
| serialization | Specifies whether objects that instantiate the generated classes are serializable; if this option is not used, "none" is assumed | /serialization:unidirectional |
| parameters | Identifies the path and name of an XML file that contains overrides of SPMetal default settings | /parameters:ParameterFile.xml |

**Table 14-1** SPMetal Command Line Arguments

Once the project has been created, we need to take a few steps to make it compatible with SharePoint 2010. First, we need to set the build type to be 64-bit. SharePoint 2010 is 64-bit only, and by default Windows Forms Application projects are configured for 32-bit builds.

1. From the Build menu, select Configuration Manager.

2. Under Platform, select <New…>.

3. In the New Project Platform dialog, select x64 from the New Platform drop-down list. Click OK to save the changes.

Next, we need to add references to the SharePoint object model:

1. In the Solution Explorer pane, right-click References and then select Add Reference.

2. In the dialog that appears, select Microsoft.SharePoint and Microsoft.SharePoint.Linq.

3. Click OK to add the references.

### Generate Entity Classes

We're now ready to use SPMetal to generate entity classes for our extranet sample. Open a command prompt, change the current directory to C:\Code\Chapter14\LinqSampleApplication, and then execute the following command (note that this command should be entered on a single line, not on two lines as shown here):

```
%SPROOT%\bin\SPMetal.exe /web:http://localhost/Chapter14/CustomerTemplate / →
code:HireSample.cs
```

> **TIP** Define a system variable to point to SharePoint root; it saves a whole load of time instead of typing C:\Program Files\Common Files\Microsoft Shared\Web Server Extensions\14\. Instead you can simply type %SPROOT% as a shortcut. See Chapter 2 for a step-by-step guide.

SPMetal will create a new file named HireSample.cs in the project directory for our LinqSampleApplication. To add it into the project, select Add Existing Item from the Project menu, and then select the file named HireSample.cs.

Have a look at the code in HireSample.cs. You'll notice that each class is declared using the **partial** keyword. This allows you to extend the functionality of the auto-generated classes using additional files so that if the classes are automatically regenerated using SPMetal, any customizations are not lost.

Figure 14-4 shows the objects that are defined in HireSample.cs. You'll notice that a **HireSampleDataContext** class that's derived from **DataContext** has been defined and has properties corresponding to each of the three lists: AssetNotes, HireContracts, and OnHireAssets. Additionally, there are two classes derived from AssetNote and OnHireAsset, named **AssetNotesAssetNote** and **OnHireAssetsOnHireAsset**. These derived classes contain the additional lookup values that we added to define the relationships between the content types. Since the lookup values were not added to the content type for reasons mentioned earlier, a new derived class exists containing only the lookup field.

### Controlling Entity Creation Using a Parameters File

To save any confusion, it would be nice to rename a few of the entities, particularly the derived entities containing the additional columns. While it's perfectly possible to do this manually in code, the next time SPMetal is used to regenerate the entities, all changes will be lost and any code that refers to the old entity names will fail to compile. Instead, SPMetal allows for the use of a parameters file.

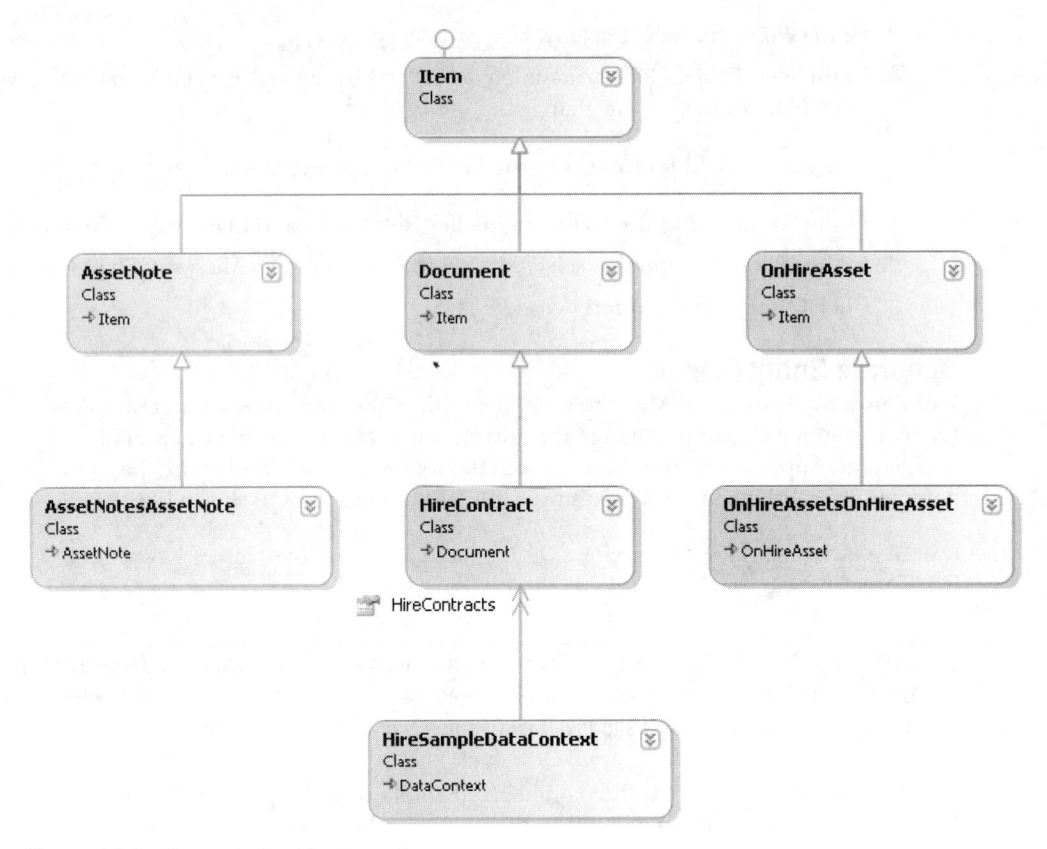

**Figure 14-4** Generated entity class diagram

In Visual Studio, add a new XML file named SPMetalParameters.xml. Insert the following XML into the file:

```xml
<?xml version="1.0" encoding="utf-8" ?>
<Web AccessModifier="Internal"
    xmlns="http://schemas.microsoft.com/SharePoint/2009/spmetal">
  <List Name="Asset Notes" Type="AssetNote">
    <ContentType Name="Asset Note" Class="AssetNote" />
  </List>
  <List Name="On-Hire Assets" Type="OnHireAsset">
    <ContentType Name="On-Hire Asset" Class="OnHireAsset" />
  </List>
  <ContentType Name="Asset Note" Class="BaseAssetNote"/>
  <ContentType Name="On-Hire Asset" Class="BaseOnHireAsset"/>
</Web>
```

Save the file, and then rerun SPMetal using the following command line (as before, this command should be entered on one line):

```
%SPROOT%\bin\spmetal.exe /web:http://localhost/Chapter14/ →
customertemplate /code:HireSample.cs /parameters:SPMetalParameters.xml
```

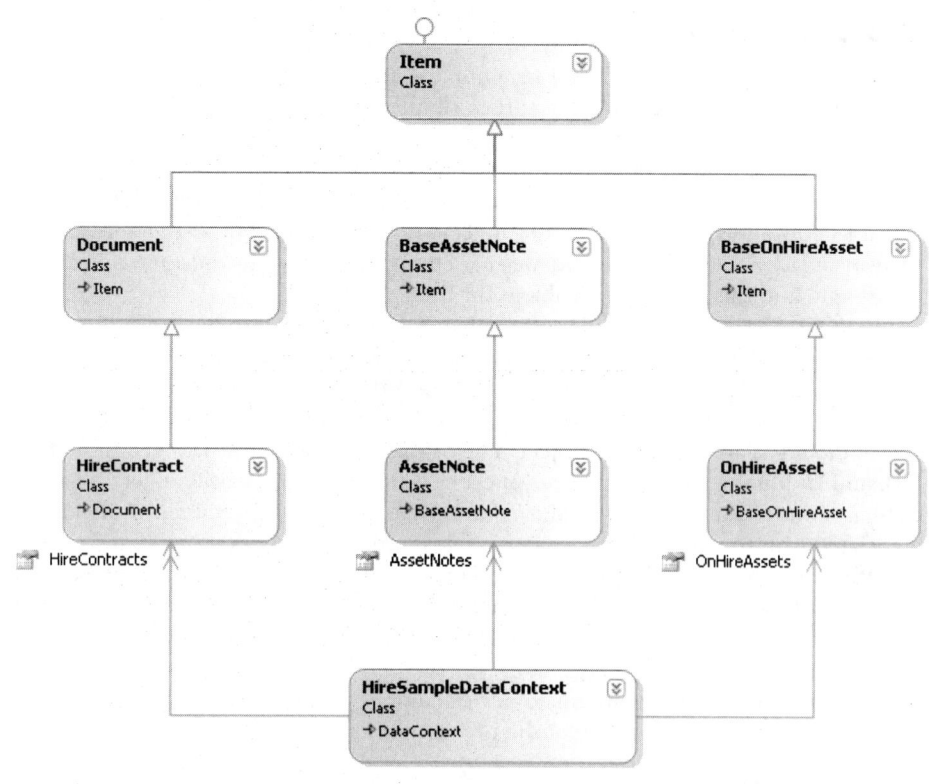

**Figure 14-5** Revised entity class diagram

If you now examine HireSample.cs, you'll notice that the objects have been renamed as specified in the parameters file. Figure 14-5 shows the new object model.

## Incorporate a Build Script to Regenerate Entities Automatically

Rather than having to rerun SPMetal manually each time your data structure changes, you can incorporate a build script into your Visual Studio project that calls SPMetal automatically each time the project is built.

In Visual Studio, in the Project menu, select LinqSampleApplication Properties. In the Properties pane, select Build Events, and then click the Edit Pre-Build button. In the dialog that appears, enter the following script (in one continuous line; line breaks are added here for readability):

```
%SPROOT%\bin\spmetal.exe /web:http://localhost/Chapter14/customertemplate →
/code:"$(ProjectDir)HireSample.cs" →
/parameters:"$(ProjectDir)SPMetalParameters.xml"
```

Build the project. You'll notice that when the build has completed, you're notified that HireSample.cs has been modified. This confirms that the prebuild script has automatically regenerated the file as part of the build process.

## Adding Data Using LINQ

Our data structure consists of two lists, On-Hire Assets and Asset Notes, and a document library, Hire Contracts. Recall from earlier chapters that the difference between a document library and a list is the type of content contained in each. Document libraries contain document-based content, and as a result, content types that are used in a document library must be derived from the built-in Document content type. When we created our Hire Contract content type, we based it on the Document content type to meet this requirement. By using a Document content type, we're dictating that all items must have an associated document, and this presents a problem for LINQ.

LINQ to SharePoint is a data manipulation tool designed to deal with the actual data that's associated with an individual item. The entity classes are created based on the fields defined in the associated content types as opposed to the properties of the object that manages the content. For example, most data items in SharePoint are represented by the object model as an **SPListItem** object. The **SPListItem** has many properties, such as **Title**, **Url**, and **UniqueId**. None of these properties is mapped to an entity object for use by LINQ to SharePoint; instead, LINQ to SharePoint focuses only on the values of the fields that are associated with the **SPListItem**. As a result, it's impossible to manipulate any properties of an **SPListItem** object (or any other object) using LINQ to SharePoint. In the case of a Document-based item, we can't create an object using LINQ, because items stored in a document library must have an associated file. Since **File** is a property of the **SPListItem** object, we cannot set it via LINQ.

Since we can't add documents to our document library using LINQ, we can write some SharePoint code that makes use of the object model to insert some sample data quickly.

### Add Data Generation Buttons to LinqSampleApplication

In the LinqSampleApplication project, open Form1.cs. From the toolbox, drag three button controls, a textbox, and a label onto the design surface. The form designer should look like this:

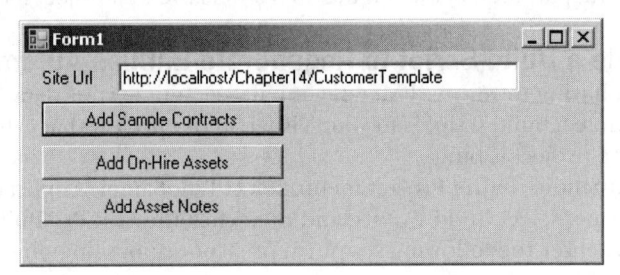

### Add Sample Contracts

Double-click the Add Sample Contracts button to add some code for the on-click event, and then add the following code:

```
private void button1_Click(object sender, EventArgs e)
{
    //Add some sample data to the hire contracts document library
```

```csharp
//disable the button to prevent concurrency problems
button1.Enabled = false;
using (SPSite mySite = new SPSite(SiteUrl.Text))
{
    using (SPWeb myWeb = mySite.OpenWeb())
    {
        for (int x = 0; x < 3; x++)
        {
            //Since we're not interested in the document contents,
            //create a simple text document
            string test = x.ToString("This is test contract" +
                                    " number 000");
            byte[] content = System.Text.Encoding.UTF8.GetBytes(test);

            //Get a reference to the Hire Contracts list

            SPList HireContracts=myWeb.Lists["Hire Contracts"];

            //Generate a sequential file name

            string filename=x.ToString("SampleContract000.txt");

            //Upload the file to the document library
            SPFile newFile = HireContracts.RootFolder.Files.Add(filename,
                                                                content);

            //Get a reference to the SPListItem that is automatically
            //created when the document is uploaded

            SPListItem item =newFile.Item;

            //populate the mandatory fields with sample data

            item["ContractId"] = x.ToString("CONT-000");
            item["Contract Start Date"] = DateTime.Now.AddMonths(0-x);
            item["Contract End Date"] = DateTime.Now.AddMonths(x+12);

            //Persist the changes to the content database
            item.SystemUpdate();
        }
    }
}
//change the text on the button so that we know the job's done
button1.Text += " - Done";
}
```

As you'll see from the comments, this code simply creates a few dummy Hire Contract documents in our document library. Once the documents have been uploaded, the properties are set using indexed properties on the **SPListItem** object. You'll notice that the field names and the name of the document are not strongly typed. This is the problem we are addressing by using LINQ.

## Add On-Hire Assets

Now that we have documents in our document library, we can move on and create list items that refer to those documents. Double-click the Add On-Hire Assets button on the form designer to add an on-click event handler. Add the following code:

```
private void button2_Click(object sender, EventArgs e)
{
    //Add some assets for our contracts
    //disable the button to prevent concurrency problems
    button2.Enabled = false;
    using(HireSampleDataContext dxWrite = new HireSampleDataContext(SiteUrl.Text))
    {
        //since we'll be making changes, we must set ObjectTrackingEnabled to true
        //This is the default value but is explicitly included here
        //for the sake of clarity
        dxWrite.ObjectTrackingEnabled=true;
        int counter = 0;
        //loop through the contracts in our Hire Contracts document library
        foreach (HireContract contract in dxWrite.HireContracts)
        {
            //Add new assets for each contract
            for (int x = 0; x < 3; x++)
            {
                OnHireAsset newAsset = new OnHireAsset();

                //generate sequential sample data
                newAsset.AssetId = counter.ToString("ASSET000");
                newAsset.AssetTag = counter.ToString("TAG-000");
                newAsset.ContractReference = contract;
                //set the new asset entity to be added into the OnHireAssets list
                dxWrite.OnHireAssets.InsertOnSubmit(newAsset);
                counter++;
            }
        }

        //Submit the changes. This will actually add the items to the list
        dxWrite.SubmitChanges();
    }
    //change the text on the button so that we know the job's done
    button2.Text += " - Done";
}
```

Notice first, and most importantly, that everything is strongly typed, meaning that if the code contained any errors, it would not compile. Second, the code is much more descriptive than the preceding example. It's apparent which data entities we're dealing with and what actions we're performing on them purely from the syntax of the code. Finally, as you'll remember from our data structure in Figure 14-2, each On-Hire Asset must have an associated Hire Contract. In this code, the assignment of a parent Hire Contract is done by simply assigning an appropriate **HireContract** entity to the **ContractReference** property that defines the relationship. There's no need to know exactly which field is used to define the foreign key since all of that information is automatically determined by the configuration of the lookup field.

### Add AssetNotes

We've created sample contracts and associated assets; the next thing to add is Asset Notes for each asset. Double-click the Add Asset Notes button to add an on-click event handler. Add the following code:

```
private void button3_Click(object sender, EventArgs e)
{
    //disable the button to prevent concurrency problems
    button3.Enabled = false;

    //Add some notes for our sample assets
    using(HireSampleDataContext dxWrite = new HireSampleDataContext(SiteUrl.Text))
    {
        dxWrite.ObjectTrackingEnabled = true;
        foreach (OnHireAsset asset in dxWrite.OnHireAssets)
        {
            for (int x = 0; x < 3; x++)
            {
                AssetNote newNote = new AssetNote();

                newNote.LocationCode = x.ToString("Location000");
                newNote.AssetReference = asset;
                dxWrite.AssetNotes.InsertOnSubmit(newNote);
            }
        }
        dxWrite.SubmitChanges();
    }
    //change the text on the button so that we know the job's done
    button3.Text += " - Done";
}
```

You should now have a Windows Forms application with three buttons that can be used to generate some sample data. Run the application, clicking each of the three buttons in turn to add some sample data.

## Deleting Data Using LINQ

Although we couldn't use LINQ to add document items to a document library, we can use LINQ to delete such items. Delete works because LINQ provides a DeleteOnSubmit method that makes use of the unique identifier for the entity object to delete the corresponding object from the data store.

### Deleting Sample Data

Add a new button to the sample application and name it *Delete Sample Data*.

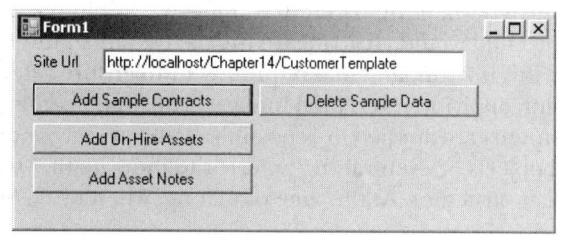

Add the following code in the on-click event handler:

```
private void button4_Click(object sender, EventArgs e)
{
    //disable the button to prevent concurrency problems
    button4.Enabled = false;

    using(HireSampleDataContext dxWrite = new HireSampleDataContext(SiteUrl.Text))
    {
        dxWrite.ObjectTrackingEnabled = true;
        //loop through the Hire Contracts
        foreach (HireContract contract in dxWrite.HireContracts)
        {
            //for each contract, loop through the assets
            foreach (OnHireAsset asset in contract.OnHireAsset)
            {
                //for each asset loop through the notes
                foreach (AssetNote note in asset.AssetNote)
                {
                    //delete the note
                    dxWrite.AssetNotes.DeleteOnSubmit(note);
                }
                //delete the asset
                dxWrite.OnHireAssets.DeleteOnSubmit(asset);
            }
            //finally delete the contract
            dxWrite.HireContracts.DeleteOnSubmit(contract);
        }

        dxWrite.SubmitChanges();
    }

    //change the text on the button so that we know the job's done
    button4.Text += " - Done";
}
```

It should be apparent from the comments that this code will delete all the sample data that we created in the preceding code examples. It uses three nested loops to ensure that referential integrity is maintained, and all associated child data is deleted before the parent element is deleted.

## Ensuring Referential Integrity

Since we defined relationships for which participation was mandatory—that is, each child object must have a parent object—you may wonder why the child objects were not automatically deleted when the parent was removed, because removing the parent object while leaving the child would clearly leave the data set in an invalid state. In relational database terms, this is a fundamental requirement to ensure referential integrity.

In SharePoint, applying referential integrity constraints on a lookup field is optional. Where no constraints are applied, it is possible to delete parent objects without cascading deletes to child objects or even raising an error to indicate that such a delete would invalidate the data structure. At the time of writing, when using SharePoint Designer

2010 Beta 2 to create lookup columns, there is no option to configure referential integrity options. Of course, this issue may be resolved by the time this book goes to print.

## Programmatically Configure Referential Integrity Options

For the moment, we can set referential integrity options using only the SharePoint user interface or programmatically. Let's consider the programmatic option first. Add another button to the sample application and name it *Enforce Integrity Checks*. In the on-click event handler, add the following code:

```
private void button5_Click(object sender, EventArgs e)
{
    //disable the button to prevent concurrency problems
    button5.Enabled = false;

    using (SPSite mySite = new SPSite(SiteUrl.Text))
    {
        using (SPWeb myWeb = mySite.OpenWeb())
        {
            //Get a reference to the On-Hire Assets list
            SPList assets = myWeb.Lists["On-Hire Assets"];

            SPFieldLookup contractRef;
            contractRef = assets.Fields["Contract Reference"] as SPFieldLookup;

            //there are three options for relationship delete behaviour:
            //None - the default, when this option is select referential
            //       integrity is not enforced
            //Cascade - where a parent object is deleted, all child objects
            //          are automatically deleted
            //Restrict - where an attempt is made to delete a parent object
            //           without first deleting child objects, an
            //           exception is raised

            contractRef.RelationshipDeleteBehavior = SPRelationshipDeleteBehavior.Restrict;

            //in order to enforce referential integrity, the lookup
            //column must be indexed
            contractRef.Indexed = true;

            contractRef.Update();

            //Get a reference to the Asset Notes list
            SPList notes = myWeb.Lists["Asset Notes"];

            SPFieldLookup assetRef;
            assetRef = notes.Fields["Asset Reference"] as SPFieldLookup;

            assetRef.RelationshipDeleteBehavior = SPRelationshipDeleteBehavior.Restrict;
            assetRef.Indexed = true;
            assetRef.Update();
        }
    }

    //change the text on the button so that we know the job's done
    button5.Text += " - Done";
}
```

This code updates the lookup column properties to enforce referential integrity by throwing an exception if an attempt is made to delete a parent object while child objects still exist. The other option for ensuring referential integrity is to cascade deletes automatically. In that case, when a parent object is deleted, any child objects are also automatically deleted.

To see the effects of this change, review the code for the Delete Sample Data button. Either comment out or delete the middle loop so that the code reads as follows:

```
private void button4_Click(object sender, EventArgs e)
{
    //disable the button to prevent concurrency problems
    button4.Enabled = false;

    using(HireSampleDataContext dxWrite = new HireSampleDataContext(SiteUrl.Text))
    {
        dxWrite.ObjectTrackingEnabled = true;
        //loop through the Hire Contracts
        foreach (HireContract contract in dxWrite.HireContracts)
        {
            //for each contract, loop through the assets
            foreach (OnHireAsset asset in contract.OnHireAsset)
            {
                //delete the asset
                dxWrite.OnHireAssets.DeleteOnSubmit(asset);
            }
            //finally delete the contract
            dxWrite.HireContracts.DeleteOnSubmit(contract);
        }

        dxWrite.SubmitChanges();
    }

    //change the text on the button so that we know the job's done
    button4.Text += " - Done";
}
```

Run the sample application, re-creating the sample data first if you've deleted it. This time, before clicking the Delete Sample Data button, click the Enforce Integrity Checks button to apply our constraints. When you click the Delete Sample Data button, an exception will be thrown, as illustrated. Furthermore, if you stop execution of the sample application and check your data in the SharePoint user interface, you'll find that no changes have been made.

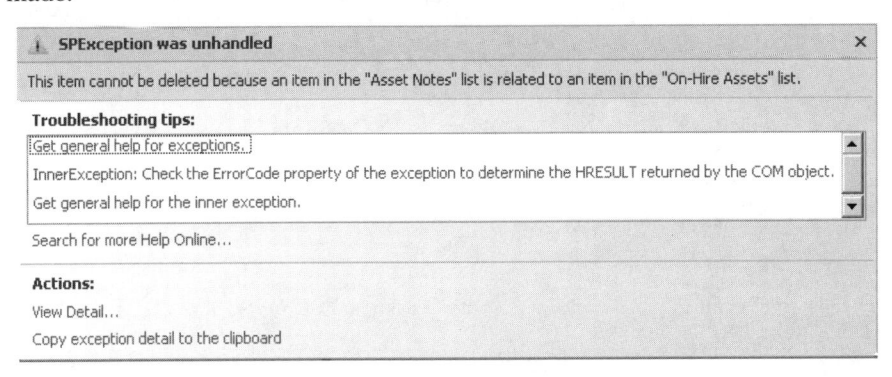

```
SPException was unhandled                                                    X
This item cannot be deleted because an item in the "Asset Notes" list is related to an item in the "On-Hire Assets" list.
Troubleshooting tips:
Get general help for exceptions.
InnerException: Check the ErrorCode property of the exception to determine the HRESULT returned by the COM object.
Get general help for the inner exception.
Search for more Help Online...

Actions:
View Detail...
Copy exception detail to the clipboard
```

### Configure Referential Integrity Options Using the User Interface

You've seen how to enforce constraints on lookup fields programmatically. Let's now look at how this can be done using the SharePoint user interface. Navigate to the Asset Notes list using Internet Explorer. From the ribbon, under List Tools, select List | List Settings. In the page that appears, find the Columns section, and then select Asset Reference. You should now see the Change Column page:

At the bottom of the page is a Relationship section with option buttons for restricting and cascading delete and a checkbox to enable or disable referential integrity. The options are currently set as specified by the code in our sample application; however, so that our Delete Sample Data function works properly, we need to change the selected option from Restrict Delete to Cascade Delete. Make the change and click OK to save it.

Run the sample application. As before, click the Delete Sample Data button. This time, the function completes without error, and a quick check of the lists using Internet Explorer will confirm that all data has been deleted as expected.

## Querying Data Using LINQ to SharePoint

One of the primary functions of LINQ is querying data. In this section, we'll dig a little deeper into how LINQ works before looking at how to retrieve data using LINQ to SharePoint.

## Query Limitations

As you saw earlier, LINQ works by passing lambda expressions to extension methods that have been declared to extend the **IEnumerable** and **IEnumerable<T>** interfaces. By chaining together these extension methods, you can create complex queries, all with compile-time syntax checking and type-safe return values. Earlier we looked at LINQ to Objects as a simple starting point to discuss how LINQ works. In the case of LINQ to Objects, parsing queries is relatively straightforward since the objects are in memory and LINQ is simply being used as a shortcut for more traditional programming techniques. Ultimately, behind the scenes, LINQ to Objects simply expands the query into the more verbose code that we would have written in a non-LINQ world.

There is one major difference between LINQ to Objects and LINQ to SharePoint, however, and that is the location of the data being queried. For LINQ to SharePoint, the data exists not in memory—as is the case for LINQ to Objects—but in the SharePoint content database. Because of this, LINQ to SharePoint has to work a bit harder in parsing the LINQ queries. Rather than simply expanding the queries, the parser must convert them to a syntax that can be used to query the SharePoint content database directly. Since the SharePoint platform defines its own query language in the form of the XML dialect CAML, LINQ to SharePoint must translate all LINQ queries into CAML. These CAML queries can then be processed directly by the SharePoint platform. Once the results are returned, they are mapped onto strongly typed entity objects, which are then returned as the query results.

## Expression Trees

It's worthwhile for you to understand how this process works, because it has implications when it comes to creating more complex queries—as you'll see later. To find out a bit more, let's start with one of the extension methods that we'd commonly use in a LINQ query. If we examine the **Where** extension method in more detail, we find the following method signature:

```
public static IQueryable<TSource> Where<TSource>(this IQueryable<TSource>
source, Expression<Func<TSource, bool>\> predicate)
```

At first glance, you may think there's too much information in this statement and decide to skip ahead a few paragraphs—but bear with me, because only one part of the signature is actually important for the purposes of this discussion.

The method accepts two parameters: the first being an **IQueryable** data source and the second being a generic **Expression** object of type **Func**. The **Func** object is a delegate that references the code that's been entered as the lambda expression, and this is passed as a parameter to the **Expression** object. The **Expression** object, however, converts the lambda expression into an **ExpressionTree**. The **ExpressionTree** is where the magic that is LINQ takes place. By using expression trees, you can programmatically analyze lambda expressions. As a result, you can convert compiled expressions into something completely different by applying logic to the expression tree. By using this process, LINQ to SharePoint converts the lambda expressions that make up a query into valid CAML syntax that can then be directly executed against the content database. (As an aside, this is exactly the same way that LINQ to SQL works—the only difference is the target query syntax.)

All very interesting, you may be thinking, but why is this relevant? Well, here's the thing: Many extension methods are defined for LINQ, they all have a default implementation in LINQ to Objects, and it's down to the creator of a new LINQ provider to override them with a platform-specific implementation. However, CAML doesn't support all the available extension methods. Some things in there simply can't be translated into CAML. In other implementations such as LINQ to SQL, where a method can't be implemented directly in SQL, the standard LINQ to Objects method is used, meaning that a portion of the query is performed using SQL, the results are then loaded into memory, and any remaining operations are performed using LINQ to Objects extension methods. Of course, this is all done behind the scenes and is completely transparent to the user.

The issue with LINQ to SharePoint is that CAML is a very limited language when compared to SQL, and as such a significant number of the standard LINQ operations are not possible. If such operations were left to revert to their default implementation in LINQ to Objects, significant performance issues could result due to the amount of in-memory processing that could be required. Without an in-depth understanding of how LINQ works, an uninitiated developer could easily create a LINQ query that, if executed concurrently by many users, could severely degrade system performance.

### Inefficient Queries

At the time of writing, this problem has been highlighted by having the LINQ to SharePoint provider throw an error if an unimplemented extension method is used in a query. In previous versions, this behavior could be controlled by setting the **AllowInefficientQueries** flag on the **DataContext** object; however, the current version—at the time of writing, Beta 2—no longer allows this flag to be publically altered and therefore unimplemented expressions will not work with LINQ to SharePoint. This may change in future releases of the product.

The following extension methods are considered inefficient due to inability to convert to CAML and are therefore not implemented by LINQ to SharePoint:

| Aggregate | All | Any | Average | Distinct | ElementAt |
|---|---|---|---|---|---|
| ElementAtOrDefault | Except | Intersect | Join | Max | Min |
| Reverse | SequenceEqual | Skip | SkipWhile | Sum | |

## Performing a Simple Query

Now that I've discussed the dos and don'ts of LINQ to SharePoint, let's get started on creating a few queries using our sample application.

We'll extend our user interface to make it easier to view our results and the CAML that's being generated behind the scenes. On Form1.cs in LinqSampleApplication, add a SplitContainer under the buttons that we added earlier. Set it to anchor to all sides. Within the left panel, drop a WebBrowser control, and set its Dock property to Fill. In the right panel, drop a DataGridView control, and set its Dock property to Fill. Add another button next to those created earlier, and label the button *Basic Query*. Once you've finished, your form should look like this:

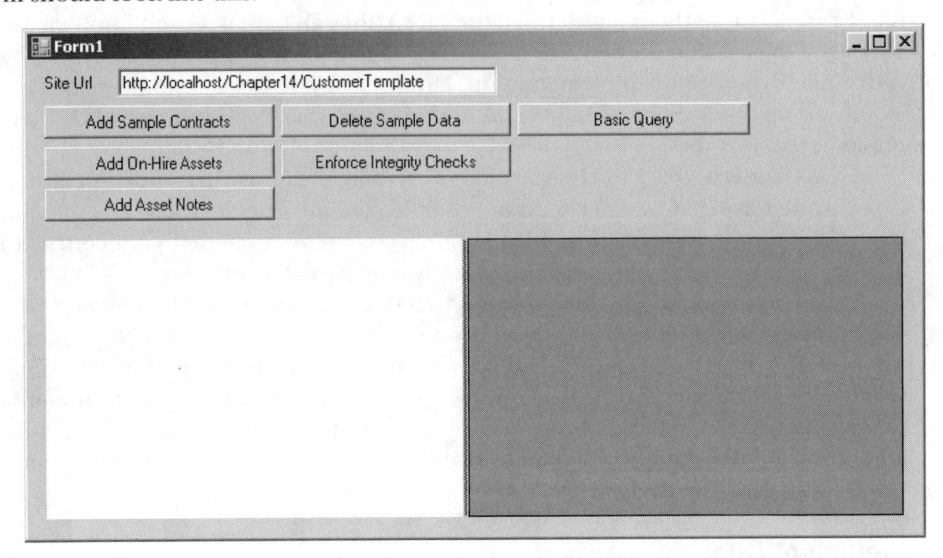

In the on-click event handler for the Basic Query button, add the following code:

```
private void button6_Click(object sender, EventArgs e)
{
    using(HireSampleDataContext dxRead = new HireSampleDataContext(SiteUrl.Text))
    {
        //create a stringbuilder to store the CAML query
        StringBuilder sb = new StringBuilder();

        using (StringWriter logWriter = new StringWriter(sb))
        {
            //log the generated CAML query to a StringWriter
            dxRead.Log = logWriter;

            //Since we're only reading data, disabling object tracking
            //will improve performance
            dxRead.ObjectTrackingEnabled = false;

            var basicQuery = from c in dxRead.HireContracts
                             where c.ContractStartDate.Value < DateTime.Now
                             orderby c.ContractStartDate
                             select c;

            //DataGridView can't bind to IEnumerable. Calling ToList
            //executes the query and returns a generic List
            dataGridView1.DataSource = basicQuery.ToList();
        }
        //create a temporary file for the generated CAML
        string fileName = Path.Combine(Path.GetTempPath(), "tmpCaml.xml");
```

```
        XmlDocument doc = new XmlDocument();
        doc.LoadXml(sb.ToString());
        doc.Save(fileName);

        //point the browser control to the temporary generated CAML file
        webBrowser1.Navigate(fileName);
    }
}
```

Notice a few interesting things about this code sample. First, notice the use of the **Log** property on the **DataContext** object. When a **TextWriter** object is assigned to this property, the CAML that is generated by the LINQ provider will be output to the **TextWriter** when it is executed. In this sample, we've made use of that functionality to generate a temporary XML file that we can view using our WebBrowser control.

Another thing to highlight is the **ObjectTrackingEnabled** flag: since we're planning to execute queries only using this DataContext, setting this flag to *false* will improve performance, because the provider doesn't need to track references to the underlying **SPListItem** objects that are represented by the result set.

Finally, the last thing to note is the use of the **ToList** extension method when assigning the query as the data source for our **DataGridView**. LINQ queries are not actually executed until the result set is enumerated. Since the **DataGridView** control doesn't support the **IEnumerable** interface for data sources, the result set is never enumerated, and therefore the query is never executed. The **ToList** extension method enumerates the result set to convert the results into a generic list; this list is then passed to the **DataGridView**, enabling us to view the results in the user interface.

Running the sample application and then clicking the Basic Query button should yield the following result:

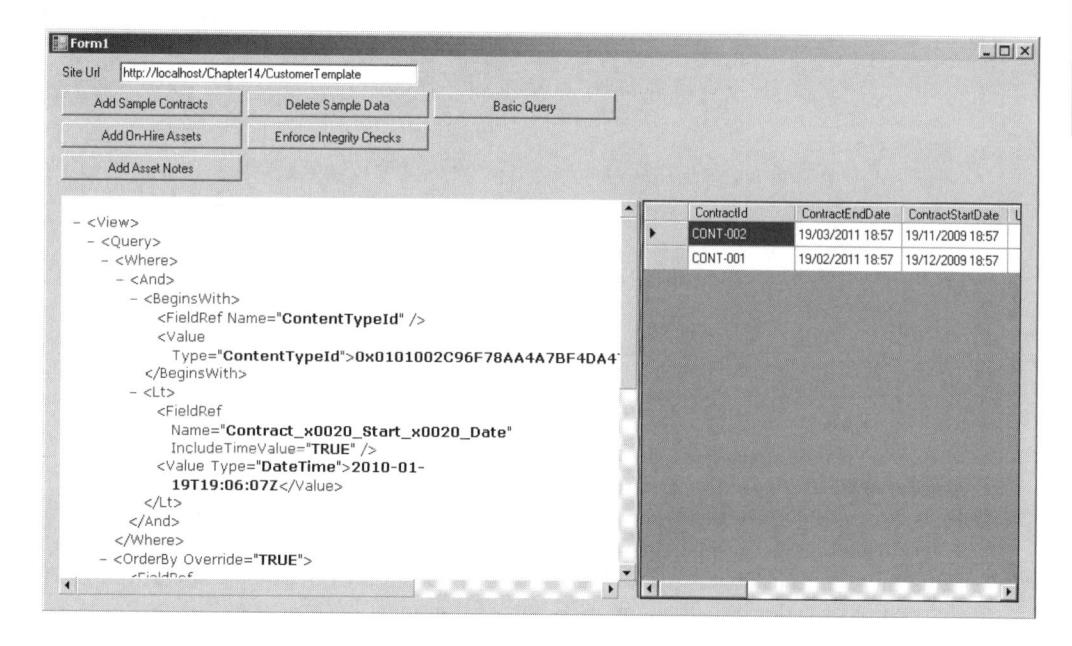

## Result Shaping Using LINQ

One of the benefits of LINQ is its ability to shape result sets while still retaining a type-safe output. We can explore this functionality by adding another button to our sample application; this time, label it *Basic Result Shaping* and add the following code:

```
private void button7_Click(object sender, EventArgs e)
{
    using(HireSampleDataContext dxRead = new HireSampleDataContext(SiteUrl.Text))
    {
        //create a stringbuilder to store the CAML query
        StringBuilder sb = new StringBuilder();

        using (StringWriter logWriter = new StringWriter(sb))
        {
            //log the generated CAML query to a StringWriter
            dxRead.Log = logWriter;

            dxRead.ObjectTrackingEnabled = false;

            var basicQuery = from c in dxRead.HireContracts
                             where c.ContractStartDate.Value < DateTime.Now
                             orderby c.ContractStartDate
                             select new{
                                 c.ContractId,
                                 c.ContractStartDate,
                                 c.ContractEndDate,
                                 Creator = c.DocumentCreatedBy.Substring(
                                     c.DocumentCreatedBy.LastIndexOf('\\')+1),
                                 Version = "v" + c.Version.Value.ToString("0.000")
                             };

            dataGridView1.DataSource = basicQuery.ToList();
        }

        string fileName = Path.Combine(Path.GetTempPath(), "tmpCaml.xml");

        XmlDocument doc = new XmlDocument();
        doc.LoadXml(sb.ToString());
        doc.Save(fileName);

        //point the browser control to the temporary generated CAML file
        webBrowser1.Navigate(fileName);
    }
}
```

Notice the creation of a new anonymous type as part of the LINQ query. The new type consists of fields from the returned entity together with some string manipulation functions to get the results into the appropriate format.

Notice when examining the generated CAML for this query that the string manipulations have not been translated. Although CAML does not support these operations, the LINQ to SharePoint provider still allows them as part of the query because they are performed on the results and are therefore unlikely to cause significant performance issues.

## Joining Tables Using LINQ

You may have noticed in the preceding code that the **Join** extension method is included in the list of inefficient extension methods earlier in the chapter and as such is not permitted within LINQ to SharePoint. However, this does not mean that retrieving related data isn't possible, only that arbitrary joins are not supported. Where the relationship between two entities is defined by a lookup column, retrieving related data is permitted and in fact is actually achieved using a much simpler syntax than is required by the **Join** operator.

### Simple Join

Let's add a new button to enable us to execute a basic join query. Label the button *Basic Join Query* and in the event handler add the following code:

```
private void button8_Click(object sender, EventArgs e)
{
    using(HireSampleDataContext dxRead = new HireSampleDataContext(SiteUrl.Text))
    {
        StringBuilder sb = new StringBuilder();

        using (StringWriter logWriter = new StringWriter(sb))
        {
            //log the generated CAML query to a StringWriter
            dxRead.Log = logWriter;

            dxRead.ObjectTrackingEnabled = false;

            var basicQuery = from a in dxRead.OnHireAssets
                             where a.ContractReference.ContractStartDate.Value
                                 < DateTime.Now
                             orderby a.AssetTag,
                                 a.ContractReference.ContractStartDate
                             select new
                             {
                                 a.AssetTag,
                                 a.AssetId,
                                 a.ContractReference.ContractId,
                                 a.ContractReference.ContractStartDate,
                                 a.ContractReference.ContractEndDate
                             };

            dataGridView1.DataSource = basicQuery.ToList();
        }

        //create a temporary file for the generated CAML
        string fileName = Path.Combine(Path.GetTempPath(), "tmpCaml.xml");

        XmlDocument doc = new XmlDocument();
        doc.LoadXml(sb.ToString());
        doc.Save(fileName);

        //point the browser control to the temporary generated CAML file
        webBrowser1.Navigate(fileName);
    }
}
```

From this code example, you can see that the join is performed by making use of the lookup field. Within the LINQ query, the lookup field is of the same type as the item to which it refers. In this case, the **ContractReference** lookup field is implemented as a property of type **HireContract**. This allows you to deal with entity objects within a logical hierarchy, ignoring the underlying data structure implementation. This is much simpler than the **Join** extension method syntax, which relies on your knowledge of the data structure to know which tables to join together and which fields to use for the join.

## Complex Join

Using this syntax, you can join multiple lists together as long as appropriate lookup fields have been defined. To explore this, we'll add another button, this time labeled *Complex Join Query* with the following code:

```
private void button9_Click(object sender, EventArgs e)
{
    using(HireSampleDataContext dxRead = new HireSampleDataContext(SiteUrl.Text))
    {
        StringBuilder sb = new StringBuilder();

        using (StringWriter logWriter = new StringWriter(sb))
        {
            //log the generated CAML query to a StringWriter
            dxRead.Log = logWriter;

            dxRead.ObjectTrackingEnabled = false;

            var basicQuery = from n in dxRead.AssetNotes
                    where int.Parse(n.LocationCode.Substring(8))==2
                    && n.AssetReference.ContractReference.ContractStartDate.Value
                        < DateTime.Now
                    orderby n.LocationCode,
                        n.AssetReference.AssetId,
                        n.AssetReference.ContractReference.ContractStartDate
                    select new
                    {
                        n.LocationCode,
                        n.AssetReference.AssetTag,
                        n.AssetReference.AssetId,
                        n.AssetReference.ContractReference.ContractId,
                        n.AssetReference.ContractReference.ContractStartDate,
                        n.AssetReference.ContractReference.ContractEndDate
                    };

            dataGridView1.DataSource = basicQuery.ToList();
        }

        //create a temporary file for the generated CAML
        string fileName = Path.Combine(Path.GetTempPath(), "tmpCaml.xml");

        XmlDocument doc = new XmlDocument();
        doc.LoadXml(sb.ToString());
        doc.Save(fileName);
```

```
            //point the browser control to the temporary generated CAML file
            webBrowser1.Navigate(fileName);
        }
}
```

In this sample, we've joined all three lists together and have also performed some string processing as part of the Where clause. You'll notice from the generated CAML that the Location Code filter is not included in the query; that's because the LINQ provider brings back the resulting rows and then programmatically applies the additional filter in memory before returning the results. Again, this can be done efficiently because only one CAML query is required, so the resource usage is minimal.

## Combining LINQ to SharePoint and LINQ to Objects

Although the join syntax in LINQ to SharePoint is very powerful, in some situations you won't be able to retrieve the data that you need using this syntax. Some operations that you require are not permitted on the LINQ to SharePoint provider, because they are considered inefficient.

### Performing an In-Memory Subquery

Here's an example of an in-memory subquery: Suppose that our sample application requires a list of asset tags and locations codes for a particular contract, but only where the locations are also being used to store assets that are subject to another contract. If you were writing this query using SQL, it would be relatively straightforward—something along the lines of this:

```
SELECT AssetTag, LocationCode
FROM    AssetNotes as n
INNER JOIN OnHireAssets as a
ON A.AssetId=n.AssetId
INNER JOIN HireContracts as c
ON c.ContractId=a.ContractId
WHERE n.LocationCode in (
SELECT LocationCode
FROM AssetNotes as n1
INNER JOIN OnHireAssets as a1
ON a1.AssetId=n1.AssetId
INNER JOIN HireContracts as c1
On c1.ContractId=a1.ContractId
Where c1.ContractId=CONT-002'
)
AND c.ContractId='CONT-001'
```

OK—maybe this is not that straightforward with all the joins, but you get the picture. You could use a subquery to filter the results to suit your requirements.

Unsurprisingly, given its similarity to SQL, LINQ syntax also supports a similar operation. Let's use our sample application to try it out. As usual, add a new button, label it *Sub Query* and add the following code:

```
private void button10_Click(object sender, EventArgs e)
{
```

```csharp
using(HireSampleDataContext dxRead = new HireSampleDataContext(SiteUrl.Text))
{
    StringBuilder sb = new StringBuilder();

    //since we-re using subqueries, more than one CAML query
    //will be generated.
    //add a root element to ensure that the logged output is valid XML
    sb.Append("<Queries>");

    using (StringWriter logWriter = new StringWriter(sb))
    {
        //log the generated CAML query to a StringWriter
        dxRead.Log = logWriter;

        dxRead.ObjectTrackingEnabled = false;

        var subquery=from note2 in dxRead.AssetNotes
                    where note2.AssetReference.ContractReference.ContractId
                        == "CONT-002"
                    select note2.LocationCode;

        var results = from note in dxRead.AssetNotes
                    where note.AssetReference.ContractReference.ContractId
                        == "CONT-001"
                    && subquery.Contains(note.LocationCode)
                    select new
                    {
                        note.AssetReference.AssetTag,
                        note.LocationCode
                    };

        dataGridView1.DataSource = results.ToList();
    }

    sb.Append("</Queries>");

    //create a temporary file for the generated CAML
    string fileName = Path.Combine(Path.GetTempPath(), "tmpCaml.xml");

    XmlDocument doc = new XmlDocument();
    doc.LoadXml(sb.ToString());
    doc.Save(fileName);

    //point the browser control to the temporary generated CAML file
    webBrowser1.Navigate(fileName);
}
```

In this code sample, we've defined the subquery, and then used it within the main query. I've split up the queries for the sake of clarity; LINQ syntax allows you to combine them within a single query if required.

When you run this query using the sample application, an exception will be thrown, because the LINQ to SharePoint parser can't convert the statement into CAML, because the CAML syntax doesn't support subqueries. However, it is still possible to execute this query by making a small modification. Modify the subquery declaration to render the results to a List, as follows:

```
var subquery=(from note2 in dxRead.AssetNotes
          where note2.AssetReference.ContractReference.ContractId
              == "CONT-002"
          select note2.LocationCode).ToList();
```

This time, clicking the Sub Query button will return the expected result set, and an examination of the generated CAML queries will reveal that two queries were generated. The first query corresponds to the subquery and the second corresponds to the main query without the inclusion of the subquery.

So how does this work? Using **ToList** in the definition of the subquery forces the query to be executed immediately, returning the results as a generic list. The generic List object implements **IEnumerable<T>** and can therefore be used within a LINQ expression. The main LINQ query then performs the subquery using LINQ to Objects as opposed to LINQ to SharePoint, yielding the expected results. In effect, adding **ToList** to a query allows you to process the results using the full power of LINQ to Objects. However, as discussed earlier, this approach has drawbacks, and efficiency must be given serious thought before you adopt this technique.

# Updating Information Using LINQ to SharePoint

LINQ provides an efficient, transactional way to update data. Either all modifications made to a given data context are applied or all are rolled back. The update process also supports checking for concurrent updates, allowing for long-running processes to create and hold references to disconnected entity objects without the overhead of maintaining references to heavyweight objects such as **SPWeb** and **SPSite**.

## Disconnecting Entities

To see disconnected entities in action, let's add another button to our sample application. Label the button *Update and Disconnect*, and add the following code:

```
//Define a member variable to store the query
IQueryable<AssetNote> _basicQuery;

private void button11_Click(object sender, EventArgs e)
{
    using(HireSampleDataContext dxWrite = new HireSampleDataContext(SiteUrl.Text))
    {
        StringBuilder sb = new StringBuilder();

        sb.Append("<Queries>");
```

```csharp
using (StringWriter logWriter = new StringWriter(sb))
{
    dxWrite.Log = logWriter;

    //Since we're updating data, object tracking must be enabled
    dxWrite.ObjectTrackingEnabled = true;

    _basicQuery = from n in dxWrite.AssetNotes
                  select n;

    foreach (var n in _basicQuery)
    {
        //Edit each location code
        n.LocationCode += "-Edit";
    }

    //disconnect from the datacontext
    //remove the logger to prevent problems when the reference
    //is missing on reconnect
    dxWrite.Log = null;
    dxWrite.Dispose();

    dataGridView1.DataSource = _basicQuery.ToList();
}

sb.Append("</Queries>");

//create a temporary file for the generated CAML
string fileName = Path.Combine(Path.GetTempPath(), "tmpCaml.xml");

XmlDocument doc = new XmlDocument();
doc.LoadXml(sb.ToString());
doc.Save(fileName);

//point the browser control to the temporary generated CAML file
webBrowser1.Navigate(fileName);
    }
}
```

Notice a few important things in this code. First, a member variable is required to store the updated entities between function calls. Second, it's important that you disconnect the **DataContext** object properly. If a logger is attached to the **DataContext**, the logger must be detached before disposing of the **DataContext**; otherwise, an error will occur when the entities attempt to reconnect, since the **DataContext** entity has an internal reference to the logger. This issue may be resolved in the final version of the code.

## Reconnecting Entities

Now that we have created some code to update items and disconnect the updated entities, we need some code to reconnect the entities and save the changes. Before we do that, we need to consider error handling for our sample application.

Since we have the facility to create disconnected updates, it's possible that another user will change an item that we have disconnected before our update has been applied. Indeed, even if our update was not performed in a disconnected manner and was made in near real-time, the web-based nature of the SharePoint platform means that it is still likely that data will have changed before the update completes.

As mentioned earlier in this chapter, LINQ to SharePoint provides functionality to deal with this type of error via the **ChangeConflicts** property of the **DataContext** object. So that we can see the **ChangeConflicts** property in action in our sample application, we need to make a few changes to the user interface:

1. In the form designer, un-dock the DataGridView from the SplitContainer and add a second SplitContainer in the right pane.
2. Set the Orientation of this new SplitContainer to *Horizontal*.
3. In the top pane of the new SplitContainer, place the original DataGridView control, and again set the Dock property to *Fill*.
4. Drag a new, second DataGridView onto the bottom pane of the new SplitContainer.
5. Again, set the Dock property of this new DataGridView to *Fill*.

Once you've made these changes, add a new button labeled *Reconnect and Save*. Your updated form should look like this:

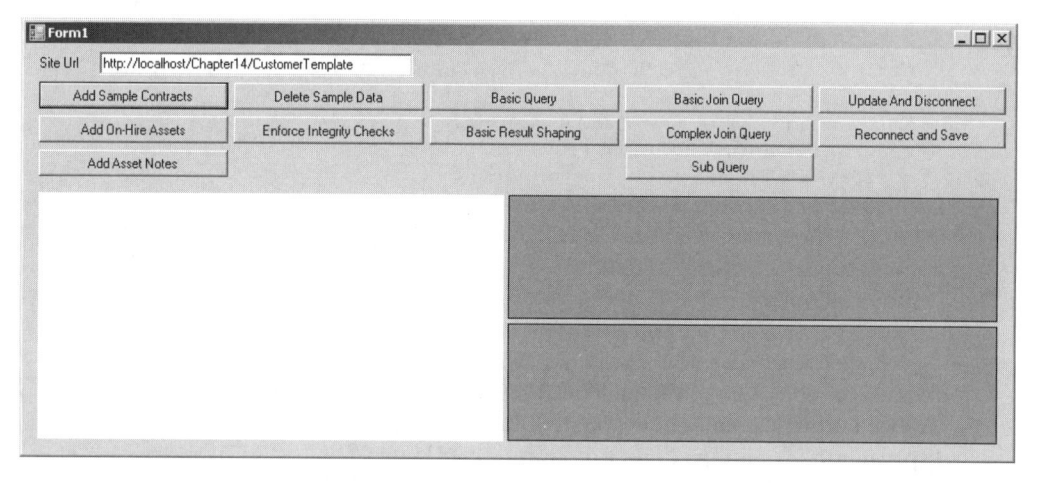

Double-click the Reconnect and Save button and in the code file add the following:

```
private void button12_Click(object sender, EventArgs e)
{
    using(HireSampleDataContext dxWrite = new HireSampleDataContext(SiteUrl.Text))
    {
        StringBuilder sb = new StringBuilder();

        sb.Append("<Queries>");

        using (StringWriter logWriter = new StringWriter(sb))
        {
            dxWrite.Log = logWriter;
```

```csharp
            //Since we're updating data, object tracking must be enabled
            dxWrite.ObjectTrackingEnabled = true;

            foreach (var n in _basicQuery)
            {
                dxWrite.AssetNotes.Attach(n);
            }

            //always define a catch for ChangeConflictException
            try
            {
                dxWrite.SubmitChanges();
            }
            catch (ChangeConflictException ex)
            {
                //bind any conflicts to a data grid so that we can see them
                dataGridView2.DataSource = dxWrite.ChangeConflicts.ToList();
            }

            dataGridView1.DataSource = _basicQuery.ToList();
        }

        sb.Append("</Queries>");

        string fileName = Path.Combine(Path.GetTempPath(), "tmpCaml.xml");

        XmlDocument doc = new XmlDocument();
        doc.LoadXml(sb.ToString());
        doc.Save(fileName);

        webBrowser1.Navigate(fileName);
    }
}
```

Notice the try/catch block around the **SubmitChanges** statement. You should always define a handler for the **ChangeConflictException** since, by its very nature, the exception can occur any time an item is updated. In this sample code, the exception is handled by displaying the resulting conflicts in our user interface.

We can use the two new buttons that we added to simulate a disconnected update. First, click the Update and Disconnect button to make updates to a set of records. Using the SharePoint user interface, verify that the updates have not yet been applied to the list. Then go back to the sample application and click Reconnect and Save. This time, checking the SharePoint user interface will confirm that the updates have been applied as expected.

## Handling Concurrency Errors when Updating Data

Let's add another button to our sample application so that we can simulate concurrent updates. Label the button *Concurrent Update* and add the following code in the on-click event handler:

```csharp
private void button13_Click(object sender, EventArgs e)
{
    using(HireSampleDataContext dxWrite = new HireSampleDataContext(SiteUrl.Text))
    {
        //Disable deferred loading, so that all data is
        //loaded when the query is parsed
        dxWrite.DeferredLoadingEnabled = false;

        StringBuilder sb = new StringBuilder();

        sb.Append("<Queries>");

        using (StringWriter logWriter = new StringWriter(sb))
        {
            dxWrite.Log = logWriter;

            dxWrite.ObjectTrackingEnabled = true;

            _basicQuery = from n in dxWrite.AssetNotes
                          select n;

            //enumerate the query to populate the entity objects
            //with the current data
            foreach (var n in _basicQuery)
            {
                //Edit each location code
                n.LocationCode += "-Edit";
            }

            //Perform a concurrent update
            using(HireSampleDataContext dxWrite2 =
                new HireSampleDataContext(SiteUrl.Text))
            {
                var concurrentQuery = from n in dxWrite2.AssetNotes
                                      select n;

                foreach (var n in concurrentQuery)
                {
                    n.LocationCode = n.LocationCode += "-Concurrent";
                }

                dxWrite2.SubmitChanges();
            }

            try
            {
                dxWrite.SubmitChanges();
            }
            catch (ChangeConflictException)
            {
                //bind any conflicts to a data grid so that we can see them
                dataGridView2.DataSource = dxWrite.ChangeConflicts.ToList();
            }
```

```
            dxWrite.Log = null;

            dataGridView1.DataSource = _basicQuery.ToList();
    }

    sb.Append("</Queries>");

    //create a temporary file for the generated CAML
    string fileName = Path.Combine(Path.GetTempPath(), "tmpCaml.xml");

    XmlDocument doc = new XmlDocument();
    doc.LoadXml(sb.ToString());
    doc.Save(fileName);

    webBrowser1.Navigate(fileName);
    }
}
```

Notice a few significant aspects of this sample code: First, notice the introduction of the **DeferredLoadingEnabled** property. By default, deferred loading is enabled on a **DataContext** object. This means that child entities are loaded dynamically if and when they are required. So, for example, our LINQ query returns a collection of **AssetNote** objects. Each **AssetNote** object has an **AssetReference** property that refers to an **OnHireAsset** object. Since the **OnHireAsset** object is not used by the query, it isn't loaded until it's required. Our code doesn't need this property, so to prevent it from being loaded we've set **DeferredLoadingEnabled** to *false*.

Next, a separate **DataContext** object has been used to simulate a concurrent update, because if we were to use the same **DataContext** object to attempt a concurrent update, the **DataContext** object itself would merge the updates internally, resolving the concurrency issue. Internally, the **DataContext** object uses a dictionary type object known as the **EntityTracker** to manage all changes that have occurred to entities attached to the **DataContext**. Attempting to apply concurrent updates to the same **DataContext** would effectively be handled internally by the **EntityTracker**.

By using a second **DataContext** object, when **SubmitChanges** is called, the changes are committed to the content database. This is significant because each entity implements an interface named **ITrackOriginalValues**, and this interface defines an **OriginalValues Dictionary** object that is used to store the values of each property when the entity is created. A change conflict occurs when the original value for a property does not match the current content database value before an item is updated.

By clicking the Concurrent Update button, you'll see that an error row appears in the lower DataGridView, similar to the illustration. Checking the contents of the Asset Notes list using the SharePoint user interface will confirm that, other than the simulated concurrent update of adding *"–Concurrent"* to each location code, no other updates have been performed. In effect, the change conflict has aborted any additional changes.

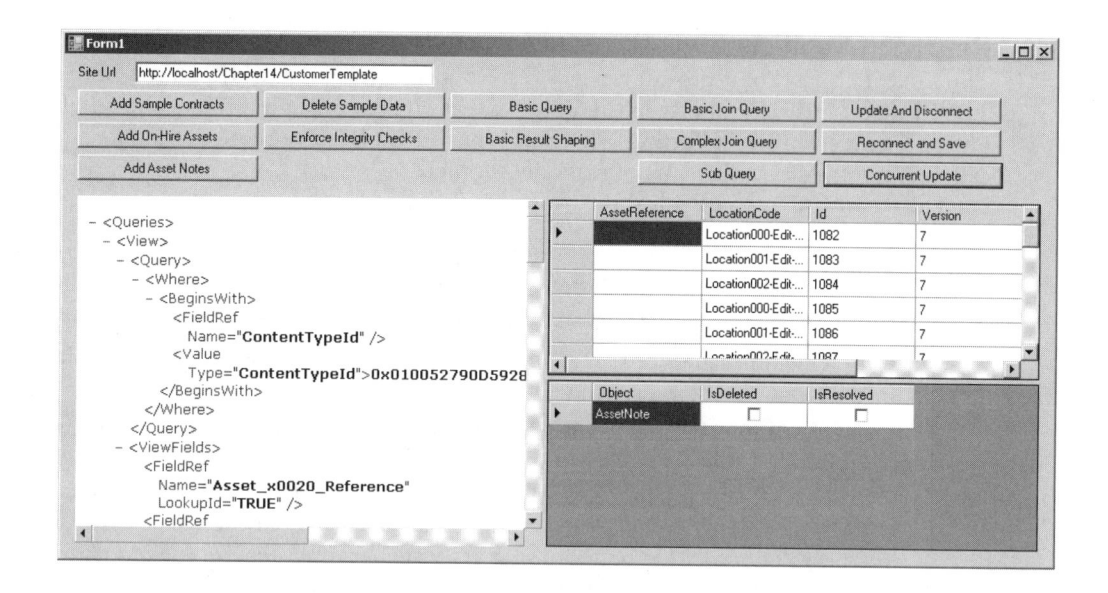

You may be wondering why there is only one row in the **ChangeConflicts** data grid. Earlier, when we covered the properties and methods of the **DataContext** object, we found that **SubmitChanges** has three overloads. The overload that our sample code uses does not specify a value for **ConflictMode** and so the default value of **ConflictMode.FailOnFirstConflict** has been used. This is the reason for us only seeing one conflict. As soon as the first conflict is found, the update is aborted and all changes are rolled back.

So that we can see all of the change conflict messages, we can change the **SubmitChanges** method call to this:

```
dxWrite.SubmitChanges(ConflictMode.ContinueOnConflict);
```

Rerunning the application will now show all the conflicts in the lower **DataGridView**. As before, checking the list using the SharePoint user interface will confirm that no changes have actually been made. By setting **ConflictMode** to **ContinueOnConflict**, we've instructed the LINQ to SharePoint provider to attempt all updates before rolling back the changes if any conflicts occurred.

## Resolving Change Conflicts

Alerting users to change conflicts would be pretty pointless if there was no way to resolve the conflicts in question. There are a few approaches that we can take when resolving change conflicts.

## Resolving Conflicts Globally

The LINQ to SharePoint provider makes resolving conflicts a relatively painless process. The **ChangeConflicts** property of the **DataContext** object returns a reference to an object of type **ChangeConflictCollection**. This object provides a **ResolveAll** method that can be called to resolve all conflicts. What could be simpler?

The **ResolveAll** method has three overloads:

- **ResolveAll( )**   This overload is used when the default resolution behavior is acceptable. Effectively, this is the same as calling **ResolveAll** with the **RefreshMode** parameter set to **KeepChanges** and the **autoResolveDeletes** parameter set to *true*.

- **ResolveAll(RefreshMode)**   This overload is used when a **RefreshMode** setting of **KeepChanges** is not appropriate.

- **ResolveAll(RefreshMode, Boolean)**   This overload is used when delete conflicts should not be automatically resolved. The Boolean parameter is a flag that determines whether or not to delete conflicts that should be resolved automatically. By allowing delete conflicts to be automatically resolved, any delete conflicts are effectively ignored. This behavior makes sense, because the item to be updated no longer exists, so other than notifying the user, no other options are available. Setting this value to *false* will cause an InvalidOperationException to be thrown if any delete conflicts exist when **ResolveAll** is called.

The **ResolveAll** methods make use of a **RefreshMode** enumeration to specify how conflicts should be resolved. The enumeration has three possible values:

- **KeepChanges**   When this option is selected for the **RefreshMode** parameter of the **ResolveAll** method, any updated values are maintained even if they conflict with the current database values. All other values that were not specifically updated are changed to match the current database values. In effect, this option merges fields that were specifically updated with the latest values in the database.

- **KeepCurrentValues**   When this option is selected for the **RefreshMode** parameter of the **ResolveAll** method, all field values are applied regardless of whether they match the current database values. In effect, this option disregards all concurrent changes, overwriting them with the current state of the object being updated.

- **OverwriteCurrentValues**   When this option is selected for the **RefreshMode** parameter of the **ResolveAll** method, all field values are updated to reflect the current state of the database. Any updates that do not correspond with the current state are lost. This option disregards any changes, replacing all values with the current values from the database.

To see the effects of calling **ResolveAll**, change the sample code for the Concurrent Update button to this:

```
retry:
    try
    {
        dxWrite.SubmitChanges(ConflictMode.ContinueOnConflict);
    }
```

```
catch (ChangeConflictException)
{
    //bind any conflicts to a data grid so that we can see them
    dataGridView2.DataSource = dxWrite.ChangeConflicts.ToList();
    dxWrite.ChangeConflicts.ResolveAll();
    goto retry;
}
```

You'll notice that after the **ResolveAll** method is called, a call to **SubmitChanges** must again occur to retry the changes. Running the sample application and clicking the Concurrent Update button now returns the same list of change conflicts—but this time each conflict is flagged as resolved. Also, checking the Asset Notes list using the user interface will confirm that all updates have been applied. Try re-running this test to see the operation of the other **RefreshMode** options.

### Resolving Conflicts Individually

I'm sure you'll agree that the **ResolveAll** method works well when you need to resolve all conflicts en masse, but what happens if you want to apply different rules to some of the conflicts? Or what if you want to apply different rules to specific fields? The LINQ to SharePoint conflict resolution model allows for this behavior.

And what if you want to go further? What if you want to handle change conflicts on a field-by-field basis? Again, the LINQ to SharePoint provider allows for this.

**Record Level Conflict Resolution** Along with a **ResolveAll** method on the **ChangeConflictCollection** object, which allows you to resolve all conflicts on all objects with one method call, is a **Resolve** method on the **ObjectChangeConflict** object. As mentioned earlier, the **ObjectChangeConflict** object represents a change conflict for a single entity. Remember that in relational database parlance, an entity corresponds to a record. By selecting specific **ObjectChangeConflict** objects from the **ChangeConflictCollection**, you can apply different resolution options for each record.

For example, if you wanted to ignore any updates where the **LocationCode** contained Location001, you could change the preceding code sample as follows:

```
retry:
    try
    {
        dxWrite.SubmitChanges(ConflictMode.ContinueOnConflict);
    }
    catch (ChangeConflictException)
    {
        //bind any conflicts to a data grid so that we can see them
        dataGridView2.DataSource = dxWrite.ChangeConflicts.ToList();
        dxWrite.ChangeConflicts.ResolveAll();
        goto retry;
    }
```

**Field Level Conflict Resolution** As illustrated in Figure 14-1, each **ObjectChangeConflict** object has a **MemberConflicts** property that returns a reference to a collection of **MemberChangeConflict** objects. As described earlier, a **MemberChangeConflict** object represents a change conflict at the individual field level, and again, like the

**ObjectChangeConflict** object, the **MemberChangeConflict** object has a **Resolve** method. The difference this time is that there are only two overloads: The first accepts a **RefreshMode** parameter and behaves in a similar fashion to the **Resolve** method on the higher level objects. The second override accepts an object, and rather than attempting to resolve the conflict based on the values that have been set, it simply sets the field value to the object.

For example, if we wanted to flag fields where new value contained the original value but a conflict had been detected, we could do this by appending the text *Disputed* to the new field value. Using the preceding code sample, we could achieve this with the following:

```
retry:
    try
    {
        dxWrite.SubmitChanges(ConflictMode.ContinueOnConflict);
    }
    catch (ChangeConflictException)
    {
        //bind any conflicts to a data grid so that we can see them
        dataGridView2.DataSource = dxWrite.ChangeConflicts.ToList();

        //Select the conflicts that we're interested in
        var keepChanges = (from c in dxWrite.ChangeConflicts
                           from m in c.MemberConflicts
                           where m.CurrentValue.ToString().Contains(
                                 m.OriginalValue.ToString())
                           && m.CurrentValue is string
                           select m).ToList();

        //Resolve by appending some text
        keepChanges.ForEach(m => m.Resolve(m.CurrentValue + "-Disputed"));

        //Call ResolveAll to resolve everything else using the default values
        dxWrite.ChangeConflicts.ResolveAll();
        goto retry;
    }
```

You can see that handling change conflicts using LINQ to SharePoint is flexible enough to accommodate practically any requirement.

### Considerations when Setting ConflictMode

You may have noticed in the past few code samples that **SubmitChanges** is being called with **ConflictMode.ContinueOnConflict**. This is useful when more than one item is being updated, because it allows you to deal with all conflicts at once. Changing this value to **ConflictMode.FailOnFirstConflict** would allow only one conflict to be detected each time **SubmitChanges** was called. The code in the sample would still work, but it would do so by calling **SubmitChanges** many times, each time resolving one conflict.

One thing to bear in mind when resolving conflicts is that in the time it takes to resolve a conflict, more concurrent updates may have occurred. In heavy traffic situations where many concurrent updates present a problem, resolving conflicts individually may be more effective, because it takes less time to apply changes to one item than it does to apply changes to many, so the likelihood of more concurrent updates occurring is reduced.

## Summary

This chapter introduced LINQ as the preferred way of programmatically working with SharePoint data. LINQ to SharePoint is a powerful tool that allows developers to write strongly typed code to create, edit, update, and delete data from SharePoint lists and libraries, all using a syntax that is familiar to developers with experience of LINQ to SQL or indeed with experience of SQL syntax itself. SPMetal is an easy to use, flexible tool that quickly creates entity types for each list and library within a SharePoint site.

As discussed at the beginning of the chapter, the two main problems with data layer development in SharePoint are a lack of compile time validation for CAML and the extensive use of indexed properties to access data. By using strongly typed entity objects to contain data and LINQ syntax to perform queries, you can write and test your code much more effectively, all with full design-time validation and IntelliSense support in Visual Studio 2010.

This chapter also discussed how content types can be shared across multiple sites and compared the SharePoint data structure and the more traditional relational database structure with which we developers are very familiar. There's no doubt that making the jump from relational database to SharePoint requires a bit of thought and planning, but with the introduction of useful new tools like LINQ to SharePoint and SPMetal, designing and building data-driven applications using SharePoint 2010 is hopefully much easier than ever before.

# CHAPTER 15

# Business Connectivity Services

When it comes to building business applications, one thing has become universally true: no application is an island. Every organization, no matter what its size, uses more than one tool to manage data. The big challenge in software engineering today is the unification of these disparate business systems to provide a consolidated platform for managing an organization.

Of course, each of the many possible solutions to this problem has its own strengths and weaknesses. However, no matter which set of tools and technologies you use, ultimately, the answer is a mash-up—a consolidation of various components and data to create a new application to serve a particular function.

SharePoint is an application development platform that has mash-up embedded in its architecture. As you've seen in the preceding chapters, SharePoint is all about providing a framework that allows developers to include components and data from many different sources. From the use of web parts for creating customizable user interfaces right through to Business Connectivity Services, a tool for interfacing with any kind of data, from any source, SharePoint makes it easy to build new applications that leverage existing business systems.

## Business Data Catalog in MOSS 2007

SharePoint 2007 introduced the Business Data Catalog, which existed as a tool to allow line-of-business data to be surfaced within SharePoint web sites. Using a collection of specially designed web parts, it was easy to integrate business data with other content created and managed by SharePoint. For example, a connection could be made to a customer relationship management (CRM) system to allow customer contact details to be retrieved and displayed within an intranet site.

With the release of SharePoint 2010, things have moved on considerably. The biggest shortfall with Business Data Catalog was its inability to update data. Information imported using Business Data Catalog was read-only—meaning users had to go back to the source system if they wanted to make changes. Of course, this makes sense if you consider that the aim of Business Data Catalog was to allow the incorporation of business data within SharePoint-managed content. However, having to go back to the source system to make changes is an anathema in the age of the mash-up.

SharePoint 2010 introduces Business Connectivity Services (BCS), which can be used to amalgamate business data with SharePoint-managed content. BCS can also be used as an abstraction layer for practically any data source. It's now easy to create mash-up applications with full read and write access to all business systems using a single data access platform.

## Components of BCS

Business Connectivity Services is the generic name for a set of services and components that enable connectivity between disparate business systems. Several key components are involved in the delivery of BCS, which is included as a component of Microsoft Office 2010, providing universal data access for Office client applications.

### External Content Types

*New in 2010*

Content types are a core part of the SharePoint data structure, as you've already seen in previous chapters. External content types, as the name suggests, extend the content type metaphor to content stored in other systems and accessed via BCS.

Although external content types share a lot of common functionality with standard content types, there are a few important differences. First, external content types are created and managed by BCS. It's not possible to add columns or make changes to columns in an external content type without redefining the underlying BCS model. Second, external content types can't be used in ordinary lists or attached to ordinary lists in the same way that standard content types can. You can create external lists that look and behave in much the same way as a regular list, but those lists are bound to a single external content type only.

> **TIP** In the MSDN documentation for BCS, you'll often find references both to entities and external content types. To save any confusion, both are effectively the same thing. An external content type is created by defining an entity using BCS. Strictly speaking, an entity is the definition of a particular item of data using Business Data Connectivity metadata, whereas an external content type is a SharePoint implementation of that representation.

### External Lists

*New in 2010*

As mentioned, external content types can't be used in regular lists. SharePoint 2010 introduces a new type of list, known as the *external list*, that provides full read/write functionality for external data. Each external list is bound to a single external content type and allows the user to create, read, update, and delete data in the external system in much the same way as a regular list does for SharePoint-managed data. Of course, the actual capabilities of the list are dependent on the BCS configuration for the data source. For example, if the underlying model doesn't support deletion, then delete functionality will be unavailable in the external list.

### External Data Column

*New in 2010*

The external data column is an enhancement of the Business Data List column in SharePoint 2007. It's basically a lookup column that can be included in any SharePoint list, where it will allow the user to select items from an external data source. For example, in a list containing employee reviews, if a company's HR system is linked via BCS, an external column can be added to the list that allows employee details to be attached to review data. The external data column allows one record to be selected, but any number of fields from that record can be included. So in our example, we could bring through employee name, payroll number, and contact telephone all by selecting the employee from a searchable list.

## External Data Search

Included in the SharePoint Server 2010 product is External Data Search, a service that allows data linked using BCS to be indexed and returned in search results in the same way as SharePoint managed data. External Data Search gives an organization the ability to search and index all business data regardless of the source, as long as an appropriate BCS model can be defined.

## Secure Store Service

The Secure Store Service replaces the Single Sign On Service that was included with MOSS 2007. Because BCS allows connectivity with a number of different systems, one of the problems that can arise is the maintenance of multiple sets of credentials for each user. It's quite common for each line-of-business application to require users to authenticate, often using different credentials each time. Secure Store Service resolves this problem by securely storing credentials for each line-of-business application and mapping those credentials to a particular SharePoint login. So, for example, Joe Bloggs is automatically logged into SharePoint using his username *domain\jbloggs*. However, when he accesses the company's enterprise resource planning (ERP) system, he has to log in with the username *bloggs-j* and a different password. By using the Secure Store Service, when he needs to access business data via BCS in SharePoint, his credentials for the ERP system are automatically retrieved and used transparently by BCS.

## Profile Pages

In MOSS 2007, the main mechanism for viewing business data in SharePoint was the profile page. Profile pages were automatically generated from a set of specially designed web parts to provide full details of the business data in question as well as any related items. In SharePoint Server 2010, this functionality is still present and offers a quick and easy way to present a read-only view of business data.

## External Data Web Parts

As mentioned, SharePoint Server 2010 includes the functionality to generate profile pages for BCS entities automatically. This functionality is provided by the following web parts, which can be connected together to provide a comprehensive view of a particular entity and any related entities:

- **External Data List** The External Data List web part (formerly known as the Business Data List web part) is used to display a read-only list of data relating to a particular external content type.

- **External Data Item** This web part (formerly known as the Business Data Details web part) is used to display the details of a single item of a particular External Content Type. This web part is particularly useful since it uses Extensible Stylesheet Language Transformations (XSLT) to transform the data, allowing a great deal of flexibility in terms of how the data is presented.

- **External Data Item Builder** This web part (formerly known as the Business Data Item Builder web part) is used to retrieve a particular item based on parameters passed via the query string. This web part is then connected to other web parts, such as the External Data Item, to display the data to the user.

- **External Data Related List**   This web part (formerly known as the Business Data Association web part) can be used to retrieve a list of items automatically from a related External Content Type. Again, by connecting this web part to others such as the External Data List, associated data is automatically retrieved based on the item selected in the External Data List web part.

- **External Data Connectivity Filter**   While the External Data Item Builder web part is used to identify an item based on parameters from the query string, the External Data Connectivity Filter (formerly known as the Business Data Filter web part) can be used to capture criteria on the page. This web part can then be connected to other web parts to display associated data.

## Rich Client Integration

One of the major features of BCS is its ability to present a common platform for accessing business data. By using this model, SharePoint Server 2010 provides the facility to surface business data in rich client applications such as Microsoft Outlook. For example, a list of employees located in an HR system can be accessed via BCS in an external list. However, with rich client integration, the external list can also be accessed as a contacts list in Microsoft Outlook. In a similar fashion to external lists, full read/write functionality is also available in the client application. It's possible to update a contact record in Outlook and have it automatically cascaded through to the HR system. Furthermore, all clients connected to the data via Outlook will see the effects of the update through an automatic synchronization process.

## Rich Client Components

As well as the features present in SharePoint 2010, Office 2010 applications also include additional functionality to use BCS data, including the following:

- **External data parts**   Controls that display items or lists of items retrieved from BCS in a client application.

- **Actions**   When creating BCS models, custom actions can be associated with each external content type. These actions are carried through to rich client applications and appear in the ribbon, allowing for seamless integration with the BCS system from the client application. For example, the BCS model may define a Submit Order action that creates and submits an order based on a particular entity. The order can then be created using a rich client application and submitted using a custom action, all without any specific coding requirements on the rich client side.

## Business Data Connectivity Service

The Business Data Connectivity (BDC) service is the successor to the Business Data Catalog service in MOSS 2007. The name was changed because "Catalog" suggests a read-only collection of business data, whereas the new BDC service provides full read/write capability. BDC provides the engine for BCS by creating and managing metadata describing possible interactions with the source data systems as well as providing an extensible connector framework.

**Connector Framework**   By default, BDC provides connectivity to a number of different systems:

- **Databases**   By making use of ADO.NET, the BDC provides access to any database for which ADO.NET drivers exist. Since the ADO.NET provider model is extensible, it's possible to create ADO.NET drivers for practically any database system.
- **Windows Communication Foundation (WCF) endpoints**   WCF provides a framework for accessing web services. By using WCF endpoints, the BDC is able to communicate with external data systems via appropriately designed web services.
- **.NET Connectivity Assemblies**   Even though using ADO.NET and WCF provides the flexibility to talk to the vast majority of data systems, sometimes neither of these methods is appropriate. For systems such as these, using .NET Connectivity Assemblies is the answer. Since the assemblies are written in managed code, they can perform whatever actions are required to access the source system.

**NOTE**   At the time of writing, SharePoint Designer supports the creation of SQL Server connections only. It is possible to create a connection for other ADO.NET data providers, but manual generation of the BDC metadata will be required. Some third-party tools offer a much higher degree of customization of BDC metadata, such as BCS Meta Man from Lightning Tools.

Clearly, these three options cover virtually every imaginable scenario; however, just in case a hitherto unimagined scenario crops up in the future, BDC also provides a pluggable connector framework that lets developers plug in a new connector for systems of different types. The three connectors described here are examples of out-of-the-box connectors.

**TIP**   Although BDC provides a connector for WCF endpoints, unless the web service meets very specific requirements, it can't be configured using the WCF Connection wizard. Having tried to configure several well-known web services via the wizard, I found it to be practically impossible. The WCF connector is best used to communicate with custom-designed WCF or Simple Object Access Protocol (SOAP) services. For any other web service, a .NET Connectivity Assembly will provide the configuration flexibility required.

## Demonstration Scenario

To demonstrate the capabilities of BCS, we'll design and build a simple application based on the following scenario:

You've been asked to develop an application for the marketing department of Adventure Works Corp. that will assist them in building a repository of competitive analysis data. The repository will consist of a series of reports comparing the company's product models with competing products from other vendors. Adventure Works has an ERP system in place that maintains details of all product models and associated products.

Since product data is maintained in a separate ERP system, we'll use BCS to surface this data in SharePoint. Additionally, we'll attach Internet-based content by developing a connectivity assembly for Bing.com. Once these connections have been defined, we'll be able to create a new document library to hold the reports. We'll add columns to the reports library to allow the selection of the appropriate product model from the ERP system and a link to the competing product on an external web site.

## Prerequisites

To provide some sample data to work with in our various examples, you'll need to download and install the SQL Server 2008 sample databases, which can be found at www.codeplex.com/MSFTDBProdSamples. Our code examples make use of the AdventureWorks OLTP database installed on the local instance of SQL Server 2008.

As well as connecting to a database, we also need to retrieve search results from Bing.com. To make use of the Bing.com web service API, we must first generate a unique application ID (AppID) that can be used within our code. To generate a new AppID, follow the process detailed at www.bing.com/developer.

To create a new site for our sample application, take the following steps:

1. Open SharePoint Designer.
2. Click the New Blank Web Site button.
3. In the dialog that appears, enter the name **http://<*your server name*>/Chapter15**.
4. Click on OK to create the site.

# Connecting to BCS Data Using SharePoint Designer

As discussed earlier in this chapter, BCS data is surfaced in SharePoint via external content types. Regardless of the mechanism used to connect to the data, whether it's via an out-of-the-box connector such as ADO.NET or WCF or via a connectivity assembly or custom connector, the end result is a series of external content types, each of which represents a single entity definition in the source system. So, for example, in an underlying CRM system, entities may be defined for Customer, Address, and Sales Order.

## Associations

Naturally, in any data system, entities have relationships—for example, a Customer entity may be related to a Sales Order entity. BCS allows for the modeling of such relationships using *associations*. It's possible to create associations between any two external content types provided they have appropriate identifiers.

To take our CRM example a bit further, let's say we also had an ERP system with stock information on individual products. The product stock level was defined in an entity called Product in the ERP model. If the Sales Order entity in our CRM model contained a ProductId field of type Int32 and the Product Entity in our ERP model contained an identifier named ManufacturedProductId, also of type Int32, it would be possible to create a relationship between these entities regardless of the fact that they exist in separate systems.

## Stereotypes

You may wonder how a system that's capable of retrieving data from practically any data source works. In general programming terms, where an object must communicate with other objects of unknown type, a common standard is adopted, either via the implementation of a known interface or via inheritance, which requires that all objects inherit from a common base class. The BDC service, the engine behind BCS, employs a similar mechanism known as *stereotyping*.

You may also be wondering, why call it stereotyping? Why not use an established term that makes more sense to developers? There is a very good reason for this: The BDC service is all about defining the connections between two systems, not physically making the connections. None of the code in the BDC service actually sends or receives data between A and B; instead, the BDC service simply delegates the request to the appropriate endpoint. As a consequence, there is nowhere to implement an interface and no abstract classes to inherit from—it's all about metadata. Stereotyping denotes a particular endpoint and configuration as being appropriate for a particular operation. For example, one important stereotype is **SpecificFinder**. A model may contain metadata that specifies that requests should be sent to the **ReadRecordFromDataBase** function in the **MyBDCModel** assembly whenever a **SpecificFinder** operation is executed.

The BDC Service defines a number of stereotypes covering every data access operation supported by the platform. Not all of these operations are commonly required, although the following operations are used in most models to provide create, read, update, delete, and query (CRUDQ) functionality:

| Operation | Description |
| --- | --- |
| Creator | Creates a new item in the external data store. |
| SpecificFinder | Returns a single specific item from the underlying data store. The parameters for this operation are defined by the identifiers that are associated with the external content type. |
| Updater | Updates items in the external data store. |
| Deleter | Deletes items in the underlying data store. |
| Finder | Returns a list of items from the external data store usually based on some criteria. |

The following operations provide additional functionality for use in specific circumstances:

| Operation | Description |
| --- | --- |
| AccessChecker | Retrieves the permissions of the calling security principal for each of a collection of items. |
| AssociationNavigator | Retrieves a collection of items that are associated with a single specified item. |
| Scalar | Calls a method on the external system that returns a single value (for example, use a scalar operation to get the total sales made to date from the external system). |
| Associator | Associates two specific items. |
| BinarySecurityDescriptorAccessor | Retrieves a sequence of bytes from an external system. The byte sequence describes a set of security principals and the associated permissions of each security principal for a specified item. |
| BulkAssociatedIdEnumerator | Retrieves pairs of source and destination items for a specified association. |

| Operation | Description |
| --- | --- |
| BulkAssociationNavigator | Retrieves destination items that are associated with multiple specified items for each of the sources of the specified association. |
| BulkIdEnumerator | Retrieves a set of instance IDs and a small subset of important fields of items that are identified by the specified set of Instance IDs. |
| BulkSpecificFinder | Returns a set of instances of an entity, given a set of instance IDs. |
| ChangedIdEnumerator | Retrieves a collection of items that were modified in an external system after a specified time. |
| DeletedIdEnumerator | Retrieves a collection of items that were deleted from an external system after the specified time. |
| Disassociator | Removes an association between two specified items. |
| GenericInvoker | Performs a specific task in an external system. |
| IdEnumerator | Returns a collection of identifiers for entities of a specific type. Works similar to the Finder operation, except that IdEnumerator returns identifiers only. |
| StreamAccessor | Retrieves a field of an item as a data stream of bytes. |

## Create an External Content Type

Now that you understand what BCS is and how the BDC service uses metadata to connect to external systems, you're ready to put this knowledge into practice by creating an external content type using SharePoint Designer.

1. In SharePoint Designer, connect to the new site that we created earlier. From the Site Objects menu, choose External Content Types:

2. From the ribbon, in the New section, select External Content Type. In the page that appears, double-click New External Content Type next to the Name label and change the name to **Model**.

3. From the ribbon, select Operations Design View. You'll notice that the title of the window changes to Model, confirming that the name change has been

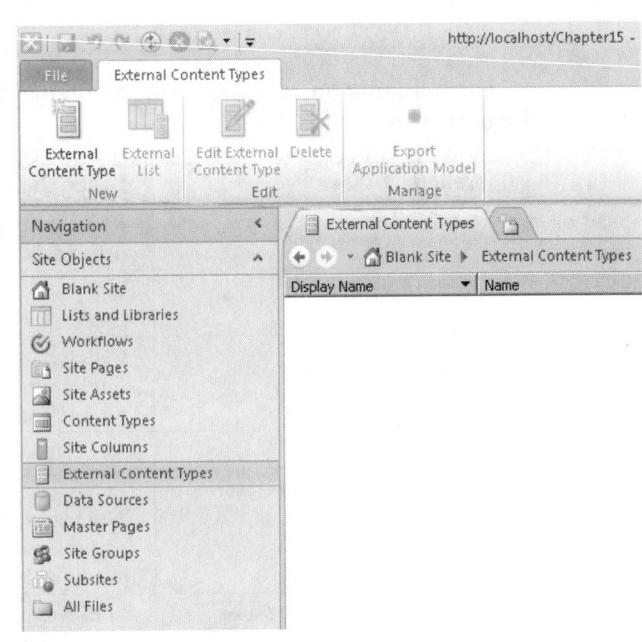

applied. In the window that appears, click the Add Connection button. In the dialog that appears, set the Data Source Type to SQL Server, as shown; then click OK to continue.

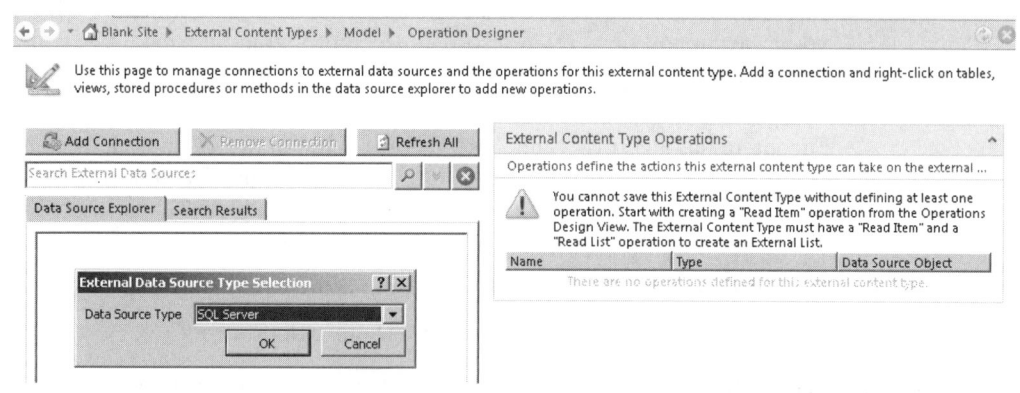

4. In the SQL Server Connection dialog, enter the name of your SQL server in the Database Server text box. For example, if you're using the local SQL Express instance, you will type **.\SQLExpress**. In the Database Name text, type **AdventureWorks.** Accept the default connection option of Connect With User's Identity. Click on OK to create the connection.

## Define SpecificFinder Operation

1. After the connection has been verified, in the Data Source Explorer tab, you'll be able to see the objects in the database. Expand the Tables node and then scroll down to the ProductModel table. Right-click the table, and in the context menu, you'll see a number of options for defining operations on the ProductModel entity. Select New Read Item Operation.

2. The Read Item Wizard will start, where you can define the metadata for a new SpecificFinder operation. In the Operation Name text box, type **Read Item.** Click Next to continue.

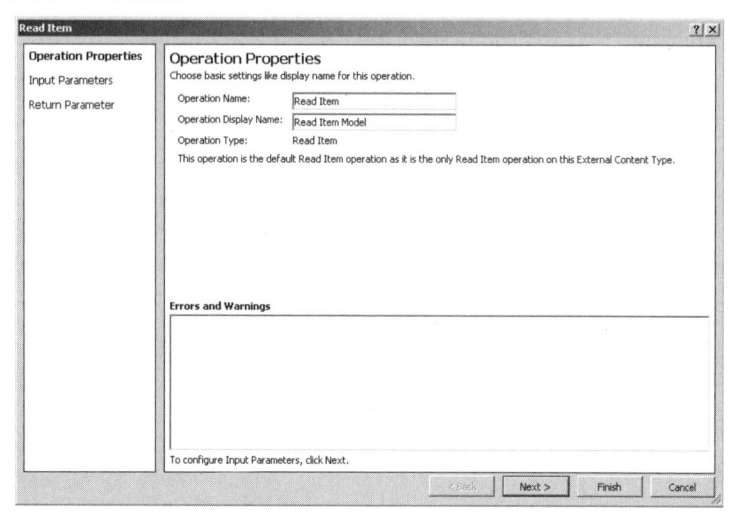

3. On the Input Parameters page, you'll notice a few important things:

    - ProductModelID is highlighted as an identifier. Each entity must define at least one identifier, though more than one identifier can be defined. For example, if you have a many-many relationship between two tables in a database, you may have a join table with a compound primary key. In this case, you'd have two identifiers.
    - Each item has a Display Name and Default Value option. Changing the Display Name in this page has no effect when creating external lists since the display name used by SharePoint is taken from the return values. Changing the Default Value will apply a default if the input parameter is null.

    Accept the default settings by clicking Next to move to the next page.

4. On the Return Parameter page, notice a few more options:

    - Each field can be checked or unchecked, although unchecking the ProductModelID yields an error since each entity must have an identifier. Unchecking other fields may raise a warning if the field is not nullable in the underlying table, because updates and additions will be impossible since a value is required by the database schema.
    - Remember that even though we're defining a SpecificFinder operation, unchecking columns here affects the overall definition of the entity. This means that it will not be possible to add or update values in fields that are unchecked even though the operations to perform these actions are defined separately. In effect, the SpecificFinder defines the columns of any external lists created from the External Content Type and consequently the columns used when adding and editing data.
    - A number of parameters appear for each field, including a Map to Identifier checkbox. Identifiers are defined in metadata separately and must be mapped to fields using this option.
    - The Display Name property defines the column name as it appears in External Lists created from the external content type. It also defines the text on the label that appears next to the item in add and edit forms.

    Click Finish to complete the creation of the Read Item operation.

---

**NOTE** If we had an additional entity that could be correlated by using a particular field—such as Name—you would imagine that we could flag Name as an identifier, allowing associations between the entities to be made. However, this change has some undesirable implications: since Name is now an identifier, we effectively have a compound primary key. This means that all associations would be created based on both the Name and ProductModelID fields. It would not be possible to create an association based on one field or the other in isolation, thus defeating the object of the change.

## Define Finder Operation

Now that we have defined a SpecificFinder operation to retrieve individual items from our data source, the next requirement for creating an external list is to define a Finder operation. The external list, like all other lists in SharePoint, makes use of the XsltListViewWebPart to render the contents of the list. However, rather than retrieving the list contents from the SharePoint database, the View definition contains a Method element specifying the name of a Finder operation that's been defined on the external content type.

Creating a Finder operation follows a similar process to the creation of the SpecificFinder operation:

1. Right-click a table on which to define the operation and then select the type of operation from the context menu. In this case, we'll create a new Read List operation on the ProductModel table.

2. In the wizard that appears, set the Operation Name to Read List, and then click Next to continue.

3. On the Filter Parameters Configuration page, you'll notice in the Errors and Warnings section a warning message relating to the creation of a limit filter. By default, a limit filter is not created, and this has implications when creating external lists. The default maximum number of rows that can be supported by an external list is 2000 (although this value is configurable, as detailed in Chapter 20). If the Finder operation returns more rows than this, we'll end up with a pretty cryptic web part error when we try to view the data in our external list.

**TIP** Even when external lists are not required, by not setting a filter, we're allowing the BDC service to return all rows in a table. In most cases, this would represent a significant waste of system resources.

## Add a Limit Filter

1. To add a limit filter, click the Add Filter Parameter button. A new filter will be added to the list of Filter Parameters.

2. From the Data Source Element drop-down, select the field that contains the data to be filtered. In this case, it doesn't matter which column we select since we're applying a limit filter. Leave the default of ProductModelID selected.

3. Next to Filter, click the Click To Add hyperlink to display the filter configuration dialog.

4. In the New Filter text box, enter **Limit Filter** as the name. Select Limit from the Filter Type drop-down and <<None>> from the Filter Field drop-down. Click OK to create the filter.

5. In the Properties section of the Filter Parameters Configuration page, in the Default Value combo box, enter **2000** as the default. The completed page should look as illustrated next:

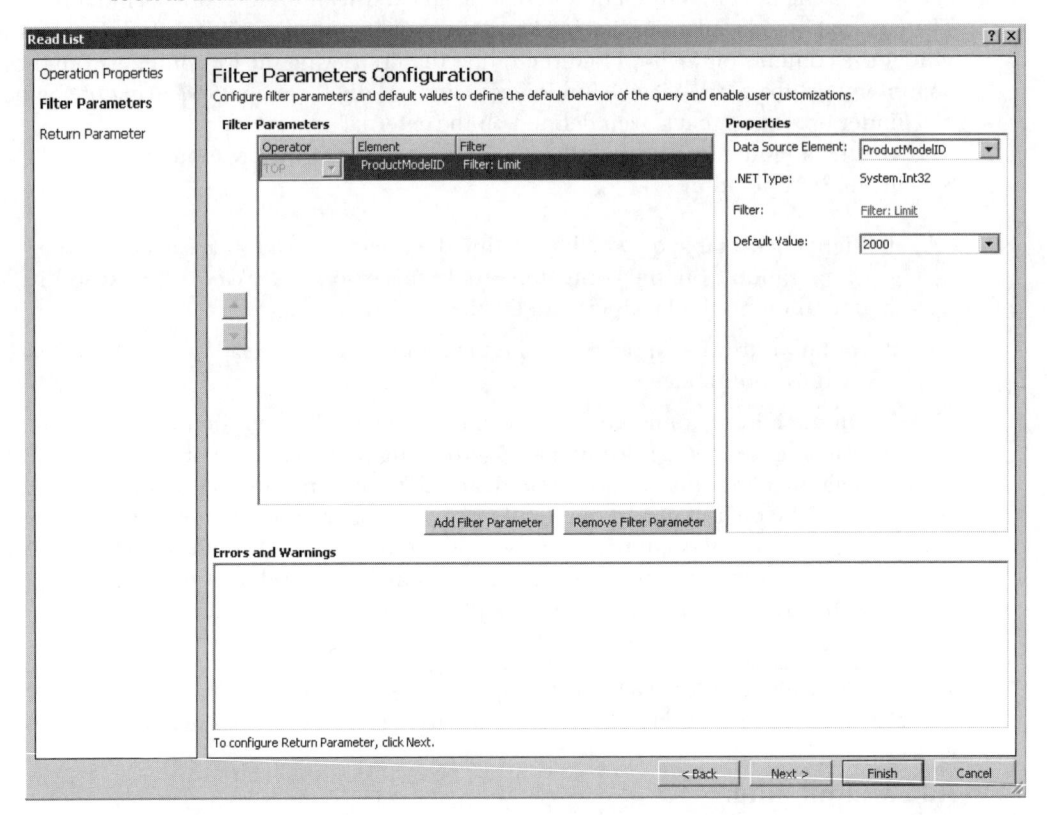

6. Click Next to move on to the Return Parameter Configuration step. You'll notice that this page is similar to the Return Parameter page used when creating a SpecificFinder method. However, there is one significant difference: the inclusion of the Show In Picker checkbox in the properties for each field. As you'll see later, the External Data Picker control allows the user to search for an item from an external data source. Selecting the Show In Picker flag will include the associated field as a column in the results displayed in the External Data Picker control. Set the Show In Picker flag for the Name field only. Click Finish to complete the wizard.

**TIP** By default, none of the fields have Show In Picker selected. Since the External Data Picker doesn't know which fields to include, it simply includes all of them. A much better user experience can be gained by displaying only useful columns in the picker control.

## Create All Operations

We've now added the minimum operations required to generate an external list. If we generate a list using only these operations, users will be able to view data in a list but will not be able to add, edit, or delete since we haven't defined those operations.

We manually created the Finder and the SpecificFinder to give us a chance to review the various configuration options. Thankfully, in the real world, you don't need to go through the same steps for each operation; you can simply select Create All Operations from the context menu. A wizard will automatically generate the required operations to allow users to read and write to the external data store.

1. Use the Create All Operations wizard to add additional operations to the Model content type. Once the wizard has completed, delete both the Read Item 2 operation and the Read List 2 operation since these are duplicates of the operations that we manually created. When using SharePoint Designer, items can be deleted using the Remove command.
2. Save the changes by clicking the Save icon in the upper-left corner of the window.

### Create an External List

1. Select the Model External Content Type, and then click the Create Lists & Form button in the ribbon.
2. In the dialog that appears, make sure that Create New External List is selected.
3. In the List Name text box, enter **Product Models**. Read Item Operation should be set to Read Item and System Instance should be set to AdventureWorks. You can add a List Description if you're feeling particularly conscientious.
4. Click OK to create a new external list based on our Model External Content Type.

Once the list has been created, navigating to http://localhost/Chapter15 will show a link to the new list on the left side of the page. When you open the list, you can see that it's populated with data from our AdventureWorks database, as expected.

Since the list is rendered directly from the AdventureWorks database whenever the page is loaded, any changes made in the database will have immediate effect. By the same token, any changes made in SharePoint are applied directly to the database.

### Create an Associated External Content Type

Now that you're familiar with the tools used to create external content types, you're ready to create another external content type for product information. Then we'll define a parent-child relationship between our new Product content type and our existing Model content type.

1. Follow the steps detailed earlier to create a new external content type named Product based on the AdventureWorks Product table. Rather than manually configuring each operation, select Create All Operations from the context menu to allow the wizard to do most of the work. This time flag the Name and ProductNumber fields to appear in the picker. Remember to include a Limit filter to restrict the number of rows returned.
2. In the Operations Design View, right-click the Product table to show the operations context menu. This time, select New Association to create an association between this entity and our Model entity.

3. In the Association wizard, change the Association Name and the Association Display Name to Product Model. The Association Display Name is shown in any form as the label for the External Data Picker control.

4. Click the Browse button and in the dialog that appears, select Model. When an entity is selected, its identifiers are listed in the Related Identifier column. To the right is a Field column that contains drop-down lists, where we can select the field in our content type that maps to the identifier in the associated entity. In effect, the Related Identifier column contains the primary key columns of the entity that we're associating with, and by selecting a matching field in our entity, we're creating a foreign key relationship.

5. Click Next to proceed to the Input Parameters page. Even though in the preceding step we defined the relationships between the entities, in the Input Parameters page we have to select the foreign key field from the list of Data Source Elements, and then check the Map To Identifier checkbox to create the foreign key relationship physically. Click Finish to complete the wizard. The list of external content type operations should be populated, as shown here:

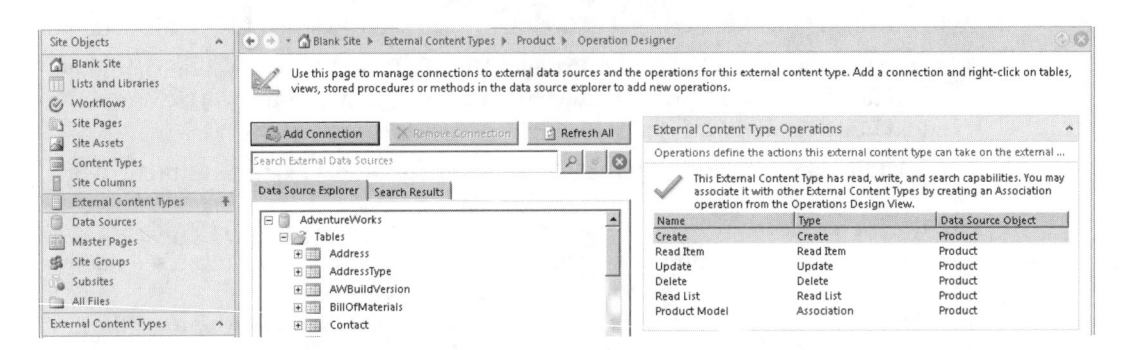

## External Data Picker Control

We've now created a new Product external content type that has a relationship with our existing Model content type. To see the effects of this association in action, create a new external list based on the Product content type. In the Create List and Form dialog, set the List Name to Products.

By browsing to the new Products list using Internet Explorer, you'll see that when editing an item in the list, models can be selected from a list using an External Data Picker control, as shown here:

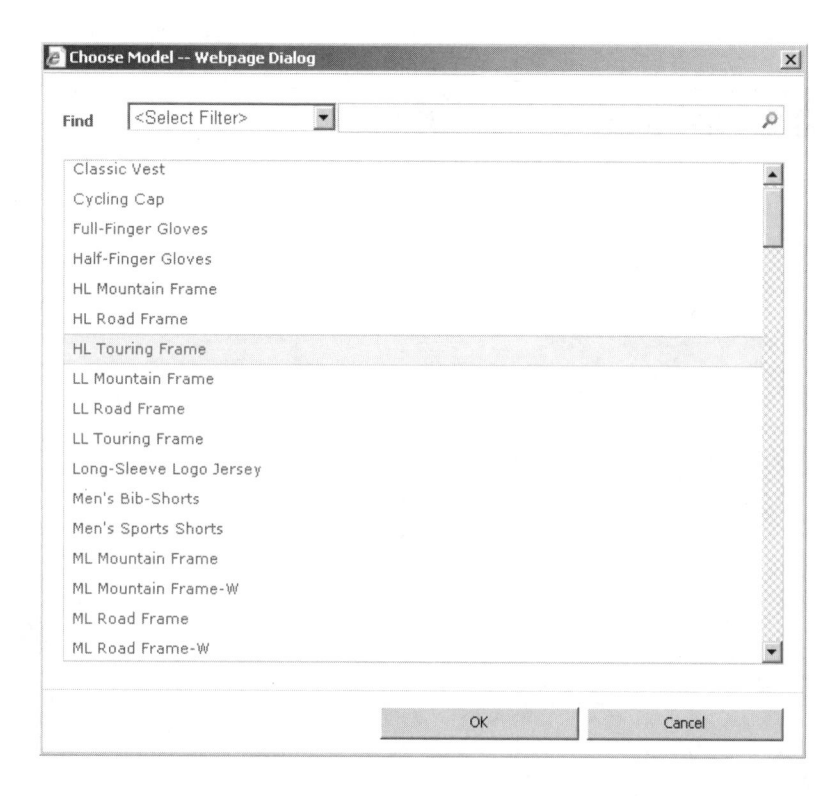

```
Choose Model -- Webpage Dialog

Find  <Select Filter>  ▼  [                    ] 🔍

Classic Vest
Cycling Cap
Full-Finger Gloves
Half-Finger Gloves
HL Mountain Frame
HL Road Frame
HL Touring Frame
LL Mountain Frame
LL Road Frame
LL Touring Frame
Long-Sleeve Logo Jersey
Men's Bib-Shorts
Men's Sports Shorts
ML Mountain Frame
ML Mountain Frame-W
ML Road Frame
ML Road Frame-W

        [ OK ]        [ Cancel ]
```

You should notice a few things when you're using the data picker. First, the list displays all rows from the Models table. If you enter criteria in the Find box, you'll get an error message, as shown next. Second, if you select an item from the list and then click OK, the

Product Model control contains the ID of the selected item rather than the user-friendly text you might expect.

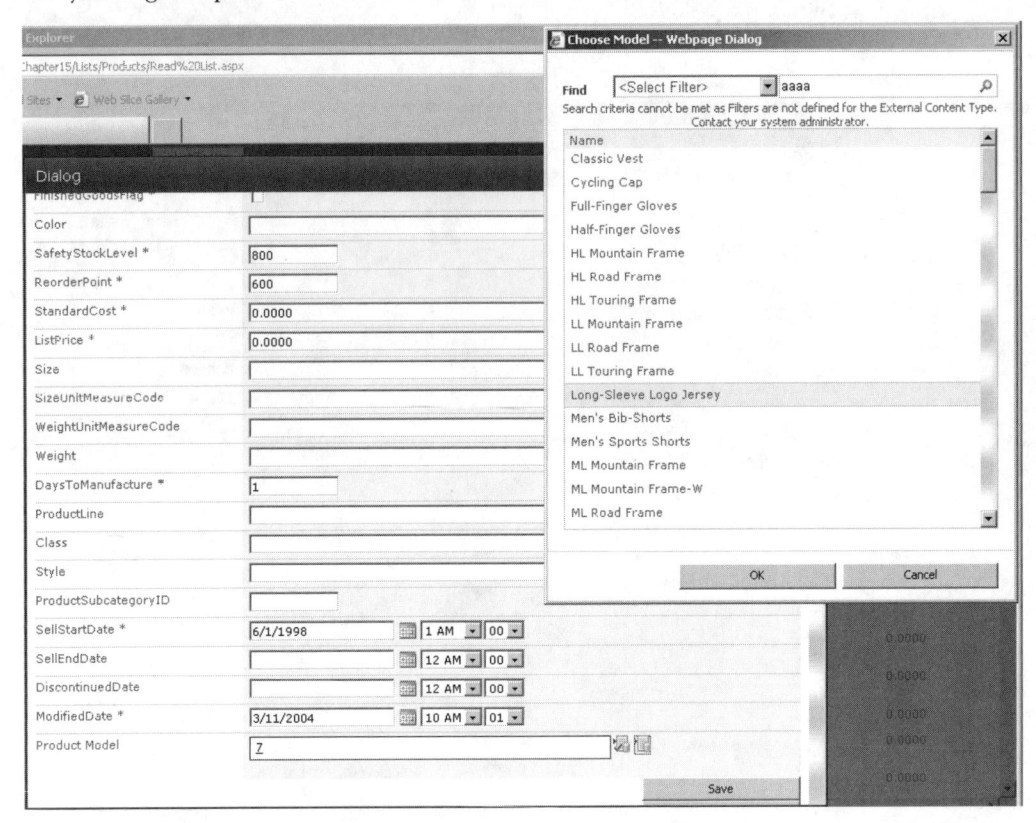

Both of these problems are easy to resolve and take us back to our Model content type.

## Setting Picker Display Text

When opening the Model content type in Summary View, you'll notice a list of fields on the right side of the page.

1. Select the Name field, and from the ribbon, click the Set As Title button.
2. Save the changes to the external content type, and then review the Products list in Internet Explorer.

This time, when editing an item, the model name is displayed when a model is selected rather than the ID.

Each external content type can have a title column defined. If no title is defined, the ID is used instead. Any column in the entity can be flagged as the title.

## Adding Picker Search Functionality

The next problem requires a few more mouse clicks to resolve. Open the Model content type in Operations Design View. Since we want to change the way lists of items are returned, we need to adjust the settings for the Finder operation.

1. In SharePoint Designer, Finder operations are created using the Read List type. Highlight the Read List operation, and then select Edit Operation from the ribbon.
2. In the Filter Parameters step of the Edit Operation wizard, click Add New Filter Parameter to add an additional filter.
3. Set the Data Source Element to Name, and then click the Click To Add link to show the Filter Configuration dialog.
4. Create a new filter named **Search Filter** and set the Filter Type to Wildcard.
5. Since we don't want to apply this filter where no criteria have been entered, check the Ignore Filter If Value Is checkbox. The default option of Null is fine.

   A couple additional checkboxes warrant some explanation:

   - The Is Default checkbox determines whether the filter should be selected by default in the picker control. You'll remember that the picker control contains a drop-down list of search types as well as a text box for the user to enter search criteria. A check in the Is Default checkbox means the filter will automatically be selected as the default in the search types drop-down.

   - The Use To Create Match List In Data Picker checkbox also relates to the default search. However, rather than setting the default search in the search types drop-down, the checkbox defines which filter should be used when the user types a value in the External Data Picker control without clicking the picker button. So, for example, on an edit page containing an External Data Picker control, the control is rendered as a text box with two buttons. The rightmost button opens up the picker, and the left button performs a behind-the-scenes search using the value entered in the text box. If a single match is found, the item is selected. If not, a list of suggestions are presented.

   With an understanding of the Is Default and Use To Create Match List In Data Picker options, set both of these options to *true*.

6. Click Finish to apply the changes, and then save the external content type.

This time, when viewing the changes in the edit form, try entering **jersey** in the product model text box, and then click the button to the immediate right. You'll see an error message indicating that no exact match was found, and you can click the underlined text to see a list of suggestions, as illustrated here:

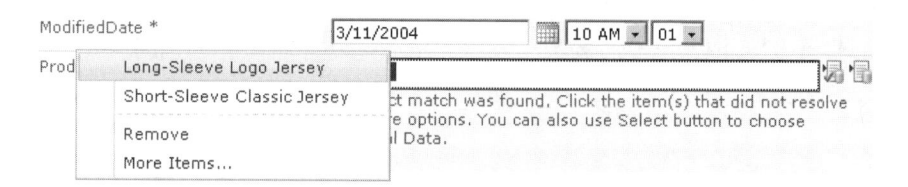

The picker now behaves as expected, filtering results based on the criteria entered in the textbox and allowing search within the pop-up dialog.

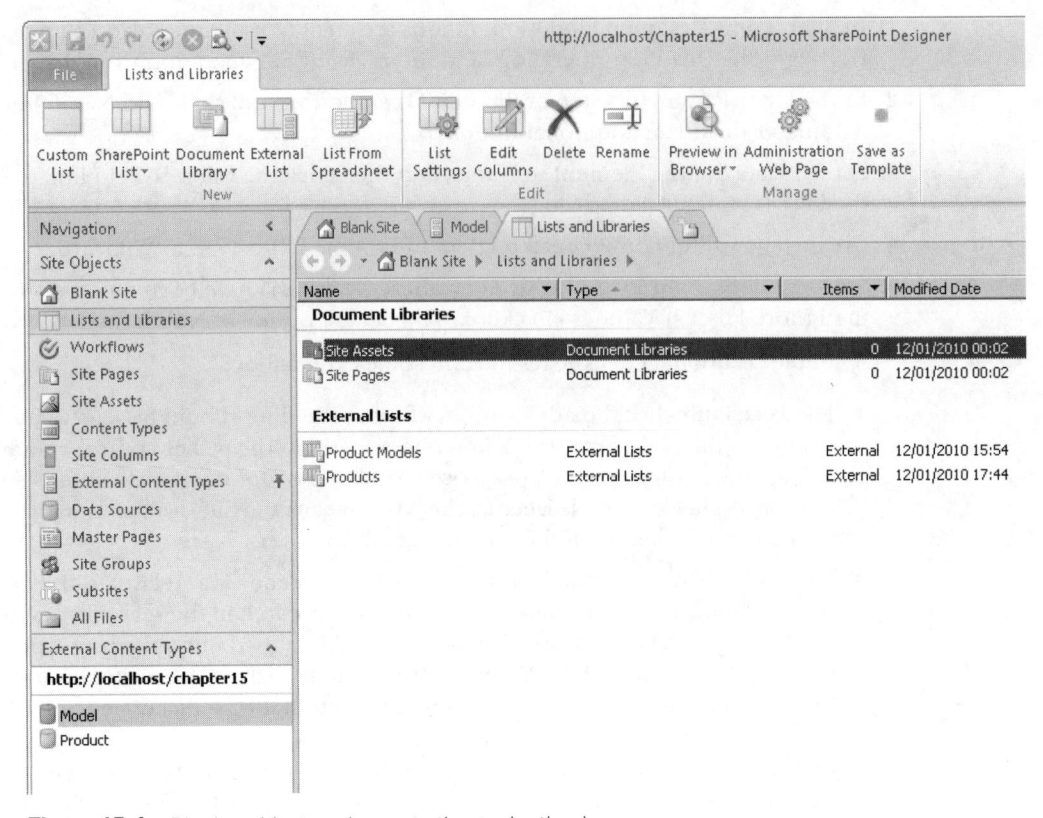

**Figure 15-1** Pinning object explorers to the navigation bar

> **TIP** When moving between different object types in SharePoint Designer, it's possible to pin one category of objects to the left sidebar. In Figure 15-1, the External Content Types explorer is pinned to the navigation bar while the List and Libraries explorer is visible in the main pane, making it easy to switch to a particular external content type without first having to bring up the explorer.

## Building a .NET Connectivity Assembly

You've seen how to connect to a business system using SharePoint Designer. The wizards make it simple to connect to SQL Server databases or appropriately designed WCF services. But what happens if you want to connect to something a bit more exotic? The answer is to create a .NET connectivity assembly. By creating a connectivity assembly, you can write code to handle any of the operation stereotypes supported by the BDC service. As mentioned earlier, BDC itself doesn't read or write to the external data store; it simply delegates to an appropriate endpoint. By creating a connectivity assembly, you can effectively create custom endpoints to do whatever is appropriate for your application.

## Pluggable Connector Framework

As briefly covered earlier in the section "Connector Framework," BCS makes connections to external systems via a pluggable connector framework. It is therefore possible to create custom connectors to interface with external systems. While creating custom connectors is beyond the scope of this chapter, it's worthwhile for you to know the differences between creating a custom connector and using a connectivity assembly.

Connectivity assemblies encapsulate an entire data access model. In the preceding section, we worked through configuring the metadata for the database connector; with connectivity assemblies, such configuration isn't required since the metadata is installed with the connectivity assembly. Naturally, this lack of configurability can also be considered a drawback where the APIs for the external data store are likely to change frequently.

When you're building custom connectors, you should be aware of some installation considerations. Connector assemblies must be manually installed in the Global Assembly Cache (GAC) on each server or rich client that intends to use the connector. By contrast, a connectivity assembly is stored within the BDC data store and is therefore automatically available to the BDC service on every server. Where the assembly is required by a rich-client interface, it is seamlessly installed via ClickOnce.

## Business Data Connectivity Model Project

From our demonstration scenario, we require the functionality to attach product information retrieved from Internet search results to our competitive analysis reports. Of course, we could achieve this result by using a web browser and simply cutting and pasting the URL into a text field, but in the age of the mash-up, switching between applications in such a fashion would almost certainly lead to a disciplinary hearing of the International Association of Mash-up Artists—not to mention the fact that it would deprive us of the opportunity to explore Business Data Connectivity Model projects in Visual Studio 2010.

### Create a New Project in Visual Studio 2010

To create a new Business Data Connectivity Model project, take the following steps:

1. Open Visual Studio 2010. Choose File | New | Project.

2. In the New Project window, select SharePoint in the left pane and Business Data Connectivity Model in the middle pane, as illustrated next. In the Name text field, type **BingConnectivity**.

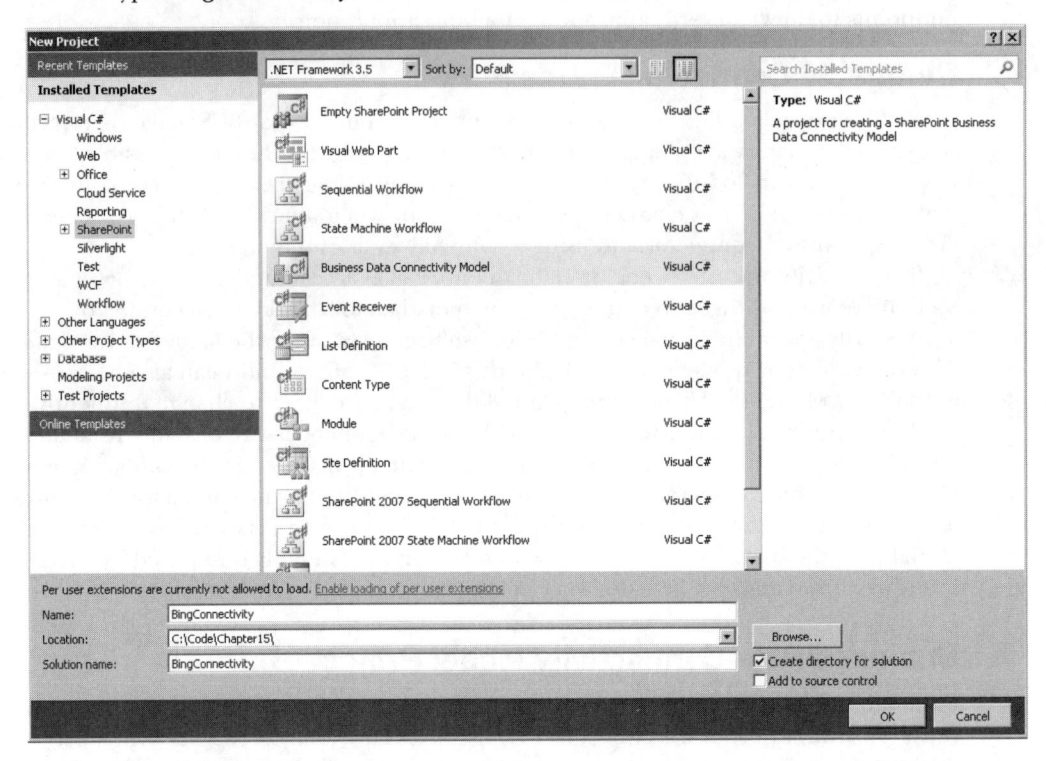

3. In the SharePoint Customization Wizard, select your local server for use when debugging.
4. Click Finish to create the project. A new project will be created containing a BDC Model and a single sample entity, as shown in Figure 15-2.

The Visual Studio 2010 design surface for creating connectivity assemblies includes a number of specific tools. First, the entity view, shown in the middle of the page in Figure 15-2, lets you see all of the entities defined in your data source and the identifiers and methods defined on them. By clicking a method or identifier in the entity view, the BDC Method Details pane, shown below the entity view in the figure, is populated with details about the methods and identifiers defined in the entity. Finally, the upper-right pane in Figure 15-2 is the BDC Explorer pane. This control presents a hierarchical view of your BDC model.

**NOTE** At the time of writing, the BDC design tools are visible only when you're viewing files with a .BDCM extension.

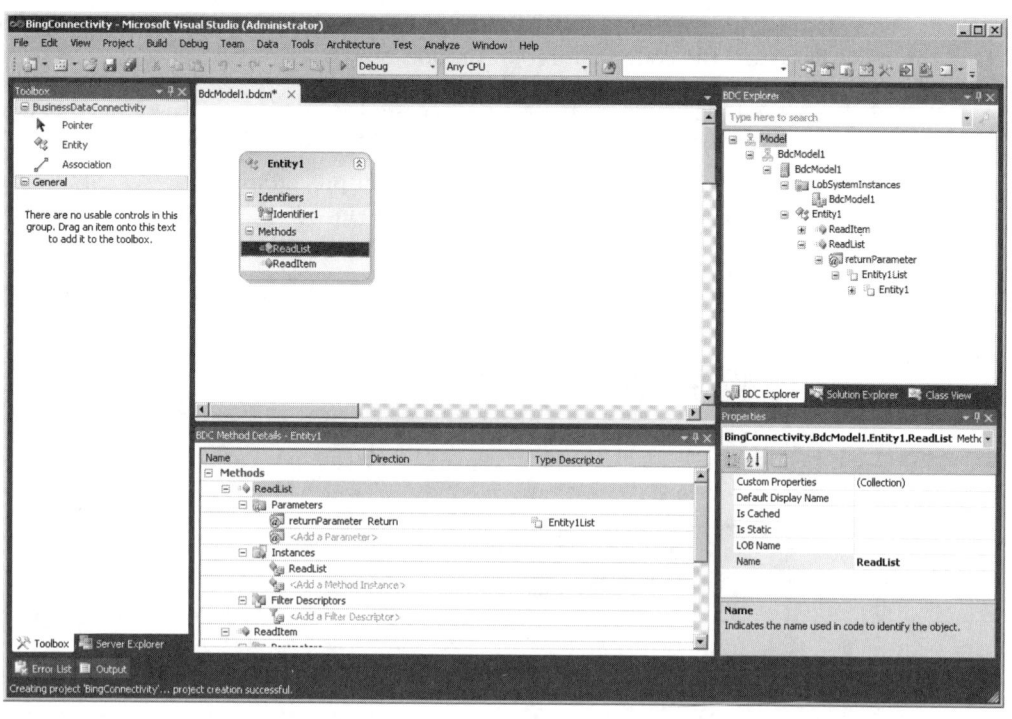

**Figure 15-2** The Business Data Connectivity Model design surface

## Create a Custom Entity Service Object

Before we jump into creating a new Entity Service object, it's worth discussing what an Entity Service object is and how it relates to the rest of the items in our model. A BDC model project consists of three things:

- A BDCM file that contains the configuration metadata for the connection
- An Entity Service class that contains the methods that will be the endpoints of the operations defined in the metadata
- An Entity class that contains the data to be processed by the Entity Service methods

To relate this back to the connection we made earlier via SharePoint Designer, the BDCM file contains the configuration details that we entered in the Operations Design View of the External Content Type. The Entity Service object is the equivalent of the ADO.NET provider for SQL Server and the Entity class represents a row of data.

**NOTE** These relationships and their representation in the design tools can cause some confusion at first glance. In the Entity View, it appears as though the methods are defined on the entity object. In fact, the methods are declared as static methods on the Entity Service object.

Now that you have a clear understanding of the purpose of the Entity Service object, we can move on to add the code required to support our data source.

1. Since the Bing.com search service is accessed via a web service, we need to add a new service reference. Choose Project | Add Service Reference.
2. In the Add Service Reference dialog, enter **http://api.bing.net/search .wsdl?AppID=<*Your App ID Goes Here*>&Version=2.2**.
3. Click Go to download the service WSDL.
4. Set the Namespace to **Microsoft.Bing**, and then click OK to create proxy classes for the service, as shown here:

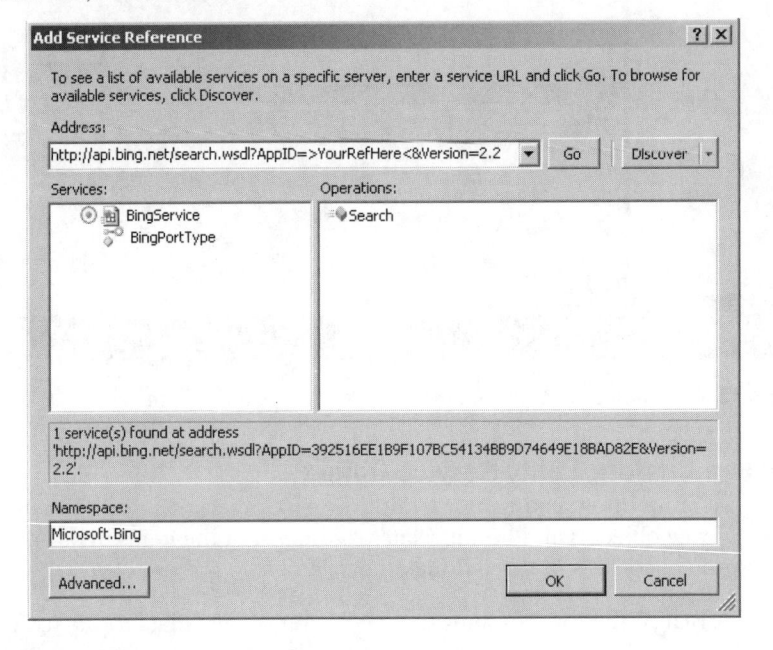

**Define a Method to Support the Finder Stereotype**  Our next step is to implement methods that will be called by BCS clients to interact with the data source. In our demonstration scenario, we need to be able to query the data source using a wildcard query and retrieve a single specific result.

First of all, let's take a look at the query method. You'll remember from earlier examples that the operation for retrieving a list of data is referenced using the Finder stereotype. We'll start by creating a new method for this stereotype.

1. In the Entity viewer in Visual Studio, delete the default Entity1 object, and then drag a new Entity from the toolbox onto the design surface. Change the Entity name to **WebResult**.
2. In the BDC Methods Details pane, click <Add a Method> to create a new method. From the drop-down that appears, select Create Finder Method. This will automatically add a method named ReadList.

3. Since our Finder method needs to be able to perform wildcard searches, we need to add a wildcard filter. We're effectively performing the same configuration that we did earlier when we set up a search filter on the Model External Content Type—you'll no doubt recognize some of the configuration objects that we're dealing with. To add a new filter, we first need a parameter to which we can attach the filter. We'll add a new query parameter to the **ReadList** method. Expand the parameters node in the BDC Method Details pane, and then click Add a Parameter. Select Create A Parameter to add a new parameter to the method. You'll notice that although the default parameter name is selected in the BDC Method Details pane, it's not possible to overtype it with a new value. To add a new value, we need to use the Properties pane, as shown next. Type **query** for the new parameter name.

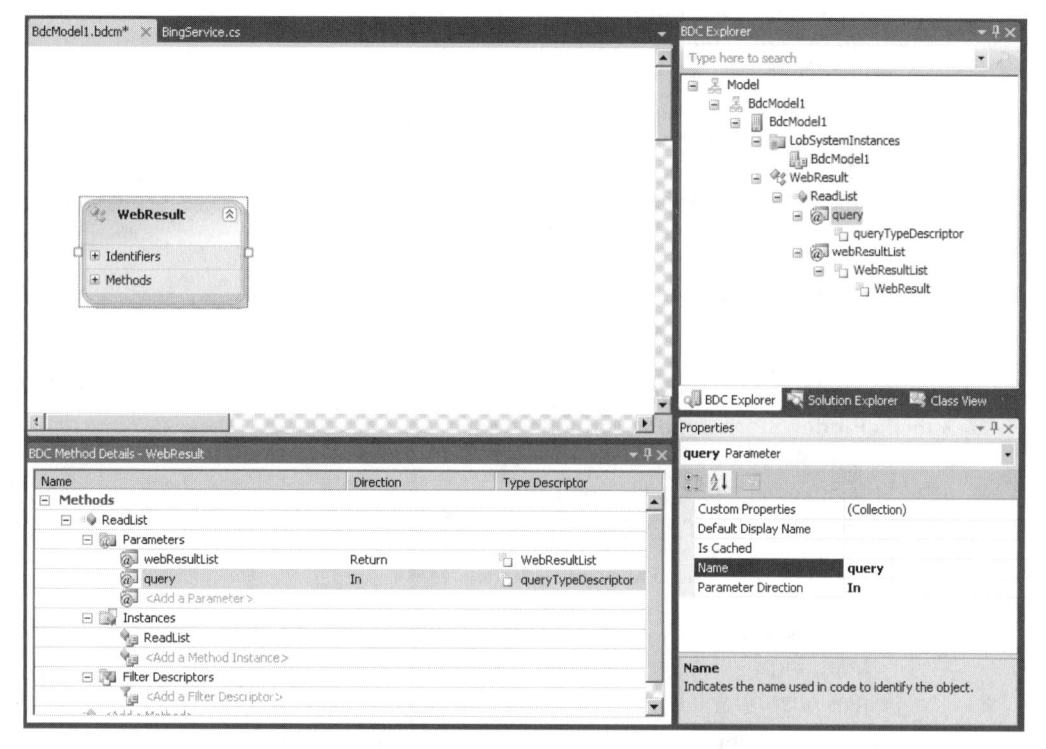

4. With this new parameter in place, we're now free to add a new filter. Under the Filter Descriptors node, click <Add a Filter Descriptor>, and then select Create a Filter Descriptor. As before, use the Properties pane to change the Name to **Search Filter** and the Type to **Wildcard**. To make this filter the default, we need to add an additional property. Click the ellipsis next to Custom Properties in the Properties pane to add another property. Type **IsDefault** for the Name, **System.Boolean** for the Type, and **true** for the Value.

5. Now that we have a filter, we need to associate it with our **ReadList** method. We can do this by selecting an associated type description. You'll notice in the BDC Method Details pane that each parameter has a type descriptor attached. A *type descriptor* is

metadata that defines the type of the parameter as well as a number of properties that control how the type should be handled, such as whether the type is an identifier or should be read-only. When we added our additional parameter to the **ReadList** method, a new type descriptor was automatically created. We need to attach our Search Filter to this type. From the BDC Explorer pane, expand the ReadList node and the query node beneath it. Select the queryTypeDescriptor node to define the properties of the parameter. First, let's change the name to something more succinct: In the Properties pane, change the Name to **simply query**. To attach the filter to this type, select the filter name (Search Filter) from the drop-down list next to the Associated Filter property, as illustrated next:

**Define a Method to Support the SpecificFinder Stereotype**   With our Finder operation in place, the next thing we need to add is a SpecificFinder operation to allow clients to retrieve a single specific entity.

1. Follow steps 2 and 3 above to add a new method, but this time select Create a SpecificFinder in the BDC Method Details pane. By default, the new method will be named ReadItem.

2. Since this method returns only a single item, we don't need to create any filters. However, we do need to add a parameter that will uniquely identify the item to be returned. Since the results will consist of web pages, the most sensible identifier is the URL. Follow steps 4 and 5 above to add a new parameter named *itemUrl*.

3. A new Type Descriptor of itemUrlTypeDescriptor is added. For the sake of brevity, rename this as **itemUrl** using the BDC Explorer:

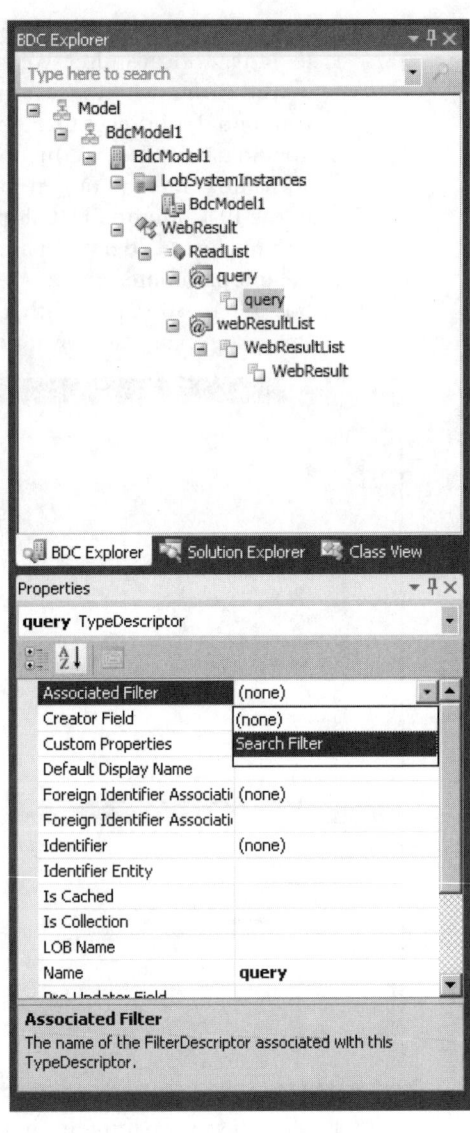

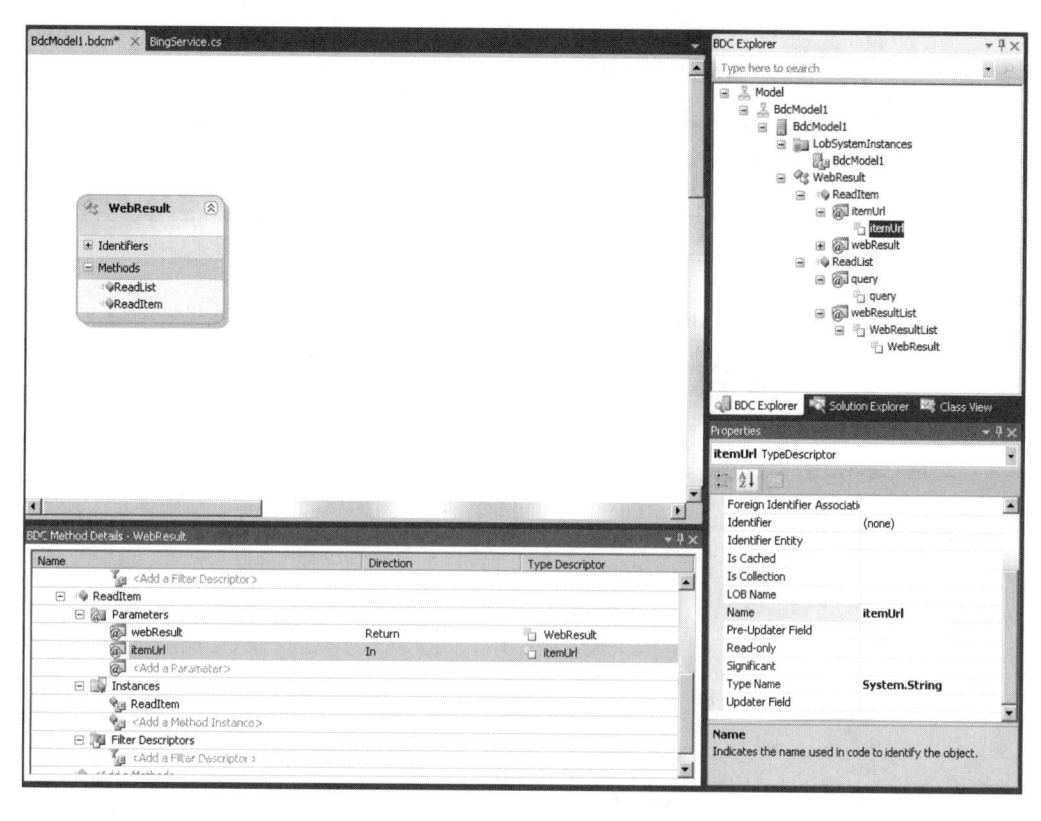

[Screenshot of Visual Studio showing BdcModel1.bdcm with WebResult entity, BDC Explorer, and BDC Method Details panes]

4. Before we move on to add the code to support these new methods, we need to add one more piece of metadata to the model: we need to declare our identifier. Right-click the WebResult entity and select Add | Identifier, as shown next. Change the default name to **itemUrl**.

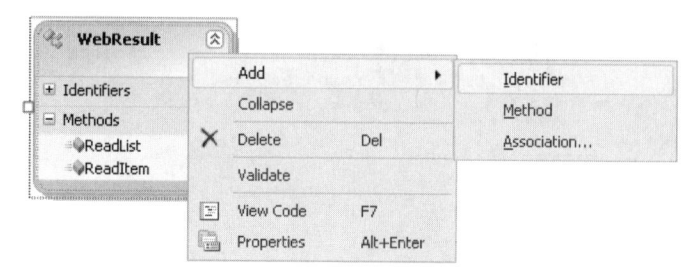

[Screenshot of context menu showing Add | Identifier option on WebResult entity]

5. With this identifier created, we can now update the metadata for the itemUrl descriptor that we're using to define the parameter for the **ReadItem** method. In the BDC Explorer pane, select the itemUrl type descriptor (ReadItem | itemUrl | itemUrl), and then, in the Properties pane, change the Identifier property to **itemUrl**.

Now that we have the metadata in place for our model, we can start fleshing out our **ReadList** and **ReadItem** methods.

1. Save the BDC model, and then switch to the Solution Explorer pane in Visual Studio. You'll notice that a WebResultService.cs file has been added. Open this file, and you can see that as we've been making changes to the model, Visual Studio has automatically created stub methods with the appropriate parameters for us. Since we don't need them, delete the Entity1.cs and Entity1Service.cs files that were added to the project by default.

2. In the WebResultService class, add the following code:

```
using System.Collections.Generic;
using System.Linq;
using System.ServiceModel.Channels;
using System.ServiceModel;
using BingConnectivity.Microsoft.Bing;

namespace BingConnectivity.BdcModel1
{
    public partial class WebResultService
    {
        public static IEnumerable<string> ReadList(string query)
        {
            //We can't perform a web search with no query
            if (!string.IsNullOrEmpty(query))
            {
                //Get an instance of the Bing proxy class
                BingPortTypeClient client;
                SearchRequest request = GetRequestProxy(out client);

                //Setup the request parameters
                request.Query = query;

                //Execute the search
                SearchResponse response = client.Search(request);

                //Shape the results to suit our requirements
                var results = from r in response.Web.Results
                              select r.Url;

                return results;
            }
            else
            {
                return null;
            }

        }
        public static string ReadItem(string itemUrl)
        {
            if (!string.IsNullOrEmpty(itemUrl))
            {
                BingPortTypeClient client;
```

```
            SearchRequest request = GetRequestProxy(out client);
            request.Query = itemUrl;

            SearchResponse response = client.Search(request);

            //Since urls are globally unique this query will
            //only return one result
            return response.Web.Results.Single().Url;
        }
        else
        {
            return null;
        }

    }

    private static SearchRequest GetRequestProxy(out
                                                BingPortTypeClient client)
    {
        //When we added the service reference. Visual Studio automatically
        //added configuration information to app.config.
        //However since this assembly may be called from a number of processes
        //app.config won't be available. As a result we need to manually
        //configure the service.

        Binding b = new BasicHttpBinding();
        EndpointAddress address = new
                    EndpointAddress("http://api.bing.net:80/soap.asmx");

        client = new BingPortTypeClient(b, address);

        SearchRequest request = new Microsoft.Bing.SearchRequest();

        request.AppId = "ENTER YOUR APPID HERE";

        //We're only interested in search the Web source
        //See Bing SDK for more details on this parameter

        request.Sources = new SourceType[] { SourceType.Web };

        return request;
    }

}
}
```

3. With the methods fleshed out, we can now build and deploy the model to SharePoint to see the results of our actions. Choose Build | Deploy BingConnectivity. The project will be built, packaged, and automatically installed on the SharePoint server that we specified when creating the project.

4. In SharePoint Designer, navigate to the External Content Types explorer. You can see that a new WebResult content type has been added with type .Net Assembly. By opening the content type, you can see whether the metadata configuration is as expected and the appropriate operations have been added.

> **TIP** The SharePoint server that's used as the target for deployments can be changed by clicking the Project node in Solution Explorer and changing the Site URL property in the Properties pane.

## Create a Custom Entity Object

One of the things you may notice when reviewing the properties of the WebResult External Content Type in SharePoint Designer is that no fields are defined. Of course, there is a perfectly reasonable explanation for this. If you look back at the return types for the **ReadLst** and **ReadItem** methods, you'll see that they return values of type **IEnumerable<string>** and **string**, respectively. While this is a valid configuration, SharePoint Designer can't break down a single string into multiple fields; therefore, no fields are shown.

This is where the Entity object comes into play. An Entity object, as you'll remember, defines an individual row of data; it stores individual field data as properties. To show individual fields in SharePoint, we need to create an appropriate object.

Earlier in the chapter, we added a service reference to allow us to communicate with the Bing service. By examining the details of the service contract, we can determine what fields are returned from the service. From the Bing Web Service definition Language (WSDL), we see that the **Search** method returns an array of **WebResult** elements:

```
<xsd:complexType name="WebResult">
<xsd:sequence>
  <xsd:element minOccurs="0" maxOccurs="1" name="Title" type="xsd:string" />
  <xsd:element minOccurs="0" maxOccurs="1" name="Description" type="xsd:string" />
  <xsd:element minOccurs="0" maxOccurs="1" name="Url" type="xsd:string" />
  <xsd:element minOccurs="0" maxOccurs="1" name="CacheUrl" type="xsd:string" />
  <xsd:element minOccurs="0" maxOccurs="1" name="DisplayUrl" type="xsd:string" />
  <xsd:element minOccurs="0" maxOccurs="1" name="DateTime" type="xsd:string" />
  <xsd:element minOccurs="0" maxOccurs="1"
               name="SearchTags" type="tns:ArrayOfWebSearchTag" />
  <xsd:element minOccurs="0" maxOccurs="1"
               name="DeepLinks" type="tns:ArrayOfDeepLink" />
</xsd:sequence>
</xsd:complexType>
```

By creating an object with a property for each of these elements, we'll be able to pass the results back to our client application without any loss of data. However, rather than create a new entity class from scratch, we can simply hook up our metadata to the **Microsoft.Bing.WebResult** object that was created automatically when we added the service reference. This eliminates the unnecessary step of reading the data from the proxy class into a custom entity class before passing it back to the client.

> **TIP** Although we could jump straight in and change the return types of our **ReadList** and **ReadItem** methods, it's always a good idea to make changes to the metadata first, since these changes are automatically cascaded to the Entity Service. Following this procedure helps to eliminate mismatches in data types since the assembly won't build if a type copied from the metadata model into the Entity Service code isn't valid.

1. Open the BdcModel1.bdcm model to display the Entity viewer. Since we want to change the data type for the return parameter of the **ReadItem** and **ReadList** methods, start by expanding the **ReadItem** method in the BDC Explorer pane.

Select the WebResult Type Descriptor, and then in the Properties pane, change the Type Name to **BingConnectivity.Microsoft.Bing.WebResult, BdcModel1**.

2. Repeat this process for the **ReadList** method, except change the Type Name for the WebResultList Type Descriptor to **System.Collections.Generic .IEnumerable`1[[BingConnectivity.Microsoft.Bing.WebResult, BdcModel1]]** and the Type Name for Type Descriptor WebResult to **BingConnectivity.Microsoft .Bing.WebResult, BdcModel1**.

3. Save the changes to the model, and then return to the WebResultService class. You'll notice that the method signatures have been updated accordingly.

4. As a result of these updates, our project no longer builds, because our code returns items of the wrong type. To fix this, update the **ReadList** method as follows:

```
public static IEnumerable<WebResult> ReadList(string query)
    {
      //We can't perform a web search with no query
      if (!string.IsNullOrEmpty(query))
      {
        //Get an instance of the Bing proxy class
        BingPortTypeClient client;
        SearchRequest request = GetRequestProxy(out client);

        //Setup the request parameters
        request.Query = query;
        try
        {
          //Execute the search
          SearchResponse response = client.Search(request);

          return response.Web.Results;
        }
        catch(System.Exception)
        {
          return null;
        }
      }
      else
      {
        return null;
      }

    }
```

5. To resolve the errors in the **ReadItem** method, update the code as follows:

```
public static WebResult ReadItem(string itemUrl)
{
  if (!string.IsNullOrEmpty(itemUrl))
  {
    BingPortTypeClient client;
    SearchRequest request = GetRequestProxy(out client);
    request.Query = itemUrl;

    SearchResponse response = client.Search(request);
```

```
    //Since urls are globally unique this query will only return one result
    return response.Web.Results.Single();
  }
  else
  {
    return null;
  }
}
```

Our project will now build correctly.

**Define Entity Metadata**  Before we redeploy our assembly, we need to make another important change. Even though we've updated the metadata to use the WebResult object as our Entity class, we haven't added metadata defining the properties of the WebResult object. We need to update the WebResult Type Descriptor with details of the fields on the object that we want to allow clients to use.

1. Open up the model. In the BDC Explorer pane, navigate to the WebResult Type Descriptor defined on the **ReadItem** method. Right-click the Type Descriptor node and select Add Type Descriptor. This will add a child-type descriptor object that we can use to declare details of a field.

2. Add the following type descriptors:

| Name | Type Name |
|---|---|
| DateTime | System.DateTime |
| Description | System.String |
| DisplayUrl | System.String |
| Title | System.String |
| Url | System.String |

3. In the properties for the Url type descriptor, set the Identifier to **itemUrl** to declare this as the identifier for the entity.

4. Now that we've updated the WebResult type descriptor for the ReadItem method, we need to copy this information to the ReadList method. Thankfully the BDC Explorer tool allows us to copy and paste descriptors. Delete the existing WebResult descriptor from the ReadList method, and then copy the WebResult descriptor node on the ReadItem method.

5. Navigate to the WebResultList node on the ReadList method. Click to highlight it, and then paste the WebResult node.

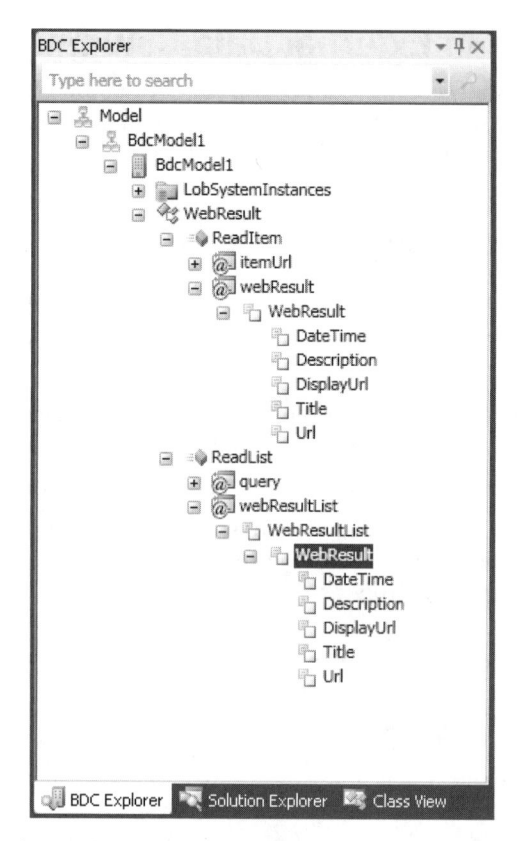

6. We're now good to redeploy our completed connectivity assembly. Choose Build | Deploy BingConnectivity.

Once the solution has been deployed, we can see in SharePoint Designer that the fields are now available as expected. (You might need to press F5 to refresh the view to see the changes.) We can test our model by creating an External List from it. Follow the procedure discussed in the section "Create an External List."

When navigating to your new list for the first time, you'll notice that it's empty. This is expected, because the ReadList method requires a query property. So how do you set the property? In External Lists, data source filters can be defined as part of the view. If you modify the default ReadList view, you'll find a Data Source Filters section containing a text box to enter a parameter for our Search Filter. Type a search query in the Search Filter text box and save the view to see the results displayed in the list:

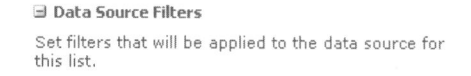

## Using BCS Data in External Data Columns

We've now successfully created connections to our sample ERP system and an external web service that can be used to retrieve web results relating to competing products. With these connections in place, our next step in completing the user interface for our application is to define a new document library in which to store competitive analysis documents.

1. Using Internet Explorer, navigate to our sample SharePoint site. Then, from the Site Actions menu, select New Document Library. In the dialog that appears, type the name of the document library: **Competitive Analysis**. Click Create to continue.

2. Make sure that the Library menu is visible in the ribbon, and then select Library Settings.

3. To add an External Data Column that can be used to select a product to associate with the Competitive Analysis document, click Create Column.

4. Set the name of the new column to **Model**; then select the External Data type.

5. In the Additional Column Settings section, in the External Content Type Picker, enter **Model**. Then click the Verify button (with a checkmark) that appears to the immediate right of the text box, as shown here:

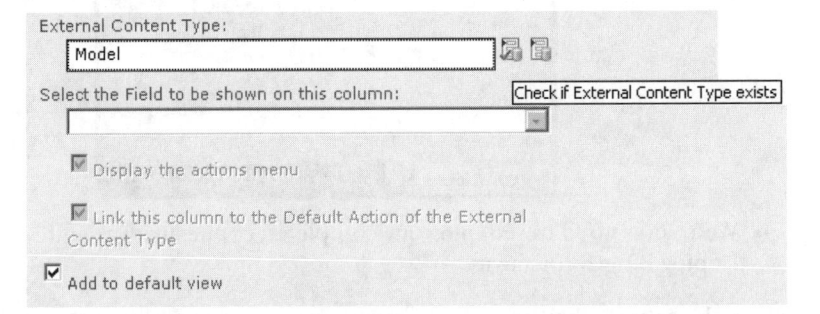

6. From the drop-down labeled Select The Field To Be Shown On This Column, choose Name. As well as the Name field, we also want to include ModifiedDate as a field in our list. Select this from the list of additional fields.

7. Click OK to create the new column.

8. Repeat steps 3 to 7 to add a link to the web-based content. This time, name the column **Competing Model**. Set the External Content Type to WebResult. Show the Title field in the column and include the DateTime field.

With these new columns in place, we're ready to start uploading or creating documents. As you'll see when you upload a document, you are prompted to select a Model and a Competing Model before you can save the document. In both cases, you can make use of the External Picker Control to select the item from a list.

Once your document is saved to the document library, you'll notice that additional fields have been carried through from the external content type, such as Model: Modified Date and Competing Model: Date Time.

**NOTE** At the time of writing, creating External Data Columns is not supported using SharePoint Designer 2010 Beta 2.

## Profile Pages

By using External Data Columns, you can easily combine data from external systems with SharePoint-generated data, allowing for data consistency throughout your applications. But what happens when you want to drill down into the data that's associated with External Data Column?

The answer is profile pages. This feature is available in SharePoint Server 2010 only, and before it can be used, it must be configured via SharePoint 2010 Central Administration. Let's do that now:

1. Open SharePoint 2010 Central Administration. In the Application Management section, select Manage service applications.

2. From the list of Service Applications, select Business Data Connectivity with type Business Data Connectivity Service Application.

3. On the Service Application Information page, select Edit from the top menu to show the Edit ribbon. Then select Configure.

4. Check the Enable Profile Page Creation checkbox. For the Host URL, enter **http://localhost/Chapter15**.

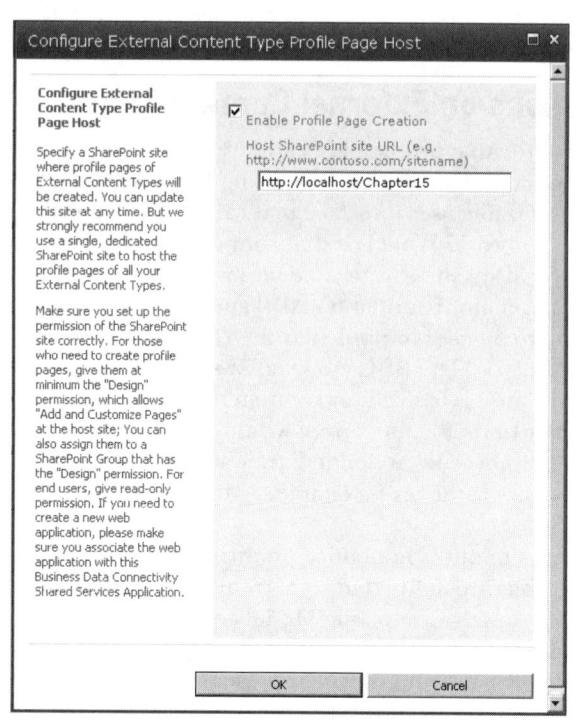

> **NOTE** As you saw in Chapter 9, service applications can be shared between multiple applications. Generally where profile pages are being used by multiple sites, a dedicated site to host the pages will be set up. For the sake of simplicity, we've used our demonstration site, but this is not indicative of best practice.

Now that we have the facility to create profile pages, we need to do the work to create a page for our Model external content type. Using SharePoint Designer, this is simple:

1. In SharePoint Designer, navigate to the Model External Content Type.
2. From the ribbon, select Create Profile Page.

That's all there is to it. A new profile page has been created that will be automatically linked to our Model content type wherever it appears in lists.

To see this in action, navigate to the Competitive Analysis document library that we created earlier. You'll notice that items in the Model column are now hyperlinks instead of plain text. Clicking the hyperlink will take you to the auto-generated profile page for that item.

The profile page presents a read-only view of the entity together with any associated entities. In this case, you can see the Model together with any Products that are based on the model. As mentioned earlier, the profile page is generated using External Data Web Parts and as such can be customized further to meet specific requirements.

For example, in the Model profile page, let's say we wanted to hide the rowguid and ProductModelID columns. By selecting Edit Page from the Site Actions menu, and then editing the properties of the Business Data Item web part, we can easily hide these fields.

## Default Actions on External Content Types

I'm sure you'll agree that profile pages are pretty useful stuff. Not only can we easily attach data to our SharePoint lists and libraries using BCS, but with a few mouse clicks we can generate a customizable user interface that can be used to drill down into that data.

But how does it work? What is it that connects the content type to the profile page? What if the external system is web-based and we want to link to a page there instead? What if we're using SharePoint Foundation 2010 and don't have the profile pages feature?

It's all about *actions* and in particular the *Default Action* that's been defined for our External Content Type. The BDC model allows multiple actions to be defined for each entity, where an action is basically a parameterized URL that can be used to connect to an external system or to redirect to a page within the SharePoint site, as is the case with profile pages. Once actions have been defined, they are available wherever the content type is presented. As we saw earlier, for example, actions are automatically attached to External Data Columns.

If we look back to our Competitive Analysis document library, one of the things we can see is that no actions are defined for our WebResult content type. By clicking the icon to the left of the text in our Competing Model column, you can see that no actions are available on the context menu.

Since our WebResult content type represents a web page, it would be useful if our default action was simply to connect to the associated web page. We can make this change in Visual Studio 2010, as follows:

1. Open the BingConnectivity project. In the Solution Explorer pane, right-click the BdcModel1.bdcm file, and then select Open With. From the list that appears, select XML Editor.

2. At the time of writing, the SharePoint BDC Designer tool in Visual Studio doesn't support the creation of actions, so we need to edit the underlying metadata file directly. Make the highlighted changes:

```xml
<?xml version="1.0" encoding="utf-8"?>
<Model xmlns:xsi="http://www.w3.org/2001/XMLSchema-instance" xmlns:xsd="http://www
.w3.org/2001/XMLSchema" xmlns="http://schemas.microsoft.com/windows/2007/Business-
DataCatalog" Name="BdcModel1">
  <LobSystems>
    <LobSystem Name="BdcModel1" Type="DotNetAssembly">
      <LobSystemInstances>
        <LobSystemInstance Name="BdcModel1" />
      </LobSystemInstances>
      <Entities>
<!--IMPORTANT: Increment the Version number of the Model won't deploy-->
        <Entity Name="WebResult" Namespace="BingConnectivity.BdcModel1"
                                 Version="1.0.0.49">
          <Properties>
            <!-- Clipped for brevity -->
<!-- The name of the DefaultAction is defined as a property on the Entity-->
<Property Name="DefaultAction" Type="System.String">ViewWebPage</Property>
          </Properties>
          <Identifiers>
            <!-- Clipped for brevity -->
          </Identifiers>
          <Methods>
            <!-- Clipped for brevity -->
          </Methods>
<!-- A new action section is added containing details of each action-->
          <Actions>
            <Action Name="ViewWebPage" DefaultDisplayName="View Web Page"
               Url="{0}" IsOpenedInNewWindow="true" Position="1">
              <ActionParameters>

<!-- The ActionParameter must be the name of a field returned from -->
<!-- the SpecificFinder method-->
<!-- The Index attribute related to the replacement index in the -->
<!-- Action Url attribute, in this case {0}-->
                <ActionParameter Index="0" Name="Url"/>
              </ActionParameters>
            </Action>
          </Actions>
        </Entity>
      </Entities>
    </LobSystem>
  </LobSystems>
</Model>
```

3. Deploy the updated metadata by selecting Deploy BingConnectivity from the Build menu.

Now when you reload the Competitive Analysis document library, the Competing Model column is hyperlinked. Clicking the link takes you to the URL originally returned from our Bing search.

## Summary

This chapter aimed to provide an overview of the Business Connectivity Services functionality available in 2010. Through our demonstration scenarios, you've been able to take an in-depth look at a lot of the key features and gain some experience with various tools.

As a standard platform for interfacing with business data, BCS offers unparalleled functionality. Using the tools available in SharePoint Designer and Visual Studio 2010 as well as third-party tools such as BCS Meta Man, it's easy to surface business data in SharePoint. Of course, it's fair to say that programmatically using the data can be somewhat challenging at first, but once you get into the way the abstraction works, you will really begin to see the power of BCS as a platform for accessing data in any client application.

# CHAPTER 16

# Enterprise Search

When modern computing was still young, the vast majority of processing power was used for generating content—performing calculations, analyzing input, and producing useful output. Today, although a sizeable percentage of processing power is still used in assisting users in producing content in the form of word processing applications and spreadsheet applications, an ever-increasing slice is now used to manage the content being created. In fact, these days, the role of the IT professional is often more about managing user-created content than it is about creating content itself.

This is where SharePoint 2010's *enterprise search* technology enters the picture. Enterprise search is the one feature that delivers immediate business benefit in SharePoint 2010. Organizations have scattered content far and wide, with more and more being created every minute of every day. Enterprise search provides a platform that can crawl and index content from practically any source. After all, a document that nobody can find may as well not exist. Using SharePoint 2010, organizations can easily implement a scalable search portal where users can find the information they need.

Of course, there's much more to enterprise search than simply crawling and indexing content, and as you'll see in this chapter, custom development can create powerful business applications that leverage the capabilities of the platform.

## Components of Enterprise Search

Enterprise search comprises many components—some were mentioned briefly in earlier chapters; others have been specifically designed to provide enterprise-class search functionality and are covered here.

### Architecture

Before we delve into the components that we, as developers, are most likely to use to meet the specific requirements of our application, let's take a brief look at how enterprise search works in SharePoint. Every search solution has three main elements: the front end web server, query architecture, and crawl architecture. In that respect, SharePoint 2010 is not remarkably different from MOSS 2007. However, as you'll see when we drill down a bit, the way in which these three elements are implemented by SharePoint Server 2010 offers a higher degree of flexibility.

The first element in which most of our development work will be done is the *front-end web server*. The web server acts as the presentation layer for our search solution and hosts the pages and controls that will be used to capture queries and display results.

The next element in the solution is the *query architecture*, which consists of one or more query servers, each responsible for directly servicing all or part of a search query. This is the business logic layer of our search solution.

The final element is the *crawl architecture*. While the query architecture is responsible for servicing end user queries, the crawl architecture is responsible for scanning connected data sources and producing indexes of the content found. In addition to producing the index, the crawl architecture also generates a properties database. As you'll see when we get into how queries are executed, there's a big difference between the index file and the property database.

## Enhancements in SharePoint 2010

Within MOSS 2007, although enterprise search was capable of supporting a large corpus and tens of thousands of users, the overall topology suffered a few problems. For example, each shared service provider could use only a single index server. Notwithstanding the hardware requirements for this single server on very large farms, this was a major issue because the index server became a single point of failure. Another major drawback was the physical size of the index files. Although this was somewhat mitigated by using a number of smaller shadow index files, ultimately all the index files had to be merged into a single master file, and the master file had to be present on all query servers in the farm. The physical hardware required to support this was significant.

With SharePoint 2010, these problems have been addressed by subdividing the query architecture and the crawl architecture into a number of smaller, more scalable components. For example, rather than a single index server, SharePoint 2010 introduces the concept of a crawl component. Using crawl components, you can add multiple index servers to a farm, each running one or more crawl components.

## Indexing Components

Now that you understand how an enterprise search solution is implemented using SharePoint Server 2010, let's look at some of the configurable components—starting with how the crawl architecture can be extended by adding indexing components.

### Search Connector Framework

From our perspective as software developers, one of the most significant aspects of the crawl architecture is the Search Connector Framework, the preferred mechanism used by the crawler component when accessing data to be indexed. The Search Connector Framework should be familiar to you at this point in the book, since it's based on Business Connectivity Services (BCS), covered in Chapter 15.

A number of different properties can be attached to Business Data Connectivity (BDC) metadata when you're creating a search connector. At a minimum, however, the following additions need to be made to configure a search connector properly.

First, to make sure that the BDC adaptor is visible in the Search user interface, the ShowInSearchUI property must be set on the LobSystemInstance object.

1. In the BDC Explorer pane, select the LobSystemInstances node for the model, and then click the ellipsis next to Custom Properties in the Properties window, as shown:

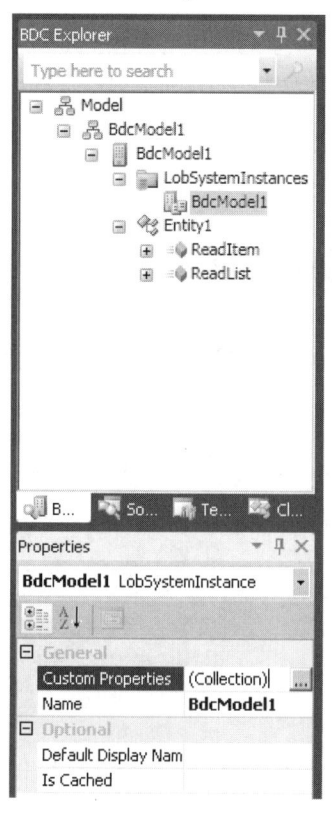

2. In the Property Editor, add a new property named ShowInSearchUI with a Type of System.String and a Value of x, as shown:

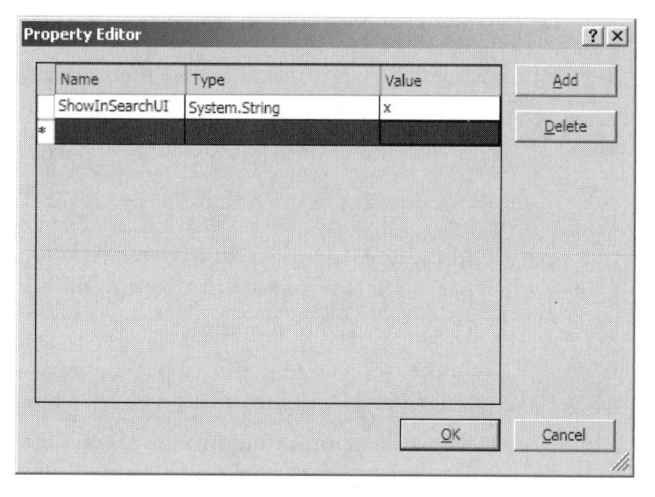

The next property that needs to be added is RootFinder, which is attached to the finder method that will be called to enumerate the items to be crawled. For example, if our search connector were crawling data in a database table, the RootFinder method would return a list of identifiers for all items to be crawled. The crawl process would then make use of the SpecificFinder method to perform the actual crawl of each field in the row.

1. In the BDC Explorer pane, select the ReadList node (or whichever finder method you're planning to use for enumeration), and then click the ellipsis next to Custom Properties in the Properties window.
2. In the Property Editor, add a new property named RootFinder with a Type of System.String and a Value of x:

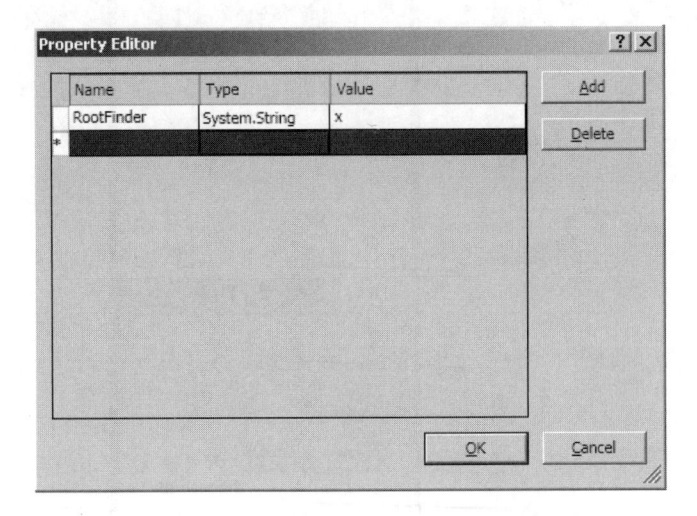

To support incremental crawls, entities should include a LastModifiedTimeStamp column. So that the crawler knows which column is the time stamp, the LastModifiedTimeStampField property should be added to the finder method instance.

1. Select the appropriate finder method instance, and then open the Property Editor.
2. Add a RootFinder property as above, and then add an additional property named LastModifiedTimeStampField with a Type of System.String and a Value of x.

You can then configure a Search Connector for a content source as follows:

1. In Central Administration, navigate to the Search Service Application management page. Select Content Sources from the Crawling menu on the left-hand side.
2. Click New Content Source.
3. In the Add Content Source page, enter a suitable name for the new content source, and then select Line of Business Data from the list of Content Source Type options.
4. Select the appropriate Business Data Catalog Service application, and then select the external data source, as shown:

# CHAPTER 16

# Enterprise Search

When modern computing was still young, the vast majority of processing power was used for generating content—performing calculations, analyzing input, and producing useful output. Today, although a sizeable percentage of processing power is still used in assisting users in producing content in the form of word processing applications and spreadsheet applications, an ever-increasing slice is now used to manage the content being created. In fact, these days, the role of the IT professional is often more about managing user-created content than it is about creating content itself.

This is where SharePoint 2010's *enterprise search* technology enters the picture. Enterprise search is the one feature that delivers immediate business benefit in SharePoint 2010. Organizations have scattered content far and wide, with more and more being created every minute of every day. Enterprise search provides a platform that can crawl and index content from practically any source. After all, a document that nobody can find may as well not exist. Using SharePoint 2010, organizations can easily implement a scalable search portal where users can find the information they need.

Of course, there's much more to enterprise search than simply crawling and indexing content, and as you'll see in this chapter, custom development can create powerful business applications that leverage the capabilities of the platform.

## Components of Enterprise Search

Enterprise search comprises many components—some were mentioned briefly in earlier chapters; others have been specifically designed to provide enterprise-class search functionality and are covered here.

### Architecture

Before we delve into the components that we, as developers, are most likely to use to meet the specific requirements of our application, let's take a brief look at how enterprise search works in SharePoint. Every search solution has three main elements: the front end web server, query architecture, and crawl architecture. In that respect, SharePoint 2010 is not remarkably different from MOSS 2007. However, as you'll see when we drill down a bit, the way in which these three elements are implemented by SharePoint Server 2010 offers a higher degree of flexibility.

The first element in which most of our development work will be done is the *front-end web server*. The web server acts as the presentation layer for our search solution and hosts the pages and controls that will be used to capture queries and display results.

The next element in the solution is the *query architecture*, which consists of one or more query servers, each responsible for directly servicing all or part of a search query. This is the business logic layer of our search solution.

The final element is the *crawl architecture*. While the query architecture is responsible for servicing end user queries, the crawl architecture is responsible for scanning connected data sources and producing indexes of the content found. In addition to producing the index, the crawl architecture also generates a properties database. As you'll see when we get into how queries are executed, there's a big difference between the index file and the property database.

## Enhancements in SharePoint 2010

Within MOSS 2007, although enterprise search was capable of supporting a large corpus and tens of thousands of users, the overall topology suffered a few problems. For example, each shared service provider could use only a single index server. Notwithstanding the hardware requirements for this single server on very large farms, this was a major issue because the index server became a single point of failure. Another major drawback was the physical size of the index files. Although this was somewhat mitigated by using a number of smaller shadow index files, ultimately all the index files had to be merged into a single master file, and the master file had to be present on all query servers in the farm. The physical hardware required to support this was significant.

With SharePoint 2010, these problems have been addressed by subdividing the query architecture and the crawl architecture into a number of smaller, more scalable components. For example, rather than a single index server, SharePoint 2010 introduces the concept of a crawl component. Using crawl components, you can add multiple index servers to a farm, each running one or more crawl components.

## Indexing Components

Now that you understand how an enterprise search solution is implemented using SharePoint Server 2010, let's look at some of the configurable components—starting with how the crawl architecture can be extended by adding indexing components.

### Search Connector Framework

From our perspective as software developers, one of the most significant aspects of the crawl architecture is the Search Connector Framework, the preferred mechanism used by the crawler component when accessing data to be indexed. The Search Connector Framework should be familiar to you at this point in the book, since it's based on Business Connectivity Services (BCS), covered in Chapter 15.

A number of different properties can be attached to Business Data Connectivity (BDC) metadata when you're creating a search connector. At a minimum, however, the following additions need to be made to configure a search connector properly.

Use this page to add a content source.

* Indicates a required field

| Name | Name: * |
|---|---|
| Type a name to describe this content source. | MyExternalDataSource |

| Content Source Type | Select the type of content to be crawled: |
|---|---|
| Select what type of content will be crawled.<br><br>Note: This cannot be changed after this content source is created because other settings depend on it. | ○ SharePoint Sites<br>○ Web Sites<br>○ File Shares<br>○ Exchange Public Folders<br>⦿ Line of Business Data<br>○ Custom Repository |

| External Data Source | Select the Business Data Catalog Service Application: |
|---|---|
| A Line of Business Data content source crawls external data sources defined in an Application Model in a Business Data Catalog Service Application. | Business Data Connectivity |
| Select whether to crawl all external data sources in the Business Data Catalog Service Application, or include only selected external data sources.<br><br>Crawl Rule: To create a crawl rule for an external data source, use the following pattern:<br>bdc3://*ExternalDataSourceName* | ○ Crawl all external data sources in this Business Data Catalog Service Application<br>⦿ Crawl selected external data source<br>☑ BdcModel1 |

## Protocol Handlers and IFilters

In earlier versions of SharePoint, the index server made use of components known as *protocol handlers* to connect to content to be indexed. Although protocol handlers are still used in SharePoint 2010, their inclusion is mainly for backward compatibility. The preferred solution for accessing external content is via the Search Connector Framework. As a result, I won't cover building these components in detail.

> **TIP** In SharePoint 2010, when you're configuring search connectors, the terminology used in the user interface can be confusing. For example, when you're adding a new content source, the options available include Line of Business Data and Custom Repository. It would be reasonable to assume that selecting Custom Repository would be the correct way to use the Search Connector Framework; however, this isn't the case. The Custom Repository option is used to reference custom protocol handlers. To make matters more confusing, the user interface often refers to protocol handlers as "custom connectors." The thing to bear in mind is that the Search Connector Framework is a set of extensions to BCS, and from a user interface perspective, we're still using BCS. As you'll see later, the correct way to use the Search Connector Framework is to select a Content Source Type of Line of Business Data.

## Working with Content Sources

Building on our understanding of how connections are made to index content physically, let's look at what happens to that content as part of the indexing process.

You know that the Search Connector Framework can be used to crawl and index content from a wide variety of sources. Each source is defined as a separate entity within SharePoint known as a *content source*. As well as defining content retrieved via specific connectors, content sources can also be used to subcategorize content within the wider SharePoint *farm*. For example, a farm may use a content source to define a set of data from a particular site collection.

You should be aware that it's impossible to create overlapping content sources. For example, it's impossible to create a content source with a start address of *http://myroot* and then create another content source with a start address of *http://myroot/subsite*.

> **TIP** When configuring a search on larger farms, it's important that you determine which content is most likely to be updated frequently. Since content crawls run on a schedule, it's good practice to split the corpus into a number of smaller content sources. Doing this will allow greater control over how frequently particular content is indexed and therefore how current search results are for that content.

As well as content sources, which define the starting point of any search crawl, SharePoint also allows us to define *crawl rules*. You can use crawl rules to exclude certain files or folders, or to specify that particular credentials should be used when accessing particular files or folders. An important new feature in SharePoint 2010 is the ability to use regular expressions when defining crawl rules.

### Working with Managed Properties

As mentioned earlier, when content is crawled, an index of the content is created along with a property database. Generally speaking, the index contains the main body of the content, whereas the property database contains metadata. So to give an example, when a Word document is crawled, the contents of the document are included in the index, and any properties of the document such as the title, author, or the creation date are added to the property database. The property database contains details of all metadata properties for each item indexed by the crawler process. However, since different items may define the same metadata in different ways, SharePoint incorporated the notion of managed properties.

A *managed property* is a logical grouping of crawled properties from one or more indexed content types. For example, when an Excel spreadsheet is crawled, author metadata will be retrieved and stored in the property database; however, if an MP3 file is crawled, artist metadata will be retrieved. Logically, both artist and author could be grouped into a managed property named Creator, for example. By making the grouping, it becomes possible for you to search multiple content types using a common set of attributes without your having to understand how those attributes map to the underlying metadata of the content.

Mapping crawled properties to managed properties is particularly important when you're indexing SharePoint content, since each column in a list or library is stored as a crawled property. When it comes to properties such as Title or Created By, the mapping is straightforward, since these properties are present on every item and therefore the mapping is simply one-to-one. However, as you create custom content types to accommodate your application data structure, the mapping becomes a bit more involved. Mapping crawled properties to managed properties does not occur automatically. If, for example, you have a list named Product containing a Product Name column and a second list named Orders also containing a column named Product Name, these two columns will not be automatically mapped to a managed property. You would physically need to map both crawled properties to a new managed property.

> **TIP** When using site columns, each instance of the column makes use of the same crawled property. So, in our example, if Product Name was a site column, you'd need to map only one property to your managed property rather than two.

The key thing to be aware of with respect to managed properties versus crawled properties is that only managed properties can be displayed in search results or used for filtering or refining results.

## Working with Scopes

We've covered how content can be split up using content sources and how metadata can be used by created managed properties; let's move on to consider one important use of content sources and managed properties: the creation of scopes. For now let's build up an understanding of what Scopes are and why we might use them.

When a query is executed using the Query Object Model, it's performed against the entire search index. Sometimes this behavior doesn't make sense for a number of reasons: if we already know the type of content that we're looking for, it makes sense to search content of only that type, or if we already know which web site contains the content that we're looking for, it doesn't make sense to search all web sites.

Search scopes allow us to define subsets of the search index based on a series of rules. These rules can include only content from a particular content source, only content where a managed property has a specific value, or only content from a specific URL. Additionally, complex combinations of rules can be created to restrict the scope to the content that is appropriate for our search application. For example, if we were implementing a search feature for retrieving technical specification documents, and we knew that these documents existed only within the engineering department web site, we could define a scope that included only content of type technical specification and included only results from the engineering department content source.

We could refine this example further if necessary. Let's say that some of the technical specifications were flagged as confidential. We could exclude those from search results by creating a managed property that referred to the confidential flag, and then using that managed property in a rule that specifically excluded those documents from the scope. As you can see, by using scopes, you can increase the relevance of search results by restricting the search area to an appropriate subset of the entire index.

## Query Components

As you can imagine, the most important requirement for a search solution is the ability to perform queries. Let's move on to take a look through the various components available to us as developers. As you'll see, SharePoint 2010 delivers a number of interfaces covering a range of scenarios.

### Query Object Model

Enterprise search in SharePoint 2010 provides a Query Object Model that allows developers to use the capabilities of search programmatically within custom applications. The core class of the Query Object Model is the Query abstract class, which has two concrete implementations: the FullTextSqlQuery class, which can be used to issue full-text SQL syntax queries to the search provider, and the KeywordQuery class, which can be used to issue keyword syntax queries. The Query Object Model can be used to query any SharePoint Search application, whether it's a default SharePoint Search provider or a FAST Search for SharePoint provider.

One thing to bear in mind is that SQL syntax queries are supported only when using SharePoint Search. The examples that follow focus on keyword syntax queries.

> **NOTE** For more information on SQL syntax queries, see http://msdn.microsoft.com.

Using the Query Object Model is relatively straightforward, as this example illustrates:

```
static void Main(string[] args)
{
  using (SPSite thisSite = new SPSite("http://localhost"))
  {
    Console.WriteLine("Enter search query");
    String queryText = Console.ReadLine();
    KeywordQuery q = new KeywordQuery(thisSite);
    q.RowLimit = 10;
    q.QueryText = queryText;
    q.ResultTypes = ResultType.RelevantResults;
    ResultTableCollection results = q.Execute();
    ResultTable relevantResults = results[ResultType.RelevantResults];
    Console.ForegroundColor = ConsoleColor.DarkGreen;
    relevantResults.Table.WriteXml(Console.Out);
    Console.ReadLine();
  }
}
```

Notice a few interesting things about this code sample. First, take a look at the **ResultTableCollection** object that's returned by the **Execute** method. The **ResultsTableCollection** is an **IEnumerable** collection of **ResultTable** objects. Each query can therefore return multiple result sets as defined by the **ResultTypes** property of the **Query** class. In this code sample, only **RelevantResults** are selected, but multiple result sets can be retrieved by performing a bitwise combination of two or more **ResultType** enumerations, as shown:

```
q.ResultTypes = ResultType.RelevantResults & ResultType.HighConfidenceResults;

ResultTableCollection results = q.Execute();

ResultTable relevantResults = results[ResultType.RelevantResults];
ResultTable hiConfidenceResults = results[ResultType.HighConfidenceResults];
```

**Result Types Returned by the Query Object Model** Let's take a look at the various types of results that can be included in the ResultTableCollection:

- **None** The query is performed but no results are returned.
- **RelevantResults** A result set containing the main search results from the content index matching the search query is returned.
- **SpecialTermResults** A result set containing best bet results matching the search query is returned. Best Bet results are manually configured mappings between keywords and specific results. For example, users may frequently search for "permission" to find documentation on how to obtain permissions for a particular resource. Since many documents may contain the word "permission," it may not be

easy to find the relevant document. Best Bets allow the administrator to specify that a particular document is always returned in the search results for a particular keyword.

- **HighConfidenceResults**  High-confidence results are generated when the keywords entered exactly match items in the search index.
- **DefinitionResults**  A result set containing definitions for keywords matching the search query is returned.
- **VisualBestBetsResults**  A result set containing Visual Best Bets matching the search query is returned. Visual Best Bets work like Best Bet results, except that an image is displayed rather than a text result. Visual Best Bets are available only when FAST Search is configured.
- **RefinementResults**  A result set containing refined results matching the search query is returned. Refinements are a new addition in SharePoint 2010 and make use of property filters to refine search results further. The important difference in SharePoint 2010 is that refinements now have a specific user interface, whereas previously property filters had to be included as part of the search query. You'll see some examples of this later in the chapter.

## Common Query Language

One of the benefits of the Query Object Model is the availability of a common query language that works across all services supported by the Query Object Model. In practice, two query languages are available to the Query Object Model, keyword syntax and SQL syntax, although only keyword syntax is supported across all services.

Keyword syntax is relatively straightforward and will be familiar to users of any search engine. In its simplest form, a query consists of one or more keywords. For example, to return all documents containing the words "SharePoint" or "Search," a user would enter this:

```
sharepoint search
```

If the results contained links pertaining to "MOSS 2007", the user could exclude these results by changing the query to this:

```
sharepoint search -"MOSS 2007"
```

If the result set contained documents relating to Google search, for example, the user could alter the query to return only documents containing the words "SharePoint" and "search" by changing the query like so:

```
+sharepoint +search -"MOSS 2007"
```

As you can see, basic keyword syntax is pretty intuitive.

**Using Property Filters**  As mentioned, when crawling content, an index and a property database are created. From the database of crawled properties, you can create managed properties, which, as you discovered earlier, are logical groupings of crawled properties. One of the main uses of managed properties is for filtering search results. As well as the basic keyword syntax, the common query language allows you to use property filters to return only results in which a managed property is set to a particular value.

So to pick up on the earlier example, if you wanted to return only Word documents matching your keywords, the query could be changed to this:

```
+sharepoint +search -"MOSS 2007" (FileExtension="doc" OR FileExtension="docx")
```

This example uses the **FileExtension** managed property to filter the result set. One important thing to note about property filters is that they apply to the entire result set. So, referring back to the original keyword syntax example, this query

```
sharepoint search
```

returns all results matching either "sharepoint" or "search". However, if the Word document property filter is applied, here's how it would look:

```
sharepoint search (FileExtension="doc" OR FileExtension="docx")
```

You might expect, given the syntax of keyword queries, that this query would return results matching "SharePoint" or "search", or having a **FileExtension** of doc or docx. Instead, the query actually returns results containing either "SharePoint" or "search" where the **FileExtension** is doc or docx. Effectively, the property filter is applied to the result set of the keyword query.

There are many default managed properties in SharePoint 2010 that allow search results to be filtered using metadata such as CreatedBy, ContentType, Department, or even things like PictureHeight. By using these built-in properties and defining domain-specific properties, you can easily build targeted search queries.

## Federation Object Model

Earlier I discussed how the query architecture is responsible for servicing end-user queries. As mentioned, this is done using one or more query components, right? Usually yes, but I have to admit that I wasn't telling the whole truth. It is true to say that queries performed against content that's crawled by SharePoint are serviced via query components. However, SharePoint 2010 also incorporates the concept of *federation*, meaning that search queries can be serviced directly by external search providers.

Strictly speaking, the functionality of the Federation Object Model is implemented on the web front end, but logically it dictates how queries are performed and therefore I've listed it as a query component. The Federation Object Model provides a layer of abstraction between the front-end web parts, used to process search queries, and the physical destination of the query server. In plain English, this means that the front-end web parts can be used to query and retrieve results from any search engine that is supported by the Federation Object Model. For example, it's possible to use the out-of-the-box search web parts to perform queries against the product catalog at Amazon.com. To take the example even further, it's possible to perform queries against the Amazon.com product catalog as well as the content index from our SharePoint farm and return the highlights of the combined result set in a single web part. Figure 16-1 illustrates where the Federation Object Model sits relative to other components.

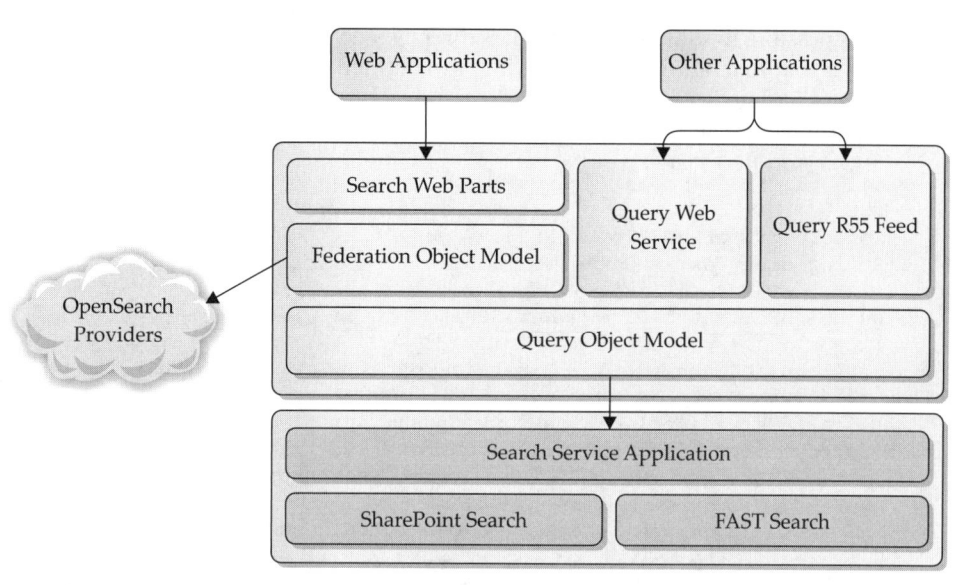

**Figure 16-1** The Federation Object Model relative to other search components

As illustrated, the Federation Object Model exists as an abstraction layer between web parts that implement search functionality and the Query Object Model. As you've seen, the Query Object Model provides a standard mechanism for communicating with search service applications within SharePoint. The Federation Object Model takes this abstraction a step further by allowing external search engines to be used to service search queries.

Out of the box, SharePoint 2010 allows you to connect to three types of locations:

- **SharePoint Search**   The default search provider that's installed with SharePoint.
- **FAST Search**   An add-in search provider that enhances the capabilities of SharePoint Search.
- **OpenSearch 1.0/1.1**   This is where the real power of federated search comes in. OpenSearch is an open standard for communicating with search engines. The standard was originally proposed by Amazon.com but is now used by hundreds of search engines under the terms of a creative commons license. By using OpenSearch, you can query and retrieve results from practically every major search engine. As an aside, OpenSearch is used in Internet Explorer 8 to add search providers to the Instant Search list.

As discussed earlier, the Query Object Model is a common interface for all SharePoint Search applications. Although the Federation Object Model makes use of distinct runtime classes for SharePoint Search and FAST Search, namely the **FASTSearchRuntime** class and the **SharePointSearchRuntime** class, both of these classes use the Query Object Model to communicate with the underlying search application.

It's possible to use the runtime class directly from within our code. One of the benefits of this is that federation location settings are defined at the search service application level and these settings are used automatically by the runtime. This is much simpler than manually configuring each property when using the Query Object Model.

```
static void Main(string[] args)
{
    Console.WriteLine("Enter search query");
    String queryText = Console.ReadLine();

    using (SPSite thisSite = new SPSite("http://localhost"))
    {
        SPServiceContext ctx = SPServiceContext.GetContext(thisSite);

        SearchServiceApplicationProxy proxy;
        proxy= SearchServiceApplicationProxy.GetProxy(ctx) as
                                    SearchServiceApplicationProxy;

        Location sp = new Location("LocalSearchIndex", proxy);

        SharePointSearchRuntime runtime = new SharePointSearchRuntime();
        runtime.Location = sp;
        Console.Write(runtime.SendRequest(queryText).InnerXml);
    }
}
```

## Query Web Service

As shown in Figure 16-1, the Query Web Service communicates with SharePoint Search via the Query Object Model. As a result of this, search federation functionality is not available when issuing queries via web service.

```
static void Main(string[] args)
{
    DoSearch("sharepoint", "http://localhost/sites/Chapter16/_vti_bin/search.asmx");
    Console.ReadLine();
}

static void DoSearch(string query, string url)
{
    EndpointAddress address = new EndpointAddress(url);
    SPSearchWebservice.QueryServiceSoapClient proxy = new
                              SPSearchWebservice.QueryServiceSoapClient();
    proxy.Endpoint.Address = address;
    proxy.ClientCredentials.Windows.AllowedImpersonationLevel =
                                TokenImpersonationLevel.Impersonation;

    string myQueryXml = "<QueryPacket><Query><Context><QueryText type=\"STRING\">" +
                    query +
                    "</QueryText></Context></Query></QueryPacket>";

    string result=proxy.Query(myQueryXml);

    Console.Write(result);
}
```

## Query RSS API

As well as the Query Web Service, SharePoint 2010 also provides a Really Simple Syndication (RSS) application programming interface (API) for retrieving search results. Again, since the RSS API uses the Query Object Model, federation functionality is not available.

Using the RSS API is relatively straightforward. It's simply a case of building a query string that contains the appropriate search criteria. Following are the main values for the query string:

- **k** The search query text (that is, `+sharepoint +search (FileExtension=docx)`)
- **s** The search scope to use (that is, All Sites)
- **start** The number of the first result to return (that is, 10)

The RSS API can be accessed at http://<SiteUrl>/_layouts/srchrss.aspx. For example, the following URL can be used to create an RSS feed for results matching "sharepoint" and "search":

```
http://<SiteUrl>/_layouts/srchrss.aspx?k=%2Bsharepoint%20%2Bsearch&s=All%20Sites
```

## Custom Ranking Model

When determining the order of search results, SharePoint uses two types of ranking: *query-dependent ranking*, also known as *dynamic ranking*, and *query-independent ranking*, also known as *static ranking*. A full discussion on the nuances of these ranking models is outside the scope of this book. However, one thing that does merit some discussion is the ability to use custom ranking models in SharePoint 2010.

In MOSS 2007, it was possible to alter the ranking model using the Search Administration Object Model. In effect, this meant altering the weights for particular managed properties in the case of query-dependent ranking. The problem with this approach was two-fold: it was possible to make changes only programmatically, and it applied across the board to all searches performed using a particular Shared Service Provider.

With SharePoint 2010, it's now possible to create custom ranking models using XML and apply them on an individual query basis. For example, when using the Core Results Web Part, setting the DefaultRankingModelId to the identifier for a custom ranking model will apply that model to all results rendered in the web part.

## Front-End Components

To make it quick and easy to generate a search user interface, SharePoint 2010 provides a number of web parts out of the box. All of the web parts target the Federation Object Model and therefore support many different types of search results.

### Capturing Search Queries

The following web parts provide a user interface that allows the user to build search queries:

- **SearchBoxEx** This web part provides a basic search query interface. It provides a scopes drop-down and a textbox for entering keywords. A link can also be provided to a page containing an AdvancedSearchBox web part.

- **AdvancedSearchBox**   This web part expands on the user interface of the SearchBoxEx web part to allow the user to create complex queries by selecting from a range of options, including language and result type. The AdvancedSearchBox web part also supports the addition of property filters.

Both query web parts work in a similar fashion—they build up a query string that is then used when redirecting to a results page.

## Displaying Search Results

Earlier we looked at the Query Object Model and the various types of results that are returned. The main factor in deciding which web part to use to display search results is the type of results to be displayed and the default formatting of the results. The following web parts can be used to display search results:

- **CoreResultsWebPart**   Used to render results of type RelevantResults.
- **FederatedResultsWebPart**   Used to render results of type RelevantResults. The key difference between the FederatedResultsWebPart and the CoreResultsWebPart is that results in the latter can be paged by including a SearchPagingWebPart on the page. Also, the FederatedResultsWebPart requires that a location is specified, whereas, to provide backward compatibility, the CoreResultsWebPart automatically uses the default search provider defined by the Search Service Application.
- **PeopleCoreResultsWebPart**   Used to render the results of people searches. Derived from the CoreResultsWebPart, results are displayed in a specific format and have different sort options more appropriate to a people search.
- **TopFederatedResultsWebPart**   Returns an aggregated set of top results from a number of federated locations.
- **VisualBestBetWebPart**   Displays results of type VisualBestBets. As described earlier, Visual Best Bets are a feature of FAST Search, and although this web part can be added to sites without FAST Search enabled, no results will be displayed.
- **HighConfidenceWebPart**   Displays results of type HighConfidenceResults as well as SpecialTermResults.
- **SearchStatsWebPart**   Displays information about the last query executed in the CoreResultsWebPart.
- **SearchSummaryWebPart**   Includes a summary of the search query. In effect this implements "Did you mean" functionality, whereby if you start entering a keyword, suggested keywords will be shown that will generate more results.
- **SearchPagingWebPart**   Supports paging of the results displayed in a CoreResultsWebPart.

## Shared Query Manager

One significant change between MOSS 2007 and SharePoint 2010 is in the way search web parts are implemented. With SharePoint 2010, each page containing search web parts has a single instance of the **SharedQueryManager** object that is shared between all web parts on the page. Through this object we can easily create custom web parts that can hook into the query pipeline at a few different points.

The following code snippet shows how to data bind search results to a repeater control rather than using the traditional XSLT-based rendering approach. Such a technique is useful if controls are required within search results that have post-back functionality. For example, in a shopping cart application, an Add to Basket button may be required.

```
using System;
using System.Web.UI;
using Microsoft.Office.Server.Search.Query;
using Microsoft.Office.Server.Search.WebControls;

namespace RefinerWebPart.MySearchWebPart
{
  public partial class MySearchWebPartUserControl : UserControl
  {

    private QueryManager _manager;

    protected override void OnInit(EventArgs e)
    {
      _manager = SharedQueryManager.GetInstance(this.Page).QueryManager;
    }

    protected void Page_Load(object sender, EventArgs e)
    {
      if (!this.IsPostBack)
      {
        LocationList list = _manager[0];
        Location loc = list[0];
        Repeater1.DataSource= loc.GetResults(_manager);
        Repeater1.DataBind();
      }
    }
  }
}
```

## Refining Search Results

The RefinementWebPart can be used to generate a series of refinement filters automatically for a given result set. Refinements are basically property filters that are automatically derived from a result set. So, for example, if a result set contains results of different types such as web pages and Word documents, the refinement web part will show refinement option for web pages or Word documents.

Let's look at how the RefinementWebPart works in a bit more detail since a good understanding of the inner workings will make it easier for you to configure.

From the following class diagram, you can see that a number of objects are involved in rendering the RefinementWebPart. The first object to consider is the RefinementManager, the engine that processes the configuration for the web part. Refinement configuration can be done at the web part level, by changing the value of the Filter Category Definition property.

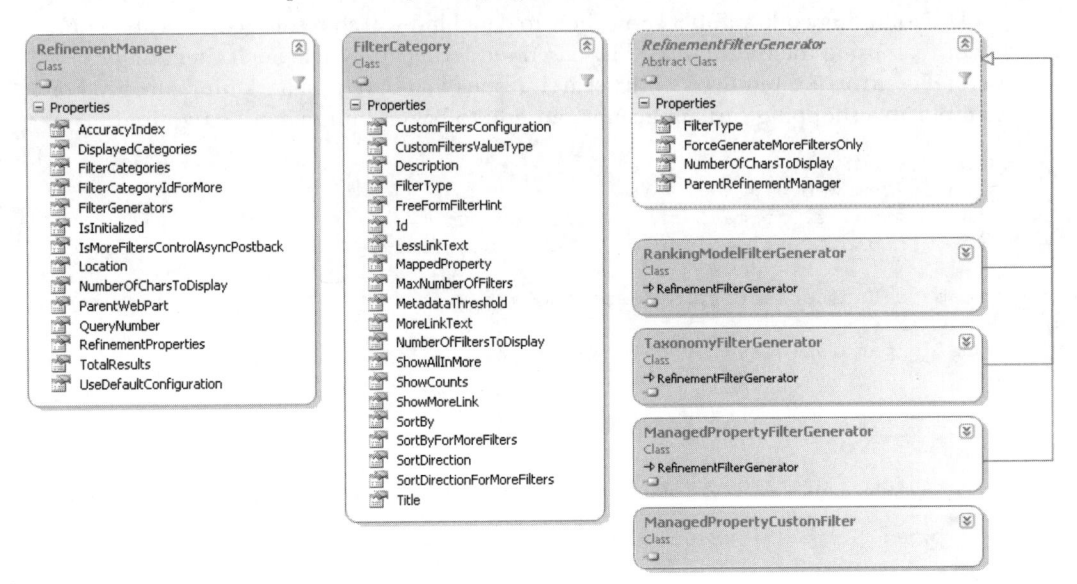

**RefinementManager**
Class
- Properties
  - AccuracyIndex
  - DisplayedCategories
  - FilterCategories
  - FilterCategoryIdForMore
  - FilterGenerators
  - IsInitialized
  - IsMoreFiltersControlAsyncPostback
  - Location
  - NumberOfCharsToDisplay
  - ParentWebPart
  - QueryNumber
  - RefinementProperties
  - TotalResults
  - UseDefaultConfiguration

**FilterCategory**
Class
- Properties
  - CustomFiltersConfiguration
  - CustomFiltersValueType
  - Description
  - FilterType
  - FreeFormFilterHint
  - Id
  - LessLinkText
  - MappedProperty
  - MaxNumberOfFilters
  - MetadataThreshold
  - MoreLinkText
  - NumberOfFiltersToDisplay
  - ShowAllInMore
  - ShowCounts
  - ShowMoreLink
  - SortBy
  - SortByForMoreFilters
  - SortDirection
  - SortDirectionForMoreFilters
  - Title

**RefinementFilterGenerator**
Abstract Class
- Properties
  - FilterType
  - ForceGenerateMoreFiltersOnly
  - NumberOfCharsToDisplay
  - ParentRefinementManager

**RankingModelFilterGenerator**
Class
→ RefinementFilterGenerator

**TaxonomyFilterGenerator**
Class
→ RefinementFilterGenerator

**ManagedPropertyFilterGenerator**
Class
→ RefinementFilterGenerator

**ManagedPropertyCustomFilter**
Class

The Filter Category Definition property accepts XML and typically will have the following structure:

```
<FilterCategories>
  <Category>
    <CustomFilters>
      <CustomFilter>
        <OriginalValue></OriginalValue>
        ....
      </CustomFilter>
      ....
    </CustomFilters>
  </Category>
  ....
</FilterCategories>
```

Each **Category** element is represented by the **FilterCategory** class. When the control is rendered, a **Category** is displayed as a section title in the refinement panel. The **FilterCategory** class defines various properties for controlling the presentation of the section title, such as the text to be displayed and the maximum number of child elements to display. Probably the most important property of the **FilterCategory** class is the **FilterType**; this property contains the type name of a class derived from **RefinementFilterGenerator** that is used to generate a list of child elements to appear within the section. So, for example, if the section was titled Modified

Date, the child elements would probably be a list of dates. To generate these dates from the result set, a **ManagedPropertyFilterGenerator** is used. Effectively the filter generator extracts the values of a particular managed property from the query result set and displays the distinct values in the refinement control.

```
Result Type
Any Result Type
Webpage
Excel

Site
Any Site
win-hs8gzgtapbh

Author
Any Author
win-hs8gzgtapbh\cha...

Modified Date
Any Modified Date
Past 24 Hours
Past Month

Tags
Any Tags
sample
```

Because managed properties may have a wide range of values, the **ManagedPropertyFilterGenerator** allows results to be further grouped before displaying them by introducing an additional **ManagedPropertyCustomFilter** class. So continuing with our Modified Date example, if we wanted to show a refinement for all documents modified within the past 24 hours rather than a list of the exact times of each modification, we could use a **ManagedPropertyCustomFilter** class configured to show results only within the past day. Here's a typical example of custom filter configuration:

```
<CustomFilters MappingType="RangeMapping" DataType="Date"
ValueReference="Relative" ShowAllInMore="False">
  <CustomFilter CustomValue="Past 24 Hours">
    <OriginalValue>-1..</OriginalValue>
  </CustomFilter>
```

```
  <CustomFilter CustomValue="Past Week">
    <OriginalValue>-7..</OriginalValue>
  </CustomFilter>
  <CustomFilter CustomValue="Past Month">
    <OriginalValue>-30..</OriginalValue>
  </CustomFilter>
  <CustomFilter CustomValue="Past Six Months">
    <OriginalValue>-183..</OriginalValue>
  </CustomFilter>
  <CustomFilter CustomValue="Past Year">
    <OriginalValue>-365..</OriginalValue>
  </CustomFilter>
  <CustomFilter CustomValue="Earlier">
    <OriginalValue>..-365</OriginalValue>
  </CustomFilter>
</CustomFilters>
```

## Custom Refinement Controls

We've looked at the out-of-the-box refinement web part; and you should be able to see how it can be easily configured to generate refinement options automatically using XML. However, with SharePoint 2010, we can take the concept of refinement a step further and create our own refinement controls. The **RefinementManager** object is shared between all web parts on a page. This means that we can create a web part that picks up a reference to this object and uses it for providing further data visualization support to refinement data.

The following code sample generates a simple web part that renders a pie chart with slices for each type of document returned in the search results. A pie chart is shown in the illustration that follows the code sample.

```
using System;
using System.ComponentModel;
using System.Linq;
using System.Web.UI.DataVisualization.Charting;
using System.Web.UI.WebControls.WebParts;
using System.Xml;
using System.Xml.Linq;
using Microsoft.Office.Server.Search.WebControls;

namespace RefinerWebPart.VisualWebPart1
{
  [ToolboxItemAttribute(false)]
  public class MyWebPart : WebPart
  {
    private Microsoft.Office.Server.WebControls.Chart _chart;
    protected override void CreateChildControls()
    {
      _chart = new Microsoft.Office.Server.WebControls.Chart();
```

```
            _chart.Width = 120;
            _chart.Height = 120;

        ChartArea area = new ChartArea("File Types");

            _chart.ChartAreas.Add(area);
            _chart.EnableViewState = true;
        Controls.Add(_chart);

    }

    protected override void OnPreRender(EventArgs e)
    {
      RefinementManager mgr = RefinementManager.GetInstance(this.Page);

        XmlDocument refinements = mgr.GetRefinementXml();
        if (refinements != null)
        {
          Series theSeries = new Series();
          theSeries.ChartType = SeriesChartType.Pie;

          XDocument doc = XDocument.Parse(refinements.OuterXml);

            var values = from documentTypes in doc.Descendants("Filter")
                         where documentTypes.Parent.Parent. →
Attribute("ManagedProperty").Value == "FileExtension"
                         && documentTypes.Element("Count").Value != "0"
                         && documentTypes.Element("Count").Value != string.Empty
                         select new
                         {
                            Name = documentTypes.Element("Value").Value,
                            Count = documentTypes.Element("Count").Value,
                            Url = documentTypes.Element("Url").Value
                         };

            foreach (var docType in values)
            {
              int point = theSeries.Points.AddY(docType.Count);
              theSeries.Points[point].Label = docType.Name;
              theSeries.Points[point].Url = docType.Url;
            }

            if (theSeries.Points.Count > 0)
              _chart.Series.Add(theSeries);
        }
      }
    }
  }
}
```

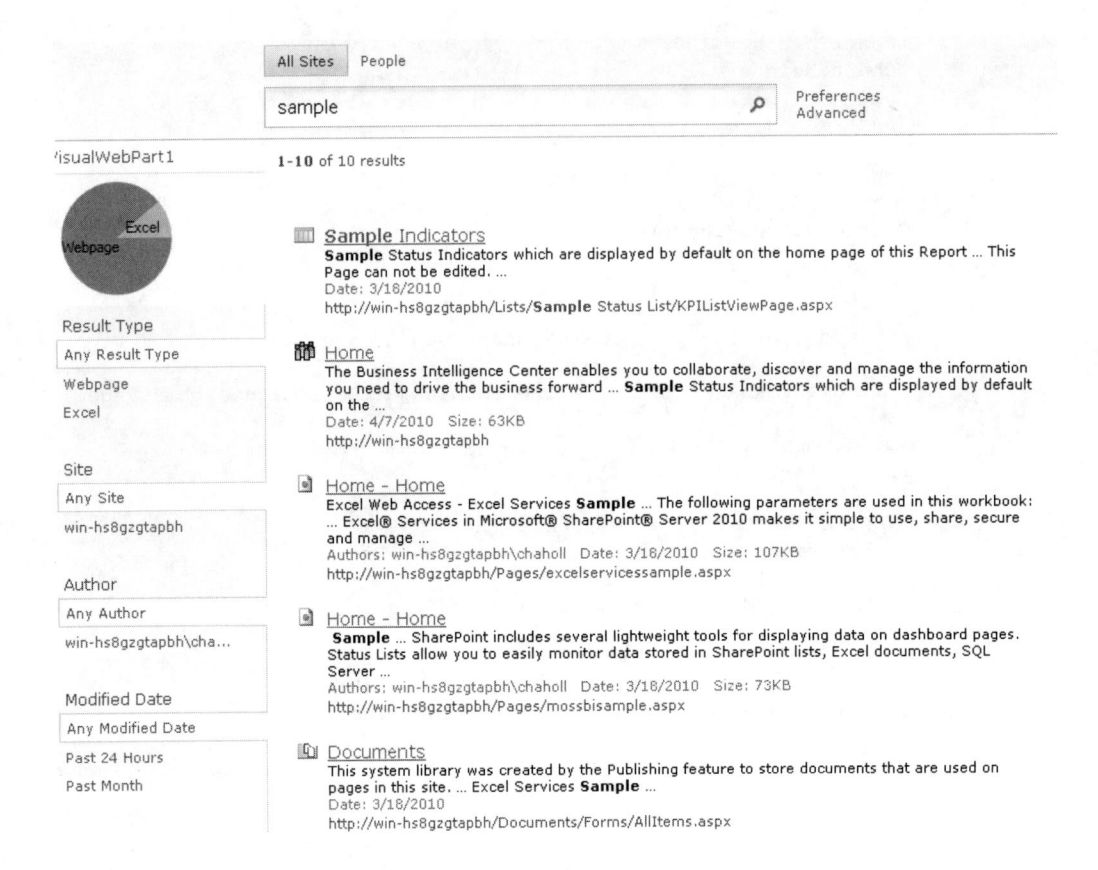

## Summary

In this chapter, we looked at how enterprise search works in SharePoint 2010. We've also looked at the rich object models that are available to us as developers that allow us to leverage the powerful capabilities of the platform.

# CHAPTER 17
# User Profiles and Social Data

In the beginning, there was Hypertext Markup Language (HTML), a language that allowed anybody with a text editor to create pages and post them on the Internet for everyone to see. Back then, the Internet was all about finding information. Surfing the Web, as it came to be known, was a pretty solitary pursuit. Fast-forward 20 years and things have changed dramatically. With social computing giants such as Facebook, MySpace, and Twitter, the Internet is no longer just a vast electronic library; it has become a communications platform allowing for rich social interactions with contacts the world over.

Many organizations, aware of the growing use of social computing sites, seek to block access to such sites because they believe that employee productivity will be affected as employees are distracted from important work tasks. Although there may be a case for this argument, a flip side might not be so apparent. Social computing, by its very nature, is about people, and every organization is reliant on one thing above all else: customers. By blocking access to social computing sites, an organization is missing the opportunity to communicate with customers to understand how they feel about its products and services. If an angry mob on Facebook is cursing your company's latest product, surely it's better to know about it. These people won't take the time to call to tell you that the power light on your latest electronic gizmo is irritatingly bright; they'll simply take their business elsewhere. Is having access to this kind of information really a distraction from more important tasks?

The social computing phenomenon has taken over the Internet for one simple reason: it works—not just as a tool for sharing holiday snaps and personal gossip, but as a means of identifying and accessing a community of experts in any given field and getting answers to questions that would otherwise be impossible to answer. No organization can hire every smart person in a given field, but social computing allows organizations to tap into the skills of these people as and when required.

So what's this got to do with SharePoint 2010? Setting aside the question of whether organizations should allow access to public social networking sites, I'm sure we can all agree that social computing is an effective way to share knowledge and to identify and communicate with specialists in a given field. Such capabilities are just as useful within an organization as they are outside. Everybody has a unique set of skills and interests that often stretch far beyond their job description, but this knowledge goes untapped because it can't be identified.

SharePoint 2010 offers a number of features to allow users to build and manage their own personal profiles. User profiles are accessible throughout an organization and make it possible to identify users with particular skills or interests. Blogs and wikis make it possible for users to create and collaborate on content.

In an age in which products and services have become increasingly commoditized, the key to building and maintaining competitive advantage is organizational intelligence. Social computing is a viable answer. In this chapter, you'll see how this thread is woven into the fabric of the SharePoint 2010 platform.

## Folksonomies, Taxonomies, Tagging, and Rating

When it comes to structuring information, you can employ one of two approaches: You can either organize the information within a well-defined and widely understood hierarchical structure so that users know where to look for something, or you can build an index that can be scanned to find relevant content.

There are pros and cons to both approaches. In the hierarchical approach, content creators must understand and adhere strictly to the hierarchy; changing the structure over time causes confusion. In the indexed approach, the usefulness of the index will vary depending on the context of the searcher. For example, if a collection of sales invoices are indexed by date, but the searcher wants to retrieve all invoices for a particular customer, the index won't be much help.

In the past, SharePoint has adopted a hierarchical approach to information architecture. Recognizing that such an approach doesn't address every requirement, search functionality has traditionally picked up the slack. However, this combination of approaches doesn't address the biggest downsides of both techniques: rigid hierarchies offer no flexibility and deviation causes confusion, whereas an index that is useful to a broad audience cannot truly take searcher context into account. Useful search results are lost in a deluge of irrelevant matches.

With SharePoint 2010, in addition to the traditional approaches to managing content, the power of social computing has been leveraged in the form of *tagging* and *rating*. Rating will be familiar to anyone who's used Amazon or eBay: users have the option to rate content. Consolidated ratings are then visible to other users of the content, and over time these ratings become an indicator of the content's usefulness. Such ratings can then be used in conjunction with an index to rank useful content more prominently within search results.

While the rating approach works well, it doesn't address the issues of relevance and searcher context. This is where tagging comes in. Each page in SharePoint 2010 has a Tags & Notes button in the upper-right corner, as shown next. Users can click this button to add their own tags to each page. These tags are then shown in the user's profile page and can be used in search results to find content.

In addition to allowing user-defined tags, SharePoint 2010 also provides a Managed Metadata column that can be added to lists and libraries. The Managed Metadata column allows users to select from a collection of predefined tags. (The Managed Metadata column is covered in more detail in Chapter 15.)

You know that there are two distinct approaches to tagging content: administrator-defined and user-defined. After content is tagged using administrator-defined terms, the content can be organized into a taxonomy. Generally speaking, taxonomy is a well-defined system of classification, and it's a word of which most of us are aware.

So what is folksonomy? Coined by information architecture guru Thomas Vander Wal, a *folksonomy* is a system of classification based on the collaborative collection of keywords attached to documents. As more users attach their own specific tags to a document, more and more contexts can be taken into account when classifying the content. Incorporating this context into search results and other features makes it easier for users to find what they are looking for, and at the end of the day, that is the purpose of any classification system.

In a folksonomy, as users view content, they do so from their own perspective, and as a result the tags they attach are unique to their perspective. For example, a document may contain financial forecasts for sales of a particular product. Someone viewing the document from a financial perspective may tag the document "Q3 Forecast," whereas someone viewing the document from a marketing perspective may tag the document "Widget Sales Projections." These are pretty obvious examples, but what about somebody viewing the document from a corporate communications perspective? They may be more interested in the layout of the document than the actual content and may tag the document "Corporate Logo."

# User Profile Service Application

As mentioned, users of the SharePoint 2010 platform can create and use their own user profiles. Although the primary interface for managing these profiles at the user level is the My Sites site collection, the actual user profile content is maintained and managed by the User Profile Service application. As well as storing user profile information, the User Profile Service application provides a number of additional features that enable social computing on SharePoint 2010.

## Synchronization

SharePoint 2010 is an enterprise product that's designed to be installed in organizations with an existing infrastructure for supporting many users. One common feature of such an infrastructure is the presence of a user database. In the case of the Windows platform, such a user database is provided by Active Directory; if the organization is using a Sun-based infrastructure, the user database may exist as a Sun ONE LDAP (Lightweight Directory Access Protocol) server.

One thing that all user database implementations have in common is that they contain information on users, and it is likely that the same user accounts will be used to access content within a SharePoint farm. Rather than duplicating user information between the user database and SharePoint, the User Profile Service provides full two-way synchronization capabilities that allow user information to be synchronized automatically between systems.

## User Properties

Active Directory and its LDAP counterparts from other vendors provide a user database that can be extended to include additional information. Custom fields can be added to user accounts, which can then be synchronized with SharePoint. However, the synchronization process is not limited to a single data source. User profiles in SharePoint can include user properties from a number of different data sources. For example, while data such as username, first name, and last name will most likely come from an LDAP system, other properties such as past projects or cost center will likely come from a line-of-business application. By making use of Business Connectivity Services (covered in Chapter 15), the User Profile Service can import data from practically any data source and include it within a user profile.

User properties can be added using code, as this snippet shows:

```
void AddUserProperty(string siteUrl)
    {
      using (SPSite site = new SPSite(siteUrl))
      {
        SPServiceContext ctx = SPServiceContext.GetContext(site);

        UserProfileConfigManager mgr = new UserProfileConfigManager(ctx);
        UserProfileManager upm = new UserProfileManager(ctx);
        ProfilePropertyManager ppm = mgr.ProfilePropertyManager;

        //Create Core property
        CorePropertyManager cpm = ppm.GetCoreProperties();
        CoreProperty p = cpm.Create(false);
        p.Name = "MyName";
        p.Type = "string";
        p.Length = 50;
        p.DisplayName = "MyDisplayName";
        cpm.Add(p);

        //Create ProfileType property
        ProfileTypePropertyManager ptpm = →
ppm.GetProfileTypeProperties(ProfileType.User);
        ProfileTypeProperty pt = ptpm.Create(p);
        pt.IsVisibleOnEditor = true;
        ptpm.Add(pt);

        //Create ProfileSubType property
        ProfileSubtypePropertyManager pspm = →
upm.DefaultProfileSubtypeProperties;
        ProfileSubtypeProperty pst = pspm.Create(pt);
        pst.DefaultPrivacy = Privacy.Public;
```

```
        pspm.Add(pst);
    }
}
```

Notice a few things about this code. At first glance, it may seem that we're adding the same property many times: first, using the **CorePropertyManager**, then with the **ProfileTypePropertyManager**, and finally with the **ProfileSubtypePropertyManager**. In fact, user properties are multi-layered, and each layer is managed using its own object. The following class diagram shows the objects involved.

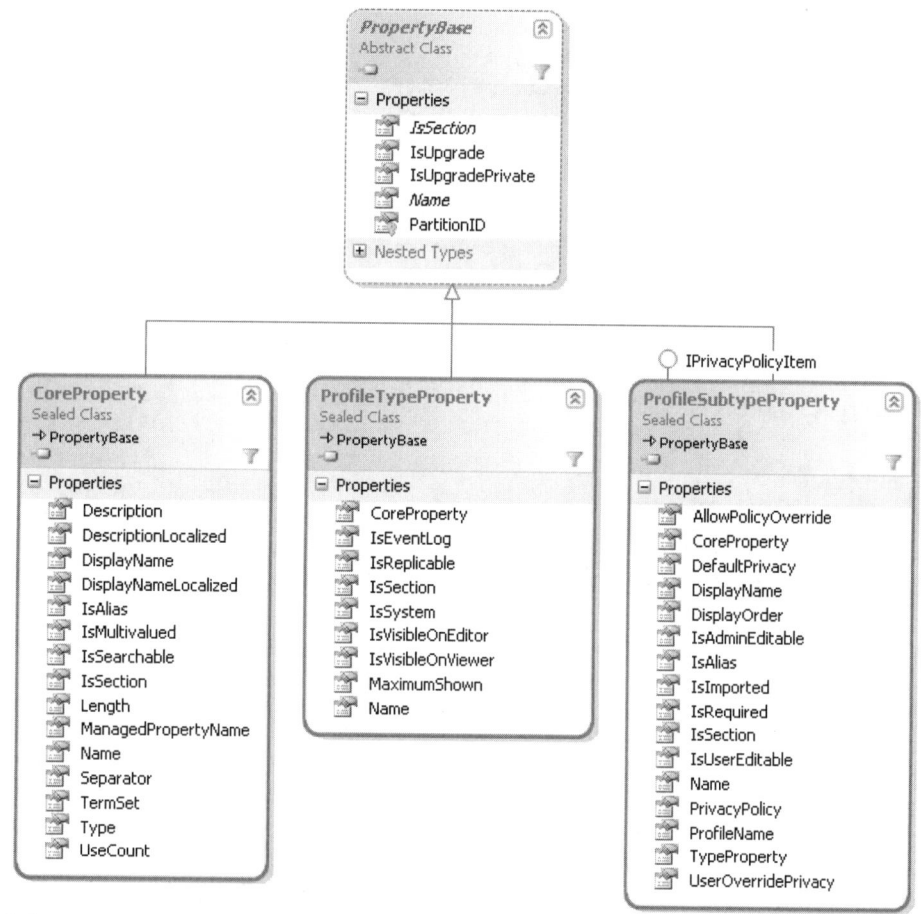

## Subtypes

Subtypes are an interesting addition in SharePoint 2010. They allow user profiles to be grouped. For example, within an organization, not all users may use a particular line-of-business application, and for those users, it doesn't make sense to include data from that application within the user's profile (since it would be blank anyway). By creating a subtype for users of the line-of-business application, user properties from the application can be added only to members of the subtype.

The following code shows how to add profile subtypes:

```
void AddProfileSubtype(string siteUrl, string name,string description)
    {
      using (SPSite site = new SPSite(siteUrl))
      {
        //Get the manager object
        SPServiceContext ctx = SPServiceContext.GetContext(site);
        ProfileSubtypeManager mgr  = ProfileSubtypeManager.Get(ctx);

        //Add a new user subtype
        ProfileSubtype newSubtype = mgr.CreateSubtype(name,
                                                     description,
                                                     ProfileType.User);
        //list the subtypes
        Console.WriteLine("SubTypeID\tName\t\tDisplayName");
        Console.WriteLine(new string('=',60));
        foreach (ProfileSubtype subType in →
mgr.GetSubtypesForProfileType(ProfileType.User))
        {
            Console.WriteLine ("{0}\t\t{1}\t{2}",subType.SubtypeID, →
subType.Name,
                                                      subType.DisplayName);

        }
        //delete the new type
        newSubtype.Delete();
      }
    }
```

## Audiences

Audiences are a useful feature introduced in SharePoint 2007. When it comes to building content management systems, or indeed any system for presenting information to end users, it's important that you display the right information to the right users. On the surface, this may seem like a job for application security—after all, security is partly about determining whether a user is authorized to perform a particular action.

In some circumstances, this is the case; however, consider the following scenario: A company provides an intranet application that displays relevant data and links to commonly used applications. Users in one department are likely to have requirements different from users in another. Both groups of users have access to all of the information, but certain items are more relevant to each group and should therefore be featured on the intranet site. Clearly, this is not a security requirement, because both groups are authorized to view all content. It's more of a personalization requirement, and this is where audiences come in useful. By applying criteria to user properties, audiences can be easily compiled and used for personalizing content. For example, to pick up on our line-of-business subtype, all users who have a particular cost center code can be grouped into a single audience. Content related to that cost center can then be displayed where appropriate.

## Organizations

Although user profiles can contain properties that define where a specific user sits within an organizational hierarchy, sometimes it's more useful to know how an organization is structured at a higher level. For example, if a user reports to a marketing manager, it's reasonable to assume that the user works within the marketing organization. However, if you're looking for information in the marketing organization itself, this information doesn't help you.

If, however, the marketing organization has its own profile, you can easily locate the information that you need and understand how the marketing organization fits within the wider enterprise structure. Organization profiles, new in SharePoint 2010, can also use custom properties and subtypes in the same way as user profiles.

Adding properties to organization profiles is similar to adding properties to user profiles—the main difference is the manager objects that are used. Here's an example:

```
void AddOrganizationProperty(string siteUrl)
    {
      using (SPSite site = new SPSite(siteUrl))
      {
        SPServiceContext ctx = SPServiceContext.GetContext(site);

        UserProfileConfigManager mgr = new UserProfileConfigManager(ctx);
        OrganizationProfileManager opm = new OrganizationProfileManager(ctx);
        ProfilePropertyManager ppm = mgr.ProfilePropertyManager;

        //Create Core property
        CorePropertyManager cpm = ppm.GetCoreProperties();
        CoreProperty p = cpm.Create(false);
        p.Name = "MyOrgName";
        p.Type = "string";
        p.Length = 50;
        p.DisplayName = "MyOrgDisplayName";
        cpm.Add(p);

        //Create ProfileType property
        ProfileTypePropertyManager ptpm = →
ppm.GetProfileTypeProperties(ProfileType.Organization);
        ProfileTypeProperty pt = ptpm.Create(p);
        pt.IsVisibleOnEditor = true;
        ptpm.Add(pt);

        //Create ProfileSubType property
        ProfileSubtypePropertyManager pspm = →
```

```
    opm.DefaultProfileSubtypeProperties;
        ProfileSubtypeProperty pst = pspm.Create(pt);
        pst.DefaultPrivacy = Privacy.Public;
        pspm.Add(pst);
      }
    }
```

# My Sites

One of the first steps in configuring user profiles for use within SharePoint is to set up a My Sites host by following these steps:

1. In Central Administration, under Application Management, create a new Site Collection using the My Site Host template from the Enterprise category.

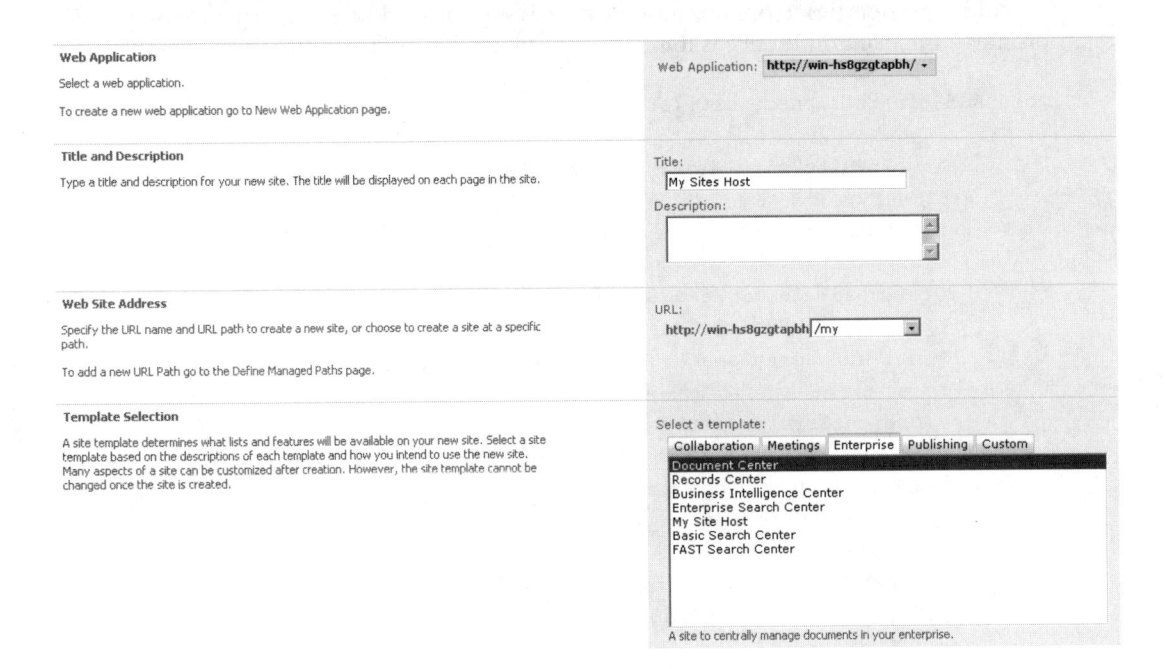

2. Once the My Sites site collection is up and running, we can configure the User Profile Service application and use it to create sites for each user. In Central Administration, choose Manage Service Applications | User Profile Service Application | Setup My Sites. In the My Site Host Location text box, enter the URL of the site collection that we just created:

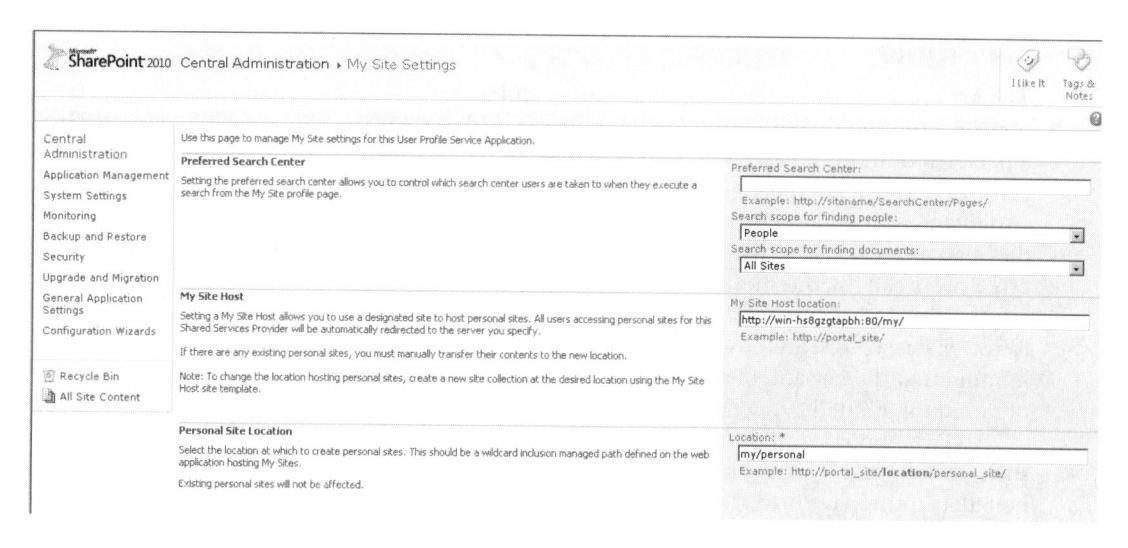

3. As well as providing a user interface for managing user profile information, users have the option of creating their own personal sites. This is covered in a bit more detail later. However, since each personal site is effectively a site collection in its own right, before users can create these sites, self-service site creation must be enabled on the web application that hosts the My Sites site collection. To enable self-service site creation, from Central Administration, select Application Management. In the Site Collections section, select Configure Self-Service Site Creation and then select the On option, making sure that the My Site host web application is selected first.

> **TIP** Self-service site creation is defined at the web application level. Creating a separate web application to host My Sites will allow greater administrative control over the sites that can be created within a SharePoint farm. If My Sites is enabled on an existing web application, users with the appropriate permissions will be able to create other types of site collections, potentially leading to fragmented distribution of content and an ineffective use of resources.

4. Now that we've configured My Sites, users can manage their profiles and access their personal sites by clicking their username in the upper-right corner of the page and then selecting My Profile:

   After selecting My Profile, the user is automatically directed to the My Sites site collection. Across the top of the page are three links: My Profile, My Network, and My Content. Let's take a look at each of these.

## My Profile

The My Profile page contains a number of useful features and is the main access point for social computing in SharePoint 2010. Users can add to their profile information, including a personal description and a picture as well as contact details. These are pretty standard features that you'd expect to find in any user profile application. However, SharePoint 2010 also includes new features such as Ask Me About, where a user can list subjects in which they have relevant expertise. These subjects are then listed on the user's profile page, and other users can ask questions based on the subject by clicking a hyperlink. This feature is not trivial—this additional data is included in the people search index, making it possible for others users to search for experts in a particular field and easily ask questions. Bearing in mind that the key aim of social computing in the enterprise is the development of organizational intelligence, you can begin to see how this feature can be very powerful.

Ask Me About is just one property that users can complete on their profile. Other data such as Skills and Interests can be used in a similar manner. In effect, these tags are used as metadata to help users find other users who can assist with problems or who are interested in a particular topic regardless of where they sit within an organizational hierarchy. The properties that are available within the Edit Profile page are defined by the User Profile Service application and can therefore be extended to meet any requirement.

Earlier I discussed taxonomies and the Managed Metadata column. You can add profile properties that make use of the managed metadata column, as shown below, allowing users to select from a range of predefined tags. Functionality such as this is useful for allowing users to manage their geographic location—and, again, this data can be used to refine search results.

## Status Messages

As well as providing links to a user's profile information, the My Profile page also includes a number of social computing features that are new to SharePoint 2010. Probably the most obvious of these is the status message, shown next:

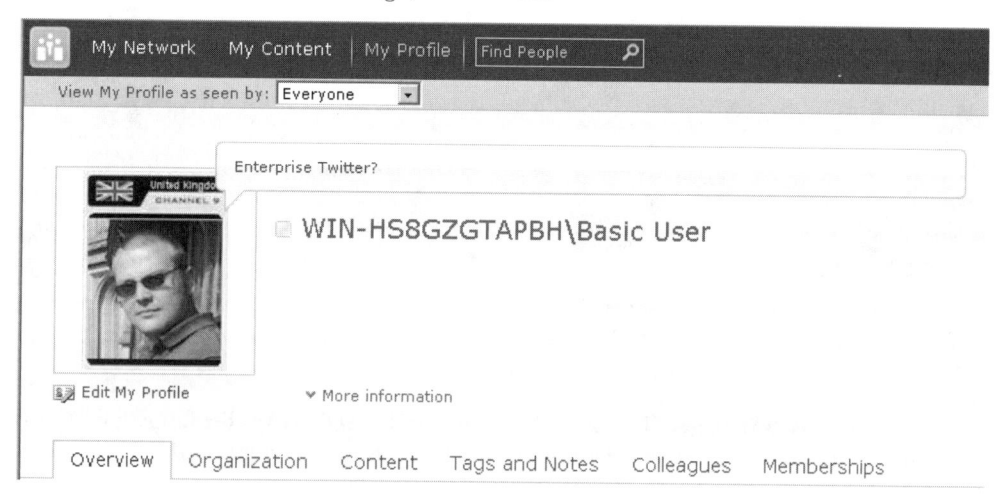

![Screenshot of My Profile page showing status message "Enterprise Twitter?" for WIN-HS8GZGTAPBH\Basic User]

Status messages work similarly to Twitter, the only difference being that the messages are not posted to the public Internet. A user can enter short messages that are then visible by all users viewing the user's profile; these messages are automatically shown on the profile page of other users in their network (more on networks later).

> **NOTE** I've got a confession to make when it comes to Twitter. When I was first introduced to the service, I thought, "Who's got the time to waste posting inane comments on the Web that nobody will ever read?" I was missing the point. Status updates in SharePoint or Twitter provide a record of your thoughts, ideas, musings, and findings over time, which can be referred to at a later date. Not only that, but they help to spread information quickly throughout an organization—or, in the case of Twitter, throughout the world. Everything you ever type is stored, indexed, and made available for searching. Why is this a good thing? How many times do you find yourself saying, "I vaguely remember a conversation about that, but I can't remember the details"? Now you don't need to remember the details—"Note to self" has been superseded by status update.

## Activities

Most things that you do within SharePoint appear in your activity feed. Whether it's creating a new document or updating your user profile, it all ends up in your activity feed, and anybody who's interested can view it. In a sense, the activity feed is like the news feed in Facebook.

As developers, we're likely to be involved in writing data to and retrieving data from the activity feed for our custom applications. Before we get into some code snippets that illustrate how we can tackle these tasks, let's look at how activities are represented by the object model:

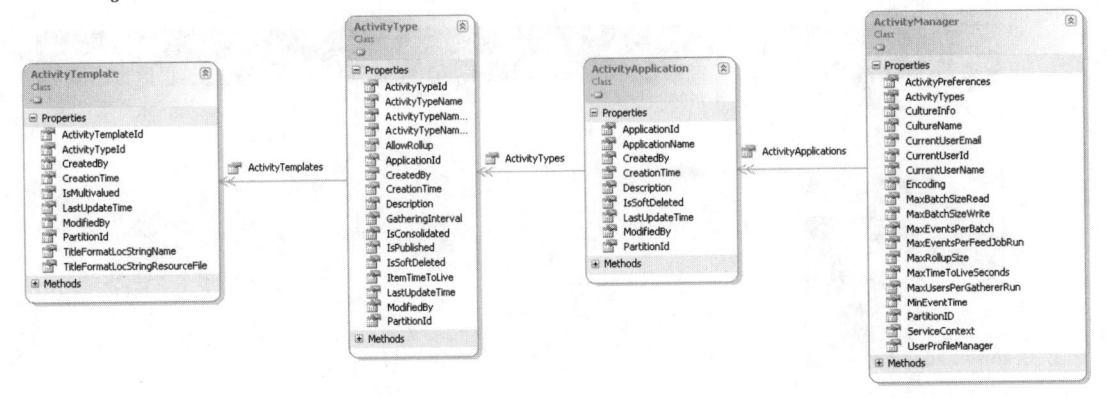

The **ActivityManager** class is used to manage the **ActivityApplications** that are registered with the User Profile Service. Configuration of a custom application that adds events to the activity feed will begin with the **ActivityApplication** class:

```
public ActivityApplication CreateOrGetApplication(ActivityManager mgr,
                                                   string applicationName)
{
  ActivityApplication app = mgr.ActivityApplications[applicationName];
  if (app == null)
  {
    app = mgr.ActivityApplications.Create(applicationName);
    app.Commit();
    app.Refresh(true);
  }
  return app;
}
```

Each application will have one or more **ActivityTypes**, where an **ActivityType** is the type of event that's written to the feed. For example, if we develop a custom helpdesk application and we want activities to be written when a case is assigned to a user, we would add an **ActivityType** for CaseAssignment. We may also add ActivityTypes for CaseClosed or ReachedSLATimeout.

```
public ActivityType CreateOrGetActivityType(ActivityApplication app,
                                             string typeName,
                                             string resourceFile,
                                             string resourceName)
{
```

```
      ActivityType theType = app.ActivityTypes[typeName];
      if (theType == null)
      {
        theType = app.ActivityTypes.Create(typeName);
        theType.ActivityTypeNameLocStringResourceFile = resourceFile;
        theType.ActivityTypeNameLocStringName = resourceName;
        theType.IsPublished = true;
        theType.IsConsolidated = true;
        theType.Commit();
        theType.Refresh(true);
      }
      return theType;
    }
```

Once we've defined our ActivityType, the next part of the configuration is the ActivityTemplate, which defines the template that will be populated when adding an event using our custom ActivityType. Each ActivityType may have one or more ActivityTemplates. Here's an example:

```
public ActivityTemplate CreateOrGetActivityTemplate(ActivityType type,
                                                    string resourceFile,
                                                    string resourceName,
                                                    bool isMultiValued)
{
  ActivityTemplate theTemplate = type.ActivityTemplates[ActivityTemplatesCollection. →
CreateKey(isMultiValued)];

  if (theTemplate == null)
  {
    theTemplate = type.ActivityTemplates.Create(isMultiValued);
    theTemplate.TitleFormatLocStringResourceFile = resourceFile;
    theTemplate.TitleFormatLocStringName = resourceName;
    theTemplate.Commit();
    theTemplate.Refresh(isMultiValued);
  }
  return theTemplate;
}
```

Both ActivityType and ActivityTemplate objects make use of resource files to retrieve the content that is included in a user's activity feed. This allows the content to be localized based on the user's language preferences.

For the ActivityType object, the resource file is configured using the following properties:

- **ActivityType. ActivityTypeNameLocStringResourceFile**   Contains the name of the resource file. All resource files are stored in the %SPRoot%\Resources folder.

- **ActivityType.ActivityTypeNameLocStringName**   Contains the name of a data element within the resource file that defined the name that will be displayed for the ActivityType.

A sample resource file containing details for an ActivityType might look like this:

```
<root>
  <data name="My_Activity_Key">
    <value xml:space="preserve">My Sample Activity Type Name</value>
  </data>
</root>
```

For the ActivityTemplate object, configuration is performed by using two similar properties:

- **ActivityTemplate.TitleFormatLocStringResourceFile**   Contains the name of the resource file.

**NOTE** Resource filenames should not contain the path or extension. For example, a resource file named myresources.en-us.resx would be used by setting the appropriate property to **myresources**.

- **ActivityTemplate.TitleFormatLocStringName**   Contains the name of the data element within the resource file that contains the event template.

A sample resource file containing two activity templates, one with a single value and another multi-value template, might look as follows:

```
<root>
  <data name="My_SingleValue_Template">
    <value xml:space="preserve">
    {Owner} has performed a new activity: {Link}
    </value>
  </data>
  <data name="My_MultiValue_Template">
    <value xml:space="preserve">
    {Owner} has performed {Size} new activities:   {List}
    </value>
  </data>
</root>
```

**TIP** Templates can contain entity escaped HTML if additional formatting is required.

Making use of these functions, we can write some setup code that adds the appropriate ActivityType and ActivityTemplate elements as follows:

```
static void Main(string[] args)
{
```

```
      string siteName = "http://localhost";
      using (SPSite site = new SPSite(siteName))
      {
        SPServiceContext context = SPServiceContext.GetContext(site);
        UserProfileManager profileManager = new UserProfileManager(context);
        string username = Environment.UserDomainName + "\\" + Environment.UserName;

        UserProfile p = profileManager.GetUserProfile(username);
        ActivityManager manager = new ActivityManager(p,context);

        Program prog = new Program();
        string applicationName = "MyHelpdeskApp";
       string resourceFile = "MyHelpdeskAppResources";
        prog.Setup(manager, applicationName,resourceFile);
    }
}
public void Setup(ActivityManager mgr, string applicationName,
                  string resourceFile)
{
    mgr.PrepareToAllowSchemaChanges();
    ActivityApplication app = CreateOrGetApplication(mgr, applicationName);
    ActivityType assignedType = CreateOrGetActivityType(app, "CaseAssignment",
                          resourceFile, "MyHelpdesk_Assignment_Display");
    ActivityTemplate assignedSVT = CreateOrGetActivityTemplate(assignedType,
                          resourceFile, "MyHelpdesk_Assignment_SVT", false);
    ActivityTemplate assignedMVT = CreateOrGetActivityTemplate(assignedType,
                          resourceFile, "MyHelpdesk_Assignment_MVT", true);
    ActivityType closedType = CreateOrGetActivityType(app, "CaseClosed",
                          resourceFile, "MyHelpdesk_Closed_Display");
    ActivityTemplate closedSVT = CreateOrGetActivityTemplate(closedType,
                          resourceFile, "MyHelpdesk_Closed_SVT", false);
    ActivityTemplate closedMVT = CreateOrGetActivityTemplate(closedType,
                          resourceFile, "MyHelpdesk_Closed_MVT", true);
    ActivityType timeoutType = CreateOrGetActivityType(app, "ReachedSLATimeout",
                          resourceFile, "MyHelpdesk_Timeout_Display");
    ActivityTemplate timeoutSVT = CreateOrGetActivityTemplate(timeoutType,
                          resourceFile, "MyHelpdesk_Timeout_SVT", false);
    ActivityTemplate timeoutMVT = CreateOrGetActivityTemplate(timeoutType,
                          resourceFile, "MyHelpdesk_Timeout_MVT", true);
}
```

If we run this code sample and then click the Edit My Profile link on the My Profile page for a user, we'll see that three additional options in the Activities I Am Following section, as shown next. These new activities correspond to the ActivityType objects that we configured in our code sample.

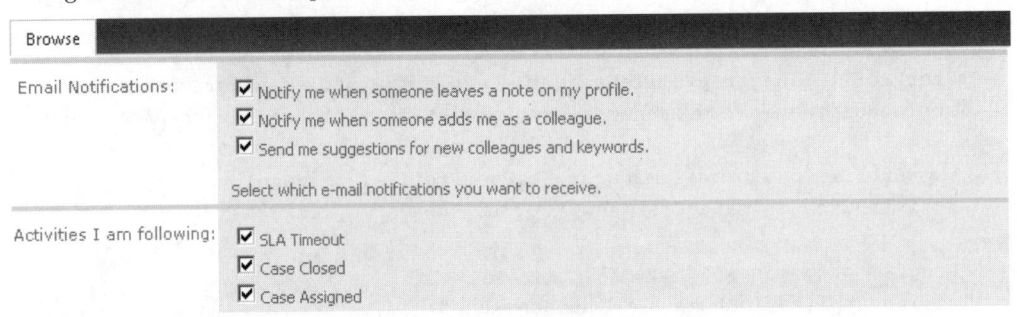

Now that we know how to configure custom activities for our applications, let's move on to take a look at how to make use of these configured activities. The following class diagram shows the classes that are involved in creating activity events:

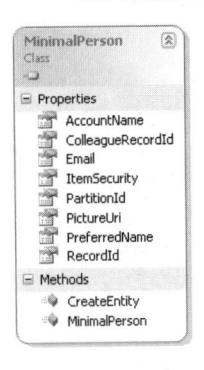

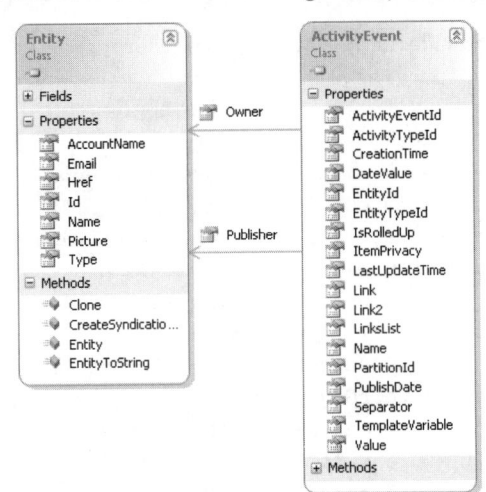

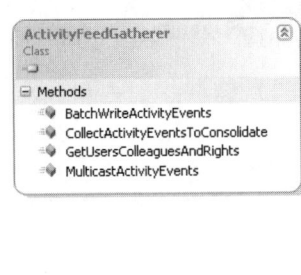

Using ActivityEvents is a two-step process. First, the events are generated and written to the appropriate user's activity feed using the ActivityFeedGatherer. The ActivityFeedGatherer object makes use of batching to write events. This allows for scheduled jobs to scan periodically for changes and write activity events in batches while at the same time allowing for more traditional event-driven activity generation. For example, in the case of our helpdesk application, the CaseCreated event would most likely be event-driven, whereas the SLATimeout would probably be generated by a scheduled task.

```
public ActivityEvent GenerateActivityEvent(ActivityManager mgr,
                                           UserProfile p,
                                           ActivityType activityType,
                                           string nameText,
                                           string siteUrl)
{
```

```
  Entity owner = new MinimalPerson(p).CreateEntity(mgr);
  Entity publisher = new MinimalPerson(p).CreateEntity(mgr);
  ActivityEvent activityEvent = ActivityEvent.CreateActivityEvent(mgr,
                                 activityType.ActivityTypeId, owner, publisher);
  activityEvent.Name = activityType.ActivityTypeName;
  activityEvent.ItemPrivacy = (int)Privacy.Public;

  Link link = new Link();
  link.Href = siteUrl;
  link.Name = nameText;
  activityEvent.Link = link;
  activityEvent.Commit();

  return activityEvent;
}

public void RaiseActivityEvent(ActivityManager mgr,
                               UserProfile p,
                               ActivityType type,
                               string nameText,
                               string siteUrl)
{
  List<ActivityEvent> events=new List<ActivityEvent>();
  ActivityEvent newEvent = GenerateActivityEvent(mgr, p, type, nameText, siteUrl);
  events.Add(newEvent);
  ActivityFeedGatherer.BatchWriteActivityEvents(events,0,1);

  WriteMulticastEvents(mgr, events, newEvent);
}
```

The second step in the process, once the events have been written to the user's activity feed, is to broadcast the events to colleagues who have elected to receive them. This is where the terminology gets a bit confusing and warrants some further explanation. Looking at the code above for GenerateActivityEvent, we can see that the **CreateActivityEvent** method accepts two properties of type Entity: **owner** and **publisher**.

First, let's consider what an Entity is. An Entity object represents the owner or publisher of a feed. The feed part is significant. Earlier you learned that each user has an activity feed and that other users can subscribe to that feed; when we're generating activity events, the owner should always be the owner of the feed to which we're trying to add the event.

Second, now that we're clear on what an Entity is and the significance of the owner, let's take a look at the publisher. You'd think that publisher would be the user or application that published the event. In some cases, this is true, but as a rule of thumb the assumption doesn't work. A more accurate definition of *publisher* is the user who is the target of the activity—or maybe an easier way to picture it is the user whose activity feed will contain the activity.

These two properties are significant when looking at broadcasting events to subscribers. Consider this template as an example:

```
<data name="MyHelpdesk_Closed_SVT" xml:space="preserve">
  <value>{Publisher} has closed a case: {Link}</value>
</data>
```

This same template will be used for the event when written to the originating user's activity feed as well as the My Network feed of colleagues who have elected to receive updates. We're using the **{Publisher}** property in the description because, unless it is changed programmatically, the publisher will remain the user that originated the event. If instead of **{Publisher}** we were to use **{Owner}**, the value would change to the user viewing the My Network feed. **{Publisher}** is the originator or source of the activity, whereas **{Owner}** is the current consumer of the feed

In the preceding code snippet, notice that when calling GenerateActivityEvent, both the owner and the publisher are set to the same user. This is necessary to have the activity appear in the user's activity feed.

The following code broadcasts an **ActivityEvent** to all subscribed colleagues:

```
private static void WriteMulticastEvents(ActivityManager mgr,
                             List<ActivityEvent> events, ActivityEvent newEvent)
{
  List<long> ownerIds = new List<long>();
  Dictionary<long, MinimalPerson> owners;
  Dictionary<long, List<MinimalPerson>> colleaguesOfOwners;
  Dictionary<long, List<ActivityEvent>> eventsPerOwner;
  List<ActivityEvent> multicastEvents;

  ownerIds.Add(newEvent.Owner.Id);

  ActivityFeedGatherer.GetUsersColleaguesAndRights(mgr, ownerIds, out owners,
                                        out colleaguesOfOwners);

  ActivityFeedGatherer.MulticastActivityEvents(mgr, events, colleaguesOfOwners,
                                        out eventsPerOwner);

  ActivityFeedGatherer.CollectActivityEventsToConsolidate(eventsPerOwner,
                                        out multicastEvents);

  ActivityFeedGatherer.BatchWriteActivityEvents(multicastEvents, 0,
                                        multicastEvents.Count);
}
```

The important thing to note about this code snippet is that it uses the same **BatchWriteActivityEvents** method to generate the subscriber events. The main difference between the events being generated by this process and the original event is that the entities that represent the owner and the publisher will be different. The owner will be the colleague who has elected to subscribe, whereas the publisher will be the originating user.

## Memberships

Memberships in SharePoint 2010 are a central component of fostering community-based social computing. Two types of membership are built in:

- **Distribution List Membership**   These groups and members are retrieved directly from Active Directory as part of the User Profile synchronization process.
- **SharePoint Site Membership**   These groups can be created within individual sites and are commonly used for assigning rights and permissions.

As well as built-in membership types, you can create custom groups programmatically and add users to those groups. When developing social computing applications, this functionality is very useful. Here's an example:

```
void CreateMembership(UserProfileManager mgr, UserProfile p,
                string groupName, string mailName,
                string description, string url, string source)
{
  MemberGroupManager groupManager = mgr.GetMemberGroups();
  Guid policyId=PrivacyPolicyIdConstants.MembershipsFromDistributionLists;
  MemberGroup newGroup = groupManager.CreateMemberGroup(policyId,groupName,
                                  mailName, description, url, source);

  p.Memberships.Create(newGroup, MembershipGroupType.UserSpecified, groupName,
                Privacy.Organization);
}
```

## Tags and Notes

As mentioned, the ability to add tags and notes to SharePoint content is available by default for most content. When tags and notes are added, although they are visible on the page containing the content, the main reason for adding them is to make the content easier to find for the user attaching the tags and notes. This functionality is implemented using the Tags and Notes section of the My Profile site. In addition, tags and notes can be added to external content such as public web sites or other web-based content not managed by SharePoint.

## My Network

The My Network application is another key social computing element of SharePoint 2010. Although the My Profile page allows users to manage their own profiles, the My Network page provides a consolidated view of relevant data that's specific to the current user. For example, by specifying additional users as colleagues, content from their activity feeds will automatically become visible in the user's My Network page. By the same token, if interests are specified in a user profile, when any content is tagged matching those interests, a link to the content is also available on the My Network page.

The My Network application is where social computing works its magic in SharePoint 2010. By making use of user profile data, users have access to information that is relevant to them and their interests at any time. The net effect of this is that users converge into a collaborative community, where ideas and information can flow freely among interested members. Documents move from being a source of reference to a focus for collaborative endeavor.

## My Content

In a sense, SharePoint has come full circle. Originally with SharePoint Team Services 2001, the aim was to provide a web-based alternative to the ubiquitous network file share. This allowed teams to collaborate on documents with the benefit of the additional context information that could be made available using HTML. So rather than a document on a network share named ProjectHooHaTechnicalSpec.doc, the document could be stored in a document library named Technical Specifications, on a team site name Project HooHa. The team site could contain other relevant information such as an overview of the project or a list of team members and relevant contacts. Of course, all of this information could still be contained in various documents on a network file share, but using a web application made it much simpler to keep together related information and to add context easily in the form of lists and other content.

To get back to SharePoint 2010, clearly this functionality has moved on over the years. The same is also true of the requirements of knowledge workers. Nowadays, it is common practice for users within a large organization to have a dedicated network file share that can be used for storing documents. Using network file shares facilitates backups and ensures that documents can be made available regardless of the physical hardware that the user is using. My Content takes this idea a step further and applies the rationale behind SharePoint Team Services to all user-generated content. Rather than storing content on a personal file share, all documents can be uploaded to a user's My Content site, where they can be freely shared with anybody within an organization.

## Summary

Social computing is not a checkbox on a feature list. Having the ability to engage in social computing does not deliver on its true potential unless, as a concept, social computing is embraced by the organization. Of course, for most organizations, embracing a change will be gradual and will require some incremental payback if it is to succeed. SharePoint 2010 accommodates this requirement by providing features that are immediately useful, such as My Content, People Search, and Audiences. As more and more users realize the utility of these features and become engaged in the creation of content, other social computing features such as tagging, notes, and user profiles will become more useful. The final step in truly adopting social computing within an organization is the user-driven creation of blogs and wikis and the widespread use of features such as status messages and activity feeds.

For us, as developers, the challenge is to gauge where social computing fits within our organization currently and to predict how it will feature in the future. By leveraging the capabilities of the SharePoint 2010 platform, we can easily incorporate social computing features that will deliver immediate benefits to our users while allowing for future improvements that will take advantage of additional platform functionality as organization adoption increases.

# CHAPTER 18

# Business Intelligence

*Business Intelligence (BI)* is an interesting term. You could ask ten people within ten different organizations what it means in practice, and you'd probably get ten completely different answers. That's probably a good thing though, because by its very nature, BI is specific to a particular business. One organization may see BI as the analysis of sales and manufacturing data for a range of products being produced, whereas another organization—and this is particularly true in the public sector—may see BI as the analysis of social and demographic data.

Although at a practical level, implementations of BI are usually quite different, most organizations agree that as a general concept, BI is an important part of day-to-day management. Without appropriate data, modern scientific management principles are impossible. Of course, that's not to say that BI is the be-all and end-all of management information; in fact, BI as a concept has gained widespread acceptance only in the past 20 years or so. But when it comes to building and maintaining a competitive market position, organizations need a crystal ball, and BI as a concept is all about building the intelligence required to make confident predictions.

Conceptually, we all have a good idea of what BI is, and as you've seen, practically it means something different to every organization. Technically, however, the tools used to deliver BI are pretty well established and easy to define. Commonly, BI solutions make use of a data warehouse that acts as a central repository of data. Using approaches such as Online Analytical Processing (OLAP), data can be effectively analyzed in many different dimensions. As well as providing a mechanism for ad hoc analysis of data, BI also commonly provides well-defined performance management data. This may include measures such as actual sales performance versus sales target or statistical measures such as capacity utilization. For organizations in the public sector, this data are more likely to relate to social factors such as socioeconomic distribution or cost per interaction.

Regardless of the type of data required and the nature of organization, the underlying principles remain the same. BI can be subdivided into two categories: *business analytics (BA)*, which refers to the analytical use of data to facilitate better long term planning and decision making; and *business performance management (BPM)*, which refers to the short-term management of an organization using defined metrics and targets. This chapter looks at the tools available within the SharePoint Server 2010 platform for facilitating both of these approaches.

# Microsoft Business Intelligence Solution

Before we dive into what SharePoint can do to help us implement a BI solution, let's spend a bit of time considering where SharePoint fits into the bigger picture. If there's such a thing as a BI mantra, it's this: "One version of the truth." That is, every BI system within an organization should provide exactly the same answer when asked the same question. Addressing this problem is undoubtedly one of the biggest considerations of a BI solutions architect, and to address this issue, Microsoft provides a single enterprise-ready BI solution. Where there's one single, all-encompassing platform, maintaining one version of the truth is a much more realistic goal.

## Business User Experience

Microsoft Office applications are ubiquitous on the desktop PCs and laptops of knowledge workers. Using applications such as Excel and Outlook to surface and manipulate BI data makes it easy for users to consume BI data without having to adopt a new way of working or learn new tools. Furthermore, using applications such as Excel, users can achieve a much higher level of integration than would be possible if BI data were available only via reports or other static data media. Custom workbooks can be created that directly access and utilize data from the BI platform.

## Business Productivity Infrastructure

"Business productivity infrastructure" is something of a marketing term that relates to the infrastructure and applications that an organization uses to facilitate the use of business information by knowledge workers. Business productivity is all about making the right information available to the right people at the right time. It's also about allowing people to create and collaborate on the creation of new information as effectively as possible. Clearly, when viewed from this perspective, SharePoint fits in. Centrally managed and created content can be easily surfaced using portal sites, and self-service BI applications can be created using tools such as Excel Services. Furthermore, BI can be integrated with other sources of information, increasing the overall visibility of important business metrics.

## Data Infrastructure

The user experience is all about how the user interacts with the data provided, whereas the productivity infrastructure is about providing a platform that allows centralized storage, collaboration, and content creation. One important element that we haven't looked at is the actual data itself—where it's stored and how it's processed. Although SharePoint is a great tool for storing documents and document-related content, when it comes to processing and analyzing large volumes of data, a more specialized tool is required.

Offering tried-and-tested OLAP functionality via Analysis Services and a comprehensive reporting platform via Reporting Services, SQL Server is the obvious choice for hosting and managing both the data warehouse aspect of a BI solution and the analysis and report-generation aspects.

# SharePoint Server 2010 Business Intelligence Platform

Now that you know how SharePoint fits into the bigger picture, let's look at the features and tools that are available to us when developing BI solutions.

## Excel Services

Excel Services were discussed in Chapter 12, where its uses within the BI domain were mentioned. One of the things about Excel is that it's commonly used to hold a lot of vital management information within an organization. In an ideal world, every useful piece of data would be found in a data warehouse and would be accessed via OLAP or some other reporting mechanism. In the real world, that just isn't the case. Despite the best efforts of BI professionals the world over, business users simply find Excel to be easy to use and an essential tool for performing their day-to-day jobs. In the real world, some vital data will always live in Excel.

Rather than chasing some data warehousing utopia, a more effective approach is to allow users to continue to use Excel. By taking advantage of the features offered by Excel Services, data managed and stored in Excel workbooks can play an important part in an organization's BI strategy. All the tools available within SharePoint can make use of Excel data as readily as OLAP data or relational data from SQL Server.

As well as making effective use of data stored within Excel workbooks, you've seen how the Excel application forms a key part of the Microsoft BI solution. The analytical and display capabilities coupled with a general familiarity with the product represent an unbeatable combination that should always form a core part of any BI strategy. By allowing workbooks to be hosted in Excel services and used via a web browser, SharePoint extends the reach of the powerful features of Excel beyond the desktop.

## Business Intelligence Web Parts

SharePoint provides a few basic BI web parts out of the box. As a platform that's often used for creating intranet sites and other organizational portals, the web parts allow users to include important performance metrics within portal pages easily. Along with web parts that are used to display information, SharePoint also defines a number of content types specifically for storing BI data. Based on the Common Indication Columns content type, these additional content types all describe business metrics that can be displayed using the built-in web parts.

The indicator types available out of the box include the following:

- **Excel-based status indicator**  This indicator is used for retrieving values from an Excel workbook hosted using Excel services. The indicator can refer either to a cell address such as *Sheet1!$A$1* or a named range such as *MyIndicator*.

- **Fixed Value–based status indicator**  The Fixed Value indicator has been designed to be manually updated. However, it's particularly useful to us as developers, because its value can be manipulated programmatically as the following code sample shows:

```
static bool SetIndicatorValue(SPWeb web, string listName,
                              string indicatorName, double newValue)
{
  SPList list = web.Lists.TryGetList(listName);

  if (list != null)
  {
    SPContentTypeId myct = new
                 SPContentTypeId("0x00A7470EADF4194E2E9ED1031B61DA088401");

    bool supportsContentType = (from SPContentType ct in list.ContentTypes
                                where ct.Id.IsChildOf(myct)
                                select true).First();
    if (supportsContentType)
    {
      //Note: Only use this technique on very small lists. For larger lists a
      //CAML query will offer much better performance

      SPListItemCollection listItems = list.Items;

      SPListItem item = (from SPListItem indicator in list.Items
                         where indicator.Title == indicatorName
                         select indicator).First();

      if (item != null)
      {
        if (item.Fields.ContainsField("Value"))
        {
          item["Value"] = newValue;
          item.Update();
          return true;
        }
      }
    }
  }
  return false;
}
```

- **SharePoint list–based status indicator** While a fixed value indicator makes use of a single value stored within SharePoint, the SharePoint list–based indicator makes use of all items in a SharePoint list. The value of the indicator can be either the number of the items in the list or the percentage of the items where a particular condition is met or even a calculation based on the values of particular fields in the list. This indicator is especially useful for showing metrics for data that is created and managed within SharePoint.

- **SQL Server Analysis Service–based status indicator**  As you've seen, most BI data is processed using OLAP. The SQL Server Analysis Services indicator allows you to display an indicator easily from an OLAP cube.

---

NOTE  At the time of writing, on SharePoint 2010 Beta 2, it's not possible to create a custom list with the facilities to add new indicators. Although the appropriate content types can be added to the list, they're not displayed in the New Item menu and therefore can't be created. To resolve this problem, enable the SharePoint Server Enterprise Site Features option within Site Settings, and then create an indicator list using the Status List template, as shown next:

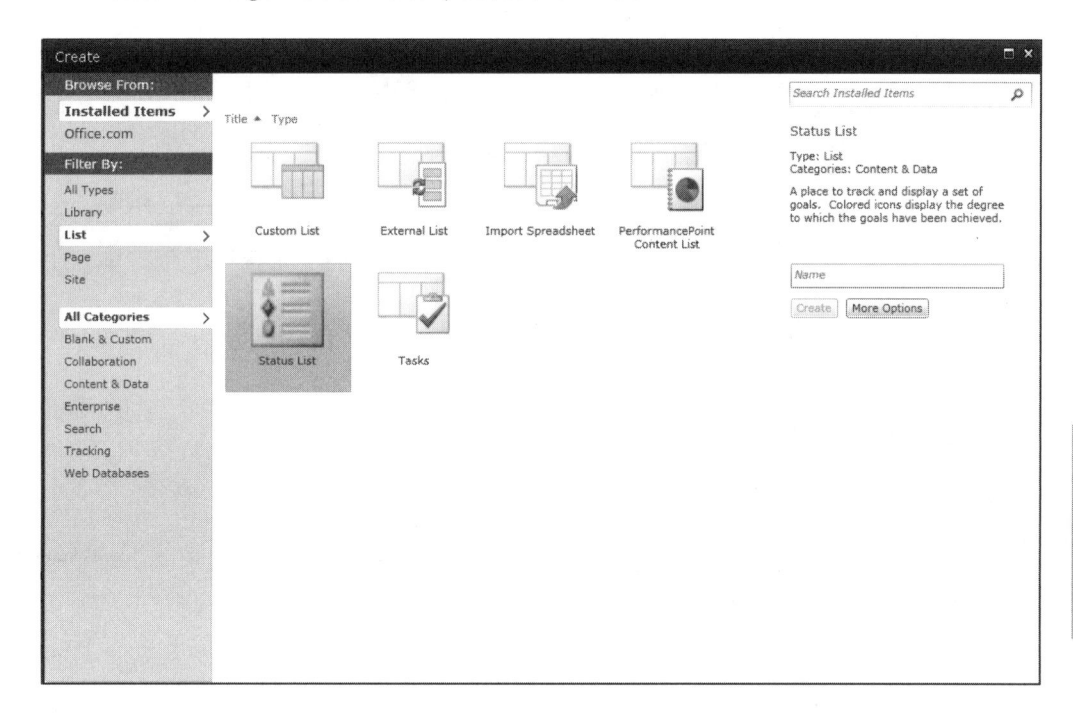

---

Several built-in web parts are available out of the box and are discussed in the following sections.

## Indicator Details Web Part

The Indicator Details web part can be used to display details of a single indicator value. As you've seen, all indicator values are derived from the Common Indicator Columns content type, and each of these types can be appropriately rendered using the Indicator Details web part.

The following screenshots show the configuration settings and rendered output of an indicator derived from an Excel workbook:

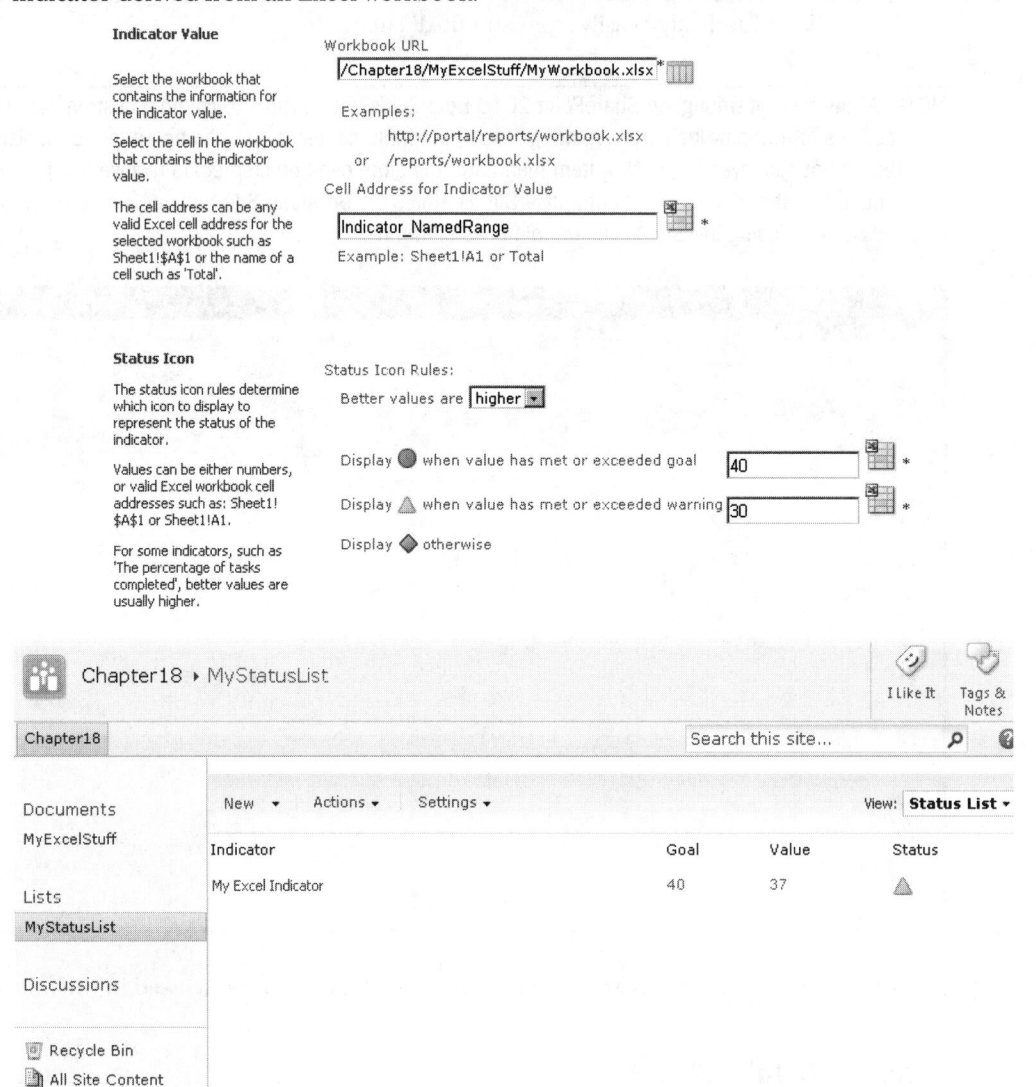

**Indicator Value**

Select the workbook that contains the information for the indicator value.

Select the cell in the workbook that contains the indicator value.

The cell address can be any valid Excel cell address for the selected workbook such as Sheet1!$A$1 or the name of a cell such as 'Total'.

Workbook URL: /Chapter18/MyExcelStuff/MyWorkbook.xlsx *

Examples:
    http://portal/reports/workbook.xlsx
 or /reports/workbook.xlsx

Cell Address for Indicator Value: Indicator_NamedRange *

Example: Sheet1!A1 or Total

**Status Icon**

The status icon rules determine which icon to display to represent the status of the indicator.

Values can be either numbers, or valid Excel workbook cell addresses such as: Sheet1!$A$1 or Sheet1!A1.

For some indicators, such as 'The percentage of tasks completed', better values are usually higher.

Status Icon Rules:
Better values are [higher]

Display ● when value has met or exceeded goal [40] *

Display △ when value has met or exceeded warning [30] *

Display ◆ otherwise

| | | Goal | Value | Status |
|---|---|---|---|---|
| Indicator | | | | |
| My Excel Indicator | | 40 | 37 | △ |

## Status List Web Part

The Status List web part works in a similar fashion to the Indicator Details web part, except the Status List web part shows all indicators from a specific SharePoint list. Indicators derive from a common content type, and by creating a list based on this content type, we can store a number of different indicators in a single location. The Status List web part renders each indicator appropriately based on its underlying source.

The Status List web part is useful for displaying a range of important metrics on an intranet page or other portal site, as shown here:

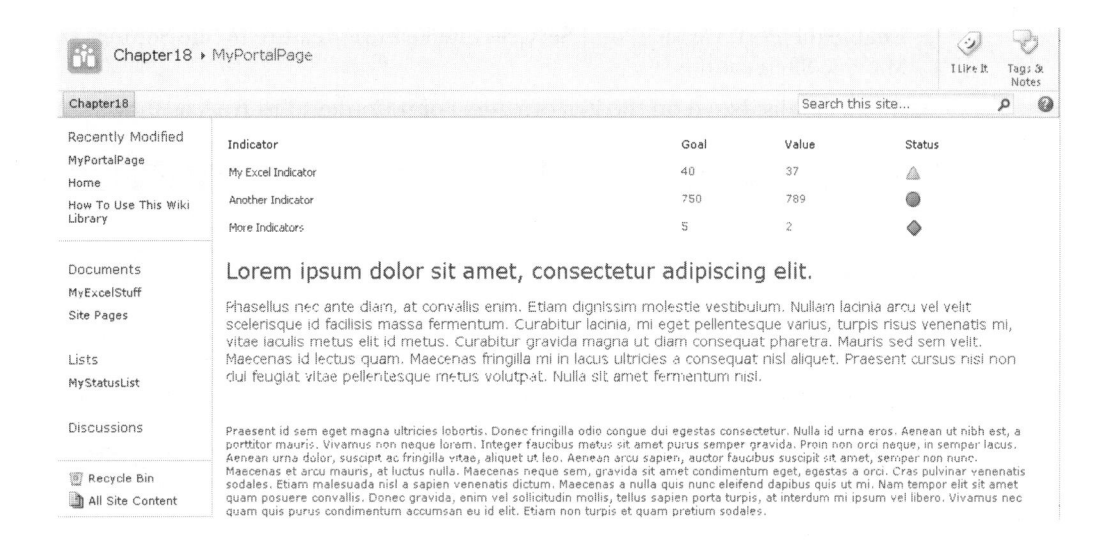

## Chart Web Part
The Chart web part is a useful new addition in SharePoint 2010. Data can be retrieved from Lists, Business Connectivity Services, or Excel Services. Alternatively, the chart control can be connected to another web part, which can act as a data source for the control.

## PerformancePoint Services
The web parts that are available out of the box are great for adding basic BI functionality to portal sites or other SharePoint applications. However, when it comes to building a dedicated BPM portal, the real jewel in the SharePoint 2010 crown is PerformancePoint Services, with features that allow developers and BI professionals to create highly interactive BPM portals.

Ultimately, PerformancePoint solutions are delivered as a series of SharePoint web part pages and can therefore be completely integrated into a larger portal solution in the same way as any other SharePoint content. Although the pages consist of a collection of PerformancePoint-specific web parts, a rich client editing experience is provided via the Dashboard Designer, which is accessed as a ClickOnce-deployed application from any PerformancePoint-enabled site.

### Using PerformancePoint Within a Site
To use PerformancePoint within a site, you must create a few specific lists and libraries. In much the same way as the Status Indicator web parts, PerformancePoint content is based on a few custom content types. Data based on these content types is then stored in specific lists and libraries, which are referenced in turn by the custom web parts. To add PerformancePoint functionality to an existing site, take the following steps:

1. Enable the PerformancePoint Services Site Collection Features at the Site Collection level. From Site Settings, choose Go To Top Level Site Settings | Site Collection Features.

2. Enable the PerformancePoint Services Site Features feature in Site Settings | Manage Site Features.
3. Add a new list based on the PerformancePoint Content List type, as shown:

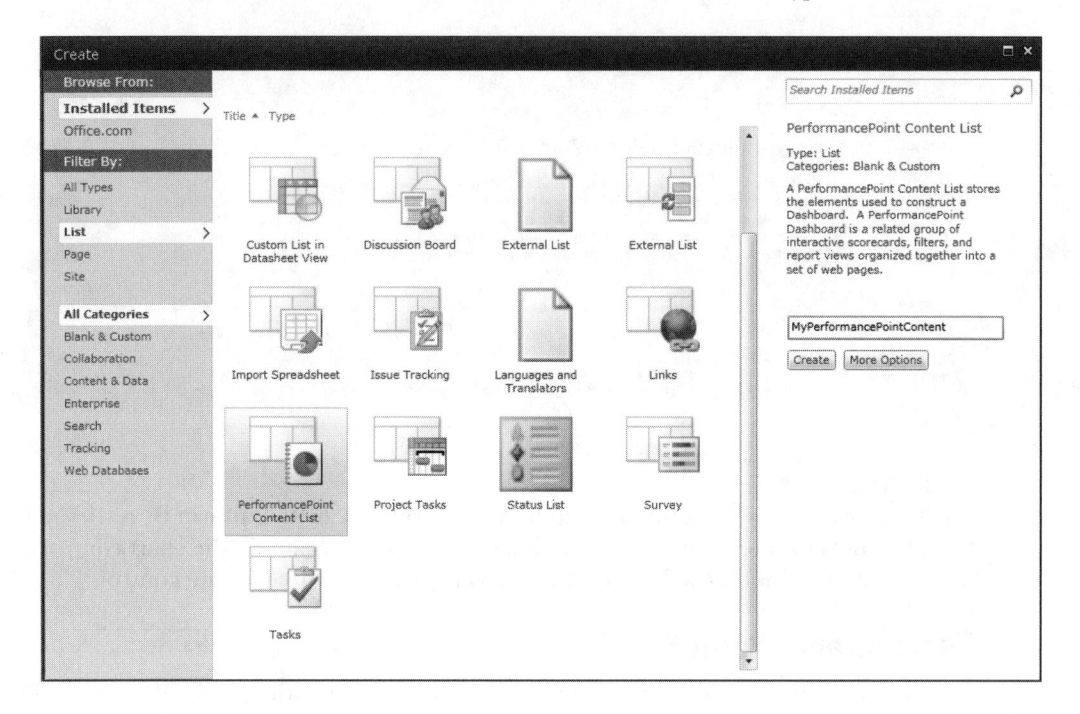

4. Add a new data connections library based on the DataConnections Library for PerformancePoint type.

> **NOTE** The PerformancePoint data connection library uses a different template to the standard data connection library that is generally used by Office applications. Be sure to select the correct type when creating the library. The difference between the two is that the standard data connection library can contain only Office Data Connection files as used by Excel or Universal Data Connection files as used by InfoPath, whereas the PerformancePoint library can also include the PerformancePoint Data Source content type. Bearing this in mind, you can convert an existing data connection library to support PerformancePoint simply by adding the PerformancePoint Data Source content type.

5. Add a new library based on the Dashboards library type.

## Dashboard Designer

To start using the PerformancePoint Dashboard Designer, navigate to the PerformancePoint content list and then add a new item. The Dashboard Designer will start automatically, as shown here:

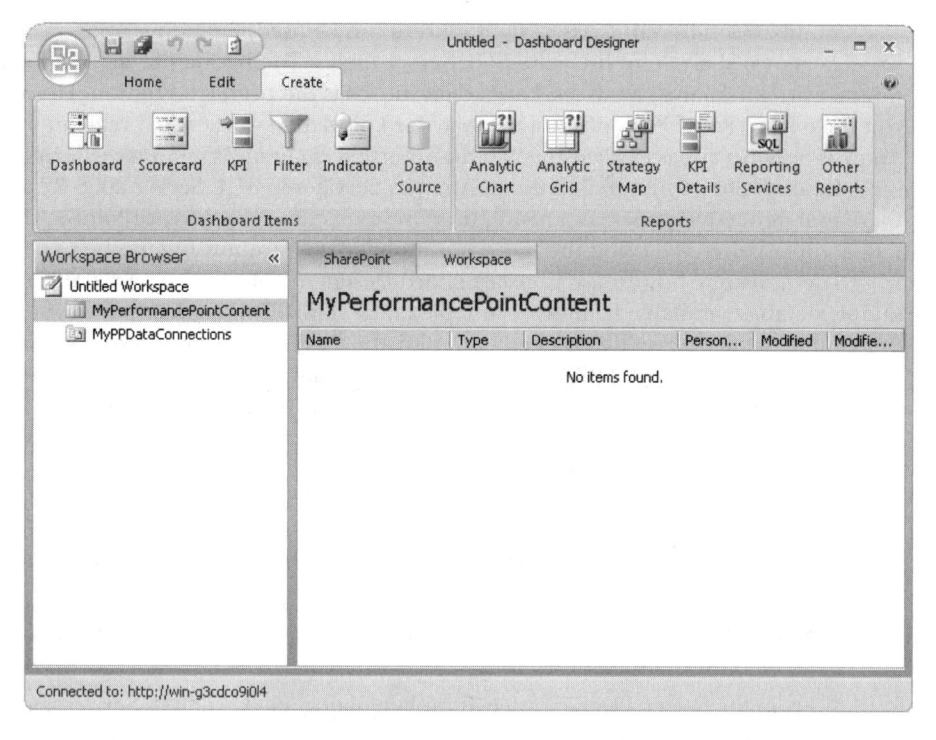

The Workspace Browser performs a similar function to the Solution Explorer in Visual Studio: it allows you to see all the items that are available for use within the project. One important difference here, however, is that two views are available for each of the items listed in the Workspace Browser: the SharePoint view, which lists all the items in the associated SharePoint list, and the Workspace view, which lists all the items in use in the current workspace. An item from SharePoint can be added to the current workspace by double-clicking it.

One thing to bear in mind about the Dashboard Designer is that workspace files can be saved to the file system. You can open these files using the Open command in the Dashboard Designer or by double-clicking the filename to view the workspace, which will be automatically bound to the appropriate SharePoint lists. However, it's also possible to use the file to export a workspace to another site. Rather than opening the file directly, you can click the Import Items button in the Home menu of the Dashboard Designer application to allow artifacts from the workspace file to be imported and automatically added to a new SharePoint site.

## PerformancePoint Data Connections

In much the same way as Office Data Connections (ODCs) are created and managed via the Excel client application and Universal Data Connection (UDCX) connections are managed via InfoPath, PerformancePoint connections are created and managed using the Dashboard Designer application.

A number of different types of data sources can be used, including Analysis Services, Excel Services, SharePoint lists, and SQL Server tables. To provide the highest degree of interactivity, an Analysis Services–based data source is the preferred option. However, as you'll see later, PowerPivot offers a new way for knowledge workers to create in-memory Analysis Services cubes easily using an add-in for Excel client. When PowerPivot integration is configured, SharePoint makes use of Analysis Services in SQL Server 2008 R2 to host these user-generated cubes; as a result, they are usable by PerformancePoint in the same way as cubes generated using the more traditional data warehousing method.

To demonstrate how to use the Dashboard Designer, consider the AdventureWorks sample database available from www.codeplex.com/MSFTDBProdSamples. In addition to the sample databases, we'll also need to deploy the OLAP sample project that can be found at C:\Program Files\Microsoft SQL Server\100\Tools\Samples\AdventureWorks 2008 Analysis Services Project\standard after the AdventureWorks sample project has been installed. For full details of how to set up the sample databases, please see the instructions that are available from the CodePlex site.

To create a connection to an OLAP data source, take the following steps:

1. In Dashboard Designer, select the Data Connections folder that we created earlier when we enabled PerformancePoint functionality for our site.

2. Select the Create tab on the ribbon, and then click the Data Sources button in the Dashboard Items section.

3. From the Select a Data Source Template dialog, click Analysis Services, as shown, and then click OK:

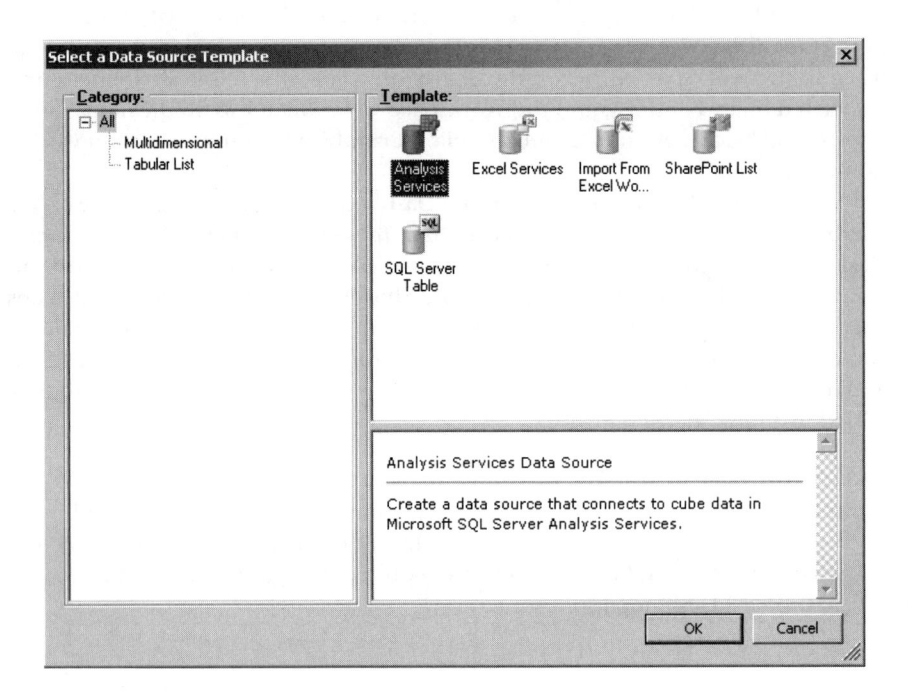

4. In the Properties tab, set the name of the new connection to **AdventureWorksOLAP**. Then in the Editor tab's Connection Settings section, enter the name of the Analysis Services instance that hosts the AdventureWorks OLAP sample cube. Select the Adventure Works DW 2008 SE database and the Adventure Works Cube.

```
Connection Settings                                                    ≈
  ⦿ Use Standard Connection
       Server:       .\standard
       Database:     Adventure Works DW 2008 SE                ▼
       Roles:
  ○ Use the following connection
       Connection String:

       Cube:         Adventure Works                            ▼
```

The three options in the Data Source Settings section warrant some explanation:

- **Unattended Service Account**  This generic account is used by the PerformancePoint Service application to access data sources where no specific credentials are provided. In practice, the unattended service account works in a similar fashion to the unattended account discussed in Chapter 12 on Excel Services. The Unattended Service Account is configured via Central Administration and can be found in the PerformancePoint Service Application Settings section of the PerformancePoint Service Application management page. This can be accessed by choosing Central Administration | Manage Service Applications | PerformancePoint Service Application | PerformancePoint Service Application Settings | Secure Store And Unattended Service Account. To use the Unattended Service Account, the Secure Store Service must also be properly configured. The steps required to do this are covered in Chapter 12.

- **Unattended Service Account and Add Authenticated User Name In Connection String**  For some data sources, the username is useful for providing a personalized view of the data. By selecting this option, the data source is still accessed using the unattended service account credentials, but the username of the requesting user is also passed to the data source via the CustomData connection string property. CustomData is an Analysis Services–specific connection string property and can contain any string value. The value of the property can then be picked up within the OLAP project by using the **CustomData()** Multidimensional Expressions (MDX) language function.

- **Per-user Identity**  By selecting this option, the identity of the requesting user is used to access the data source. This option offers a more granular approach to security but does so at the expense of having to manage requesting user access directly on the data source.

5. Now that we have some understanding of the options available, we'll use the default value of Unattended Service Account. As mentioned earlier, in order for this to work the account must be appropriately configured in Central Administration.
6. Click Test Data Source to confirm connectivity. Once connectivity has been confirmed, click the Save icon to persist the changes.

Although we've used only one data connection for this demonstration, you can use any number of data connections within a PerformancePoint workspace. For example, if our application captured data using a survey in SharePoint 2010, we could easily include the results of the survey in our dashboard by creating a connection to the appropriate SharePoint list. As you saw when creating our Analysis Services connection, available options include Excel Services, SharePoint lists, and SQL Server tables.

## PerformancePoint Content

With a connection set up and ready to go, we can move on and take a look at creating our first dashboard using PerformancePoint. Before jumping into this, however, you'll find it worthwhile to develop an understanding of how everything hangs together behind the scenes. Select the PerformancePoint Content folder that we created earlier, and then click the Create tab in the ribbon. This time, you'll see a much wider range of options, as shown next:

Dashboards are essentially a collection of web pages. As mentioned earlier, PerformancePoint dashboards are made up of web parts, which are discussed in the following sections.

**PerformancePoint Filter** When the Filter item is added to a dashboard from the Dashboard Items section of the ribbon, behind the scenes the PerformancePoint Filter web part is added to the underlying page. As you'll see, the Filter control can be used to filter other elements on the page.

**PerformancePoint Report** The PerformancePoint Report web part does most of the heavy lifting within a dashboard. Whenever a report is added to a dashboard, behind the scenes a PerformancePoint Report web part is added to the underlying page. This means that each of the options available from the Reports section of the ribbon are implemented using a PerformancePoint Report web part.

**PerformancePoint Scorecard** Scorecards are implemented using a specific web part. Scorecards work in a similar fashion to the Status List web part discussed earlier. The major difference is that PerformancePoint scorecards are managed by the PerformancePoint Service Application, as opposed to being rendered from a SharePoint list.

**PerformancePoint Stack Selector** The PerformancePoint stack selector web part is used to provide a navigation mechanism between the dashboard pages. When creating a dashboard, the Stack Selector is added automatically.

## Create a Dashboard

Now that you know how PerformancePoint weaves its magic, let's create a simple dashboard:

1. From the Dashboard Items section, click Dashboard to add a new dashboard to the workspace.
2. From the Select a Dashboard Page Template dialog, select the 2 Columns template.
3. Type the name of the dashboard as **MySampleDashboard**.
4. In the Series box, click the Product Categories drop-down. When the Select Members dialog appears, uncheck the Default Member (All products) checkbox, and then expand the All Products branch and select Accessories, Bikes, Clothing, and Components.
5. You can see in the editor that three sections are shown. The top section allows you to add additional pages to the dashboard, and the bottom section represents the dashboard content and contains two columns, as shown next, because we selected the 2 Columns template. We can add content to the Dashboard Content section by dropping the appropriate item from the Details section on the right side of the page. Of course, before we do this, we'll need to create some content to add!

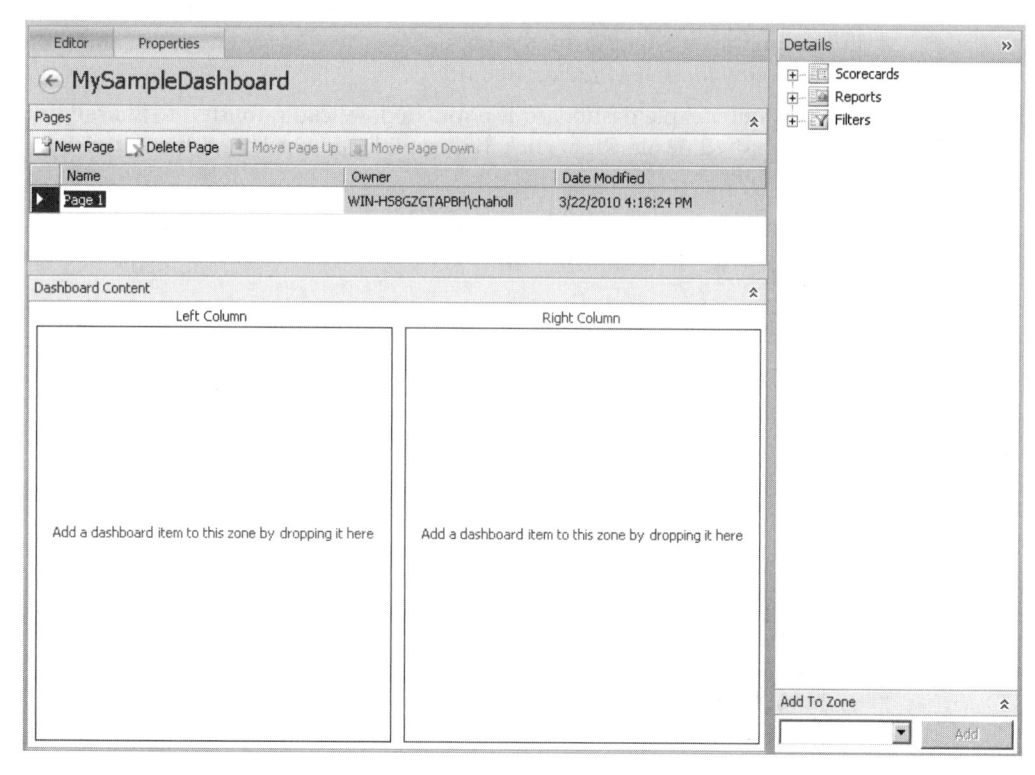

6. From the Reports section of the ribbon, click Analytic Chart. In the Select a Data Source step of the wizard, select the AdventureWorksOLAP data source and then click Finish.

7. Type the name of the new report as **MyChartReport**. You'll see the Analytic Chart designer interface. To create a chart, you can drag measures, dimensions, or named sets from the Details section on the right side of the page onto the design interface.

8. Drag the Product dimension into the Series section and the Date dimension into the Bottom Axis section.

9. Rather than displaying our data using the default bar chart, change the layout to Pie Chart by right-clicking anywhere on the chart and selecting Report Type | Pie Chart.

10. Save the finished report, and then switch back to MySampleDashboard.

11. Drag the finished report onto the dashboard. Under the Reports heading in the Details pane, drag MyChartReport onto the left column of the dashboard.

The next thing we need to add is some content for the right column. This time, we'll use an Analytic Grid report to allow users to examine the details that make up the chart.

1. As before, click the Analytic Grid icon in the Reports section of the ribbon. Select the AdventureWorksOLAP data source, and then name the report **MyGridReport**.

2. This time we want to show a bit more detail. Drag the Product dimension into the Rows section, the Geography dimension into the Columns section, and the Date dimension into the Background section. Save the completed report, and then add it to the right column of the dashboard.

3. Now that our sample dashboard is populated, we can publish it to SharePoint to see the finished result. Right-click MySampleDashboard, and then select Deploy to SharePoint.

Once the dashboard has been deployed, it will automatically be opened in a new browser window and will look similar to this:

| Product Categories | All Geograph... | Australia | Canada | France | Germany | United Kingd... | United States |
|---|---|---|---|---|---|---|---|
| All Products | $80,450,596.98 | $1,594,335.38 | $14,377,925.60 | $4,607,537.94 | $1,983,988.04 | $4,279,008.83 | $53,607,801.21 |
| Accessories | $571,297.93 | $23,947.53 | $118,127.35 | $48,031.73 | $35,083.07 | $42,593.03 | $303,515.23 |
| Bikes | $66,302,381.56 | $1,323,820.73 | $11,636,380.59 | $3,560,665.65 | $1,548,015.65 | $3,405,747.21 | $44,832,751.73 |
| Clothing | $1,777,840.84 | $42,915.80 | $378,947.63 | $128,092.22 | $71,619.43 | $118,828.80 | $1,037,436.95 |
| Components | $11,799,076.66 | $203,651.31 | $2,244,470.02 | $870,748.34 | $334,269.89 | $711,839.79 | $7,434,097.31 |

## Time Intelligence

Before we look at some of the advanced functionality of the PerformancePoint Report web part, let's take a look at another important aspect of most BI solutions: *time intelligence*. Practically every dataset has some aspect of time involved, and more often than not, data is analyzed over specific time periods. To show how this works in PerformancePoint, we'll add a filter to our report that will allow us to select a specific time period and will automatically update our reports accordingly.

1. Switch back to Dashboard Designer. Time intelligence must first be configured on the data connection before it can be used. Double-click the AdventureWorksOLAP connection, and then switch to the Time pane.

2. Our sample cube has various dimensions that we can use for time intelligence. For the purposes of this demonstration, select Date.Date.Calendar from the Time Dimension drop-down.

3. With the dimension defined, we can set a reference member. All we're doing here is selecting a specific value from our chosen time dimension and then specifying to what actual value it corresponds. Click the Browse button, and then select a single day from the Date.Date.Calendar hierarchy.

4. In the Hierarchy Level drop-down, select Day and then enter the corresponding date in the Reference Date text box, as shown next:

**Reference Data Mapping**

Time Dimension:
Date.Date.Calendar

Reference Member:
Member:
November 1, 2006

Hierarchy level:
Day

MAPS TO...

Reference Date:
Enter a date that is equal to the period specified by the reference member above:
11/ 1/2006

PerformancePoint has its own time aggregation levels that need to be mapped to the corresponding levels in our dimension hierarchy. In our case, this is pretty much a one-to-one mapping.

5. In the Time Member Associations section, select the appropriate Time Aggregation values, as shown:

| Time MemberAssociations | |
|---|---|
| Member Level | Time Aggregation |
| Month | Month |
| Date | Day |
| Calendar Year | Year |
| Calendar Semester | Semester |
| Calendar Quarter | Quarter |

6. Save the changes to the AdventureWorksOLAP data connection.

We can now make use of our time intelligence functionality to create a filter for our sample dashboard.

1. Switch to MySampleDashboard, and then click Filter from the Dashboard Items section of the Create ribbon.
2. In the Select a Filter Template dialog, select Time Intelligence, as shown:

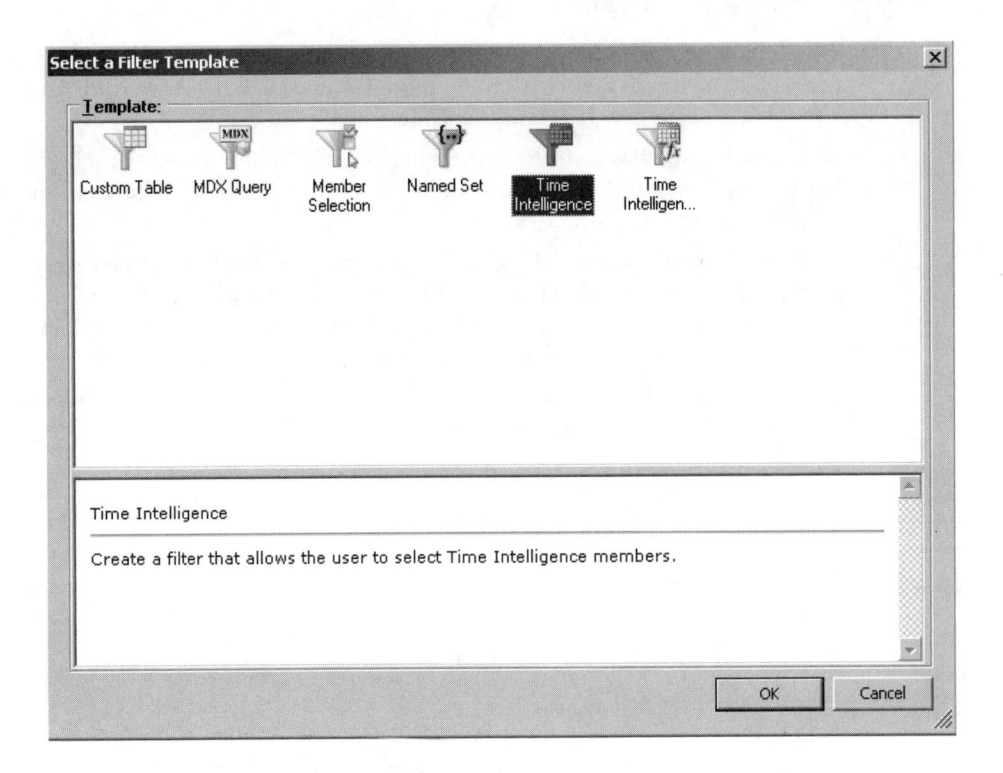

[Select a Filter Template dialog showing templates: Custom Table, MDX Query, Member Selection, Named Set, Time Intelligence (selected), Time Intelligen... Description reads: "Time Intelligence — Create a filter that allows the user to select Time Intelligence members."]

3. Click Add Data Source, and then select AdventureWorksOLAP.
4. Add formulae as shown in the following illustration. This step warrants a bit of further explanation. Time, of course, is always changing. By tomorrow, today will have become yesterday. To accommodate this constant change, values shown in the time selector are calculated using simple formulas that take the current date into account. You'll see this in action by creating a selector that shows how to select from one of the previous four quarters.

## Create a Filter

### Enter Time Formula
Each formula will be one value that the user can select in the filter.

Select a data source
**Enter time formula**
Select display method
Create a filter

Add Formula | Remove Selected Formulas

| Formula | Display Name |
|---|---|
| Quarter-15 | This Quarter |
| Quarter-16 | Last Quarter |
| Quarter-17 | 2 Quarters ago |
| Quarter-18 | 3 Quarters ago |
| Quarter-15,Quarter-16,Quarter-17,Quarter-18 | Year |
|  |  |

Preview — Formula example: "Year", "Quarter-1", "Month:Month-5", "Day+1,Day+2,Day+3", and "Year.FirstQuarter:Quarter"

< Previous | Next > | Finish | Cancel

---

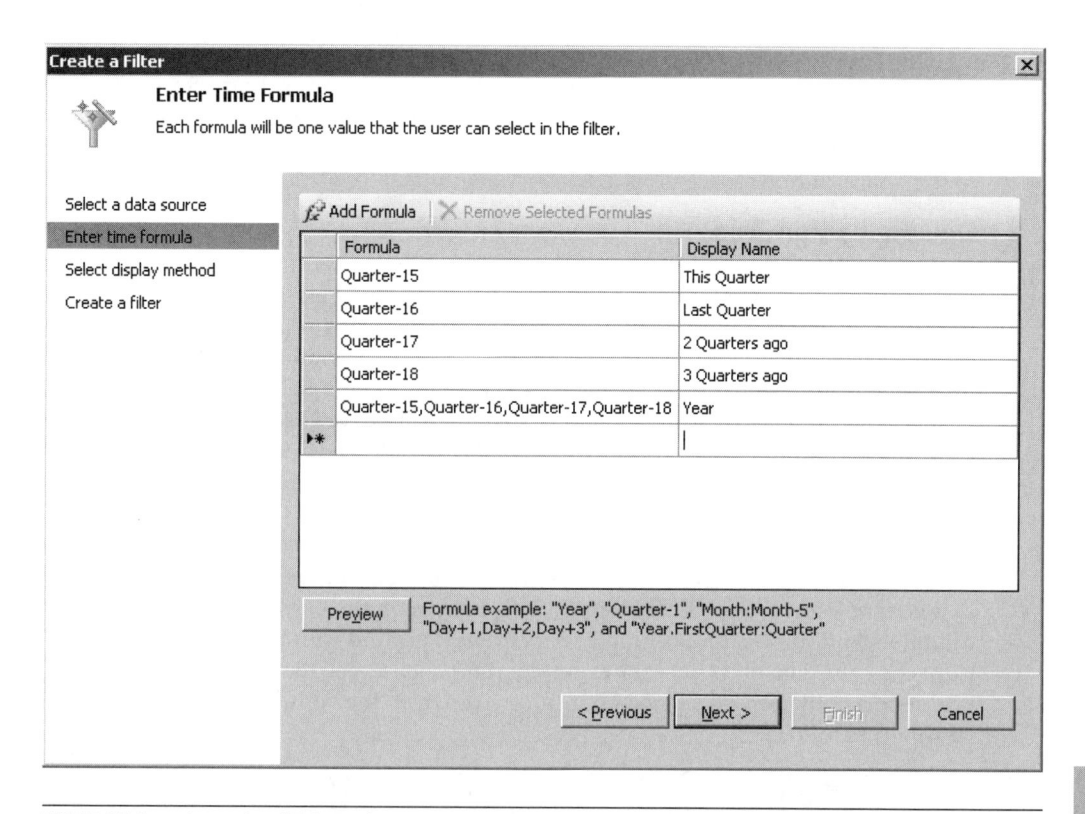

**NOTE** We're subtracting 15 from the current quarter because the AdventureWorks data set contains data from 2001 through to 2006, so subtracting 15 quarters will ensure that we've got something to see in our report. Depending on the version of the sample data that you're using, you may need to adjust the formulae accordingly.

5. Click Next, and then select List as the Display Method. Click Finish to create the new filter. Type the name **MyTimeFilter**.
6. Switch back to the MySampleDashboard item and drag the new filter from the Details pane onto the left column.
7. We can hook the filter up to our reports by dragging the AdventureWorksOLAP field onto the Drop field to create a connections section of the appropriate report. In the Connection dialog, accept the default values of Connect To: Date Calendar and Source Value: AdventureWorksOLAP.
8. Do this for both reports, and then deploy the updated dashboard to SharePoint.

Our dashboard now contains a drop-down selector that we can use to select the date range for our reports. Notice that when we select Year, a chart is drawn for each quarter in the year rather than a single chart covering the entire period. This happens because we defined year as a series of quarters rather than a single time period, and our chart is bound to use a time period as one of its axis.

### Decomposition Tree

**New in 2010**

Although we specified which dimensions and measures were to be used on our reports together with the layout and other options, all of this stuff can be changed dynamically by the user so that he or she can further analyze the data being represented. In reality, when we create a dashboard, we're simply defining the starting point for further analysis by the user. When a user right-clicks any PerformancePoint Report web part, a context menu appears and presents an array of options, such as drill up/drill down and measure selection. Covering the entire range of options available is outside the scope of this chapter. However, of these options, one of the new additions in SharePoint 2010 is the *Decomposition Tree*.

The Decomposition Tree is a Silverlight control that allows users to drill down visually into data using any of the dimensions and measures that are available within the cube. Clicking each data item presents a list of dimensions that can be used to expand the dataset as well as relevant properties and rollup information on the current selection. The best way to understand the Decomposition Tree is to mess around with it. To show the control, right-click any data element—for example, right-click a pie chart slice or a number on the grid report, and then select Decomposition Tree from the context menu. The control will be shown as follows:

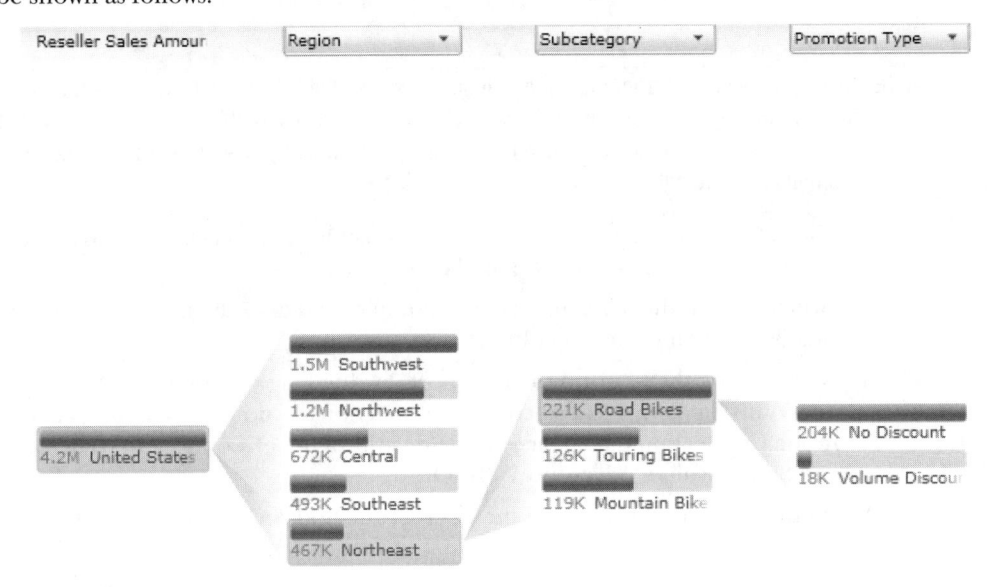

| Reseller Sales Amour | Region ▼ | Subcategory ▼ | Promotion Type ▼ |

4.2M United States
  1.5M Southwest
  1.2M Northwest
  672K Central
    221K Road Bikes
      204K No Discount
      18K Volume Discou
    126K Touring Bikes
    119K Mountain Bike
  493K Southeast
  467K Northeast

### PowerPivot

We've looked at PerformancePoint and how it can be used to build powerful business process management solutions using the SharePoint platform. Such solutions are excellent for providing day-to-day management information or other business information, for which the requirements can be easily defined and implemented. However, one of the common stumbling blocks in large-scale BI projects is that too often the project becomes a victim of its own success. A project may start off with a range of commonly used line-of-business reports, but over time, more and more requests for additional reports or changes to existing reports can overwhelm available development resources. When this happens, users who are unable or unwilling to wait until a suitable resource is available often resort to cobbling together their own solutions using Excel, Access, or some other tool. Each homegrown solution is a step farther away from the BI mantra of one version of the truth, and over time, a lot of the good work done on the project is lost.

Thankfully, it doesn't have to be this way. The solution to this problem is to empower users to create their own ad hoc reports using a series of common data sources. Historically, solutions to this problem have focused on the front end, presentation layer of report generation. Tools such as Reporting Services include a report builder with which users can create reports from published data sources. Although this approach does go a long way toward reducing the burden on development resources, the presentation layer is probably the least time-consuming aspect of report generation. Where the hard work comes in is at the data warehousing and OLAP layers, and tools such as Report Builder don't provide any assistance here.

With SQL Server 2008 R2, Microsoft includes a new product known as *PowerPivot*. PivotTables are a well-known and widely used feature of Excel, especially when it comes to analyzing business data. However, PivotTables have their limitations, and one of the most significant with respect to this discussion is in the selection of data sources. PivotTables can either make use of data within a workbook or they can be connected to a predefined data source. You've seen that a fair bit of work is involved in predefining data sources, especially when attempting to meet specific reporting requirements. PowerPivot addresses these issues by allowing users to create their own data sources from a mash-up of existing sources. Additionally, PowerPivot lets users work with much larger datasets that would normally be possible using PivotTables.

In effect, PowerPivot is a user-driven OLAP tool. It allows users to create in-memory OLAP cubes and uses those cubes within Excel in the same way as external data sources. Now, the implications of that are pretty significant, but when coupled with the fact that the resulting Excel workbooks can then be hosted using Excel services and accessed as OLAP data sources in their own right, you can see that PowerPivot truly opens the door to collaborative BI solutions.

## PowerPivot Excel Add-In

Users can create PowerPivot data sources using an add-in for Excel 2010 that can be downloaded from www.microsoft.com. Let's work through an example to see how the add-in works. As earlier, we'll make use of the AdventureWorks sample databases.

1. PowerPivot data is created using Excel 2010, as mentioned. Open the Excel application and then, from the PowerPivot tab, select PowerPivot Window from the ribbon, as shown here:

PowerPivot can import data from a variety of sources, including traditional sources such as SQL Server and other database systems, as well as other sources such as Reporting Services reports, ATOM feeds, and other PowerPivot workbooks. For the purposes of this demonstration, we'll use the AdventureWorks database running on SQL Server.

2. From the Home tab, select From Database in the Get External Data section of the ribbon, and then select From SQL Server.

3. Configure the connection to connect to the AdventureWorks sample database, and then select the Product and ProductInventory tables, as shown:

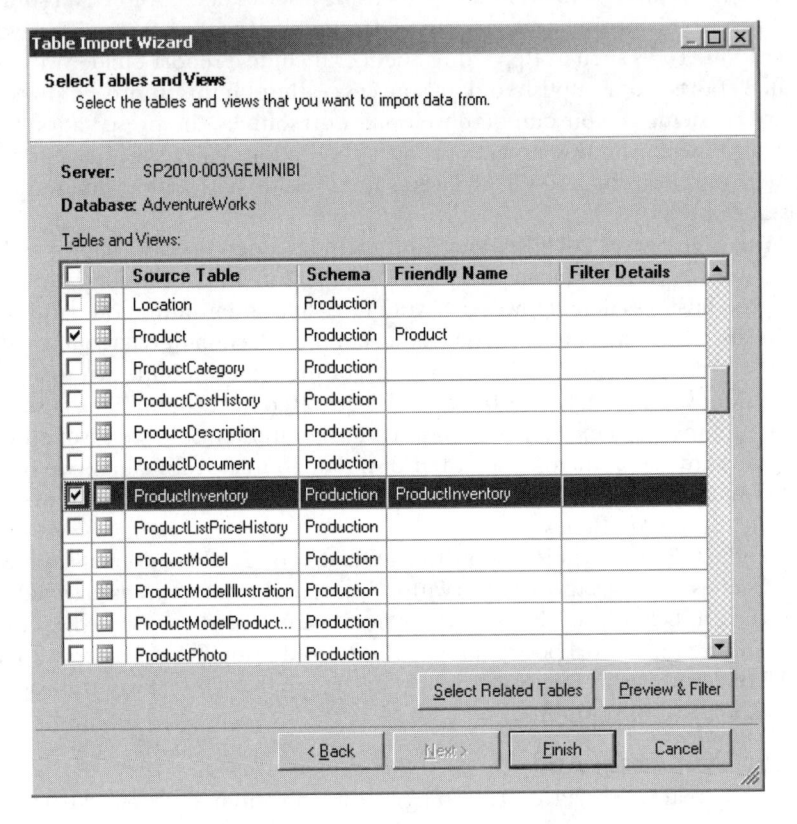

4. Data from the selected tables will be imported into PowerPivot and will be displayed as data grids within individual tabs. As part of the import process, PowerPivot automatically creates relationships between the two tables. We can check that these relationships are correct by clicking the Table tab and then clicking the Manage Relationships button from the ribbon.

**TIP** Creating relationships within PowerPivot is an important feature. You can import data from a variety of sources and create relationships between tables from different sources.

## Data Analysis Expressions (DAX)

In the Manage Relationships dialog, you can see that the ProductInventory table is related to the Product table using ProductId. This relationship was picked up from the underlying database. We'll make use of this relationship to illustrate the use of the new DAX language. DAX uses a syntax that's similar to Excel formulae. The main difference is that DAX functions generally operate on multiple rows of data. In our example, our function summarizes quantity values from a related table.

1. In the Product table, select the Column tab, and then click the Add Column button.
2. In the formula bar, enter the following DAX expression:

```
=SUMX(RELATEDTABLE('ProductInventory'),
             'ProductInventory'[Quantity])*'Product'[StandardCost]
```

3. Right-click the CalculatedColumn1 header, and then select Rename Column. Change the column name to **InventoryCost**.
4. To make use of this data in Excel, switch back to the Home tab and then select PivotTable | Single PivotTable from the ribbon.

We can now create a PivotTable in the usual manner by adding columns to the appropriate sections. Notice that our calculated InventoryCost column appears in the list and can be used in the same way as other columns. We can drag the InventoryCost column into the Values section of the Gemini Task Panel to create a new summary value named Sum of InventoryCost, as shown here:

## PowerPivot for SharePoint

In addition to the Excel add-in that allows users to create and use PowerPivot enabled workbooks, another feature of SQL Server 2008 R2 provides SharePoint integration for PowerPivot. This allows PowerPivot-enabled workbooks to be hosted by Excel services in the same way as regular workbooks. Instead of the in-memory version of Analysis Services that's used when accessing a PowerPivot-enabled workbook via the Excel client, when SharePoint integration is configured, PowerPivot cubes are hosted on-demand by Analysis Services.

---

**NOTE** For more information on configuring PowerPivot for SharePoint, see http://msdn.microsoft.com/en-us/library/ee637439.aspx and http://msdn.microsoft.com/en-us/library/ee637271(v=SQL.105).aspx.

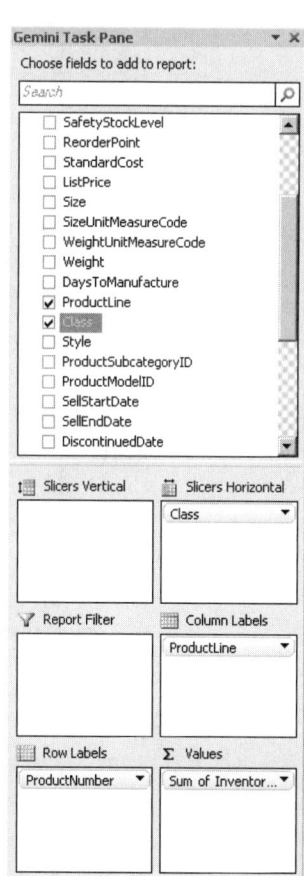

Making use of the simple PowerPivot workbook that we created earlier, we can publish the workbook to SharePoint. Before we do this, we need to create a PowerPivot Gallery document library to contain our workbook.

1. You publish PowerPivot workbooks in exactly the same way you publish other Excel content to Excel Services. Select the File tab to enter the backstage area, and then select Share.

2. Click Publish To Excel Services, and then navigate to the PowerPivot gallery that we created earlier. If everything is set up properly, the workbook will be uploaded to the library. Navigating to the PowerPivot gallery will show details of the workbook together with previews of each page:

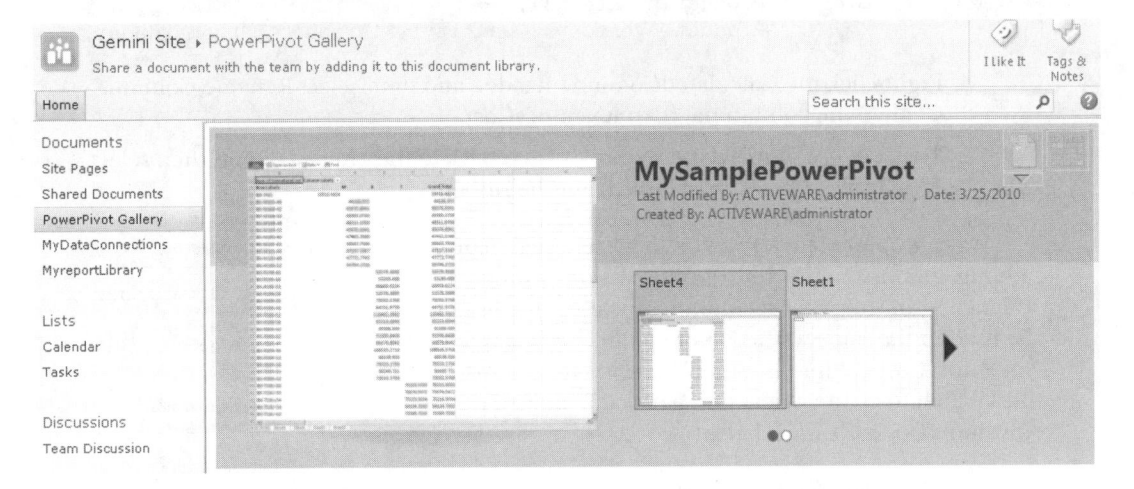

Now that we've published our PowerPivot data source, we can make use of it as a data source anywhere that can utilize Analysis Services data. Let's see this in action by creating a PerformancePoint dashboard based on our PowerPivot workbook.

1. In Dashboard Designer, create a new data source by selecting Data Source from the Create tab.

2. In the Select a Data Source Template dialog, select Analysis Services.

3. In the Connection Settings section, set the Server to the URL for our sample PowerPivot workbook, and then choose the default Database and Cube values from the respective drop-downs.

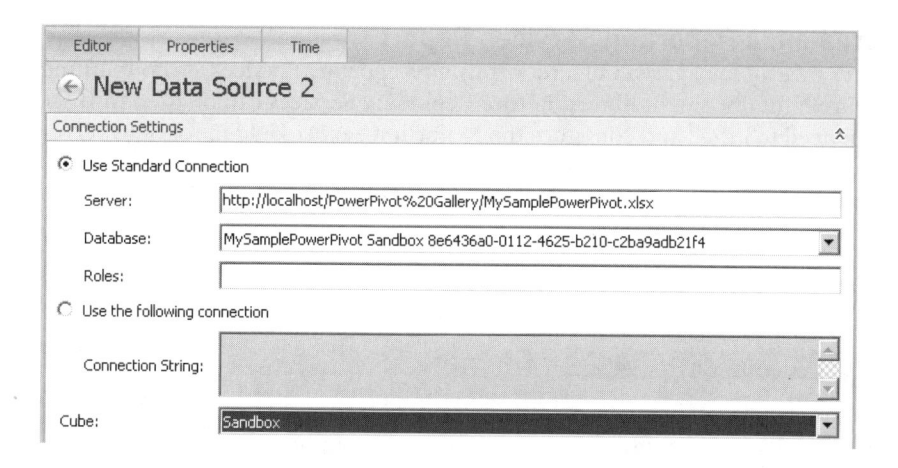

NOTE I've used **localhost** as the server name for illustrative purposes. Enter the actual name of your server to prevent security errors.

4. Using this new data connection, we can now create dashboards and reports in the same way we did earlier when addressing the AdventureWorksOLAP data source.

The real power of PowerPivot on SharePoint is that a workbook published to Excel Services can be treated in the same way as a regular OLAP cube. Instead of development resources being tied up designing and developing every cube using Business Intelligence Studio, you can now build simple cubes using Excel and PowerPivot. Since the data is easily accessible, it can be integrated into a wider BI solution with relatively little effort. As you've seen, for example, PowerPivot data can be used to generate the same dynamic PerformancePoint reports as OLAP data hosted using Analysis Services.

## Reporting Services

Reporting Services are generally used in conjunction with SQL Server and Analysis Services to generate all manner of reports. A standard installation of Reporting Services will provide a web-based portal where users can browse through a collection of published reports. As an alternative to a stand-alone portal, Reporting Services can also be installed in SharePoint integration mode. As the name suggests, this mode provides a much higher degree of integration with SharePoint. All report data, rather than being stored in a dedicated Reporting Services database and presented via a stand-alone portal, is now stored directly within SharePoint lists and libraries.

## Creating a Reporting Services Report

Let's take a look at creating a report using Reporting Services and publishing it to a SharePoint document library. Before Reporting Services can be used with SharePoint, you need to install and configure the Reporting Services add-in for SQL Server 2008 R2. The add-in can be downloaded from www.microsoft.com/downloads/details. aspx?FamilyID=16bb10f9-3acc-4551-bacc-bdd266da1d45&displaylang=en. After you've installed the add-in, do the following:

1. Start the SQL Server Business Intelligence Studio application, and then create a new project using the Report Server Project Wizard template, as shown next:

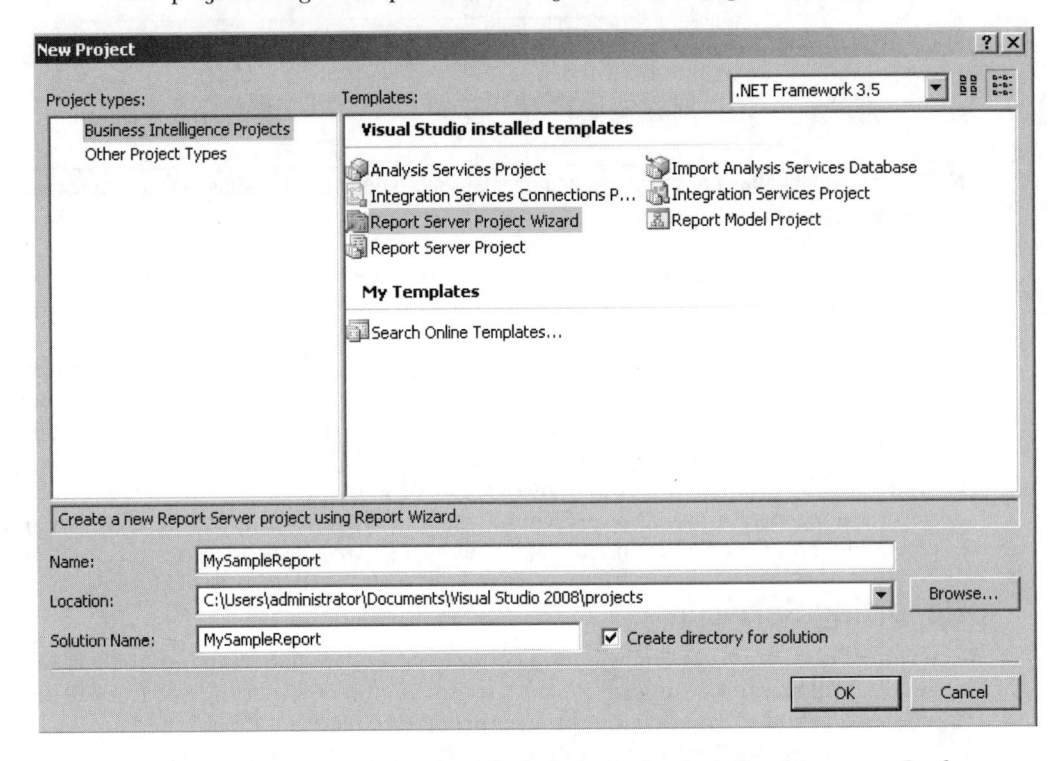

2. We'll make use of the AdventureWorks sample database for this report. In the Report Wizard dialog, click Next to move to the Select the Data Source step. Create a new data source and name it **AdventureWorks**. Set the connection string to point to the AdventureWorks sample database.

3. Click the Make This A Shared Data Source checkbox. By making the data source shared, it will be published as a separate data source item in SharePoint; this will allow it to be reused by other reports. The alternative to a shared data source is an embedded data source, where the details are embedded within the report.

4. Either click the Query Builder button to create the following query or manually enter it into the Query string text box:

```
SELECT     C.FirstName,
           C.LastName,
           C.Phone,
           E.Title
FROM       HumanResources.Employee as E
INNER JOIN Person.Contact as C
ON         E.ContactID = C.ContactID
```

5. Create a Tabular report grouped by Title with FirstName, LastName, and Phone in the Detail section, as shown here:

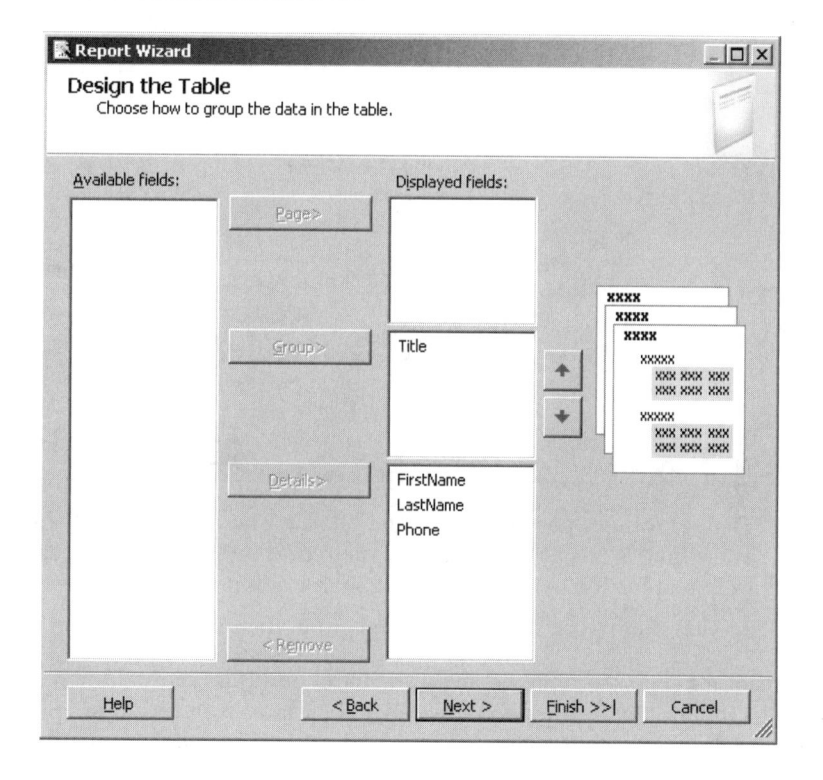

6. Click Finish and then name the report **Telephone Directory**.
7. Before we can publish the new report to SharePoint, we need to let the project know where to store the various components, such as the data connection and the report definition. To set these options, choose Project | MySampleReport Properties.

8. In the Deployment section, specify appropriate values for each target folder and the TargetServerURL, as shown next. Notice that the folders must be fully qualified URLs and the TargetServerURL must be the URL to the SharePoint site where the reports will be deployed.

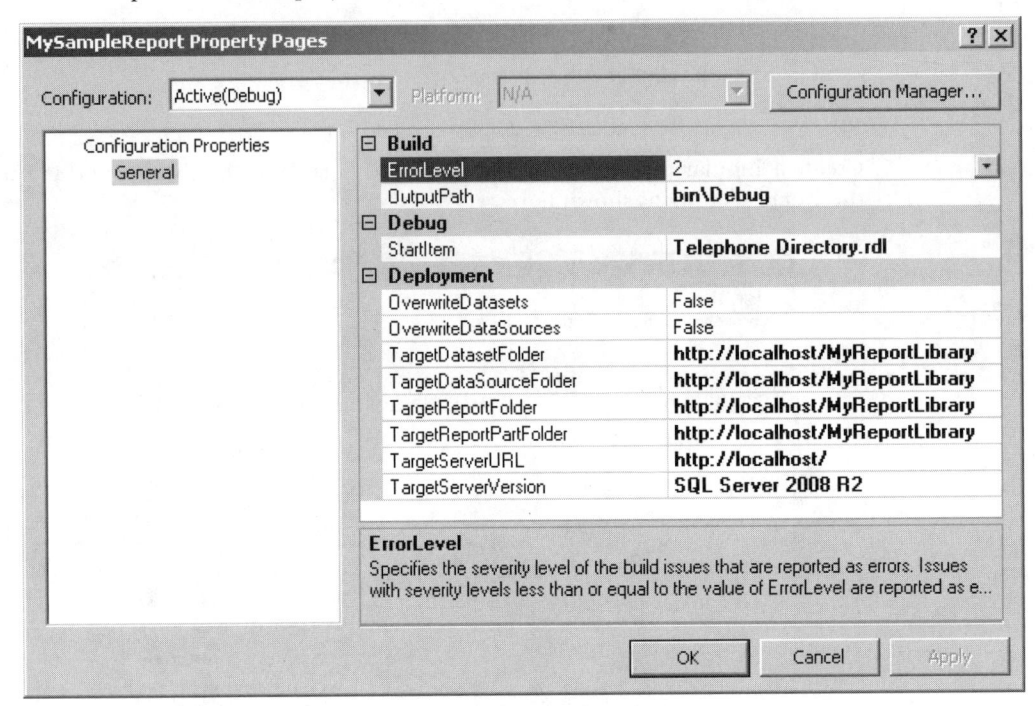

9. To deploy the report to SharePoint, choose Build | Deploy MySampleReport. If everything is properly configured, the report and its associated data connection will be uploaded to the configured SharePoint document library.
10. To view the report, simply click the item in the document library.

Creating a report and publishing it to SharePoint is no more difficult than creating a Word document or any other content. Since the report is stored within SharePoint, it is automatically subject to the same security and information management policies as other content.

## Report Builder

After a report has been published to SharePoint, it can be modified by users who have the appropriate permissions by using the Report Builder tool. Like the PerformancePoint Dashboard Designer, the Report Builder is a click-once application that can be accessed directly from within SharePoint. To open a report using the Report Builder, select Edit in Report Builder from the context menu, as shown here:

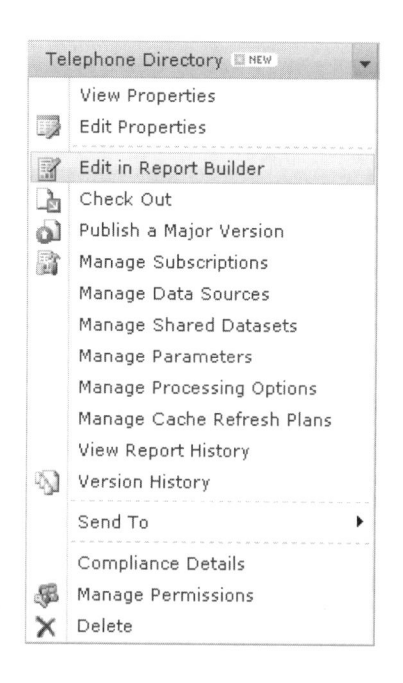

### Reporting Services Web Part

When a user clicks a report in a SharePoint library, the report is automatically rendered on the page. It should come as no surprise to learn that this is done using a Reporting Services–specific web part. However, having such a web part available presents the opportunity to integrate Reporting Services content with other content on pages within a SharePoint application.

For us developers, being able to amalgamate Reporting Services content with application-generated content greatly increases the flexibility of our applications. When it comes to displaying or printing application data, offloading the task to Reporting Services provides a whole host of functionality that would be very time-consuming to build from scratch.

## Summary

The groundbreaking BI capabilities enabled by SharePoint 2010 offer many exciting possibilities for developers. You've seen how PerformancePoint offers powerful BPM capabilities while PowerPivot delivers a whole new level of self-service business analytics. There's no doubt that this is all great stuff if you're building a BI application. Even if your application doesn't require any BI functionality, by leveraging the capabilities available for building BI solutions, such as the Reporting Services web part, the Chart web part, or the status indicators, you can address a lot of user interface requirements without having to resort to custom coding.

# PART V

# Configuration

**CHAPTER 19**
Packaging and Deployment Model

**CHAPTER 20**
PowerShell

# CHAPTER 19

# Packaging and Deployment Model

In the various examples in this book, we've made extensive use of Visual Studio and SharePoint Designer to create and deploy custom code to SharePoint. By now you should have a good idea of how projects are structured in Visual Studio and how this structure relates to the entities that are created in SharePoint.

The projects we've worked on so far have been relatively small, and we've deployed to a single development server. Although we've been using the SharePoint packaging and deployment model, we haven't explored it's full potential. In the real world, a knowledge of how packaging and deployment works in a SharePoint farm is an essential skill. This chapter will help you use the knowledge you've gained so far to understand how the SharePoint packaging and deployment model fits into the bigger picture.

## Working with Packages

What may not be apparent in the projects that we've created so far is that when we're deploying a solution to SharePoint, the artifacts in our Visual Studio project are collated into a package file that is then copied to the server. The SharePoint deployment process then uses the contents of the package to install our customization. We can see this process in action by monitoring the output window in Visual Studio.

So far we've been working on a single server development machine, but what happens if a farm includes several servers? How can we deploy our customization to all servers? The answer is, of course, to use a package that can be stored centrally and automatically rolled out to all servers in the farm as part of the installation process. As new servers are added to the farm, centrally stored packages are automatically deployed as required. Furthermore, farm administrators have the ability to deploy and retract packages from the Central Administration console.

## Package Structure

SharePoint packages are created as cabinet (CAB) files with a .wsp extension. We can, however, rename a .wsp file, such as myproject.wsp, to myproject.cab and view the contents in Windows Explorer.

Each package file contains many different elements, mostly consisting of XML files and resources such as dynamic link libraries (DLLs), script files, or images. One thing that package files have in common, however, is a manifest.xml file. This file is basically the setup guide for the package and contains a list of the deployable items within the package.

Each solution consists of one or more deployable item. A number of different types of deployable items exist, such as an assembly, a resource file, or a site definition file. However, for the most part, deployable items are defined using feature manifests.

## Package Designer

Let's see how these ideas jibe with our understanding of the Visual Studio project structure.

1. Create a new blank site named Chapter19.
2. Using Visual Studio, create a new Empty SharePoint Project named Chapter19, as shown:

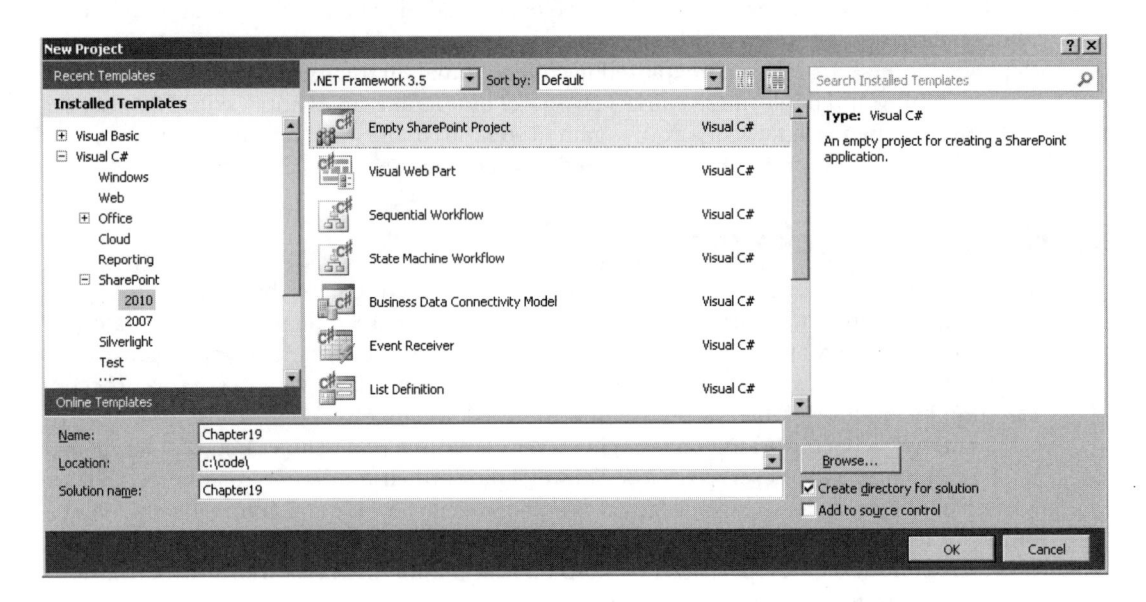

3. In the SharePoint Project Wizard, set the site to use for debugging as the site created in step 1, and then select the Deploy As Farm Solution option.
4. Choose Project Add New Item. Then in the Add New Item dialog, select Empty Element, as shown. Name the element **FirstElement**.

## Chapter 19 Packaging and Deployment Model 495

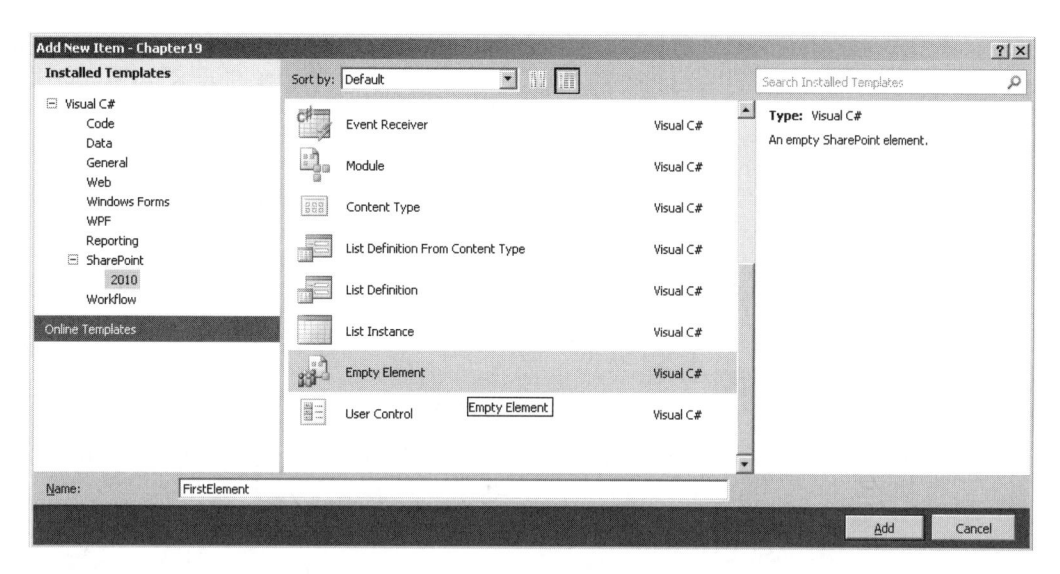

Let's take a look at what's happened in Visual Studio. We have a Features folder and a Package folder. If we double-click Package.package within the Package folder, we'll see the package designer shown here:

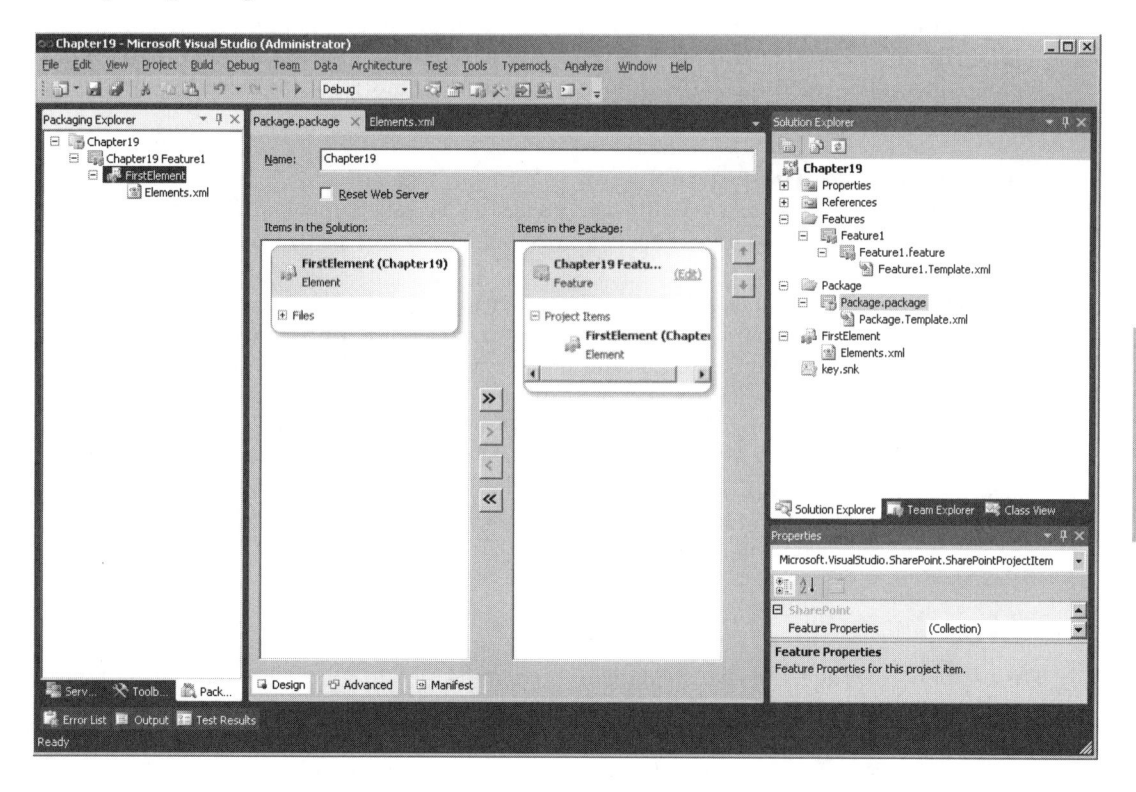

The package designer gives us a visual tool we can use to modify the manifest.xml for a package file. Click the Manifest button at the bottom of the page to see the underlying manifest.xml file:

```
<Solution xmlns="http://schemas.microsoft.com/sharepoint/"
          SolutionId="--snipped--" SharePointProductVersion="14.0">
  <Assemblies>
    <Assembly Location="Chapter19.dll"
              DeploymentTarget="GlobalAssemblyCache" />
  </Assemblies>
  <FeatureManifests>
    <FeatureManifest Location="Chapter19_Feature1\Feature.xml" />
  </FeatureManifests>
</Solution>
```

In this manifest are two deployable items: an assembly that will be the build output of our Visual Studio project and a FeatureManifest that points to a Feature.xml file.

## Deploying Assemblies

By default, the build output assembly will always be added to the solution file. This means that any code that we add within our project will be compiled and the resultant DLL will be deployed to SharePoint in the solution package. In some situations, however, we may need to add another assembly. By clicking the Advanced button in the Solution Designer, we can either add an assembly or add the compiled output of another project within the solution. Along with adding additional assemblies, we can also add any resource assemblies that should be included.

### Adding Safe Controls

When adding assemblies to a solution, we can also add a safe control entry. Safe control entries were mentioned in preceding chapters, but I'll clarify exactly what they are and why you might need them here.

SharePoint makes use of a custom page parser to assemble the user interface, and this parser is known as the *Safe-Mode Parser*. Its primary function is to prevent users from executing code on the server that hasn't been specifically approved by an administrator. The mechanism by which an administrator approves code for execution is the SafeControl entry, which is ultimately applied as a web.config entry on each front-end server. If our assembly contains user controls or web parts or any other component that can be declaratively added to a page, a SafeControl entry is required. If a user attempts to add a component that does not have a corresponding SafeControl entry, an error will be thrown detailing the absence of the SafeControl entry as the problem.

## Features

In a solution package, the FeatureManifest element is used to specify the reference to the manifest file for a particular feature. To a certain extent, features work in a similar way to solutions in that they can contain a number of individual components and make use of a manifest file to specify what should be done with these components.

## Feature Designer

Using the Chapter19 project that we created earlier, double-click the Feature1 node in the Features folder to display the Feature Designer:

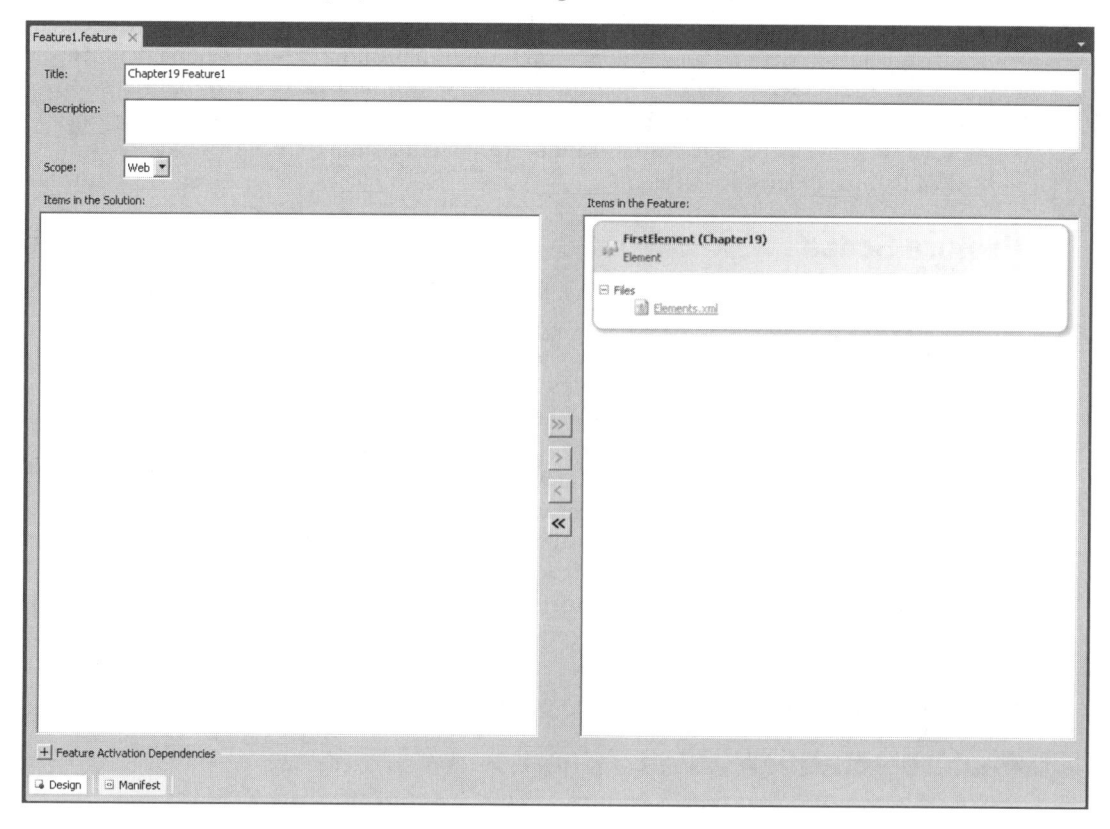

As you know, features are individual items of functionality that can be activated or deactivated within a SharePoint farm. You can see in the Feature Designer that features comprise one or more elements, where an element may be a web part, a list definition, a workflow, or a number of different components. Using the Feature Designer, we can select which elements should be included in a feature and therefore specify which functionality will be enabled when the feature is activated.

## Activation Dependencies

For the most part, we don't need to think about feature elements, because Visual Studio automatically creates features for us and adds our project items to them. However, in the real world, this default behavior may not be appropriate. For example, rather than having many features, each with a different project item in it, we may want to consolidate related items into a single feature. This makes it easier for users to activate our customization since they need to activate only one feature rather than many separate items. It also makes it easier for us to ensure that all the parts of our solution are activated.

We can consolidate related items in a few ways: We can use the Feature Designer to specify which elements should be included in a feature, or we can define feature dependencies. Where a dependency is defined, a feature cannot be activated unless its dependencies have also been activated. This may seem like a poor solution, because it means that users still have to activate a load of individual features, but we can take this a step further. Under some circumstances, dependency features will be automatically activated when a feature that depends upon them is activated. Furthermore, we can hide features so that they don't appear in the feature activation user interface. Effectively, this brings us back to the idea of a single activation click for our customization, while at the same time allows us to keep individual features relatively simple.

## Feature Scope

The activation dependency approach has a few limitations, but before we look at those, we need to consider feature scope. Again, this is something that we've been able to ignore because Visual Studio handles it for us automatically; in the real world, an understanding of scope is essential when building complex solutions.

In the Feature Designer, under the Description text box is a drop-down that we can use to select the scope of a feature: Farm, WebApplication, Site, and Web. As you've probably guessed, these options determine the level at which the components are activated. Components within a feature scoped as Web will be activated for a single site only, whereas components within a feature scoped as Farm will be available to the entire farm. However, it's not quite as straightforward as that. Not all types of component can be installed in all scopes. For example, if we're creating a content type, we can deploy it only using a feature scoped at the Site level; if we're adding an event receiver, it can be scoped only at the Web level. You can find a complete list of what goes where at http://msdn.microsoft.com/en-us/library/ms454835.aspx.

## Feature Activation Rules

To return to our discussion of the limitations of feature dependencies, the first limitation concerns scope. Features cannot be dependent on features of a more restrictive scope—that is, a feature scoped at the site collection (Site) level cannot depend on a feature scoped at the site (Web) level. This makes sense when you think about it, because a site collection can contain multiple sites, each with its own set of activated features—so there's no way to satisfy such a dependency properly. The opposite is not true, however. Features scoped at the site level can depend on features at the site collection level. There is one caveat to this rule: A feature can't depend on another feature at a higher scope if the higher level feature is not visible. So a site feature can't be dependent on a site collection feature that's hidden. There is a good reason for this: Although we can automatically activate dependent features, we can do so only within the same level. So we would be unable to activate our site feature because there would be no way to activate the site collection feature upon which it depended if the site collection feature were hidden.

The second limitation concerns dependency chains. Generally speaking, activations can be only one level deep. For example, if feature A depends on feature B, then feature B cannot have any dependencies. This is true only for visible dependencies, however. If feature B is dependent upon feature C, which is hidden, then the dependency chain is allowed. Hidden features cannot have any dependencies; therefore, the maximum chain depth is two levels.

## Feature Properties

With the Feature Designer open, we can set feature properties using the Properties pane in Visual Studio. For example, we can hide a feature by setting the Is Hidden property to True. Many of the properties are set automatically by Visual Studio, but the following properties can also be used to meet specific configuration requirements:

- **Activate on Default**   This Boolean value dictates whether the feature should be activated when the solution package is deployed.

- **Always Force Install**   The SharePoint deployment mechanism is pretty clever when it comes to installing features. Because features can be shared by many solutions, only features that are not already installed are installed when a package is deployed. Each feature has a unique identifier that's used as the reference for activation dependencies and so on. To force an installation when the solution is deployed, this value can be set to True.

- **Deployment Path**   All features are deployed to their own folder at %SPROOT%TEMPLATE\FEATURES\. By default, Visual Studio creates folders named *ProjectName_FeatureName*. In our project, our feature will be deployed in a folder named Chapter19_Feature1. We can change the name of this folder by changing the Deployment Path. (The name Deployment Path is something of a misnomer; it more accurately contains the Deployment folder name.)

- **Image URL & Image Alt Text**   In the Manage Features page, an icon appears to the left of each feature's description. These properties can be used to specify an alternative image file and appropriate alternative text if required. In no alternative is specified, the default feature icon will be used.

We'll look at few other properties, such as Receiver Assembly, Upgrade Actions Receiver Assembly, and Version in more detail in later sections.

## Feature Elements

With a few exceptions, almost all the items we can add to a project using Visual Studio are packaged as feature elements. In our demonstration project, we added an empty element named FirstElement; in the Solution Explorer page, we can see that it contains a single file named Elements.xml. In the Feature Designer, we can click the Manifest button at the bottom of the page to see the manifest file for the feature:

```
<Feature xmlns="http://schemas.microsoft.com/sharepoint/"
         Title="Chapter19 Feature1" Id="5fcd733e-2cc9-4363-85fd-dfe7893cb195"
         Scope="Web">
  <ElementManifests>
    <ElementManifest Location="FirstElement\Elements.xml" />
  </ElementManifests>
</Feature>
```

Similar to how the manifest file for the solution was made up of FeatureManifest elements, we can see that the feature manifest is made up of ElementManifest elements.

Let's add a more complex element to our project to see how this is represented:

1. In Visual Studio, choose Project | Add New Item. In the Add New Item dialog, select List Definition and name the element **SampleList**.

2. In the SharePoint Customization Wizard dialog, accept the defaults and then click Finish. A new SampleList folder will be added to the project, as shown:

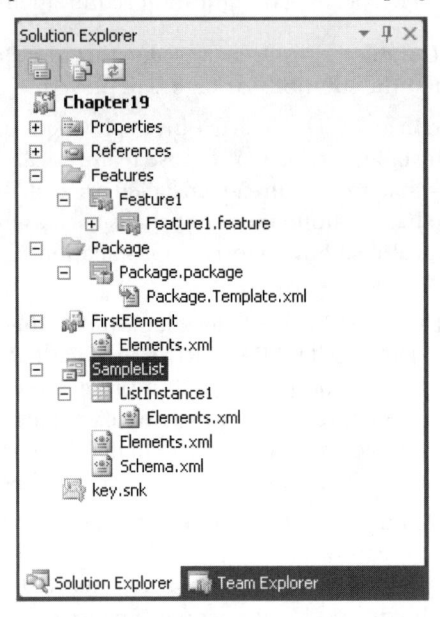

If we look at the feature manifest file again, we can see that three new elements have been added:

```
<Feature xmlns="http://schemas.microsoft.com/sharepoint/"
      Title="Chapter19 Feature1" Id="5fcd733e-2cc9-4363-85fd-dfe7893cb195"
      Scope="Web">
  <ElementManifests>
    <ElementManifest Location="FirstElement\Elements.xml" />
    <ElementManifest Location="ListInstance1\Elements.xml" />
    <ElementManifest Location="SampleList\Elements.xml" />
    <ElementFile Location="SampleList\Schema.xml" />
  </ElementManifests>
</Feature>
```

Two new ElementManifest elements point to the new Elements.xml files that were added and an ElementFile element. This prompts the question, What's the difference between an ElementManifest and an ElementFile? We'll find the answer by examining the Elements.xml file in the SampleList folder:

```
<Elements xmlns="http://schemas.microsoft.com/sharepoint/">
    <ListTemplate
        Name="SampleList"
```

```
            Type="10000"
            BaseType="0"
            OnQuickLaunch="TRUE"
            SecurityBits="11"
            Sequence="320"
            DisplayName="Chapter19 - SampleList"
            Description="My List Definition"
            Image="/_layouts/images/itann.png"/>
</Elements>
```

In our Elements file, we're specifying that we are creating a new ListTemplate. Our Elements file is effectively issuing a command to the deployment framework. If we open the Schema.xml file, we find much more information contained within it. The Schema file is effectively a resource file that's used by the deployment framework to provision our list template. Another way to look at it is that our ElementManifest files dictate what should be done, whereas our ElementFile files provide the required resources to do the job.

A number of commands can be issued using ElementManifest files, and although these are mostly wrapped by a SharePoint Project Item in Visual Studio, a complete list can be found at http://msdn.microsoft.com/en-us/library/ms414322.aspx.

Although covering the various resource files that can be used by features is beyond the scope of this chapter (and could fill a book), one very important point needs to be made here: Although most of the content within a SharePoint site is stored in a content database, the same is not true for configuration. Much of the configuration for a site is defined within features, and the element files within the features are actually used to deliver the appropriate functionality.

To get a better understanding of the significance of this, we can navigate to %SPROOT%TEMPLATE/FEATURES and then open the TaskList folder. In the folder, we'll find a Feature.xml manifest file, which refers to the Tasks.xml ElementManifest file in the ListTemplates folder. When this feature is activated, the Task List list template is added to the list of lists that can be created for a SharePoint site. If we examine the contents of the Tasks folder, we'll find a schema.xml file. This file defines the schema for every task list that's currently in use on the SharePoint farm. Looking through the contents of the Features folder, we'll find that much of the functionality of the SharePoint platform is defined here.

## Feature Receivers

We've used a few feature receivers in some of the example projects in this book. A *feature receiver* is basically an event handler responsible for handling installation and activation events for a feature. We can add feature receivers to any type of feature by right-clicking a Feature node in the Solution Explorer pane and selecting Add Event Receiver. When we perform this action, Visual Studio adds a new code file to our project and sets the Receiver Assembly and Receiver Class properties of the feature to reference the new code file. Let's do this now:

1. Right-click the Features node and select Add Feature. A new feature named Chapter 19 Feature 2 will be added to the project.

2. Right-click the Feature2 node in the Features folder and select Add Event Receiver.

3. Double-click Feature2.feature in the Feature 2 folder. In the Properties pane, the Receiver Assembly and Receiver Class have been automatically set.

In the Feature2.EventReceiver.cs file are five commented methods representing the events that can be handled by the feature receiver. By uncommenting these methods, we can add custom code to do whatever we need to do. As you embark on more complex SharePoint projects, you'll find that although you can perform much configuration using the SharePoint Project Items available in Visual Studio, a lot of configuration still needs to be done programmatically. In these situations, the feature receiver is the tool of choice. Bearing that in mind, let's look at how feature receivers work and how we can best make use of them.

1. Add the following code to Feature2.EventReceiver.cs:

```
public override void FeatureActivated(SPFeatureReceiverProperties properties)
{
  if (properties.Feature.Parent is SPWeb)
  {
    SPWeb web = properties.Feature.Parent as SPWeb;

    Guid listId=web.Lists.Add("My New List",
                              "This is a demonstration list",
                              SPListTemplateType.Contacts);
    SPList newList = web.Lists[listId];
    newList.OnQuickLaunch = true;
    newList.Update();
  }
}

public override void FeatureDeactivating(
                            SPFeatureReceiverProperties properties)
{
  if (properties.Feature.Parent is SPWeb)
  {
    SPWeb web = properties.Feature.Parent as SPWeb;

    SPList myList = web.Lists.TryGetList("My New List");

    if (myList != null)
    {
      myList.Delete();
    }
  }
}
```

2. Deploy the solution by selecting Deploy Chapter 19 from the Build menu.

If all is well, we'll find that our blank demo site now contains two new lists: one named Chapter 19 - ListInstance1, which has been created by the ElementManifest in Feature1, and another named My New List, which has been created programmatically by our feature receiver in Feature 2.

Notice in this code snippet that we're using the properties.Feature.Parent property to obtain a reference to the SPWeb object on which our feature is being installed. Some investigation of the Parent property will reveal that it's of type object, and for that reason we're checking its type before casting it to a variable of the correct type. To understand why this is the case, you can take a look at how features are defined within the server object model, as shown here:

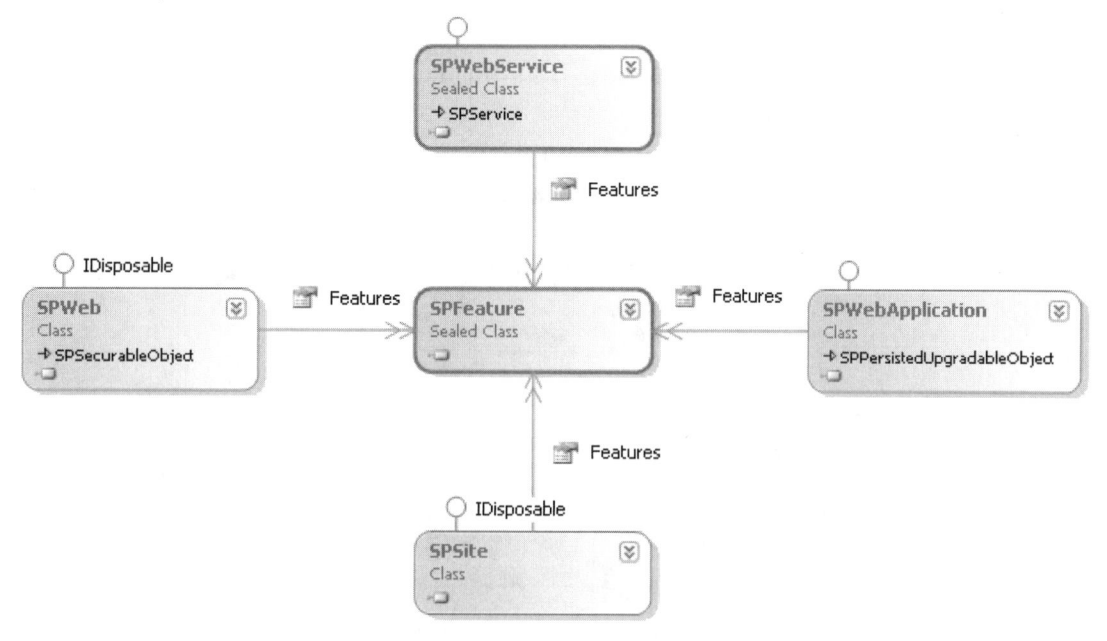

Features can have four possible scopes. When a feature of a particular scope is installed, it's added to the Features collection of the appropriate object. For example, a site collection–scoped feature would be added to the Features collection of the appropriate SPSite object. The SPFeature object that is returned by properties.Feature can therefore have one of four possible parents, depending on the scope of the feature.

To confirm that our receiver is working as expected, we can take the following steps:

1. From the Site Actions menu, select Site Settings, and then select Manage Site Features from the Site Actions section.
2. Both Chapter 19 Feature 1 and Chapter 19 Feature 2 are active. Deactivate Chapter 19 Feature 2. Notice that My New List is removed from the site. This confirms that our feature receiver is working as expected.

## Debugging Feature Receivers

Feature receivers can be difficult to debug because they are often executed within a separate process. To see an example of this problem, put a breakpoint on the first line of our FeatureActivated method and try debugging using Visual Studio. The code will be deployed and the feature will be activated, but execution will not stop at the breakpoint. Visual Studio makes use of a separate process, VSSPHost4.exe, to automate the deployment process. The Visual Studio debugger, however, is set up to attach to a W3SVC.exe process only, and therefore the breakpoint is never hit but the code still executes.

We can work around this issue in one of two ways: we can either attach a debugger to the appropriate process, or we can ensure that our feature receiver runs in the W3SVC process. To ensure that a debugger is attached to the correct process, we can take the following steps:

1. Add the following line of code to the method to be debugged:

   `Debugger.Break();`

2. Start the debugging process as normal. An error dialog will be displayed:

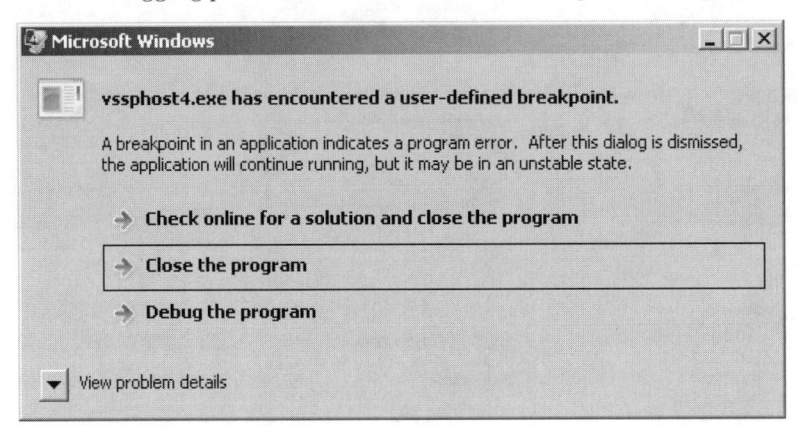

3. Click Debug The Program, and then in the Visual Studio Just-In-Time Debugger select the appropriate instance of Visual Studio. Click Yes to begin debugging.

This technique will work regardless of the host process. For example, if PowerShell is used to install a package, the same error dialog will be displayed.

Our second option is to ensure that the feature receiver code runs in the W3SVC process. This is relatively easy to do. Earlier when we looked at feature properties, we saw that the Activate On Default value is used to determine whether a feature should be automatically installed. We can use this setting as follows:

1. Remove the line of code that we added in the preceding example.

2. Double-click the Feature 2 node and set the Activate On Default property to False.

3. Debug the solution as normal. This time, when the solution is deployed, our feature will not be automatically activated.

4. When the web site being debugged is shown in the browser, select Site Settings from the Site Actions menu, and then select Manage Site Features from the Site Actions section. Manually activate the feature being debugged. The debugger will now stop on the breakpoints.

This method works because when features are activated via the user interface, the feature receiver runs under the W3SVC process, and Visual Studio has attached a debugger to this process as part of the standard debugging mechanism.

## Passing Parameters to Feature Receivers

You've seen how to create feature receivers and how to pick up references to the object that you need in order to access the server object model. We've looked at a few ways to enable debugging. Let's move on to look at more complex feature receivers.

As mentioned, practically every real-world SharePoint project will require some custom feature receivers. This is especially true when code being developed must be shared among multiple developers or deployed to testing or staging environments. As a result, it is sensible to create a library of feature receivers that perform specific configuration tasks. For example, I have a collection of feature receivers that perform actions such as configuring security for a site or setting up search scopes. These are actions that are common to many SharePoint projects but that can't be performed declaratively.

One essential aspect of creating reusable feature receivers is the ability to pass configuration into the receiver. Let's look at a few ways to solve this problem.

The first method is appropriate if a collection of name/value pairs is sufficient for our purposes.

1. Open the Feature Designer for Feature 2.
2. Add the FirstElement element that we created earlier to the feature, as shown:

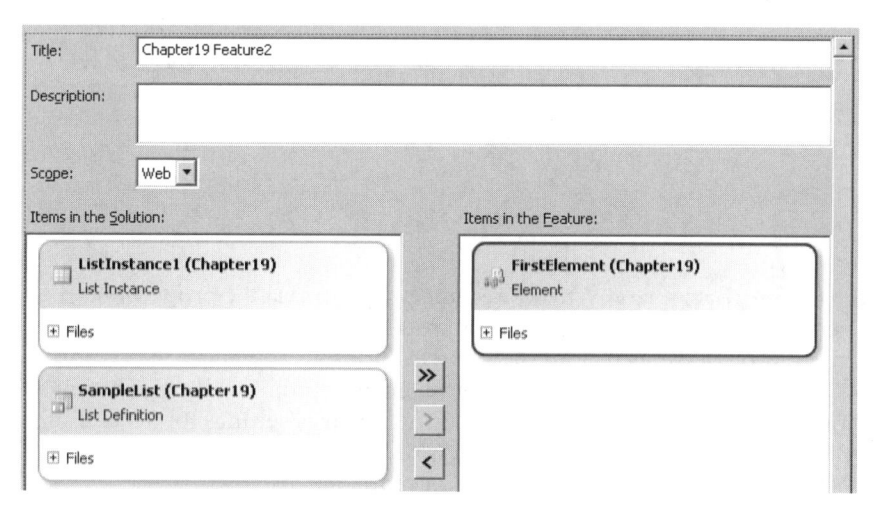

3. In the Solution Explorer pane, select the First Element node. Then in the Properties pane, click the ellipsis next to Feature Properties.

4. Add two new properties, ListName and ListDescription. Set the values to Another New List and This is Another list, respectively.

5. Click OK to close the dialog.

   Although every element in a feature has a Feature Properties property, in reality the properties are applied at the feature manifest level—that is, the combination of all the properties that are added to each element in Visual Studio are actually written within a single Properties element in the feature manifest.

6. Update the code in Feature2.EventReceiver.cs as follows:

```
public override void FeatureActivated(SPFeatureReceiverProperties properties)
{
   if (properties.Feature.Parent is SPWeb)
   {
      SPWeb web = properties.Feature.Parent as SPWeb;
      string listName = properties.Definition.Properties["ListName"].Value;
      string listDescription = properties.Definition.Properties["ListDescription"].Value;
      Guid listId = web.Lists.Add(listName,
                                  listDescription,
                                  SPListTemplateType.Contacts);
      SPList newList = web.Lists[listId];
      newList.OnQuickLaunch = true;
      newList.Update();
   }
}

public override void FeatureDeactivating(
                            SPFeatureReceiverProperties properties)
{
   if (properties.Feature.Parent is SPWeb)
   {
    SPWeb web = properties.Feature.Parent as SPWeb;
    string listName = properties.Definition.Properties["ListName"].Value;
    SPList myList = web.Lists.TryGetList(listName);
    if (myList != null)
    {
       myList.Delete();
    }
   }
}
```

You can see that we're able to address the properties via the properties.Definition object. The Definition object is of type SPFeatureDefinition and is an object representation of the various XML elements that make up the feature.

The next method for solving the problem is appropriate if more complex configuration is required. For example, when configuring security settings for a site using a feature receiver, I use this approach to load an XML file containing the security configuration (see http://spsecurity.codeplex.com/ for more details).

1. Add an XML file named MyConfig.xml to the FirstElement folder. Add the following code:

```
<Lists>
   <List name="1st List" description="1st list description"
         type="Contacts"/>
   <List name="2nd List" description="2nd list description"
         type="Announcements"/>
   <List name="3rd List" description="3rd list description"
         type="Events"/>
</Lists>
```

2. To specify that the MyConfig.xml should be included as an element file, select the MyConfig.xml node in the Solution Explorer. Then, in the Properties pane, change the Deployment Type to ElementFile, as shown here:

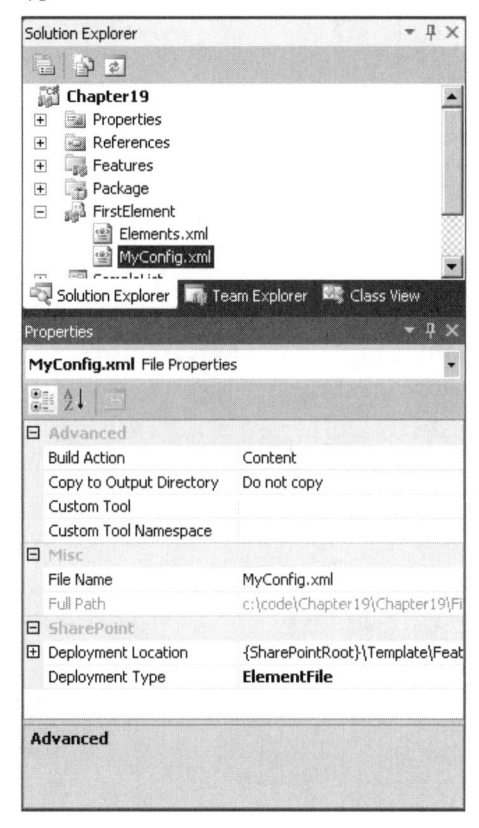

3. Update the code in Feature2.EventReceiver.cs as follows:

```
public override void FeatureActivated(
                    SPFeatureReceiverProperties properties)
{
  if (properties.Feature.Parent is SPWeb)
  {
    SPWeb web = properties.Feature.Parent as SPWeb;
    using (Stream s = properties.Definition.GetFile(
                                "FirstElement\\MyConfig.xml"))
    {
      using (XmlReader rdr = XmlReader.Create(s))
      {
        rdr.ReadToDescendant("List");
        do
        {
          string listName = rdr.GetAttribute("name").ToString();
```

```
                    string listDescription = rdr.GetAttribute(
                                                "description").ToString();
                    string listType = rdr.GetAttribute("type").ToString();
                    SPListTemplateType typeEnum = (SPListTemplateType)Enum.Parse(
                                    typeof(SPListTemplateType), listType);
                    Guid listId = web.Lists.Add(listName,
                                        listDescription, typeEnum);
                    SPList newList = web.Lists[listId];
                    newList.OnQuickLaunch = true;
                    newList.Update();
                  } while (rdr.ReadToNextSibling("List"));
                }
            }
         }
      }
   }

   public override void FeatureDeactivating(
                            SPFeatureReceiverProperties properties)
   {
      if (properties.Feature.Parent is SPWeb)
      {
         SPWeb web = properties.Feature.Parent as SPWeb;
         using (Stream s = properties.Definition.GetFile(
                                    "FirstElement\\MyConfig.xml"))
         {
            using (XmlReader rdr = XmlReader.Create(s))
            {
               rdr.ReadToDescendant("List");
               do
               {
                  string listName = rdr.GetAttribute("name").ToString();
                  SPList myList = web.Lists.TryGetList(listName);
                  if (myList != null)
                  {
                     myList.Delete();
                  }
               } while (rdr.ReadToNextSibling("List"));
            }
         }
      }
   }
```

When we deploy the solution and activate the feature, three new lists will be added to the site as specified in the MyConfig.xml file. In this example, we've used an XmlReader to parse the configuration file for the sake of keeping the example simple. In a real-world solution, using an XmlSerializer to deserialize the configuration file into an appropriate collection of objects would be more robust.

## Upgrading Features

In SharePoint 2010, one of the important new capabilities from a packaging and deployment perspective is the ability to upgrade features. In previous versions, an upgrade was possible, but it was more a case of replacing an old feature with a new version. This could leave a system in an indeterminate state, because actions performed by the old feature would not necessarily be undone when a new version of the feature was installed. For example, if a feature created a list that users subsequently populated with data and then a new version of the feature created a new version of the list with a different name, the result of deploying the new feature would be two lists. A better approach would be to rename the old list.

With the upgrade capabilities in SharePoint 2010, we can define a number of upgrade actions declaratively in the feature manifest, and for more complex upgrade processes we can also use a feature receiver to make any changes programmatically.

## Using PSCONFIG.EXE

We can trigger an upgrade in a few different ways, including using the psconfig tool to upgrade all features within a farm. This tool is useful when many features have been updated, since it's a pretty lengthy process. For example, if a service pack updates many system features, running psconfig will ensure that instances of the updated features are upgraded where appropriate.

Let's look at several possible psconfig commands. This command performs a version-to-version upgrade:

```
psconfig.exe -cmd upgrade -inplace v2v
```

Feature versions are in the format *major.minor.build.build*. When using a version-to-version upgrade, only features in which the major or minor version number has changed will be upgraded. So for a feature with version 1.0.0.0, if we deploy a new build with the version 1.0.1.234, no upgrade will be performed. However, if we deploy version 1.1.1.234, an upgrade will be performed because the minor version number has changed.

This command performs a build-to-build upgrade:

```
psconfig.exe -cmd upgrade -inplace b2b
```

By using this mode, we ensure that any changes to the version number will trigger an upgrade. So, for example, version 1.0.0.0 will be upgraded if version 1.0.0.1 is deployed.

## Using PowerShell

A quicker way to upgrade an individual feature instance is to use PowerShell. Follow these steps to see the upgrade process in action:

1. Open the Feature Designer for Feature2. In the Properties pane, set the version number to 1.0.0.0. Where no version number is specified, a default of 0.0.0.0 is assumed. Version numbers must contain four components.

2. From the Build menu, select Deploy. This will deploy our version 1 solution to the farm.

3. In the Feature Designer, click the Manifest button at the bottom of the page. Expand the Edit Options section to display the Manifest Template. Replace the template XML with the following:

```xml
<?xml version="1.0" encoding="utf-8" ?>
<Feature xmlns="http://schemas.microsoft.com/sharepoint/">
<UpgradeActions>
<VersionRange>
<CustomUpgradeAction Name="MyUpgrade"/>
</VersionRange>
</UpgradeActions>
</Feature>
```

By attaching this XML to the feature definition, we're defining the steps that should be taken to upgrade existing features. The CustomUpgradeAction element specifies that we're using a feature receiver to perform the upgrade programmatically. In this example, we haven't specified a version range, so this upgrade action will apply for all versions. If we needed to include different upgrade actions for different versions we could add this:

```xml
<Feature xmlns="http://schemas.microsoft.com/sharepoint/">
  <UpgradeActions>
    <VersionRange BeginVersion="1.0.0.0" EndVersion="2.0.0.0">
      <CustomUpgradeAction Name="V2Upgrade"/>
    </VersionRange>
    <VersionRange BeginVersion="2.0.0.0" EndVersion="3.0.0.0">
      <CustomUpgradeAction Name="V3Upgrade"/>
    </VersionRange>
  </UpgradeActions>
</Feature>
```

4. In the Properties pane, change the Version number for Feature 2 to 2.0.0.0.

**NOTE** Within the Properties pane are options to set the Upgrade Actions Receiver Assembly and Class properties. These properties allow a feature to use a separate assembly for handling standard feature events such as Activate and Deactivate and a separate assembly for handling upgrade events. This facility is useful for retrofitting upgrade capabilities to a feature if the existing receiver assembly isn't available or can't be altered for some reason.

5. For the sake of simplicity, we'll implement our upgrade code in our existing feature receiver. In the Feature2.EventReceiver.cs file, add the following code:

```csharp
public override void FeatureUpgrading(
                    SPFeatureReceiverProperties properties,
                    string upgradeActionName,
                    IDictionary<string, string> parameters)
{
  switch (upgradeActionName)
  {
    case "MyUpgrade":
      if (properties.Feature.Parent is SPWeb)
      {
        SPWeb web = properties.Feature.Parent as SPWeb;
        using (Stream s = properties.Definition.GetFile(
                                     "FirstElement\\MyConfig.xml"))
        {
          using (XmlReader rdr = XmlReader.Create(s))
          {
            rdr.ReadToDescendant("List");
            do
            {
              string listName = rdr.GetAttribute("name").ToString();
              SPList myList = web.Lists.TryGetList(listName);

              if (myList != null)
              {
                myList.Description += "- Updated";
```

```
                myList.Update();
            }
        } while (rdr.ReadToNextSibling("List"));
        }
    }
  }
  break;
default:
  break;
  }
 }
}
```

Notice the use of a switch block in this code snippet to handle the upgradeActionName. This value is specified in the Name attribute of the CustomUpgradeAction element in the feature manifest.

6. If we deploy our updated feature using Visual Studio, our existing version will be removed first, which will make it impossible to test our upgrade process. Instead, we'll package our solution using Visual Studio and deploy it manually. From the Build menu, select Package.

7. To test our upgrade process quickly, we can use PowerShell to upgrade a single feature. Choose Start | SharePoint 2010 Management Shell, and then enter the following script:

```
update-spsolution -identity Chapter19.wsp -literalpath c:\code\chapter19\→
chapter19\bin\debug\chapter19.wsp -gacdeployment
```

**NOTE** This command should be entered as a single line.

8. This command will upgrade the Chapter19 solution package to the latest version. We can confirm this by entering the following script:

```
$featureName="Chapter19_feature2"
$latestVersion=(get-spfeature|where {$_.DisplayName -eq $featureName}).Version
$web=get-spweb http://<your Server Name>/chapter19
$theFeature=$web.Features|Where {$_.Definition.DisplayName -eq $featureName}
$currentVersion=theFeature.Version
write-host "Current Version: $currentVersion, Latest Version: $latestVersion"
```

If all is well, the resultant output should be this:

```
Current Version: 1.0.0.0, Latest Version: 2.0.0.0
```

9. We can upgrade a single feature using the following script:

```
$web=get-spweb http://<your Server Name>/chapter19
$theFeature=$web.Features|Where {$_.Definition.DisplayName -eq $featureName}
$theFeature.Upgrade($false)
```

10. Any errors that occur as part of the upgrade process will be shown in the PowerShell window. However, we can confirm that our upgrade was successful by issuing the following command:

```
write-host ($theFeature).Version
```

The new version number should be reported as 2.0.0.0.

## Site Definitions

So far in this chapter, you've seen how we can package our customizations using features and solutions. By using these methods, we can activate and deactivate particular features to achieve our desired level of functionality. This process works well if we're adding functionality to an existing site, but what happens if we want to create a new site that uses functionality that's encapsulated in a number of features? As we did in an earlier example, we could start out with a blank site and enable the appropriate features. However, SharePoint provides a better way to achieve this result. We can create a custom site definition.

To understand how a custom site definition fits into the overall picture, select New Site from the Site Actions menu on any SharePoint site. Each of the items listed in the Create dialog is an example of a site definition. Basically, a site definition is a template that can be used to create new sites. By creating a custom site definition, we can specify how a new site is provisioned, including which features should be activated and which lists and libraries should be created by default.

> **NOTE** Regarding site definitions versus site templates, from SharePoint Designer, we can save a site as a site template. When using this function, we're actually creating a WSP package that contains a list of customizations to whatever site definition the site was created from. This type of site template can then be applied to other sites that are derived from the same site definition. This functionality differs from that of creating a custom site definition because site definitions can be used only when creating new sites.

Confusingly, site definitions as stored on each front-end server in the %SPROOT%TEMPLATE\SiteTemplates folder. In a similar manner to features, each site definition has its own folder. The site definition configuration is stored in a file named onet.xml within the XML folder.

Site definitions have been part of SharePoint since day 1, whereas the feature framework was introduced in Windows SharePoint Services 3.0 to provide a higher degree of flexibility. As a result of this, site definitions come with some serious baggage and can be pretty complex. The recommended approach with SharePoint 2010 is to factor as much configuration into features as possible. This helps to keep site definition files maintainable while still allowing a high degree of flexibility.

> **TIP** When creating site definitions, bear in mind that future service packs for SharePoint may overwrite out-of-the-box files. Always create a separate folder for any customized site definitions. As you'll see when using Visual Studio, this approach is adopted automatically.

### Creating Site Definitions Using Visual Studio

Let's look at how we can create a new site definition using Visual Studio.

1. Choose File | Add | New Project.
2. In the Add New Project dialog, select Site Definition and name the new project **Chapter19DemoSite**, as shown:

A new project is added containing the following files:

- **onet.xml**   Contains the site definition markup. Each onet.xml file can contain more than one configuration, where a configuration is for all intents and purposes a site definition.
- **webtemp-Chapter19DemoSite.xml**   The SharePoint platform builds a list of available templates by examining the %SPRoot%Template\1033\xml\ folder for XML files with names beginning with *webtemp*. These files act as a table of contents for the site definitions that are stored in each onet.xml file.
- **default.aspx**   As you'll see when we look at the onet.xml file, the default.aspx file is deployed to the root of a new site that's created using our custom site definition. Without this file, there would be no home page for the site.

If we examine the onet.xml file that's been added to our project automatically, we'll find the following XML:

```
<Project Title="Chapter19DemoSite" Revision="2"
        ListDir="" xmlns:ows="Microsoft SharePoint"
        xmlns="http://schemas.microsoft.com/sharepoint/">
  <NavBars>
  </NavBars>
  <Configurations>
    <Configuration ID="0" Name="Chapter19DemoSite">
      <Lists/>
      <SiteFeatures>
      </SiteFeatures>
      <WebFeatures>
      </WebFeatures>
      <Modules>
```

```xml
            <Module Name="DefaultBlank" />
        </Modules>
      </Configuration>
    </Configurations>
    <Modules>
      <Module Name="DefaultBlank" Url="" Path="">
        <File Url="default.aspx">
        </File>
      </Module>
    </Modules>
</Project>
```

> **NOTE** Site definitions can get pretty complex. A full discussion of each of the elements in the onet.xml file and how each can be used is beyond the scope of this chapter. For more information, see http://msdn.microsoft.com/en-us/library/ms474369.aspx.

## Configurations

The most important element in the onet.xml file is the Configuration element. Each file can contain more than one Configuration element, and each element must have a unique ID. The Configuration element effectively defines a distinct site definition. Our file has a single site definition named Chapter19DemoSite, which refers to a module named DefaultBlank.

## Modules

Our onet.xml file also contains a Modules section that is outside the Configurations section. These modules can be shared between all configurations in the file. Modules are used to provision files to a SharePoint site and can also be added as feature elements by adding a Module item to a project. In our sample, the default.aspx file is being provisioned to the root of the new site.

## Site Features/Web Features

As mentioned, with SharePoint 2010, the recommended approach to creating site definitions is to use features as much as possible. We can specify which features are automatically activated when a site is created by adding Feature nodes to the SiteFeatures and WebFeatures elements. These elements represent features that should be activated at the Site collection level and features that should be activated at the site level.

Add the following XML to the WebFeatures node:

```xml
<WebFeatures>
  <!--Chapter19_Feature2-->
  <Feature ID="69d95a17-8c35-4bbb-9a79-4154fc55be6a" />
  <!--Chapter19_Feature1-->
  <Feature ID="5fcd733e-2cc9-4363-85fd-dfe7893cb195" />
</WebFeatures>
```

Features are referenced using their unique identifier. To find the identifier for a particular feature, you can use a few techniques. If the feature is a custom feature, the identifier can be found in the Feature ID property that can be seen in the Properties pane in the Feature Designer. If the feature is an out-of-the-box or third-party feature that's already installed on a server, the following PowerShell command can provide a list:

```
get-spfeature|select DisplayName,Id
```

Our site definition will now automatically activate our two features when a new site is created. Deploy the solution by choosing Build | Deploy in Visual Studio.

After the deployment process has completed, navigate to the sample site that we created earlier, and then select New Site from the Site Actions menu. In the Create dialog, select Chapter19DemoSite from the SharePoint Customizations category. Name the new site Demo and then click Create. A new site will be created, as shown, that contains the lists defined by our features:

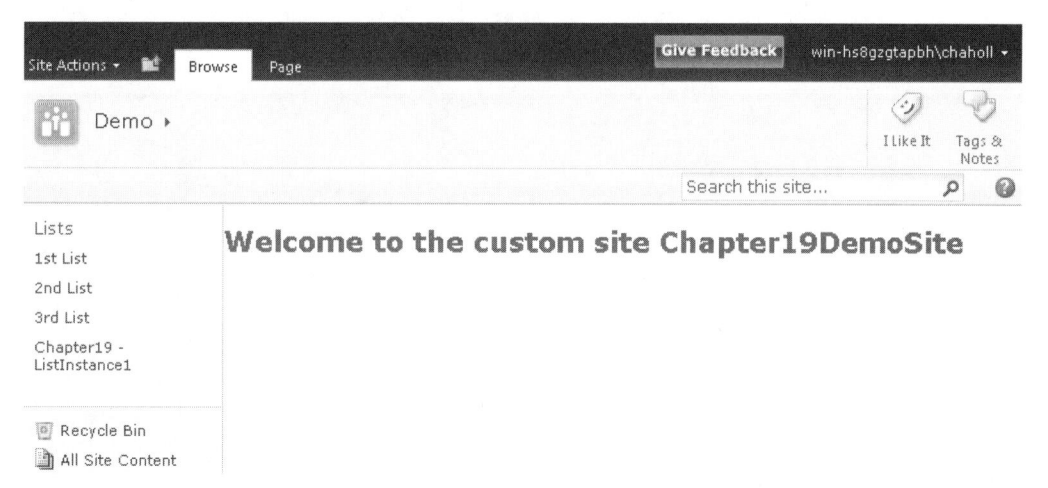

## Summary

In the real world, packaging and deployment is a big part of any SharePoint project. The new tooling in Visual Studio makes it much easier for developers to create packages automatically to manage our custom solutions, but in all but the simplest projects, some aspect of coding will be involved in deploying a SharePoint solution. In this chapter, you've seen how to make use of the feature framework to deploy solutions as a series of modular components. You also learned about the new feature upgrade functionality in SharePoint 2010 that will allow users to upgrade older versions of our applications seamlessly.

# CHAPTER 20

# PowerShell

In previous versions of SharePoint, command line configuration was available via the STSADM tool. Although the tool is still available for use with SharePoint 2010, the recommended approach for managing a SharePoint farm via the command line is to use the new SharePoint 2010 Management Shell. This shell is a PowerShell instance with a collection of SharePoint-specific cmdlets (pronounced *command-lets*) installed. In this chapter, we'll take a look at the new command shell and a few of the main cmdlets.

## PowerShell Primer

PowerShell is a powerful scripting environment that leverages the flexibility of the .NET Framework to allow command line users to develop scripts and utilities that can automate administrative tasks. Unlike many command line tools, PowerShell has been designed to deal with objects rather than plain text output. Most command line tools are effectively executables and as such can read only text-based input from the command line and return only text-based output to the console. PowerShell introduces the concept of a *cmdlet*, PowerShell-specific commands that are derived from the System.Management.Automation.Cmdlet class and are created using the .NET Framework. PowerShell uses an object pipeline to pipe the output of one cmdlet to the next cmdlet in a chain so that objects can be passed between functions simply.

Many cmdlets are available for use with PowerShell, and users are free to create their own cmdlets using tools such as Visual Studio. To make it easier for you to manage cmdlets, they are commonly packaged together as snap-ins. Snap-ins usually contain all of the cmdlets for managing particular products or services. For example, the Microsoft.SharePoint.PowerShell snap-in contains the out-of-the-box snap-ins for SharePoint 2010.

When using legacy command line tools, you may find it difficult to remember the names of the various tools. No standard is used for naming or passing parameters. For PowerShell cmdlets, a verb-noun naming convention has been adopted, which makes it easier for users to guess the name of a command. By using the **get-***command* cmdlets, you can get a list of the commands that are available. This command also accepts **-verb** or **-noun** as parameters for filtering the output. For example, you could enter the following command to retrieve a list of commands relating to the SPWeb object:

```
get-command -noun spweb
```

As well as a standard naming convention for cmdlets, PowerShell also imposes a standard convention for passing parameters. Parameters are always preceded with a hyphen. You can see this in the preceding example. You can view help for a particular cmdlet by passing the parameter **-?**.

One really useful feature of the PowerShell command line interface is the ability to use *tab expansion*. As developers, we've become used to having tools such as IntelliSense to remind us of our options as we enter code. The same idea works with PowerShell: When entering a command name, if we enter part of the name and then repeatedly press the TAB key, we can cycle through the available commands matching our input. When entering parameters for a command, if we enter the preceding hyphen we can also cycle through the list of available parameters. These two features, combined with a standard naming convention, make learning PowerShell scripting a relatively straightforward process.

## Using Objects

As mentioned, PowerShell deals with objects rather than text. This means that you can often set or query properties or execute methods on the object that is returned by a particular cmdlet. For example, the following command returns an SPWeb object :

```
Get-SPWeb -Identity http://localhost
```

If we execute this command, we'll find that a URL is returned. This is the default output when no specific property has been called.

We can get a list of the available members for the resultant SPWeb object by passing the output of this command to the **get-member** command using the pipe character, as follows:

```
Get-SPWeb -Identity http://localhost|get-member
```

After we've found the property in which we're interested, we can either retrieve the value by placing parenthesis around the command or by assigning the output of the command to a variable and then querying the variable:

```
(Get-SPWeb -Identity http://localhost).Title
```

or

```
$web=Get-SPWeb -Identity http://localhost
$web.Title
```

PowerShell variables are always prefixed with $ and persist for the duration of a session. We can examine the type of a variable by using the GetType method as shown:

`$web.GetType()`

If we need to view more than one property from an object or collection of objects, you can use the **Select-Object** cmdlet to specify the properties that you require:

`(Get-SPFarm).Service|Select-Object -Property TypeName,Status`

This command will return a list of services on a farm along with their statuses. Here's another way to write the same command:

`(Get-SPFarm).Service|select TypeName,Status`

This shortened version of the **Select-Object** command uses a technique known as *aliasing*. Many commonly used commands have simpler aliases, and a full list can be retrieved using the following command:

`Get-Alias`

As well as being able to specify which properties are shown when displaying a collection of objects, we can also filter which objects appear in the collection by using the **Where-Object** cmdlet. Again, this cmdlet has an alias: Where.

Let's consider the properties that are available for this cmdlet. Table 20-1 shows the comparison operators.

| Comparison Operator | Meaning | Example (Returns True) |
| --- | --- | --- |
| -eq | is equal to | 1 -eq 1 |
| -ne | Is not equal to | 1 -ne 2 |
| -lt | Is less than | 1 -lt 2 |
| -le | Is less than or equal to | 1 -le 2 |
| -gt | Is greater than | 2 -gt 1 |
| -ge | Is greater than or equal to | 2 -ge 1 |
| -like | Is like (wildcard comparison for text) | "file.doc" -like "f*.do?" |
| -notlike | Is not like (wildcard comparison for text) | "file.doc" -notlike "p*.doc" |
| -contains | Contains | 1,2,3 -contains 1 |
| -notcontains | Does not contain | 1,2,3 -notcontains 4 |

**Table 20-1** Comparison Operators

| Logical Operator | Meaning | Example (Returns True) |
|---|---|---|
| -and | Logical and; true if both sides are true | (1 -eq 1) -and (2 -eq 2) |
| -or | Logical or; true if either side is true | (1 -eq 1) -or (1 -eq 2) |
| -not | Logical not; reverses true and false | -not (1 -eq 2) |
| ! | Logical not; reverses true and false | !(1 -eq 2) |

**Table 20-2** Logical Operators

As well as comparison operators, we can combine comparison by using the logical operators shown in Table 20-2.

Using these two techniques, we can create queries such as this:

```
(Get-SPFarm).Services|Where {$_.TypeName -Like "*data*"}|Select TypeName, Status
```

Note the use of the **$_** variable. This is a system-defined variable that evaluates to the current object in the object pipeline—in other words, the output of the preceding command. When the preceding command returns an enumerable collection, the **where** command will iterate through the collection; therefore, **$_** will evaluate to an instance of an object in the collection rather than the entire collection.

## Using Functions

As well as being able to execute command chains and use variables, we can also define functions using PowerShell. These functions work similarly to those in any other programming language—the only minor difference is that all uncaptured output within a function is returned to the caller. For example, we can create the following simple function:

```
function addNumbers($first,$second)
{
"Adding numbers"
return $first + $second
}
```

We can call this function by entering the command (note the method of passing named parameters):

```
addNumbers -first 1 -second 2
```

Here's the resultant output:

```
Adding numbers
3
```

This is expected. However, what isn't expected is that if we examine the data type of the return value by piping the output to **Get-Member,** we find two return types, string and int32. If we want to use our function in a chain, this is not ideal. The reason this has happened is that the Adding Numbers message is uncaptured output—that is, it isn't assigned to a variable or passed to a cmdlet—and as a result it forms part of the output. We can prevent this from occurring by modifying the function as follows:

```
function addNumbers($first,$second)
{
Write-Host "Adding numbers"
return $first + $second
}
```

## PowerShell for SharePoint

Now that you understand what PowerShell is and how it works, let's move on to look at its uses in administering SharePoint. More than 530 cmdlets are included in the Microsoft. SharePoint.PowerShell snap-in, so we won't cover all of them. Hopefully, the discussion so far has given you the tools you need to be able to find the correct command for a particular task.

First things first. Where can we find PowerShell? When running on a SharePoint server, two possibilities exist: either select the SharePoint 2010 Management Shell from the Start menu or open a command prompt and enter the following:

```
PowerShell
```

If we're using the SharePoint management shell, the SharePoint snap-in will already be installed. If we're using a standard PowerShell console, we can install the snap-in by entering the following command:

```
Add-PSSnapIn Microsoft.SharePoint.PowerShell
```

We can check the list of installed snap-ins by using this command:

```
Get-PSSnapIn
```

### Connecting to SharePoint Remotely

One of the real benefits of PowerShell is its ability to connect to remote machines. We can open a PowerShell session on a client machine and then use *remoting* to connect to a SharePoint server. To enable remoting on the server, enter the following command:

```
Enable-PSRemoting
```

This command will enable the WinRM service and set up the firewall to allow incoming sessions.

After the server has been configured, we can connect from any client machine by entering the following command:

```
Enter-PSSession "Server Name" -Credential (Get-Credential)
```

> **NOTE** If the client machine is running on a domain and your SharePoint server is running as a stand-alone server, a few other steps are necessary to enable remote connectivity, such as configuring Secure Sockets Layer (SSL) connectivity on the server. A full discussion of these steps is outside the scope of this chapter. See http://msdn.microsoft.com/en-us/library/aa384372(VS.85).aspx for more information.

After a remote connection has been established, the SharePoint snap-in can be added with the command:

```
Add-PSSnapin Microsoft.SharePoint.PowerShell
```

## PowerShell Permissions

To use SharePoint cmdlets, a user must be a member of the SharePoint_Shell_Access role for the farm configuration database as well as a member of the WSS_ADMIN_WPG group on the SharePoint front-end server. To grant users the appropriate permissions, use the following command:

```
Add-SPShellAdmin -Username domain\username -database (Get-SPContentDatabase →
-webapplication http://Web app name)
```

Each user must be explicitly granted permissions to every database to which he or she needs access. By default, only the account used to set up SharePoint will have permission to execute this command.

## Working with Site Collections and Sites

Most of the cmdlets commonly used in the management of site collections or sites end in *SPSite* or *SPWeb*. To pick up a reference to a site collection, we can use the following:

```
$site=Get-SPSite -Identity http://siteurl
```

Or we can return a list of all site collections by using this:

```
Get-SPSite
```

When it comes to managing site objects (SPWeb), we can pick up a specific web site using this:

```
$web=Get-SPWeb -Identity http://weburl/
```

To return a list of sites, we need to use either the Site parameter or an SPSite object:

```
Get-SPWeb -Site http://SiteUrl
```

or

```
Get-SPWeb -Site $site
```

### Creating Site Collections and Sites

We can create a new site collection using the **New-SPSite** cmdlet:

```
New-SPSite -Url http://localhost/Sites/NewSiteCollection - OwnerAlias username
```

We can also add new sites using the **New-SPWeb** cmdlet:

```
New-SPWeb -Url http://localhost/Sites/NewSiteCollection/NewWeb -Name MyNewWeb
```

### Deleting Site Collections and Sites

We can delete site collections and sites by using the **Remove-SPSite** or the **Remove-SPWeb** cmdlet:

```
Remove-SPWeb -Identity http://localhost/Sites/NewSiteCollection/NewWeb
```

or

```
Remove-SPSite -Identity http://localhost/Sites/NewSiteCollection
```

### Setting Properties on SharePoint Objects

When setting properties on the objects returned by SharePoint management cmdlets, we need to call the Update method in the same manner as when updating properties using the Server Object Model. Here's an example:

```
$web=SP-GetSPWeb -Identity http://myweburl
$web.Title="My New Title"
$web.Update()
```

## Working with Lists and Libraries

Similarly to how lists and libraries are accessed in the Server Object Model, they can be accessed via SPWeb objects. For example, we can enumerate the lists on a site using the following:

```
Get-SPWeb -Identity http://myweburl | Select -Expand lists| Select Title
```

We can add new lists using the Add method of the Lists property:

```
Get-SPWeb -Identity http://myweburl | ForEach {$_.Lists.Add("My Task List", "", $_.ListTemplates["Tasks"])}
```

### Changing the Business Connectivity Thresholds

The maximum number of rows that can be retrieved via a Business Connectivity Services (BCS) connection is limited. The only way to change this value is via PowerShell. We can use the following command to retrieve the current settings:

```
$proxies=Get-SPServiceApplicationProxy | Where {$_.TypeName -like "Business Data*"}
$rule=Get-SPBusinessDataCatalogThrottleConfig -ServiceApplicationProxy $proxies -Scope →
Database -ThrottleType Items
$rule
```

We can then update the value using the following:

```
Set-SPBusinessDataCatalogThrottleConfig -Identity $rule -Maximum 10000 -Default 10000
```

## Working with Content

We can retrieve a list of all items in a site using the following:

```
Get-SPWeb -Identity http://myweburl | Select -Expand Lists | Select -Expand Items | →
select Name, Url
```

Or we can apply a filter to show only documents:

```
Get-SPWeb -Identity http://myweburl | Select -Expand Lists | Where {$_.BaseType -eq →
"DocumentLibrary"} | Select -Expand Items | select Name, Url
```

We can also make use of filters to search for a specific item:

```
Get-SPWeb -Identity http://myweburl | Select -Expand Lists | Select -Expand Items | →
Where {$_.Name -like "foo*"} | select Name, Url
```

### Creating New Documents

To create a new document in a document library, use the following:

```
function New-SPFile($WebUrl, $ListName, $DocumentName,$Content)
{
$stream = new-object System.IO.MemoryStream
$writer = new-object System.IO.StreamWriter($stream)
$writer.Write($content)
$writer.Flush()
$list=(Get-SPWeb $WebUrl).Lists.TryGetList($ListName)
$file=$list.RootFolder.Files.Add($DocumentName, $stream,$true)
$file.Update()
}
New-SPFile -WebUrl "http://myweburl" -ListName "Shared Documents" -DocumentName →
"PowerShellDocument.txt" -Content "Document Content"
```

## Working with Timer Jobs

As you've seen in a few of the chapters in this book, SharePoint makes use of timer jobs to perform a lot of back-end processing. We can use PowerShell to get a list of all timer jobs:

```
Get-SPTimerJob
```

Or we can get a list of job failures grouped by the job name:

```
Get-SPTimerJob | Select -Expand HistoryEntries | Where {$_.Status -ne "Succeeded"} | →
group JobDefinitionTitle
```

## Summary

PowerShell lets us manage SharePoint from the command line. We can perform many of the same actions using PowerShell that we performed using the Server Object Model. Users who are unfamiliar with PowerShell will need to take time to learn the language, but as developers we're already familiar with the basic concepts and general syntax of the language largely due to its similarity to C#.

Although this was not covered in this chapter, we can easily create custom PowerShell cmdlets to assist in the management of our custom SharePoint applications. These custom cmdlets can then be integrated into other SharePoint administration scripts by system administrators, making our custom applications configurable and maintainable using a familiar toolset.

For those of us who "grew up" with STSADM, we may be tempted to put off learning PowerShell, but as you've seen in this chapter, the level of flexibility that it offers is well worth the effort. Farewell STSADM; you served us well, but you had your day!

# Index

## A

abstract classes, 173
Action rules, 101
actions, 226, 390, 420–422
activation dependencies, 497–498
AdditionalPageHead control, 47
administration classes, 20–21
administrators, 115
Advanced mode, 35
anonymous delegates, 340
AppId, 101, 175, 392
application pages, 33, 35–36
Application Services
    event receivers, 8:9–167
    handling events, 153–158
    overview, 153–167
application-level integration, 6
applications
    console. *See* console applications
    custom activities for, 455–461
    debugging. *See* debugging
    Office. *See* Office applications
    remote, 174
    rich client, 64, 124, 390
    service. *See* service applications
    web, 6, 14, 86, 269
ASP.NET framework, 122, 123, 153–154
ASP.NET pages, 37
assemblies
    deploying, 496
    third-party, 10
associations, 215, 316, 392, 396
audio files, 121
authentication, 389

## B

BA (business analytics), 463
backup/restore functionality, 15–16
BaseFieldControl class, 328–330
BCS (Business Connectivity Services), 387–422
    Business Data Catalog, 387–391
    changing thresholds, 523–524
    components, 388–391
    demonstration scenario, 391–392
    described, 388
    .NET connectivity assemblies, 404–417
    rich client integration, 390
BCS data
    associations, 392
    connecting to via SharePoint Designer, 392–404
    in external data columns, 418–422
BDC (Business Data Connectivity), 426–427
BDC metadata, 391
BDC Model projects, 405–417
BDCM files, 407
BI (Business Intelligence), 463–489
    business user experience, 464
    Microsoft BI solution, 464–465
    overview, 463–464
    PerformancePoint Services, 469–480
    PowerPivot, 480–485
    Reporting Services, 485–489
    SharePoint BI platform, 465–489

BI solutions, 464, 469–480
BLOB data, 121–122
BPM (business performance management), 463–464
BrowserForm web part, 81–86
build script, 357
business analytics (BA), 463
Business Connectivity Services. *See* BCS
Business Data Association web part, 390
Business Data Catalog, 387, 390. *See also* BDC
Business Data Connectivity. *See* BDC
Business Intelligence. *See* BI
business performance management (BPM), 463–464
business productivity infrastructure, 464
business user experience, 464
buttons
    data generation, 358–361
    disabling, 47
    Hello World, 46–47

## C

CAB (cabinet) files, 494
cabinet (CAB) files, 494
CAML (Collaborative Application Markup Language), 10, 337
CAML queries
    considerations, 10, 332, 333, 366
    example of, 332–333
    retrieving, 65–68
    vs. SQL, 367
CAML Query Builder, 10

CAML syntax, 337, 375
canHandleCommand method, 50
CAS (custom code access security), 29
Cascading Style Sheets (CSS),
    137–139
change conflicts, 381–384
ChangeConflictException property,
    343, 378
ChangeConflicts property, 343, 377,
    381, 382
Chart web part, 469
charts
    analytic, 278
    date range, 282
    PivotCharts, 280–281
child objects, 362–364
child sites, 15, 17
classes. *See also* specific classes
    abstract, 173
    administration, 20–21
    client-side, 179–181
    configuration, 20–21
    content access, 20–21
    entity, 353–357
    receiver base, 154–155
    server-side, 176–179
    site provisioning, 20–21
client object model, 53–77
    adding data, 71–72
    architecture, 53–54
    client-side objects, 61–64
    deleting data, 74–75
    demonstration environment,
        55–61
    described, 53
    dialogs, 76–77
    JavaScript, 53, 60–61, 64
    namespaces, 61
    notifications, 76
    retrieving data, 65–71
    Silverlight, 53–60
    status bar, 75–76
    updating data, 72–74
ClientContext object, 61–64
client/server communication, 173
client-side implementation, 171–172
client-side objects, 61–64
Client.svc service, 54
cmdlets, 517–518
code-behind file, 36, 103–105
Collaborative Application Markup
    Language. *See* CAML

ColorPicker control, 46
columns, 321–330. *See also* site
    columns
    associating content types with,
        322–323, 349–350
    external data, 388–389,
        418–422
    field controls, 123–124
    field types, 323–330
    indexing, 335–336
    libraries and, 331–332
    lists and, 331–332
    lookup, 322, 352–353, 450, 457
    overview, 321–323
    types of data used in, 322
    validation, 330
COM component, 25
COM errors, 257
Command attribute, 46
CommandPreview attribute, 46
CommandRevert attribute, 46
CommandUIHandler element, 46
common query language, 431–432
comparison operators, 519–520
concurrency errors, 378–381
configuration classes, 20–21
Configuration element, 514
configuration files, 24
conflict resolution objects, 344
ConflictMode setting, 381, 384
connections. *See* data connections
connectivity assemblies, 391,
    404–417
connector frameworks
    BDC, 391
    pluggable, 391, 405
    search connector, 424–427
console applications
    configuring, 19–20
    creating, 18–19
    debugging, 12–13
    unit testing, 12–13
content
    considerations, 107
    containers for, 331
    custom content types, 118,
        208–209, 348–350
    JSON, 299–300
    organizing, 112–114
    overlapping, 428
    PerformancePoint, 474–475
    PowerShell, 524

publishing, 124–130
rich media, 121
updates to, 428
user-generated, 34
users of, 114–115
content access classes, 21–25
content creators, 115
content deployment, 130
Content Editor web part, 298–299
content fields, 127
Content Management Server, 3
Content Organizer feature, 112–114
content pages, 34, 35
Content Query web part, 131
content sources, 427–428
content types, 311–321
    associating columns with,
        322–323, 349–350
    associating with lists, 351
    associating workflows with,
        239–240, 316
    creating, 348–350
    custom, 118, 208–209,
        348–350
    document sets, 116–118
    enterprise, 318–321
    grouping, 315–316
    identifiers, 312–315
    libraries, 331–332
    lists and, 331–332, 349
    media, 120–121
    metadata, 316–318
    multiple, 332
    overview, 311–316
    page layouts and, 123–125
    PerformancePoint, 465,
        467–470
    relationships between,
        352–353
    site, 118, 125, 209, 332
ContentTypes collection, 331–332
controls. *See also* specific controls
    adding to ribbon, 42–45
    disabling on ribbon, 47
    examples of, 41
    field, 123–124, 324–330
    groups of, 41
    predefined, 46
    safe, 496
    ScriptLink, 48
    server, 34, 127, 140, 145
crawl architecture, 424

crawl components, 424, 426, 427
crawl rules, 428
Create All Operations wizard, 398–399
credentials, 389
cross-site scoping, 319
CSS (Cascading Style Sheets), 137–139
custom code access security (CAS), 29
custom entity objects, 414–417
custom ranking models, 435
CustomAction elements, 43–44, 48

# D

Dashboard Designer, 470–472, 477, 484–485
dashboards, creating, 475–476
data. *See also* external data entries; metadata
    adding via client object model, 71–72
    adding via LINQ, 358–361
    BCS. *See* BCS data
    BDC, 391
    BLOB, 121–122
    change conflicts, 381–384
    concurrency errors, 378–381
    deleting via LINQ, 361–365
    deleting with Client Object Model, 74–75
    filtering, 68–70
    locating via anonymous delegates, 340
    locating via iterators, 339–340
    locating via Lambda expressions, 340–341
    locating via LINQ, 341
    OLAP, 472–474, 476, 481
    querying. *See* queries
    retrieving, 64–71
    social, 443–462
    structuring, 444–445
    synchronizing, 445–446
    updating via Client Object Model, 72–74
    updating via LINQ to SharePoint, 375–384
data access
    columns. *See* columns
    considerations, 311
    content types. *See* content types
    document libraries. *See* document libraries
    lists. *See* lists
    overview, 311–336
    performance, 333–336
    stereotyping, 392–394, 408–414
data access layer, 311, 338
Data Analysis Expressions (DAX), 483
data connection libraries, 99, 272, 300–308
data connections
    configuring, 276
    exporting, 261, 276, 308
    ODC, 302, 303, 470
    PerformancePoint, 471–474
    restricting, 301–302
    trusted, 272, 301, 303, 304
    UDCX, 471
    used by Excel, 276
data generation buttons, 358–361
data infrastructure, 464–465
data picker, 398, 400–404
data providers, 272
data structures, 346–353
Data View controls, 127
databases
    Access, 6
    BDC and, 391
    multiple, 14
    user, 445–446
DataContext objects, 342–344, 376, 380–381
DAX (Data Analysis Expressions), 483
De Smet, Bart, 338
debug script files, 49
debugging
    console applications, 12–13
    Developer Dashboard, 28–29
    feature receivers, 503–505
    sandboxed solutions, 30
    Sysinternals DebugView, 11
    user-defined files, 294–295
    Visual Studio Debugger, 295, 503–504
.debug.js extension, 49
DebugView, 11, 29
decomposition tree, 480
delegate controls, 47–49, 136–137
dependency chains, 498–499
deployment. *See* packaging/deployment model

Desktop Experience feature, 12
Developer Dashboard, 28–29
Developer toolbar, 28–29
development environment
    defining SPRoot environment variable, 12
    development server configuration, 11–13
    enabling Desktop Experience feature, 12
    platform development tools, 9–11
    setting up, 11
development server configuration, 11–13
Dialog framework, 76–77
digital asset management, 120–122
disk-based caching, 121–122
Document content type, 113, 331, 348, 358
Document ID service, 118–119
Document Information Panels, 93–96
document libraries. *See also* libraries
    creating, 220
    LINQ and, 358
    overview, 331–333
document management, 114–120
Document Set feature, 116–118
document sets
    custom, 207–222
    overview, 116–118
    welcome page, 118, 219
documents. *See also* files
    combining with OpenXML, 215–217
    converting to alternative formats, 204–205, 217–218
    creating with PowerShell, 524
    creation/collaboration tool for, 207–222
    permissions. *See* permissions
    storing on team site, 462
    templates. *See* templates
    uploading, 222, 271, 303, 418, 462
    Word. *See* Word documents
    XML, 316–318
DocumentSetProperties web part, 210–214

# E

ECM. *See* Enterprise Content Management
editor parts, 144–145
editors, 115
element files, 57, 165, 501, 507
ElementManifest element, 500–501, 502
e-mail events, 167
EnabledScript attribute, 47
Enterprise Content Management (ECM), 107–131
    described, 107
    digital asset management, 120–122
    document management, 114–120
    managed metadata, 107–114
    page templates, 34
    publishing content, 124–130
    web content management, 122–131
enterprise content types, 318–321
enterprise search technology, 423–442
    architecture, 423–424
    capturing search queries, 435
    custom ranking models, 435
    custom refinement tools, 440–442
    displaying search results, 436
    FAST Search, 433
    front-end components, 435–442
    indexing components, 424–429
    OpenSearch, 433
    order of search results, 435
    query components, 429–435
    refining search results, 437–440
    SharePoint Search, 433
entities. *See also* external content types
    considerations, 345
    creating with SPMetal, 353–357
    custom, 414–417
    disconnecting, 375–376
    metadata, 416–417
    reconnecting, 376–378
entity classes, 353–357
Entity Service object, 407–414
EntityTracker object, 380
environment variables, 12
error handling, 27–28
errors
    COM, 257
    concurrency, 378–381
    data entry, 312
    debugging. *See* debugging
    Developer Dashboard, 28
    JSOM, 300
    logging, 27–28
    runtime, 338
    sandboxed solutions and, 29
    security, 485
    spelling, 130
    strongly typed code and, 360
    tracking, 28
    try-catch blocks, 27
    during upgrade process, 511
    validation and, 226
    workflow, 233
event handling
    advanced techniques, 47–52
    Application Services, 153–158
    from ribbon, 46–47
    server-side, 50–52
event hosts, 154
event receivers, 111, 154–167
events
    asynchronous, 155, 162–163
    binding, 165–167
    deployment, 158
    e-mail, 167
    enabling/disabling, 163–165
    packaging, 158
    post-back, 153
    properties, 157–158
    security issues, 156–157
    synchronous, 155, 161–163
    workflow services, 255–256
Excel Calculation Services, 266, 267
Excel Services, 265–308
    Application Services, 266
    business intelligence strategy, 464
    Calculation Services, 266, 267
    Client Service, 266–269
    configuring, 270–273
    data connection libraries, 99, 300–308
    demonstration scenario, 273–285
    JavaScript Object Model, 268, 297–300
    named ranges, 277–278
    overview, 265–266
    PivotCharts, 280–281
    PivotTables, 270, 275–280, 286–287, 293
    PowerPivot, 270, 472, 481–485
    publishing to, 281, 284, 287
    REST API, 268–269, 285–288, 293–294
    Slicer, 282–285
    user-defined functions, 266, 272–273, 288–297
    Web Services, 268
    workbooks. *See* workbooks
Excel Web Access web part, 267–268
Excel Web Apps, 269
Excel-based status indicator, 465
exceptions, 27–28
exporting
    connections, 261, 276, 308
    sites, 15–16
    themes, 137
    workflows, 231, 233, 238
expression trees, 366–367
eXtensible Application Markup Language (XAML), 225
Extensible Markup Language. *See* XML
Extensible Stylesheet Language Transformations (XSLT), 389
extension methods, 340
external content types. *See also* entities
    associations, 392, 399–400
    considerations, 404
    creating, 394–410
    default actions on, 420–422
    described, 388
    stereotyping, 392–394, 408–414
external data columns, 388–389, 418–422
External Data Connectivity Filter web part, 390
External Data Item Builder web part, 389–390
External Data Item web part, 389
External Data List, 276–277, 388, 389, 390
External Data List web part, 389
external data parts, 390
External Data Picker Control, 398, 400–404
External Data Related List web part, 390
External Data Search, 389
External Data web parts, 389–390

external lists
considerations, 89, 276–277
creating, 396, 397, 399
described, 388, 389
rich client integration, 390
ExternalDataExchange attribute, 250–251
ExternalDataExchangeService attribute, 251–252

## F

Facebook, 443
farms. *See* SharePoint farms
FAST Search, 433
Feature Designer, 497
feature elements, 499–501
feature receivers, 501–508
FeatureManifest element, 496, 500
features, 496–511
    activation dependencies, 497–498
    activation rules, 498–499
    identifiers, 514–515
    properties, 499
    scopes, 497–498, 503
    upgrading, 508–511
    versions, 509
federation, 432
Federation Object Model, 432–434
field controls, 123–124, 324–330
field types, 323–330
FieldRenderingControls, 328
fields
    adding formulae to, 91
    content, 127
    described, 131
    indexed, 338
    page, 127
Fields collection, 331–332
file size, 121
file-level integration, 5–6
files. *See also* documents
    audio, 121
    BDCM, 407
    CAB, 494
    debug script, 49
    element, 57, 165, 501, 507
    image, 121
    ODC, 302, 303, 470
    permissions. *See* permissions
    resource, 455–456
    script, 49
    templates. *See* templates
    trusted, 272, 301

UDC, 99–101
UDCX, 471
uploading, 222, 271, 303, 418, 462
video, 121
ZIP, 138, 206–207
filters
    IFilters, 427
    limit, 397–398, 399
    property filters, 431–432
    wildcard, 409
Finder operations, 396, 402–403
Finder stereotype, 408–410
Fixed Value-based status indicator, 465–466
folders
    enumerating, 24–25
    organizing with, 24–25, 111–112
    system, 24
folksonomies, 109, 445
Formatting rules, 101
forms, InfoPath. *See* InfoPath forms
forms, workflow, 96, 105
front-end web server, 424
functions
    in PowerShell, 520–521
    user-defined, 266, 272–273, 288–297

## G

GAC (Global Assembly Cache), 48, 405
gateway objects, 342
getGlobalCommands method, 50
ghosting/unghosting, 35
Global Assembly Cache (GAC), 48, 405
Groove tool, 3, 6
Group element, 44
groups, 41, 315–316

## H

handleCommand method, 50
Hello World button, 46–47
HTML (Hypertext Markup Language), 268, 443
HTTP (Hypertext Transport Protocol), 268
Hypertext Markup Language (HTML), 268, 443
Hypertext Transport Protocol (HTTP), 268

## I

IDisposable interface, 25
IDisposable objects, 25–26
IFilters, 427
IIS (Internet Information Services), 5, 195
image files, 121
importing
    Excel data, 275
    PowerPivot data, 482
    sites, 15–16
    workflows, 228, 233–234, 238
indexed columns, 335–336
indexed fields, 338
indexing components, 424–429
Indicator Details web part, 467–468
indicators, 465–467
InfoPath forms
    accessing data in, 96–101
    adding formulae to fields, 91
    creating for lists, 92–93
    issues, 99–100
    publishing to SharePoint, 82, 84, 91–92
    responding to events in, 101–105
    rules engine, 101–103
    tables, 90–91, 97–98
    templates, 83, 86–92
    using in SharePoint, 86–96
InfoPath Forms Services, 79–105
    BrowserForm web part, 81–86
    configuring, 80–81
    overview, 79–81
inheritance
    from BaseFieldControl class, 328–330
    content types, 312–316
    from SPField, 324–328
in-memory subqueries, 373–375
integer values, 322
IntelliSense, 30
interactivity, 53, 265, 282–285, 472
Internet, 107
Internet Information Services (IIS), 5, 195
iterators, 339–340, 341

## J

JavaScript, 298–299
JavaScript Client Object Model, 53, 60–61, 64

JavaScript Object Model (JSOM), 268, 297–300
JavaScript Object Notation (JSON), 54
JavaScript test page, 60–61
job definitions, 214–215
joins, table, 371–373
JSOM (JavaScript Object Model), 268, 297–300
JSON (JavaScript Object Notation), 54

## L

Lambda expressions, 340–341
layouts, creating web pages with, 128–130
libraries. *See also* document libraries
    columns and, 331–332
    content types and, 331–332
    data connection, 99, 272, 300–308
    maximum number of items in, 114
    PerformancePoint, 469–470
    permissions, 301
    in PowerShell, 523–524
limit filter, 397–398, 399
LINQ
    joining tables, 371–373
    locating data via, 341
    overview, 338–341
    result shaping, 370
LINQ queries, 71, 366, 367, 369–370
LINQ to Objects, 70, 339–340, 342, 366
LINQ to SharePoint
    adding data, 358–361
    deleting data, 361–365
    demonstration scenario, 344–357
    objects, 373–375
    overview, 341–344
    querying data, 365–373
    updating information via, 375–384
    vs. LINQ to Objects, 366
LINQ to SQL, 342
LINQ to XML, 341
list content types, 332, 349
list throttling, 334–335
lists
    associating content types with, 351
    columns and, 331–332
    content types and, 331–332
    creating custom forms for, 92–93
    external. *See* external lists
    overview, 331–333
    in PowerShell, 523–524
ListViewWebPart component, 40
Location attribute, 43, 44
locations, 43, 44
logs
    history list, 261–262
    ULS, 11, 27–28
lookup columns, 322, 352–353, 450, 457

## M

Managed Metadata column, 109, 445, 452
Managed Metadata service, 107–114, 173–174, 319–320
managed properties, 428–429, 431, 432
master page tokens, 135–136
master pages, 34, 123, 133–136
MaxSize element, 44
Media Content types, 120–121
memory
    in-memory subqueries, 373–375
    performance and, 333
metadata. *See also* data
    BDC, 391, 424
    content types, 316–318
    default, 110–111
    entities, 416–417
    managed, 107–114
    navigation, 111–112
    rich media content, 121
    XML, 316–318
Microsoft BI solution, 464–465
Microsoft Office. *See* Office
Microsoft Office SharePoint Server (MOSS), 3
Microsoft SQL Server, 5
mobile browsers, 40, 316
mobile devices, 40, 316
mobile pages, 40, 316
Module items, 514
MOSS (Microsoft Office SharePoint Server), 3
MOSS 2007, 387–391, 424
My Network application, 461–462
My Profile page, 452–461
My Sites host, 450–462

## N

NCompass Labs, 3
.NET assemblies, 10
.NET connectivity assemblies, 391, 404–417
.NET Framework, 3–4
.NET Reflector, 10
network load, 64
networks
    download time, 121, 333
    My Network application, 461–462
    performance issues, 333
notes, 461

## O

objects. *See also* specific objects
    child, 362–364
    client-side, 61–64
    conflict resolution, 344
    custom entity, 414–417
    DataContext, 342–344, 376, 380–381
    gateway, 342
    LINQ to Objects, 70, 339–340, 342, 366, 373–375
    LINQ to SharePoint, 373–375
    parent, 362–364
    in PowerShell, 518–520
    properly disposing of, 25–26
    properties, 523
    setting properties on, 523
ODCs (Office Data Connections), 46, 47, 470, 471
Office applications
    integrating with SharePoint, 5–6, 120
    using with Windows 2008 Server, 12
    web-based, 6, 14, 86, 269
Office Data Connections (ODCs), 46, 47, 470, 471
Office Web Applications, 6, 14, 86, 269
OLAP (Online Analytical Processing), 463, 464–465, 467
OLAP cubes, 467, 471, 485
OLAP data sources, 472–474, 476, 481

Online Analytical Processing. *See* OLAP
OpenSearch, 433
OpenXML, 137, 138, 203, 206–222
operation batching, 64

## P

package designer, 494–496
packaging/deployment model, 493–515
    activation dependencies, 497–498
    deploying assemblies, 496
    features. *See* features
    package structure, 494
    safe controls, 496
    service packs, 509, 512
    site definitions, 511–515
    upgrades, 508–511
    working with packages, 493–496
page components, 49–52
page content type, 123–125
Page directive, 36
page fields, 127
page layouts, 123, 125–130
page model, 122–124
PageParserPath entry, 35–36
pages. *See also* web pages
    adding custom functionality, 140–149
    application, 33, 35–36
    ASP.NET, 37
    attached/detached, 35
    editing, 130
    ghosted/unghosted, 35
    master, 34, 123, 133–136
    modifying title, 40
    profile, 389, 419–420, 452–461
    site, 34
    standard, 34
    structure, 494
    templates, 34
    web part, 34
    working with, 133–139
parameters file, 355–357
parent objects, 362–364
parsing queries, 337, 366
passwords, 100, 305, 306, 389
PDF, converting Word documents to, 204–206
performance
    coding practices and, 26–27
    data access, 333–336
    list throttling and, 334–335
PerformancePoint Services, 3, 469–480
permissions
    forms, 99
    item-level, 115
    libraries, 301
    PowerShell, 522
per-user identity, 473
PivotCharts, 280–281
PivotTables
    considerations, 481, 483
    in Excel Services, 270, 275–280, 286–287
placeholders, 123
platform development tools, 9–11
pluggable connector framework, 391, 405
pluggable workflow services, 240–257
    configuring, 256
    creating, 240–257
    external activities via, 227
    overview, 250–251
PowerPivot, 270, 472, 481–485
PowerPivot for SharePoint, 483–485
PowerPivot reports, 270, 481, 482, 485
PowerShell, 517–525
    basics, 517–521
    objects in, 518–520
    upgrading features with, 509–511
    using functions, 520–521
    using objects, 518–520
PowerShell for SharePoint, 521–524
    activating Developer Dashboard, 28–29
    creating documents, 524
    permissions, 522
    remote connections, 521–522
    timer jobs, 524
    working with content, 524
    working with lists/libraries, 523–524
    working with site collections/sites, 522–523
presentation layer
    application pages, 33, 35
    executing server-side code, 35–40
    mobile pages, 40
    overview, 33–52
    site pages, 34, 35
problems. *See* troubleshooting
ProClarity, 3
profile pages, 389, 419–420, 452–461
projects. *See* SharePoint projects
properties
    crawled, 428–429, 431
    events, 157–158
    features, 499
    managed, 428–429, 431, 432
    objects, 523
    service applications, 201–202
    users, 446–447
property filters, 431–432
protocol handlers, 427
psconfig tool, 509
publishing content, 124–130
publishing items
    to Excel Services, 281, 284, 287
    workflows, 239, 263

## Q

queries
    CAML, 10, 65–68, 337, 366
    capturing search queries, 435–436
    common query language, 431–432
    components, 429–442
    custom refinement tools, 440–442
    inefficient, 367
    in-memory subqueries, 373–375
    LINQ, 71, 366, 367, 369–370
    overview, 332–333
    parsing, 337, 366
    performing simple, 367–369
    ranking, 435
    refining search results, 437–440
    Shared Query Manager, 437
    SQL, 332, 333, 430
query architecture, 424
query limitations, 366
Query Object Model, 429–431, 433–435
Query RSS API, 434
Query Web Service, 434
queryable load, 71
QueryCommand attribute, 46

## R

ratings, 444
RBS (Remote BLOB Storage), 122
readers, 115
receiver base classes, 154–155
records management, 120
Red Gate .NET Reflector, 10
referential integrity constraints, 362–365
relationships
    between content types, 352–353
    defining, 352–353
    within PowerPivot, 482, 483
remote applications, 174
Remote BLOB Storage (RBS), 122
remote connections, 521–522
Report Builder, 488
Reporting Services, 485–489
Reporting Services web part, 489
reports
    BCS, 391, 405
    creating with Reporting Services, 485–489
    in Dashboard, 476
    modifying with Report Builder, 488–489
    PerformancePoint, 474, 480, 485
    PowerPivot, 270, 481, 482, 485
    time intelligence, 477–480
    via Decomposition Tree, 480–481
Representational State Transfer. *See* REST
ResolveAll methods, 382–383
resource files, 455–456
REST (Representational State Transfer), 268–269
REST API, 268–269, 285–288, 293–294
result shaping, 370
ribbon, 40–52
    adding controls to, 42–45
    adding custom tab, 42–45
    architecture, 40–42
    disabling controls, 47
    extending, 42–45
    handling events from, 46–47
    key elements in, 41–42
    scaling, 42
ribbon controls, 41
ribbon tabs, 41–42
rich client applications, 64, 124, 390
rich client integration, 390
rich media content, 121
root site, 15, 17
RootFinder method, 426
RSS API, 434
rules, workflow, 225
rules engine, 101–103

## S

safe controls, 496
SafeControl entry, 496
Safe-Mode Parser, 496
sandboxed solutions, 29–30
Scale element, 44
scopes, 429, 497–498, 503
script files, 49
script links, 47–49
ScriptLink controls, 48
Search Administration Object Model, 435
Search Connector Framework, 424–427
search connectors, 426–427
search queries, 435–436
search results
    displaying, 436
    refining, 437–440
searches
    External Data Search, 389
    Finder operations, 396, 402–403
    picker search functionality, 402–404
    SpecificFinder operations, 395–396, 410–414
Secure Store Service, 272, 305–308, 389
security
    events, 156–157
    passwords, 100, 305, 306, 389
    web parts, 140
security errors, 485
sequential workflows, 224
server controls, 34, 127, 140, 145
server farm architecture, 4–5
server object model, 17–28
    administration classes, 20–21
    best practices, 25–27
    configuration classes, 20–21
    content access classes, 21–25
    error handling, 27–28
    overview, 17–20
    performance issues, 26–27
    saving changes, 25
    site provisioning classes, 21–25
server-side code, executing, 35–40
server-side event handling, 50–52
server-side implementation, 169–171
Service Application Framework, 169–202
    adding client-side classes, 179–181
    adding server-side classes, 176–179
    calling service applications, 196–199
    capturing user input, 190–193
    client/server communication, 173
    client-side implementation, 171–172
    configuring service applications, 173–175
    connecting to remote applications, 174
    creating SharePoint projects, 176
    demonstration scenario, 175–202
    installing components, 185–187
    managing service applications, 199–202
    provisioning instances, 187–195
    server-side implementation, 169–171
    topology service, 175, 198
service applications
    calling, 196–199
    configuring, 173–175
    managing, 199–202
    properties, 201–202
    provisioning instances of, 187–195
    remote connections, 174
service packs, 509, 512
Shared Query Manager, 437
SharePoint 2010, 3–7
    architecture, 4–5
    business experience platform, 465–489
    enhancements, 424
    fundamentals, 14–17
    hierarchy, 14–20

integration with Office, 5–6, 120
overview, 3–4
remote connections, 521–522
services architecture, 170–171
user features, 5–7
vs. SharePoint product, 9
SharePoint Designer, 126–128
connecting to BCS data, 392–404
creating workflows with, 227, 262–264
implementing workflows, 233–238
overview, 10
SharePoint farms
custom code and, 29
farm solutions, 6, 30
farm-level configuration, 14
security issues, 130
server farm architecture, 4–5
SPFarm object, 20, 170, 172
system instability in, 29
SharePoint list-based status indicator, 466
SharePoint lists. *See* lists
SharePoint Portal Server, 3
SharePoint product, 9
SharePoint projects
creating, 176
installing Service Application components, 185–187
naming, 176
translation functionality, 183–185
SharePoint Search, 433
SharePoint Server 2010
BI platform, 465–489
considerations, 11, 21
features, 389, 390
SharePoint Workspace, 6
Silverlight Client Object Model
hosting in SharePoint, 55–59
overview, 53–54
Silverlight test page, 55–60
Silverlight web part, 59–60
Simple Object Access Protocol (SOAP), 269
Single Sign On Service, 389
site collections
creating, 15, 523
deleting, 523
document sets within, 116–117
in PowerShell, 522–523

site columns. *See also* columns
associating content types with, 349–350
creating, 346–348
described, 332
site content types, 118, 125, 209, 332
site definitions, 512–515
site pages, 34, 35–36
site provisioning, 14–17
site provisioning classes, 21–25
SiteFeatures element, 514–515
sites
child, 15, 17
creating, 15–17
deleting, 523
importing/exporting, 15–16
mobile versions of, 40, 316
in PowerShell, 522–523
root, 15, 17
templates, 15–17, 350–353, 512
Slicer, 282–285
SOAP (Simple Object Access Protocol), 269
social computing, 443–462
SPContentTypeId object, 314–315
SPContext.Current property, 23
SPDocumentLibrary class, 23
SPDocumentLibrary objects, 23
SpecificFinder operations, 395–396, 410–414
SPException class, 27–28
SPFarm object, 20–21, 170, 172
SPField class, 324–328
SPFieldFile type, 324
SPFieldLookup type, 324
SPFieldType enumeration, 322, 323
SPFile object, 23–24
SPFolder object, 24–25
SPItemEventReceiver class, 154
SPList object, 23, 27, 331
SPListEventReceiver class, 154–155
SPListItem object, 23, 26, 358
SPLongOperation object, 193, 208
SPMetal, 338, 353–357
SPMonitoredScope object, 29
SPQuery object, 26–27
SPRequest object, 25
SPRequestModule component, 40
SPRoot environment variable, 12
SPServer object, 21
SPService class, 21
SPServiceApplication object, 170, 171, 172–173, 199

SPServiceApplicationProxy object, 172, 173, 175
SPServiceInstance object, 21, 170
SPSite object, 22, 25–26
SPUCWorkerProcess.exe process, 30
SPView objects, 332
SPWeb objects, 22, 25–26
SPWebApplication object, 22
SPWebEventReceiver class, 155
SPWebService, 21
SPWorkflowEventReceiver class, 155
SQL (Structured Query Language), 338–339
SQL connections, 97
SQL queries, 332, 333, 367, 430
SQL Server, 5
SQL Server Analysis Service-based status indicator, 467
SQL Server connections, 391
standard pages, 34
standards compliant web interface, 6–7
state, visualizing in workflows, 238–240
state machine workflows, 224–225
Status List web part, 468–469
stereotyping, 392–394, 408–414
strongly typed code, 360
Structured Query Language. *See* SQL
STSADM tool, 28, 517, 525
subtypes, 447–449
.svc files, 248
synchronization, 445–446
Sysinternals DebugView, 11
system folders, 24
System.IO.FileNotFound exception, 13

# T

tab expansion, 518
tables
joining, 371–373
in LINQ, 342
tags/tagging, 444–445, 461
taxonomies, 109, 445
Template element, 44
TemplateAlias attribute, 45
templates
activity, 455–457
for compilation process, 220–222
documents, 220–222, 316
forms, 83, 86–92

templates *(continued)*
  groups, 41
  pages, 34
  sites, 15–17, 350–353, 512
  TemplateAlias attribute, 45
  Word documents, 220–222
  workflows, 231, 232–233
term sets, 108
terms, 108, 110–111
text
  alternative, 499
  in columns, 322
  command, 276
  description, 498
  translating, 183–185, 198–199
text boxes, 237, 240
text values, 260
themes, 137–139
throttling, 26
time intelligence, 477–480
timer jobs, 524
toolbox behavior, 227
topology service, 175, 198
Trace.Write, 11
translation functionality, 183–185
troubleshooting
  performance issues, 11
  with SPMonitoredScope, 29
trusted data connections, 272, 301, 303, 304
trusted data providers, 272
trusted files, 272, 301
try-catch blocks, 27
Twitter, 453–460
type descriptor, 409–410
TypeMock Isolator, 10

## U

U2U CAML Query Builder, 10
UDC (Universal Data Connection), 99–101, 471
UDC files, 99–101
UDCX files, 471
UDFs (user-defined functions), 266, 272–273, 288–297
ULS (Unified Logging Service), 11, 27–28
Unattended Service account, 272, 305, 307–308, 473
Unified Logging Service (ULS), 11, 27–28
uniform resource indicators (URIs), 198, 268
uniform resource locators (URLs), 269
Universal Data Connection (UDC). *See* UDC
Update method, 25
upgrading features, 508–511
uploading documents, 222, 271, 303, 418, 462
URIs (uniform resource indicators), 198, 268
URLs (uniform resource locators), 269
user database, 445–446
user features, 5–7
user interface customization, 133–149
User Profile Service, 445–462
user profiles, 443–462
user-defined functions (UDFs), 266, 272–273, 288–297
usernames, 15, 305–307, 389, 473
users
  activities, 455–461
  business user experience, 464
  capturing input from, 190–193
  of content, 114–115
  memberships, 461
  organizations, 449–450
  personal sites, 450–462
  pre-user identity, 473
  properties, 446–447
  status messages, 453
  subtypes, 447–449

## V

validation
  activities, 226
  columns, 330
Validation rules, 101
variables
  environment, 12
  PowerShell, 519
  workflow, 225, 226, 235, 237, 259
video files, 121
Visio 2010
  creating workflows with, 228, 257–262
  designing workflows with, 231–240
Visio Services, 238–240
Visual Studio 2010
  considerations, 3–4
  creating BDC Model projects, 405–417
  creating site definitions, 512–515
  creating workflows with, 228
  replaceable tokens, 248–249
  SharePoint Designer and, 10
  workflow designer tool, 258–262
Visual Studio Debugger, 295, 503–504
Visual Studio IntelliSense, 30
Visual Studio Tools for Applications, 103
visual web parts, 145–149

## W

WCAG (Web Content Accessibility Guidelines), 6–7
WCF (Windows Communication Foundation), 54
WCF calculation service, 241–250
WCF components, 181–183
WCF Connection wizard, 391
WCF endpoints, 181, 391
WCF messages, 254–256
WCF proxy class, 196–198
WCF services
  calling (pluggable service), 253–254
  calling (SharePoint-hosted), 256–257
  SharePoint-hosted, 246–250
  Windows Forms-hosted, 241–245
web applications, 6, 14, 86, 269
web browsers
  BrowserForm web part, 81–86
  mobile, 40, 316
Web Content Accessibility Guidelines (WCAG), 6–7
web content management, 122–131
web pages. *See also* pages
  creating with layouts, 128–130
  dashboards, 475–476
  dynamic generation of, 131
  "standard," 56
web part pages, 34, 287–288

web parts. *See also* specific web parts
   business intelligence, 465–469
   creating, 140–144
   custom, 140–144
   described, 131
   infrastructure, 140
   Reporting Services, 489
   security, 140
   Silverlight, 59–60
   visual, 145–149
Web Service Definition Language (WSDL), 97, 414
web sites
   collaborative, 4
   creating, 16–17
   events raised by, 155
   hosting, 170
   root site method, 16–17
   searching. *See* searches
WebFeatures element, 514–515
WF. *See* Workflow Foundation
wildcard filter, 409
Windows 2008 Server, 12
Windows Communication Foundation. *See* WCF
Windows Forms, 241–245
   sample application, 353–355
Windows Workflow Foundation. *See* Workflow Foundation
Word Automation Services, 203–222
Word documents
   conversion jobs, 204–206, 217–218
   converting to alternative formats, 204–205, 217–218
   converting to PDF, 204–205
   custom content types, 208–209
   templates, 220–222
Workbook object, 297
workbooks
   business intelligence, 464, 465, 485

   creating dashboards from, 484–485
   Excel, 274–275, 284–285, 293
   PowerPivot, 483–485
workflow activities
   configuring, 259–262
   custom, 226–227
workflow forms, 96, 105
Workflow Foundation (WF), 223–264. *See also* workflows
   creating workflows with SharePoint Designer, 227, 262–264
   creating workflows with Visio 2010, 228, 257–262
   demonstration scenario, 228–231
   designing workflows with Visio 2010, 231–240
   fundamentals of, 223–228
workflow services, 255–256
workflows, 223–264. *See also* Workflow Foundation
   associating with content types, 239–240, 316
   considerations, 229
   content creation, 115–116
   creating with SharePoint Designer, 227, 262–264
   creating with Visio 2010, 228, 257–262
   creating with Visual Studio 2010, 228
   custom designer, 227
   demonstration scenario, 228–231
   designing with Visio 2010, 231–240
   design-time behavior, 226–227
   errors, 233
   exporting, 231, 233, 238

   implementing with SharePoint Designer, 233–238
   importing, 228, 233–234, 238
   overview, 223–224
   pluggable. *See* pluggable workflow services
   publishing, 239, 263
   reusable, 234, 239–240, 263
   rules, 225
   runtime behavior, 226
   sequential, 224
   state, 238–240
   state machine, 224–225
   templates, 231, 232–233
   toolbox behavior, 227
   types of, 224–225
   variables, 225, 226, 235, 237, 259
   working with, 225–226
WSDL (Web Service Definition Language), 97, 414
.wsp extension, 494

# X

XAML (eXtensible Application Markup Language), 225
XML (Extensible Markup Language), 137, 138, 203, 206–222
XML documents, 316–318
XSLT (Extensible Stylesheet Language Transformations), 389

# Z

ZIP files/archives, 138, 206–207

# Practical Guides for Microsoft SharePoint 2010 Users of Every Level

Mc Graw Hill
Learn more. Do more.
MHPROFESSIONAL.COM

Available everywhere books are sold, in print and ebook formats.